# The Sixties in America

# The Sixties in America

## Volume II

Giovanni, Nikki — SANE (National
Committee for a Sane Nuclear Policy)

*Editor*

## Carl Singleton

**Fort Hays State University**

*Project Editor*

## Rowena Wildin

SALEM PRESS, INC.
PASADENA, CALIFORNIA
HACKENSACK, NEW JERSEY

*Managing Editor:* Christina J. Moose

*Project Editor:* Rowena Wildin      *Production Editor:* Janet Long

*Research Supervisor:* Jeffry Jensen      *Research Assistant:* Jun Ohunki

*Acquisitions Editor:* Mark Rehn      *Graphics and Design:* James Hutson

*Photograph Editor:* Karrie Hyatt      *Layout:* William Zimmerman

*Title page photo:* Express Newspapers/Archive Photos

∞ The paper used in these volumes conforms to the American National Standard for Permanence of Paper for Printed Library Materials, Z39.48-1992

**Library of Congress Cataloging-in-Publication Data**

The Sixties in America / editor, Carl Singleton ; project editor, Rowena Wildin.
     p.   cm.
     Includes bibliographical references and index.
     ISBN 0-89356-982-8 (set : alk. paper). — ISBN 0-89356-983-6 (v. 1 : alk. paper). — ISBN 0-89356-984-4 (v. 2 : alk. paper). — ISBN 0-89356-985-2 (v. 3 : alk. paper)
     1. United States — History — 1961-1969 — Encyclopedias.
   I. Singleton, Carl.   II. Wildin, Rowena, 1956-

E841.S55     1999
973.92—dc21                                                98-49255
                                                                           CIP

Second Printing

PRINTED IN THE UNITED STATES OF AMERICA

# ■ Contents

# ■ Alphabetical List of Entries

## Volume I

# Volume II

# Volume III

# The Sixties in America

# ■ Giovanni, Nikki

**Born** June 7, 1943, Knoxville, Tennessee

*An African American poet who first gained fame in the 1960's. Her poetry addresses issues ranging from the black revolution to love.*

**Early Life** Born in Knoxville, Tennessee, Yolande Cornelia "Nikki" Giovanni and her family moved to Cincinnati, Ohio, when she was still an infant. Because her grandparents remained in Knoxville, she spent short periods there during her formative years and considered Knoxville her home. As a teenager, she returned to Knoxville to live with her grandparents and attended Austin High School. She was heavily influenced both socially and intellectually by her grandmother and her high school English teacher. Because of their efforts, Giovanni entered Fisk University in 1960 at age sixteen.

**The 1960's** Giovanni proved to be a serious student with strong political views, concentrating on writing and politics. At Fisk, she met and worked with novelist and writer-in-residence John O. Killens, a leader of the Black Arts movement. In addition to editing the university literary publication, she helped reinstate the Student Nonviolent Coordinating Committee, which had earlier been banned.

After earning her degree in 1966, she returned to Cincinnati, where she wrote many of the poems for her first published collection, *Black Feeling, Black Talk* (1968). At this time, Giovanni edited *Conversation*, a local publication, and organized the first Black Arts Festival in Cincinnati. Following the successful festival, Giovanni became acquainted with leaders of several important movements within the African American community. She did not always agree with them, however, especially concerning violence, and often became embroiled in controversy.

Giovanni published her second volume of poems, *Black Judgement*, in 1969, with financial assistance from the Harlem Council of the Arts. By this time, she had become firmly entrenched as a poet and voice of the ordinary African Americans of the urban areas of the United States.

**Later Life** Giovanni has remained a controversial figure. Although she gained a level of popularity virtually unknown for an African American female poet, Giovanni has endured both professional and personal attacks from people in the male-dominated Black Arts movement, including LeRoi Jones (Amiri Baraka) and Don L. Lee. Because of this rift, she pursued success alone throughout the 1970's and 1980's and received it, winning numerous awards, earning honorary degrees, and publishing several volumes of poetry, essays, and children's poetry.

**Impact** As a successful female poet of the 1960's, Giovanni has effectively communicated what it meant to grow up black and female in post-World War II United States. Though openly criticized for her opinions and actions, the outspoken poet continues to write, speak, and teach new generations of Americans through her unique and controversial poems, essays, and recordings.

**Subsequent Events** In 1984, Giovanni was again targeted by her critics. She came under intense fire because she refused to take part in the boycott of South Africa and defended other artists who were blacklisted for performing there. Rumors accusing her of performing in South Africa endangered her career. However, as she had earlier, she withstood the criticism and continued her work. In 1989, Giovanni joined the teaching staff of Virginia Polytechnic Institute and State University as an English professor.

**Additional Information** In 1976, Giovanni published *Gemini: An Extended Autobiographical Statement on My First Twenty-five Years of Being a Black Poet*, which provides information about her role as a 1960's activist from her own viewpoint.

*Kimberley H. Kidd*

**See also** Poetry.

# ■ Goldwater, Barry

**Born** January 1, 1909, Phoenix, Arizona
**Died** May 29, 1998, Phoenix, Arizona

*One of the founders of the modern conservative movement in the United States. Goldwater helped conservatives capture the Republican Party in the 1960's. Despite losing the 1964 presidential election, his efforts solidified a conservative coalition that helped future Republicans win presidential elections.*

**Early Life** A member of one of the most prominent families in Arizona, Barry Morris Goldwater was heir to a local chain of department stores that helped fund his entry into politics. Goldwater's political

*Barry Goldwater, 1964 Republican presidential candidate, shakes some hands along the campaign trail.* (AP/Wide World Photos)

involvement helped build the Arizona Republican Party in a state traditionally dominated by Democrats. He began a thirty-eight-year political career by winning a seat on the Phoenix City Council in 1949. Goldwater's continued presence in state politics resulted in a successful run for the United States Senate in 1952. His dedication to the party and his ability to raise money led to Goldwater's appointment as chairman of the Republican senatorial campaign committee in 1955. This prominent position bolstered Goldwater's status and helped him become one of the most visible conservatives in the United States. The lack of a unifying conservative figure at the end of the 1950's ensured that Goldwater would take a prominent place in the Republican Party in the following decade.

**The 1960's** Richard M. Nixon's loss in the 1960 presidential campaign left a leadership void in the Republican Party that Goldwater quickly filled. The Arizonan gained national attention by hitting the lecture circuit, appearing on television talk shows,

and writing a nationally distributed newspaper column. However, it was his book, *Conscience of a Conservative* (1962), which sold 3.5 million copies, that defined Goldwater and the movement he represented. The book advocated individualism, limited government, a strict constructionist view of the U.S. Constitution, federalism, and anticommunism. Through his appearances and book and by chiding many members of the Republican Party for being too liberal and accommodating the growing influence of government in American society, Goldwater gained credence with party conservatives.

Conservative intellectuals and emerging conservative youth organizations such as Young Americans for Freedom and the Young Republicans started a "draft Goldwater" movement in an attempt to get the Arizonan to run for the Republican presidential nomination in 1964. Goldwater won the party's nomination over liberal Republican Nelson A. Rockefeller. However, Goldwater's archconservatism, his opposition to the Civil Rights Act of 1964, and several campaign gaffes helped to paint him as an extremist on social welfare and nuclear warfare. Goldwater was wounded by his fights with liberal and moderate Republicans in the divisive primary campaign and entered the general election against President Lyndon B. Johnson without the support of business and key Republican leaders. This, combined with Johnson's political strength in the wake of John F. Kennedy's assassination, resulted in a crushing defeat for both Goldwater and the Republicans in the 1964 elections. Goldwater captured only 38.8 percent of the vote and won only Arizona and five southern states. Republicans lost thirty-eight seats in the House of Representatives and two in the Senate. Goldwater was wounded by the loss, but remained an active participant in Republican politics. The party rebounded with a significant victory in the 1966 congressional elections, and closed the decade by electing Richard M. Nixon as president. Goldwater's candidacy had helped to solidify a conservative base in the Republican Party, which led to additional electoral victories in the decades that followed the 1960's.

**Later Life** Goldwater remained a force in Republican politics until his retirement from the Senate in 1986. However, he became increasingly uncomfortable with the social agenda of the New Right organizations that became active in the Republican Party in the 1970's and 1980's. Goldwater's belief in the primacy of individual rights led him to oppose much of the new conservative social agenda and therefore limited his importance to the new conservative cause that championed Ronald Reagan.

**Impact** Goldwater helped launch the modern U.S. conservative movement by uniting intellectuals, youth, and grassroots movements of the political right. Through his 1964 presidential run, Goldwater helped transform the Republicans from a moderate, Eastern-dominated party into a national coalition that was decidedly conservative. The immediate electoral effects of his crushing defeat at the hands of Johnson in 1964 were less important than Goldwater's influence on the future of the Republican Party. His *Conscience of a Conservative* helped define the agenda of the right, mobilized future leaders of the party, and helped build a national base of financial support for conservative Republicans. Goldwater's focus on winning conservative states led to the Republican "southern strategy," which helped the party gain a foothold in the Democrat-dominated

South and led to the elections of Republican presidents in the following decades.

**Additional Information** Goldwater published his memoirs, *Goldwater*, in 1988. Lee Edwards published the comprehensive biography, *Goldwater: The Man Who Made a Revolution*, in 1995.

*J. Wesley Leckrone*

**See also** Buckley, William F., Jr.; Conservatism in Politics; Johnson, Lyndon B.; Nixon, Richard M.; Presidential Election of 1960; Presidential Election of 1964; Young Americans for Freedom.

---

# ■ Golf

*A game that lost its elitist image during the 1960's. Golf became popular largely because of television and big-name stars.*

Despite its humble origins among Scottish shepherds and the caddyshack roots of aging stars such as Ben Hogan and Sam Snead, golf began the 1960's with a snobbish country club image. Golf courses were seen as private places for status seekers, while bowling and fishing were much more popular with the general public. In the ensuing decade, however, the situation changed, as golf began a process of democratization that would continue into the 1990's.

The decade began with the dramatic victories of Arnold Palmer in the 1960 U.S. Open and Masters. A muscular greenskeeper's son, his charisma and slashing style soon made him golf's first television icon. Palmer won six major professional tournaments and many other events from 1960 to 1964, acquiring immense popularity among varied fans who either watched the "Palmer Charge" on television or cheered their hero firsthand as part of "Arnie's Army."

Jack Nicklaus, a talented collegian, turned pro in 1962 and quickly won his first U.S. Open. Like Palmer, Nicklaus won six major tournaments in the 1960's, while among the other men pros only Gary Player won as many as three. The supporting cast of Palmer and Nicklaus included many excellent players such as Julius Boros, Billy Casper, Ray Floyd, and Ken Venturi, but Palmer remained "the king," and Nicklaus was "the crown prince." Palmer won no more major championships after 1964, but the perceived rivalry between Palmer and Nicklaus was still the big story in men's pro golf at the end of the decade. Palmer was the hero of the masses, many of whom had begun to play the game, and Nicklaus with his more methodical approach and more bourgeois image was grudgingly granted co-hero status.

The popularity of golf grew rapidly. Golf could be seen on television most weekends, and made-for-TV golf events began with the series "Wonderful World of Golf." At the end of the decade, Lee Trevino emerged as a new popular hero, adding his jocular persona to the golf boom. Participation in golf grew as well.

Women's golf languished behind men's golf in popularity and status for most of the 1960's, partly as a consequence of the early death of its first big star, Mildred (Babe) Zaharias. Veterans such as Patty Berg, Louise Suggs, and Betsy Rawls were soon joined by the likes of Mickey Wright, Kathy Whitworth, and Carol Mann; Rawls and Wright were pupils of the legendary teacher Harvey Penick. Yet Wright, whose dominance directly paralleled Palmer's in the early 1960's, went into semiretirement in 1965. The next-best player of the decade may have been JoAnne Gunderson (later JoAnne Carner), who long remained an amateur until increasing purses finally tempted her to turn pro. Lack of media exposure kept the women pros out of the limelight, and the elitist values long associated with golf did not appeal to the early women's movement. It remained for Nancy Lopez in the late 1970's to become the "Arnold Palmer of women's golf," drawing media attention and new fans to the sport.

**Impact** Very few golfers of either gender could make a decent living at the game in the early 1960's. This situation changed quickly, especially for the men, as Palmer's popularity began to revolutionize the sport. Yet amateur golf grew as well, at an even faster rate. New courses, including many public courses, were rapidly built. The pull cart and the motor cart gradually replaced the caddy, even at private courses, and caddies eventually became nearly obsolete at the local level. Yet golf carts continued to be prohibited in most professional and major amateur events, while some pro caddies such as Trevino's Herman Mitchell became stars in their own right.

**Subsequent Events** Since its 1960's democratization, golf has continued to experience a boom that turned into a virtual explosion with the late 1990's popularity of Tiger Woods; the growth of women's and junior golf have proceeded accordingly. A major development of the 1980's was the establishment of the Senior Tour by Palmer and others as they began to pass their fiftieth birthdays. By the 1990's, a television Golf Channel allowed fans to engage in full-time viewing, and new made-for-television events such as the various Skins Games filled the off-season.

**Additional Information** *Golf in America: The First One Hundred Years* (1994), edited by George Peper, Robin McMillan, and James A. Frank, provides information about the history of golf, its rules and equipment, championships and tournaments, and its most noteworthy American players.

*Tom Cook*

**See also** Nicklaus, Jack; Palmer, Arnold; Rawls, Betsy; Sports; Wright, Mickey.

───────────────────────────────

## ■ *Graduate, The*

**Released** 1967
**Director** Mike Nichols (b. Michael Igor Pechkowsky, 1931-    )

*An immensely successful film that celebrated new discoveries and values of the youth culture. It criticized the affluent, empty, and plastic lifestyles and traditional ways of the older generation.*

**The Work** *The Graduate* is a wonderful blend of humor and sadness that shrewdly depicts the emptiness of the affluent suburban lifestyles of the 1960's. The film communicates the alienation of the young from the older generation, which has reaped the full material rewards of the American Dream. As it celebrates the honesty and vision of youth, it also calls into question the sanctity of marriage.

The plot involves a successful graduate, Benjamin Braddock, played by Dustin Hoffman, who returns to California from his school on the East Coast and is bored and humiliated by his proud, well-to-do parents. He is seduced by Mrs. Robinson, the middle-aged wife of his father's colleague, brilliantly played by Anne Bancroft. He discovers that sex can at least check boredom for a time. He then falls in love with Mrs. Robinson's daughter, Elaine, played by Katherine Ross, who spurns him when she finds out about the affair. He then pursues Elaine with demonic intensity finally running off with her in the middle of her wedding to someone else. The film ends as the bride—still wearing her wedding gown—

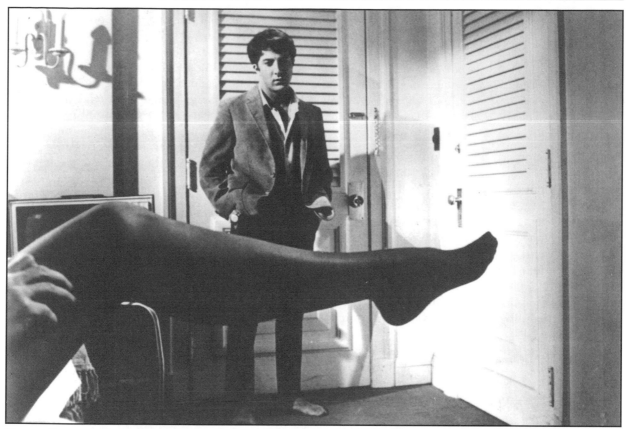

*Recent college graduate Benjamin Braddock (Dustin Hoffman) gazes at the leg of Mrs. Robinson (Anne Bancroft), an older woman who has seduced him, in the 1967 film* The Graduate. *(Museum of Modern Art/Film Stills Archive)*

and Benjamin ride off together on a public bus.

The film, produced by Lawrence Turfman, was both a critical and commercial success. It became the number-one money maker of 1968, earning fifty million dollars at the box office. Mike Nichols won the Academy Award for Best Director, and the film received six other nominations. The film gave Dustin Hoffman, then an unknown actor, the first big break of his career. The film's soundtrack by Simon and Garfunkel, a popular singer-songwriter duo, became a long-selling hit.

**Impact**  *The Graduate* was released at a time when the war in Vietnam was escalating and young people were increasingly questioning the values of the older generation. It appealed to many high school and college-age youths, marking their increased sophistication. As a protest film, it was relatively mild; however, it did depict the "plastic" world of adults as a bore, based on a crumbling value system upheld by predatory and foolish people. *The Graduate*

showed the gulf between the younger and the older generation by endowing the young couple with integrity and energy that contrasted with the emptiness of their parents' lives and marriages. The language and sexual explicitness of the film were marked, as was the departure from the normal morals long depicted by Hollywood. After *The Graduate*, the film industry targeted the youth market with many more films of a sophisticated nature, most with a more intense message of protest. Language and sexuality also followed *The Graduate*'s lead and became much more explicit.

**Additional Information**  Leonard Quart and Albert Auster's *American Film and Society Since 1945* (second edition, 1991) helps place *The Graduate* in perspective.

*Henry Weisser*

**See also**  Film; *Midnight Cowboy*; Simon and Garfunkel; Social Satires.

# ■ Grape Workers' Strike

**Date** September 16, 1965-July 29, 1970

*A milestone event in the farmworkers' movement. This strike successfully established, for the first time in U.S. history, the right of farmworkers to organize and bargain collectively and helped in the development of many effective union strategies.*

**Origins and History** At the beginning of the 1960's, the situation for U.S. farmworkers was much as it had been throughout the post-World War II era. In California and the Southwest, the largely Mexican American agricultural labor force was subjected to blatantly exploitative policies. Growers were confident that law enforcement agencies and lawmakers would continue to ignore their often violent intimidation of striking workers and their engineering of labor surpluses in order to maintain a large pool of desperate unemployed workers who would cross picket lines.

In the 1960's, John F. Kennedy's administration and the Civil Rights movement extended support to U.S. farmworkers, who were predominantly members of minority groups and one of the most oppressed occupational groups in the country. The unique political climate of the 1960's made the effective organization of farmworkers possible for the first time in U.S. history. For an effective farmworkers' movement to come into being, a charismatic leader who could unify farmworkers into a community of common interests had to appear. César Chávez was that leader.

**The Strike** The seminal events in the farmworkers' movement were strikes by workers in Delano, California, vineyards and a nationwide consumer boycott of grapes and products made from them or marketed by vineyard-owning corporations. In the fall of 1965, Filipino grape pickers associated with the Agricultural Workers Organizing Committee (AWOC) went on strike against Delano-area growers to protest excessively low wages. The remainder of the farmworkers in the area were represented by the National Farm Workers Association (NFWA), which was headed by Chávez, so AWOC asked the NFWA to join them.

Although Chávez expressed serious reservations, the members of the NFWA voted overwhelmingly to join the strike. Chávez knew his union had no resources to sustain striking workers, so he sought and received financial and moral support from grassroots sympathizers, religious leaders, civil rights organizations, labor unions, and college students. He initially raised funds by going on a speaking tour of California universities, returning with $6,700 in dollar bills and change donated by students. Walter Reuther, head of the United Automobile Workers, pledged $5,000 a month to the strike, and others followed with similar offers of support. People from the various groups that supported the grape workers' strike stood on the picket lines with farmworkers and were beaten, sprayed with insecticide and fertilizer, and struck by vehicles driven through their lines by growers' associates. Local police did little to intervene and made mass arrests of pickets when injunctions restricting the number of pickets were issued by local courts.

Chávez knew that it would take substantive financial pressure on growers, who were still operating using nonunion workers, to achieve a victory for the farmworkers. In October, 1965, he called for a nationwide consumer boycott of California table grapes, products made from them, and products marketed by corporations that owned vineyards. The public had witnessed how the striking workers had been treated through media coverage of the events, and they responded. In 1966, Chávez, inspired by the 1965 voting-rights march led by Martin Luther King, Jr., from Selma to Montgomery, Alabama, organized a twenty-five-day, three-hundred-mile march from Delano to Sacramento, the state capital, which further heightened the nation's awareness of the boycott and strike. Boycott organizations sprang up in every city in the country; the strategy began to have a significant economic impact on the growers.

The early success of the boycott drew the strongest possible response from politically and financially powerful growers and their associations. A battle ensued between some of the nation's most powerful politicians and associations, and grassroots political activism grew to epic proportions. Growers' organizations mounted an expensive national public-relations campaign to promote grape consumption, thinking that they could entice the public with slogans such as "Eat grapes, the forbidden fruit." California governor Ronald Reagan characterized the boycott and strike as being immoral and illegal, and while campaigning for Richard M. Nixon during his 1968 bid for the presidency, he called Chávez and the strikers "barbarians." After Nixon was elected, the new president helped growers by increasing Defense Department purchases of grapes to be sent to troops in Vietnam from half a million pounds in 1968 to more than two million pounds in 1969. The boycott continued to cost growers millions of dollars, and on July 29, 1970, all the Delano growers signed contracts with the United Farm Workers Organizing Committee (UFWOC, later the United Farm Workers of America, UFW); these contracts contained the worker health and safety provisions and wages sought by the union.

**Impact** The movement's leaders brought the grape workers' strike to the attention of the national media, and the entire nation became aware of the living and working conditions that led to the strike and the growers' response: violent intimidation of strikers, the use of strike-breaking workers, and petitions for court injunctions against the strikers. The heightened public awareness of the brutality and injustice suffered by farmworkers and Chávez's absolute insistence on nonviolence gained sympathy for the farmworkers' movement from organizations and individuals whose financial contributions and political clout made the movement's accomplishments possible. The cooperation of large numbers of Americans who did not consider themselves political or labor activists during the grape boycott helped workers gain many concessions from growers. The Delano grape workers' strike and boycott were so successful that by the mid-1970's, 85 percent of California's grapes were picked by workers covered by UFW contracts. Nearly three decades after the strike, the UFW was still the largest union for farm laborers in California.

**Additional Information** Detailed accounts of the Delano, California, grape workers' strike and the events surrounding it are found in the following books: *César Chávez: A Triumph of Spirit* (1995), by Richard Griswald del Castillo and Richard A. Garcia; *The Politics of Insurgency: The Farm Worker Movement in the 1960's* (1985), by J. Craig Jenkins; *César Chávez: Autobiography of La Causa* (1975), by Jacques E. Levy; *Sal Si Puedes: César Chávez and the New American Revolution* (1971), by Peter Matthiessen; and *Farmers' and Farm Workers' Movements: Social Protest in American Agriculture* (1995), by Patrick H. Mooney and Theo J. Marjka.

*Jack Carter*

**See also** Chávez, César; Chicano Movement; Unions and Collective Bargaining.

---

# ■ Grateful Dead

*A rock band inextricably linked to a time and place—San Francisco in the 1960's. The presence and influence of the Grateful Dead were felt musically and culturally.*

The Grateful Dead and their distinctive blend of traditional and experimental music date to the summer of 1961, when bluegrass banjo player Jerry Garcia joined with blues harmonica player Ron "Pigpen" McKernan and folksinger-songwriter Robert Hunter to play in Northern California. The group broke up, and Garcia, McKernan, and rock drummer Bill Kreutzmann joined in a band called the Zodiacs. By 1964, Garcia, McKernan, guitarist Bob Weir, and a few others were playing in San Francisco Bay Area bars and coffeehouses as Mother McCree's Uptown Jug Champions. In 1965, Garcia, McKernan, Weir, Kreutzmann, and jazz bassist Phil Lesh formed an electric blues band called the Warlocks. A year later, they changed their name to the Grateful Dead. Percussionist Mickey Hart joined in 1967. The Dead had a few additional members, but these six formed the band's core.

Musically, the Grateful Dead were made up of contradictions. Although they were at the center of the hippie movement, they played an eccentric fusion of folk and blues rather than psychedelic music. First known as a studio band unable to duplicate their sound on stage, they are usually remembered as an energetic, even meandering, spontaneous live act. They released the album *The Grateful Dead* in 1967, followed by *Anthem of the Sun* in 1968.

Culturally, the Dead were a social institution, often living communally and crossing paths with such 1960's icons as novelist Ken Kesey, musician Bob Dylan, LSD (lysergic acid diethylamide or acid) manufacturer Augustus Owsley Stanley III, and promoter Bill Graham. As the Warlocks, they performed at Kesey's acid tests, which were multimedia LSD parties. They lived for about seven months at 710 Ashbury Street in San Francisco and played many free shows and benefits. Some of their performances—a 1966 benefit to legalize marijuana, an anti-Vietnam War moratorium show on November 15, 1969, and fund-raisers for the Black Panther Party—showed their support of key issues of the

*Jerry Garcia, pivotal member of the Grateful Dead, which made its home in the Haight-Ashbury district in the mid-1960's, performs with the group at the Woodstock Festival in 1969. (Tucker Ranson/Archive Photos)*

1960's. They also played on the roof of the student union at Columbia University not long after the student strike there.

In 1968, the Grateful Dead moved to Marin County north of San Francisco to concentrate on recording. They released four albums in four years—including 1969's studio record *Aoxomoxoa* and 1970's concert recording *Live Dead*. At the end of the decade, the group produced two of their most enduring recordings, *Workingman's Dead* (1970) and *American Beauty* (1970).

**Impact** The Grateful Dead became forever associated with Haight-Ashbury, acid tests, and the 1967 Summer of Love. Their lives in the 1960's epitomized the hippie movement and their music, although not acid rock, has come to embody the spirit of that time. Their mellow sound and the group

members' frequent collaborations with other musicians have had a great influence on rock music.

For some time, the Grateful Dead was the only American pop band to partially control concert ticketing and to invite fans to record concerts despite a potential loss of record revenues. This resulted in extraordinarily loyal fans, dubbed Dead Heads, who ranged from basketball star Bill Walton and U.S. Senator Patrick Leahy to anonymous fans and followers who trailed the tours. These fans carried on some of the traditions of the 1960's by using hallucinogenic drugs, donning tie-dyed clothing, and rejecting the materialism of the society around them.

**Subsequent Events** In the 1970's, the Grateful Dead's concert popularity grew, forcing them into larger venues and compelling them to develop a massive sound system dubbed "the Wall." The group stopped touring in 1974, then resumed in 1976, eventually becoming one of the top concert draws in the United States. In 1977, the band released *The Grateful Dead Movie*, footage of performances at San Francisco's Winterland Auditorium in 1974. In 1987, the Grateful Dead had a top-ten hit, "Touch of Grey." That same year, their sixty-minute video, *So Far*, was a top-selling music video. McKernan died in 1973, and in 1995, after Garcia died of heart failure, the group disbanded.

**Additional Information** A thorough chronicle of the group's first twenty years is Blair Jackson's *Grateful Dead: The Music Never Stopped* (1983). *Grateful Dead: The Official Book of the Dead Heads* (1983), edited by Paul Grushkin, combines photos and anecdotes with a list of more than twenty years of concert dates and places.

*Bill Knight*

**See also** Be-ins and Love-ins; Counterculture; *Electric Kool-Aid Acid Test, The*; Haight-Ashbury; Hippies; Jefferson Airplane; LSD; San Francisco as Cultural Mecca; Summer of Love.

# ■ Great Society Programs

*A term coined by Lyndon B. Johnson to describe and promote his agenda and vision for the nation. His attempt to realize changes was manifested in more than two hundred pieces of enacted federal legislation.*

Lyndon B. Johnson first used the phrase "Great Society" to describe his domestic agenda in a commencement speech delivered at the University of Michigan on May 22, 1964. In his inaugural address in 1965, Johnson spelled out his vision of the United States as a "great society" and challenged the American public to address society's most pressing social, economic, educational, and environmental concerns. His vision was to be achieved by assigning each problem to a specific presidential task force that develop a solution. This approach meant that Great Society programs would be implemented as they were developed rather than as part of a grand strategic plan.

Much of the welfare-oriented legislation that Johnson proposed followed in the tradition established by Franklin D. Roosevelt's New Deal and Harry S Truman's Fair Deal. Johnson's civil rights legislation built upon modest antidiscrimination laws passed in 1957 and 1960. In civil rights, welfare, and several other areas, the scope of activity initiated by the Johnson administration far surpassed the activity of any other administration.

The bulk of Johnson's legislative program was passed after his landslide election to the presidential office in 1964. As a result of the coattails effect produced by his decisive victory, the Democratic Party added to its majority in both the House and Senate, and Congress was sympathetic to Johnson's programs. Johnson's tendency to use consensus building—ensuring that all major interest groups affected by a certain policy received some benefit—also helped minimize opposition. For example, the Food Stamp Act of 1964, besides helping low-income families buy food, purchased surplus crops from U.S. farmers and included higher support prices for other crops. In this way, Johnson attempted to ensure that the poor would be fed and farmers would be fairly compensated.

**Civil Rights and Voting** The first significant piece of civil rights legislation was originally proposed by President John F. Kennedy. After Kennedy's assassination, President Johnson worked with fellow Democrats Senator Hubert Humphrey and Attorney General Robert F. Kennedy to secure passage of this legislation. However, the bill stalled in the Senate when southern Democrats initiated a filibuster on March 26, 1964, to prevent a final vote on the measure. Because the northern Democrats did not have enough votes for cloture (a parliamentary device that would end a filibuster), Johnson was forced to

turn to the Senate minority leader, Everett Dirksen, for support. In exchange for his efforts, Dirksen was given full credit for the passage of the Civil Rights Act of 1964. The act, signed into law on July 2, forbid discrimination in regard to race, color, religion, sex, or national origin.

However, the 1964 Civil Rights Act had little impact on voting rights. By 1965, this deficiency was obvious, and calls for additional federal legislation rang out. In March, 1965, violence surrounding a civil rights march from Selma to Montgomery, Alabama, received national television coverage. Johnson responded by proposing new voting rights legislation in one of the most moving speeches of his presidency. Johnson successfully secured passage of the Voting Rights Act of 1965 using the coalition created with Dirksen. This act created federal examiners who would determine if a person was qualified to vote, abolished literacy tests required of voters, and provided federal monitoring of registration and voting.

**Poverty and Health** One of the most significant pieces of legislation in fighting the War on Poverty was the Economic Opportunity Act of 1964. It was designed to eliminate poverty by creating employment opportunities through education and training. This law created the Office of Economic Opportunity (OEO), initially headed by R. Sargent Shriver, a holdover from the Kennedy administration who became Johnson's chief adviser on poverty in the United States. The OEO created a number of innovative programs, including the Community Action Programs (CAP), which included funding for job training, legal counseling, health care, housing, welfare reform, and education. CAP was designed to empower community groups by providing them with grants and by requiring that the poor be represented on local planning boards. Other programs initiated by the OEO included the Job Corps, Volunteers in Service to America (VISTA, a domestic version of the Peace Corps), college work-study jobs, and neighborhood health centers.

Health care was extended to Americans age sixty-five and older in 1965 when Medicare legislation was enacted. This legislation also included Medicaid, which provided health care coverage for individuals on welfare. Both programs were funded by the Social Security payroll tax.

**Education** A major focus of Johnson's Great Society program was improving education. A task force appointed by President Kennedy recommended increased federal support for nursery, elementary, and secondary schools in impoverished areas. In response, the OEO created Head Start, a community action preschool program in 1965.

The Elementary and Secondary Education Act of 1965 authorized more than one billion dollars in grants to impoverished school districts to pay for more teachers, textbooks, and new buildings. The goal was to equalize educational opportunities for children from low-income families, which it did on a limited basis, although it also provided newly allocated federal funds to middle-class communities.

Colleges and universities were also supported by the Higher Education Act of 1965 and the National Defense Education Act of 1965. The former provided grants to libraries and insured college student loans, and the latter financed increased enrollments in undergraduate and graduate schools. This legislation did little to fight poverty, but it provided unprecedented opportunities for the middle class and strengthened colleges and universities.

**Housing** One of Johnson's goals was to enable impoverished people to live in better housing. The Housing and Urban Development Act of 1965 created the Department of Housing and Urban Development (HUD), which oversaw the Federal Housing Administration, Urban Renewal Administration, and Public Housing Administration. The act's provisions included rent supplements and low-interest and no-down-payment mortgages designed to help lower-income families purchase housing. Three years later, Congress passed the Housing and Urban Development Act of 1968, which provided funds for the construction of millions of new homes and apartments to replace substandard dwellings. Unlike the Model Cities Act of 1966, which funded city development projects but got bogged down in squabbles between federal and local agencies, the 1968 housing act was successful in providing improved housing to many low- and middle-income people.

**Environment** Many of the Great Society's environmental policies were guided through Congress by Senator Edmund Muskie of Maine, who introduced water and air pollution control legislation. The Water Pollution Control Authority, created in 1965 by the Water Quality Act, established federal standards for water treatment facilities. The Clean Water Restoration Act of 1966 increased federal aid for sewage treatment plants and provided grants for pollution control programs for the nation's rivers and lakes. After a number of delays caused by the automobile industry, the Motor Vehicle Air Pollution Act of 1965 added federal controls for motor vehicle emissions to existing clear air legislation. The Air Quality Act of 1967 strengthened these federal standards and provided funding for fuel combustion research.

**Impact** The success of the Great Society programs was limited because of the relatively limited funding the programs received. Though authorized to spend tens of billions of dollars on various programs, Congress appropriated only a fraction of this amount. This gap was caused by pressures to finance the United States' growing involvement in the Vietnam War and intensified by Johnson's reluctance to ask Congress for a tax increase to pay for the war effort. Johnson did seek a tax surcharge in 1967, but his bill died in committee. It became increasingly clear that the nation could not afford both guns and butter.

Although the Great Society programs failed to end poverty in the United States, they did alleviate many of the problems faced by the nation's poor by taking a multifaceted approach. The federal government's regulatory role increased markedly as it took responsibility for the well-being of the nation's poor, elderly, consumers, and students and for the state of the environment and cities. The number of programs and the amount of aid transferred by the federal government to states, localities, and community organizations more than doubled.

In civil rights, federal intervention changed the face of southern society and politics by ending legal segregation and by ensuring that African Americans were allowed to vote. In addition, Johnson issued an executive order in 1965 requiring that federal contractors adopt affirmative action hiring guidelines. The urban riots of 1967 and 1968 drew attention to the economic and housing problems of city-dwelling African Americans, and these problems were addressed by a provision in the Civil Rights Act of 1968 that outlawed housing discrimination. Through these policies, the legal status of African Americans was secured in a relatively short period of time.

**Subsequent Events** During the 1980's and 1990's, many of the Great Society programs were reassessed. In 1994, the Republican Party captured control of both chambers of Congress for the first time in forty years. One of the principal components of the Contract with America, the platform upon which many House Republicans were elected, was the promise to reform the welfare system. In 1995, Congress passed the Welfare Reform Act, which transferred much of the responsibility for determining welfare eligibility and benefits to the states. States responded in various ways, some opting to reform as others attempted to disassemble many of the Great Society programs.

**Additional Information**  A number of biographies of Johnson address his vision of a great society, including Doris Kearns's *Lyndon Johnson and the American Dream* (1976) and Paul K. Conkin's *Big Daddy from the Pedernadales: Lyndon Baines Johnson* (1986). His War on Poverty is described in James T. Patterson's *America's Struggle Against Poverty, 1900-1980* (1981) and in John Morton Blum's *Years of Discord: American Politics and Society, 1961-1974.*

*Joseph R. Marbach*

**See also**  Air Pollution; Civil Rights Act of 1964; Civil Rights Act of 1968; Economic Opportunity Act of 1964; Food Stamp Program; Head Start; Higher Education Act; Housing Laws, Federal; Job Corps; Johnson, Lyndon B.; March on Selma; Medicare; Motor Vehicle Air Pollution Act of 1965; Urban Renewal; Voting Rights Legislation; War on Poverty; Water Pollution; Welfare State.

---

# ■ Greenwich Village

*A neighborhood in lower Manhattan known since the early twentieth century as a home to eccentrics, artists, and social reformers. In the 1960's, "the Village" was home to some of the most vital artistic activity in New York City.*

Greenwich Village got its name in pre-Revolutionary War years when the British took over New York from the Dutch. It developed sporadically in the eighteenth and nineteenth centuries, escaping the symmetrical grid street plan that dominates the rest of Manhattan. By 1910, Greenwich Village's low rents, lively ethnic life, and growing spirit of tolerance attracted the artists, writers, and political radicals who gave the Village its unique cultural ambience.

By 1960, the rise of the Beat generation, the raffish coffeehouse culture, and the proliferation of small, intimate theaters had set the stage for some of the 1960's most important radical cultural movements.

No art form in Greenwich Village in the 1960's

was more dynamic or varied than theater. Joseph Papp founded both the New York Shakespeare in the Park festivals and the Public Theater in Greenwich Village, two institutions of tremendous influence in the life of the city. Other pioneers include Judith Malina and Julian Beck, founders of the Living Theater; Al Carmines, director of the Judson Poets' Theater; and Off-Off-Broadway, Joe Cino of the Caffe Cino, and Ellen Stewart, founder of the Café La Mama. Playwrights who got their start in the 1960's in Greenwich Village include Edward Albee, LeRoi Jones (Amiri Baraka), Arthur Kopit, Sam Shepard, John Guare, and Lanford Wilson. Happenings and various forms of street theater added further color to the avant-garde scene.

In music and dance, avant-garde composer John Cage and choreographer Merce Cunningham continued their history of individual and collaborative achievement. In addition to composing, Cage was an influential teacher and writer. The Merce Cunningham Dance Company studio produced experimental works with Cage, David Tudor, and painters such as Robert Rauschenberg and Jasper Johns. Cunningham protégé Robert Dunn founded the innovative Judson Dance Theater. Bob Dylan brought his unique folk style to MacDougal Street in 1961, and jazz greats Thelonius Monk, Charles Mingus, and John Coltrane explored new paths at Max Gordon's Village Vanguard.

A visible and long-lasting social movement associated with Greenwich Village in the 1960's was the gay rights movement. In the 1960's, gay and lesbian groups began to fight official and unofficial harassment in and out of the courts. The most dramatic moment in this struggle was the Stonewall Inn riots on Christopher Street in 1969. Subsequently, the Gay Liberation Front was organized, and the first annual Lesbian and Gay Pride Parade took place in June, 1970.

*The Village Voice*, which featured Norman Mailer and Jules Fieffer among its contributors, and the *East Village Other* chronicled the political and artistic activities of the era.

**Impact**  Always friendly to nonconformity, individualism, and experiment in life and the arts, in the 1960's, Greenwich Village had a special energy and synergy that fostered free, mobile interaction between individuals and groups stretching the boundaries in art, music, and cultural politics.

**Additional Information** Sally Banes's *Greenwich Village 1963* (1993) provides an excellent overview of the topic.

*Roger J. Stilling*

**See also** Albee, Edward; Art Movements; Beat Generation; East Village; Gay Liberation Movement; Minimalism; Stonewall Inn Riots; Theater; Theater of the Absurd.

---

# ■ Gregory, Dick

**Born** October 12, 1932, St. Louis, Missouri

*A stand-up comedian who promoted civil rights causes in his nightclub acts and college speeches before becoming a prominent civil rights activist. Gregory's involvement in the Civil Rights movement, antiwar campaign, and political arena won him national acclaim.*

**Early Life** Richard Claxton "Dick" Gregory was born and raised in a poor neighborhood in St. Louis, Missouri, where he often shined shoes to help sup-

*Comedian and civil rights and antiwar activist Dick Gregory raises his arms in a peace gesture as he addresses protesters on Moratorium Day in 1969. (Archive Photos)*

port his family. After attending Sumner High School, where he set state track records, Gregory entered Southern Illinois University in 1951. After two years in the U.S. Army, he returned to college from 1955 to 1956 and began working at a post office in Chicago. This job was short-lived because of his amusing antics and impersonations of coworkers. Using these talents, Gregory began a career as a stand-up comedian. He performed in several nightclubs in Illinois before making guest appearances on national television shows. In 1959, he married Lillian Smith. Later, they had ten children.

**The 1960's** In his acts, Gregory used racial satire to emphasize negative and contradictory aspects of racial segregation. Prompted by Dr. Martin Luther King, Jr., Gregory became a full-time civil rights activist and participated in many nonviolent demonstrations and antiwar protests.

In 1965, Gregory was shot while attempting to prevent looting after the Watts riot in Los Angeles. A year later, he joined other civil rights leaders in completing a 220-mile freedom walk from Memphis, Tennessee, to Jackson, Mississippi, begun by James H. Meredith, the African American student who integrated the University of Mississippi in 1962. Meredith, who had planned a solo march, was shot and wounded by a white gunman on June 6, one day after beginning his march.

Gregory is widely known for his active involvement in antiwar campaigns. Although his role in teach-ins and seminars was significant, he attracted national attention with two prolonged fasts in protest of the United States' increased involvement in the Vietnam War. In 1967, he fasted for forty days and, in 1968, for forty-seven days.

Gregory's activism embraced many arenas. In 1967, he ran as a write-in candidate against incumbent Richard Daley for Chicago's mayoral seat. A year later, he spoke on one hundred fifty college campuses and became the presidential nominee for the Peace and Freedom Party. Gregory demonstrated his support for peace by attending the World Assembly of Peace meeting held in East Germany in 1969. He wrote several books whose content often reflected civil rights issues. Titles included *Nigger: An Autobiography* (1964), *What's Happening* (1965), *The Shadow that Scares Me* (1968), and *Write Me In!* (1968).

**Later Life** By the 1970's, Gregory had ended his career as a nightclub entertainer and devoted himself to lecturing on college campuses across the nation. He continued to write politically charged books such as *Up from Nigger* (1976), *Code Name Zorro: The Murder of Martin Luther King, Jr.* (1977), and *Dick Gregory's Bible Tales, with Commentary* (1974). He also started his own business after publishing *Dick Gregory's Natural Diet for Folks Who Eat: Cooking with Mother Nature* (1983). He publicly promoted health and nutrition nationwide. His ventures in these two areas were extremely successful as his line of Bahamian dietary and natural food products were widely sold. In 1989, Gregory constructed drug and alcohol rehabilitation centers in Missouri and Louisiana.

**Impact** Gregory's ability to present the horrors of segregated life and racial discrimination in an amusing manner helped spread civil rights causes all over the country. His personal sacrifices as a civil rights activist and antiwar protester provide useful models of protest for future generations. Over a twelve-year span, he was jailed twenty times for his participation in demonstrations.

**Subsequent Events** Gregory's activism continued in the 1990's. In 1996, he was arrested outside the headquarters of the Central Intelligence Agency (CIA) while protesting against charges that the CIA's Contra armies in Nicaragua shipped tons of cocaine into Southern California. That same year, he joined several demonstrators in a fast to repeal welfare-restricting legislation.

**Additional Information** *Nigger: An Autobiography* (1964) chronicles Gregory's life and activism. An insightful discussion of Gregory's involvement in civil rights protests is presented in *We Shall Overcome: The Civil Rights Movement in the United States in the 1950's and 1960's* (1989).

*Phyllis M. Jones-Shuler*

**See also** Carmichael, Stokely; Civil Rights Movement; Watts Riot.

# ■ Griffith-Paret Fight

**Date** March 24, 1962

*A nationally televised championship fight between welterweight champion Benny Paret and former champion Emile Griffith ended in tragedy when Paret was knocked unconscious and died ten days later.*

*The referee holds back Emile Griffith as Benny "Kid" Paret slumps to the canvas in Madison Square Garden in New York during the welterweight championship match. Griffith regained the title, and Paret died ten days later. (AP/Wide World Photos)*

Benny "Kid" Paret became the world's welterweight boxing champion in May, 1960, only to lose the title to Emile Griffith the next year. In a rematch, Paret defeated Griffith in a close decision and regained the championship. A much-publicized third fight was scheduled for March 24, 1962. Three months before the nationally televised fight, Paret was severely beaten in a match with Gene Fullmer; only three weeks before the event, featherweight champion Davey Moore died from injuries received in a televised fight. During the twelfth round of the rematch, Griffith knocked out Paret with a flurry of twenty-five furious and mostly unanswered blows. Paret was pinned on the ropes so that he could not fall, and he took many hits before the referee stopped the fight. Paret was taken from the ring on a stretcher and died ten days later without regaining consciousness.

**Impact** The fight provoked national concern about the future of boxing, including calls for greater controls on the sport. Griffith recovered from his role in the tragedy and was named fighter of the year in 1964; he was later inducted into the Boxing Hall of Fame.

**Additional Information** For a discussion of the moral implications of Paret's death in the ring, see Norman Cousins's essay entitled "Who Killed Benny Paret?" in the May 5, 1962, issue of the *Saturday Review*.

*Joe Blankenbaker*

**See also** Ali, Muhammad (Cassius Clay); Liston, Sonny; Patterson, Floyd; Sports.

---

# ■ Griswold v. Connecticut

*Supreme Court case that in 1965 established a constitutional right to privacy. The case would later be cited as authority for the right of minors and unmarried individuals to use contraceptives and the right of women to terminate unwanted pregnancies.*

An 1879 Connecticut law made it a criminal offense to use any type of birth control in the state. The statute had been unsuccessfully challenged twice before the Planned Parenthood League of Connecticut decided to appeal the conviction of its executive director, Estelle T. Griswold, and its medical director, Dr. Charles Lee Buxton, for violating the anticontraceptive legislation by opening a birth control clinic in New Haven in 1961.

This time, the United States Supreme Court agreed to consider the constitutionality of the Connecticut statute. Griswold and Buxton, the Court declared, had standing to sue because of their professional relationship with the persons whose rights (patrons of the clinic) were at issue. Thomas I. Emerson, the appellants' attorney, argued before the Court that the law abridged both his clients' and their patients' right to liberty without due process of law, in violation of the Fourteenth Amendment. Additionally, he argued that the Ninth Amendment protected privacy as one of the unenumerated rights retained by the people. Privacy was, therefore, one of the fundamental rights guaranteed by the Bill of Rights.

On June 7, 1965, the Court voted seven to two to strike down the Connecticut law. Writing for the Court, Justice William O. Douglas, while admitting that the Constitution did not spell out a right to privacy, nevertheless proclaimed that, "specific guarantees [in the Bill of Rights] . . . have penumbras, formed by emanations from those guarantees that

help give them life and substance." Just as the Court had earlier found that the First Amendment right to freedom of speech extends to protect freedom of association, so Douglas found, do the First, Third, Fourth, Fifth, and Ninth Amendments imply that there are "zones of privacy" protected by the Constitution.

In separate concurring opinions, Justice Arthur Goldberg supported the theory that the Fourteenth Amendment incorporated into the Constitution additional rights—such as the right to privacy—"so rooted in the traditions and conscience of our people as to be ranked fundamental," while Justices John M. Harlan and Byron White argued that the Connecticut law violated basic values "implicit in the concept of ordered liberty."

**Impact** *Griswold v. Connecticut* was a landmark case because it invested an unenumerated right with constitutional status. The activist Court headed by Chief Justice Earl Warren helped bring about enormous social change in the 1960's by such means, and it has been theorized that this case sparked the sexual revolution that was one of the hallmarks of the era.

**Subsequent Events** The most important outgrowth of *Griswold v. Connecticut* has proven to be *Roe v. Wade* (1973), in which the Court, citing the constitutional right to privacy, upheld a woman's right to abortion. Also, in *Carey v. Population Services International* (1977), *Griswold* served as precedent for upholding the right of unmarried persons to purchase contraceptives.

**Additional Information** *The Right to Privacy: Essays and Cases* (1976), edited by Allan Dionisopolous and Craig Ducat, provides an excellent overview of the issues surrounding *Griswold v. Connecticut*.

*Lisa Paddock*

**See also** Abortion; Sexual Revolution; Supreme Court Decisions; Warren, Earl.

---

# ■ Gross National Product (GNP)

*The dollar value of all final goods and services produced in the economy. The gross national product measures economic activity in a country.*

Following a slump in economic activity beginning in 1957, the 1960's opened with a mild economic recession. The slump lasted from April, 1960, to February, 1961. This downturn in economic activity, in which real gross national product (GNP) declined by 7.2 percent, lasted ten months and corresponded with a peak unemployment rate of 7.1 percent. The downturn was not considered severe and lasted the typical length of time for a post-World War II recession.

During most of the 1960's, the growth rate of the GNP was positive and strong. The 1960's were a boom period (a period of rapid expansion of economic activity). The expansion can be attributed to increases in government spending, changes in tax policies, and the monetary policy pursued by the Federal Reserve System.

In 1961, government expenditures increased. This expanded the economy (boosted GNP) by putting more money in the hands of consumers. In the mid-1960's, continued growth in government spending, including expenditures for President Lyndon B. Johnson's War on Poverty, helped to prolong the expansion. In mid-1965, the escalation of the Vietnam War led to rapid rises in spending on the military, further expanding the economy.

The growth in GNP during the 1960's can also be attributed to changes in the tax code and federal income tax cuts. In 1962, revisions of tax laws to encourage investment led to increased purchases of new equipment, contributing to employment and GNP expansion. In March, 1964, a federal income tax cut was passed, leaving consumers with increased incomes and contributing to economic expansion.

Finally, Federal Reserve monetary policy contributed to the economic boom of the 1960's. During 1961 to 1966, the Federal Reserve enlarged the money supply by a mildly expansionary 3.1 percent per year. Money-supply growth was halted briefly and then increased for the remainder of the decade. Expanding the money supply put more money into the economy, allowing greater economic expansion.

**Impact** Economic growth in the 1960's due to fiscal policy (changes in taxes and government spending) and monetary policy (Federal Reserve-initiated changes in the money supply) instilled confidence in those who favored active government intervention to stabilize the economy and prevent recessions and inflation. Many people believed, based on the experiences of the 1960's, that the government could control the economy through active fiscal policy.

The growth of the GNP and the apparent success of fiscal policy during the 1960's also contributed to a general optimism. Many of the social and economic changes during the decade came about because of the economic boom people were experiencing.

**Subsequent Events** The economy experienced a recession during the first half of the 1970's. Confidence in the ability of government to regulate the economy came into question, and the optimistic view of the economy held by many individuals through the 1960's began to change.

**Additional Information** Discussion of the economy during the 1960's can be found in *Presidential Economics* (1984), by Herbert Stein.

*Margaret A. Ray*

**See also** Business and the Economy; Inflation; Prosperity and Poverty; Unemployment; War on Poverty.

---

# ■ *Guess Who's Coming to Dinner*

**Released** 1967
**Director** Stanley Kramer (1913-     )

*The most popular Hollywood film to tackle the subject of interracial marriage. This film sought to assuage white, liberal fears of racial integration and the widening generation gap.*

**The Work** *Guess Who's Coming to Dinner* chronicles a pivotal day in the life of an interracial couple, Dr. John Prentice (Sidney Poitier) and Joanna "Joey" Drayton (Katharine Houghton). John and Joey, who met and fell in love in Hawaii, arrive in San Francisco to ask for Joey's parents' blessing before flying to Geneva, Switzerland, to be married. Twenty-one-year-old Joey naively assumes that her upper-middle-class, liberal parents will have no objection to the relationship, but she soon learns otherwise. Although initially shocked, Joey's mother, Christina (Katherine Hepburn), quickly comes to share her daughter's excitement; however, her irascible father, Matt (Spencer Tracy), views John with anxiety and suspicion. Sensing this, John privately informs the Draytons that he will end the relationship if they do not approve. The rest of the day, Matt wrestles with his fear, hypocrisy, and racism, struggling to come to terms with the impact of an interracial marriage on his family and society at large.

To add to the drama, Joey has invited the Prentices to dinner. The Prentices assume that Joey is

*Joey (Katharine Houghton) introduces her fiancé, John, (Sidney Poitier) to her father (Spencer Tracy) in the 1967 film* Guess Who's Coming to Dinner, *a popular film that looked at interracial marriage.* (Museum of Modern Art/Film Stills Archive)

African American, so when they arrive, the tension builds. John argues with his father (Roy E. Glenn, Sr.), who vehemently opposes the match. Christina and John's mother (Beah Richards) fear that their husbands' disapproval will destroy the couple.

Joey, however, excitedly packs for Geneva, unaware that her future hangs in the balance. At last, Matt assembles everyone in the living room to announce his decision. With pent-up emotion, he declares that he does not object to the marriage and hopes John and Joey's love is strong enough to overcome the hurdles they will face. Having given his blessing to the union, Matt escorts the still grumbling Mr. Prentice, the relieved wives, and the happy couple into the dining room for the long-awaited dinner.

**Impact** Amid widespread social upheaval and militant calls for civil and economic rights for African

Americans, the melodramatic *Guess Who's Coming to Dinner* with its sentimental aura and well-known stars made racial integration palatable to a white, middle-class audience. John and Joey's union reinforces rather than threatens the social order. Poitier, an established symbol of integration, plays the perfect man—an extremely successful Harvard-educated doctor—who just happens to be African American. Joey, innocent and unable to see race as a problem between people, represents the idealism of 1960's youth. The Draytons and the Prentices are the older generation, bewildered and frightened by the rapid pace of social change but able to adapt given time. Although the Draytons find their liberal principles tested, they ultimately live up to them. Despite the refusal of many southern theaters to show the film, it was a popular and critical success. Hepburn won an Oscar for Best Actress and the film won the Best Screenplay Award.

**Related Work** *In the Heat of the Night* (1967), also starring Poitier, dealt with race relations in the South.

**Additional Information** *A Special Kind of Magic* (1967), by Roy Newquist, chronicles the making of the film and includes interviews and candid photos taken on the set.

*Cynthia Young*

**See also** Civil Rights Movement; Film; *In the Heat of the Night*; Interracial Marriage Laws.

---

# ■ Guevara, Che

**Born** June 14, 1928, Rosario, Argentina
**Died** October 9, 1967, La Higuera, Bolivia

*Argentine-born Marxist revolutionary and companion of Cuban leader Fidel Castro. Guevara's romantic career, ideals, and dramatic end made him a major icon for radical movements of the 1960's.*

**Early Life** The offspring of upper-middle-class parents with leftist leanings, Ernesto "Che" Guevara de la Serna displayed adventurous traits as a youngster. After receiving a medical degree, Guevara took an extended tour through Latin America, eventually reaching Mexico City in 1955. There, he joined Cuban revolutionary Fidel Castro, who was preparing to overthrow the dictatorship of Fulgencio Batista. Guevara, who now went by the Argentine nickname of "Che," served Castro's guerrilla movement with distinction during its two-year struggle, earning the rank of major. In January, 1959, the new revolutionary regime made Guevara a Cuban citizen.

**The 1960's** From 1959 to 1965, Guevara held ministerial posts in economic planning and finance and undertook foreign diplomatic and commercial missions for the revolutionary government. Next to Castro, "El Che" was the regime's most prominent personality. In addition, the Argentine physician turned Cuban revolutionary wrote classic treatises on revolutionary guerrilla warfare that projected the successful Cuban model of armed struggle based in the countryside on other Latin American countries.

In March, 1965, Guevara suddenly disappeared from public view, not to resurface until his capture and death two and one-half years later. After an unsuccessful revolutionary venture in Africa, Guevara took up his dream of establishing an insurrectionary center in the Andean region of South America. Captured following a skirmish on October 8,

*After his death in 1967, Cuban revolutionary Che Guevara became a cult figure and popular hero for rebels and revolutionaries throughout the world.* (Archive Photos)

1967, the wounded guerrilla chief was executed the next day and his burial site kept secret.

**Impact** After his death, Guevara became a popular hero and legendary symbol for rebellious youth and revolutionary sympathizers throughout the world. The Cuban regime set forth "El Che" as a model for school children to emulate for his idealism, revolutionary dedication, and courage in giving his life for the cause of uplifting exploited peasants and workers. In the United States, New Left groups and black militants of the 1960's adopted Guevara as a cult figure and symbol; his likeness appeared on demonstrators' banners and lapel pins and decorated many apartment walls.

**Subsequent Events** Guevara maintained his cult hero status in Cuba and the outside world into the late 1990's. The revolutionary continued to be a subject for books and Hollywood films, including the 1996 motion picture version of the famous Broadway musical *Evita*, starring Madonna and Antonio Banderas. Ironically, capitalist marketers have exploited Guevara's image to sell compact discs, watches, and beer to rebellious American youth. In early July, 1997, Guevara's secret burial site was found. His body was moved to a mausoleum in Santa Clara, Cuba, where Guevara led Cuban guerrillas to a decisive victory in 1958.

**Additional Information**  Consult *Che: The Making of a Legend* (1969), by Martin Ebon, for a relevant but hostile biographical treatment and Hans Koning's *The Future of Che Guevara* (1971) for a more sympathetic view. A more recent look at the revolutionary's life can be found in Jorge G. Castaneda's *Companero: The Life and Death of Che Guevara* (1997).

*David A. Crain*

**See also**  Castro, Fidel.

## ■ Gulf of Tonkin Incident

**Date** August 2-4, 1964

*An attack and an alleged attack by North Vietnamese torpedo boats on U.S. destroyers off the coast of North Vietnam. These incidents were used by President Lyndon B. Johnson to obtain the Gulf of Tonkin Resolution, which became the legal basis for U.S. military involvement in Vietnam.*

**Origins and History**  Early in his administration, President Lyndon B. Johnson had decided that South Vietnam's survival required increased U.S. military involvement. In preparation, U.S. military and Central Intelligence Agency (CIA) forces began two covert operations in the Tonkin Gulf off the coast of North Vietnam, code-named DeSoto (an electronic reconnaissance mission conducted by U.S. naval forces) and 34A (CIA-trained commando hit-and-run attacks against North Vietnamese island and shore installations). Though ostensibly separate operations, U.S. naval commanders also monitored and responded to 34A actions. One such operation, hit-and-run attacks against the North Vietnamese offshore islands of Hon Me and Hon Ngu on the night of July 30-31, resulted in the U.S. destroyer *Maddox* being sent on a reconnaissance mission into the Tonkin Gulf near these islands. Two days later, the *Maddox* encountered the enemy.

**The Incidents**  On August 2, North Vietnamese torpedo boats from Hon Me unsuccessfully attacked the *Maddox* and then fled. The *Maddox* also withdrew. This confirmed attack is referred to as the "first incident." U.S. officials responded by ordering the *Maddox* and a second destroyer, the *C. Turner Joy*, to return to the gulf and resume operations. On August 2-3, while the destroyers patrolled, 34A operations continued and included an August 2 bombing of North Vietnamese villages and an August 3 guerrilla commando raid. Meanwhile, on August 3, the two destroyers made runs toward the North Vietnamese coast, coming within eight miles of shore. On the night of August 4, in bad weather, low clouds, and darkness, the destroyers claimed their radar had picked up high-speed attacking vessels and that they were under torpedo attack. This attack, referred to as the "second incident," remains unconfirmed and probably never happened. Hours after the initial report, FLASH messages from the *Maddox* arrived in Washington, D.C., indicating that overeager sonar operators and the effects of bad weather on sonar and radar had led to error. Moreover, the *Maddox*'s commander, Captain John J. Herrick, admitted that no visual sightings of enemy vessels or weaponry had occurred.

President Johnson, held hostage by his domestic reform program and by election-year politics, saw in these incidents an opportunity to increase the United States' military commitment in Vietnam and to silence Republican presidential candidate Barry Goldwater's criticism of Johnson's foreign policy. On August 5, Johnson declared the incidents to have been "deliberate attacks" and "open aggression on the high seas," and he sent Congress the text of a resolution actually drawn up two months earlier that would allow him officially to commit U.S. forces in Vietnam. In explaining the Gulf of Tonkin incidents to a Senate hearing on August 6, Secretary of Defense Robert McNamara claimed that the North Vietnamese attacks were unprovoked, that the United States had not been engaged in any recent attacks on North Vietnam, and that the destroyers were there for defensive purposes only. Such statements were at best disingenuous, since McNamara had approved the DeSota and 34A operations.

On August 7, Congress, with only two dissenting votes—Senators Ernest Gruening and Wayne Morse—passed the Gulf of Tonkin Resolution, which allowed Johnson to take "all necessary measures to repel any armed attacks against the forces of the United States and to prevent further aggression" and to defend any Southeast Asia Treaty Organization member.

**Impact** Although no evidence exists suggesting Johnson and McNamara engineered the incidents, their less than candid reporting of events later led many members of Congress and the general public to feel that they were misled. By the late 1960's, journalist I. F. Stone and others had begun calling the incidents a hoax, which contributed to the Johnson administration's growing "credibility gap." Many people believed that if the government had misled the nation about the Tonkin Gulf incidents, it might be less than honest about the events of the Vietnam War. This distrust of the U.S. government greatly aided the antiwar movement. Certainly the administrations of Johnson and Richard M. Nixon had used the Gulf of Tonkin Resolution as the basis for escalating military operations in Vietnam, and Nixon even invoked the resolution to justify his invasion of Cambodia. In December, 1970, Congress repealed the resolution. To prevent future presidential misuse of U.S. military power, Congress passed the War Powers Act in 1973.

**Additional Information** Edwin E. Moïse's *Tonkin Gulf and the Escalation of the Vietnam War* (1996) and Robert McNamara's *In Retrospect: The Tragedy and Lessons of the Vietnam War* (1995) provide two perspectives on the Gulf of Tonkin incident.

*Ken Millen-Penn*

**See also** Cold War; McNamara, Robert; Vietnam War.

# H

## ■ Haight-Ashbury

*Twenty-five-block district near Golden Gate Park in San Francisco, California, known as the birthplace of hippies. Haight-Ashbury became a cultural center attracting young people who were searching for a way of life different from that of their parents.*

During the early 1900's, the Haight-Ashbury district contained many lavish homes built by local politicians. By the 1940's, the district's glamour had subsided considerably. After World War II, several local

*The Haight-Ashbury district of San Francisco, first a mecca for hippies, became overcrowded and over commercialized, and by 1970 had turned into a dangerous slum.* (AP/Wide World Photos)

groups attempted to reestablish its former splendor, but their efforts were largely unsuccessful. By the early 1960's, the Haight-Ashbury district offered attractive housing at extremely modest prices. This combination proved irresistible to a bohemian community consisting of Beatniks and other nonconformists.

The first hint that something noteworthy was occurring in Haight-Ashbury was provided by the September 6, 1965, *San Francisco Examiner.* On that day, the newspaper published an article entitled, "A New Haven for Beatniks," in which the reporter referred to the local residents as "hippies." The thrust of the article was that the 1950's Beatniks—and the rebellious nonconformity that they symbolized—had not just faded away; instead, the members of the Beat generation had relocated to Haight-Ashbury and magically transformed themselves.

The "new rebels" in Haight-Ashbury were young people who were part of the leading edge of the baby-boom generation (people born between 1946 and 1964), which represented a sizable segment of the U.S. population. By 1965, half of the people in the United States were under age thirty. Young people gravitated toward the Haight-Ashbury district because the area not only tolerated alternative ways of living but also actively encouraged them.

The "magic transformations" occurring in Haight-Ashbury were primarily fueled by one drug: LSD (lysergic acid diethylamide or acid). LSD is classified as a psychedelic or mind-altering drug because it affects the brain's capacity to process sensory impressions. Among the psychedelic effects attributed to the drug are its ability to heighten the vividness of colors and to distort the clarity of sounds. For many residents of Haight-Ashbury, LSD was a quick way to discover "reality uncensored." According to proponents of the drug, the insights provided by LSD transformed any individual into a more loving, caring, and understanding human being.

Several Haight-Ashbury endeavors developed around the use of LSD. Acid rock and psychedelic-tinged groups, such as the Grateful Dead and Jefferson Airplane, were keystones of the Haight-Ashbury economy. The Grateful Dead, who lived at 710 Ashbury Street, epitomized the Haight-Ashbury experience. Their concerts seemed to duplicate the LSD experience by simultaneously employing rock music, sound distortion, and flashing strobe lights. The success enjoyed by the Grateful Dead and other groups encouraged many Haight-Ashbury residents to capitalize on related enterprises. Many exotic shops began to open in the Haight-Ashbury district. Merchants eventually formed their own association, the Hip Independent Proprietors (HIP). Businesses such as the Psychedelic Shop, the Blushing Peony, and the I/Thou Coffee Shop sold clothing, posters, books, incense, food, and drug paraphernalia. The new hippie businesses revived the Haight Street shopping district. By 1967, the Haight-Ashbury community was essentially self-contained in that all of the residents' needs—from music and clothing to medical treatment—could be satisfied within the district.

The Haight-Ashbury community began to disintegrate in 1967 because its popularity led to the inflow of too many people, too much media attention, and over-commercialization. Tourists clogged the district, rents escalated, and rapes, murders, and drug overdoses began to dominate the local news. Some of the early arrivals began to feel that the only thing left for the community was a proper burial, which took form as a Death of Hippie ceremony on October 6, 1967. A cardboard coffin was carried down Haight Street. The contents of the coffin included an effigy designated "Hippie" and copies of daily newspapers. All were consigned to fire in Golden Gate Park.

**Impact** The hippies of Haight-Ashbury represented only one aspect of the 1960's youth movement; however, they had a visible and auditory impact on American society during the decade. The Haight-Ashbury style influenced popular music and fashion. It promoted drug use and created a greater tolerance for alternative lifestyles. It even was adopted by professional advertising campaigns that wanted to capitalize on the large youth market. Perhaps the most lasting effect of the Haight-Ashbury experience was to demonstrate convincingly that the baby-boom generation would continue to influence American society.

**Subsequent Events** During the late 1960's, the Haight-Ashbury district became a dangerous, drug-infested slum. Through the efforts of local residents, the district rebounded during the mid-1970's, and Haight-Ashbury became a livable area again in the 1980's. The district's 1960's history and mystique were two of the prime reasons that the area was considered worthy of revitalization.

**Additional Information** A comprehensive history of the district is provided in Charles Perry's *The Haight-Ashbury: A History* (1984).

*Ernest Rigney, Jr.*

**See also** Death of Hippie; Flower Children; Grateful Dead; Hippies; Jefferson Airplane; LSD; San Francisco as Cultural Mecca.

---

# ■ *Hair*

**Produced** 1967
**Writers** Gerome Ragni (1942-1991), James Rado (1939-    ), and Galt MacDermot (1928-    )

*The musical that embodies hippie messages of peace, protest, and freedom. The show punctuates its loosely structured, presentational narrative with a rock music score and confronts almost every major social controversy of the late 1960's.*

**The Work** *Hair: The American Tribal Love-Rock Musical* premiered at the Public Theater on December 2, 1967 (producer Joseph Papp, director Gerald Freedman). On April 29, 1968, a fully rewritten, recast, and restaged *Hair* opened at the Biltmore Theater, Broadway (producer Michael Butler, director Tom O'Horgan). The show could vary with each performance and, as it toured, with each location. Actors frequently changed parts from performance to performance and made ad libs. The musical numbers evoke character traits, introduce issues, illustrate context, and set mood rather than advance a traditional story line. However, in the underlying narrative of the early Broadway version (generally considered the most "authentic"), Claude, the central character, faces induction into the military service the following morning and the likelihood that he will be sent to fight in Vietnam. He resolves not to go but burns his library card rather than his draft card. Claude's friend, the hedonistic Berger, urges him not to go. Romance complicates things: Claude loves New York University freshman peace protester Sheila, who loves Berger although he mistreats her; Jeanie, who is pregnant, loves Claude

*A young man jumps on a formal dining table in the 1979 film adaptation of the highly successful 1967 musical* Hair. *(Museum of Modern Art/Film Stills Archive)*

but sees that Claude loves Sheila and Berger; and Claude's friend Woof loves a Mick Jagger poster. At a be-in, the "tribe" members take drugs inspiring a hallucinogenic trip about war's absurdity. Later, at the induction station, they call for Claude's release. Claude, who approaches them in uniform, hair shorn ("Like it or not, they got me"), has become invisible to them. The tribe leads the audience in singing "Aquarius/Let the Sunshine In." Berger holds his drumsticks to form a glowing cross above Claude's corpse as the lights fade. The Grammy Award-winning score's thirty-two numbers include "Aquarius/Let the Sunshine In," "Good Morning Starshine," "Easy to Be Hard," and "Hair."

**Impact** *Hair* broke artistic barriers for Broadway and theater nationally. It was the first Broadway musical to use rock music, include full male and female nudity, and emerge from a production con-cept and collectively creative rehearsal process rather than a conventional script. It was also unusual because it moved to Broadway from off-Broadway, used a cast of nonstars (all young, many amateurs, and one-third African Americans), involved direct actor-audience interaction, drew youthful audiences through positive television (instead of newspaper) reviews, and deliberately embraced controversy. As cast member Lorrie Davis wrote, "*Hair* was different from other shows because what was happening on-stage was happening at that particular moment on the streets." What was happening included the hip-pie and peace movements, recreational use of psy-chedelic and other drugs, and rejection of conven-tional sexual morality (*Hair* made reference to interracial, gay/bisexual, nonmarital, and non-monogamous couplings) and fashion (*Hair* further popularized long hair for men and blue jeans). *Hair*'s backers won Supreme Court First Amendment battles to stage the show in Boston, Massachusetts, and Chattanooga, Tennessee. Ultimately, *Hair* was commercial and successful, totaling 1,750 Broadway performances, 14 national touring companies, and roughly 4 million tickets sold and $22 million grossed between 1968-1970.

**Additional Information** For a full critical and historical discussion, see *The Age of Hair: Evolution and Impact of Broadway's First Rock Musical* (1991), by Barbara Lee Horn, and for an original cast member's reminiscences, see *Letting Down My Hair: Two Years with the Love Rock Tribe—From Dawning to Downing of Aquarius* (1973), by Lorrie Davis with Rachel Gallagher.

*Ben Furnish*

**See also** Be-ins and Love-ins; *Boys in the Band, The*; Censorship; Hairstyles; Hippies; Music; *Oh, Calcutta!*; Rock Operas; Theater; *Tommy*.

# ■ Hairstyles

*A physical manifestation of rebellion among members of the youth culture. The 1960's began with button-down shirts, scrubbed faces, and crew cuts; it ended with tie-dyed shirts, bearded faces, and shaggy-dog hairstyles.*

In the early 1960's, the clean-cut image of President John F. Kennedy and his family was reflected in the hairstyles of the period, especially the bouffant hairdo of First Lady Jacqueline Kennedy. With the death of Camelot, however, longer hairstyles began to reflect the turmoil in the country, especially among disaffected youth.

The decade started with "big hair," best represented by the bouffant and the beehive, which were popular well into the middle of the 1960's despite being quite time-consuming. These styles were created by curling the hair on curlers, back-combing the hair with a rat-tail comb (to create height), lifting a smooth layer over the top of the rat's nest, and applying ample hair spray to keep the style in place. In the beehive, all the hair was pulled back, but in the bouffant, the lower part of the hair was simply curled. By the mid-1960's, women began to imitate the long, straight "natural" hairstyles of celebrities such as folksingers Joan Baez and Mary Travers of Peter, Paul and Mary; many ironed their hair to straighten it.

The popularity of the 1950's crew cut faded as men began to prefer a neat, well-styled haircut. To achieve this, many men stopped going to barbershops and instead frequented hairstyling salons that serviced both men and women. After the Beatles led the British invasion in 1964, mop-top haircuts like those favored by the group became popular, especially among the younger generation. The mod haircut, worn by such 1960's icons as the Rolling Stones and model Twiggy, became a symbol of rebellion and independence.

By 1967, the same year the musical *Hair* opened, the hippie movement peaked with the birth of an alternative society where hair—the longer the better—represented freedom from the responsibilities of convential adulthood. Men and women wore their hair in longer, "natural" styles, influenced by the back-to-nature attitudes of the flower children. Many men grew beards and mustaches. Many African American men and women symbolized their pride in being black by wearing their hair in an Afro, a

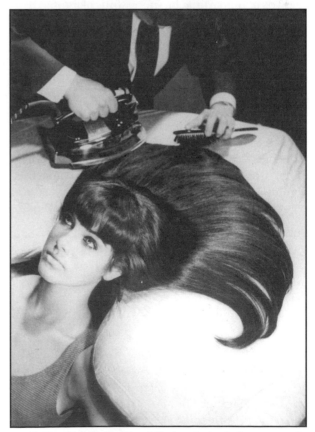

*In 1965, a New York stylist, following the lead of teenagers who iron their hair straight, develops a specially designed board on which to brush and iron his clients' hair.* (AP/Wide World Photos)

"natural" style featuring tight, unstraightened curls trimmed into a rounded shape.

However, not everyone was happy with long hair and what it represented. Newspapers often reported incidents in which young men were expelled from school or banned from sports teams until their hair was cut to an "acceptable" length, despite the protests of their parents, who sometimes resorted to legal action.

An influential figure during this decade was British hairstylist Vidal Sassoon, who revolutionized women's hairdressing by reinventing the bob to complement the miniskirt, creating a close-to-the-head, often asymmetrical blunt cut that exposed the nape of the neck. He also initiated the natural look, a reaction to the sculpted look of previous decades. His unisex salons featured male and female hairstylists who used blow dryers in a stylish setting complete with rock music. To increase the financial rewards of hairstyling, he successfully marketed haircare products and established a profitable chain of hairdressing schools.

**Impact** The evolution of hairstyles in the 1960's from the clean-cut, neatly styled look of the Kennedy administration to the long, shaggy hippie look was the result of both changing fashions and rebellious youth seeking to express themselves. As men began to favor long hair and get their hair cut by hairstylists at unisex salons rather than barbers, many barbers either went out of business or became hairstylists. Similarly, beauticians in beauty parlors learned the new styles and reemerged as hairstylists in salons.

**Subsequent Events** The trend toward longer hair on men continued through the 1970's but decreased in the 1980's as conservatism spread under the administration of Republican Ronald Reagan. Short haircuts were suddenly popular again among men, although women continued to favor more natural styles.

**Additional Information** Wendy Cooper's *Hair: Sex, Society, Symbolism* (1971) discusses the social aspects of hair, and Dylan Jones's *Haircults: Fifty Years of Styles and Cuts* (1990) celebrates styles from the 1940's to the present, with good illustrations of 1960's styles.

*Martin J. Manning*

**See also** Fashions and Clothing; Flower Children; *Hair*; Hippies; Youth Culture and the Generation Gap.

# ■ Hampton-Clark Deaths

**Date** December 4, 1969

*A concerted effort by law enforcement to destroy New Left and African American radical organizations. Black Panther members Fred Hampton and Mark Clark were killed by Illinois state police officers.*

**Origins and History** Twenty-one-year-old Fred Hampton and twenty-two-year-old Mark Clark were leaders in the Illinois branch of the Black Panther Party, a radical African American organization that had a reputation for militancy and was dedicated to equality between whites and blacks; the group was particularly active in Chicago, where it had a large membership.

**The Killings** On December 4, 1969, Clark and Hampton were killed during an early-morning raid on their apartment by members of the Illinois state police. The police fired between eighty-two and one hundred shots through the door at the apartment's inhabitants. Hampton, chairman of the Illinois branch of the Black Panther Party, was hit four times, twice in the head. Clark, a Panther leader from Peoria, Illinois, fired a single shot at the police (the only shot fired during the incident by those inside) before being killed. Four of the seven other Panthers in the apartment, including Hampton's pregnant girlfriend, were wounded. Hampton was probably drugged the previous evening by police and Federal Bureau of Investigation (FBI) informant William O'Neal, who had provided police and members of the FBI with a map of the apartment showing where Clark and Hampton slept.

After the killings, the Panthers opened the apartment for public viewing. Thousands walked through the quarters and saw for themselves the damage the police had done. The Illinois attorney general filed charges of attempted murder against the surviving Panthers. His office supported police attempts to characterize the attack as a shootout in which police acted in self-defense. These attempts included lying to the media about a gun Hampton was said to have fired (paraffin tests later proved Hampton had not fired any weapon) and stating that nail holes in the apartment door were actually bullet holes from weapons fired by the Panthers.

**Impact** The Hampton-Clark killings convinced many Americans that the U.S. government meant to eradicate the Panthers and other African American radicals. That police would kill citizens as they slept and execute a concerted coverup dramatized the extremes to which government agencies would go. The overall, eventual effect of the murders was to create sympathy for the Panthers among whites and blacks.

**Subsequent Events** A federal grand jury was empaneled in January, 1970, and was subsequently disbanded four months later without indicting anyone. Charges against the Panthers were dropped soon after. A state grand jury was empaneled and in April, 1971, indicted twelve police officers, the state attorney general, and another member of his office for obstruction of justice. The case went to trial in July, 1972. In October, 1972, the judge acquitted the defendants on all charges without requiring them to present their case.

Hampton and Clark's families sued the state of Illinois, the state attorney general, and the police in 1970, but the case was delayed until all criminal proceedings were through. A third criminal trial began in 1976 and ended in another acquittal by the bench, despite a deadlocked jury. This acquittal was overturned in a federal appeals court in 1979 and was upheld by the U.S. Supreme Court in June, 1980. Meanwhile, declassified FBI files revealed the existence of a concerted FBI offensive against the Panthers and other African American and left-wing organizations. The civil trial brought by the slain men's families began in 1976 after a series of government delays. On February 28, 1983, the families of Hampton and Clark received a settlement of $1.85 million.

**Additional Information** Journalist Paul Engleman wrote a long article twenty-five years after the raid entitled "Night of the Hunters" for *Chicago Magazine* (November, 1994).

*Ron Jacobs*

**See also** Black Panthers; Civil Rights Movement.

---

# ■ Hansberry, Lorraine

**Born** May 19, 1930, Chicago, Illinois
**Died** January 12, 1965, New York, New York

*The first African American woman to have a play produced on Broadway. For that play, Hansberry received the New York Critics Circle Award.*

**Early Life** Although born on the Southside of Chicago and surrounded by the poverty of the black

*Playwright Lorraine Hansberry's* A Raisin in the Sun *was produced on Broadway and won the New York Critics Circle Award.* (AP/Wide World Photos)

ghetto, Lorraine Vivian Hansberry, nevertheless, had a privileged upbringing. Her father, a successful property owner, and her mother, a trained teacher, nurtured a home life rich with books and an appreciation of learning. However, the cruel fact of racism was early ingrained in her when her father sought to move his family into a predominately white neighborhood. They met with intense and often violent white resistance, forcing her father to fight a winning case before the Supreme Court for the right to raise his family where he chose.

After being educated in the Chicago public schools, Hansberry attended the University of Wisconsin. In 1950, she headed to Harlem and to work on Paul Robeson's progressive newspaper, *Freedom*. There she came in contact with influential African American writers and thinkers.

**The 1960's** By 1959, drawing on her experiences of growing up on the Southside of Chicago, her work on *Freedom*, and her intense social commitment to racial equality, Hansberry completed what would become her award-winning play, *A Raisin in the Sun.* This powerful drama dealt with the effects of racism and bigotry on an African American family seeking to move from a cramped Chicago apartment to a larger house in a white neighborhood. Issues concerning African American family life and women and the race's celebration of its African roots were portrayed on stage as never before. These themes came across with equal force in the 1961 film version.

In 1964, *The Sign in Sidney Brustein's Window* became Hansberry's second Broadway production. She surprised her audience with an unsentimental play populated mostly by white people, including a homosexual, set in Greenwich Village. It explored issues of social commitment, political corruption, human relationships, and sexual orientation.

After her death in 1965, Hansberry's former husband, Robert Nemiroff, helped turn her various published and unpublished writings into the 1969 off-Broadway hit, *To Be Young, Gifted, and Black.* The play explored virtually all facets of Hansberry's genius while articulating her personal and political commitment to social and artistic freedom. It also highlighted her African heritage, as did *Les Blancs*, a 1970 posthumous production of a play dealing with African struggles for liberation and the evils of colonialism.

**Impact** Hansberry was a powerful African American voice. Through her plays, she helped articulate and press issues of racial and social equality, pan-Africanism, and black pride. Her works unsentimentally explore family life, racism, civil rights, and gender issues.

**Subsequent Events** In 1973, *Raisin*, a musical version of *A Raisin in the Sun*, was produced on Broadway.

**Additional Information** Details concerning Hansberry's life and work may be found in Richard M. Leeson's *Lorraine Hansberry: A Research and Production Sourcebook* (1997) and Steven Carter's *Hansberry's Drama: Commitment and Complexity* (1991).

*Richard M. Leeson*

**See also** Civil Rights Movement; Theater; Women's Identity.

# ■ Happenings

*A type of theatrical/artistic event. Happenings were free-flowing performances, generally involving the audience in a barrage of sensory impressions.*

Happenings grew out of several earlier movements, including existential philosophy, Surrealist painting, and Theater of the Absurd. The most direct precursor to the happenings of the 1960's was artist Allan Kaprow's experimental 1959 *Eighteen Happenings in Six Parts*, which combined movement, sight, and sound.

Happenings in the 1960's were highly varied, but they generally shared certain features. Though theatrical in nature, they seldom took place in theaters and rarely relied on scripts or trained actors. Rather, they began with a concept and unfolded in an improvised fashion, with emphasis on spontaneous expression. Happenings could contain music, movement, creation of visual art, or display and manipulation of symbols. They tended not to draw sharp distinctions between audience and performers, and unlike plays, which rely on language, happenings often drew their power from visual spectacle, nonlinguistic sounds, and sense impressions. Because each performance of a given work was unique, few records exist documenting the content of particular happenings.

**Impact** Like much art of the 1960's, happenings were controversial: They often contained nudity and sometimes included irreverent treatment of religious or political symbols. They were products of and contributed to changing social norms.

**Subsequent Events** By the 1970's, happenings had evolved in several directions and were renamed "performance art." Performance art ranges from confessional monologues to musical performances and multimedia extravaganzas. Like its predecessor, performance art is controversial.

**Additional Information** Allan Kaprow's *Assemblage, Environments, and Happenings* (1965) describes individual happenings and discusses the movement's history.

*Janet E. Gardner*

**See also** Art Movements; Music; Theater; Theater of the Absurd.

## ■ Hard, Darlene

**Born** January 6, 1936, Los Angeles, California

*A tennis champion who achieved the top rank in the sport during the early 1960's. She overcame an impoverished background to master the game.*

**Early Life** Born into a poor family and a broken home in Los Angeles during the Depression, Darlene Ruth Hard had to support herself as a waitress to pay her way through high school and Pomona College. By age eighteen, she was nationally ranked in tennis, and she won the intercollegiate singles title in 1958. Hard, who was five feet, six inches tall and weighed one hundred and forty pounds in her prime, was agile and quick on the court and for a decade was one of the leading women players when the sport was dominated by amateurs. She was a finalist in the Wimbledon championships in 1957 and 1959.

**The 1960's** Hard won the French Open in 1960 and captured the U.S. Open in 1960 and 1961. Her skills in doubles earned for her twelve titles at the French Open, U.S. Open, and Wimbledon tournaments from 1957 through 1963. She won another Wimbledon doubles title in 1969, five years after her retirement, when she reached back for one last victory after she and her partner lost the first set 0-6. Hard was well-known for her emotional displays. In 1960, she walked off the court for seven minutes during a doubles match that she was losing, and in 1962, when she lost to Margaret Smith at the U.S. Open, her dismay at line calls led to tears on the court, a tactic that was highly criticized by the press.

**Later Life** In 1973, Hard was inducted into the International Tennis Hall of Fame. She was married in 1977 and has spent most of her retirement from competition coaching tennis.

**Impact** Despite her tempestuous personal style and unorthodox appearance, Hard was partly responsible for the growing popularity of women's tennis at the end of the 1960's.

**Additional Information** *We Have Come a Long Way: The Story of Women's Tennis* (1988), by Billie Jean King with Cynthia Starr, contains a passage about Hard, and an entry on the tennis player is included in Joseph Layden's *Women in Sports: The Complete Book on the World's Greatest Female Athletes* (1997).
*Karen K. Gould and Lewis L. Gould*

**See also** Ashe, Arthur; King, Billie Jean; Sports; Tennis.

## ■ Hare Krishnas

*Members of the International Society for Krishna Consciousness (ISKCON), who believe salvation is attained by chanting the praises of the Hindu god Krishna. The Hare Krishna movement spread consciousness of Krishna through bhakti yoga, or self-sacrificing devotion.*

The spiritual movement of the Hare Krishnas is rooted in the sixteenth century teachings of Bengali religious ascetic Sri Krishna Caitanya, who devoted his entire life to the Hindu god Krishna. The recognized founder of the movement in the United States is A. C. Bhaktivedanta Swami Prabhupada, born in Calcutta in 1896 and initiated as a disciple of guru Bhaktisiddhanta.

Swami Prabhupada arrived in New York City in 1965 and began to teach people to become conscious of Krishna through devotional chanting, singing, and dancing. The appeal of transcending the mundane world and escaping maya (the illusory world) through devotion led many young people, especially those who identified with the counterculture, to join the Hare Krishnas. Within one year of his arrival, Swami Prabhupada founded the International Society for Krishna Consciousness (ISKCON). The organization focused its efforts on recruitment, disseminating information, and establishing Krishna temples. By the late 1960's, it had moved its headquarters to San Francisco, then to Los Angeles.

Reflecting basic Hindu religious practices, Hare Krishnas followed a daily schedule of discipline to attain the ultimate union with Krishna. To free the self of all material pleasures and purify the soul, devotees did not drink alcoholic beverages, gamble, engage in premarital sex, or eat meat, fish, or eggs. They regularly worshiped in temples, offering spiritual food to Krishna. Devotees wore distinctive Indian-style clothing, saffron-colored dhotis for men and saris for women. Disciples shaved their heads except for a tuft of hair, marked their bodies in thirteen places with wet clay, and wore sacred prayer beads. Their practice of chanting the Hare Krishna, Hare Ram mantra in public places was their means of preaching Krishna consciousness, enlisting members, and raising funds.

**Impact** During the 1960's, the Hare Krishna movement had its greatest impact on the growing number of young, urban middle-class white Americans who were dissatisfied with traditional organized religions and frustrated by the changing cultural values. These young people, attracted by the theosophical teachings of Indian religion, chose the alternative path of spiritualism that ISKCON offered. Their joining the Hare Krishna movement, which usually resulted in a drastic alteration in their appearance and activities, appeared to be a form of cult indoctrination to critics of counterculture religions.

**Subsequent Events** Before Swami Prabhupada's death in 1977, the Hare Krishna movement grew to include five thousand members in the United States and ten thousand worldwide, thirty ISKCON communities and preaching centers, and several publishing houses distributing millions of copies of writings on the Vedic scriptures. In the 1980's and 1990's, ISKCON began to suffer from dwindling funds, decreasing membership, a series of conflicts in the governing body commission, anticult pressures, and unfavorable press coverage.

**Additional Information** A thorough look at the growth and development of the Hare Krishna movement in the United States is found in E. Burke Rochford's *Hare Krishna in America* (1991). A dated but worthwhile examination of the religion appears in J. Stillson Judah's *Hare Krishna and the Counterculture* (1974).

*Tamara M. Valentine*

**See also** Counterculture; Cults; Religion and Spirituality.

## ■ Haynsworth, Clement, Jr.

**Born** October 30, 1912, Greenville, South Carolina
**Died** November 22, 1989, Greenville, South Carolina

*A conservative appeals court judge. His was the first of two consecutive nominations to the Supreme Court by President Richard Nixon to be rejected by the Senate.*

**Early Life** Clement Furman Haynsworth, Jr.'s family was part of the professional and social elite of Greenville, South Carolina. One of Haynsworth's forbears established Furman University, from which he graduated summa cum laude in 1933. He earned his law degree from Harvard University in 1936,

served in the U.S. Navy during World War II, and practiced law in Greenville after the war. Although fairly inactive in politics, he was among the Democrats who actively supported Dwight D. Eisenhower in 1952. In 1957, President Eisenhower appointed Haynsworth to the Court of Appeals for the Fourth Circuit.

**The 1960's** Judge Haynsworth's performance as a member of a small federal appeals court won him respect from other legal professionals but criticism from organized labor representatives and civil rights activists. When Justice Abe Fortas resigned from the Supreme Court on May 14, 1969, Haynsworth appeared to be the kind of replacement who would permit President Richard M. Nixon to redeem his pledge to the South to appoint a conservative southerner. Nixon nominated Haynsworth on August 18, 1969, and the American Bar Association rated him "highly qualified."

During Senate hearings regarding his confirmation, Haynsworth was criticized by representatives of labor and civil rights organizations. They charged him of being racist and antilabor and of participating in cases in which he had a financial interest. He was, indeed, conservative, and his decisions had been reversed by the Supreme Court in some labor and race cases; however, he also decided numerous appeals in favor of labor and civil rights interests. He had participated in *Brunswick v. Long* (1968) while owning stock in Brunswick Corporation; however, although it appeared to be a conflict of interest, the facts in the case were clear and the decision in favor of the corporation was unanimous. Because of these political and ethical uncertainties, the Senate rejected Haynsworth's nomination.

**Later Life** After his Supreme Court nomination was rejected by the Senate, Haynsworth resumed his position on the court of appeals, which he held until his death. The federal courthouse in Greenville was named for him while he was still alive, an honor that some people believe constituted an unofficial government apology.

**Impact** The fight between the Nixon administration and the Democratic Senate over the Haynsworth nomination continued the combative nature of judicial politics that had surrounded President Lyndon B. Johnson's nomination of Fortas for chief justice. The politics of Supreme Court nominations became increasingly ideological and retaliatory. Haynsworth's rejection invigorated Democrats, and they were again able to defeat Nixon when he followed the Haynsworth nomination with a less worthy southern nominee, G. Harold Carswell. These nominations, though unsuccessful, made Nixon's southern strategy more effective in drawing the South to the Republican Party.

**Subsequent Events** After a period of continued ideological judicial politics during the presidency of Ronald Reagan, the politics of Supreme Court nominations became less ideological and less bitter, as presidents sought to nominate moderates who were "confirmable" in an era when the Senate and the presidency were controlled by different political parties.

**Additional Information** A thorough study of the Haynsworth nomination is provided by John P. Frank's *Clement Haynsworth, the Senate, and the Supreme Court* (1991).

*Patricia A. Behlar*

**See also** Fortas, Abe; Nixon, Richard M.

# ■ Head Start

*A comprehensive national preschool program designed to enhance the opportunities for disadvantaged children in the United States. Head Start was a symbol for success among Great Society programs of the 1960's.*

In the early 1960's, poverty in the United States was "rediscovered," and the Civil Rights movement focused the country's attention on the many needs of children growing up in impoverished households. With a booming economy and a new spirit of liberalism dominating the mood of the country, the nation's politicians turned their attention to correcting these inequities. This atmosphere for change coincided with research that demonstrated the special needs of disadvantaged children. Some of the most influential research was conducted at the Upstate Medical Center in Syracuse, New York, under the direction of the center's dean, Julius B. Richmond.

When Lyndon B. Johnson assumed the presidency in 1963, he immediately moved to direct the nation's resources toward improving the quality of life for disadvantaged Americans. In 1964, Johnson signed the Economic Opportunity Act, legislation

that provided the funds for a number of programs designed to help impoverished people and established the Office of Economic Opportunity, headed by R. Sargent Shriver, John F. Kennedy's brother-in-law. Shriver appointed a committee to develop a program for children growing up in poverty. That committee's recommendations included teaching children cognitive skills and social competence and providing health and dental services, better nutrition, and social services. Providing these services to impoverished children during the preschool years would enable them to start school on an equal footing with children from middle-class families.

The resulting project, Head Start, was placed under the direction of Richmond, who set out to develop a nationwide program to be in place by summer, 1965. Head Start targeted the nation's three hundred poorest counties, and its staff worked with enormous energy and commitment to bring the program to fruition. An outline of the program had been created between November, 1964, and January, 1965, but the community planning, funding, and orientation took place over a period of just four months. Although the implementation of the program that summer was not without controversy—especially in Mississippi—Head Start was an unqualified success. The first comprehensive national preschool program in U.S. history, it served approximately 561,000 children in 13,000 centers in 2,400 communities. Nearly 41,000 teachers, each with two assistants, were employed, with more than 100,000 people participating as volunteers.

**Impact** Although in the early years of Head Start, controversy arose as to whether the gains children made were maintained after they entered school, subsequent studies have demonstrated the program's effectiveness. Some of the early critics focused their attention solely on cognitive skills rather than on the multiple goals of the original committee and the program. Under Head Start, hundreds of thousands of children received (many for the first time) medical and dental attention and developed better diets. The local Head Start programs also sought the involvement of the children's parents. By providing the parents with a voice in their children's programs, Head Start ensured its success and was a model for the way programs should be run. In the 1990's, thirty years after the program was initiated, buses with "Head Start" emblazoned on their sides

*Students in Head Start, one of the more successful War on Poverty programs, practice counting.* (Library of Congress)

were still common sights in communities across the United States.

**Subsequent Events** Although Head Start received bipartisan support from Congress and became institutionalized by legislation in the 1970's, it was inadequately funded, partly because of the costly ongoing Cold War. Despite the program's demonstrated benefits, it remained underfunded throughout the twentieth century, providing services for only about 25 percent of the nation's eligible children in the 1990's.

**Additional Information** For a more detailed analysis of Head Start's origin, see "Julius B. Richmond and Head Start," by Charles J. Bussey in the spring, 1993, issue of *Perspectives in Biology and Medicine* and *Head Start: A Legacy of the War on Poverty* (1979), by E. Ziegler and K. Valentine.

*Donna Bussey and Charles J. Bussey*

**See also** Economic Opportunity Act of 1964; Johnson, Lyndon B.; War on Poverty.

# ■ Heart of Atlanta Motel v. the United States

*One of the first major legal actions concerning the public accommodation section of the Civil Rights Act of 1964. This case was instrumental in the push for equality for African Americans.*

*Heart of Atlanta Motel v. the United States* resulted directly from disagreements over the Civil Rights Act of 1964. A motel operator was required to rent rooms to African Americans and sued to challenge the constitutionality of the public accommodation section that made it illegal to use race as a basis to refuse to rent rooms. The validity of these provisions was upheld unanimously by a three-judge circuit court, prompting an appeal to the U.S. Supreme Court by the plaintiff.

Argument began on October 4, 1964, in the Supreme Court. The plaintiff claimed the public accommodation section did not apply to business conducted by the motel and that requiring it to make rooms and services available to African Americans subjected the motel operator to involuntary servitude, a violation of the Thirteenth Amendment. The defendants, however, argued that because the motel had advertised to and conducted business with interstate travelers, its activity did fall within the parameters of the Civil Rights Act through the commerce clause.

On December 14, 1964, the Supreme Court unanimously decided in favor of the defendants by ruling that the public accommodation provisions of the Civil Rights Act are valid under the commerce clause. The court deemed that the actions of the motel operator were of potential harm to interstate commerce and that racial discrimination could be prohibited as a result. It also maintained that economic loss as a result of the prohibition of racial discrimination had no effect on the validity of the public accommodations section. In the view of the court, the motel operator was in no way being deprived of personal liberties or properties guaranteed by the Fifth or Thirteenth Amendments.

**Impact** Prior to the 1960's, travel for African Americans was made difficult by the strong presence of discrimination, especially in the southern portion of the country. In fact, this problem was so prevalent that many individuals and families were forced to design travel that corresponded with areas willing to accept African Americans. Although the Civil Rights Act of 1964 was created to address difficulties like these, actual relief did not come until the laws were tested in courts and enforced. *Heart of Atlanta v. the United States* was significant in that it upheld one aspect of civil rights and led to its enforcement, making travel more realistic for African Americans.

**Subsequent Events** From the 1960's through the 1990's, the validity of the Civil Rights Act of 1964 was tested in a wide variety of cases. The U.S. Supreme Court repeatedly upheld the act.

**Additional Information** A comprehensive review of civil rights litigation can be found in Henry J. Abraham's *Freedom and the Court* (1994). An important account of the Civil Rights movement is Richard Kluger's *Simple Justice* (1975).

*Brandon Raulston*

**See also** Civil Rights Act of 1964; Housing Laws, Federal; *Katzenbach v. McClung*; Supreme Court Decisions.

# ■ Heart Transplants

*A spectacular accomplishment in the history of cardiac surgery. In the 1960's, surgeons first proved that they could successfully transplant a human heart.*

The idea of transplanting a heart can be found in ancient myths and legends. Actual transplantation, however, had to wait for the development of vascular surgical techniques, cardiopulmonary bypasses, and medications to manage the body's rejection of a new healthy heart. In the early twentieth century, Alexis Carrel and Charles Guthrie performed the first heart-lung transplantations on animals in the Hull Laboratories of the University of Chicago. Later studies by Frank Mann, director of the experimental medical laboratories at the Mayo Clinic, demonstrated the rejection phenomenon.

In the 1940's and 1950's, Vladimir Demikhov, a Soviet scientist, made major contributions to knowledge of cardiac surgery. Historians credit him with being the first person to implant an auxiliary heart within the chest, to replace the heart, and to perform a complete heart-lung transplant. In 1962, *Experimental Transplantation of Vital Organs*, the English translation of his 1960 book, was published.

Animal experimentation conducted by Stanford University's Norman E. Shumway, Adrian Kantrowitz, James Hardy, and South African Christiaan Barnard helped develop a technique by which a human heart could successfully be transplanted. The research showed that a surgeon could cut a heart out of a donor dog and preserve it in a cold, 40-degree saline solution. Then, surgeons could attach a heart-lung machine to the recipient dog to keep circulation going while its heart was removed and the donor heart sewn in place. After the stitching was done and the clamps released, blood would flow through the heart but not normally until the heart was given an electric shock.

In 1964, Hardy, a professor of surgery at the University of Mississippi, transplanted the heart of a large chimpanzee into a human patient. The patient, Boyd Rush, died two hours after receiving the heart.

Cardiac surgeon Barnard attempted the first human heart transplant on December 3, 1967, at Groote Schuur Hospital in Cape Town, South Africa. His patient was a fifty-five-year-old grocer, Louis Washkansky, who had experienced several heart attacks since 1960. Upon waking up after surgery,

Washkansky proclaimed, "I am the new Franken-stein." He died of a bacterial infection eighteen days later. Three days after Barnard operated on Washkansky, cardiac surgeon Kantrowitz performed a heart transplant on an infant at Maimonides Hospital in Brooklyn, New York. The infant died two hours after surgery.

Barnard's second patient, a dentist named Philip Blaiberg who received a new heart on January 2, 1968, survived seventeen months, stimulating a rash of transplant activity. Shumway, through additional canine experiments, developed a way to simplify the operative technique. He showed how to leave about 5 percent of the old heart—part of the walls of the heart chambers to which six veins are attached—which cut the length of an operation in half. On September 15, 1969, Denton Cooley of the Texas Heart Institute of Houston performed the first heart-lung transplant on an infant. The infant lived only fourteen hours, dying of respiratory insufficiency. By the end of 1970, approximately three years after Barnard operated on Washkansky, 166 heart transplants had been attempted worldwide. Only

twenty-three of those patients, however, were still alive, which was a mortality rate of 85 percent.

Shumway's research also proved that the major challenge of heart transplants was rejection after the surgery. In 1969, the key that helped resolve this problem was discovered in a soil sample in an isolated highland plateau called Hardanger Vidda in southern Norway. Jean-François Borel, a microbiologist for Sandoz Limited, a pharmaceutical company based in Basel, Switzerland, discovered a compound called "cyclosporine." Research would show that it could control rejection, and the drug became widely used in the early 1980's.

**Impact** The 1960's was a significant and spectacular period in the history of cardiac surgery. Without the combined daring, efforts, imagination, and skill of medical scientists, physicians, and surgeons, heart transplantation would not have become a reality. The transplants performed in the 1960's created the foundation for later surgeries that enabled many deathly ill patients to extend their lives.

**Subsequent Events** Because of the limited availability of suitable donor hearts and problems with rejection, efforts to create an artificial heart began as early as 1969 and continued into the following decades. By the 1990's, more heart recipients were living longer, healthier lives, in part because of advances in preventing rejection of the transplanted organ.

**Additional Information** An exhaustive history of heart transplantation can be found in *The Evolution of Cardiac Surgery* (1992), by Harris B. Shumacker, Jr.

*Fred Buchstein*

**See also** Kidney Transplants; Medicine; Science and Technology.

# ■ Heiss, Carol

**Born** January 20, 1940, New York, New York

*Ladies figure skating gold medalist. Heiss's courage and determination captured America's heart and imagination at the 1960 Winter Olympics.*

Carol Heiss enjoyed early success as a skater, winning the National Junior Ladies Championship at age twelve. In 1954, she suffered a career-threatening injury and in 1955 learned that her mother suffered from cancer. Despite these setbacks, she placed second in the 1955 World Championships and finished

*Figure skater Carol Heiss displays the gold medal she won at the 1960 Winter Olympics. (AP/Wide World Photos)*

a very close second at the 1956 Winter Olympics.

After her mother's death in October, 1956, Heiss put all her efforts into obtaining the one skating honor she had yet to achieve—an Olympic gold medal. She prepared for the Olympics by winning four straight world and national titles. Finally, in Squaw Valley, California, in 1960, she won an Olympic gold medal, dazzling the world with a spectacular display of skating.

She was welcomed back to New York City with a ticker-tape parade attended by two hundred and fifty thousand people and received a medal from the mayor. Four weeks after her victory, she announced her retirement from amateur skating, married figure skater Hayes Alan Jenkins, and made a film, *Snow White and the Three Stooges* (1961). In the film, Snow White, played by Heiss, meets the Three Stooges instead of the seven dwarfs.

**Impact** Heiss was one of the most celebrated female athletes of the 1960's. The intense interest in her personal struggles as well as her career prefigured the public's increasing attention to athletes as role models and celebrities throughout the 1960's and beyond.

**Additional Information** For more information on figure skating, see *The Fine Art of Ice Skating: An Illustrated History and Portfolio of Stars* (1988), by Julia Whedon.

*Mary Virginia Davis*

**See also** Fleming, Peggy; Olympic Games of 1960; Sports.

## ■ Hell's Angels

*A California motorcycle gang that gained notoriety in the 1960's, first for a confrontation with peace marchers in Berkeley and later for its part in the violence at the Altamont Music Festival.*

**Origins and History** The Hell's Angels motorcycle club was started in San Bernardino, California, in 1947 by a biker named Otto Friedli, to encourage biker solidarity after a brawl in the town of Hollister, California, in which almost a hundred motorcyclists were jailed. Many of the original members were Air Force veterans, and they took the name "Hell's Angels" from the Howard Hughes film about military flyers. When motorcycle clubs wishing to improve the image of bikers publicly stated that 99 percent of motorcycle riders are good citizens, the Hell's

*Members of the Hell's Angels motorcycle gang follow the casket of a club member who was killed in a car crash to a Napa, California, cemetery in 1968. (AP/Wide World Photos)*

Angels proudly called themselves "One Percenters." Several chapters of the club were organized in the 1950's, and after founder Friedli was imprisoned in 1958, new president Ralph "Sonny" Barger took over and eventually brought the club to national prominence.

The 1954 film *The Wild One*, starring the young Marlon Brando as a misunderstood motorcyclist, improved the image of bikers in general and the Hell's Angels in particular. It also may have been responsible for the belief that the Hell's Angels, like the bikers in the film, wore leather jackets. In fact, the club disdained leather because of its protective aspects and forbade the wearing of leather, just as it did not allow its members to wear helmets while riding until state laws required it. Club members instead wore "colors": a sleeveless denim jacket bearing the group's death's-head symbol.

The club had a strong macho code, demanding shows of respect, if not submission, from all they met, and going to the aid of any fellow Angel in a fight, regardless of who started it. The public image of the organization tended to be polarized, with some seeing them as underappreciated individualists, while others viewed them as thugs, beating and raping wherever they went. Both pictures were exaggerated, but the latter seems to have been closer to the truth.

**Activities** The Hell's Angels came to national prominence in 1965, when members of the Oakland chapter battled with demonstrators protesting the Vietnam War. The club loudly proclaimed its patriotism and indeed offered to go over to Vietnam and help in the military effort.

Counterculture leaders such as Ken Kesey (himself a motorcyclist) and Allen Ginsberg eventually persuaded the club to agree not to interfere with further peace demonstrations. This led to a rapprochement and some social contact between the bikers and the counterculture.

The Angels were, in fact, a drug-taking counterculture, but they used amphetamines and barbiturates, often mixed with alcohol, rather than the marijuana and hallucinogenic drugs the hippies favored. Unlike the hippies, the club was also seriously racist and sexist; African Americans were never permitted to join, and women in their presence were not safe from harassment or even assault unless they were clearly identified as the property of another member.

**Impact** The mid-1960's contacts between the Hell's Angels and the counterculture led some hippie leaders to believe that because the bikers were drug-using fellow rebels, they could be allies in the war against straight society. This required a certain amount of denial of important aspects of the Hell's Angels culture, including the bikers' violent tendencies and lack of tolerance.

On December 6, 1969, the Rolling Stones gave a free concert at Altamont Speedway in California. Preparations for the concert were hasty and ill-organized, and because of the romanticized image many hippies had of the Hell's Angels, the biker club was hired to provide security. This was a mistake. The concert was marred by violence, including the fatal stabbing and beating of one audience member; most of the incidents appeared to originate in the motorcycle club's actions.

**Subsequent Events** In the 1970's, the Hell's Angels were widely believed to have engaged in the wholesale manufacture and distribution of methamphetamine and other drugs. Many were convicted of drug-trafficking charges.

**Additional Information** In 1967, two years after the events he described, Hunter S. Thompson published *Hell's Angels: The Strange and Terrible Saga of the Outlaw Motorcycle Gangs.* Despite some exaggerations, the book offers a thorough first-person account. *Freewheelin' Frank* (1968), written by Hell's Angel Frank Reynolds with the aid of Beat poet Michael McClure, offers a somewhat defensive look at the club from the inside. *Hell's Angels: Three Can Keep a Secret if Two Are Dead* (1987), by Yves Lavigne, is a sensationalistic treatment of the group that emphasizes the club's drug-dealing activities in the 1970's and 1980's.

*Arthur D. Hlavaty*

**See also** Altamont Music Festival; Counterculture; Drug Culture; Rolling Stones.

---

# ■ Hendrix, Jimi

**Born** November 27, 1942, Seattle, Washington
**Died** September 18, 1970, London, England

*Guitarist, singer, and songwriter. Hendrix's innovations were both technical and creative.*

**Early Life** Jimi Hendrix, born Johnny Allen Hendrix and renamed James Marshall Hendrix at age three, learned to play guitar at age twelve. His earliest musical influences were the great blues musicians, as is evident in his renditions of songs by Howlin' Wolf, Willie Dixon, and Muddy Waters, as well as his on-stage dramatics, which were inspired by Aaron "T-Bone" Walker. After a brief stint in the army, Hendrix worked as a backup guitarist for various musicians including Little Richard, the Isley Brothers, Curtis Knight, and Wilson Pickett.

**The 1960's** Hendrix was brought to England by Chas Chandler of the Animals in 1966. Hendrix formed the Jimi Hendrix Experience with bass player Noel Redding and percussionist Mitch Mitchell, and their debut record, *Are You Experienced?*, was released in 1967. The first single was an evocative version of William Roberts's "Hey Joe," and the album featured numerous songs that would become Hendrix classics, including "Purple Haze,"

"Manic Depression," "Fire," "The Wind Cries Mary," and "Foxy Lady." A hit in England, Hendrix's stateside reputation exploded into the hippie and psychedelic rock consciousness with his performance at the 1967 Monterey International Pop Festival in California, which he capped off by burning his guitar. His version of the Troggs' "Wild Thing," which featured pantomimed masturbation and a sacrificial guitar burning, cemented Hendrix's place in the iconography of rock and roll.

Hendrix's second album *Axis: Bold as Love* (1968) pointed toward his increasing experimentation. Ballads such as "Little Wing" and "Castles Made of Sand" were countered with hard-driving numbers such as "Spanish Castle Magic" and "If Six Was Nine," which was featured on the *Easy Rider* (1969) film soundtrack. His studio output peaked later in 1968 with the release of the monumental *Electric Ladyland*. Perhaps the pinnacle of 1960's psychedelic rock, this double album ran the gamut from blues jams such as "Voodoo Chile" and "Voodoo Chile (Slight Return)," to avant-garde songs such as "1983" and "Moon, Turn the Tides," to straight-ahead rock such as "All Along the Watchtower" and "House Burning Down," and highlighted his innovative uses of feedback, distortion, and other effects. The band was augmented with performances by Steve Winwood and Chris Wood of Traffic, Jack Casady of Jefferson Airplane, Al Kooper of Blood, Sweat, and Tears, and drummer Buddy Miles.

His performance at the Woodstock Music and Art Fair in August, 1969, was momentous for the guitarist's brilliantly artistic interpretation of "The Star Spangled Banner." It was the first time a popular artist had taken serious liberties with the national anthem, and he was subjected to widespread criticism for breaking this ground.

By the end of 1969, Hendrix had formed a new group, The Band of Gypsies, with drummer Miles and bassist Billy Cox. Their only album is a live effort from New Year's Eve, 1969, recorded at Bill Graham's Filmore East. The music represented a new direction, incorporating funk rhythms, jazz improvisation, and overtly political lyrics, as evidenced by the song "Machine Gun." Posthumously released jazz-fusion work with musicians ranging from Miles Davis to Larry Young indicated yet another direction being pursued by this boundless artist. A promising future, however, including plans to enroll at the Juliard School of Music in order to learn to read

*Guitarist, singer, and songwriter Jimi Hendrix plays his Fender Stratocaster guitar in a 1968 concert.* (Archive Photos)

music, was cut short when Hendrix died from inhalation of vomit after barbiturate intoxication on September 18, 1970.

**Impact**  His musicianship popularized Marshall Amplifiers in the United States and the Fender Stratocaster guitar worldwide. His blending of blues, jazz, funk, rock, and psychedelic elements influenced countless musicians in various genres.

**Additional Information**  Harry Shapiro and Caesar Glebbeek published a biography of the musician, *Jimi Hendrix, Electric Gypsy* (1995).

*Akim D. Reinhardt*

**See also**  Joplin, Janis; Monterey Pop Festival; Music; Woodstock Festival.

## ■ Hesse, Eva

**Born** January 11, 1936, Hamburg, Germany
**Died** May 29, 1970, New York, New York

*Sculptor known for using nontraditional materials and forms in pieces that often have an emotional content and for emphasizing the process of creation. Hesse's youthful success, gender, and early death increased interest in her work.*

**Early Life** Eva Hesse's early years were difficult. Her German-Jewish parents sent her and her sister to an Amsterdam orphanage in 1939 to prevent their being taken to concentration camps. Reunited the same year, the family moved to New York City. There, Hesse's parents divorced, and in 1946, her mother committed suicide. From 1954 to 1957, Hesse studied drawing and painting at Cooper Union in New York City and, in 1959, at Yale University. She married sculptor Tom Doyle in 1961; they divorced in 1965. Hesse thought her narrow escape from Nazi terror and family tragedies affected both her personality and her work.

**The 1960's** Hesse established a reputation early in the 1960's, exhibiting her drawings in New York. A year in Germany exposed Hesse to avant-garde European work by artists such as Joseph Beuys and reforged links with her past. She began to experiment with three-dimensional forms. Between 1964 and 1970, she made more than one hundred sculptures. Most were designed to hang from ceilings and walls or to be placed on the floor. Though nonrepresentational, Hesse's sculptures seem almost human, organic in form. They are charged with emotion and are innovative in their use of materials. Hesse and other 1960's artists used industrial materials such as rope, string, felt, and rubber. She also emphasized her working method, or process, as did other 1960's artists such as Beuys, Richard Serra, Robert Morris, and Lynda Benglis. As part of her concern for process, Hesse kept notebooks and diaries recording her emotions and how they related to her productions. Like her contemporaries, the minimalists, she often worked in series, believing that repetition enhanced the effects of her sculptures.

**Later Life** Hesse's career was brief. She was diagnosed with a brain tumor in April, 1969. With the help of studio assistants, she continued to work. She died in May, 1970, at the age of thirty-four. That year, the School of Visual Arts in New York exhibited a survey of her sculptures. In 1972, the Guggenheim Museum organized a retrospective show.

**Impact** Hesse's lifelike sculptures contrasted with the geometric, constructed work of 1960's minimalist sculptors. Her use of nontraditional materials and organic forms affected many later artists, as did her unconventional installation techniques. The connections she made between personal feeling and sculptural form influenced feminist artists in the 1970's. A concern for process and a rejection of traditional ideas about art's appearance characterizes much post-1960's art. Hesse's intense, tragic life, like that of photographer Diane Arbus, has attracted as much attention as her work. Her sculptures are featured in most major museum collections in Europe and the United States.

**Subsequent Events** Process art and minimalism remained strong into the early 1970's. They have continued to influence artists as part of a long-term general trend to reject established ideas about materials, form, and meaning in art.

**Additional Information** Lucy Lippard's *Eva Hesse* (1976) is still the standard overview of Hesse's life and work. Bill Barrette's *Eva Hesse: Sculpture* (1989) is an illustrated catalog of Hesse's three-dimensional work, with a brief biographical introduction.

*Susan Benforado Bakewell*

**See also** Arbus, Diane; Art Movements.

# ■ Higher Education Act

*Landmark legislation passed in 1965 that greatly increased the federal role in higher education as a keystone to the Great Society and War on Poverty.*

In 1960, the federal government supported about 9 percent of U.S. higher education funding, mostly through the G.I. Bill, the National Defense Education Act of 1958 (NDEA), and various social security programs. One billion dollars went to support land-grant universities, veterans, science education, libraries, and college housing in 1961. That year, President John F. Kennedy introduced a bill to support $2.8 billion in faculty loans and $892 million in merit- and need-based loans to students at four-year institutions; it was defeated.

By 1965, the climate had changed. Both President Lyndon B. Johnson (a former teacher) and the heavily Democratic Congress considered education key to their antipoverty and Great Society programs. The bill passed the House by 368 to 22 and the Senate by 79 to 3. Johnson signed the Higher Education Act at his old college in San Marcos, Texas, on November 9, 1965, to "strengthen the educational resources of our colleges and universities and to provide financial assistance for students in post-secondary and higher education."

The act's fifty-two pages are divided into eight titles. The first title allotted $25 million to establish "urban land-grant" programs of community service, including continuing education. The second appropriated $50 million for building up library and media collections and training specialists. Title III set aside $55 million to help "developing institutions"—largely southern African American schools—that were "struggling for survival and are isolated from the main currents of academic life." Potential faculty were to be encouraged with special fellowships, and "cooperative" partnerships with stronger northern schools were also envisaged.

Title IV was revolutionary in its restructuring of federal aid to students. NDEA needs-tested loans were extended and complemented by an additional $70 million in aid to schools for Educational Opportunity Grants to undergraduates "of exceptional financial need," insurance for $700 million in commercial loans (to be doubled two years hence), and $129 million for work-study programs, an extension of the Economic Opportunity Act of 1964.

Title V sought to improve the preparation of teachers and established the National Teacher Corps, an analog to President Kennedy's Peace Corps, "to strengthen the educational opportunities available to children in areas having concentrations of low-income families." Experienced teachers and inexperienced teacher-interns were to be enrolled and sent to these areas to augment teaching staffs. The title also approved $40 million for forty-five hundred fellowships to support training for school teachers. Title VI authorized $40 million for classroom televisions and training of media specialists. Title VII expanded the funding of the Higher Education Facilities Act of 1963, while Title VIII prohibited "federal control of education."

**Impact** General aid increased tenfold between 1964 and 1971, and by 1970, two million students, or one in four, were receiving federal aid. The triad of grants, loans, and work-study—all enormously expanded—remains the principal platform of federal aid to students. Though they had played an insignificant role in 1965, education lobbyists soon became a powerful force behind the ever-increasing flow of funds, and Congress eagerly took over where the president had left off. Through rules for student funding, the federal government could now gain compliance with antidiscrimination policies, even from private schools. The 1968 amendments added six new programs—including aid to "disadvantaged students" and the Law School Clinical Experience Program—and appropriations of $2.46 billion: more than twice the amount Johnson requested.

**Additional Information** For further background on this act, see H. D. Graham's *The Uncertain Triumph* (1984).

*Joseph P. Byrne*

**See also** Education; Great Society Programs; Job Corps; Student Loans; War on Poverty.

## ■ Hippies

*A group of young people who rejected mainstream culture in favor of an alternative lifestyle. This optimistic, easygoing group favored love, peace, and mind-altering drugs.*

The hippie movement was born in 1965 in the Haight-Ashbury district of San Francisco, California. Students, artists, and dropouts had streamed into this area, attracted by the cheap rents and bohemian way of life that offered an alternative to the middle-class lifestyle of mainstream America. By mid-1966, boutiques, head shops (shops selling drug paraphernalia, incense, and psychedelic posters and pins), and coffeehouses with colorful names such as I/Thou, Blushing Peony, and In Gear crammed the Haight-Ashbury district.

Haight-Ashbury's hippie community consisted largely of teenagers and young people who were rebelling against their conservative middle-class backgrounds. According to scholars who have studied the hippie movement, its members were alienated and distrustful of social and political institutions. The hippies rejected authority and the status quo and believed their best chance of changing society was to drop out of the competitive, materialistic world of their parents. They were peace loving, nonmaterialistic, and noncomformist. They believed in free love and hoped to expand and open their minds to new possibilities by using psychedelic drugs.

The hippies adopted their own look: long, often scraggly hair, bowler hats, love beads, bells, colorfully designed clothing, bell-bottoms pants, and Victorian shawls, for starters. Typically, they wore flowers in their hair, painted their bodies in Day-Glo bright colors, and took drugs, especially LSD, calling themselves "acid heads." To survive, many sold marijuana and LSD or panhandled on the street for spare change. To celebrate their growing sense of community, the hippies held happenings, be-ins, acid tests (parties where LSD was distributed, often featuring music), and concerts featuring acid rock played by groups such as the Grateful Dead and Jefferson Airplane. In Haight-Ashbury, the hippie lifestyle reached a peak during the much publicized 1967 Summer of Love, when thousands of young people went to San Francisco seeking to live the countercultural lifestyle.

Because of the national media attention given to these new residents of Haight-Ashbury, hundreds of thousands of youth across the country duplicated the hippie lifestyle. It became fashionable to quit school, smoke marijuana, enjoy free love, wear loud clothes, and grow long hair. Many Americans disap-

*Hippies, like this man at a 1967 gathering, favored long hair, beads, and flowers, which they believed expressed their message of love and peace.* (Express Newspapers/Archive Photos)

proved of the lifestyle these young people led. Ronald Reagan, then governor of California, defined a hippie as someone "who looked like Tarzan, walked like Jane, and smelled like Cheetah."

By 1967, Haight-Ashbury and its hippie residents had become internationally known, but soon after, the scene deteriorated. The sheer numbers of young people pouring into the area strained its resources. Drug arrests and rapes increased as criminals moved in to take advantage of the young people gathered there. The hippie lifestyle became increasingly commercialized as advertisers and marketers picked up on its images and colors. Some hippies sought enlightenment through meditation and took trips to India in search of spiritual truth; others turned to rural communes to practice their lifestyle and live close to nature.

**Impact** By the early 1970's, the hippie movement began to decline, as most of its members came to realize it was difficult to reform society by "dropping out." Many became involved in various movements—political, environmental, and religious. Others left the hippie period of their lives behind them, while retaining the ideals and principles that once motivated them. Most of them either returned to school or joined the labor force. They cut their hair, gave up free love and drugs, and married, slowly adopting mainstream lifestyles. Many of those who had joined communes left them.

However, each year since 1971, an informal network of hippies and self-styled anarchists have used computers and word of mouth to organize the Rainbow Family Peace Gatherings, multiday festivals that bring together craftspeople, artists, and others who enjoy the hippie lifestyle.

**Additional Information** For more information on the hippies and their lifestyle, see *Sixties People* (1990), by Jane and Michael Stern.

*Ron Chepesiuk*

**See also** Counterculture; Death of Hippie; Drug Culture; Flower Children; Haight-Ashbury; LSD; Marijuana.

## ■ Hitchcock Films

*The most recognizable American director in the 1960's. Hitchcock made five films during the decade and broke new ground in the horror genre.*

*Anthony Perkins and Janet Leigh star in Alfred Hitchcock's immensely popular 1960 horror film* Psycho. *(Museum of Modern Art/Film Stills Archive)*

Alfred Hitchcock was born in 1899 in London, England, and began directing films in 1927. He made ten silent films between 1927 and 1929 and fourteen talkies before moving to Hollywood in 1940. He established his reputation in the United States with thrillers such as *Rebecca* (1940), *Suspicion* (1941), *Lifeboat* (1944), and *Notorious* (1946) and hit his stride as a director in the 1950's with films such as *Rear Window* (1954), *To Catch a Thief* (1956), *The Man Who Knew Too Much* (1956), *Vertigo* (1958) and *North by Northwest* (1959). By the 1960's, he had become known as the "Master of Suspense" and was widely recognized for his trademark cameos and for the introductions he made for his television series, *Alfred Hitchcock Presents*, which ran from 1955 to 1965.

***Psycho*** (1960)  Hitchcock was acutely aware of the marketability of cheap horror films and felt that a high-quality horror film might be even more profitable. *Psycho* confirmed his belief and contains some

of the most infamous scenes of all of Hitchcock's films. The film opens with Marion Crane (Janet Leigh) embezzling a large sum of money. On the run, she stops at the Bates Motel, where she encounters hotelier and amateur taxidermist Norman Bates (Anthony Perkins). In one of the most horrifying scenes in the history of cinema, Marion is stabbed to death while showering. The forty-five second scene was composed from seventy-eight pieces of film. The editing jumps disturbingly from one camera angle to another while the soundtrack shrieks along with the motion of the blade. When Marion's lover and her sister arrive at the Bates Motel, it is revealed that Norman's mother is a withered corpse, and Norman has taken on her personality as well as his own. *Psycho* was filmed in black and white so that Hitchcock could avoid splashing garish red all over the screen, but many viewers were convinced that the film jumped to color for the shower scene. *Psycho* received mixed reviews from critics, many of whom considered it to be beneath Hitchcock's talent, but it was a huge success at the box office, and the elements of *Psycho*—the shower scene, the Bates Motel, and the word "psycho"—all became part of the cultural lexicon.

**The Birds (1963)** Hitchcock returned to the genre of the suspense thriller with *The Birds*, an apocalyptic vision of nature gone awry. Melanie Daniels (Tippi Hedren) meets Mitch Brenner (Rod Taylor) in a bird shop in San Francisco and decides to surprise him by delivering a pair of love birds to his home in the quiet coastal town of Bodega Bay. Returning to her car, she is struck by a gull—an odd occurrence that puzzles all who witness it. The incident is just the first in a series of escalating attacks that eventually take on epic proportions. The menacing accumulation of gulls and crows and their seemingly random attacks on the citizens of Bodega Bay were filmed with innovative special-effects techniques. The apocalyptic overtones were an attempt on Hitchcock's part to attract more sophisticated viewers. Many of his loyal viewers were disappointed with the film, confused by the cause of all of the mayhem and disturbed by the grisly images of birds attacking people.

**Marnie (1964)** This film is one of Hitchcock's most uneven projects. The title character is a compulsive thief, and the action uncovers the psychological traumas of her childhood that cause her to steal. Communication between Hitchcock and Tippi Hedren (who plays Marnie) broke down in the course of filming, compromising her performance and his effectiveness. The psychoanalytic structure of the film was a deliberate and somewhat ineffective attempt to please film critics, and the conventional ending an attempt to appease his popular audience. Both audiences gave the film a cool reception.

**Torn Curtain (1966)** Hitchcock returned to the espionage thriller format that he had perfected in the 1950's with *Torn Curtain*, the story of American physicist Michael Armstrong (Paul Newman) who defects to East Germany and is followed there by his suspicious fiancé (Julie Andrews). Though the film was very similar to Hitchcock films of the 1950's, it looked old-fashioned and simplistic to audiences who had become accustomed to the fast pace and self-parody of James Bond films such as *From Russia with Love*.

**Topaz (1969)** Hitchcock's final film of the decade was another espionage thriller. The plot centers around a Soviet intelligence officer who defects to the United States in the midst of the Cuban Missile Crisis. Hitchcock went to great lengths to preempt comparisons to James Bond films, emphasizing the factual basis of the Leon Uris novel from which the script was derived. Though more warmly received than *Torn Curtain*, *Topaz* was not significantly more successful.

**Impact** Hitchcock's sense of timing and suspense have been adopted by many directors. Many Americans were afraid of their showers after seeing *Psycho* and suspicious of crows and gulls after seeing *The Birds*. The respectability that Hitchcock brought to the horror genre with these films is in part responsible for the American desensitization to images of violence that started in the 1960's. Hitchcock invented the modern notion of the director as a public figure. His films were defined by complex characters, masterful camera work, and Hitchcock's superb sense of timing.

**Subsequent Events** Hitchcock made only two more films, *Frenzy* (1972) and *Family Plot* (1976) before his death in 1980. Though he insisted early in his career that he made films solely to entertain audiences, in the late 1960's, he launched an effort to redefine himself as a director of cinemagraphic art. By the 1970's, his reputation as a serious director was firm, and film scholars of the 1970's and 1980's found more merit in *Marnie* and *Torn Curtain* than the critics and audiences of the 1960's had.

**Additional Information** For a treatment of Hitchcock's place in the history of cinema, see *Hitchcock: The Making of a Reputation* (1992), by Robert Kapsis. For studies of Hitchcock's films, see *Hitchcock's Films Revisited* (1989), by Robin Wood, and *The Films of Alfred Hitchcock* (1993), by David Sterritt. For details on Hitchcock's life, see *Hitch: The Life and Times of Alfred Hitchcock* (1981), by John Russell Taylor.

*Craig Sean McConnell*

**See also** Film; *Hush . . . Hush Sweet Charlotte*; *Rosemary's Baby*; *What Ever Happened to Baby Jane?*

## ■ Holmes, Hamilton

**Born** July 8, 1941, Atlanta, Georgia
**Died** October 26, 1995, Atlanta, Georgia

# ■ Hunter, Charlayne

**Born** February 27, 1942, Due West, South Carolina

*On January 10, 1961, Holmes and Hunter became the first African Americans to desegregate the University of Georgia.*

**Early Life** Hamilton Earl Holmes and Charlayne Hunter (later Charlayne Hunter-Gault) both graduated from Turner High School in Atlanta; Holmes was valedictorian of their class and Hunter was ranked third. Hunter's father was a chaplain in the military, but when her parents separated, Hunter and her mother moved to Atlanta, where Holmes was born and raised. Holmes's father owned various businesses in Atlanta, and his grandfather practiced medicine on Atlanta's famous Auburn Avenue.

Hunter had written for Atlanta's African American newspaper, *The Inquirer*, during high school and wished to pursue a degree in journalism, and Holmes intended to follow his grandfather into medicine. The University of Georgia had reputable programs in medicine and journalism and seemed a logical choice for both students—except that the university had not desegregated, despite the 1954 Supreme Court ruling in *Brown v. Board of Education* that had declared racial segregation in public education unconstitutional. As local attorneys and leaders worked out a case to force desegregation of the facility, Holmes entered Morehouse, part of the prominent Atlanta University Center, and Hunter attended Wayne University in Detroit, Michigan.

**The 1960's** In January, 1961, federal district court Judge William Bootle ordered that Hunter and Holmes be admitted to the University of Georgia for the winter academic quarter, which began the next week. Although it seemed likely that Governor S. Ernest Vandiver (who earlier had promised "not one, no, not one" African American would enter public schools) would close the university to prevent desegregation of its facilities, the school stayed open, and Hunter and Holmes registered and attended classes.

Holmes stayed with an African American family in Athens during his tenure at Georgia, and Hunter lived in dorms. Both initially experienced difficulty on the campus. A mob gathered outside Hunter's dorm the first night, threatening violence, and administrators—not friendly to the idea of integration from the start—suspended both Hunter and Holmes "for their own safety." Hunter, the more outgo-

ing of the two, eventually enjoyed acceptance and many friendships, particularly within the college of journalism. Holmes, who studied chemistry in preparation for medical school, largely kept to himself, feeling rebuffed by the white college community throughout his stay at the university. Both students spoke extensively on their experiences to community and religious groups around the South and occasionally in the North.

After graduation in 1963, Hunter accepted a secretarial position at *New Yorker* magazine on the condition that she would eventually be considered for writing assignments. Holmes continued study at Emory University School of Medicine, receiving his degree in 1967.

**Later Life** Hunter gained national recognition in journalism through her work for *New Yorker* magazine, the *New York Times*, National Broadcasting

*Hamilton Holmes and Charlayne Hunter (now Hunter-Gault) desegregated the University of Georgia in January, 1961.* (Library of Congress)

Company (NBC) News, and the *MacNeil/Lehrer News-hour*. She received two Emmy awards, for national news and a documentary film, was named Journalist of the Year in 1986, and received the 1986 George Foster Peabody Award. Hunter married Ronald Gault in 1971, becoming Charlayne Hunter-Gault.

After graduating from Emory University School of Medicine, Holmes remained on staff at the university, garnering recognition for his work as an orthopedic surgeon. He died in 1995.

**Impact** The first assault on segregation in the Deep South focused on higher education. The desegregation of the University of Georgia by Holmes and Hunter combined with that of the University of Mississippi by James H. Meredith and of the University of Alabama by Autherine Lucy, Vivian Malone, and James Hood to effect a region-wide breakdown of official and unofficial policies preventing African Americans from attending most colleges and universities. As intended, the desegregation of major universities helped destroy the walls of segregation at all public schools and at other public facilities.

**Additional Information** Journalist Calvin Trillin revised his original *New Yorker* articles covering the integration of the University of Georgia into *An Education in Georgia: The Integration of Charlayne Hunter and Hamilton Holmes.* The revised edition, published in 1991, includes a new foreword by Charlayne Hunter-Gault. Hunter-Gault published her autobiography, *In My Place*, in 1992.

*LeeAnn Bishop Lands*

**See also** Civil Rights Movement; Malone, Vivian; Meredith, James H.; School Desegregation.

# ■ Hoover, J. Edgar

**Born** January 1, 1895, Washington, D.C.
**Died** May 2, 1972, Washington, D.C.

*Director of the Federal Bureau of Investigation who opposed the Civil Rights movement as subversive. His policies grew out of his racial and anticommunist bias and conservative social outlook.*

**Early Life** J. Edgar Hoover was born in Washington, D.C., of Swiss parents, who settled there in the early 1800's. The dominant influence in his Southern conservative upbringing was his mother, Annie M. Scheitlin Hoover, with whom he lived until her death in 1938. Entering the Justice Department in 1917,

he organized surveillance activities in the recently established Federal Bureau of Investigation (FBI). Known for his honesty and integrity, he became director of the bureau in 1924. Under his leadership, the bureau became a professional agency of career civil servants appointed and promoted on merit. Clear lines of authority were established, with control in the director's office. During his long career, he did as much as any man to professionalize policing in the United States.

**The 1960's** Hoover set out during the Cold War to combat not only communists but also other organizations he deemed subversive. Under Hoover, the FBI blurred the line between dissent and disloyalty, often focusing its attention on legitimate political opposition.

Among the most objectionable weapons employed by Hoover against this opposition was electronic surveillance. His use of this technique was governed by three concerns. The first was to discover "subversive" influence. This led to placing taps and bugs, for example, on leaders of leftist or civil rights organizations, including Martin Luther King, Jr. His second concern was to prevent "violent activity." To this end, he ordered the surveillance of Malcolm X, the Black Panther leaders, the Ku Klux Klan, and the Jewish Defense League. His third concern was to detect the sources of leaks of classified information. He ordered, for example, the so-called "Kissinger taps" of 1969-1971 on seventeen journalists and government employees suspected of receiving information about the government's policy of secretly bombing Cambodia. Even the highest levels of government were suspect. After Hoover's death in 1972, a scandalous dossier on Eleanor Roosevelt was found in his "Official and Confidential" files.

**Later Life** His last years were embittered and isolated. Despite mounting criticism that his leadership of the FBI was arbitrary and misguided, he continued his policies unabated until his death in 1972. He left the FBI ill-prepared to carry on without him or to deal with new issues of gender, race, and civil liberties.

**Impact** In the long run, Hoover's antisubversive campaign undermined the FBI's reputation among Americans for professional impartiality. He failed to recognize that American attitudes toward African Americans and their civil rights had altered. His

*Federal Bureau of Investigation director J. Edgar Hoover (center) confers with President John F. Kennedy (left) and Attorney General Robert F. Kennedy in February, 1961.* (AP/Wide World Photos)

customary charge, therefore, that communists were behind civil rights demonstrations no longer worked. His policies also distracted the FBI from investigating more pressing problems, such as organized crime.

**Additional Information**  In 1987, Richard Gid Powers published *Secrecy and Power: The Life of J. Edgar Hoover*, a thorough, well-balanced, and critically acclaimed work that deals at great length with Hoover's role in the 1960's.

*Charles H. O'Brien*

**See also**  Black Panthers; Civil Rights Movement; King, Martin Luther, Jr.; Ku Klux Klan (KKK); Malcolm X.

## ■ *House Made of Dawn*

**Published** 1968
**Author** N. Scott Momaday (1934-      )

*The first novel by an American Indian author to receive the Pulitzer Prize. It inaugurated a renaissance in American Indian writing.*

**The Work**  *House Made of Dawn* is set in the pueblo of Walatowa, New Mexico, and in Los Angeles, California, between 1945 and 1952. The narration includes a brief prologue and four dated sections. After a prologue describing a man running in open country, the story opens on July 20, 1945, when a young Pueblo Indian named Abel returns to Walatowa after serving in World War II. Alienated and troubled,

Abel works for Angela St. John, a stranger visiting the area, and has an affair with her. At a village festival, an ominous-looking albino man attacks Abel and humiliates him. Meanwhile, Father Olguin, the village priest, studies the diary of his predecessor, Fray Nicolás, and makes an awkward overture to Angela. On August 1, Abel stabs the albino to death in a cornfield. This section of the novel concludes the next day, as Francisco, Abel's grandfather, hoes his cornfield alone. The second section, dated January 27 and 28, 1952, is set in Los Angeles and centers on John Big Bluff Tosamah, a Kiowa peyote priest. On January 27, Tosamah preaches a sermon asserting that white people have debased language; meanwhile, Abel lies on a beach, recovering consciousness after a severe beating. The narration moves back and forth in time, interspersing the sermon with fragments from Abel's past: trial testimony, prison, his affair with a social worker named Milly, and a peyote ceremony. In the part dated January 28, Tosamah meditates, in his second sermon, on his grandmother's life and the magnificent Kiowa culture. The third section of the novel, dated February 20, 1952, is narrated by Ben Benally, a relocated Navajo who has befriended Abel in Los Angeles. Benally's reverie reflects Abel's life in Los Angeles: his work in a cardboard carton factory, a problem with a sadistic police officer, conversations with Tosamah and Milly, and an encounter with Angela. Benally recalls singing verses from Navajo ceremonies, including the poem that begins with the phrase "House made of dawn." In the novel's fourth section, dated February 27 and February 28, 1952, Abel returns to Walatowa as Francisco is dying. Abel buries his grandfather; then arises before dawn and runs, singing silently.

**Impact** Publication of *House Made of Dawn* and its subsequent receipt of the Pulitzer Prize led to the first book of criticism on literature written by American Indians. This critical study inaugurated an ever-increasing number of books, scholarly articles, and university courses on works by American Indians. More important, Momaday's novel inspired a new generation of American Indian writers to begin producing a wealth of poetry, fiction, autobiography, essays, and performance scripts.

**Related Work** Vine Deloria's *Custer Died for Your Sins* (1969) is a nonfiction treatment of many of the issues raised in *House Made of Dawn*.

**Additional Information** The most thorough study of *House Made of Dawn* is *Landmarks of Healing: A Study of House Made of Dawn* (1990), by Susan Scarberry-Garcia.

*Helen Jaskoski*

**See also** Literature; Silko, Leslie Marmon; *Way to Rainy Mountain, The.*

# ■ Housing Laws, Federal

*Laws that involved the federal government in the housing market. They established public housing, slum clearance, urban renewal, and fair housing programs and policies.*

President John F. Kennedy inherited from his predecessors a legacy of federal involvement in the housing market. The Housing Act of 1934, part of Franklin D. Roosevelt's New Deal, was the cornerstone of all federal housing programs because it established the Federal Housing Administration (FHA) and federal mortgage insurance for single-family and multi-family homes. Two additional laws—the Housing Acts of 1937 and 1949—created the basic framework of low-rent public housing, slum clearance, and urban renewal, and the Servicemen's Readjustment Act of 1944, known as the G.I. Bill of Rights, guaranteed home mortgage loans for veterans.

The construction of homes for Americans able to afford private housing benefitted from federal involvement. Pent-up demand generated during the Great Depression and World War II drove housing starts to record levels by the end of the 1940's. Despite the Korean War (1950-1953), which produced temporary shortages of building materials, housing starts averaged 1.5 million per year during the 1950's. In contrast, federal performance in the field of public housing and urban renewal was relatively feeble. Although the Housing Act of 1949 had proclaimed the ambitious goal "of a decent home and suitable living environment for every American family," public housing and urban renewal efforts had fallen far short of that objective.

**Kennedy's Efforts** When he took office in January, 1961, President Kennedy made a new housing law part of his legislative agenda. The result was the Housing Act of 1961, which attempted to enhance and supplement the private housing market. Among other provisions, the Housing Act of 1961 reduced down payments for FHA mortgage loans and extended the loan period to thirty-five years, furnished

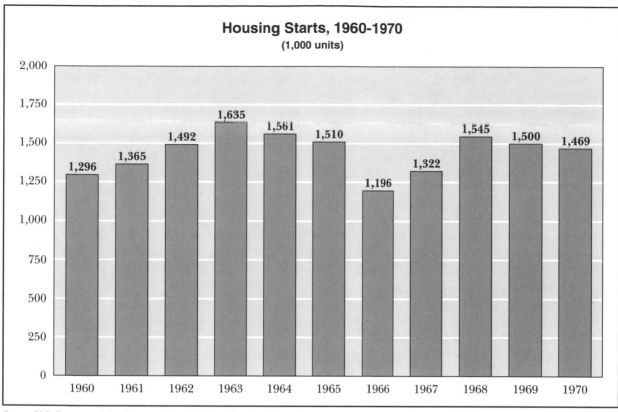

**Housing Starts, 1960-1970**
(1,000 units)

*Source:* U.S. Bureau of the Census. *Historical Statistics of the United States, Colonial Times to 1970.* New York: Basic Books, 1976.

federal aid for repair of dilapidated housing in urban areas, and increased funds for low-cost veterans mortgages. The most controversial section of the 1961 law was that creating a costly below-market-rate FHA insurance program for subsidized middle-income rental housing.

Praising the 1961 law as "a giant step toward better cities and improved housing," Kennedy appointed Robert C. Weaver, an impressively credentialed African American, to take charge of federal housing policy as head of the Housing and Home Finance Agency. The president also urged Congress to create a cabinet-level department to deal with the problems of America's cities. He failed, however, to overcome Republican and conservative Democratic opposition to his urban affairs bill. Blocked by the conservative coalition, Kennedy, on November 20, 1962, issued Executive Order 11063 on Equal Opportunity in Housing, which prohibited racial discrimination in new housing built with federal assistance. The executive order, though limited in scope and widely ignored by builders and lenders, marked the beginnings of federal fair housing policy. It fulfilled a promise that Kennedy had made during the 1960 election campaign to wipe out discrimination in federal housing programs with "a stroke of the pen."

**Great Society Legislation** Following the death of President Kennedy, Lyndon B. Johnson capitalized on the nation's post-assassination mood and urged Congress to adopt Kennedy's legislative agenda as a memorial to the slain president. Johnson's landslide victory in the 1964 presidential election increased Democratic majorities in Congress and made possible a deluge of Great Society legislation, including the Housing and Urban Development Act of 1965. As Kennedy had earlier proposed, the new law created a cabinet-level department of urban affairs, the Department of Housing and Urban Development (HUD). The core of the new cabinet department was the Housing and Home Finance Agency, which included the Federal Housing Administration, Urban Renewal Administration, and Public Housing Administration. Johnson chose Weaver to fill the secretary of HUD position, making Weaver the first African American cabinet officer in U.S. history.

In calling for passage of the Housing and Urban Development Act of 1965, Johnson had declared that "the ultimate goal in our free enterprise system must be a decent home for every American family." Like most other Great Society programs, the law failed to achieve Johnson's purpose, but it did create new "leased housing" and rent-supplement plans to assist the poor. Other features of the 1965 housing act included FHA loans without down payments for veterans, lower down payments on other FHA mortgage loans, and low-interest loans for rural housing.

The following year, Congress passed the Model Cities Act of 1966. To improve the quality of urban life, the federal government funded comprehensive model cities projects that included construction of low- and middle-income housing. Soon, however, the model cities program bogged down in squabbling between federal and local agencies. It had scant effect on urban housing.

Undismayed by the troubles afflicting model cities, in 1968, Johnson submitted another sweeping bill to Congress. The Housing and Urban Development Act of 1968, called the most ambitious housing program in U.S. history, was designed to eradicate substandard housing within ten years through the construction of twenty-six million new homes and apartments. The law extended interest-rate subsidy and rent-supplement programs to increase the construction and repair of low-rent housing and to expand home ownership by low-income Americans. It also created the Government National Mortgage Association to purchase mortgage loans written at below-market rates and allowed the privatization of the Federal National Mortgage Association, formed during the 1930's by the Federal Housing Administration to provide a secondary market for home mortgage loans. Finally, the housing law of 1968 contrived an assortment of other programs, including "new communities," neighborhood development, housing rehabilitation, and "national housing partnerships" intended to facilitate the investment of corporate money in low-income housing in blighted urban areas.

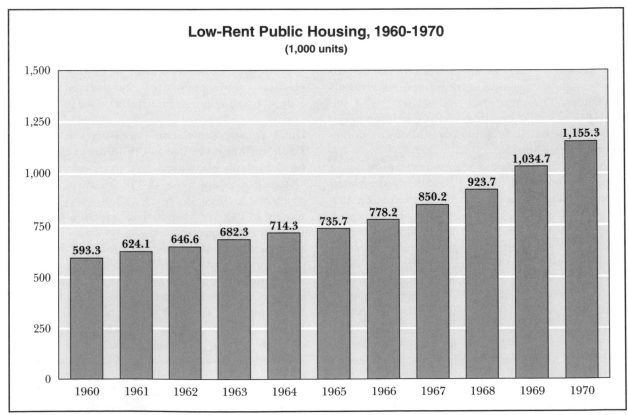

**Low-Rent Public Housing, 1960-1970**
(1,000 units)

| Year | Units |
|------|-------|
| 1960 | 593.3 |
| 1961 | 624.1 |
| 1962 | 646.6 |
| 1963 | 682.3 |
| 1964 | 714.3 |
| 1965 | 735.7 |
| 1966 | 778.2 |
| 1967 | 850.2 |
| 1968 | 923.7 |
| 1969 | 1,034.7 |
| 1970 | 1,155.3 |

*Source:* Kurian, George, *Datapedia of the United States, 1790-2000, America Year by Year.* Lanham, Maryland: Bernam Press, 1994.

**Impact** Taken together, the various provisions of the Housing and Urban Development Act of 1968 constituted a heightened federal commitment to public housing. The effects of the 1968 law would not be felt until after President Richard M. Nixon took office in 1969. Despite abuses and scandals that plagued the public housing program, by 1972, 1.3 million low- and moderate-income housing units had been completed. Although the 1968 housing act did not lift many Americans out of poverty, it did allow some moderate-income families to become home owners. Additionally, as was the case with earlier housing legislation dating back to the 1930's, the 1968 law provided not only profits for lenders, developers, and builders but also jobs for workers.

Civil rights legislation also affected housing in the United States during the 1960's. The Civil Rights Act of 1964 moved in the direction of fair housing policy by prohibiting racial discrimination in federally subsidized housing programs. The private, non-federally assisted housing market remained largely untouched, and in January, 1966, President Johnson urged Congress to adopt a fair housing law to eliminate racial discrimination. Following the assassination of Martin Luther King, Jr., Congress in April, 1968, adopted the Civil Rights Act of 1968, which included Title VIII, a fair housing statute that outlawed racial discrimination in virtually all public and private housing.

**Subsequent Events** The 1960's were a decade of strong housing growth, with more than fourteen million homes constructed. Of those homes, 97.5 percent were produced by the private sector. That astonishing statistic furnished ammunition for radical critics of public housing who complained that federal housing policy continued to be skewed in favor of the affluent, especially by the federal income tax deduction for home mortgage interest, which was much more advantageous for the wealthy. In the radical view, federal policy had aided lenders, developers, and builders in their profit-making endeavors and had promoted suburbanization for the largely white middle and upper classes, while public housing programs for the poor remained underfunded and wholly inadequate. According to radical critics, urban renewal meant removal of slum housing and displacement of racial minorities without replacement of the housing units that were demolished.

Conservative critics were equally harsh in their evaluation of Great Society housing laws and programs. In the conservative view, public housing and urban renewal were expensive and wasteful, ran contrary to the logic of the private marketplace, and probably made conditions in urban areas worse instead of better. Conservatives concluded that the federal government should cease its messy, meddlesome intervention and allow the private market to function. In January, 1973, partly in response to the conservative critique and alarmed about multiplying scandals, President Nixon suspended all federally subsidized public housing programs. The public housing and urban renewal programs of the 1960's, enacted with such great expectations, proved disappointing in operation and, for many Americans, had come to symbolize the failure of the Great Society.

**Additional Information** Useful studies of federal housing legislation include *History of Housing in the U.S., 1930-1980* (1982), by Joseph B. Mason; *Critical Perspectives on Housing* (1986), edited by Rachel G. Bratt, Chester Hartman, and Ann Meyerson; *The Builders: Houses, People, Neighborhoods, Governments, Money* (1978), by Martin Mayer; *The Politics of Federal Housing* (1971), by Harold Wolman; and *Housing: Federal Policies and Programs* (1980), by John C. Weicher.

*Richard N. Chapman*

**See also** Great Society Programs; Johnson, Lyndon B.; Kennedy, John F.; Nixon, Richard M.; Urban Renewal.

# ■ Hughes, Howard

**Born** December 24, 1905, Houston, Texas
**Died** April 5, 1976, in an airplane en route from Acapulco, Mexico, to Houston, Texas

*The United States' premier tycoon, financial genius, aviator, filmmaker, and celebrity enigma. Hughes enjoyed fame and fortune equaled by few others during his complex life but endured numerous hardships, including phobias and other disorders, a near-fatal plane crash, and wrenching drug addiction.*

**Early Life** A brilliant but withdrawn only child, Howard Robard Hughes, Jr., briefly attended Rice Institute, ending his education after his father died in 1924. At age twenty, he inherited his late father's patents and tool company, worth millions of dollars. He married and moved to Hollywood to make films, including the box-office hit *The Outlaw* (1941). By 1938, Hughes, a world-class pilot and aircraft designer, held nearly every aviation record. In 1946, Hughes's XF-11 crashed and sent him to the hospital, where he developed a hopeless addiction to morphine, which led to other dependencies that would hamper him for life and cause him to become an eccentric recluse in the 1960's. In 1947, he suffered from an embarrassing Senate investigation into his wartime financial conduct, which ended after the dramatic flight of his gigantic seaplane, named *Hercules* but called *Spruce Goose*, which many doubted could fly. The flight captured the nation's attention and admiration. In 1948, there was a failed effort to draft Hughes for president. Throughout the 1950's, Hughes concentrated on expanding his business empire.

**The 1960's** During the 1960's, Hughes's personal behavior became increasingly erratic, but his businesses had lives of their own. Hughes was a billionaire by the mid-1960's. His holdings included a charitable medical institute, media outlets, and Hughes Aircraft Corporation. In 1960, a Hughes Research Laboratory scientist created the first laser, and in 1963, Hughes Electronics produced some of the earliest communications and spy satellites. His companies were essential in the lunar landing of 1969.

Although his financial empire flourished, Hughes languished personally, becoming a reclusive shell of a person, paranoid and dependent. In 1966, Trans World Airlines, one of his companies, was sold after lengthy litigation. That same year, Hughes went to Las Vegas, Nevada, and rented the entire top floor of the Desert Inn. He would not leave the hotel room for years. Remarried, Hughes rarely allowed even his wife to see him. A one-time celebrity and Hollywood star, he detested the limelight that followed him and made few public appearances and seldom granted interviews after the 1950's.

**Later Life** Hughes remained reclusive, fleeing his Las Vegas refuge for the Bahamas in 1970. Political involvement became a hobby for him. From obscurity, he had been affecting presidential elections since the early 1960's, some in favor of Republicans and others in favor of Democrats. The billionaire recluse became the focus of much speculation, innuendo, and attack. Rumors of Hughes's death were common by the 1970's. Hughes, in

dreadful physical condition, died while being flown to Houston in 1976.

**Impact** Hughes, through his wealth and genius, had a significant impact on the 1960's. In aviation and space travel, communications, and medicine, Hughes profoundly affected U.S. history. Despite his wishes, his celebrity status persisted decades after his death. He is most known, however, as an eccentric, billionaire recluse.

**Additional Information** In 1985, Michael Drosnin wrote *Citizen Hughes*, which chronicles the life of Howard Hughes and is based upon the billionaire's internal documents and papers.

*Brett Eric Smithson*

**See also** Business and the Economy; Gross National Product (GNP).

---

# ■ Human Sexual Response

**Published** 1966

**Authors** William H. Masters (1915-       ) and Virginia E. Johnson (1925-       )

*A scholarly book that became a national best-seller in 1966. The authors were professionals who provided the first detailed descriptions of bodily physiology before, after, and during the sexual act.*

**The Work** Alfred Kinsey had completed and published two volumes of research concerning the attitudes of Americans toward sex and issues related to sex, *Sexual Behavior in the Human Male* (1948) and *Sexual Behavior in the Human Female* (1953). These books were widely quoted, frequently stolen from libraries, and banned in many communities. Their popularity demonstrated a desire among many individuals and groups to discuss openly issues relating to sex, a subject that was simply not discussed in polite company. Human sexuality was poorly understood by both the general public and the medical community, which could diagnose diseases but lacked information on sexual disorders.

William H. Masters and Virginia E. Johnson's seminal work, *Human Sexual Response*, directly examined the subject of human sexuality. Masters was a practicing physician and Johnson was trained as a nurse. For several years, they gathered data for the book by observing more than six hundred volunteers age eighteen to eighty-nine engaged in various sexual acts in laboratory conditions rather than by interviewing people, as Kinsey had done.

In their book, Masters and Johnson documented the physiology of sex in great detail. They provided a broad, detailed view of the female sexual response, with chapters on the clitoris, vagina, uterus, and female orgasm, and of the male sexual response, examining in turn the penis, scrotum, and male orgasm. The book, meant for practicing professionals, was well-written but scholarly and somewhat dry. To the amazement of most social critics and the book's publishers and authors, *Human Sexual Response* became a national best-seller.

Masters and Johnson were largely responsible for destroying the myth that sexual activity had to cease with advancing age. They published data demonstrating that older people were physiologically capable of normal sexual functioning. They also demonstrated that the sexual response was similar in men and women. The book provided measurements of the physiological patterns in the sexual response cycle.

**Impact**  Masters and Johnson's findings enabled medical and therapeutic professionals to better treat sexual dysfunctions and helped the general public have open discussions about sex by providing factual information that made these conversations more socially acceptable. In addition, they fostered an entire generation of self-help books, videos, and seminars by making sex therapy a legitimate mode of therapy.

Masters and Johnson also probably contributed to the sexual experimentation of the late 1960's and the subsequent decade by focusing their studies on the mechanics of sex rather than its social aspects. The 1960's were a time of unheralded revolution and experimentation during which traditional sexual mores were first questioned and then challenged. However, much of the information regarding interpersonal and sexual relationships was flawed. Kinsey's pioneering work concerning the attitudes of adult Americans toward sex and sexuality in the late 1940's and early 1950's reflected the dominant beliefs and cultural standards that had been widely held for decades.

**Related Works**  Subsequent research conducted by Masters and Johnson was published as *Human Sexual Inadequacy* (1970) and *Masters and Johnson on Sex and Human Loving* (1986). The public's heightened interest in human sexuality is reflected in the popularity of works such as Alex Comfort's *The Joy of Sex* (1974).

**Additional Information**  *An Analysis of "Human Sexual Response"* (1966), edited by Ruth Brecher and Edward Brecher, provides a look at the Masters and Johnson work. The effect of their work on sex research and study is described in Paul Robinson's *The Modernization of Sex: Havelock Ellis, Alfred Kinsey, William Masters, and Virginia Johnson* (1988).

*L. Fleming Fallon, Jr.*

**See also**  Birth Control; Pill, The; Sexual Revolution.

# ■ Humphrey, Hubert

**Born** May 27, 1911, Wallace, South Dakota
**Died** January 13, 1978, Waverly, Minnesota

*Known as the "Happy Warrior" of U.S. politics. Humphrey was much beloved for his unfailing optimism about the future of the country; as a senator and as vice president, Humphrey was a driving force behind most of the 1960's outstanding social legislation.*

**Early Life**  Hubert Horatio Humphrey, Jr.'s political philosophy was forged largely through a mix of South Dakota populism; the influence of his father, who had been devoted to the politics of Woodrow Wilson; and the hard times his family experienced during the Depression. Humphrey was an outstanding high school student who, inspired by his father, a small-town pharmacist and drugstore owner, became exceptionally well read. He matriculated to the University of Minnesota in 1929. The depression interrupted his studies in 1931, but after a stint as a registered pharmacist in his father's store, he returned to Minnesota to follow a curriculum in political science. While an undergraduate student, he married Muriel Faye Buck on September 3, 1936, and eventually they had four children. He received his B.A. degree in 1939 from Minnesota and a year later his M.A. from Louisiana State University. His year in Louisiana put him in touch with African Americans for the first time, and he was appalled by the segregated circumstances in which they lived. In 1940, he returned to Minneapolis to pursue a doctorate but soon became involved in local politics. After one failed attempt, he was elected mayor of Minneapolis in 1945. He was a brilliant reforming mayor, and his success led to a love affair with Min-

*Democrat Hubert Humphrey, vice president under Lyndon B. Johnson, ran for president in 1968 but lost to Republican Richard M. Nixon.* (Archive Photos)

nesotans that continued until his death. In 1948, he became the first Democrat elected to the U.S. Senate from Minnesota. He was reelected in 1954.

**The 1960's** By 1960, Humphrey was considered the most liberal, optimistic, compassionate, and effective senator in Washington, D.C. He had a phenomenal memory and a thorough knowledge of legislative procedure and was reputed to be the best orator in the Senate. He challenged John F. Kennedy for the Democratic presidential nomination in 1960 but retired from the race after a dispiriting defeat in the West Virginia primary. In the same year, he was returned to the Senate from Minnesota.

As a senator in the 1960's, Humphrey was a stalwart in the Civil Rights movement, a champion of equal employment opportunity, an eloquent spokesman for improved medical care, a fierce opponent of nuclear testing, and a voice for those who were left out of the American Dream. In 1964, Lyndon B. Johnson, Humphrey's political tutor, selected him as

his running mate on the Democratic ticket. Humphrey's liberal associates began to abandon the vice president when he refused to openly oppose Johnson's expansion of the Vietnam conflict, a position he felt he could not take because of his loyalty to the president and his own anticommunist beliefs.

Humphrey's selection as the Democratic Party's nominee for president at the tumultuous 1968 Chicago convention was met with loud and coarse abuse from many elements of the antiwar campaign. Stunned, hurt, and confused by this venomous assault, which cost him considerable financial support, Humphrey was unable to focus his campaign until mid-October. The "politics of joy" that Humphrey espoused seemed out of tune with the reality of the nation's travail over Vietnam. In the end, many of his liberal followers came back to the fold but not enough. He lost the election by a razor-thin margin to Richard M. Nixon.

**Later Life** Following his defeat in 1968, Humphrey lectured in politics at Macalester College and the University of Minnesota. He again was elected to the U.S. Senate in 1970. In 1972, he unsuccessfully challenged South Dakota senator George McGovern for the Democratic presidential nomination. Although showing signs of weakened health, he was reelected to the Senate for a fifth term in 1976. He died on January 13, 1978.

**Impact** Humphrey's biggest impact in the 1960's revolved around his contributions toward shaping and passing vital social legislation. He was the senator that President Kennedy depended on to get his legislative program through a divided Senate. In 1964, Humphrey took charge of the civil rights bill and guided the measure through the Senate, whose membership included enough segregation diehards to make it a close affair. Humphrey worked day and night to maintain the necessary bipartisan alliance that ultimately ended the prolonged filibuster of southern senators. It was the greatest triumph Humphrey had in Washington. As vice president and therefore president of the Senate, Humphrey was put in charge of ensuring that Johnson's Great Society legislation came out of Congress intact. At the time of Humphrey's death, *The Times* (London) commented that the Minnesota senator was the most important person in making the achievements of the Kennedy-Johnson era possible.

*In September, 1965, Hurricane Betsy slammed ashore in Louisiana, leaving massive destruction along this highway through Delacroix Island near New Orleans.* (AP/Wide World Photos)

**Additional Information**  Humphrey's autobiography, *The Education of a Public Man* (1976), is outstanding, and Charles L. Garrettson's *Hubert H. Humphrey and the Politics of Joy: A Case Study in Religious-Political Ethics* (1993) offers an interesting interpretation of Humphrey's career.

*Ronald K. Huch*

**See also**  Civil Rights Act of 1964; Civil Rights Act of 1968; Civil Rights Movement; Democratic National Convention of 1968; Great Society Programs; Nixon, Richard M.; Presidential Election of 1964; Presidential Election of 1968; Voting Rights Legislation.

## ■ Hurricane Betsy

**Date** September 6-10, 1965

*One of the most destructive natural disasters of the 1960's. Hurricane Betsy killed seventy-four people and did more than one billion dollars of property damage.*

**Origins and History**  Hurricane Betsy began as a tropical storm off the northeast coast of South America. It was detected on August 27, 1965, by ships, aircraft, weather satellites, and astronauts Gordon Cooper and Charles Conrad aboard the spacecraft Gemini V. After moving northwest for several days without approaching land, the hurricane turned southwest on September 4 and began heading for populated areas.

**The Hurricane** Hurricane Betsy struck the Bahamas, a chain of islands southeast of Florida, on September 6, 1965. Winds of up to 145 miles per hour did extensive damage to the capital city of Nassau. On September 7, the hurricane moved east to the southern tip of Florida. The cities of Miami and Fort Lauderdale were flooded by the highest tides to hit the area since a previous hurricane in 1926. At least six deaths in Florida were blamed on the hurricane. Property damage in the state was estimated at one hundred million dollars.

On September 9, the hurricane entered the Gulf of Mexico, where it began to move northwest. At about midnight on the morning of September 10, the hurricane struck New Orleans with winds of up to 150 miles per hour. Tides ranging from six to twelve feet high flooded coastal areas of eastern Louisiana, Mississippi, Alabama, and western Florida. More than ten thousand homes were without electricity, and more than 185,000 people were housed in emergency shelters. By September 11, when the hurricane dissipated into a heavy rainstorm moving north over Louisiana into Arkansas, it had caused more than fifty deaths and more than one billion dollars of property damage. President Lyndon B. Johnson and Louisiana Governor John J. McKeithen visited the area on September 11. Under their direction, federal and state agencies began repairing the extensive destruction.

During the worst part of the hurricane, a barge loaded with six hundred tons of liquid chlorine, a highly poisonous substance, sank into the Mississippi River near Baton Rogue, Louisiana. A potential disaster was avoided when the barge was recovered safely on November 12, in a salvage operation that required the evacuation of most of the city's population.

**Impact** Compared with previous large hurricanes, which had sometimes killed hundreds or thousands of people, Hurricane Betsy's final death toll of seventy-four was considered to be quite low. The relatively small number of deaths was credited to early warnings given by radar equipment and weather satellites and quick responses by rescue workers. The $1.4 billion dollars worth of property damage caused by Hurricane Betsy made it the most costly hurricane up to that time.

**Additional Information** A detailed account of Hurricane Betsy and photographs of the destruction it caused can be found in *Hurricanes: Weather at Its Worst* (1967), by Thomas Helm.

*Rose Secrest*

**See also** Alaska Earthquake; Hurricane Camille; Weather Satellites.

---

# ■ Hurricane Camille

**Date** August, 1969

*The most intense hurricane to strike the United States in the 1960's. Camille killed hundreds and caused enormous damage to property.*

**Origins and History** Many residents of the Central Gulf Coast had lived through Hurricane Betsy, a powerful hurricane that came ashore in 1965, and some through a severe, unnamed hurricane in 1947. Therefore, although some people fled, others believed they could safely remain home.

**The Storm** On August 9, 1969, about 480 miles east of the Leeward Islands, a tropical disturbance formed and brought rain the following day. On August 14, the disturbance in the Caribbean Sea became tropical storm Camille, with strong, counterclockwise winds. On August 15, about 60 miles southeast of the western tip of Cuba, Camille, with winds of 115 miles per hour, became a category three hurricane on the Saffir-Simpson scale. That evening, Camille crossed far-western Cuba, producing ten inches of rain.

The next day, the hurricane moved north-northwest in the Gulf of Mexico toward the Florida panhandle. Early in the morning of Sunday, August 17, however, Camille was 250 miles south of Mobile, Alabama, and threatened the coast west of Florida. Early in the afternoon, a U.S. Air Force reconnaissance flight revealed a surface atmospheric pressure of 26.61 inches at the center of Camille; that measurement indicated surface wind speeds as great as 201.5 miles per hour, placing this hurricane far up in category five and foretelling catastrophic damage.

Many residents on the coasts of Alabama, Mississippi, and eastern Louisiana had begun evacuating. Others returned from attending church services, gathered supplies, boarded windows, listened to weather reports, and remained in their homes. With

*In August, 1969, Hurricane Camille struck the Central Gulf Coast, destroying property such as this motel in Biloxi, Mississippi, and killing more than one hundred people.* (AP/Wide World Photos)

increasing rain, wind, and waves, Camille brushed the Mississippi River delta and struck the Mississippi coast directly, its eye moving ashore between 10:30 P.M. and 11:00 P.M., a few miles west of Pass Christian, where the storm surge rose to 24.2 feet.

The storm traveled farther inland on August 18, gradually weakening, and by the time Camille reached far-northern Mississippi, it was only a depression. The storm passed through Tennessee and Kentucky and on August 19 and early the next morning produced heavy rain in far-southern West Virginia and Virginia, where twenty-seven inches of rain fell in only a few hours. The downpour caused flash floods and landslides in the mountains and flooding downstream in Richmond, Virginia, and elsewhere. On August 21, having reached the Atlantic Ocean, Camille briefly regained the status of a tropical storm but disappeared the next day southeast of Newfoundland.

**Impact** Besides causing property damage of $1.42 billion in the United States, Camille killed 3 people

in Cuba, 143 in Louisiana and Mississippi, and 113 in West Virginia and Virginia. President Richard M. Nixon voiced his concern about a supposed failure on the federal level to forecast the severity of the hurricane. Black and white storm refugees harmoniously shared barracks at Camp Shelby. However, during and soon after the huge relief campaign in Mississippi, black storm victims complained about the originally all-white governor's emergency council and about what they considered an anti-poor and therefore anti-African American bias in the policies of the American Red Cross and the Small Business Administration.

**Additional Information** Jim Y. Davidson's *Camille . . . She Was No Lady* (1969) furnishes photographs and maps.

*Victor Lindsey*

**See also** Civil Rights Movement; Hurricane Betsy; Nixon, Richard M.

## ■ *Hush . . . Hush Sweet Charlotte*

**Released** 1964
**Director** Robert Aldrich (1918-1983)

*A shocker that continued in the tradition of an earlier Aldrich film featuring Bette Davis and Joan Crawford. Although the film was intended as a vehicle for these two stars, only Davis appeared.*

**The Work** *Hush . . . Hush Sweet Charlotte* opens with the 1927 bloody ax murder of John Mayhew (Bruce Dern), then jumps forward thirty-seven years to a shadow-filled Louisiana plantation house where neurotic Charlotte Hollis (Bette Davis) lives. Charlotte was suspected of murdering Mayhew, her married lover, but was spared arrest because of her late father's prominence. Charlotte, an aging, single

*Bette Davis (right) and Olivia de Havilland star in the 1964 suspense film* Hush . . . Hush Sweet Charlotte. *(Museum of Modern Art/Film Stills Archive)*

woman, becomes further isolated by her fight to save the house from being razed for construction of a highway. Cousin Miriam Deering (Olivia de Havilland, in the role meant for Joan Crawford) arrives, supposedly to help. This intrusion is regarded with suspicion by the slatternly housekeeper, Velma (Agnes Moorehead), who is later murdered. Dr. Drew Bayliss (Joseph Cotten), with whom Miriam is secretly having an affair, also comes to help Charlotte. Despite their facade of concern for Charlotte, Miriam and the doctor are plotting to get her money. To convince the half-crazed Charlotte that she has gone insane, they plant phony body parts that seem to be from Charlotte's murdered lover, and Miriam tries to convince Charlotte that the elderly woman has murdered the doctor. Charlotte is almost driven into insanity but overhears their gloating and pushes an immense planter off a balcony, crushing them. Charlotte's return to some sort of normality is further aided when she learns that the wife of her long-ago lover (Mary Astor in her last film appearance) has confessed to killing her unfaithful husband.

**Impact** Although not quite as successful as its predecessor, *What Ever Happened to Baby Jane?* (1962), starring Bette Davis and Joan Crawford, *Hush . . . Hush Sweet Charlotte* was a worthy follow-up. It owed a debt to the Grand Guignol grotesquerie exemplified in such classics as *Gaslight* (1944) and *Diabolique* (1955) but was a departure in that the horror was caused as much by the protagonist's own psyche as by outside occurrences. Robert Aldrich's 1962 film touched off a brief revival of interest in films dealing with elderly ladies in jeopardy (the 1964 film *Lady in a Cage*, starring de Havilland, being another example), but *Hush . . . Hush Sweet Charlotte* more or less ended that subgenre. The bravura lighting effects, with their foreboding shadows, were developed using new techniques, and they made the old mansion one of the main characters. The film was somewhat of a watershed in black-and-white filmmaking, which gradually declined thereafter. The film garnered an Academy Award nomination for black-and-white cinematography and received a total of seven nominations. Although criticized at the time, its scenery-chewing overindulgences and mossy *mise en scène* contribute to its enduring qualities.

**Related Work** *What Ever Happened to Baby Jane?* (1962), directed by Robert Aldrich, was this psychological horror film's progenitor.

**Additional Information** For interpretations of *Hush . . . Hush Sweet Charlotte* and information about Aldrich as a filmmaker, see *The Films and Career of Robert Aldrich* (1986), by Edwin T. Arnold, and *What Ever Happened to Robert Aldrich?: His Life and Films* (1995), by Alain Silver.

*Roy Liebman*

**See also** Film; Hitchcock Films; *What Ever Happened to Baby Jane?*

# I

## ■ *I Am Curious—Yellow*

**Released** 1967
**Director** Vilgot Sjöman (1924-    )

*The infamous film that captured the attention of both the public and censors. The release of the film in Sweden in 1967 and in the United States in 1969 abetted the sexual revolution of the 1960's.*

**The Work**   In *I Am Curious—Yellow*, twenty-two-year-old Lena (Lena Nyman), a self-appointed sociologist, attempts to study the class structure in Sweden by a series of interviews, all the while attempting to emulate the nonviolent activities of Martin Luther King, Jr., with meditation, diet, and participation in marches and demonstrations. She takes a lover (Börje Ahlstedt), her twenty-fourth to this point. This is the story within a story: Lena, a drama student, and her lover are characters within a documentary studying various aspects of life in Sweden. The film makes use of newsreels and television voice-overs. Lena the character becomes convinced that the Ten Commandments are no longer relevant and that new ones need to be created. She declares that Sweden needs to stop supporting U.S. involvement in the Vietnam War. Lena the actress is involved with the forty-two-year-old director, Vilgot Sjöman, who has the role of the director in the documentary. All of these characters inhabit a black-and-white film-in-film world that uses a loose narrative structure with

*A woman wraps a rope around a tree and numerous men in* I Am Curious—Yellow, *which was banned for its sex scenes before its eventual release in the United States in 1969, two years after its release in Sweden.* (Museum of Modern Art/Film Stills Archive)

some cinema verité interviews, as with the poet Yevgeny Yevtushenko. The film ends with the characters breaking off their relationships, the documentary being completed, and Lena turning in her key to the front door of the studio. Fade-out comes after the Make Love Not War button is displayed on the screen with the subtitle of "Buy our film."

**Impact** *I Am Curious—Yellow* was a commercial success. "Offensive," "obscene," and "pornographic" were the words used most often to describe the film, which included simulated sexual intercourse, full frontal nudity, fondling of genitalia, and a nude romp. The film was seized by U.S. customs and was not released to Grove Press, its U.S. distributor, until after several court battles involving the film's artistic merits. The legal wrangles generated a great deal of publicity, and the public filled New York theaters when the film was released there in March, 1969. The film's contents—the film within a film and all the politics—was a letdown for those who expected lurid footage. What audiences got instead was an interpretation of the colors of the Swedish flag, new definitions for obscenity and sexuality, and the end of an era of censorship.

**Related Work** In 1968, Sjöman made a second version of the film entitled *I Am Curious—Blue*. This second film is a retelling of the first; the characters and incidents are the same.

**Additional Information** For information on the Swedish political issues in the film, see *The Labor Movement, Political Power, and Workers' Participation in Western Europe* (1982), by John and Evelyne Stephens, and *Interest Groups in Sweden* (1974) by Nils Elvander.

*James F. O'Neil*

**See also** *Blow-up*; Censorship; *Medium Cool*; Sexual Revolution.

## ■ "I Have a Dream" Speech

**Date** August 28, 1963

*The best-known and most-quoted address of Martin Luther King, Jr. Delivered before the Lincoln Memorial on August 28, 1963, it was the keynote speech of the March on Washington, D.C.*

**Origins and History** Along with Abraham Lincoln's Gettysburg Address, delivered one hundred years

earlier, Martin Luther King, Jr.'s "I Have a Dream" speech is one of the most memorable in U.S. history. It was delivered on the steps of the Lincoln Memorial in Washington, D.C., on August 28, 1963, where nearly a quarter of a million people gathered for a March for Jobs and Freedom to urge Congress and President John F. Kennedy to pass a national civil rights bill.

**The Speech** King's remarks were the keynote address of the rally and capped off a day of speeches and musical presentations. The large crowd was charged with emotion and enthusiasm as King took the podium. The three major television networks were to provide live television coverage of the speech, so King had carefully prepared a formal text. In an interview a few months after giving the speech, he recalled he was so moved by the emotion of the crowd spread out before him on that August afternoon in the nation's capital that he abandoned the prepared text and began to preach from the heart, using the phrase, "I have a dream." He had previously used this phrase in speeches given at mass meetings in Birmingham, Alabama, in April and in Detroit in June, 1963. In one of the speech's most memorable passages, King said, "I have a dream that my four little children will one day live in a nation where they will not be judged by the color of their skin but by the content of their character." He drew inspiration from the prophet Isaiah in the Old Testament, mixing his "I have a dream" phrase with phrases from the Bible. After speaking a few sentences from his prepared conclusion, he picked up on a new theme, reciting the first stanza of "My Country, 'Tis of Thee" and ending with the line "from every mountainside, let freedom ring." King spoke forcefully to make himself heard over the growing roar of the crowd. His conclusion powerfully summarized his dream for the United States and his hope for the future. He looked forward to a day "when all God's children—black men and white men, Jews and Gentiles, Catholics and Protestants—will be able to join hands and to sing in the words of the old Negro spiritual, 'Free at last, free at last; thank God almighty, we are free at last.'"

**Impact** Although he did not know it at the time, King had delivered the greatest speech of his life. His words conveyed, to a television audience of millions, the moral power of the great crusade for civil rights in the 1960's. No longer could the country ignore the injustices of poverty, segregation, and violence against African Americans in the United States. King's eloquent plea for justice and freedom was one of the decade's shining moments; however, it also served as a powerful reminder that much still needed to be done.

**Additional Information** *Certain Trumpets* (1994), by Garry Wills, contains a chapter on King that carefully analyzes the origins and influences of this famous speech. The text of the speech can be found in *A Testament of Hope: The Essential Writings and Speeches of Martin Luther King, Jr.* (1986), a one-volume collection of King's writings, speeches, interviews, and reflections edited by James M. Washington.

*Raymond Frey*

**See also**  King, Martin Luther, Jr.; March on Washington.

---

# ■ Immigration

*Influx of people into a nation. Immigration to the United States was on the rise in the 1960's, with the largest group of newcomers arriving from Cuba.*

Immigration to the United States has occurred in waves, one of the largest of which consisted of nearly 28 million people between 1880 and the late 1920's. The numbers of newcomers dropped dramatically in 1924, when Congress passed highly restrictive immigration legislation. The Depression and World War II contributed to low immigration. However, the 1960's saw the beginning of an increase in immigration that continued through the 1990's. Two major patterns of immigration are evident during this decade. One is the large number of Cubans who immigrated to the United States, and the other is the large number of arrivals from different geographical areas following the passage of new immigration legislation in 1965.

**Cuban Immigration**  Throughout the twentieth century, Cuba had maintained close ties with the United States. By the mid-1950's, U.S. business interests had come to dominate many major industries in Cuba. Many wealthy and middle-class Cubans worked for U.S. businesses and consumed North American products. Those Cubans who had money to invest often invested it in the United States.

In 1959, Fidel Castro succeeded in overthrowing the government of Cuban dictator Fulgencio Batista

and began to nationalize U.S. property and to redistribute the wealth. Redistribution involved using force; therefore, many Cubans opposed Castro, who, in turn, viewed those who opposed him as enemies. In addition, many middle-class Cubans had worked for U.S. companies, and Castro's policies deprived them of their livelihoods. During the early years of Castro's revolutionary government, middle- and upper-class Cubans poured into the United States. Between January, 1959, and October, 1962, about 215,000 Cubans left their island for the United States. The majority of these people came from large cities, especially from Havana, not from the impoverished countryside where the majority of Cuba's citizens lived. About 37 percent of Cuban heads of household arriving in the United States between 1960 and 1962 were business owners, managers, and professionals, even though only 10 percent of the Cuban population worked in these occupations.

In 1961, a group of Cuban exiles living in the United States attempted to invade Cuba with help from the Central Intelligence Agency. Although the invaders hoped to topple Castro, they were immediately and decisively defeated by Castro's forces at the Bay of Pigs. This promoted further migration to the United States by making Castro less tolerant of opposition and by convincing many of those who were critical of the Cuban leader's government that they could not look forward to its disappearance in the near future.

In 1962, a new crisis ended the first wave of Cuban migration to the United States. Acting on evidence that Soviet missiles were in Cuba, President John F. Kennedy imposed a naval blockade around the island until the Soviet Union withdrew the missiles. In response, the Cuban government suspended all flights to the United States and exercised strict border controls. From 1962 until the end of 1965, only about 30,000 Cubans managed to reach the United States, either by traveling first to a third country or by sailing to the southern coast of Florida on small boats and rafts.

In the autumn of 1965, another wave of immigration began. Castro publicly invited his critics to leave the country, and President Lyndon B. Johnson gave a speech in front of the Statue of Liberty, in which he said that Cubans could find freedom in the United States. The two nations reached an agreement that allowed "freedom flights" to leave Cuba twice a day. In this second wave, which lasted until

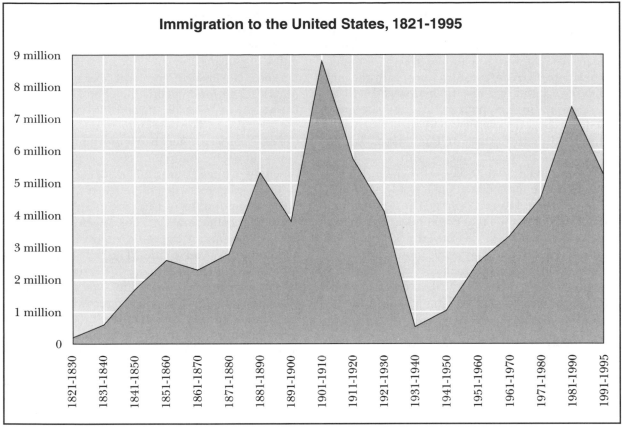

**Immigration to the United States, 1821-1995**

*Source:* Adapted from Immigration and Naturalization Service, *An Immigrant Nation: U.S. Regulation of Immigration, 1798-1991.* Washington, D.C.: U.S. Department of Justice, 1991.

Castro ended the airlift in 1973, 340,000 Cubans made their way to the United States.

These patterns of Cuban immigration were shaped by U.S. government policy. Castro took power during the height of the Cold War, the global rivalry between the United States and the communist states of the Soviet Union and China. After Castro seized power in 1959, it quickly became clear that he was a communist, and his political beliefs led many Americans to support the influx of Cuban refugees.

During the first wave of Cuban immigration, from 1959 to 1962, the U.S. government used Voice of America radio to broadcast anti-Castro messages that encouraged Cubans to flee. All Cubans arriving in the United States were granted "parolee" status, which exempted them from regular immigration quotas and allowed them to be admitted temporarily without giving them legal claims to remain permanently.

In 1960, the United States created the Cuban Refugee Program to handle the processing and re-

settlement of refugees from the island nation. After refugees were screened by the Immigration and Naturalization Service, an emergency center helped them with educational programs, medical treatment, job training and placement, and other social services. In addition, the program attempted to relocate refugees from the Miami area where they were heavily concentrated because it was believed that they placed too much pressure on the Miami economy.

The Kennedy administration convinced Congress to pass the Migration and Refugee Assistance Act in June, 1962, providing continued funds for assistance to refugees from Cuba. The Cuban Adjustment Act, passed in 1966, facilitated the transition from temporary refugee to permanent U.S. resident by virtually guaranteeing that any Cuban reaching the United States could apply for regular immigrant status within one year.

**Immigration Laws** Large-scale Cuban settlement in the United States was followed by a great expansion in the size and diversity of the overall immigrant population. The Immigration Act of 1924 not only limited immigration but also established quotas for immigrants that were heavily biased in favor of people from northern and western Europe. By the mid-1960's, civil rights and discrimination had become central topics in U.S. political life, and the quota system had begun to be viewed as discriminatory.

In 1965, Congress passed an Immigration Act that replaced nation-specific quotas with a worldwide ceiling on immigration. Some immigrants, such as refugees or the immediate families of U.S. citizens, were not counted in this ceiling. The act equalized the number of people that could be accepted from each country and also prioritized potential immigrants. The goal of family reunification was given the highest priority, so family members of both citizens and noncitizens living in the United States were given preference over all others wishing to immigrate.

**Asian Immigration** The Immigration Act of 1965 had two consequences. First, overall immigration increased sharply in the late 1960's and continued to rise steadily in the decades that followed. Second, immigration from Asia and Latin America—areas from which few people had arrived in the first half of the twentieth century—began to increase.

Asians, largely barred from settling in the United States since the nineteenth century, became the fastest growing segment of the population under the new immigration policy. For example, from 1960 to 1970, the number of Chinese living in the United States increased from 237,292 to 436,062; the Filipino population grew from 181,614 to 336,731; and the number of Koreans climbed from about 32,000 to 69,130. These and other Asian American groups continued to grow rapidly through the 1990's.

**Impact** The influx of Cubans in the 1960's created a large Cuban American population. New York City, Chicago, Los Angeles, and the New Jersey cities of Newark and Jersey City all developed substantial Cuban American communities. However, about 60 percent of all Cuban Americans lived in Florida, primarily in Miami, which was home to more Cubans than any other city in the world except Havana.

In Miami and the municipalities adjoining it, Cubans established Little Havana, a bustling neighborhood with thousands of Cuban businesses and its own radio and television stations, newspapers, and social halls. Miami, which had been a declining tourist center in 1960, enjoyed an economic revival partly as a result of Cuban activity. However, the influx of Cubans also gave rise to racial and ethnic tensions, particularly between Cubans and African Americans in lower-income neighborhoods, whose frustration occasionally turned into anger against the newcomers. The development of a large bloc of Cuban American voters had a great impact on U.S. policy and was a source of continued tension between the United States and Cuba.

The immigrants who entered after the passage of the Immigration Act of 1965 also established ethnic residential concentrations. Los Angeles, in particular, became one of the world's most international and ethnically diverse cities. The full impact of this legislation did not become evident until after the 1960's, particularly during the 1980's and 1990's when legal immigration reached record levels. However, much of the later increase in the size and diversity of the immigrant population of the United States can be traced to the 1965 change in policy.

**Subsequent Events** The second wave of Cuban migration ended in 1973, when Castro canceled the airlifts to the United States. A few thousand Cubans continued to reach the United States every year, often in small boats, but it was generally believed that large-scale Cuban immigration was over. Then, in April, 1980, Castro announced that anyone who wished to leave Cuba would be free to do so, and he opened the Mariel harbor as their place of exit. In the following five-month period, more than 130,000 Cubans arrived in south Florida, with 85,000 entering in May alone.

Most of the "Marielitos," as those in this third wave of immigrants were called, were working-class and lower-class people. However, they also included a large number of hardened criminals. Antisocial acts committed by some Marielitos undermined popular support for ready admittance of Cuban refugees and stigmatized responsible Marielitos within the Cuban American community. In 1995, the United States came to an agreement with Cuba under which those wishing to migrate to the United States would have to apply for visas.

By 1990, the Cuban American population exceeded one million, about 72 percent of which had been born in the United States. As the numbers grew, Cuban American political power continued to increase, especially in Florida. Cuban-born Xavier Suarez was elected mayor of Miami in 1985. By 1987, a majority of Miami's registered voters were Hispanic, and Cubans controlled Miami's city commission and held many of municipal positions.

Immigration stemming from the Immigration Act of 1965 climbed steadily in the decades following the 1960's. Legal immigration increased from about 250,000 per year before the act to 1,827,167 in 1991. As a consequence of this immigration, the Asian population of the United States grew from less than 1 percent of all Americans in 1970 to 3 percent of all Americans in 1990, and the Hispanic population increased from 4.5 percent in 1970 to 9.0 percent in 1990. Although immigrants accounted for just under 10 percent of U.S. population growth in 1960 and just over 10 percent of population growth in 1970, by 1990, fully 37 percent of U.S. population growth was due to immigration.

**Additional Information** *Latin Journey* (1985), by Alejandro Portes and R. L. Bach compares the settlement of Cubans in the United States with the settlement of Mexicans and is the authoritative description of the Cuban refugee economy in Florida. Felix R. Masud-Roberto's *From Welcome Exiles to Illegal Immigrants: Cuban Migration to the U.S., 1959-1995* (1996) provides a comprehensive history of Cuban immigration. Philippe Lorrin's *Freedom Flights: Cuban Refugees Tell About Life Under Castro and How They Fled* (1980) gives the testimonies of exiles from Cuba. David J. Rieff's *The Exile: Cuba in the Heart of Miami* (1993) offers a view of Florida's Little Havana. *Challenges of a Changing America: Perspectives on Immigration and Multiculturalism in the United States* (1994), edited by Ernest R. Myers, is a collection of articles that give different views on the problems and opportunities created by the immigration that followed the Immigration Act of 1965.

*Carl L. Bankston III*

**See also** Bay of Pigs Invasion; Castro, Fidel; Central Intelligence Agency (CIA); Cold War; Cuban Missile Crisis; Kennedy, John F.

---

## ■ *In Cold Blood*

**Published** 1966
**Author** Truman Capote (1924-1984)

*A national best-seller and literary experiment, based on a multiple murder, adapted into a motion picture. In this*

*work, Capote combined his abilities as stylist, storyteller, and reporter to tell the story of two drifters and their four murder victims in a new form: the nonfiction novel.*

**The Work** Originally published as a four-part article in *The New Yorker*, *In Cold Blood* had made Truman Capote a millionaire and a national celebrity even before the book's highly touted publication. Capote was fascinated by the mystery of the brutal, seemingly unmotivated 1959 murders of respected, prosperous Kansas farmer Herbert Clutter, his wife, Bonnie, and their two teen-age children, Nancy and Kenyon. Encouraged by *New Yorker* editor William Shawn, Capote followed the case for years, living in Kansas much of the time, interviewing scores of people (at first accompanied by his friend, the novelist Harper Lee), and eventually becoming confidant to Dick Hickock and Perry Smith, the two men convicted of the murders, as they waited on death row during a series of appeals. Capote became especially close to Smith, whose lonely childhood, physical self-consciousness, and artistic aspirations resonated with the writer. Published serially just months after the executions of Smith and Hickock, Capote's project had accumulated unprecedented interest, partly because of its sensational subject matter but also because of Capote's established literary reputation, his personal flamboyance, and his widely publicized claims that he was creating a paradoxical new literary form, the nonfiction novel. In 1967, Pax Enterprises/Columbia produced a film adaptation of *In Cold Blood* that closely follows Capote's narrative design, his interest in the psychological makeup of the criminals (especially Smith), and his commitment to realism (director Richard Brooks even staged the murder scene at the Clutter's home). However, the film omits much of Capote's close, almost anthropological attention to the Clutter family's small-town life, focusing instead on the flight and subsequent capture, trial, and execution of Hickock and Smith. As in the novel, the film waits until deep into the narrative to present the Clutter murders, which are "recalled" by Smith as a testimonial flashback. In contrast to Capote's subtle rhetorical stance, Brooks adds the character of a reporter, who operates as the film's conscience, questioning the morality of capital punishment, thus making explicit the implied irony of the title.

**Impact** Although described as nonfiction on trade lists, *In Cold Blood* won the 1966 Mystery Writers of

America's Edgar Allan Poe Award. Capote's precise methods would be almost impossible to replicate—he claimed a self-taught ability to recall and thus transcribe, with nearly perfect accuracy, hours of interview material and insisted that he had constructed his novel exclusively from observed or recorded detail—but his interest in blurred genres was shared by other novelists, journalists, and filmmakers committed to exploring American social life in new ways. Capote's aggressive self-promotion and extravagant literary claims fostered a situation in which the use of fictional techniques in nonfiction forms and the ethics of making art (and money) from murder could be debated. The strong sense of "two Americas" that characterized *In Cold Blood* became emblematic of an increasingly polarized nation, split apart by suspicion, intolerance, and violence.

The film version of *In Cold Blood* was more revision than experiment, a solid, capably produced studio film in content reminiscent of the earnest social problem films of the 1950's, driven by psychological explanation and liberal argument (in this case, against capital punishment), and in form characterized by moody, highly stylized black-and-white photography evocative of 1940's *film noir*. Although sufficiently admired to have been nominated for four major Academy Awards—Brooks, for both Director and Original Screenplay; Conrad Hall, for Cinematography and Quincy Jones, for Original Musical Score—the film received none and was overshadowed in 1967 by another story of a criminal couple loosely based on fact: the more popular, more violent, more radical, and thus far more controversial *Bonnie and Clyde*. *In Cold Blood* did launch the careers of a pair of talented, previously unknown young actors, Scott Wilson (Hickock) and Robert Blake (Smith), who portrayed, with sensitivity and imagination, the two damaged, ruthless men who intrigued Capote and much of the nation in the mid-1960's.

**Related Work**  In *Armies of the Night* (1968), Norman Mailer offers his version of a fact-based literary experiment, labeling the form novel-as-history, history-as-novel. Although personally antagonistic and publicly dismissive of each other's work, Mailer and Capote nevertheless shared many goals.

**Additional Information**  For a collection of contemporaneous reviews, interviews, and related essays, see *Truman Capote's "In Cold Blood": A Critical Handbook* (1968), edited by Irving Malin; for a return,

decades later, to memories of the project by many participants, see "Capote's Long Ride," by George Plimpton, in the October 13, 1997, issue of *The New Yorker*. In both sources, Capote's methods and his accuracy are both praised and questioned.

*Carolyn Anderson*

**See also**  Crimes and Scandals; *Electric Kool-Aid Acid Test, The*; Film; Literature; Mailer, Norman.

---

# ■ *In the Heat of the Night*

**Released** 1967
**Director** Norman Jewison (1926-     )

*A motion picture that illustrates the changing portrayal of African Americans in films in the 1960's. A winner of five Academy Awards, it was received differently by blacks and whites.*

**The Work**  At the start of *In the Heat of the Night*, an African American police detective, Virgil Tibbs (Sidney Poitier), from Philadelphia, Pennsylvania, is visiting his mother in Mississippi. He is accused of a local murder because of his race and is humiliated and interrogated. After proving his identity, he is still mocked and patronized but decides to stay in the town and work with Bill Gillespie (Rod Steiger), the racist police chief of the small southern town, to solve the murder. Although the police chief finds it hard to think of an African American as a colleague, Tibbs rapidly demonstrates his expertise in criminal investigation procedures, and the police chief turns to Tibbs for assistance in solving the murder. Other examples of white racism are shown. When a local white aristocrat, enraged at being questioned by Tibbs, slaps the detective across the face, Tibbs slaps him back. Tibbs is also ambushed twice, but he persists and singles out the murderer from a mob of youths. At the end of the film, Gillespie takes Tibbs's suitcase to the train station, indicating a grudging acceptance of Tibbs.

**Impact**  *In the Heat of the Night* affected white and black audiences very differently. To liberal whites, Poitier was a strong, well-educated and well-mannered superhero who made justice triumph over racism, and his "courageous" slap became known as the "slap heard around the world." Most of the southern white characters were portrayed as prejudiced and not well-educated. The film was viewed as attacking racism without descending into liberal mawkishness and lecturing. The African American reaction was divided, largely along class lines. Middle-class and lower-middle-class African Americans generally accepted Poitier as someone who embodied African American middle-class values and virtues, lacked any "ghetto baggage," and changed the previous practice of almost always portraying African American characters negatively. Other African Americans, especially intellectuals, referred to Poitier as a straight-arrow assimilationist, an integrationist hero, a black who was liked by whites because he met white standards in manners and was nonthreatening. After criticism following *In the Heat of the Night* and other films, Poitier appeared in more politicized hero roles. Steiger won an Academy Award for Best Actor, but his role aroused little controversy.

**Related Work** The 1967 film *Guess Who's Coming to Dinner*, starring Poitier and directed by Stanley Kra-

mer, dealt with an interracial marriage. It also received mixed reactions from white and black Americans.

**Additional Information** For an analysis of the racial interaction depicted in *In the Heat of the Night*, see *Blacks in American Films: Today and Yesterday* (1972), by Edward Mapp.

*Abraham D. Lavender*

**See also** Film; *Guess Who's Coming to Dinner.*

---

## ■ *Indians*

**Produced** 1968
**Playwright** Arthur Kopit (1937-    )

*A play about the legendary Indian fighter and showman "Buffalo Bill" Cody. Although set in the late 1800's, the play is Kopit's vehicle for exploring contemporary American mythology and its supposed "historical amnesia," a mind-*

*Northern African American police detective Virgil Tibbs (Sidney Poitier) helps the racist police chief of a small southern town (Rod Steiger) solve a local murder in the 1967 film* In the Heat of the Night. *(Museum of Modern Art/Film Stills Archive)*

*set Kopit believed led the United States into the morass of the Vietnam War.*

**The Work** *Indians* opens with an eerie onstage tableau of three glass museum display cases: the first contains an effigy of Buffalo Bill in riding costume, the second a plainly dressed Sitting Bull, and the third an assortment of artifacts—a buffalo skull, a rifle, a bloody Indian shirt. In a sudden cacophony of light and sound, the display cases recede and are replaced by the "real" Cody, riding his white horse inside a show ring and waving his Stetson hat to the crowd. Then, from the darkness at the edge of the stage, ghostly Indians begin appearing. The horse shies, and Cody looks around in terror. He desperately proclaims to the audience, "I am a fine man. And anyone who says otherwise is wrong. . . . " The twelve scenes that follow, in flashback, represent twenty-four years in the life of Cody—during a time when the U.S. government killed or displaced numerous tribes of Native Americans from their land. Between Geronimo's surrender and the Wounded Knee Massacre, Cody meets up with Ned Buntline, a dime-novel writer who helps create the "Buffalo Bill" myth that will become the basis for his popular Wild West Show. The show, ironically, features Sitting Bull and other real-life characters playing themselves, though the events they portray are rewritten for public consumption. Near the end of the play, an army officer who has just taken part in a group slaughter of Indians is being interviewed by the press; he tells them "Of course, our hearts go out to the innocent victims of this . . . " The line is identical to one spoken by General William Westmoreland, commander of U.S. forces in Vietnam. Kopit credited the Vietnam War as being the impetus for writing *Indians.*

**Impact** Although *Indians* was in large part a commentary on the hypocrisy of the modern United States' political and military leaders, it came at a time when U.S. society was so deeply divided over the Vietnam War that Kopit decided the play could not receive an objective viewing in its own country. As a result, *Indians* was first produced by the Royal Shakespeare Company and premiered in London—on the Fourth of July, 1968. "Even before I started to write it," Kopit said, "I knew it would have to be produced in England so that it could have a life, so that it would be done in theaters around the world . . . and judged on its merits." Kopit's strategy to "depoliti-

cize" the play apparently worked. When it was produced in New York during the 1969 theatrical season, most newspaper reviewers—regardless of their opinion of the play—failed to mention in their reviews the obvious parallel between *Indians* and the Vietnam War. The play is generally considered Kopit's best work. It ran for only one season in New York—apparently not from lack of audience interest but from the tremendous staging costs involved. Director Robert Altman bought the film rights to *Indians,* and the play was the basis for his 1976 film *Buffalo Bill and the Indians,* with Paul Newman in the role of Cody.

**Related Work** Another first-class anti-Vietnam War play is David Rabe's *Sticks and Stones* (1971).

**Additional Information** For an overview of Kopit's plays and of his influence on American theater, see *Shepard, Kopit, and the Off Broadway Theater* (1982), by Doris Auerbach.

*Carroll Dale Short*

**See also** Theater; Vietnam War.

---

# ■ Inflation

*A nearly 30 percent rise in prices during the 1960's. This increase was caused in part by the pressures that President Lyndon B. Johnson's Great Society programs placed on federal budgets.*

Despite attempts to control inflation after World War II, prices had started to rise. The consumer price index—the leading indicator of inflation in the economy—rose from 19.5 in 1946 (using the year 1984=100 as a base) to 29.6 by 1960. From 1960 to 1970, the consumer price index grew by nearly 30 percent to 38.8, largely because of increased federal spending.

Government spending had accelerated considerably after President Franklin D. Roosevelt introduced his New Deal in the 1930's. In the 1960's, government expenditures grew considerably because of social welfare programs and defense. Spending on defense, which had fallen to 8 percent of the gross national product (GNP) in 1965 from 14 percent during the Korean War, rose during the Vietnam War to about 9 percent of the GNP. However, the greatest expansion in federal spending occurred in so-called social spending, which included welfare, food stamps, and medical assistance

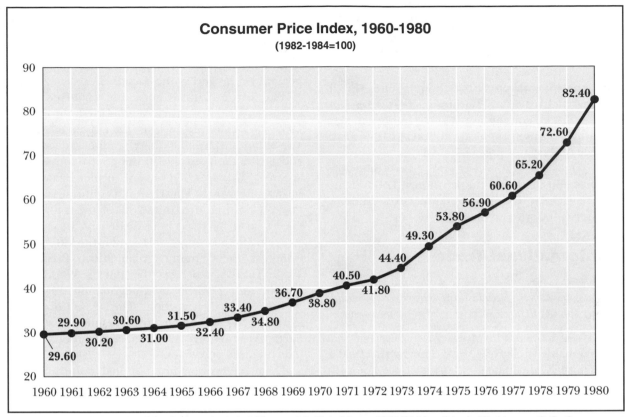

**Consumer Price Index, 1960-1980**
(1982-1984=100)

*Source:* Source: U.S. Bureau of the Census. *Statistical Abstract of the United States: 1996* (116th edition). Washington, D.C.: Government Printing Office, 1996.

to the elderly and poor. In 1964, President Lyndon B. Johnson initiated the War on Poverty and introduced the idea of the Great Society, which was to be achieved through numerous programs designed to improve the lives of Americans. The combined effect of these programs, without increased taxes or borrowing, was to increase inflation through Federal Reserve monetary policy.

In 1960, the U.S. economy, with a real GNP of $1.66 trillion, still dominated the world. Per-capita disposable income rose during the 1960's, from $6,000 to more than $8,000 by the decade's end. The tax cut and reforms proposed by President John F. Kennedy and enacted by Johnson in 1964 decreased the tax rate for individuals and substantially reduced corporate tax rates. The cuts generated a business boom; however, they primarily benefitted people in lower income groups and reduced unemployment. Contrary to predictions, the cut did not increase the federal budget deficit.

By the mid-1960's, however, other factors, including the consumer and environmental movements,

had started to affect the costs of production and, therefore, prices of products.

**Impact** Rising prices helped drive up wages, especially in manufacturing industries, where U.S. companies started to lose ground to foreign competitors. Higher wages, combined with a wave of new federal regulations on business, caused further problems for U.S. industries. Interest rates reflected the rising prices, increasing to levels three times higher in 1981 than in 1961. By the 1970's, the effects of higher interest rates, declining industrial productivity, and inflation produced a malady called "stagflation"—high inflation and high unemployment, a state thought impossible by economist John Maynard Keynes.

**Subsequent Events** In the 1970's, attempts by President Richard M. Nixon to impose wage and price controls failed to stem inflation, as did Gerald Ford's Whip Inflation Now program. President Jimmy Carter developed a measurement for the problem—a "misery index"—but could not solve it. Not until

Ronald Reagan became president in 1981 and worked with Federal Reserve Chairman Paul Volcker to stem inflation was it contained, dropping to zero percent for one quarter during his presidency.

**Additional Information**  Sidney Raner, James H. Soltow, and Richard Sylla's *The Evolution of the American Economy* (1993) contains most of the important data and provides a useful analysis, although it downplays the role of Reagan's policies.

*Larry Schweikart*

**See also**  Business and the Economy; Food Stamp Program; Great Society Programs; Gross National Product; Job Corps; Medicare.

# ■ International Trade

*Trade between the United States and other nations. During the latter part of the decade, tariff rates were gradually lowered in a bid to increase the flow of goods and services.*

The United States' involvement in international trade remained relatively steady during the 1960's. In 1960, the United States exported about 4 percent of its gross national product (GNP), and imports were about 3 percent of GNP. The export share of GNP remained roughly the same throughout the decade, but the import share increased to about 4 percent by the end of the decade.

The United States generally exported more goods and services than it imported during the 1960's. For example, in 1965, the United States had a $5 billion surplus in its merchandise trade account and $3.9 billion surplus in the goods and services account. This trend toward a surplus, which had started after World War II, would continue until the mid-1970's when the United States began to experience a steady increase in trade deficits.

From 1960 through 1961, under the authority of Congress, the General Agreement on Tariffs and Trade (GATT), which later became the World Trade Organization (WTO), held negotiations regarding multilateral tariff reductions. The Dillon Round, the fifth in the GATT negotiations, resulted in substantial tariff reductions on manufactured goods among industrialized countries.

The major event in international trade during the

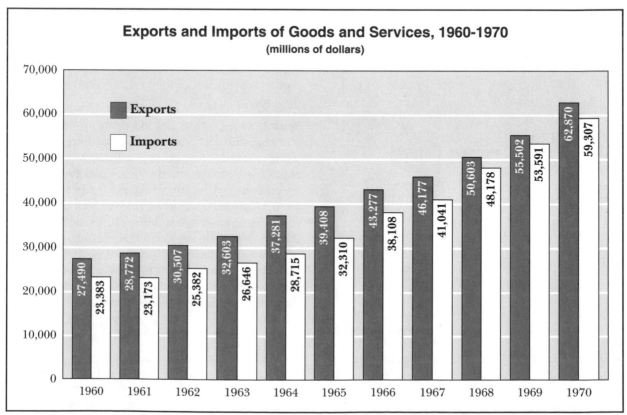

**Exports and Imports of Goods and Services, 1960-1970**
(millions of dollars)

| Year | Exports | Imports |
|------|---------|---------|
| 1960 | 27,490 | 23,383 |
| 1961 | 28,772 | 23,173 |
| 1962 | 30,507 | 25,382 |
| 1963 | 32,603 | 26,646 |
| 1964 | 37,281 | 28,715 |
| 1965 | 39,408 | 32,310 |
| 1966 | 43,277 | 38,108 |
| 1967 | 46,177 | 41,041 |
| 1968 | 50,603 | 48,178 |
| 1969 | 55,502 | 53,591 |
| 1970 | 62,870 | 59,307 |

*Source:* Kurian, George, *Datapedia of the United States, 1790-2000, America Year by Year.* Lanham, Maryland: Bernam Press, 1994.

decade was the Kennedy Round negotiations of the GATT. Congress enacted the Trade Expansion Act of 1962, once again authorizing the president to negotiate tariff cuts of up to 50 percent of their July, 1962, level. The negotiations were completed in 1967 and new lower tariff rates were phased in over a five-year period ending in 1972. A total of seventy countries participated in this round of negotiations, and tariffs on manufactured goods were reduced by an average of 35 percent. The Kennedy Round brought the average tariff rates on manufactured goods to below 10 percent. However, nontariff barriers to international trade remained, especially in agriculture.

**Impact** The successful negotiations completed during the Kennedy Round allowed for the liberalization of international trade to continue through the 1970's, and as a result, the flow of international trade increased steadily. By the mid-1970's, both the export and import shares of the GNP reached 7 percent in the United States, and by 1986, the import share grew to more than 8 percent and the export share remained at more than 5 percent.

**Subsequent Events** The Tokyo Round of the GATT negotiations was completed in 1979, and tariff rates fell below 5 percent when the newly negotiated rates came into full effect in the mid-1980's. The Uruguay Round of the GATT took effect on January 1, 1995. This round of trade negotiations addressed trade issues neglected in the previous rounds, including intellectual property rights, trade in agriculture and services, and government subsidies. The Uruguay Round also established the WTO as a replacement for the GATT.

**Additional Information** For details on the Kennedy Round of the GATT, see the Brookings Institution's *Traders and Diplomats: An Analysis of the Kennedy Round of Negotiations Under the General Agreement on Tariffs and Trade* (1970).

*Daniel Y. Lee*

**See also** Business and the Economy; Gross National Product (GNP); Japanese Imports.

# ■ Interracial Marriage Laws

*Laws prohibiting marriages between people of different races or ethnicities. These laws, some of which predated the Revolutionary War, were particularly common in southern and western states. They were declared unconstitutional by the U.S. Supreme Court in 1967.*

Interracial marriage laws, also known as antimiscegenation laws, appeared in the Americas soon after Europeans established colonies there. These laws, partly a product of the practice of slavery, prohibited people of different races from marrying. Most of the laws focused on marriages between whites and African Americans, but many also prohibited marriages between whites and Asians, Native Americans, or other nonwhites. Although interracial marriage laws had faced legal challenges as early as the 1870's, they remained widespread until the mid-twentieth century. In fact, they became especially popular in the 1920's.

The wide support that antimiscegenation laws once had is demonstrated by the number of states that passed such laws. In the 1940's, thirty states, mostly in the South and West, had laws prohibiting interracial marriages. The goals of these laws can be inferred from their structure and language: Although whites were prohibited from marrying nonwhites, nonwhites were permitted to marry other nonwhites, regardless of race. Virginia's law, which was eventually challenged before the U.S. Supreme Court, was entitled, "An Act to Preserve Racial Integrity." Proponents of antimiscegenation laws unabashedly stated that the legislation was meant to ensure the "purity" of the white race. Interracial marriages, it was argued, would result in the mongrelization or extinction of the white race. Advocates of interracial marriage laws also argued that they satisfied the Fourteenth Amendment's equal protection clause because they applied equally to all races; that is, both whites and nonwhites would be punished equally for violating the laws. Furthermore, proponents contended, the framers of the Constitution clearly did not intend it to prohibit this kind of legislation.

By the 1960's, antimiscegenation laws faced increasing opposition. Opponents of antimiscegenation laws asserted that they were unconstitutional. They argued that these laws violated the equal protection clause by creating race-based distinctions, conflicted with Americans' due process rights to marry freely, and interfered with religious freedoms. Furthermore, critics said that the laws were an attempt to promote the ideals of white supremacy. Interracial marriage laws were also criticized be-

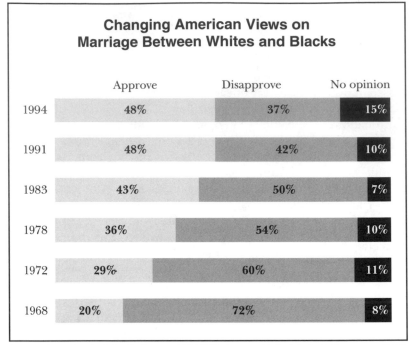

## Changing American Views on Marriage Between Whites and Blacks

| | Approve | Disapprove | No opinion |
|------|---------|------------|------------|
| 1994 | 48% | 37% | 15% |
| 1991 | 48% | 42% | 10% |
| 1983 | 43% | 50% | 7% |
| 1978 | 36% | 54% | 10% |
| 1972 | 29% | 60% | 11% |
| 1968 | 20% | 72% | 8% |

*Source: The Gallup Poll: Public Opinion 1994.* Wilmington, Del.: Scholarly Resources, 1995.

cause they required the government to determine who was white and who was not. By the 1960's, many anthropologists, biologists, and other scientists had determined that the concept of race is artificial and scientifically meaningless.

Some lower courts had declared interracial marriage laws unconstitutional as early as 1947. Before the Supreme Court's ruling in 1967, fourteen states had repealed their laws. However, the issue was not decided definitively until the U.S. Supreme Court heard the case of *Loving v. Virginia* in 1967. In that case, Richard Loving, a white man, and Mildred Jeter, an African American woman, had been convicted in 1958 of violating Virginia's laws against interracial marriage. In 1963, a Virginia court held that the antimiscegenation law was constitutional, but four years later, the Supreme Court unanimously held that the laws served no legitimate government purpose, that they were merely a vehicle to promote white supremacy, and that they violated the equal protection and due process clauses.

**Impact** The Supreme Court's opinion invalidated all remaining interracial marriage laws. Furthermore, because the Court made it clear that it would be highly skeptical of any race-based legislation, the opinion in this case spurred many states to repeal

other laws that categorized people on the basis of race. Thus, the end of antimiscegenation laws was also a significant step forward in the Civil Rights movement.

**Subsequent Events** Since 1967, interracial marriages have remained legal in all states. The rate of interracial marriages in the United States, while still relatively small, has increased since the 1960's.

**Additional Information** Walter Wadlington's "The Loving Case: Virginia's Anti-Miscegenation Statute in Historical Perspective," in the *Virginia Law Review* (issue 52, 1966) is an excellent article on the history of antimiscegenation laws. For a more modern perspective, see Peggy Pascoe's "Miscegenation Law, Court Cases, and Ideologies of 'Race' in Twentieth-Century America," in the June, 1996, issue of the *Journal of American History*.

*Phyllis B. Gerstenfeld*

**See also** Civil Rights Movement; Marriage; Supreme Court Decisions.

## ■ Interstate Highway System

*A system of limited-access highways that connect the major metropolitan areas of the United States. The system became one of the largest public works projects undertaken by the federal government. The highway system transformed not only the way Americans travel but also the culture, economy, and environment.*

The United States Congress defeated proposals for a limited-access highway system several times before President Dwight D. Eisenhower's administration pushed for a national system of efficient highways in the 1950's. Eisenhower's idea originated from his experience as an observer on a 1919 cross-country military convoy that determined how difficult and time-consuming it was to transport military vehicles and equipment. He signed the Federal Aid Highway Act on June 29, 1956, authorizing a 42,500-mile National System of Interstate and Defense Highways. Congress also created a Highway Trust Fund to finance the project. The federal government paid 90 percent of the cost, mostly from gasoline and diesel fuel taxes and usage fees. The remaining 10 percent came from the states.

In the early 1960's, many people still lived in cities surrounded by farms. Travel by car, much of it over two-lane roads with unimproved shoulders and sharp curves, remained slow and risky. As the inter-

*Freeways, like these in downtown San Francisco, enabled people to live in the suburbs and commute to work but often had deleterious effects on the city neighborhoods where they were built.* (AP/Wide World Photos)

state highway system expanded, the most obvious change was the growth of the suburbs. For many commuters and travelers, the interstate greatly diminished the frustration of crowded streets and stop-and-go traffic and decreased commute time. Private automobiles replaced the streetcar and passenger railroad systems as a major means of transportation. As many people moved out to the suburbs, businesses left the cities, creating a loss in tax revenues.

Traffic capacity on many sections of the interstate system expanded beyond levels envisioned by the highway planners. They intended the system to move existing traffic, but the new highways quickly became congested with added traffic. The interstates allowed more people to move to the suburbs, creating many areas of heavy community traffic.

Travel and leisure time also changed in the 1960's. Long weekend vacations became possible. Motel chains, restaurants, and gasoline stations developed near the interchanges, and many of the chains, including Stuckeys, Nickerson Farms, and Howard Johnson, became familiar sights to travelers. Towns along the interstates prospered, and other towns less conveniently located suffered the loss of business and tourism. People learned new meanings for words such as merging, congested areas, cloverleaf, and exit.

The interstates not only caused the cities to lose population and tax resources to the suburbs but also divided, disrupted, and destroyed some city neighborhoods. This further weakened the social fabric of some city areas. By the late 1960's, critics and environmentalists were advocating changes in further construction of interstates. Eventually, regulations required environmental impact reports before building new interstate segments.

The interstate highway system brought an increase in roadside billboard signs because of an absence of regulations governing the use of land abutting the highways. The federal government passed standards to alleviate the problem, and states that complied received bonus federal construction money. Only a few states passed legislation to comply with the standards. In 1965, President Lyndon B. Johnson, whose wife, Lady Bird, had a strong interest in highway beautification, recommended legislation for mandatory billboard control. Congress enacted the Highway Beautification Act on October 22, 1965. Under the act, 10 percent of federal aid highway funds were withheld from any state not controlling billboards within 660 feet of an interstate or primary system highway. The legislation also required screening of junkyards by natural objects or fences.

**Impact** The interstate highway system changed the pattern of commerce, work, recreation, and living in the United States. It drew regions of the country closer together, speeded the flow of people and business out of the cities, brought economic growth to states and businesses, created jobs in construction and service, and gave people more choices of places to live and work. Interstates reduced travel time, saved lives, and prevented injuries. Highway safety increased because of wider shoulders, medians, controlled accesses, and interchanges. The interstate highway system also altered commercial transportation. Delivery time for products decreased, and trucks became the primary movers of freight.

**Subsequent Events** Many older parts of the interstate system began to deteriorate in the late 1960's. Priorities shifted to repair, restoration, rehabilitation, and reconstruction. These included reconstruction of bridges, interchanges, and overpasses, and the addition of lanes. Much of this maintenance was left to the states, which could not keep up with the costs. An increase in gas taxes became a successful way to fund these needs. Cancellation of some reconstruction and new construction projects occurred because of environmental and financial problems.

**Additional Information** An in-depth study of the interstate highway system can be found in *The Motorization of American Cities* (1986), by David J. St. Clair.

*Vivian L. Richardson*

**See also** Automobiles and Auto Manufacturing; Business and the Economy; Environmental Movement.

# J

## ■ Jackson, Jesse

**Born** October 8, 1941, Greenville, South Carolina

*Civil rights advocate who promoted social activism through economic development. Jackson came of age in the 1960's Civil Rights movement.*

**Early Life** Jesse Louis Jackson's ancestors include Africans, Cherokees, and Irish landowners. Young Jackson watched his mother work as a maid and knew the man next door only as Noah Louis Robinson, a married cotton grader. However, Robinson was Jackson's biological father, a fact later revealed to a teenage Jackson.

A natural competitor, Jackson was a talented athlete. He won a football scholarship to the University of Illinois where he hoped to quarterback the football team. After learning that African American players were limited to playing linemen, he left to attend North Carolina Agricultural and Technical State College, where he quarterbacked the team and began a lifetime of advocacy.

**The 1960's** The Civil Rights movement spawned a remarkable generation of African American leaders. Jackson joined the struggle for civil rights at the most critical time in the movement and later branched out on his own to promote economic development for African Americans.

While in college in North Carolina, Jackson organized protests against segregated restaurants, theaters, and hotels. In 1963, Jackson was elected student body president and began his association with the Southern Christian Leadership Conference (SCLC). When Jackson joined SCLC, the organization was trying to raise awareness of the political potential of African Americans through nonviolent demonstrations. In 1966, he helped organize the Chicago freedom movement, which promoted local integration of schools and housing.

He became involved with one of SCLC's programs, Operation Breadbasket, designed to make African Americans economically self-sufficient. In 1967, when Martin Luther King, Jr., founder of the SCLC, asked Jackson to lead Operation Breadbas-

ket, Jackson left the seminary. When King was assassinated in Memphis in 1968, Jackson, despite his youth, hoped to be his successor. However, King's personal assistant, Ralph Abernathy, was the consensus candidate chosen to lead the SCLC.

Jackson eventually left the SCLC to form a new organization based on the economic self-sufficiency concept offered by Operation Breadbasket.

**Later Life** In 1971, Jackson founded Operation PUSH (People United to Save Humanity), a progressive economic political organization based on the concept behind Operation Breadbasket, a goal of economic self-sufficiency that served as the foundation of Jackson's political struggle for the next several decades. In 1983, Jackson founded the Rainbow Coalition, a political organization that reached out to all races and minorities, seeking a "rainbow" of races and types of people.

With the Rainbow Coalition's support, Jackson sought the Democratic presidential nomination in 1984 and 1988. He elevated his reputation as a statesman by practicing roving diplomacy for the United States. With President James "Jimmy" Carter's blessing, Jackson went to South Africa to condemn apartheid. He took a special interest in the Middle East, visiting Israel, Lebanon, the West Bank, Syria, and Egypt. Jackson intervened more than once to obtain the release of U.S. hostages held by terrorists or hostile governments.

**Impact** As the head of the Chicago branch of Operation Breadbasket, Jackson carried out a sixteen-week campaign against the A&P grocery chain that resulted in store executives signing an agreement to hire more then two hundred additional African Americans, some of them as store managers and warehouse foremen. He also was able to negotiate agreements with soft-drink bottlers and a local dairy. However, although Jackson achieved some measure of success, his efforts did not have far-reaching effects for the poor of Chicago's inner cities.

Jackson's Rainbow Coalition, the logical extension of Operation Breadbasket, was the first national attempt in the modern era to galvanize all races and

*Civil rights activist and Southern Christian Leadership Conference member Jesse Jackson is led off by police during a 1966 protest.* (AP/Wide World Photos)

socioeconomic groups. This political movement, while building on Jackson's work in the 1960's, was a forward look to the twenty-first century when shifting demographics, particularly a greater proportion of ethnic minorities in the population, will perhaps make a broad-based multiethnic coalition necessary for political success. Although Jackson has demonstrated his skills in political organizing and his ability to influence the public, he did not see the electoral success he sought. One reason may be the damage Jackson's image as a healer suffered because of his association with Louis Farrakhan, the controversial leader of the Nation of Islam, who praised Hitler and called Judaism a "gutter" religion.

**Additional Information** *Jesse* (1996), by Marshall Frady, is a valuable source of information on Jackson's life and career.

*Cathy Travis*

**See also** Abernathy, Ralph; Assassinations of John and Robert Kennedy and Martin Luther King, Jr.;

Civil Rights Movement; King, Martin Luther, Jr.; Southern Christian Leadership Conference (SCLC).

---

## ■ *Jacobellis v. Ohio*

*One of the most important obscenity cases of the 1960's. The U.S. Supreme Court held that it had the duty to make an independent judgment on the alleged obscenity of various forms of expression.*

The U.S. Supreme Court held in *Roth v. United States* (1957) that sexually explicit materials were protected by the First Amendment to the U.S. Constitution unless those materials were judged "obscene." Obscenity was defined as "whether to the average person, applying contemporary community standards, the dominant theme of the material taken as a whole appeals to prurient interest."

Nico Jacobellis was found guilty of violating Ohio's obscenity statute because he exhibited a French film called *The Lovers*. He appealed to the

U.S. Supreme Court alleging that his First Amendment right to free expression had been violated. Although on June 22, 1964, the Court overturned his conviction, six to three, the justices in the majority could not agree on a single rationale for doing so.

Justices William J. Brennan and Arthur Goldberg held that it was the duty of the Court to independently judge whether a work was obscene. Because the issue of whether a work is obscene is also an issue of whether that work is protected by the First Amendment (that is, an issue of constitutional law), the Court could not simply defer to the decisions of juries or lower court judges in such cases. They applied the *Roth* test and concluded not only that the work was not obscene but also that "community standards" referred to American society at large and not simply to a state or local community. Justices Hugo Black and William O. Douglas wrote an opinion in which they held to their belief that the First Amendment was absolute and that all speech, even obscenity, was protected. Justice Potter Stewart wrote a short opinion in which he noted that only hard-core pornography was prohibited by the First Amendment. He did not define "hard-core pornography," but noted that "I know it when I see it, and [this] is not that." The sixth member of the majority, Justice Byron White, merely agreed with the decision and wrote no separate opinion. The dissenters were Chief Justice Earl Warren and Justices Thomas Clark and John M. Harlan.

**Impact** The Court's decision meant that it would determine in the final analysis whether a work was obscene and therefore not protected by the First Amendment. It also opened the door to the Court's adopting a three-part test for obscenity in 1966 (*Memoirs v. Massachusetts*). After 1966, in addition to the *Roth* test, a work had to be patently offensive and utterly without redeeming social value to be declared obscene. The *Memoirs* test resulted in most obscenity convictions being overturned by the Court but was itself jettisoned in 1973 by a more conservative Supreme Court in *Miller v. California*.

**Additional Information** Some of the more interesting works on obscenity are John D. Emilio and Estelle B. Freedman's *Intimate Matters: A History of Sexuality in America* (1988) and Gay Talese's *Thy Neighbor's Wife* (1980).

*Michael W. Bowers*

**See also** Burger, Warren; Censorship; Free Speech Movement; *Memoirs v. Massachusetts*; Sexual Revolution; Supreme Court Decisions.

## ■ Jagger, Mick

**Born** July 26, 1943, Dartford, Kent, England

*Lead singer of the rock-and-roll group the Rolling Stones. Jagger was one of the most popular and controversial celebrities of the decade.*

**Early Life** Michael Phillip "Mick" Jagger was born into a middle-class family and grew up in the suburbs of London.

**The 1960's** While studying at the London School of Economics in 1962, Jagger and guitarist Keith Richards formed the band that was eventually to become the Rolling Stones. Other members in the original group were Brian Jones (guitar), Charlie Watts (drums), and Bill Wyman (bass). Jones was asked to leave the group in 1968 (he died the same year) and was replaced by Mick Taylor. The band drew on African American music for its sound and quickly became one of the fixtures of Britain's rhythm-and-blues movement. Jagger's unusual, provocative singing style distinguished the band from rivals such as the Animals.

The Rolling Stones had a succession of hit singles in the early 1960's, culminating in "(I Can't Get No) Satisfaction" in 1965, a number-one single in England and the United States. By the end of the decade, they were calling themselves "the greatest rock-and-roll band in the world." Many critics and millions of fans agreed with them, although the band never rivaled the Beatles' record sales. Other important songs of the 1960's were "Get Off My Cloud" (1965), "Jumpin' Jack Flash" (1968), "Sympathy for the Devil" (1969), and "Honky Tonk Woman" (1969). Important albums were *Out of Our Heads* (1965), *Aftermath* (1966), *Beggar's Banquet* (1968), and *Let It Bleed* (1969).

The Rolling Stones—in particular lead singer Jagger—were important as much for what they represented as for their music. From the beginning, the public and the media viewed them as more threatening to middle-class values than the Beatles, which is ironic given that Jagger and company were from middle-class backgrounds whereas John Lennon and Paul McCartney were from working-class backgrounds. Jagger, with his sexually ambiguous stage persona and often-explicit lyrics, was an integral part of the sexual revolution. Some critics see a misogynistic strain in Jagger's lyrics, especially in works such as "Under My Thumb" (1964).

Jagger was involved in various controversies throughout the decade. He and Richards were arrested on trumped-up drug charges in 1967. That same year, the band was forced to change the "suggestive" lyrics of the song "Let's Spend the Night Together" for an appearance on *The Ed Sullivan Show.* Jagger was involved in several high-profile romances, including one with singer Marianne Faith-

*In December, 1969, Mick Jagger, leader of the Rolling Stones rock group, and girlfriend Marianne Faithfull leave a London court after a hearing on charges of marijuana possession.* (AP/Wide World Photos)

full and another with the woman who was to become his second wife, Nicaraguan model Bianca Perez Morena de Macias. At the end of the decade, Jagger helped organize a rock festival at Altamont Speedway in California that was expected to rival the Woodstock Music and Art Fair in size and importance. Disaster marred the festival when the Hell's Angels, a motorcycle gang that had been hired as guards, murdered a young African American audience member. The concert came to symbolize the end of the 1960's.

**Later Life** Jagger continued to be controversial and popular throughout the 1970's. In the 1980's and 1990's, his cultural importance waned. He broke temporarily with the Rolling Stones in the mid-1980's and produced several unsuccessful solo albums. He and the Rolling Stones embarked on several successful world tours in the late 1980's and 1990's. His companion for much of the1980's and 1990's was American model Jerry Hall.

**Impact** Jagger had an enormous effect on the music and culture of the 1960's. He exemplified a new willingness to express sexual desire publicly. Without him, later artists such as David Bowie, Steve Tyler, and David Lee Roth would be unthinkable. He and Richards (sometimes known as "The Glimmer Twins") came to define the public's image of rock stars. Ironically, given his radical image, Jagger was one of the first to actively encourage corporate sponsorship of rock-and-roll albums and tours. In this way, Jagger was an integral part of the process whereby rock music went from being the voice of the counterculture to a billion-dollar industry.

**Additional Information** For additional information on Jagger, see *The Rolling Stone Illustrated History of Rock and Roll* (1980), edited by Jim Miller, which has a particularly informative section on Jagger and the Rolling Stones.

*Kegan Doyle*

**See also** Altamont Music Festival; Beatles, The; British Invasion; *Ed Sullivan Show, The*; Hell's Angels; Music; Rolling Stones.

# ■ James Bond Films

*A series of motion pictures that transformed the action-adventure genre. The first six James Bond films established new directions in filmmaking, created a mythos based on an immensely popular character, and gave rise to multiple imitators on screen and television.*

Ian Flemming, former British naval intelligence officer, quickly gained a following with his espionage novels featuring an agent called James Bond. His *Casino Royale* (1953) was adapted into a live television drama starring Barry Nelson as an Americanized version of Bond in 1954. The Bond character's popularity greatly expanded in 1960 when *Playboy* magazine published short stories detailing Bond's adventures. In 1961, *Life* magazine printed a list of President John F. Kennedy's favorite books, which included Fleming's *From Russia with Love*. This short mention aroused popular and media interest in the character, and all Fleming's previously published novels climbed up the best-seller lists.

In 1962, the first of the James Bond films, *Dr. No,* was released. The Bond films, based on the series of eleven novels and two short-story collections by Fleming, created a worldwide sensation, propelling Scottish actor Sean Connery (who played Bond) to international stardom and giving producers Albert R. Broccoli and Harry Saltzman command over the most lucrative franchise in film history.

*Dr. No* and *From Russia with Love* (1963) established the pattern that subsequent efforts would follow, introducing themes and motifs such as composer John Barry's signature musical themes and title songs, exotic locales, romances with alluring female costars (the "Bond girls"), technological gadgetry, elaborate chase sequences, tongue-in-cheek humor, and new techniques and advances in action adventure stunts and cinematography. In 1964, the Bond phenomenon hit full stride when the film *Goldfinger* broke box-office records in the first three weeks of its release. Many theaters screened the film twenty-four hours a day to meet public demand.

The series revolved around sophisticated, hard-bitten British secret service agent James Bond 007 (license to kill), supported by a cast of recurring characters including his chief "M" (played by Bernard Lee), M's doting secretary, Miss Moneypenny (Lois Maxwell), and eccentric quartermaster "Q" (Desmond Llewelyn). Although the Fleming novels centered on Cold War espionage between the British Secret Service and the Soviet Union's SMERSH (Russian for "death to spies"), the films from *Dr. No* through *Thunderball* (1965) had Bond and supporting characters battling larger-than-life agents of SPECTRE, the fictional "Special Executive for Counter-Intelligence, Terrorism, Revenge, and Extortion." *You Only Live Twice* (1967), *On Her Majesty's Secret Service* (1969, starring George Lazenby as Bond), and *Diamonds Are Forever* (1971) make up the Blofeld trilogy, in which Bond fights SPECTRE founder Ernst Stovro Blofeld, the murderer of Bond's wife. Cold War intrigues were magnified into a fantastic milieu that became self-parody in Bond films following *Thunderball.*

**Impact** Bond's popularity was both supported and augmented by American interest in virtually all things British, from the British invasion rock bands such as the Beatles and Rolling Stones and the fashion trends set by "swinging London's" Carnaby Street and designer Mary Quant. Merchandising sales for the films were rivaled only by the Beatles. Bond-related memorabilia, including soundtracks, toys, games, bubblegum cards, books, and toiletries, established a new level of tie-in promotions for films. The Bond novels were adapted into a long-running British comic strip, and title songs such as Shirley Bassey's "Goldfinger," Tom Jones's "Thunderball," and Nancy Sinatra's "You Only Live Twice" became major recording hits, deepening the films' penetration of the public consciousness. Actresses such as Ursula Andress, Shirley Eaton, Honor Blackman, and Jill St. John gained wide recognition as "Bond girls" and lent each film a glamorous, sensual appeal.

The film and television industry capitalized on the Bond bonanza with film series starring James Coburn as secret agent Derek Flint (*Our Man Flint*, 1965; *In Like Flint*, 1967), Dean Martin as agent Matt Helm (*The Silencers*, 1966; *Murderer's Row*, 1966; *The Ambushers*, 1968; *The Wrecking Crew*, 1968), and Michael Caine as Harry Palmer in Bond coproducer Saltzman's three-film series. Due to legal complications, the Broccoli-Saltzman team was unable to film *Casino Royale*, and the novel was instead turned into an uneven broad farce produced by Jerry Bresler and Charles K. Feldman in 1967, employing five directors and a number of actors playing Bond including Peter Sellers, David Niven, and Woody Allen.

Television shows such as *The Man from UNCLE, I Spy, Get Smart, The Avengers, The Wild Wild West,* and *Secret Agent* brought Bond-like adventures into the living room and spun off popular catalogs of tie-in merchandise with sales rivaling those of Bond col-

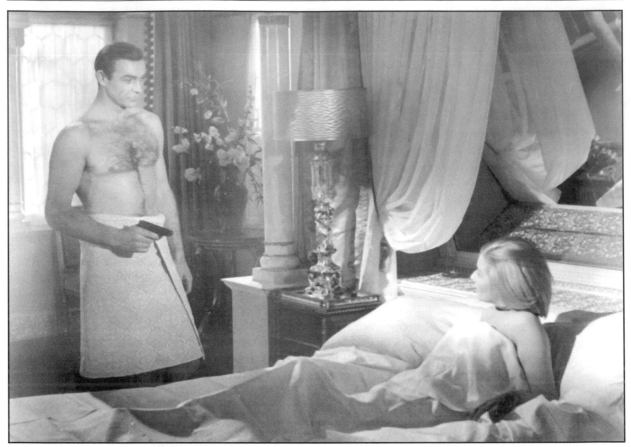

*James Bond, secret agent 007, (Sean Connery) points a gun at Tatiana Romanova (Daniela Bianchi) in the 1963 film* From Russia with Love. *(Museum of Modern Art/Film Stills Archive)*

lectibles. At the spy-craze's zenith, Sean Connery and *The Man from UNCLE* stars Robert Vaughn and David McCallum described themselves as being more like rock stars than actors because of the often-frenzied responses of young fans.

**Subsequent Events** Actor Roger Moore, who was catapulted into stardom in his role as Simon Templar on the television show *The Saint*, ultimately took over the role of Bond in the seven subsequent 007 films in the 1970's and 1980's. Other actors who have played Bond include Timothy Dalton and Pierce Brosnan.

**Additional Information** Steven Jay Rubin's *The James Bond Movie Encyclopedia* (1990), Raymond Benson's *The James Bond Bedside Companion* (1984), and Lee Pfeiffer and Philip Lasa's *The Incredible World of 007* (1992) provide detailed background on the Bond films.

*Wesley Britton*

**See also** British Invasion; Cold War; Film; Quant, Mary.

## ■ Japanese Imports

*A rapid expansion of Japanese imports that threatened domestic producers of chemicals, steel, electronics, textiles, and automobiles. The United States' trade surplus with Japan shifted to increasing trade deficits beginning in the mid-1960's, culminating in a strong protectionist challenge in 1968 and 1969.*

In the 1950's and 1960's, Japan followed a policy of channeling resources into heavy industries and actively promoting exports of basic materials and certain consumer goods. As part of post-World War II rehabilitation within the international community, Japan joined the United Nations and the General Agreement on Tariffs and Trade (GATT). The Japanese government switched its orientation from trading with China to seeking Western markets. The United States continued to be Japan's most important trading partner.

Early in the 1960's, confronting an increase in textiles, steel, and other products imported from Japan, the U.S. government requested that Japan put "voluntary restrictions" on these shipments. The Japanese replied that such restrictions would violate the GATT but nevertheless complied partially. As the two trading partners approached the 1964-1967 Kennedy Round of tariff cuts under the GATT, the United States maintained its official advocacy of free trade. However, negotiations were marred by conflicting pressures from U.S. business concerns and Japanese representatives visiting the United States. Relatively inexpensive ceramic capacitors imported from Japan and produced with low-cost labor had driven Sprague Electric Company to abandon that market. Any threat made by business concerning trade restrictions was strongly opposed by the Japanese. In a speech in early 1964 at the New York Hilton, the head of a Japanese trade mission, Yoshizane Iwasa, chairman of Fuji Bank, stated that "Japan is too valuable a [trading] partner to be discriminated against by American import restrictions."

The Kennedy Round produced substantial tariff cuts. Japan cut its high tariffs an average of 50 percent, and the United States cut its lower tariffs an average of 35 percent. Nevertheless, following its first trade deficit with Japan in 1965, the United States faced ever-increasing deficits. Businesspeople in affected industries, particularly textiles, steel, and automobiles, sought help from the U.S. government. In 1969, eighty-three bills seeking import quotas were introduced in Congress. At the end of 1969, President Richard M. Nixon introduced new trade legislation providing relief for affected industries through temporary import curbs and adjustment assistance.

**Impact** Japanese imports had an impact in the areas of consumer electronics, steel, and textiles. The Sony Corporation captured a significant share of the market for small high-quality television sets and transistor radios. In 1968, U.S. steel producers protested rising imports. In order to deter import quotas, the Japanese steel industry adopted its own company-by-company export quota plan. The United States textile industry, mindful of potential danger, fought throughout the 1960's to restrict imports of textile mill products and apparel.

**Additional Information** An in-depth study of the United States' industrial decline can be found in *Made in America: Regaining the Productive Edge* (1989), by Michael Dertouzos, Richard Lester, and Robert Solov.

*Jerome Picard*

**See also** Automobiles and Auto Manufacturing; International Trade.

# ■ Jefferson Airplane

*An acid rock band. The group embodied the culture of San Francisco's Haight-Ashbury district, and its music expressed the spirit of the young hippies who gathered there.*

In 1965, Marty Balin, a former folksinger, along with guitarists Paul Kantner and Jorma Kaukonen, drummer Skip Spence, vocalist Signe Anderson, and bassist Bob Harvey (soon replaced by Jack Casady) formed a folk-rock band called the Jefferson Airplane, which debuted at Balin's San Francisco club, the Matrix Club, in August. The group became the first of the San Francisco bands to sign with a major label when it landed a contract with RCA, and its first album, *The Jefferson Airplane Takes Off* was released in summer, 1966.

In 1966, Spencer Dryden replaced Spence, who left to form the band Moby Grape, and former Great Society vocalist Grace Slick replaced Anderson. The band, with Slick's powerful vocals, took on a somewhat harder, psychedelic sound. The Jefferson Airplane, along with other West Coast bands such as the Grateful Dead, was part of the alternative community based in the Haight-Ashbury section of San Francisco. By the summer of 1967, known as the Summer of Love, more than fifty thousand hippies lived in the area and led a bohemian lifestyle that involved free love, drugs (especially LSD—lysergic acid diethylamide—or acid), and a form of music called acid or psychedelic rock. The Jefferson Airplane released *Surrealistic Pillow* in 1967, and the album reached number three on the charts by June. Two of the songs from this album, "Somebody to Love" and "White Rabbit," both sung by Slick, reached the top ten, although "White Rabbit" was banned by some radio stations because it was about drugs. That same year, the group released *After Bathing at Baxter's*, which had no hit singles and did not sell as well.

In 1968, the Jefferson Airplane released the popular and successful *Crown of Creation*. The album reached number six on the charts and featured the single "Crown of Creation." In 1969, the group released a concert album, *Bless Its Pointed Little Head*, and the somewhat political *Volunteers*, which spoke of a revolution in its title song.

The Jefferson Airplane joined other bands such as the Grateful Dead, Big Brother and the Holding Company, and Quicksilver Messenger Service in performing many free concerts in San Francisco. One performance was in January, 1967, at the Gathering of the Tribes for a Human Be-in in Golden Gate Park, which was organized by members of the Beat generation, including writers Allen Ginsberg and Gary Snyder, and attended by more than twenty thousand hippies.

The Jefferson Airplane played at well-known San Francisco venues such as the Avalon Ballroom owned by Chet Helms, Fillmore West/East managed by Bill Graham, and at Winterland. The group also performed at the decade's most important rock music festivals, the Monterey International Pop Festival in June, 1967, and at the Woodstock Music and Art Fair and the Altamont Music Festival in 1969.

**Impact** The Jefferson Airplane, whose members lived together in the Haight at 2400 Fulton Street, epitomized the Haight-Ashbury lifestyle and gave voice to its thoughts and feelings. The band's *Surrealistic Pillow*, with its songs of love and drugs, brought the group and the hip culture that spawned it to the attention of young people throughout the nation. The group's "White Rabbit," with lyrics loosely drawn from Lewis Carroll's *Alice's Adventures in Wonderland* (1865), in which Slick exhorts people to "feed your head," became the Haight-Ashbury anthem with its drug-related message.

**Subsequent Events** The end of the 1960's brought an end to the Jefferson Airplane. In 1970, Dryden left the group to become part of the New Riders of the Purple Sage, and Kaukonen and Casady started a band of their own, Hot Tuna. In 1974, Slick,

*Jefferson Airplane, a psychedelic rock band that lived together in the Haight-Ashbury district of San Francisco, popularized the hippie lifestyle with their 1967 album* Surrealistic Pillow. *(AP/Wide World Photos)*

Kantner, and others formed the Jefferson Starship, which had a number-one album, *Red Octopus*, in 1975. In 1984, the group, minus Kantner and known as Starship, had a number-one hit with "We Built This City." It followed with two more number-one hits, "Sara" in 1986 and "Nothing's Gonna Stop Us Now" in 1987. In 1989, the Jefferson Airplane reunited for a tour and reunion album, *The Jefferson Airplane*. In 1991, Kantner brought back some former members to create Jefferson Starship—The Next Generation. In 1996, the Jefferson Airplane (with its 1967 lineup) was inducted into the Rock and Roll Hall of Fame.

**Additional Information** *A Time to Rock: A Social History of Rock 'n' Roll* (1996), by David Szatmary, and *Rock and Roll: A Social History* (1996), by Paul Friedlander, provide a closer look at the Jefferson Airplane.

*Patricia Wong Hall*

**See also** Drug Culture; Flower Children; Grateful Dead; Haight-Ashbury; Hippies; San Francisco as Cultural Mecca; Summer of Love.

## ■ *Jetsons, The*

**Produced** 1962-1963
**Producers** William Hanna (1910-     ) and Joseph Barbera (1911-     )

*A popular prime-time cartoon show featuring the Jetsons, a space age family. The program was patterned on Hanna-Barbera's successful cartoon featuring the Stone Age Flintstone family.*

**The Work** The Jetsons debuted on the American Broadcasting Company (ABC) on Sunday, September 23, 1962, at 8:00 P.M. This animated family sitcom was intended to be a twenty-first century equivalent of *The Flintstones*, which had been running in prime time on the same network since 1960. Like its predecessor, *The Jetsons* was the work of veteran cartoonists William Hanna and Joseph Barbera. The show centered around the daily lives of a "typical" space-age nuclear family: father George (voice of George O'Hanlon), mother Jane (Penny Singleton), daughter Judy (Janet Waldo), and son Elroy (Daws Butler). Regular characters also included the family dog Astro (Don Messick) and George's boss, Mr. Spacely (Mel Blanc).

The Jetsons merged two formats: the prime-time situation comedy and the children's cartoon. From the former, the program drew typical family and work situations, such as resolving parent-child conflicts, coping with workplace pressures, and meeting civic responsibilities. The cartoon format enabled the writers to create far-fetched, fantasy-filled scenarios that could be developed far beyond anything written for live-action sitcoms.

**Impact** *The Jetsons* reflected both the optimism and the anxieties surrounding new technologies and scientific breakthroughs during the early 1960's. Although the show's electronic gadgetry (from a machine to dress and groom people to a collapsible car that can be carried in a briefcase) simplified the Jetsons' lives, it inevitably proved problematic. The narrative of most of the episodes centers around the fallibility of machines. For example, one episode dealt with the emotional struggle of Rosie, the robot maid, when she was upstaged by a newer model.

Although *The Jetsons* ceased its prime-time run in September, 1963, it quickly became a Saturday morning and afterschool children's favorite, maintaining this role into the 1990's.

**Related Works** *The Jetsons* was patterned on Hanna-Barbera's highly successful prime-time cartoon show, *The Flintstones*, which ran from 1960 to 1966. An animated film, *The Jetsons*, was released in 1990.

**Additional Information** Detailed information about *The Jetsons* can be found in *The Art of Hanna-Barbera: Fifty Years of Creativity* (1989) by Ted Sennett.

*Megan Mullen*

**See also** *Flintstones, The*; Television.

## ■ **Job Corps**

*A federal government program designed to prepare economically and socially disadvantaged youth to lead productive lives in the labor market. It offers educational and vocational training, work opportunities, counseling, meals, health care, and other support services in residential living centers.*

**Origins and History** The Job Corps, which targets youth participation in conservation work, is modeled after similar programs developed during the New Deal era of the 1930's, including the Civilian Conservation Corps. Early attempts to introduce a residential youth conservation corps failed to gain full congressional support in 1958. Later, the House of Representatives rejected a proposal that promoted provisions for rural conservation projects and federal job-creation programs in urban areas.

In 1963, the presidential Task Force on Manpower Conservation published a report, entitled *One-Third of a Nation*, which highlighted the rejection rates of armed forces applicants from impoverished backgrounds. The task force's findings served as documented evidence for promoting the implementation of the Job Corps. Along with other social programs created as part of President Lyndon B. Johnson's Great Society, the Job Corps was resubmitted as part of the antipoverty bill. The Economic Opportunity Act of 1964 included Title I, which provided for the establishment of the Job Corps by which young people could gain basic and advanced skills.

**Activities**  Initially, 40 percent of participants were assigned to conservation centers, and others were placed in either rural or urban facilities. Rural centers offered enrollees general educational instruction and work opportunities on conservation projects. Urban centers provided vocational training for individuals with at least a sixth-grade education. Other centers served women, who were expected to fill one-third of Job Corps openings.

Private businesses and the Departments of Defense and Labor competed for control of the Job Corps. In 1964, President Johnson appointed R. Sargent Shriver to head the Office of Economic Opportunity. Under Shriver's leadership, the office supervised the administrative and operational aspects of the program. By 1966, the Job Corps consisted of one thousand to three thousand men's centers, more than eighty conservation centers, and seventeen women's centers. All of these facilities provided housing, health care, food, counseling, and educational and vocational programs for participants.

The escalation of U.S. involvement in the Vietnam War in the late 1960's led to budget cuts and changes in the design of the Job Corps. Congress limited the number of enrollees to forty-five thousand and reduced the amount of money allotted to each individual. Other aspects of the Job Corps also were altered. The original mandate requiring placement of 40 percent of participants in conservation centers was changed to apply to young men only. Women enrollees were increased from 23 percent to 25 percent. In 1969, President Richard M. Nixon

transferred control of the Job Corps from the Office of Economic Opportunity to the Department of Labor. Under the administration of the Department of Labor, several conservation, men's, and women's centers were closed and replaced with cost-efficient urban residential centers that ran urban manpower programs.

**Impact**  The Job Corps provides immense opportunities for disadvantaged youth to gain essential academic and employment skills. Young people with educational difficulties can earn their General Education Diploma (a high school diploma equivalency) and continue their studies in junior colleges or vocational schools for technical training. However, critics charge that the improvement in employment and wages has been too small in relation to the program's relatively high costs.

**Subsequent Events**  Federal funding for the modified Job Corps program was continued under the Comprehensive Employment and Training Act of 1973. The Department of Labor established regional offices responsible for recruitment and daily administration of Job Corps centers in local areas. In 1982, Title IV-B of the Job Training and Partnership Act authorized Job Corps services. The Nontraditional Employment for Women Act of 1991 widened the scope of the Job Training and Partnership Act, which encourages increased training and job placement of women in positions traditionally held by men. In the late 1990's, a network of more than one hundred Job Corps centers existed in forty-six states, Puerto Rico, and the District of Columbia. Eighteen centers known as the Job Corps Civilian Conservation Centers were run by the Forest Service of the U.S. Department of Agriculture.

**Additional Information**  A detailed assessment of the history and early phase of the programs can be found in *The Job Corps: A Social Experiment that Works* (1975). A brief but informative account of federal employment and training programs is outlined in *A Working Woman's Guide to Her Job Rights* (1992).

*Phyllis M. Jones-Shuler*

**See also**  Economic Opportunity Act of 1964; Great Society Programs; Prosperity and Poverty; Women in the Workforce.

# ■ John Birch Society

*A Far Right organization focused on spreading its anticommunist sentiments. This group is known for its assertions that communists had infiltrated the U.S. government and that communism gained support and membership from such people as General George Marshall, Chief Justice Earl Warren, and President Dwight D. Eisenhower.*

**Origins and History** The John Birch Society was founded in December, 1958, by Robert H. W. Welch, Jr., a wealthy businessman from Massachusetts. He named the organization after Captain John Birch, a U.S. intelligence officer killed by Communist Chinese troops just after World War II, whom Welch regarded as the first casualty of World War III. Welch gathered eleven of his friends and presented his ideologies regarding domestic and international affairs, emphasizing his belief in a communist conspiracy. He published his manifesto, *The Blue Book of the John Birch Society*, after the meeting. His eleven friends, who represented several different states, agreed to take part in Welch's war against communism and to help establish John Birch Society chapters across the nation. The society members, or Birchers, tried to recruit one million able-bodied American men whom Welch would lead in his war against communism, which he saw as a political and educational war rather than a military war.

The Birchers would not tolerate democratic representation because they thought that the nation's forefathers gave them a republic not a democracy, and they regarded democracy as the worst form of government. The society also believed that the smaller the government, the better. In the 1960's, the society focused primarily on releasing Americans from the communist conspiracy that its members thought was destroying the nation and secondly on eliminating U.S. support for communism. The Birchers believed that the communist takeovers that had been successful had been made with U.S. support, and once this support was withdrawn, the United States would win a significant battle in the war that would follow.

The John Birch Society sought to shock the American people into awareness of what it claimed was a communist conspiracy within the United States. It developed a number of ways to disseminate information, including a chain of bookstores and a publishing division. The society published the *American Opinion* monthly and *The New American* weekly. It also sought to establish reading rooms nationally, widen distribution of conservative periodicals, lead letter-writing campaigns, silence prominent "communist" speakers with questions at their lectures, supply anticommunist speakers nationwide, and introduce Bircher beliefs internationally.

**Activities** Birchers launched many strategic strikes at their opponents. They exposed "communist" liberal, artistic elitists: authors, academics, and journalists, including J. Robert Oppenheimer, Fredric March, Mark Van Doren, and Carl Sandburg. Birchers attacked the Civil Rights movement, stating that Martin Luther King, Jr.'s communistic practices needed to be exposed. They denounced President Dwight D. Eisenhower as a traitor, accusing him of being a primary agent of the communist conspiracy. They demanded that Chief Justice Earl Warren be impeached because he was a communist. Welch accused the Central Intelligence Agency of being part of the communist conspiracy and stated that 50 percent to 70 percent of the United States was under communist control.

**Impact** Although Bircher membership grew to forty thousand in 1963, the organization's main effect was to anger liberals and entertain those who were dispassionate toward its cause. Welch received a substantial amount of negative attention when he published the "black book," a supplement to *The Blue Book of the John Birch Society*, in which he accused Eisenhower of being procommunist. He published an amended version in 1963 with the most insulting passages removed. In 1967, society membership reached eighty thousand, but the movement's force had subsided. Subscriptions to the organization's *American Opinion* fell to forty thousand, and the organization had to defend itself against charges that it was a fragment of the "kook right." By the end of the 1960's, fighting communism became less of a priority to the American public.

Welch's original wealthy investors remained central figures in his crusade. Because of the society's financial power, it briefly succeeded in gaining political representation when Californian John R. Rouselot was elected to Congress and explained Bircher ideology to the House of Representatives. For a limited time, Welch's theories of communist infiltration as the root of social disorder in American society rang true with his audiences, but Welch's extreme conspiracy theories unnerved his followers.

**Subsequent Events** The John Birch Society's literature and propaganda remained afloat throughout the 1970's and mid-1980's. Some former members founded or were active in other far right movements, including Gordon Kahl, a member of the Posse Comitatus; Willis Carto, who founded the Liberty Lobby; Robert Bolivar DePugh, who established the Minutemen; and Tom Metzger, who joined the California Knights and created the White Aryan Resistance.

The John Birch Society reappeared in the 1990's, lending its support to the militia movement. The Society shifted its focus from fighting the communist conspiracy to battling an overbearing government that had created a welfare state and decrying the nation's declining moral standards. The John Birch Society's demands to keep the United States out of the United Nations and the United Nations out of the United States have been repeated throughout the militia movement.

**Additional Information** See David H. Bennett's *The Party of Fear: The American Far Right from Nativism to the Militia Movement* (1995) for a thorough account of the John Birch Society's perspectives on the quelling of America and how this organization calibrates within far right movement history. Lavern C. Hutchins interprets and analyzes Bircher ideologies in *The John Birch Society and United States Foreign Policy* (1968). James Ridgeway discusses Bircher activities and traces members' activities in other far right groups in *Blood in the Face: The Ku Klux Klan, Aryan Nations, Nazi Skinheads, and the Rise of a New White Culture* (1995).

*Gina R. Terinoni*

**See also** American Nazi Party; Conservatism in Politics; Ku Klux Klan (KKK); Minutemen; National States Rights Party.

# ■ Johnson, Lyndon B.

**Born** August 27, 1908, near Stonewall, Gillespie
 County, Texas

**Died** January 22, 1973, en route to San Antonio, Texas

*Thirty-sixth president of the United States. Johnson left a mixed legacy of the Great Society social programs and the war in Vietnam.*

**Early Life** Lyndon Baines Johnson was born in 1908 on a farm near Stonewall in the Gillespie County,

Texas. After working as a secretary for a Texas congressman in the early 1930's, Johnson was elected to fill a vacant seat in the Congress in 1937. He remained in that office through four subsequent elections. He then successfully ran for the U.S. Senate in 1948 and became the Senate Democratic leader in 1953. The Democrats became the majority party in the U.S. Senate in 1955, thus vastly increasing Johnson's power as the Senate majority leader. In this post, Johnson exercised enormous power in guiding legislation and maintaining the Democratic Party's position against the Republican-occupied White House.

**The 1960's** Johnson's political ambitions eventually led him to run for the highest office in the nation in 1960. After insisting early in the year that he was running only for reelection to his Senate seat, he eventually mounted a vigorous campaign for the Democratic Party's presidential nomination. He came in second to Massachusetts senator John F. Kennedy in the first round of convention balloting. After agonizing for twenty-four hours over his choice of a running mate, Kennedy finally selected Johnson for the vice presidential nomination. The Kennedy-Johnson ticket went on to win the general election in a close vote.

Johnson, like most vice presidents, was publicly overshadowed by the president. The effect was all the more dramatic because of Kennedy's youth and charisma. However, on November 22, 1963, the assassination of President Kennedy thrust Johnson into one of the most visible and powerful offices in the world. It was a difficult and painful period for the nation, but Johnson exhibited a resoluteness that helped to shore up public confidence in the government.

As president, Johnson expanded government social programs in the spirit of the New Deal initiated decades earlier by President Franklin D. Roosevelt. Johnson promoted his social programs under the slogan of building a Great Society. His domestic policies responded to calls by civil rights activists and advocates for the poor, whose demands reached a crescendo in the 1960's. Of particular significance was the Civil Rights Act of 1964. This legislation was introduced during Kennedy's presidency, but it was Johnson who cajoled legislators in both houses of Congress with his trademark combination of blandishments, political horse trading, and threats. The Civil Rights Act, as well as other Johnson-guided

*President Lyndon B. Johnson, born and raised in Texas, rides his Tennessee walking horse, Lady B, at the LBJ Ranch.* (Agence France Presse/Archive Photos)

Economic Opportunity Act of 1964, part of Johnson's War on Poverty. Issuing an executive order, Johnson also initiated the federal government's first "affirmative action" policy, which required institutions receiving federal assistance to make special efforts to hire women and minorities. In addition, Johnson appointed the first African American to a cabinet position when he named Robert Weaver to head the newly created Department of Housing and Urban Development.

The War on Poverty was not the only war with which Johnson had to contend. He also inherited responsibility for U.S. involvement in Indochina. The war between North and South Vietnam had intensified during Kennedy's presidency. Whereas Kennedy had evidently planned to disengage U.S. military advisers from the conflict, Johnson believed that this would lead to the fall of South Vietnam and trigger a "domino effect" in Southeast Asia. If this were to happen, he would be blamed for allowing a decisive expansion of the communist world—an especially poignant charge against the man whose path to the White House had in part depended on his anticommunist credentials. At the same time, however, Johnson sensed the dangers of becoming entangled in someone else's war. "I don't think the people of the country know much about Vietnam, and I think they care a hell of a lot less," he said privately shortly after assuming the presidency. "I don't think it's worth fighting for."

Johnson tried to balance the twin dangers of military defeat and military entanglement with an incremental approach that constantly increased U.S. military involvement. It was a prescription for

legislation, went far toward ending racial discrimination in the United States.

Johnson easily won the 1964 presidential campaign against Republican senator Barry Goldwater. With his own electoral mandate and strong backing in Congress, Johnson was able to secure passage of a raft of civil rights laws and new social programs. Significant among these were the Voting Rights Act of 1965, Medicare and Medicaid (1965), and the tragedy and failure. After committing the first U.S. fighting forces to Vietnam in 1965, Johnson found himself unable either to provide enough force for victory or to extract U.S. troops from the conflict. The deployment of U.S. troops, along with the number of American casualties, racheted ever upward. At the end of Johnson's final year in office, more than half a million Americans had been sent to Vietnam and almost fifteen thousand had been killed there.

It was the Vietnam conflict, more than anything else, that convinced Johnson to drop out of the 1968 presidential race. Antiwar protests had increased in frequency and size, and the war effort was siphoning funds and political capital from Johnson's Great Society agenda. The enthusiastic support Johnson had earlier enjoyed among younger voters and liberals eroded, and the Great Society coalition divided. Senator Eugene McCarthy of Minnesota campaigned vigorously against Johnson for the Democratic Party nomination, portraying himself as an antiwar candidate. Discouraged, Johnson withdrew from the race on March 31. He gave his support to his vice president, Hubert Humphrey, who secured the Democratic nomination. Humphrey lost the presidential election to Richard M. Nixon, who campaigned on a pledge to end the war.

**Subsequent Events** After turning over the White House to Nixon, Johnson retired to his ranch in Texas. Johnson's Great Society programs were left essentially intact by the Republican president; indeed, they would be a mainstay of American society into the 1990's.

Public opposition to the war continued to intensify after Johnson's departure, and Nixon's first term saw a further escalation of the conflict. Johnson died on January 22, 1973, one day before Nixon, two months into his second term, declared the end of the Vietnam War.

**Additional Information** Books that devote substantial attention to Johnson in the 1960's (primarily his presidency) include Robert A. Divine's *The Johnson Years* (1987) and *Lyndon Johnson Confronts the World* (1994), edited by Warren Cohen and Nancy Tucker. The secretly recorded audiotapes of Johnson's conversations offer valuable insights into Johnson's thinking during his first years in the presidency; transcripts appear in *Taking Charge: The Johnson White House Tapes, 1963-64* (1997), edited by Michael Beschloss.

*Steve D. Boilard*

**See also** Civil Rights Act of 1964; Economic Opportunity Act of 1964; Great Society Programs; Humphrey, Hubert; Kennedy, John F.; McCarthy, Eugene; Medicare; Nixon, Richard M.; Presidential Election of 1964; Vietnam War; Voting Rights Legislation; War on Poverty; Welfare State.

---

# ■ Joplin, Janis

**Born** January 19, 1943, Port Arthur, Texas
**Died** October 4, 1970, Hollywood, California

*Female vocalist who was a paragon of hedonism. Joplin was a blues-influenced rock singer who led a life unfettered by conventional morality, middle-class values, or personal constraint.*

**Early Life** Janis Lyn Joplin, the oldest of three children, was born into a fundamentalist Christian, Republican family. An early reader, as a child she exhibited extraordinary intelligence and creativity. In her early teenage years, Joplin also displayed an absolute inability to be still for any appreciable length of time and a deep need for recognition. While attending Jefferson High School in Port Arthur, she was often the victim of ridicule from her classmates because of her perceived unattractive appearance and her nearly desperate desire to be the center of attention. By the time of her 1960 graduation, she was experimenting, ominously, with drugs.

**The 1960's** Joplin believed college would be an opportunity to improve her art skills and meet fellow nonconformists, but she became disenchanted with the regimentation of school life and dropped out of Lamar State College in Beaumont, Texas, after one semester. After enrolling in, and soon leaving, two other colleges, she left academia forever and decided to make a career in music.

Heavily influenced by legendary blues singers Bessie Smith and Billie Holiday, Joplin also emulated their bawdy and raucous lifestyles. In 1966, she moved to San Francisco and was invited to join the rock group Big Brother and the Holding Company. A hugely successful album, *Cheap Thrills* (1968), and constant touring helped spread her fame. Drinking whiskey, speaking directly to the audience, and emit-

*Singer/songwriter Janis Joplin, a free spirit with an unconventional lifestyle, sings at the 1969 Woodstock Festival.* (Archive Photos)

ting ear-piercing screams were all part of the show. By the end of 1969, she was putting together another group, had achieved fame and fortune, and had a well-earned reputation for promiscuity and indiscriminate drug usage.

**Later Life** In 1970, Joplin formed the Full-Tilt Boogie band and recorded her final album. That summer, she participated in a long train tour through Canada and attended her tenth high school reunion, an event that received national media attention. She died of a heroin overdose on October 4, only three weeks after the drug-related death of fellow musician Jimi Hendrix.

**Impact** Her meteoric rise, extremely flamboyant life, and sudden death at the peak of her popularity all contributed to her enduring legend. Admirers saw her as a truly free spirit while her equally numerous detractors viewed her as a poster child of self-indulgence. She helped create the musical genre known as "blue-eyed soul," proving that a white person could sing the blues. Joplin was also a tal-

ented guitar player, song writer, and arranger who became one of the first female vocalists to play such an active role in the recording industry. Her lasting influence is apparent in the style and attitude of many performers of the late 1990's.

**Subsequent Events** The album she was finishing at the time of her death, *Pearl* (1971), was a huge posthumous hit. She has also been the subject of several books and at least one heavily fictionalized motion picture. *The Rose*, directed by Mark Rydell and starring Bette Midler and Alan Bates, is loosely based on Joplin's life and death. More than twenty years after her death, she was inducted into the Rock and Roll Hall of Fame.

**Additional Information** Two excellent sources are *Pearl* (1992), by Ellis Amburn, and *Love, Janis* (1977), by Joplin's sister, Laura Joplin.

*Thomas W. Buchanan*

**See also** Counterculture; Drug Culture; Haight-Ashbury; Woodstock Festival.

# K

## ■ *Katzenbach v. McClung*

*Case upholding Title II of the Civil Rights Act of 1964 as applied to a restaurant. Enforcement of the ruling speeded the end of racial segregation.*

The United States Congress has no constitutionally delegated power to regulate local business practices. If such practices can be shown to affect interstate commerce, however, Congress can reach them under its powers regulating commerce. In this way, Congress can use its authority to control interstate commerce to address social and economic problems. After five months of committee hearings and seven months of debate, Congress passed the Civil Rights Act of 1964. The act represented Congress's most sweeping attack on race discrimination since the Civil Rights Act of 1875. *Katzenbach v. McClung* involved a challenge to the constitutionality of Title II of the act and raised the question of whether Congress could use its authority to regulate interstate commerce to ban racial discrimination in public accommodations. The case was argued along with *Heart of Atlanta Motel v. United States*, in which the U.S. Supreme Court upheld the constitutionality of Title II's prohibitions of race discrimination in the hotel and motel industry.

*Katzenbach v. McClung* centered on Ollie's Barbecue, a small family-owned restaurant in Birmingham, Alabama, that provided sit-down service for whites but only take-out service for African Americans. If the discrimination practiced at this restaurant involved the state of Alabama, courts could intervene to enforce the Fourteenth Amendment's equal protection clause. In this case, however, no one claimed that the state supported the restaurant's practice. If large numbers of interstate travelers frequented the restaurant, Congress could intervene by using its power to regulate interstate commerce. However, Ollie's Barbecue seemed to be a local operation rarely visited by interstate travelers. Writing for the unanimous Court, Justice Thomas Clark

ruled on December 14, 1964, that Congress could regulate this restaurant because a substantial portion of the food served there had moved in interstate commerce. Clark mentioned congressional testimony that discrimination in restaurants restricted interstate travel by African Americans: "One can hardly travel without eating." He reasoned that such discrimination likewise deterred skilled professionals from moving into areas where such practices occurred. If viewed in isolation, discriminatory practices at this single restaurant would appear to have an insignificant impact on interstate commerce. However, if other "similarly situated" restaurants engaged in such practices, the cumulative effect would impose "a substantial economic effect on interstate commerce." Congress could regulate this apparently local business because it had a "rational basis" for concluding that racial discrimination in restaurants has a "direct and adverse effect on the free flow of interstate commerce." Justices Hugo Black, William O. Douglas, and Arthur Goldberg wrote separate concurring opinions.

**Impact** The Supreme Court permitted Congress to use its substantial powers to regulate interstate commerce in the battle against racial discrimination practiced by private parties. This ruling, along with the Court's decision in *Heart of Atlanta Motel v. United States*, helped end lingering segregation in the southern United States by enabling legislation to be enforced.

**Additional Information** A detailed account of the passage and implementation of the Civil Rights Act of 1964 can be found in Robert D. Loevy's *The Civil Rights Act of 1964: The Passage of the Law that Ended Racial Segregation* (1997).

*Joseph A. Melusky*

**See also** Civil Rights Act of 1960; Civil Rights Act of 1964; Civil Rights Act of 1968; *Heart of Atlanta Motel v. United States*; Voting Rights Legislation.

# ■ Kennedy, Edward "Ted"

**Born** February 22, 1932, Boston, Massachusetts

*One of the most prominent of U.S. Senators. Kennedy inherited a political legacy from his older brothers. His liberalism and personality attracted nationwide attention for several decades.*

**Early Life** Edward Moore "Ted" Kennedy was the youngest son of Ambassador Joseph P. Kennedy. His mother, Rose Fitzgerald Kennedy, was the daughter of John F. Fitzgerald, a former congressman and mayor of Boston. Following Kennedy's graduation from Milton Academy in 1950, he entered Harvard College but left when authorities expelled him for cheating on a Spanish examination in 1951. After a two-year stint in the U.S. Army, Kennedy again enrolled in Harvard where he made average grades, excelled on the football field, and graduated in 1956. He entered the practice of law in 1959 and became assistant district attorney of Suffolk County, Massachusetts, in 1961.

**The 1960's** On November 6, 1962, Massachusetts voters overwhelmingly elected Kennedy to the United States Senate seat left vacant by his brother John F. Kennedy, the new president. His other brother, Robert F. Kennedy, became attorney general. The early 1960's represented the peak of the Kennedys' power, and most commentators described them as the next U.S. political dynasty. Edward Kennedy, unlike his brother John, worked hard at being a senator and produced a solid, consistently liberal voting record. By all accounts, he was a good senator.

By the end of the decade, however, the glamour and promise had faded even though he continued to be one of the nation's hardest-working senators. The assassinations of brothers John (November, 1963) and Robert (June, 1968) had made Edward Kennedy the "keeper of the eternal flame" and heir to the Kennedy tradition. Then in July, 1969, he drove his car off a bridge on Chappaquiddick Island (off the Massachusetts coast), resulting in the death of a young woman, Mary Jo Kopechne. His inability to explain his actions on the night of the accident to the inquiring media severely damaged any presidential aspirations he might have held. Still, despite the tragedy, Kennedy remained the leading Democratic contender for the nation's highest office as the decade ended.

**Later Life** Throughout the 1970's, Kennedy symbolized American liberalism. Pundits and historians alike agreed that the Democratic Party would have nominated him for president if he had run. However, in 1980, when Kennedy challenged a weakened (but incumbent) President Jimmy Carter for the Democratic nomination, he failed to articulate why he wanted to be president and dropped his candidacy after the national convention. During the 1980's and 1990's, he continued to press liberal issues against the rising tide of conservatism that resulted in the presidencies of Ronald Reagan and George Bush. Although he supported teachers' unions and feminist issues, student loans and medical care, the Republican presidents generally denied him legislative achievements. Kennedy's position improved, however, in 1992 with the election of Bill Clinton, who was one of John F. Kennedy and Robert F. Kennedy's most enthusiastic supporters. In 1991, the senator admitted errors in his personal life and

*Edward "Ted" Kennedy lost a chance at the presidency after a 1969 accident in which a young woman died, but he remained a symbol of liberalism throughout the 1970's. (Jason Trigg/ Archive Photos)*

promised to reform. In 1994, Kennedy overcame adverse publicity stemming from his personal life (mainly a divorce and other issues resulting from alcohol abuse) and defeated Mitt Romney to win reelection by a comfortable 58 percent to 41 percent.

**Impact**  Senator Kennedy inherited a powerful political tradition from his father and older brothers. His career spanned more than one-third of the twentieth century. Although plagued by personal problems (including many of his own making), Kennedy became the leading symbol of American liberalism as the century ended.

**Subsequent Events**  Kennedy continued to champion liberal causes such as the elimination of poverty, labor issues, and equal rights that preoccupied his brother Robert before his assassination. Although some of Kennedy's bills, such as the Family and Medical Leave Act, became law, conservative presidents and Congresses blocked his national health care proposal and other legislative efforts.

**Additional Information**  For sources pertaining to the two sides of Kennedy's professional and personal life, see Richard E. Burke's *The Senator* (1992), Paul R. Henggeler's *The Kennedy Persuasion: The Politics of Style Since JFK* (1995), and Michael Barone and Grant Ujifusa's *The Almanac of American Politics 1998* (1997) and *The Almanac of American Politics 1974* (1973.)

*J. Christopher Schnell*

**See also**  Chappaquiddick Scandal; Kennedy, John F.; Kennedy, Robert F.; Liberalism in Politics.

---

## ■ Kennedy, Jacqueline

**Born** July 28, 1929, Southampton, New York
**Died** May 19, 1994, New York, New York

*Wife of President John F. Kennedy, First Lady of the United States, fashion trendsetter, and role model for women in the 1960's.*

**Early Life**  Jacqueline Lee Bouvier was born into an affluent, well-established family, but her childhood was marred by the divorce of her parents in 1940. Her father, John "Black Jack" Bouvier III, was the charming black sheep of the family. After the divorce, her mother, Janet Lee Bouvier, married Hugh Auchincloss, a wealthy businessman. Jacqueline attended private schools, Vassar College, and George

Washington University. She also spent a year at the Sorbonne, which deepened her love of France and her French heritage. After college, she worked as a photojournalist before meeting Senator John F. Kennedy, twelve years her senior. They were married in 1953 and had two children, Caroline and John.

**The 1960's**  In 1961, the Kennedys moved into the White House. Jacqueline was only thirty-one years old, and many thought her too young for the role of First Lady. Although she had not enjoyed campaign politics, she rose to the occasion in the White House. With the help of the White House Historical Association, she redecorated the aging, decaying White House, obtaining antiques and historical artifacts that would make the presidential mansion a cultural and artistic showplace. On February 14, 1962, she conducted a tour of the White House, displaying her work, which was televised by the Columbia Broadcasting System (CBS). Later that year, CBS News and Jacqueline received an Emmy Award for the program, entitled *A Tour of the White House.*

Jacqueline became the nation's fashion leader with her elegant, simple clothes, beauty, and grace. She favored Chanel suits, later switching to similar suits by U.S. designers, and Oleg Cassini gowns. Her much-copied look included simple, pared-down dresses and suits, a modified bouffant hairstyle, white gloves, a Halston pillbox hat, pumps, and a single strand of pearls.

As First Lady, she promoted cultural events, inviting artists and performers such as violinist Isaac Stern and cellist Pablo Casals to appear at social gatherings at the White House. She created a glittering social life in the presidential mansion, even holding a much-talked-about twisting party in 1961.

Publicly the Kennedys were the ideal couple although their marriage was deteriorating. Jacqueline's extravagance and her husband's indiscretions were probably the two major sources of strife, but the two had little in common. Jacqueline's cosmopolitan interests included classical music, art, and literature, and the president's tastes ran to popular culture and sports. While in the White House, the couple were saddened by the death of their son, Patrick, shortly after his birth in August, 1963.

After President Kennedy's assassination in November, 1963, Jacqueline, who was riding in the car with him when he was fatally shot, organized a

*Jacqueline Kennedy, wife of President John F. Kennedy, enjoys a moment at the White House with her son, John.* (AP/John F. Kennedy Library)

memorable, dignified funeral. Her composure and grace impressed the nation. Speaking with a journalist shortly after her husband's death, she labeled the brief Kennedy presidency an "American Camelot" after the legendary city of King Arthur's court, a term that has persisted over the decades.

After leaving the White House in early 1964, Jacqueline and her children lived first in Washington, D.C., and later in New York City. She was widely admired as a caring mother who shielded her two children from the media after her husband's death.

**Later Life**  After the assassination of her husband's brother, Robert F. Kennedy, in 1968, Jacqueline worried about the safety of her children. That year, she married her friend, Aristotle Onassis, a Greek billionaire. He provided the security she sought, but the marriage was not happy. They lived apart more than together. After Onassis died, Jacqueline settled permanently in New York. She worked as a part-time editor, first for Viking and later for Doubleday. She

successfully raised her children and remained a presence in their lives. She never remarried, but in later years, businessman Maurice Tempelsman was her companion until her death in 1994 at age sixty-four from cancer.

**Impact**  Jacqueline was perhaps the single most influential American woman of the 1960's. She set standards for fashion and elegance that were copied by millions of women. The tragic death of her husband brought further attention to an already popular woman, and she found herself subject to the media's constant scrutiny although she did not seek publicity. Her popularity and celebrity status, which endured after her death, changed the way Americans view the First Lady.

**Subsequent Events**  Jacqueline was involved in maintaining the legacy of President Kennedy, especially the Kennedy Library, and remained part of the extended Kennedy family.

**Additional Information** Two well-known sources on Jacqueline Kennedy Onassis are C. David Heymann's *A Woman Called Jackie*, published in 1989, and Richard Taylor and Sam Rubin's *Jackie: A Lasting Impression*, published in 1990.

*Norma Corigliano Noonan*

**See also** Assassinations of John and Robert Kennedy and Martin Luther King, Jr.; Camelot; Kennedy, Edward "Ted"; Kennedy, John F.; Kennedy, Robert F.

## ■ Kennedy, John F.

**Born** May 29, 1917, Brookline, Massachusetts
**Died** November 22, 1963, Dallas, Texas

*The thirty-fifth president of the United States, known for his New Frontier domestic policy and prominent role in leading the nation during the Cold War. His youth and energy symbolized a new generation of political leaders, and his assassination was a national tragedy brought home to Americans on television.*

**Early Life** Born to a wealthy and prominent family, John Fitzgerald Kennedy attended Harvard University and was graduated in 1940. He enlisted in the Navy during World War II and won a medal for heroism, an experience chronicled in the film *PT 109* (1963). After the war, Kennedy served in the U.S. House of Representatives from 1947 to 1953 and in the U.S. Senate, where he earned a reputation as a liberal, from 1953 to 1961. In 1953, he married Jacqueline Lee Bouvier, and the couple had two children, Caroline and John. He wrote a book, *Profiles in Courage*, which won the Pulitzer Prize in 1957. At the 1956 Democratic National Convention, Kennedy very nearly won the nomination for vice president of the United States. The favorable publicity from that nomination attempt made him a frontrunner for the 1960 presidential nomination.

**The 1960's** In January, 1960, Kennedy formally announced his candidacy for the presidency. He won nomination on the first ballot at the Democratic National Convention and named Lyndon B. Johnson as his vice presidential running mate. He defeated Republican opponent Richard M. Nixon by a narrow margin, becoming the first Catholic and the youngest man ever to be elected president. His 1961 inaugural address to the nation became famous for his proclamation that "the torch has been passed to a new generation of Americans." He also included the well-known directive, "Ask not what your country can do for you—ask what you can do for your country." The election of Kennedy, who symbolized young and energetic leadership, signaled a dramatic change in the nation's capital. Kennedy and his young wife, Jacqueline, brought an interest in art, culture, and fashion to the White House.

As president, Kennedy's first interest was in foreign affairs. He came to power at the height of the Cold War. In 1961, soon after he became president, a Central Intelligence Agency plan to invade Cuba at the Bay of Pigs and oust its Marxist leader, Fidel Castro—a plan Kennedy approved and implemented—ended in disaster. However, later foreign policy strategies were more successful. Kennedy led Western opposition to the building of a wall around noncommunist West Berlin, Germany, in August, 1961, and although the wall was built, the city remained open to air traffic. His confrontation with Soviet premier Nikita Khrushchev over the placing of nuclear missiles in Cuba in 1962 led to the Soviets backing down and withdrawing their weapons from the island. He coordinated the signing of the 1963 Nuclear Test Ban Treaty with the Soviet Union and England. Perhaps his most questionable foreign policy move was to increase U.S. military involvement in South Vietnam, which was battling communistic North Vietnam. One of Kennedy's proudest accomplishments was the development in 1961 of the Peace Corps, which sent young Americans around the world to promote economic and social growth in developing countries. During the first year of his presidency, he reacted to the emerging contest between the Soviet Union and the United States in developing space technology by challenging the United States to land an astronaut on the moon by the end of the decade.

Domestically, Kennedy presided over the nation as the Civil Rights movement was reaching its height. He confronted Mississippi governor Ross Barnett and made it possible for James H. Meredith to become the first African American to enroll at the University of Mississippi in September, 1962. In his last year as president, he proposed a sweeping civil rights act that was not enacted until after his death. Additionally, Kennedy proposed New Frontier programs that would promote full-employment policies, increased federal aid for education, and health in-

*President John F. Kennedy responds to reporters' questions at a Washington, D.C., press conference. The young leader's energy and the circumstances surrounding his death created a long-lasting mystique for the Kennedy family.* (AP/Wide World Photos)

surance for the aged, a policy now known as Medicare. Although these sweeping policy proposals did not become law in his lifetime, they became cornerstones in the legislative success of the Johnson administration that assumed power upon Kennedy's death.

On November 22, 1963, Kennedy was shot and killed while riding in a motorcade in Dallas, Texas.

Lee Harvey Oswald was identified as the shooter, although controversy remains about the killing. Kennedy's death and funeral were covered widely on live television and brought on a period of national mourning. He was buried in Arlington National Cemetery, where an eternal flame stands for the enduring Kennedy mystique.

**Impact** Kennedy continued to symbolize vigorous leadership after his death. Johnson, his successor, used the slain president's desire for a civil rights bill to secure passage of the Civil Rights Act of 1964. Johnson also incorporated many of Kennedy's New Frontier programs into his Great Society programs. Kennedy's challenge to land an astronaut on the moon became a rallying cry that was realized in 1969. The Kennedy mystique lived on in the political careers of his two brothers, Robert and Edward. His policy in Vietnam was greatly expanded under the Johnson administration, and the United States involved itself in a prolonged, bloody, and ultimately unsuccessful war.

**Subsequent Events** The Kennedy assassination has been the subject of continuing controversy. Many who have studied the assassination believe that Oswald did not act alone, and theories continue to abound. The Kennedy Space Center in Cape Canaveral, Florida, was named to honor the fallen president.

**Additional Information** Kennedy's early life is favorably described in James M. Burns's *John F. Kennedy: A Political Profile* (1960). A more critical biography is Nigel Hamilton's *Reckless Youth* (1992). Histories of Kennedy's public career by Kennedy associates are Theodore Sorensen's *Kennedy* (1965) and Arthur Schlesinger's *A Thousand Days: John F. Kennedy in the White House* (1965). More recently, Richard Reeves has written *President Kennedy: Profile of Power* (1993). The Kennedy assassination and surrounding events are discussed in William Manchester's *The Death of a President* (1967).

*James W. Riddlesperger, Jr.*

**See also** Assassinations of John and Robert Kennedy and Martin Luther King, Jr.; Bay of Pigs Invasion; Berlin Wall; Camelot; Civil Rights Movement; Cuban Missile Crisis; Johnson, Lyndon B.; Kennedy, Edward "Ted"; Kennedy, Jacqueline; Kennedy, Robert F.; Oswald, Lee Harvey; Peace Corps; Presidential Election of 1960; Warren Report.

# ■ Kennedy, Robert F.

**Born** November 20, 1925, Brookline, Massachusetts
**Died** June 6, 1968, Los Angeles, California

*Attorney general, senator, and candidate for United States president when assassinated. Kennedy embodied the hopes of a generation striving to find answers to the dilemma of civil rights and the disaster of the Vietnam War.*

**Early Life** Born the third son and seventh child of Rose Fitzgerald and Joseph P. Kennedy, Robert Francis "Bobby" Kennedy grew up in a large, Irish Catholic family. His parents, both products of the Irish immigrant enclave in Boston, believed firmly in responsibility and competition. When Kennedy was thirteen years old, his father was appointed ambassador to Great Britain, and the family moved to England in 1938. With the outbreak of World War II, he returned to the United States where Kennedy attended Portsmouth Priory, Milton Academy, and Harvard University, with a stint in the Naval Reserve. Kennedy attended the University of Virginia Law School and graduated in June, 1951. He married Ethel Skakel in June, 1950, and by late 1951, he had accepted a position at the Department of Justice and witnessed the birth of the first of his eleven children. He resigned the following year to manage his brother John F. Kennedy's successful campaign for senator from Massachusetts. Later, Robert Kennedy was appointed assistant counsel to Senator Joseph McCarthy but soon left that position to enter private law practice. By 1954, Kennedy was minority counsel on the Senate Investigations Committee. He participated actively in Democratic politics, working for the election of Adlai Stevenson in 1956, then becoming counsel to the Senate Rackets Committee, chaired by his brother, which was investigating the Teamsters and union leader Jimmy Hoffa. After resigning his position in 1959, he wrote *The Enemy Within* based on what he had learned of corruption. Then in 1960, when his brother decided to run for president, Kennedy again became his campaign manager.

**The 1960's** As campaign manager, Kennedy helped secure his brother's narrow victory in November, 1960. His brother promptly appointed him United States attorney general. In that position, Kennedy was a staunch supporter of the nascent Civil Rights movement and called on federal marshals to protect the Freedom Riders trying to desegregate the South.

In October, 1962, Kennedy advised his brother to ignore Nikita Khruschev's second note demanding the withdrawal of missiles from Turkey during the Cuban Missile Crisis and accept the terms of the first. This act helped bring a peaceful end to the confrontation between the world's two nuclear superpowers. However, on November 22, 1963, President Kennedy was assassinated in Dallas, Texas, as he began his push for reelection in 1964. Robert Kennedy felt the loss of his brother keenly and spent hours reading and walking, attempting to make sense of the tragedy.

Kennedy was elected United States senator from New York in 1964. Originally a supporter of the war in Vietnam, by late 1964, Kennedy was urging President Lyndon B. Johnson to order a pause in the bombing of North Vietnam. By 1968, the issues of poverty, civil rights, and the Vietnam War were tearing the country apart. After much soul searching, Kennedy decided to run for president in 1968 as an outspoken antiwar candidate. He was mobbed by supporters and successful in drawing together the voters from California to South Dakota. Kennedy was seemingly on the threshold of winning the Democratic presidential nomination when minutes after delivering his victory speech in the California primary on June 5, 1968, at the Ambassador Hotel in Los Angeles, he was shot by Sirhan Sirhan. Kennedy died the following day.

**Impact** Kennedy had become a touchstone and a unifying factor for disaffected Americans, from the farmworkers organized by César Chávez to the college students protesting the Vietnam War. With his death, Americans seemed to lose faith in the effectiveness of peaceful protests and the existing political system, and violence erupted, from the Democratic National Convention in Chicago in 1968 to the Kent State shootings in 1970. Ultimately, this disquiet forced the new president, Richard M. Nixon, to withdraw from the war in 1973. Americans turned away from the activism of the 1960's in favor of the apathy of the 1970's.

**Subsequent Events** Sirhan was convicted of single-handedly killing Kennedy. In the years following the trial, Sirhan protested his innocence, and independent investigators discovered evidence of extra bullet holes that indicated that there were two gunmen. The case came under study several times, particularly when Sirhan applied for parole.

*Robert F. Kennedy, brother to fallen president John F. Kennedy, seemed close to winning the Democratic presidential nomination when he was fatally shot in June, 1968.* (Archive Photos)

**Additional Information** Arthur M. Schlesinger, Jr.'s *Robert Kennedy and His Times* (1978) describes the man and his career. President Bill Clinton wrote the introduction to a later work by Bill Eppridge entitled *Robert Kennedy: The Last Campaign* (1993).

*Michaela Crawford Reaves*

**See also** Assassinations of John and Robert Kennedy and Martin Luther King, Jr.; Civil Rights Movement; Cuban Missile Crisis; Kennedy, John F.; Organized Crime; Presidential Election of 1968; Vietnam War.

## ■ Kennedy-Nixon Debates

**Dates** September 26, 1960; October 7, 13, 21, 1960

*The first televised presidential debates and the last for sixteen years. John F. Kennedy's relaxed style, compared with Richard M. Nixon's seeming rigidity, helped him win the election.*

**Origins and History** In August, 1960, President Dwight D. Eisenhower signed a law that allowed the free use of radio and television time by major party candidates and enabled the networks to exclude fringe candidates. John F. Kennedy, seeking wider recognition, and Richard M. Nixon, hoping to improve his image, agreed to participate in a series of four nationally televised debates.

**The Debates** Each debate was scheduled to last one hour and was structured around questions posed by a panel of four reporters. The first debate, devoted to domestic affairs, was held in Chicago, Illinois, on September 26, 1960. Immediately evident to the massive television audience was the incongruous appearance of the two candidates. Kennedy looked strong and vibrant and argued with confidence, while Nixon appeared tired and anxious and was at times evasive. Refusing facial makeup, Nixon had instead opted for powder to cover his unshaven face. As he began to sweat under the heat of the studio lights, his powdered face appeared pale. Most Americans watching on television were impressed with Kennedy, who had seemed to best the vice president. Ironically, many radio listeners believed that Nixon had done very well.

The television audience for the second debate on October 7, 1960, was considerably smaller than that for the first. Unlike in the first debate, all topics were open for discussion. Nixon appeared more poised and tried to portray Kennedy as too inexperienced to deal properly with serious foreign policy issues. In

*The 1960 televised debates between presidential candidates Democrat John F. Kennedy and Republican Richard M. Nixon may have created enough support for Kennedy to enable him to win the election.* (Copyright Washington Post. Reprinted by permission of D.C. Public Library.)

large part because of the smaller audience, the younger candidate was able to maintain his supporters despite Nixon's improved performance.

The third debate, on October 13, 1960, attempted something unprecedented. Because both candidates were campaigning around the country, they debated from separate studios, Kennedy in New York City and Nixon in Los Angeles. The reporters were able to ask questions regarding any topic. The third debate, like the second, changed few opinions.

Going into the last debate on October 12, 1960, both candidates recognized that their television audience had dwindled. Both also knew that this favored Kennedy; not until the fourth debate was the topic foreign policy. Nixon's strength.

The candidates had different reasons for entering into the unprecedented debates. Already well-known as the vice president and a former congressman, Nixon had hoped to erase his image as an ill-tempered man and inconsequential member of the Eisenhower administration. At the same time, he wanted to portray Kennedy as too young and inexperienced to guide the nation through potential Cold War crises. Nixon clearly failed in this regard during the first debate. This failure was exacerbated by the fact that the viewing audience dwindled even as Nixon improved his demeanor and effectiveness in subsequent debates.

Kennedy, though a war hero and congressman, was not as well-known as the vice president. Therefore, Kennedy's goal for the debates was not only to gain wider recognition but also to appear commanding and mature, which he succeeded in doing. Before the debates, Nixon had been ahead in the polls. Afterward, Kennedy inched ahead and eventually won the 1960 election, though by one of the slimmest margins ever.

**Impact**  Many researchers and critics believe that the televised debates directly enabled Kennedy to win the 1960 presidential election. His victory demonstrated that television could be a very powerful political weapon. The debates established that appearance could be more important than actual content, as evidenced by the different impressions the debates had on radio and television audiences. No debates were held between the candidates in the 1964 presidential election; televised debates were not resurrected until 1976, when Jimmy Carter and Gerald Ford debated under the sponsorship of the League

of Women Voters. After the Kennedy-Nixon debates, presidential candidates became much more aware of the influence of the media, especially television.

**Additional Information**  As special counsel to Kennedy, Theodore C. Sorensen was in a unique position to view these debates and discusses them at length in *Kennedy* (1965). For an interesting look at Nixon the man, see Fawn M. Brodie's *Richard Nixon: The Shaping of His Character* (1981).

*John C. Pinheiro*

**See also**  Assassinations of John and Robert Kennedy and Martin Luther King, Jr.; Camelot; Kennedy, John F.; Media; Nixon, Richard M.; Television.

# ■ Kerner Commission Report

**Published** February 29, 1968
**Author** National Advisory Commission on Civil Disorders

*A formal, governmental attempt to explain the greatest explosion of urban racial violence in the nation's history. The report, the product of a commission appointed by President Lyndon B. Johnson, blamed pervasive racist attitudes and practices for the riots in the nation's cities.*

**The Work**  Beginning in 1963, the United States experienced an unprecedented number of urban racial disorders. In 1967 alone, more than one hundred U.S. cities exploded in episodes of violence and looting. In November, 1967, President Lyndon B. Johnson appointed the Kerner Commission (formally known as the National Advisory Commission on Civil Disorders), headed by Governor Otto Kerner of Illinois, to conduct an investigation to determine exactly what had happened and why and make recommendations to solve the problem.

Because of a sense of urgency in addressing the issue before the coming of summer, the season in which most of the urban disorders took place, the commission issued its report on February 29, 1968, three months before its deadline. Although the commission members were political moderates and such commissions were often viewed as a means of postponing decision or avoiding action, the finished Kerner Commission Report was controversial and an unexpected blockbuster.

The commission reported that the basic cause of the urban disorders was white racism and that white, moderate, responsible America was where the re-

*The 1968 Kerner Commission Report analyzed the possible causes of a unprecedented large number of urban racial riots, including this summer, 1967, riot in Detroit, Michigan.* (AP/Wide World Photos)

sponsibility for the riots ultimately lay. It had conducted detailed case studies of cities where violence had erupted and found that the riots had not been caused by any single factor or precipitating incident and were not the result of an organized plan or conspiracy. Its report stated that "the single overriding cause of rioting in the cities was not any one thing commonly adduced—unemployment, lack of education, poverty, exploitation—but that it was all of those things and more, expressed in the insidious and pervasive white sense of the inferiority of black men." The commission emphasized that the source of the problems was the very structure of American society; it did not seek explanations in the psychology of individuals. The report pointed out, "What white Americans have never fully understood—but what the Negro can never forget—is that white society is deeply implicated in the ghetto. White institutions created it, white institutions maintain it, and

white society condones it." The report concluded, "Our nation is moving toward two societies, one black, one white—separate and unequal."

According to the commission, although racism was behind the riots, the more proximate causes of the unrest were pervasive discrimination and segregation in employment, education, and housing and the concentration of impoverished blacks in the inner city, produced by black migration into and white exodus from urban areas. Other contributing factors included the frustration of African Americans with civil rights legislation that failed to deliver the greater opportunity it promised; dissatisfaction with police practices that, for many African Americans, symbolized the oppression associated with racism; and society's apparent tendency to approve of violence against civil rights activists. The commission also noted enhanced racial pride, especially among young African Americans, and a feeling of powerlessness that led some to conclude that violence was the only effective means of change.

The Kerner Commission concluded that discrimination and segregation were serious problems that presented a threat to the future of the nation and must be eliminated. It indicated that three options were open to the nation: to maintain existing, admittedly inadequate policies regarding integration and the elimination of poverty; to focus on improving life in African American ghettos and ignore the goal of integration; or to pursue integration by improving conditions in the ghetto and implementing policies that would encourage movement out of the inner city.

The commission stated that the first option, to maintain existing policies, would permanently divide the United States into two separate and unequal societies and create an irreversible, polarized, police state rather than a democracy. The second option, described as "gilding the ghetto," would enrich the inner city but would further promote a separate, segregated society. Option three, a national commitment to change that involved moving a substantial number of African Americans out of the ghettos, was viewed as the most viable. This option was designed to create a single society in which all citizens would be free to live and work according to their capabilities and desires, not their color.

The Kerner Commission made a series of recommendations related to jobs, housing, education, law enforcement agencies, and nearly every aspect of American life. It asked Americans to tax themselves to the extent necessary to meet the vital needs of the nation. Specific goals included the elimination of barriers to job choice, education, and housing and an increase in the responsiveness of public institutions to relieve feelings of powerlessness. Other goals were to increase communication across racial lines to destroy stereotypes; to halt polarization, distrust, and hostility; and to create common ground for efforts toward public order and social justice.

**Impact** Shortly after the Kerner Commission Report was released, some of its dire prophecies were confirmed when massive urban disorders erupted throughout the country after the assassination of civil rights leader Martin Luther King, Jr., in April. This spasm of violence and destruction punctuated the urgent need to address racial problems.

Since the publication of the report, the passage and enforcement of major civil rights legislation erased de jure discrimination; however, major societal divisions and racial inequalities persisted into the 1990's, partly because of de facto discrimination, which is much harder to regulate away.

**Additional Information** Paul A. Gilje's *Rioting in America* (1966) provides a historical survey of the nation's urban disorders; those in the 1960's are set in the context of a national phenomenon.

*Frank E. Hagan*

**See also** Chicago Riots; Civil Rights Movement; Detroit Riot; New York Riots; Newark Riot; Washington, D.C., Riots; Watts Riot.

---

# ■ Khrushchev's UN Visit

**Date** September 20-October 13, 1960

*At the general assembly of the United Nations, Soviet premier Nikita Khrushchev attacked the West before an audience of Third World leaders and presented himself as the champion of newly independent nations.*

Nikita Khrushchev's first visit to the United Nations came at a time when the Soviet economy was experiencing difficulties. He had announced a third round of major cuts in Soviet military strength, an act resented by his generals, and the nuclear arms race was escalating to the disadvantage of the Soviet Union. By taking center stage at the United Nations, the Soviet leader hoped to deflect increasing domestic criticism. In May, 1960, a few months before Khrushchev's UN visit, U.S.-Soviet relations had soured when Soviet armed forces had shot down a U-2 spy plane belonging to the United States.

At first, Khrushchev played the role of a statesman at the United Nations. He called for disarmament and the continuation of détente. However, his visit became best known for the boorish precedents he set. During a speech by UN Secretary General Dag Hammarskjöld, he pounded his fists on his desk, interrupted other speakers with shouts, shook his finger at one delegate, and on three occasions pounded his desk with his shoe.

**Impact** His behavior undermined Khrushchev's stature as a statesman. His confrontational approach heightened Cold War tensions and led to the Cuban Missile Crisis. At home, his opponents became increasingly convinced that they were dealing with an unstable man, whom they ousted in 1964.

**Additional Information** Edward Crankshaw provides more details about this event in *Khrushchev: A Career* (1966), the standard biography of Khrushchev. In *Khrushchev Remembers: The Last Testament* (1974), edited by Strobe Talbott, the Soviet leader remains unrepentent for his behavior and maintains that his actions were in defense of Third World countries.

*Harry Piotrowski*

**See also** Arms Race; Cold War; Cuban Missile Crisis; U-2 Spy Plane Incident.

# ■ Kidney Transplants

*The implantation of a healthy kidney into a person with a failing kidney. Organ transplant techniques were standardized and defined in the 1960's.*

The transplanting of kidneys was made possible because of the development of successful techniques for rejoining blood vessels, ways to properly match donors and recipients, and effective immunosuppression.

By 1902, French surgeon Alexis Carrel had perfected the technique of vascular suture (rejoining blood vessels) and had even completely severed and then successfully reattached kidneys in animals with full resumption of function. The first human renal (kidney) graft was performed by a Ukrainian scientist in 1933. In the late 1950's, occasional unmatched renal transplants were shown to remain functioning actively for some time even when the immune system was not suppressed. On December 23, 1954, a kidney transplanted from one identical twin to the other produced long-term success. Successful transplants were also performed using kidneys donated by living or deceased relatives of the patient.

During the 1960's, renal transplantation changed from an occasional quasi-experimental exercise to an almost routine surgical procedure performed successfully in many centers. The surgical technique of placement and reattachment of the donated kidney was standardized. Improvements in technique decreased the dangerous complications of blood clotting, abnormal urine drainage, and deep-wound infections. Successful management protocols for these and other complications evolved with greater experience.

The problem of finding an appropriate donor was also made easier during the decade. In 1962, surgeons performed the first successful transplant using a kidney from someone not related to the patient, and the same year, scientists developed several new ways to preserve human kidneys. In 1966, the technique of hemodialysis (removing blood from an artery, purifying it through dialysis, and returning it to a vein) was improved, making it possible for patients with end-stage renal disease to be maintained while an appropriate donor organ was obtained. Progressive understanding of immune functions and graft rejection helped the matching of prospective donors to recipients. The first histocompatibility antigen (used in determining tissue compatibility) was described in 1958. By 1962, tissue matching of recipient and donor kidneys was being performed. Matching became a predictable, practical, and therefore routine procedure.

Advances were also made in developing methods to suppress the immune system and prevent it from rejecting the transplanted kidney. Initially, scientists used whole-body irradiation as an immunosuppressant to prevent graft rejection. This drastic measure was soon replaced by the use of steroids (such as prednisone) and chemical immunosuppressants such as those already in use in cancer chemotherapy. In 1966, a substance obtained from horses called antilymphocytic globulin was found to be useful in preventing rejection. These methods of safe immunosuppression prevented or delayed rejection of transplanted organs.

During the decade, the establishment of a National Transplant Registry helped physicians and researchers improve kidney transplants by allowing analysis of global data and quick sharing of successful strategies. Problems were defined and lessons painfully learned. An exemplary cooperation developed among physicians and scientists in different fields and countries. By the late 1960's, human kidney transplants had become quite effective. In 1967, long-term success rates of 77 percent, 71 percent, and 45 percent were reported for kidneys transplanted from siblings, parents, and deceased donors, respectively.

**Impact** Successful renal transplantation has saved lives and allowed dying patients to return to productive lives. It has also had wide impact on the transplantation of other organs such as the heart and liver and vastly increased knowledge in many fields, including human physiology, immunity, cancer chemotherapy, pharmacology, and antibiotics. An important but seldom recognized benefit has been great cooperation among scientists of diverse disciplines and countries.

In the 1960's, the importance of the biological phenomena related to transplantation was reflected in the Nobel Prizes awarded to investigators in the field in 1960 and 1966.

**Subsequent Events** In 1973, Congress mandated Medicare coverage of dialysis for end-stage renal disease, which enabled patients with damaged kidneys to wait until an appropriate organ became available. One side effect of this legislation has been the burgeoning cost of renal dialysis to the taxpayer. This and the paucity of donor organs have raised significant ethical questions regarding the determination of the suitability of recipients, the recipient selection process, and the allocation of the limited number of organs available. The definition of death also has come under ethical scrutiny, and a medico-legal assessment of death has been established.

The importance of research in transplantation and associated fields continued as evidenced by the Nobel Prizes awarded to investigators in this field in the years 1972, 1980, 1984, 1987, and 1990.

**Additional Information** Peter J. Morris's *Kidney Transplantation: Principles and Practice* (1979) takes a closer look at this medical procedure, and *Gift of Life: The Effect of Organ Transplantation on Individual, Family, and Societal Dynamics* (1987), by Roberta G. Simmons, Susan Klein Marine, and Richard L. Simmons, takes a look at the social and psychological aspects of kidney transplants.

*Ranès C. Chakravorty*

**See also** Heart Transplants; Medicine; Nobel Prizes; Science and Technology.

## ■ King, Billie Jean

**Born** November 22, 1943, Long Beach, California

*One of America's greatest women's tennis players. King is also known for working for equality for women in sports.*

Billie Jean Moffitt (known as King since her 1965 marriage to Larry King) became active in the tennis program in Long Beach, California, as a young girl. She quickly became a leading amateur player, winning her first Wimbledon doubles title in 1961, at age seventeen. She repeated the feat in 1962, 1965, 1967, and 1968, taking the mixed doubles title in

*Billie Jean King, one of the best athletes in the sport of women's tennis, plays in the Kent Lawn Tennis matches in 1967. (Popperfoto/Archive Photos)*

1967 and the singles title for three consecutive years, 1966 through 1968. In 1967, she won the singles, doubles, and mixed doubles championships at the U.S. Open (where she had taken the doubles title in 1964) and the singles title at the Australian Open. Also in 1967, King, who turned pro the following year, was named Associated Press Female Athlete of the Year, an honor she again received in 1973.

King continued winning in the 1970's, earning a record total of twenty Wimbledon titles (singles in 1972, 1973, and 1975, doubles in 1970-1973 and 1979, and mixed doubles in 1971, 1973, and 1974) and in 1971 becoming the first female athlete to earn more than one hundred thousand dollars. She won singles titles at the U.S. Opens in 1971, 1972, and 1974 and at the French Open in 1972. In the late 1970's, she cofounded a women's sports magazine that became known as *Women's Sports and Fitness*.

**Impact** King's aggressive tennis style became the standard for women's tennis. She strived to earn greater respect for women's tennis and to correct the disparity between women's and men's tournament prize money. In 1972, King became the first female *Sports Illustrated* Sportsman of the Year, and in 1973, she defeated male chauvinist Bobby Riggs in a match billed as the "battle of the sexes" and viewed on television by more than fifty million people. She founded the Women's Tennis Association in 1974 and is a member of the International Tennis Hall of Fame and the International Women's Sports Hall of Fame.

**Additional Information** William R. Sanford and Carl R. Green's *Billie Jean King* (1993) covers King's numerous championships and her famous match with Riggs.

*Jennifer Raye James*

**See also** Feminist Movement; Tennis.

## ■ King, Coretta Scott

**Born** April 27, 1927, Marion, Alabama

*One of the nation's most prominent women of the 1960's, a civil rights activist and lecturer. She is the widow of slain civil rights leader Martin Luther King, Jr.*

**Early Life** Civil rights and women's rights activist Coretta Scott King was born April 27, 1927, in Alabama. She was one of three children in the Scott family, which had farmed its own land since Reconstruction. Scott entered Antioch College in 1945, majoring in education and music. She continued her postgraduate studies at the New England Conservatory of Music in Boston, Massachusetts, where she met Martin Luther King, Jr., a graduate student at Boston University. After a whirlwind romance, the couple married June 18, 1953. In 1955, King received her degree in music and her husband received his doctorate degree. Her husband accepted the pastorate of Dexter Avenue Baptist Church, and they moved to Montgomery, Alabama, in September.

**The 1960's** King believed in the same ideals espoused by her famous husband. Early in their marriage, she focused on her children—Yolanda Denise (1955), Martin Luther III (1957), Dexter Scott (1961), and Bernice Albertine (1963)—and relinquished her career ambitions to devote herself to her family. King did some teaching and fund-raising over the years for the Southern Christian Leadership Conference (SCLC), although the bulk of her personal involvement came after the death of her husband in 1968. She gradually became involved in her husband's work and sometimes sang at his lectures. Occasionally, she participated in separate activities. In 1962, King went to the seventeen-nation Disarmament Conference in Geneva, Switzerland, as a Women Strike for Peace delegate. She also began to fill the overflow speaking engagements when the demand on her husband became too much.

After her husband's death, King filled many of her late husband's commitments and became increasingly involved in the Civil Rights movement. The Solidarity Day speech King gave in June, 1968, was considered proof that she had emerged as a civil rights leader in her own right. The profound speech called upon American women to unite to fight the evils of racism, poverty, and war. King was no longer a shadow of her husband's memory.

**Later Life** King spent much of the 1970's creating a memorial for her late husband. In 1980, the Martin Luther King, Jr., Center for Nonviolent Social Change was established. The King center is in downtown Atlanta, Georgia, in the hub of the city's National Historic Site and Preservation District. King remains an eloquent and respected speaker and is recognized for keeping her husband's dream alive.

**Impact** As founder and president of the King center, King carried on her husband's vision and unfinished work. The center promotes human rights and peace throughout the world and draws more than 3.5 million visitors yearly. King remains committed to social change and, through the center, teaches economic empowerment and promotes the elimination of poverty and racism.

**Subsequent Events** In 1997, King and her family joined with James Earl Ray, convicted killer of her husband, in requesting a new trial for Ray. William F. Pepper, Ray's attorney, alleged that the state's case against Ray was a setup and that the convicted killer was innocent. The lawyers for Ray and the King family continued to lobby for a new trial until Ray's death in April, 1998.

**Additional Information** Several book-length studies about King's life have been published. Ruth Turk's *Coretta Scott King: Fighter for Justice* (1997) provides details about her life and career and highlights on her accomplishments after her husband's death.

*Rose M. Russell*

**See also** Civil Rights Movement; King, Martin Luther, Jr.; Southern Christian Leadership Conference (SCLC).

## ■ King, Martin Luther, Jr.

**Born** January 15, 1929, Atlanta, Georgia
**Died** April 4, 1968, Memphis, Tennessee

*One of the world's most renowned advocates of nonviolence for social change, strategist, civil rights leader, and Nobel Peace Prize winner. With King's murder in 1968, the Civil Rights movement temporarily stagnated.*

**Early Life** Martin Luther King, Jr., was born Michael Luther King on January 15, 1929; later his father, also Michael Luther King, changed both his and his son's first names to Martin. King's father and grandfather, Adam Daniel Williams, were both Baptist

ministers. King began cultivating his distinct oratory skills while in high school in Atlanta. After participating in a summer work program for Morehouse College students, King was admitted to the college at age fifteen. There he began receiving oratory awards, which he continued to win throughout his life. In 1948, King received his bachelor of arts degree in sociology from Morehouse College, then received a bachelors degree in divinity from Crozer Theological Seminary in Chester, Pennsylvania, in 1951, and a doctorate from Boston University in 1955. King married Coretta Scott in Marion, Alabama, in 1953. The Kings eventually had four children—Yolanda Denise, Martin Luther III, Dexter Scott, and Bernice Albertine. In 1954, King became the pastor of Dexter Avenue Baptist Church in Montgomery, Alabama.

King became involved in one of the first and most dramatic moves toward desegregation. In 1955, seamstress Rosa Parks refused to give up her seat on a Montgomery bus to a white person. After her arrest

*Civil rights activist and leader of the Southern Christian Leadership Conference Martin Luther King, Jr., addresses the Democratic National Convention's credential committee in August, 1964, in an attempt to win accreditation for the Mississippi Freedom Democratic Party.* (AP/Wide World Photos)

for disobeying the city's segregation rules, African American community leaders formed the Montgomery Improvement Association (MIA), which elected King its president and launched a bus boycott that lasted 381 days. After a series of court cases, the buses were desegregated in 1956.

In the latter part of the 1950's and until his death, King was a dominant force in the Civil Rights movement. In 1959, King resigned his post as pastor of the Dexter Avenue Baptist Church to devote more time to the Southern Christian Leadership Conference (SCLC), a nonviolent civil rights group that he had helped organize in 1957. The SCLC sought to help African Americans obtain their rights and put an end to segregation. King moved to Atlanta and, in 1960, became the copastor of the Ebenezer Baptist Church with his father. In 1959, King, who had studied the life and teachings of Indian leader Mahatma Gandhi and was indoctrinated in his nonviolence principles, visited India as guest of Prime Minister Nehru.

**The 1960's** King's involvement with the Civil Rights movement increased, and through SCLC, he was involved in many more protests and sit-ins. King joined Atlanta students in a sit-in protest in October, 1960. King was jailed along with the student protesters for sitting at a segregated restaurant in Rich's Department Store; he refused bail in order to stay with the student protesters.

In December, 1961, King joined civil rights activists in Albany, Georgia, who were attempting to desegregate public transportation facilities. He, along with many other demonstrators, was arrested for marching without a permit. The authorities promised to negotiate with African Americans and desegregate the bus and train terminals. King, who was not part of the negotiations, was released on bond and left. However, the Albany authorities reneged on their promises.

In spring, 1963, King and the SCLC initiated a campaign to desegregate public accommodations in Birmingham, Alabama, which had gained a reputation for being opposed to desegregation. Demonstrations began in early April, and King was arrested and released. He organized demonstrations in which children, age six to eighteen, marched. At first arrests were peaceful; then on May 3, police and firefighters, using dogs and fire hoses, attacked the children. Images and stories of the event filled the television screen and appeared in newspapers throughout the nation and overseas. The event outraged millions of Americans and awakened long-slumbering African American resentments. Birmingham's public safety commissioner, Eugene "Bull" Connor, who had ordered the attacks on the protesters, came to symbolize police brutality in the minds of many Americans. Much of this sentiment helped lead to the creation and passage of the Civil Rights Act of 1964.

The most successful and inspirational civil rights event that King was involved in was the March on Washington, in August, 1963, which brought together a number of civil rights groups and attracted more than 250,000 protesters. The march culminated at the Lincoln Memorial, where King delivered his famous and powerful "I Have a Dream" speech. He spoke of his vision for a nation in which people would "not be judged by the color of their skin but by the content of their character."

King was named 1963 Man of the Year by *Time* magazine and was featured on the cover of the January, 1964, issue. He became the first African American ever to receive that distinction. In December of 1964, King became the youngest person to receive the Nobel Peace Prize for his achievements in using nonviolence to promote social change.

King organized protesters and led a march from Selma to Montgomery in March, 1965, to call attention to the need for a federal voting rights law. The Voting Rights Act of 1965 was signed into law in August. That same month, King publicly denounced the Vietnam War and urged the president to seek peaceful negotiations. King continued his antiwar protest, and in April, 1967, he delivered a speech at the Riverside Church in New York City.

He turned his efforts toward improving the quality of life for the poor. In March, 1968, King led a group of approximately six thousand protesters in support of striking Memphis sanitation workers. On April 3, 1968, King delivered his last speech, "I've Been to the Mountaintop," at the Mason Temple in Memphis. April 4, 1968, while standing on the balcony of the Lorraine Motel in Memphis, King was assassinated.

James Earl Ray was arrested and charged with the murder. Ray pled guilty and was sentenced to life in prison but later claimed to be innocent. He died of liver and kidney disease in April, 1998, still seeking a trial.

**Impact** King's nonviolent protests against segregation and racial inequality affected people around the world as well as in the United States. His words, his oratorical skill, and efforts in the field changed the attitudes of many Americans and focused attention on the rights of African Americans. His work helped enable the passage of two pieces of legislation, the Civil Rights Act of 1964 and the Voting Rights Act of 1965, both of which secured important rights for African Americans.

**Subsequent Events** Four days after King's death, Representative John Conyers of Michigan submitted the first legislation proposing to make King's birthday a national holiday. This effort failed; however, his family and followers never gave up trying. Singer-songwriter Stevie Wonder was one of the biggest proponents of making King's birthday a national holiday. He lobbied in Washington, D.C., and even wrote a song expressing his feelings for King. Through many attempts, King's birthday became a legal holiday on January 20, 1986.

**Additional Information** Taylor Branch's *Parting the Waters: America in the King Years, 1954-1963* (1988) provides a look at King and his role in the Civil Rights movement. *And the Walls Came Tumbling Down: An Autobiography* (1989), by King's close associate Ralph Abernathy, looks at the topic from a more personal angle. A close and personal view of King can be found in *My Life with Martin Luther King, Jr.* (1969), by his widow, Coretta Scott King. William F. Pepper's *Orders to Kill: The Truth Behind the Murder of Martin Luther King* (1995) takes a close look at the circumstances surrounding King's death.

*Rose M. Russell*

**See also** Assassinations of John and Robert Kennedy and Martin Luther King, Jr.; Birmingham March; Civil Rights Act of 1964; Civil Rights Movement; "I Have a Dream" Speech; Kennedy, John F.; King, Coretta Scott; March on Selma; March on Washington; Poor People's March; Sit-ins; Voting Rights Act of 1965.

## ■ Kissinger, Henry

**Born** May 27, 1923, Fürth, Germany

*A brilliant, innovative national security adviser and secretary of state. Kissinger succeeded in making U.S. foreign policy less idealistic and more realistic.*

**Early Life** The year Henry Alfred Kissinger was born, the German mark was valued one-trillionth what it had been in 1914. The inflation did much to destabilize society and bring to power the anti-Semitic Nazis. The ensuing revolution, with its terrible toll in human suffering, made a lasting impression on the young Kissinger. Despite discrimination, he managed to secure an excellent education. By 1938, conditions had become intolerable, and Kissinger and his family fled to the United States. Kissinger continued his education in New York City and later served in the U.S. Army. Kissinger, who developed an interest in history and government, attended Harvard University where he received his doctorate and began teaching in 1954. The academic life, however, could not satisfy his ambitions.

**The 1960's** Early in his academic career, Kissinger developed an interest in Klemens von Metternich, the Austrian foreign minister who at the Congress of Vienna, convened after the defeat of Napoleon in the early nineteenth century, applied the balance-of-power idea that was to give Europe a century of peace. Kissinger also admired Otto von Bismarck, the German chancellor whose "realistic" if unethical politics brought about German unification in 1871—a revolution that did not disturb the social order. Kissinger would apply the theories of both to foreign policy.

Kissinger served Presidents John F. Kennedy and Lyndon B. Johnson in an advisory capacity on foreign policy. In 1961, Kissinger was sent to Berlin to help defuse a crisis after the Soviets had cut off access to the city. The issue was resolved with a wall that bisected the city. In 1965, he was sent to Vietnam, beginning a ten-year involvement in that war. Kissinger wanted to end the war through secret negotiations. His skill and unorthodox procedures attracted the attention of Richard M. Nixon. Shortly after Nixon was elected president in 1968, he offered Kissinger the influential position of national security adviser.

**Later Life** In 1972, Kissinger accompanied Nixon to China and then to the Soviet Union where he could apply his balance-of-power idea among the three superpowers. In January, 1973, Kissinger helped to resolve diplomatically the bloody and unpopular Vietnam War. The same year, he was appointed Secretary of State, the first foreign-born person ever to assume the position. Also in 1973, Kissinger shared

*National Security Adviser and Secretary of State Henry Kissinger succeeded in making U.S. foreign policy more realistic.* (Library of Congress)

the Nobel Peace Prize with the North Vietnamese diplomat Le duc Tho. Kissinger's last diplomatic achievement was in late 1975 when he arranged a peace settlement between Egypt and Israel. He left government service early in 1977.

**Impact** Before Kissinger, idealism and isolationism influenced U.S. foreign policy. Idealism was replaced under Kissinger with realism, as evidenced by the establishment of relations with communist states. Isolationism was replaced with continued involvement in the international community and its affairs as the U.S. assumed a leadership role.

**Subsequent Events** After retirement from government, Kissinger continued to teach, serve as an adviser, and write. His 912-page *Diplomacy* (1994) is perhaps the most definitive study of the subject to date.

**Additional Information** The 1992 biography of Henry Kissinger, *Kissinger*, by Walter Isaacson is lengthy, but detailed and interesting.

*Nis Petersen*

**See also:** Johnson Lyndon B.; Kennedy, John F.; Nixon, Richard M.; Vietnam War.

## ■ Koufax, Sandy

**Born** December 30, 1935, Brooklyn, New York

*One of baseball's finest pitchers. During his career, Koufax helped lead the Los Angeles Dodgers to two World Series championships.*

Born Sanford Braun, Sandy Koufax took his stepfather's name following his parents' divorce. While attending the University of Cincinnati on an athletic scholarship, the young lefthander signed a contract with the Brooklyn Dodgers, moving with the team to Los Angeles in 1958.

In 1961, Koufax led the National League in strikeouts, a feat he would repeat in 1963, 1965, and 1966. Although he was sidelined by injuries for the better part of 1962, Koufax won two World Series games in 1963 and received the first of his three Cy Young Awards. The following year, injuries to his pitching arm forced him once again to end his season early. Aided by cortisone shots, Koufax came back in 1965 to a spectacular season that saw him pitch two more winning World Series games and a recordbreaking fourth no-hitter, the only perfect game in Los Angeles Dodger history. By 1966, Koufax had become the highest-paid player in baseball. That season marked his fifth consecutive year as the pitcher with the lowest earned run average. Plagued by progressive arthritis caused by his injuries, Koufax retired from baseball at the end of the 1966 season.

Koufax worked for several years as a sports broadcaster following his retirement. In 1972, he became the youngest player ever elected to the Baseball Hall of Fame.

**Impact** Koufax established several pitching records during his years with the Dodgers. His 1966 salary negotiation helped set the tone for a new era in player-management relations.

**Additional Information** *Baseball: An Illustrated History* (1994), by Geoffrey C. Ward and Ken Burns, provides an excellent history of the game.

*Janet E. Lorenz*

**See also** Baseball; DiMaggio, Joe; Mantle, Mickey; Maris, Roger; Mays, Willie; Sports.

---

# ■ Ku Klux Klan (KKK)

*A white supremacist movement that opposed desegregation in the South in the 1960's. The Ku Klux Klan was known for wearing white robes and hoods and using various illegal tactics including beatings, firebombings, and murder in its opposition to the Civil Rights movement.*

**Origins and History** The Ku Klux Klan, which dates back to 1866, is the best-known segregationist group in the United States. The original Klan operated in the post-Civil War era in the South and functioned as a vigilante and terrorist movement opposing Reconstruction governments and their supporters. With the end of Reconstruction, the Klan ceased to exist for several decades but resurfaced in the 1920's as a national movement opposed to African Americans, Catholics, Jews, and immigrants. The Ku Klux Klan of the 1960's was primarily a southern movement that grew in opposition to desegregation. Direct action techniques of the Civil Rights movement, including boycotts, Freedom Rides, marches, and sit-ins, resulted in significant growth of the Klan in

the first half of the 1960's. The most prominent Klan organization was the United Klans of America. This Tuscaloosa, Alabama-based group was formed in 1961 by Robert Shelton, who brought together a number of different Klan units. An estimated 90 percent of all Klansmen belonged to Shelton's Klan, which had its largest following in North Carolina.

Another high-profile Klan organization in the 1960's was the White Knights of the Ku Klux Klan of Mississippi. Its Imperial Wizard was Samuel Bowers, a Laurel, Mississippi, businessperson. Although Bowers's Klan operated only in Mississippi, it was the most violent group. Membership totaled approximately eight thousand at its peak in 1964 and 1965.

In addition to these two organizations, approximately a dozen small, independent Klan groups operated locally throughout the South. Some of the independent Klans formed a loose federation called the National Association of Ku Klux Klans. Their leader was James Venable, an Atlanta, Georgia, attorney who had been in the Klan since 1924. In 1963, Venable formed his own Klan, the National Knights of the Ku Klux Klan. His group, however, never reached the level of power of or engaged in the violence associated with the United Klans or the White Knights.

In general, those who were attracted to the Ku Klux Klan in the 1960's were blue-collar workers. Studies of Klan membership have revealed that the typical member was a skilled or unskilled worker in his thirties who had less than a high school education. These people perceived themselves as being most affected by desegregation and saw themselves losing economic, political, and social status if integration occurred.

**Activities** Although Shelton claimed that the Klan used "ballots not bullets," the Klan in the 1960's is best remembered for its violence. At the same time that traditional Klan rallies were being held throughout the South, attracting crowds as large as ten thousand, some Klansmen were engaged in terrorist activities. A common approach was for Klans to create small wrecking crews that operated independently of Klan chapters. These crews engaged in a variety of activities, including cross burnings, assaults, bombings, beatings, and murder. Numerous African American churches as well as homes and meeting places of civil rights activists were attacked and firebombed. Members of the United Klans of

America were involved in the murders of Lemuel Penn in Georgia and Viola Liuzzo in Alabama. Penn, an U.S. Army Reserve officer and Washington, D.C., educator, was murdered near Athens, Georgia, in 1964, while returning from summer training at Fort Benning, Georgia. Liuzzo, a Detroit housewife who participated in the 1965 Selma to Montgomery march, was murdered as she helped ferry marchers between the two cities. In addition, a Klansman was convicted of bombing the Sixteenth Street Baptist Church in Birmingham, Alabama, in 1963, in which four African American children attending Sunday school were killed. Bowers, Imperial Wizard of the most violent Klan, the White Knights of Mississippi, was suspected of planning at least nine murders, seventy-five bombings, and three hundred assaults.

The most infamous murder attributed to the White Knights was that of three civil rights workers—Michael Schwerner, Andrew Goodman, and James Chaney—near Philadelphia, Mississippi, in 1964.

**Impact** The Klan of the 1960's had a peak membership of fifty thousand. Despite its size and the violent activities in which some members were engaged, the Klan was unable to prevent desegregation. By the early 1970's, Klan membership had dropped below five thousand as the South was forced to adjust to desegregation and people became disillusioned with the organization.

**Subsequent Events** A modest revival of the Klan occurred in the late 1970's. New Klan leaders emerged, including David Duke, leader of the Louisiana-based

*Klansmen in Tallulah, Louisiana, burn a cross to protest civil rights activities taking place in the state in September, 1962.* (AP/Wide World Photos)

Knights of the Ku Klux Klan, and Bill Wilkinson, who broke off from Duke's Klan to create the Invisible Empire, Knights of the Ku Klux Klan. Duke's group was called a new Klan because unlike the groups of the 1960's, it admitted Catholics, created new roles for women, recruited high school students, and had extensive ties to neo-Nazi groups. In the 1970's, Klan membership reached ten thousand. By the mid-1980's, Duke and Wilkinson had left the Klan, Duke to head up the National Association for the Advancement of White People, and Wilkinson after it was revealed that he had been a Federal Bureau of Investigation informant. In the late 1990's, there were fewer than five thousand Klan members in about ten different organizations.

**Additional Information**  The activities of the Ku Klux Klan during the 1960's are covered in David M. Chalmers's *Hooded Americanism* (1981), Patsy Sims's *The Klan* (1978), and Wyn Craig Wade's *The Fiery Cross* (1987).

*William V. Moore*

**See also**  American Nazi Party; Church Bombings; Civil Rights Movement; March on Selma; School Desegregation; Schwerner, Goodman, and Chaney Deaths.

# L

## ■ Lasers

*Extraordinarily intense and coherent monochromatic light sources. Uses for lasers were found in medicine, communications, entertainment, armaments, and pure science.*

Albert Einstein showed in 1917 that stimulated emission of radiation was theoretically possible, but the first important device using stimulated emission was the maser (acronym for microwave amplification by stimulated emission of radiation), the direct precursor of the laser, developed in the 1950's mainly by Charles Hard Townes and his associates at Columbia University. The principles and general design criteria for lasers were outlined in a seminal paper by Townes and Arthur L. Schawlow in 1958, and the first functioning laser was reported two years later.

Theodore H. Maiman announced the ruby laser

*In 1963, a Hughes Aircraft Company scientist looks at the ruby rod inside glass that makes up the core of a laser.* (National Archives)

in a press conference July 7, 1960. (The word "laser" is an acronym for light amplification by stimulated emission of radiation.) The core of this laser was a ruby rod, both ends of which were flattened and silvered to make them reflective. The ruby lay on the axis of a helical glass flashlamp capable of supplying huge bursts of light energy to the rod. This energy excited, or pumped, chromium atoms in the ruby to higher energy levels. Laser action produced a beam of red light from one end of the ruby rod, the result of the excess atoms in the upper energy state reverting to the ground state and of the continual reflection of the laser light from one end of the rod to the other, which produced more and more stimulated emission. Only part of the light escaped to form the output beam.

Before the end of 1960, four other substances had been reported to undergo laser action, and by June, 1961, the number had risen to eleven, with many laboratories competing to discover new types of lasers.

By 1963, about five hundred research groups in the United States alone were engaged in laser research. Possible laser media now included gases and gas mixtures such as helium-neon or nitrogen-carbon dioxide, liquids containing soluble rare-earth compounds, and semiconducting solids such as gallium arsenide. The wide variety of media permitted laser light to be generated in various spectral ranges and with controlled intensities, in both pulsed and continuous wave modes. By the middle of the 1960's, experimenters could obtain lasers from at least twenty different vendors, and uses for lasers emerged in many fields.

The importance of stimulated emission devices was recognized in 1964 when the Nobel Prize in Physics was awarded to Charles Hard Townes, Nikolay Gennadiyevich Basov, and Aleksandr Mikhailovich Prokhorov. Soviet physicists Basov and Prokhorov had made theoretical contributions paving the way for semiconductor lasers.

**Impact** Early uses for lasers were developed in medicine, materials processing, and construction. In medicine, eye surgeons employed the intense localized heat of the laser beam to coagulate damaged retinal tissue. The heat of the laser beam was also used in cutting, welding, and drilling metals, cloth, and plastics. Even diamond, the hardest of all substances, could be drilled with a laser to make diamond dies for drawing fine wires. In 1962, a laser beam was directed at the Moon and reflected back to Earth with detectable intensity. Lasers also proved useful in construction projects such as the building of the Bay Area Rapid Transit (BART) line in San Francisco, where helium-neon lasers were used to align the equipment digging a tunnel under San Francisco Bay.

**Subsequent Events** In the 1990's, lasers were used in common, everyday products such as compact disc players, computer mice, and supermarket scanners. The generation of the new form of carbon called buckminsterfullerene was made possible by the use of a laser pulse to vaporize carbon. This discovery, made by Robert F. Curl, Harold W. Kroto, and Richard E. Smalley, earned them the 1996 Nobel Prize in Chemistry. Miniature lasers have been developed and can be inserted into blood vessels and the heart itself for surgical purposes. The telecommunications industry has been revolutionized by the advent of fiber-optic cables that transmit digitally encoded messages using laser pulses. As miniaturization and the power and spectral range of lasers progress, a wider range of applications can be expected.

**Additional Information** A thorough, nontechnical treatment of laser history is available in *The Laser in America, 1950-1970* (1991), by Joan L. Bromberg, while more technical details are found in the collection *Lasers and Light: Readings from Scientific American* (1969), with an introduction by Arthur L. Schawlow.

*John R. Phillips*

**See also** Communications; Medicine; Nobel Prizes; Science and Technology.

# ■ League of Revolutionary Black Workers

*A radical African American labor organization formed to fight racism within the United Automobile Workers union. The group was composed of the Dodge Revolutionary Union Movement and similar groups.*

In 1967, African American autoworkers at the Detroit-area Dodge main plant formed the Dodge

Revolutionary Union Movement (DRUM), a rank-and-file union caucus. DRUM accused both the company and the United Automobile Workers (UAW) of racism, citing evidence that the best positions went to whites, while blacks had the dirtiest, most dangerous jobs. The group charged that the nearly all-white local union leadership perpetuated this system by inadequately addressing the grievances of African American workers. Scores of other "RUMs" formed, including ELRUM at the Eldon Avenue plant, FRUM at the Ford plant, and UPRUM among United Parcel Service workers. The League of Revolutionary Black Workers, founded in June, 1969, acted as their umbrella group.

League organizations conducted demonstrations and wildcat strikes in response to unfair working conditions. DRUM believed racism was intentionally cultivated by employers and the union to divide African American, white, and Arab workers (who were numerous in Detroit). League members picketed the UAW International convention and ran against incumbents in union elections. The League gained broad left-wing support, but the UAW responded with red-baiting and called the League's publications "extremist hate sheets" and its members "black fascists."

**Impact** The League voiced a powerful critique of racism in the union movement. Strongly influenced by black nationalism and Marxism-Leninism, it was one of the most prominent radical labor groups of the 1960's.

**Subsequent Events** Several League activists helped launch the Black Workers Congress in 1970; shortly afterward, the League disintegrated amid internal disputes.

**Additional Information** Dan Georgakas and Marvin Surkin's *Detroit: I Do Mind Dying: A Study in Urban Revolution* (1975) recounts the activities of DRUM and the League from their beginnings through the early 1970's efforts of former League members to challenge racism in Detroit's police and judicial systems. James A. Geschwender's *Class, Race, and Worker Insurgency: The League of Revolutionary Black Workers* (1977) closely chronicles the League's ideological development and internal divisions.

*Vanessa Tait*

**See also** Detroit Riot; Unions and Collective Bargaining.

# ■ Leary, Timothy

**Born** October 22, 1920, Springfield, Massachusetts
**Died** May 31, 1996, Beverly Hills, California

*The nation's leading proponent of psychedelic drugs. Leary became a prominent figure in the emerging counterculture, touring the country and expounding on the virtues of hallucinogenic drugs.*

**Early Life** The son of a pious French Roman Catholic mother and Irish hard-drinking father, Leary grew up a rebel. He was expelled from high school, the U.S. Military Academy at West Point, and the University of Alabama before finally earning a doctorate in psychology from the University of California, Berkeley. He became a distinguished psychologist, a founding father of the new-age humanistic psychology movement in the United States, and an early proponent of the radical technique group therapy, which later became accepted as a beneficial psychotherapeutic regimen. Harvard appointed Leary to its faculty in 1959.

**The 1960's** For three years, Leary directed the Harvard Psychedelic Research Project, which involved more than fifty faculty members, graduate students, and distinguished visiting scholars, including Aldous Huxley, Arthur Koestler, Allen Ginsberg, and Jack Kerouac. While involved with the project, he began his clinical study of psychedelic drugs, including LSD (lysergic acid diethylamide), which was legal until 1966. Word spread about the project, but Leary's research created controversy, and Harvard fired him for pushing his research beyond acceptable limits. Leary then established a new research center in Middlebrook, New York, which became a beacon for many leading intellectuals, writers, and musicians of the time.

In 1965, Leary converted to Hinduism after a trip to India and, upon his return to the U.S., founded the League of Spiritual Discovery, described in its manifesto as a "legally incorporated religion dedicated to the ancient sacred sequence of tuning in, turning on, and dropping out." In 1996, Leary testified before Congress that LSD

*Timothy Leary, Harvard professor turned LSD (lysergic acid diethylamide) advocate, explains psychedelic religion to a group gathered at the University of Washington.* (AP/Wide World Photos)

could best be understood as a religious experience.

Leary's troubles with the law began in December, 1965, when he was arrested near the Mexican border on a marijuana charge. He was found guilty and sentenced to thirty days in jail, but the U.S. Supreme Court overturned his conviction three years later.

**Later Life** During the early 1970's, Leary became a leading critic of the Richard M. Nixon administration, which called him "the most dangerous man alive." In 1970, he was arrested and charged with the possession of half an ounce of marijuana, which Leary said had been planted in his car. Leary was sent to prison for ten years, but with the help of the radical Weather Underground (Weathermen), he escaped and made his way to Algeria, where he was granted political asylum. Black Panther leader Eldridge Cleaver, who was in Algeria at the time, thought Leary was dangerous and had him put under house arrest. Drug Enforcement Administration agents eventually nabbed Leary in Kabul, Afghanistan, and he was extradited to the United States. Leary was paroled in 1976.

In the 1980's, Leary became a leader in the futurist movement and president of Futique, a company that designed interactive software programs for personal computers. He used his web site to chronicle the final days of his battle with prostate cancer, dying in 1996. In April, 1997, a commercial rocket carrying his ashes and those of twenty-three others was launched from a plane after takeoff from Grand Canary Island near the Moroccan coast. The craft is expected to circle the earth every ninety minutes for ten years.

**Impact** During the 1960's, Leary was a spokesperson for the counterculture that challenged the traditional middle-class values of white American society. It was Leary who coined the 1960's phrase, "Turn on, tune in, and drop out." He was influential in the popularity and growth of yoga, Eastern religion, and drug experimentation. In fact, Leary was so influential that the Beatles wrote several songs about him, including "Come Together," which was written as Leary's campaign song when he ran against Ronald Reagan for governor of California.

**Additional Information** Leary published an autobiography, *Flashbacks: A Personal and Cultural History of an Era* (1997), describing his life and times.

*Ron Chepesiuk*

**See also** Beatles, The; Cleaver, Eldridge; Counterculture; Drug Culture; Hippies; LSD; Marijuana; Youth Culture and the Generation Gap.

# ■ Liberalism in Politics

*The 1960's revealed both the intrinsic appeal and the limitations of liberalism in national politics. The election of John F. Kennedy, which signaled a shift toward the more "liberal" side of the liberal tradition in the United States, helped usher in an era of hopeful political activism and a subsequent period of radicalization and disillusionment.*

From the constitutional convention of 1789 through the present, political thought in the United States has been dominated by liberalism—by the language of freedom, individual rights, limited government, and rule by law. Within this ideological framework, liberals have tended to advocate active national government intervention to protect individuals against the inequities and excesses of state and local governments and powerful economic interests, and conservatives have tended to advocate local autonomy and the free market against this governmental intervention. Both liberals and conservatives accept the institutional parameters of representative democracy and a capitalist economy.

The 1960's began with two events signaling the revitalization of activated, liberal politics: the civil rights sit-ins that swept through the South and brought new energy and large numbers of young people into the Civil Rights movement and the election of John F. Kennedy. Both events helped create a perception on the part of many Americans that the nation was on an historic mission to rectify ancient wrongs and to realize a more inclusive democracy.

Kennedy was not the favored candidate of Democratic Party liberals, but the Kennedy administration (and that of his successor, Lyndon B. Johnson) attracted and, in turn, was responsive to some of the more liberal elements in mainstream U.S. politics: civil rights advocates, economists who called for investment in the public sector (education, health, welfare), and defense-system analysts who sought a more flexible defense posture. Kennedy embodied two disparate features of modern liberalism in that he drew young idealists into politics with the moral rhetoric of democracy and that he preached the "end of ideology" and supported technocratic problem solving.

Although Kennedy's record of legislative accomplishment is thin, especially compared with Johnson's, many of the significant liberal acts and programs of the 1960's, including Medicare and Medicaid, the Elementary and Secondary Education Act of 1965, the War on Poverty, and the Civil Rights Act of 1964—had their roots in the Kennedy administration. These innovations expanded the national government's role in protecting equal rights and enhancing opportunities for those disadvantaged by poverty and the market economy. Similar innovations in foreign affairs—for example, the Peace Corps and the Alliance for Progress—were couched in terms of alleviating the suffering of the world's poor through U.S. intervention.

Kennedy administration innovations provided a foundation for Johnson's vast Great Society, and they, along with the young president's rhetoric, were an important catalyst for idealistic activism on the part of the young. However, the history of the 1960's reveals not only the contradictions of liberalism—seen most vividly in the tensions between the Kennedy and Johnson administrations and the decade's social and political movements—but also, by decade's end, an elite turn toward less liberalism and less democracy.

Reflecting his time, Kennedy was essentially a cold warrior in foreign policy and a technocratic problem solver in domestic policy. These traits helped set in motion growing militance in 1960's movements and the policy disasters of the 1960's: an escalated Vietnam War, an accelerated arms race, a War on Poverty that failed to liberate the poor, and an Alliance for Progress that accelerated the militarization of Latin America as it failed to help the poor in those countries. The programs of Kennedy and Johnson were shaped and constrained by the institutions of representative democracy and corporate capitalism.

Because of these constraints, the administrations of Kennedy and Johnson, although they helped inspire civil rights activism and eventually realized passage of historic civil and voting rights acts, were a source of constant frustration to civil rights activists committed to a vision of grassroots justice. Similarly, Johnson's War on Poverty contained the radically democratic Community Action Programs (CAP), designed to funnel federal assistance directly to the poor. When CAP funds became a catalyst for grassroots organizing and the empowerment of poor communities, traditional Democratic Party constituencies—urban mayors and social service professionals—found themselves the target rather than the benefactors of the poor. This somewhat radical piece of the Economic Opportunity Act was quickly reshaped to return control of CAP to the mayors. The initial steps toward community empowerment receded amid the angry flames of urban insurrection from 1965 through 1968.

**Impact** On the domestic front, Kennedy-Johnson liberalism undeniably accomplished a great deal and helped alleviate the suffering of vast numbers of people. However, this liberalism also triggered a revolt of the disillusioned and left a legacy of rising expectations and shattered dreams. The war in Vietnam undoubtedly figured centrally in these latter events. Liberals, in fact, attribute the limited successes of Kennedy-Johnson liberalism to the government's failure to extricate the United States from the war.

However, the programs themselves, and the two presidents' commitment to their progressive ends, were constrained by at least four characteristics of modern liberalism. First, in a system defined and defended by liberal ideology, one would expect to—and did—find liberals concerned primarily with system maintenance, especially when more progressive or democratic forces threatened the system (and, possibly, the electoral chances of liberal leaders). Second, the quintessentially liberal constitutionalism of limited powers, checks and balances, and federalism continually obstructed governmental responses to popular demands for justice. Third, pluralistic U.S. politics are theoretically neutral toward political demands; therefore, the moral demands for justice are no more compelling than any other political interest, and the policy process is heavily skewed toward powerful, entrenched interests. Maximizing support for change therefore requires that innovations be presented and justified in a way that is perceived as strengthening systemic features of the status quo. Also, domestic programs tend to serve the interests of the providers at least as much as those of the poor, and the idea of lifting the Third World out of poverty was sold to U.S. and Third World elites with the promise of profits, weaponry, and the idea of "containing Communism." Finally, the liberal programs of the Kennedy and Johnson administrations reflected the top-down design of technocracy. Society's problems were, in effect, exceptions to the norm. They were studied through the eyes of social scientists, leading to programs designed and staffed by trained professionals. Technocratic solutions naturally leave intact existing institutional arrangements. Corporate capitalism, service bureaucracies, two-party competition, and local government form the framework for solutions. From the perspective of democracy, the Kennedy and Johnson administrations promised the expansion of democracy as they denied or short-circuited its essence: people having effective control over their lives and environments.

With their feelings of betrayal greatly intensified by the Vietnam War, the constituencies for greater democracy became increasingly disillusioned with mainstream liberal politics and turned toward more militant action or disassociation from politics as usual. Many embraced the more radical system-critique of the Left. Political and economic elites viewed these tendencies with alarm, and with Richard M. Nixon's help, the political mainstream turned in a more conservative direction.

**Subsequent Events** Fueled by foundation and corporate funding, so-called neoconservatives authored books and studies calling for lowered expectations and less government, in part echoing the New Left's argument about what it termed "paternalistic" big government. Conservatives denounced the "democratic distemper" of the late 1960's and early 1970's and advocated a retreat from the "democratic excess" of those times. By the 1980's, with the election of Ronald Reagan to the presidency, mainstream political discourse reflected the conservatives' views. The liberalism of the Kennedy and Johnson administrations and the democratic impulses of 1960's movements became fused together in the fabric of public memory as a largely discredited time. Traditional liberals were put on the defensive, defending program after program from conservative attack. Meanwhile, largely outside the political mainstream, radical democrats and community activists agitated for change as they sustained a more radical critique of capitalism, patriarchy, and politics as usual.

**Additional Information** Louis Hartz's *The Liberal Tradition in America* (1955) presents a historical view. For a critical reading of liberalism in the Kennedy and Johnson administrations see Allen J. Matusow's *The Unraveling of America: A History of Liberalism in the 1960's* (1984); for an analysis of liberalism's relation-

ship with 1960's movements, see Edward P. Morgan's *The Sixties Experience: Hard Lessons About Modern America* (1992). For an account of liberalism's successes, see Jonathan Schwartz's *America's Hidden Success: Twenty Years of Public Policy* (1983), and for a conservative critique, see Charles Murray's *Losing Ground: American Social Policy, 1950-1980* (1984).

*Edward P. Morgan*

**See also** Civil Rights Act of 1964; Conservatism in Politics; Corporate Liberalism; Economic Opportunity Act of 1964; Great Society Programs; Johnson, Lyndon B.; Kennedy, John F.; Voting Rights Legislation; War on Poverty.

## ■ *Liberty* Incident

**Date** June 8, 1967

*Israeli forces attack the USS* Liberty. *The surprise assault provoked an international crisis and public distrust of the Israeli and U.S. authorities.*

The USS *Liberty* was sent to monitor Israeli and Arab electronic communications while patrolling off northern Sinai during the 1967 Six-Day War between Israel and the Arabs. On June 8, 1968, Israeli jets and torpedo boats strafed, napalmed, and torpedoed the *Liberty* during a two-hour assault. The attack followed six hours of repeated "close-up," aerial observations in clear visibility. During the attack, 34 men were killed and 171 were wounded. The ship's antennae were destroyed, and the ship was damaged beyond restoration to service. The USS *Andrew Jackson*, a missile submarine, accompanied the *Liberty* and photographed much of the engagement through its periscope camera according to unacknowledged reports by several independent observers. Reportedly, the strike was ordered by Israeli defense minister Moshe Dayan to prevent detection of Israel's invasion of Syria. This invasion was postponed to June 9, the day after the *Liberty* was "silenced."

Authorities soon realized that messages from the U.S. joint chiefs of staff ordering *Liberty* to withdraw from its patrol just outside of Egyptian and Israeli-claimed territorial limits were repeatedly misdirected and failed to arrive. Therefore, retaliatory bombing raids, including a first launch of nuclear-armed aircraft, from the USS *Saratoga* and USS *America*, were almost immediately recalled when the Israelis hastily claimed that poor visibility had prevented them from recognizing the ship's U.S. nationality.

Israel's formal apology on June 10, 1967, termed the incident a "tragic accident." The United States accepted the apology but refused the explanation. Israel paid $3.3 million in death benefits under duress on June, 13, 1968. Injury benefits of $3.5 million were received April 28, 1969. In December, 1980, after prolonged evasion, $6 million was paid for damage to the ship.

The *Liberty* received a Presidential Unit Citation, her commanding officer received the Congressional Medal of Honor, and thirty-six additional officers and men were decorated for their conduct.

**Impact** Suppression of information regarding the incident and persistent denial of apparently well-founded, embarrassing reports, caused widespread public and congressional complaint in the United States. In addition, U.S. public and governmental support of Israel came under heavy criticism.

**Additional Information** James M. Ennes, Jr.'s *Assault on the 'Liberty'* (1979) is an eyewitness account by one of the *Liberty*'s officers. U.S. Deputy Assistant Secretary of Defense for Public Affairs Phil G. Goulding reviews official reactions to the attack in *Confirm or Deny* (1970). Anthony Pearson's *Conspiracy of Silence* (1978) includes many rumors and contradictions in his muckraking account. Donald Neff's *Warriors for Jerusalem* (1984) discusses the *Liberty* in a general history of the Six-Day War. The *Liberty* incident is part of James Bamford's history of the U.S. National Security Agency, *The Puzzle Palace* (1982).

*Ralph L. Langenheim, Jr.*

**See also** *Pueblo* Incident; Six-Day War.

# ■ Lichtenstein, Roy

**Born** October 27, 1923, New York, New York
**Died** September 29, 1997, New York, New York

*An American painter and sculptor of pop art. Inspired by comic strips and newspaper advertisements, Lichtenstein's innovative and controversial work was a documentary on popular American culture.*

**Early Life** Roy Lichtenstein's artistic training began in 1939 at the Art Students League in New York under the instruction of Reginald Marsh. He received a B.F.A. in 1946 and an M.F.A. in 1949 from Ohio State University in Columbus, Ohio. His early paintings explored subjects drawn from U.S. history and the Far West in a figurative style influenced by cubism. After his first one-person show at the Carlebach Gallery in New York in 1951, Lichtenstein moved to Cleveland, Ohio, where he worked as a graphic designer and an engineering draftsman. Lichtenstein taught at the New York State College of Education at Oswego, 1957 to 1960, and at Douglas College, Rutgers University, 1960 to 1963. At Rutgers, he met Allan Kaprow, who introduced him to environments and happenings and stirred his interest in American consumer culture.

**The 1960's** During the 1960's, Lichtenstein relinquished the gestural abstract expressionist style that had characterized his work in the late 1950's to find new stimulation and inspiration in everyday life and popular imagery. In 1961, Lichtenstein created six epoch-making, large-scale paintings—including *Look Mickey, I've Caught a Big One*—of comic strip images that he had recently reproduced by hand, including the lettering, balloons, and Benday dots. In 1962, Leo Castelli exhibited these works at his gallery, thus launching the career of one of the major pop artists. In addition to comic strips, Lichtenstein painted black-and-white close-ups of household objects, based on images selected from newspaper advertisements. In 1963, he began to use an opaque projector to transfer his pencil sketches to canvas. Consumerism, advertising imagery, and popular culture remained at the core of Lichtenstein's art, which explored numerous themes: war and violence, love and romance, science fiction, explosions, foodstuffs, and landscapes. Lichtenstein adapted paintings by famous artists to the stylistic idioms of popular imagery.

**Later Life** In the 1970's, Lichtenstein moved to Southampton on Long Island. He expanded the range of his sources through complex compositions based on those of such modern masters as Henri Matisse, Paul Cézanne, Piet Mondrian, and Fernand Léger. He questioned assumptions about the originality of reproductions of works of art. During this period, his works became increasingly self-referential. Two large-scale murals produced in New York in the mid-1980's, at the Leo Castelli Gallery and the Equitable Building, summed up Lichtenstein's replicative system with their quotation of earlier motifs.

**Impact** By merging contemporary art, advertising, and popular art (comic strips), Lichtenstein's distinctive works document popular American culture.

In his paintings, he experimented with comic-book techniques. He used thick, black outlines, primary colors, and Benday dots to present scenes of action, violence, romance, or sentimental idealization. Some of his more famous works are the *Big Party* (1965) and *Whaam* (1963).

**Additional Information** In 1981, Jack Cowart and the St. Louis Art Museum published a book entitled *Roy Lichtenstein: 1970-1980*, which provides a thorough discussion of his work and life as well as numerous illustrations.

*Patricia Jessup-Woodlin*

**See also** Art Movements; Pop Art.

## ■ Liston, Sonny

**Born** May 8, 1932, near Forrest City, Arkansas
**Died** December 30?, 1970, Las Vegas, Nevada

*World heavyweight boxing champion from 1962 to 1964. Liston was noted for his powerful punch, his intimidating demeanor, and his associations with racketeers.*

One of twenty-five children, Charles "Sonny" Liston ran away from home at the age of thirteen to St. Louis, where he was imprisoned in 1950 for armed robbery. He learned to box and won the Chicago Golden Gloves title in 1953, but he returned to jail in 1957 for assaulting a police officer. He resumed his boxing career after his release later that year, knocking out Cleveland Williams and Nino Valdes.

Liston was managed by mob figures Frankie Carbo and Frank "Blinky" Palermo. Because of his criminal record and unsavory associations, he was denied a New York boxing license, but he destroyed heavyweight champion Floyd Patterson in one round in Chicago in 1962. In 1963, he again crushed Patterson in a rematch. Considered almost invincible, Liston was a heavy favorite over the young Cassius Clay before their 1964 fight. Clay, however, dominated the slower Liston, who failed to come out for the seventh round. In a 1965 rematch, Clay, by then known as Muhammad Ali, knocked Liston out in one round with a quick "phantom" punch that led to speculation that the fight had been fixed.

*Sonny Liston (right) delivers a right cross to heavyweight champion Floyd Patterson in the first round of a match in Chicago in 1962. Liston won the bout and the championship. (AP/Wide World Photos)*

Leotus Martin knocked out Liston for the North American Boxing Federation title in 1969. Liston's last fight was a victory over Chuck Wepner in Jersey City. On January 5, 1971, Liston was found dead in his home; officially, he died of lung congestion and heart failure, but many people suspected the cause of death was a heroin overdose.

**Impact** A member of the International Boxing Hall of Fame, Liston won fifty fights and lost four. His reputation has been diminished by his losses to Ali, his criminal record, and his associations with racketeers. He was nevertheless a major presence in the sports world of the early 1960's, and he is often recognized as the archetype of the troubled, moody, and violent fighter.

**Additional Information** Jeffrey T. Sammons treats Liston's career in *Beyond the Ring* (1967).

*John S. Reist, Jr.*

**See also** Ali, Muhammad (Cassius Clay); Frazier, Joe; Griffith-Paret Fight; Patterson, Floyd; Sports.

---

# ■ Literature

*A period of daring innovation and continuity across all genres. The literature in this period redefined both the role of the writer and the relevance of writing as a social and political act.*

**Poetry** Although it is inaccurate to describe coherent groups and movements in the 1960's poetry scene in the United States, certain strains and voices did attempt to take the poem in new directions through explicitly experimental forms. The appearances of Allen Ginsberg's *Howl and Other Poems* (1956) and Robert Lowell's *Life Studies* and *For the Union Dead* (1959) marked watersheds in poetic form and subject. Ginsberg's Beat vision made raw human experience the central spiritual focus of his work and celebrated the physical, sexual, hallucinogenic, and neurotic in all its seediness and glory. Similarly, Lowell turned inward, mixing loose cultural criticism with an analysis of domestic life, marking a new subject territory for American poetry that was distinctly personal. This confessional strain was also present in Anne Sexton's *To Bedlam and Part Way Back* (1960) and *All My Pretty Ones* (1962) and Sylvia Plath's *Ariel* (1966), which opened up the condition of the white, middle-class woman to the sharp eyes of the poet. By exploring themes such as madness,

alcoholism, and suicide, these confessional poets challenged the silence surrounding American private life.

Ginsberg's *Kaddish and Other Poems* (1961) was also highly influential in the emergence of the San Francisco poetry scene, which attempted to merge a new emotional realism with the explicitly political, a populist move to get poetry back on the streets. Lawrence Ferlinghetti's *Starting from San Francisco* (1961) and *Her* (1961) brought together anarchist and leftist strains in a blistering critique of American life. Similarly, James Scherril explored radical pacifism in *Stalingrad Elegies* (1964) and *Violence and Glory* (1969) and openly examined the crushing effects of militarized life brought about by the escalation of the Vietnam War.

However, many in the San Francisco school initiated a shift in poetic and spiritual consciousness and turned to Zen Buddhism as a truly different form of perception. Gary Snyder sought to develop a new mythology for the American spirit in *Myths and Texts* (1960) and *A Range of Poems* (1967) while openly advocating liberation from the stultifying restraints of Western logical thought in *The Back Country* (1968) and *Earth House Hold: Technical Notes and Queries to Fellow Dharma Revolutionaries* (1969). The explicit examination and transcendence of human existence could also be seen in Gregory Corso's work, which initiated a form of "automatism." By making the immediate human senses the center point for all poetry, *The Happy Birthday of Death* (1960) and *Long Live Man* (1962) switched the earlier accidental writing favored by the Surrealists in the 1920's into a direct interaction between the metaphysical and the physical world.

Corso's spiritual individualism was essentially the same in poetic nature as Charles Olson's "projective verse," a form loosely reliant on principles found in physics and aerodynamics and that placed the personal, poetic instant as the embodiment of human energy. Olson effectively became the leading intellectual voice in American poetry, and his *Distances* (1960) and monumental multivolumed *The Maximus Poems* (1960-1969) became the foundational works for the Black Mountain School of poets. Deeply influenced by Olson's voice and vision, Denise Levertov incorporated projective verse into *Jacob's Ladder* (1961) and *O Taste and See* (1964) to initiate a new phase in feminist exploration. Olson's main other disciple, Robert Creeley, tended toward the more minimalist form, and his *For Love: 1950-1960* (1962), *Words: Poems* (1967), and *Pieces* (1969) moved away from formal arrangement to a basic reliance on the rhythm of single words and phrases.

New York also served to provide the seedbed for its own school, a radically antiformalist view openly influenced by French poetry and the growing abstract expressionist school of painters. Kenneth Koch, Frank O'Hara, and John Ashbery rejected the coherency of line, syntax, and stanza for the immediacy of the open form. O'Hara's *Lunch Poems* (1965), actually scribbled down during his lunch breaks, expressed a new form of urban impressionism, focusing on the immediacy of personal vision and the intellectual uses of abstraction. Koch's *Thank You and Other Poems* (1962) and *The Pleasures of Peace and Other Poems* (1968) and Ashbery's *The Tennis Court Oath* (1962) and *Rivers and Mountains* (1966) offered an aesthetic of inconsequence and nonstatement, largely celebrating the randomness of life.

Although the flavor of poetry tended toward the openly experimental, the post-romantic formalists offered up a celebration of the traditional. William Stafford's *Traveling Through the Dark* (1962) and James Dickey's *The Early Motion: Drowning with Others and Helmets* (1962) insisted on the centrality of form and organization in poetry, a theme continued by Robert Bly in *Silence in the Snowy Fields: Poems* (1962) and *The Light Around the Body* (1967), which blended a quasi-spiritual and religious quality with the strict outlines of meter and rhythm. Elizabeth Bishop's *Questions of Travel* (1965) and Howard Nemerov's *The Next Room of the Dream: Poems and Two Plays* (1962) stressed the importance of elegance and erudition in poetry.

The tendencies toward spiritual liberation were also important in the emergence of explicitly racial and feminist poetry. With the rise of the Black Power movement, poets began to celebrate their race and explore a form of vernacular voice and culture too long ignored by the American experience. Langston Hughes was responsible for bringing forward a new range of racially attuned poets, ethnically aware and racially proud. Robert Hayden in *A Ballad of Remembrance* (1962) and LeRoi Jones (Amiri Baraka) in *The Dead Lecturer* (1964) and *Black Art* (1966) expressed a militant pride in the face of white racist oppression. In the same vein, African American women also found a voice of renewal and sexual power, sometimes countering the male vision of African Ameri-

can experience. Mari Evans's *Where Is All the Music?* (1968), Audre Lord's *First Cities* (1968), Sonia Sanchez's *Homecoming* (1969), and Nikki Giovanni's *Black Feeling, Black Talk* (1968) merged the feminist with the racial activist to produce an explosive mix of sexual outrage and ethnic pride.

**The Novel** Literary experimentation continued in the novel, which pushed subject and style to the limits of imagination. Although the novels of the period explored transformations of human consciousness, some took an inward journey to consider the very nature of perception and creative form. William S. Burroughs effectively began this transformation through a blend of surreal, hallucinatory, and frankly homosexual vignettes and experiences that wove together personal identity and political critique. In *The Soft Machine* (1961), *The Ticket that Exploded* (1962), and *Nova Express* (1964), Burroughs plotted the struggling consciousness of the writer against the oppressiveness of the almost universal authoritarian forces that existed in all organizational forms. Similarly, Ken Kesey likened American society to the madhouse in *One Flew over the Cuckoo's Nest* (1962) and pitted the lone antihero against the crushing power of the state, with tragic results.

This almost paranoid style of writing focused on the unseen in American life and hinted at the dark forces at work behind the scenes. The characters in these novels occupy a wholly irrational world that is bent on destroying them although it never actually reveals its intent. These absurd and ironic events coalesce into a series of unseen conspiracies that appear in Thomas Pynchon's *The Crying of Lot Forty-Nine* (1966) and more famously, Joseph Heller's *Catch-22* (1961). The anxiety provoked by the catch-22 situation and the inability either to prove the conspiracy or to escape it highlighted the concern with powerlessness in American life. The inevitable moral uncertainty and distrust of absolutes this produced can also be seen in Kurt Vonnegut, Jr.'s *Slaughterhouse-Five* (1969) and *Mother Night* (1961). What Pynchon, Heller, and Vonnegut effectively illustrated was the growing distrust of official doctrines and truths, a recognition that good can be quite evil and vice versa. In short, their works insisted on the paradoxical ambiguity at the heart of modern experience.

The explicit examination of reality, writing, and identity was also a focus for those concerned with metafiction. John Barth's *The Sot-Weed Factor* (1962) was a masterful copy of the eighteenth century picaresque novel, a brilliant mimicry that highlighted the effectiveness of literary theft and the power of the writer in actively shaping thought. Barth's later work, "Lost in the Funhouse" (1968), continued his fascination with the malleability and unpredictability of language. This essentially metafictional style was also employed by Robert Coover in *Pricksongs and Descants* (1969), Richard Brautigan in *Trout Fishing in America*(1967), and Pynchon in *V.* (1963). In the same vein, Donald Barthelme's *Come Back, Dr. Caligari* (1964) clearly illustrated that literature could do anything it wanted through an awareness of the contingency of literary form and function.

However, despite the room for experimental playfulness and the serious questions that emerged from this, many writers continued to work with the traditional novel. John Updike's *Rabbit, Run* (1960) and William Styron's *The Confessions of Nat Turner* (1967) continued in a familiar mode, though their material tended toward the bleak realities of empty American social life and its entrapment and the continual contradictions of racial discrimination. The dynamics of self-destructive behavior were also explored by Edward Albee in *Who's Afraid of Virginia Woolf?* (1962), *Tiny Alice* (1964), and *A Delicate Balance* (1966), which blended a new nightmare of suburban terror and the collapse of the middle-class dream. Both tense and emotionally violent, Albee's drama painted a disturbing picture of the traditional family.

In the same way, the specifically Jewish novel brought together questions of tradition and continuity. Saul Bellow's *Herzog* (1964) and Bernard Malamud's *A New Life* (1961) and *The Fixer* (1966) explored the language of poignancy and loss, melding traditional Jewish themes with the dynamics of American social change. Similarly, Philip Roth, while more contemporary in subject, comically explored Jewish sexuality and the emotional dynamics of family rearing. In *Letting Go* (1962) and *Portnoy's Complaint* (1969), Roth indulged in a comic riot that used Freudian psychology and satire to lampoon the family, guilt, sex, confusion, and thralldom to the mother figure.

If the family was one form of critical focus for literature in this period, then so were the political relations between the individual, democracy, and the structures of government. The rise of the Civil Rights and Black Power movements brought a new racial consciousness to the American scene and the clear recognition that democracy had failed many Americans. The outpouring of new voices challenged simple political clichés, offered their own lives as examples of oppression, and demanded direct action. James Baldwin's *Nobody Knows My Name* (1961) and *The Fire Next Time* (1963) put race firmly on the cultural agenda, and Eldridge Cleaver's *Soul on Ice* (1968) and Malcolm X's *The Autobiography of Malcolm X* (1965) signaled a new militancy in race relations.

**Signs of the Times** The use of the personal in social critique was also present in the writing of the New Journalism, which cut across traditional disciplines and genres, compounding poetry, prose, and biography with cultural and political analysis. Here, the writer was an engaged individual, thinking and participating in the world, having a ready ego influence. Tom Wolfe's *The Kandy-Kolored Tangerine-Flake Streamline Baby* (1965), *The Pump House Gang* (1968), and *The Electric Kool-Aid Acid Test* (1968) took personal experience as a benchmark of the real and placed the writer as an active consciousness. Although Joan Didion also inaugurated her own tremendous style in *Slouching Towards Bethlehem* (1968), perhaps the most resounding intelligence behind the New Journalism was Norman Mailer. Mailer was able to brilliantly synthesize political critique with intellectual acumen to produce landmark works such as *An American Dream* (1965), which explored the American love affair with power politics Kennedy-style. Similarly, *Why Are We in Vietnam?* (1967) laid out the underlying psychological forces for genocidal war in a complex narrative of male bonding and sexual experience. Mailer's best work, *Armies of the Night* (1968), merged fiction and history and placed Mailer as both commentator and fictional character in the Pentagon protest of the same year.

The intellectual writing of the period criticized existing social relations and offered new possibilities for thinking about culture at large. Herbert Marcuse's *One Dimensional Man* (1964) connected the American psyche to authoritarian structures, and Norman O. Brown's *Life Against Death* (1959) and *Love's Body* (1966) posited culture and civilization as antithetical to human fulfillment and genuine need. Similarly, Paul Goodman's *Growing Up Absurd* (1960) criticized the idiocy of the American value system and offered intellectual sympathy for the dropout culture. Other writers argued for a new manifesto of political action, such as Michael Harrington's *Toward a Democratic Left* (1968) and Tom Hayden's *Rebellion and Repression* (1969). Abbie Hoffman's *Revolution for the Hell of It* (1968) brought together student and youth groups in a flagrant challenge to mainstream political parties and thinking.

Marshall McLuhan celebrated the mass communications revolution in *Understanding Media* (1964), and Betty Friedan's *The Feminine Mystique* (1963) challenged the culture that stultified women's consciousness. Frantz Fanon's *The Wretched of the Earth* (1968) brought an awareness of Third World cultures in the same way that Timothy Leary's *Politics of Ecstasy* (1968) reexamined religion and spirituality. The move toward the openly sexual was fostered by the publication of William H. Masters and Virginia E. Johnson's *Human Sexual Response* (1966), which in its turn was reflected in Susan Sontag's *Against Interpretation and Other Essays* (1966), which argued for the merging of the intellectual with the erotic.

**Impact** Undoubtedly, the 1960's opened with excitement and expectation about the possibilities facing American culture. The inauguration of Kennedy and his promise of a New Frontier gave a radically youthful cast to the political scene and brought an upsurge of optimism and faith in the mission of the United States. This seeming break with the political conservatism of the 1950's was backed by strident rhetorical pledges toward social and racial equality. As a result, the literary imagination was galvanized into a renewed belief in the credo of justice for all and the possibilities of living and participating in a truly liberated and democratic society.

This utopian strain cast itself as a spiritual and moral rebirth on both the national and personal levels. The impact of Eastern religions and philosophy offered a new transcendental ideal that freed the individual from the material world to accomplish human perfection. The achievement of inner peace through outer contemplation became the bedrock of a new consciousness that was reflected at the personal and intellectual level. The belief in the liberation of consciousness was vital in the reemergence of a secular humanism, and its melding with a democratic political impulse set the mood for the 1960's. As a result, the world was seen to be both malleable and alive, fully open to the possibilities of active change. This blending of social justice and the insistence on personal authenticity was used to critique the shackles of tradition, class, race, and gender.

However, in many ways, this desire for liberation was a very familiar American trait, one that was recast into the literary experimentation of this period. It is clear that much of the literature was obsessed with an abiding dream that an authentic, unpatterned, and unconditioned life was possible. In short, many writers relied on the recasting of the individual into the most traditional figure available, that of the moral individualist capable of making right choices in the wrong conditions. However, this tendency was balanced with the countermanding suspicion that someone out there was actually patterning life, that there were secret plots afoot that actually removed autonomy of thought and action.

The stunning assassinations of John F. Kennedy and his brother Robert F. Kennedy, Martin Luther King, Jr., and Malcolm X seemed to suggest a sinister pattern at work to decapitate political and civil rights leadership. Although no hard proof existed, the Cuban Missile Crisis and the steady escalation of involvement in Vietnam proved to many writers that the forces of reaction were at work. In the same way, the growing power of the bureaucratic state and its secret information-gathering agencies only further accentuated the open contradiction of American life—that freedom has limitations. Many writers realized and explored this paradoxical existence of truth on many levels and focused on the questions of existential survival in the face of oppressive and frankly totalitarian forces. What emerged was a complex mix of hopefulness and suspicion, which oscillated between the comic and the dreadful.

The growing involvement in Vietnam brought open protest onto the streets and provided a focus for the more political writers of the period in what seemed to be a clash of official and unofficial voices. The slow but sure escalation of U.S. military power clearly illustrated the contradictions of the modern political state. That a country could claim to support democracy and freedom at home while conducting a brutal genocidal war made the need for radical change all the more necessary. The culture that produced this horror was not a fit culture; in fact, it was in thrall to totalitarian fantasies of social control and domination. As a result, some writers explored new political ideas to break the hold of the military-industrial complex and directly challenge the capitalist base of American society.

434 ■ Lombardi, Vince

Although the literature of this period generated a high degree of hope and paranoia, the link between self and society was an essential feature of all literary forms. What emerged was an extreme self-consciousness about life and writing and of the paradoxes inherent in the fluidity of structure and narrative at both the literary and political levels. The 1960's also drew attention to the fictiveness of social worlds, the propaganda that justified these systems of control, and by suggestion, the possibilities and potential of creating new social visions. By challenging the established patterns of understanding, 1960's literature insisted that society was an arbitrary fiction in which all citizens had a stake.

**Additional Information** For a useful study specifically focused on the literature of the 1960's, see *The American 1960's* (1980), by Jerome Klinkowitz. Morris Dickstein provides a broader and more personal approach in *Gates of Eden: American Culture* (1977). General studies on American literature abound, but some of the best are *American Writing Since 1945: A Critical Survey* (1983), by Robert F. Kiernan, and Ihab Hassan's *Contemporary American Literature, 1945-72* (1973). Tony Tanner's *City of Words* (1971) and Malcolm Bradbury and Richard Ruland's *From Puritanism to Postmodernism: A History of American Literature* (1991) provide detailed studies of individual authors.

*Paul Hansom*

**See also** Albee, Edward; Baldwin, James; Beat Generation; Brautigan, Richard; *Catch-22*; Cleaver, Eldridge; *Confessions of Nat Turner, The*; Didion, Joan; *Electric Kool-Aid Acid Test, The*; *Feminine Mystique, The*; Ferlinghetti, Lawrence; Friedan, Betty; Ginsberg, Allen; Giovanni, Nikki; *Human Sexual Response*; Leary, Timothy; McLuhan, Marshall; Mailer, Norman; Malcolm X; Metafiction; *One Flew over the Cuckoo's Nest*; Plath, Sylvia; Poetry; Roth, Phillip; Sanchez, Sonia; *Slaughterhouse-Five*; Sontag, Susan; Updike, John; Vietnam War; *Who's Afraid of Virginia Woolf?*

## ■ Lombardi, Vince

**Born** June 11, 1913, Brooklyn, New York
**Died** September 3, 1970, Washington, D.C.

*The Green Bay Packers lift head coach Vince Lombardi onto their shoulders after winning the National Football League title, which they did five times.* (AP/Wide World Photos)

*One of the nation's most successful professional football coaches. Lombardi's style of leadership influenced a wide public.*

Born to an immigrant Italian family, Vincent Thomas Lombardi attended parochial schools in Brooklyn. At Fordham University, he played on the school's football team, the Rams. He was a guard in the front line popularly known as the "Seven Blocks of Granite." He coached high school athletics for several years, then assisted at Fordham and West Point, where he came under the influence of Colonel Earl Blaik, whose military-style discipline he admired. In 1954, he entered professional football as offensive coach of the New York Giants.

In 1959, Lombardi became head coach and general manager of the Green Bay Packers, a Wisconsin football team that had won only one game in twelve the previous season. Lombardi weeded out the weak players, and his tough but fair coaching style got the team into great shape, physically and mentally. His quest for excellence once led him to say, "Winning isn't everything. It is the only thing." For the next nine years, the Packers dominated the National Football League, winning the league title in 1961, 1962, 1965, 1966, and 1967. They won the Super Bowl games of 1967 and 1968.

Lombardi retired from coaching in 1968 but rcmaincd with thc Packers as general manager. In 1969, he moved to Washington, D.C., and coached the Redskins to their first winning season in fourteen years. He died of intestinal cancer the next year.

**Impact**  Lombardi projected an image of discipline, commitment to excellence, and moral integrity. He had a remarkable understanding of his players and the ability to challenge them to perform often above what seemed possible. This single-minded pursuit of winning, plus his support of the Vietnam War, led some social commentators and sportswriters to criticize him in the late 1960's. However, his life and success provided the sports community in the United States a figure for all to emulate.

**Additional Information**  Michael J. O'Brien's *Vince: A Personal Biography of Vince Lombardi* (1987) takes a close look at Lombardi's life.

*Charles H. O'Brien*

**See also**  Football; Sports; Super Bowl.

# ■ *Lord of the Rings, The*

**Published** 1954, 1955, 1956
**Author** J. R. R. Tolkein (1892-1973)

*A literary trilogy that featured the fantasy world of Middle-earth and creatures known as hobbits. The three-volume fantasy caught the imagination of the 1960's generation because it presented a vision of moral struggle in a world where good and evil are clearly defined.*

**The Work**  The trilogy that featured Middle-earth, the fantasy world created by John Ronald Reuel Tolkein, became mandatory reading for many in the 1960's. *The Lord of the Rings* was published in three volumes, *The Fellowship of the Ring* (1954), *The Two Towers* (1955), and *The Return of the King* (1956). Its already significant popularity grew when Ballantine Books issued a paperback edition in 1968.

*The Lord of the Rings*, or the Tolkein trilogy, describes the struggle between good and evil in Middle-earth, a place that is simpler and more honest than the real world yet contains many of the concerns that troubled people in the 1960's. Greed, suspicion, and vanity haunt many of the characters. The evil that must be conquered is chiefly one of mind control, but it also entails destruction of the natural world. Tolkein, who was a Medieval scholar, used his familiarity with myth, language, and feudal society to create an entire world, complete with languages, theology, and political and geographical realities. In Tolkein's world, all beings control their own destinies and must freely choose their fate, often with bittersweet results. All must confront the lure and destructiveness of total power, represented by the Ring.

In the first volume, *The Fellowship of the Ring*, the wizard Gandalf discovers that a simple ring carries an overwhelming power that could be used to dominate the land. Frodo and his friends, Sam, Merry, and Pippin, set off to destroy the Ring. The four hobbits gain other companions—humans, dwarves and elves—who represent the major races helping in the struggle against the evil Dark Lord, Sauron. In *The Two Towers*, the company formed to accomplish the errand splits apart, partly because of jealousy and partly because Frodo believes he must continue on alone. Merry and Pippin meet the ents, a treelike people who help to neutralize a power-hungry wizard, Saruman. The others rouse the Riders of Rohan, Nordic-like horsemen, to add their arms to the struggle. The Riders go to help the people of Gondor, the last barrier to Sauron's conquest. In *The Return of the King*, Strider, one of Frodo's companions, is revealed as the new king. Frodo and Sam finally destroy the Ring, but only after each has faced his own weaknesses. The destruction of the Ring brings the end of the age of magic, and elves and wizards depart for another land.

**Impact** *The Lord of the Rings* was originally published in the 1950's in the United States and England. The trilogy became overwhelmingly popular in the United States when Ballantine Books issued a paperback edition in 1968. Its appeal lay partly in its description of a magical world, where people had powers beyond those of the everyday world. More significantly, it described the conflict between noble and ignoble forces in a lyrical yet concrete way. The heroes struggled not only with external forces but also with their own shortcomings. These struggles caught the imaginations of its readers, typically adolescents and young adults, who were concerned with challenging themselves and the world about them. As they stood in protest lines, they could imagine themselves engaged in a heroic struggle, much like that of the hobbits of Middle-earth.

Discussion groups, Tolkein societies, and fan magazines sprouted in the 1960's and continued with vigor throughout the remainder of the twentieth century. Fantasy as a literary genre became both more popular and more respected as adult literature. Other authors such as Anne McCaffrey and Piers Anthony, inspired by Tolkein's work, also developed trilogies and series based on fantasy themes.

**Related Work** Tolkein's prequel to the trilogy was *The Hobbit* (1937), which described the land of Middle-earth about fifty years before the time period described in the trilogy.

**Additional Information** For an analysis of the meaning of Tolkien's works, see T. A. Shippey's *The Road to Middle-Earth* (1992) or Paul H. Kocher's *Master of Middle-earth.*

*Mary Moore Vandendorpe*

**See also** Literature; *Stranger in a Strange Land.*

---

# ■ LSD

*An extremely powerful and controversial hallucinogenic drug that became a staple of the 1960's counterculture. LSD has enjoyed an enduring mystique and continues to be used illicitly by a small segment of the population.*

LSD is an acronym for lysergic acid diethylamide, a compound derived from ergot, a rye fungus. LSD, or "acid" in popular parlance, was discovered on April 16, 1943, by Albert Hofmann, a research chemist for Sandoz Pharmaceuticals in Basel, Switzerland, who accidentally ingested a minute amount of the chemical and soon experienced fascinating and vivid perceptual changes. Further tests confirmed the extraordinary potency of the substance: 250 millionths of a gram was enough to trigger profound and sometimes frightening distortions of consciousness. In 1949, LSD was introduced into the United States as a psychiatric wonder drug used to treat a variety of psychological problems: schizophrenia, depression, various kinds of sexual deviance, alcoholism, and criminality. In the late 1940's and 1950's, the U.S. military and intelligence communities (including the U.S. Army, Navy, Office of Strategic Services, and Central Intelligence Agency) experimented with LSD as a possible truth serum, incapacitant, or "unconventional warfare" agent but ultimately found its properties too unpredictable for their purposes.

Timothy Leary, a psychologist at Harvard University, ingested "magic mushrooms" (a natural hallucinogen) while on vacation in Mexico in the summer of 1960. The drug induced a powerful religious experience that launched Leary on a lifelong career as a flamboyant proselytizer for psychedelic drugs. However, the political winds soon shifted against Leary. In October, 1962, President John F. Kennedy signed legislation that strictly regulated the testing of new drugs. The Food and Drug Administration officially deemed LSD an "experimental drug" and restricted distribution to research facilities; general psychiatric use was discontinued. In the ensuing backlash, Leary and a colleague, Richard Alpert, were ejected from Harvard in May, 1963. Efforts to suppress the drug were, however, too late; LSD was already a well-established black market commodity. Other LSD gurus emerged on the scene, most notably author Ken Kesey, who, along with a group of people called the Merry Pranksters, traveled around the country in a bus, touting the visionary qualities of psychedelics. The Grateful Dead, a San Francisco rock band, became famous for extended free-form musical improvisations that were best appreciated by listeners on LSD (known as "Deadheads"). Although LSD had become illegal in 1966, it became an integral part of campus life, rock concerts, and festivals in the late 1960's and even spawned a musical genre, "acid rock," whose famous proponents included the Grateful Dead, Jefferson Airplane, and guitarist Jimi Hendrix.

**Impact** Increasingly tainted by the degeneration of the hippie subculture, the utopian aura that once surrounded LSD was decisively shattered in 1969 when LSD enthusiast Charles Manson and his cohorts went on an infamous murder rampage. A few months later, a young concert-goer was killed at a chaotic, drug-soaked Rolling Stones concert at Altamont Speedway in Northern California.

**Additional Information** Books of particular interest on this topic are *Acid Dream: The CIA, LSD, and the Sixties Rebellion* (1984), by Martin A. Lee and Bruce Shlain; *Storming Heaven: LSD and the American Dream* (1987), by Jay Stevens; *Flashbacks: A Personal and Cultural History of an Era* (1990), by Timothy Leary.

*Robert Niemi*

**See also** Altamont Music Festival; Counterculture; Drug Culture; *Electric Kool-Aid Acid Test, The*; Grateful Dead; Hendrix, Jimi; Jefferson Airplane; Leary, Timothy; Manson Murders; Marijuana.

---

# ■ *Lucky Come Hawaii*

**Published** 1965
**Author** Jon Shirota

*A darkly comic rendering of the story of an Okinawan family in Maui caught between a compelling loyalty to Japan and an appreciation for the opportunities offered by the United States.*

**The Work** *Lucky Come Hawaii* is the story of Kama Gusada, a lovable, aging drunkard and pig farmer born in the United States but raised an Okinawan to whom the news of Japanese planes attacking Pearl Harbor is almost too good to be true. Convinced that the Japanese will easily overrun the island and defeat the Americans, Kama brews sake and paints the Rising Sun (the Japanese flag) on the roof of his home to welcome the triumphant arrival of the Japanese army. For his children, however, the incursion of the Buddhaheads (Japanese) into their lives is a disaster, foreboding a return of rigid Japanese customs. To complicate matters, Kama's first-born

*A young man takes LSD (lysergic acid diethylamide or acid) on a sugar cube. The hallucinogenic drug became illegal in 1966.* (Library of Congress)

son, Ichiro, is in Japan, having only recently graduated with honors never before bestowed on a nisei (second-generation Japanese American), while his second son, Niro, is at the University of Hawaii studying to be a dentist. In the meantime, his third son, Saburo, who spends most of his time fantasizing about his American high school English teacher, slips into compulsive gambling, and his daughter, Kimiko, falls in love with a Hawaiian, who enlists in the U.S. Army, very much against the wishes of Kimiko's traditional parents. His pro-Japanese patriotic ardor dimming under such strain, Kama dreams of Ichiro and Niro meeting on the field of war, suffers a heart attack, and dies. As the novel concludes, Niro has joined the U.S. military, where he is pressed to serve as translator for the military police who terrorize Japanese Americans who fail to comply with rules of martial law. Complicitous in the racist brutalization of other Japanese immigrants, Niro is left to wonder if the distrust, hatred, and intolerance unleashed on December 7 (Pearl Harbor day) can ever be curbed, a question answered by a propitious Hawaiian rainbow that promises the return of the prewar Aloha spirit that once welcomed everyone to the islands.

**Impact** *Lucky Come Hawaii* was among the first Japanese American novels to experience critical acclaim in the United States. The book captures a tragic and poignant period in U.S. history from an unusual perspective, looking at the nation's war with Japan through the eyes of immigrants from Okinawa. In this way, Shirota's work reflects not only a canonical shift in values concerning ethnic literature but also an evolving American view of war and patriotism. Through the Vietnam experience in the 1960's, Americans, like Kama Gusada, began to recognize the moral ambiguities of modern warfare. War was no longer a matter of right versus wrong, good versus evil, civilization versus barbarianism, or, perhaps, as Shirota reveals, it never had been. It is, instead, cruelly indiscriminate, culturally complex, and darkly absurd.

**Related Work** Shirota's *Pineapple White* (1972) explores the life of a Japanese American gardener who leaves his Waipahu plantation and journeys to Los Angeles to experience a bewildering medley of adventures.

**Additional Information** *Okage Sama De: The Japanese in Hawai'i, 1885-1985* (1987), by Dorothy Ochiai Hazanna and Jane Okamoto Komeiji, provides additional information on the subject of Shirota's book, and Dennis Kawaharada's *The Rhetoric of Identity in Japanese American Writings, 1948-1988* (1988), gives details on Shirota and his works.

*Ryan A. Burrows*

**See also** Literature.

# M

## ■ McCarthy, Eugene

**Born** March 29, 1916, Watkins, Minnesota

*A staunch opponent of the Vietnam War. McCarthy was a U.S. Senator from Minnesota when he challenged for the presidency in 1968.*

Eugene Joseph McCarthy graduated from St. John's University in 1935 and received his master's degree from the University of Minnesota in 1939. He taught first at public high school and then as a university professor until 1948, when he was elected to the U.S. House of Representatives from Minnesota on the Democratic-Farmer-Labor Party ticket. He was elected to the Senate in 1958 and established himself as an independent-thinking liberal.

McCarthy served in the Senate throughout the 1960's and became a leader in the anti-Vietnam War movement. He began his maverick run for the presidency in 1968 in opposition to President Lyndon B. Johnson over the war issue. In the New Hampshire primary in 1968, McCarthy made a surprisingly strong showing against the incumbent president, although he ultimately did not receive his party's nomination.

McCarthy chose not to run for reelection to the Senate in 1970. He ran for president as an independent in 1976 but received less than 1 percent of the vote.

**Impact** McCarthy's candidacy for president in 1968 was instrumental in bringing the Vietnam War protests into the nation's mainstream, and his performance in the New Hampshire primary contributed to Johnson's decision not to seek reelection in 1968. McCarthy, because of his opposition to the war, became a sort of political hero to many young Americans.

**Additional Information** McCarthy wrote *The Limits of Power* (1967) and *The Ultimate Tyranny: The Majority over the Majority* (1980), both of which give reasons for his actions and political thought.

*James W. Riddlesperger, Jr.*

*Liberal Democrat Eugene McCarthy, who opposed the war in Vietnam, attempted to capture his party's presidential nomination in 1968 but failed. (Bernard Gotfryd/Archive Photos)*

**See also:** Johnson, Lyndon B.; Presidential Election of 1968; Vietnam War.

## ■ McGovern, George

**Born** July 19, 1922, Avon, South Dakota

*A political leader in the anti-Vietnam War movement. McGovern was the Democratic presidential candidate in 1972.*

The son of a Methodist minister, George Stanley McGovern attended high school and college in rural South Dakota. His undergraduate work was interrupted by World War II, and he served from 1942 to 1945 in the Army Air Forces, earning a Distinguished

*Liberal Democrat George McGovern, a staunch opponent of the Vietnam War, failed to win his party's presidential nomination in 1968 but was successful in 1972, although he lost to Republican Richard M. Nixon.* (AP/Wide World Photos)

Flying Cross for his service. He received a doctorate in history from Northwestern University and taught at Dakota Wesleyan University from 1949 through 1953, when he resigned to become active in politics. McGovern, a Democrat, was elected to the House of Representatives in 1956 but lost election to the Senate in 1960.

In 1961, President John F. Kennedy appointed McGovern director of the Food for Peace Program, and in 1962, McGovern won election to the Senate. McGovern became an outspoken critic of the Vietnam War and a leader of liberal Democrats. In 1968, McGovern ran unsuccessfully for the Democratic Party nomination for president.

In 1972, McGovern secured the Democratic nomination for the presidency and campaigned on a platform of opposition to U.S. involvement in Vietnam. He lost a landslide election to Republican Richard M. Nixon. McGovern stayed in the Senate until 1980, when he lost his bid for reelection.

**Impact** McGovern helped lead a popular movement to end U.S. involvement in Vietnam. He also supported the Great Society programs passed into law during the 1960's.

**Additional Information** McGovern wrote *A Time of War—A Time of Peace* (1968) and *An American Journey* (1974).

*James W. Riddlesperger, Jr.*

**See also** Kennedy, Robert F.; Presidential Election of 1968; Vietnam War.

---

## ■ McKuen, Rod

**Born** April 29, 1933, Oakland, California

*A popular and successful poet, singer, and songwriter. His sentimental poems and songs earned the love of the masses and the disdain of literary critics.*

**Early Life** Rod Marvin McKuen was born during the Depression, in a Salvation Army Hospital in California. He attended school for less than four years, mostly in one-room rural schoolhouses throughout Nevada, California, Washington, and Oregon. During his childhood, he repeatedly ran away from his mother and abusive stepfather but was always caught. At age eleven, he set off on a cross-country journey—walking, hitchhiking, and hopping trains—in an attempt to escape his past. From 1953 to 1955, he served with the U.S. Army first in Japan and then in Korea, where he wrote scripts on psychological warfare and was military assistant to the Korean Civil Assistance Command. He published *And Autumn Came*, a volume of poems, in 1954 through a vanity press. After his discharge from the service, he sang at folk clubs and worked briefly in films in Hollywood. In 1961, he had a minor hit with "Mister Oliver Twist," a rock song. In performing this song on a multistop tour of bowling alleys, McKuen would reduce his voice to the gravely sound by which later fans would know him.

**The 1960's** In 1963-1964, McKuen lived in Paris, where he developed his chanson-influenced style

of music. His 1966 English-language *Seasons in the Sun* became an award-winning album in France, and he developed a long-term relationship with French chanson artists such as Jacques Brel. In 1966, after former Limelighters singer Glenn Yarbrough recorded a collection of McKuen poems (including "Stanyan Street") set to music, McKuen self-published *Stanyan Street and Other Sorrows*. The book sold more than sixty thousand copies before publisher Random House acquired the work. McKuen's 1967 album, *The Sea*, a collection of songs about bodies of water and women, also sold well, reaching five hundred thousand copies in its first year. During the 1960's, McKuen wrote numerous concertos, symphonies, ballets, and more than a thousand songs, including "Jean," "Seasons in the Sun," and "Love's Been Good to Me." His musical score for the popular 1969 film *The Prime of Miss Jean Brodie* was nominated for an Academy Award. That

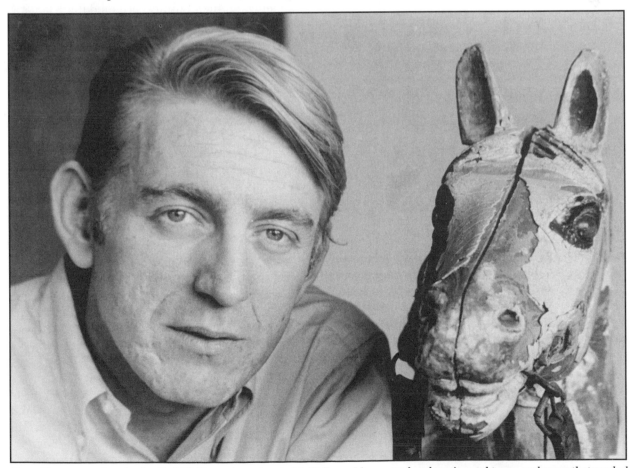

*Best-selling poet and songwriter Rod McKuen, shown here in his Hollywood home, produced sentimental poems and songs that reached the hearts of the masses but were disdained by critics. (AP/Wide World Photos)*

same year, he also scored or wrote songs for film and television productions including *Travels with Charlie*; *Me, Natalie*; *A Boy Named Charlie Brown*; and *Rod McKuen: The Loner.*

During the decade, McKuen published a number of volumes of poetry: *Listen to the Warm* (1967, collected lyrics from his songs), *Lonesome Cities* (1968, a man's quest for self-identity, which was turned into an album that won a Grammy for best spoken-word album), *The World of Rod McKuen*, (1968, which contained songs with words and music), and *In Someone's Shadow* and *Twelve Years of Christmas* (both 1969). By the end of the decade, more than three and a half million copies of his books were in print. In 1969, the popular poet and songwriter appeared before a sold-out house at Carnegie Hall.

**Later Life** McKuen's poetry and music, although extremely popular during the 1960's and early 1970's, were dismissed by poetry and music critics. The "King of Kitsch," as a 1968 *Newsweek* magazine article termed McKuen, fell into a depression in the early 1980's, and although he reportedly recovered in the early 1990's, he did not release or publish any new works.

**Impact** McKuen's broad and eclectic range of talents made him a cultural icon during the 1960's. He worked variously as an author, poet, singer, songwriter, publisher, record producer, composer, and film and television actor. At a turbulent juncture in American social history, his unabashedly sentimental poems and songs won him a vast public following, a financial fortune, and the disdain of most literary critics.

**Additional Information** The best sources of information on McKuen are his own works, including *Listen to the Warm* (1967) and *Stanyan Street and Other Sorrows* (1966).

*Carroll Dale Short*

**See also** Music; Poetry.

# ■ McLuhan, Marshall

**Born** July 21, 1911, Edmonton, Canada
**Died** December 31, 1980, Toronto, Canada

*A pioneering 1960's authority on the impact of mass media on culture. McLuhan's ideas included the concept of the global village and the notion that "the medium is the message."*

**Early Life** The young Herbert Marshall McLuhan was fascinated by technology, but at the University of Manitoba, he discovered literary studies and did graduate work at Cambridge, receiving a doctorate in 1943. In 1946, McLuhan joined the faculty at the University of Toronto and, by 1959, had founded the interdisciplinary journal *Explorations* and published *The Mechanical Bride: Folklore of Industrial Man* (1951), a study of print advertising.

**The 1960's** McLuhan's emergence as an authority on media and culture occurred through several channels simultaneously. The University of Toronto established and funded the Centre for Culture and Technology, a research institute run by McLuhan to explore and promote his ideas and topics. The National Association of Educational Broadcasters and the National Council of Teachers of English provided him with access to the education establishment, and such business-oriented think tanks as General Electric's Management Center helped him become a popular presenter at corporate meetings and executive seminars.

The intellectual center of McLuhan's work was contained in four books he published in the 1960's: *The Gutenberg Galaxy: The Making of Typographic Man* (1962), which provides the historical foundation for his theories; *Understanding Media: The Extensions of Man* (1964), in which he analyzed the specific properties of such media as clothing, comics, and television; *The Medium Is the Massage* (1967), an illustrated popularization of his main ideas; and *War and Peace in the Global Village* (1968), in which cultural conflict is examined in relation to media.

McLuhan argued that changes in information technology (media) were more important than the messages transmitted by that technology. For example, Gutenberg's press itself, rather than any book it produced, made medieval Europe's oral culture obsolete, ushering in the age of print literacy. In the 1960's, McLuhan saw the print world being made similarly obsolete by the rise of electronic media such as television and the computer. McLuhan foresaw the emergence of an electronic Global Village in which images would replace text, education would escape the traditional classroom, and information would replace manufactured goods as the foundation of economic, political, and military strength.

Additionally, the end of the decade saw McLuhan become the topic of books such as the essay collection *McLuhan: Pro and Con* (1969) and Jonathan Miller's *McLuhan* (1971), a volume in the Viking Press Modern Masters series. In the 1960's, no name was more influential or provocative in media studies than McLuhan's.

**Later Life**    In the 1970's, McLuhan was beset by professional and personal problems. His ideas were losing their freshness and appeal in academic and corporate circles, and McLuhan was having increasing trouble bringing long projects to completion. In September, 1979, a severe stroke left him partially disabled and unable to read or speak (although he could understand speech). On the morning of December 31, 1980, McLuhan was found dead by his son Micheal.

**Impact**    McLuhan, through his books, articles, interviews, presentations, and seminars, made the effect of media on culture a major theme of 1960's intellectual debate. In the 1960's, he was an intellectual celebrity with a gift for penetrating insights expressed in pungent and paradoxical style. In the 1970's, there was a backlash against both his ideas and style, but with the coming of the information revolution brought on by the computer and the Internet, his work has a renewed relevance.

**Additional Information**    Two essential sources for further study are Philip Marchand's *Marshall McLuhan: The Medium and the Message* (1989) and *Essential McLuhan* (1995), edited by Eric McLuhan and Frank Zingrone.

*Roger J. Stilling*

**See also**    Advertising; Media.

## ■ McNamara, Robert

**Born** June 9, 1916, San Francisco, California

*One of the nation's chief policymakers in the 1960's. As secretary of defense from 1961 through 1968, McNamara played a key role in such events as the 1961 crisis in Berlin, the 1962 Cuban Missile Crisis, and the Vietnam War.*

**Early Life**    Robert Strange McNamara studied economics at the University of California, Berkeley. He then earned a master's degree in business administration at Harvard and in 1940 became a member of its faculty. During World War II, he was a statistical control officer in the U.S. Army Air Corps. After the war, he joined the Ford Motor Company and in

*Secretary of Defense Robert McNamara played a large part in shaping U.S. policy in Vietnam until 1968, when he resigned from his position.* (AP/Wide World Photos)

November, 1960, became the first person outside the Ford family to be its president.

**The 1960's**    In early 1961, McNamara became secretary of defense under President John F. Kennedy. He was determined to tighten civilian control and introduce management techniques, including a new system of budgeting and systems analysis in decision making. These, however, brought unprecedented centralization and deleterious side effects. McNamara also sought to rebuild conventional military forces, neglected under President Dwight D. Eisenhower's policy of massive retaliation. The new approach was known as "flexible response." McNamara also pushed for the development of a joint army-navy fighter, the TFX. During the 1962 Cuban Missile Crisis, he proposed the naval quarantine of Cuba that was successfully adopted by the Kennedy administration.

McNamara is forever identified with the Vietnam War. He had a major role in shaping U.S. policy there and supported the U.S. commitment to South Vietnam, including the deployment of ground troops and the strategy of graduated response. By 1966, McNamara began to have doubts about the war although he did not make them public. In 1967, he began to push for a negotiated settlement. Later he admitted he had "misunderstood the nature of the conflict."

**Later Life** McNamara's divergence from President Lyndon B. Johnson's view of the Vietnam War angered the president and led him to accept McNamara's request to leave the administration. McNamara departed at the end of February, 1968, in the midst of the furor over the Tet Offensive, to become president of the World Bank, a post he held until 1982. There he set out to shift emphasis in lending from industrial projects to agriculture and education and later to population control.

**Impact** Although McNamara was certainly the most influential of post-World War II secretaries of defense, many in the U.S. military bemoan the consequences of his emphasis on management over leadership. He has also been criticized both for his role in developing U.S. policy in Vietnam and his failure to express his doubts over the outcome of the war more forcefully when he was defense secretary. He is generally regarded as the most effective of World Bank presidents.

**Subsequent Events** McNamara's 1995 book, *In Retrospect: The Tragedy and Lessons of Vietnam*, reignited debate over U.S. Vietnam policy when he admitted that the war should not have been fought and could not have been won. He subsequently made several trips to Vietnam to meet with Vietnamese leaders in an effort to identify mistakes made by the two sides, but he failed to secure any admissions from the Vietnamese.

**Additional Information** The story of McNamara's life and role in the Vietnam War can be found in Deborah Shapley's *Promise and Power: The Life and Times of Robert McNamara* (1993) and *In Retrospect: The Tragedy and Lessons of Vietnam* (1995), by Robert S. McNamara with Brian VanDeMark.

*Spencer C. Tucker*

**See also** Cuban Missile Crisis; Tet Offensive; Vietnam War.

## ■ *MAD* Magazine

**Published** 1952-
**Publisher** William M. Gaines (1922-1992)

*A widely read magazine that used cartoons to satirize everything from popular culture to emotionally charged issues such as racism and the Vietnam War. Its humor ranged from political satire to sophomoric gags.*

**The Work** *MAD* magazine was one of the first publications to use political satire in the conservative 1950's. *MAD* first appeared in 1952 as a comic book; however, in 1955 when comics were criticized for allegedly causing juvenile delinquency, it appeared in a tamer magazine form. Its parodies poked fun at comic strips, films, advertisements, and television shows and ranged from political satires to sick jokes. In *MAD*'s world, the normal and the abnormal, the American and the un-American were treated with equal zaniness.

In 1960, the magazine satirized the popular television series Lassie, which featured a boy, his all-American family, and their dog, a supersmart collie named Lassie. *MAD*'s cartoon character asked, "Can America's wholesomest TV family find happiness owning a plain, average nine-year-old collie with the intelligence of a plain average forty-year-old college professor?" In 1963, it poked fun at the television industry's attempts, prompted by the Civil Rights movement, to make its programming reflect racial diversity. The show *Julia* (starring Diahann Carroll) featured an African American nurse. *MAD*, in its version, "Jewelia," commented, "Look at that apartment she lives in and look at that fantastic wardrobe she's got. She's a member of a minority group as far as the show's audience is concerned—the majority of Americans don't live that good."

The magazine also tackled more serious subjects such as the Cold War. In 1962, the "*MAD* Guide to Russia" commented, "In America, time for a change means the citizens are going to get rid of the current government and replace it with a new one. In Russia, it means the government is going to get rid of the citizens and replace them with new ones." In 1963, the magazine's "East Side Story" transformed Nikita Khrushchev and other Eastern Bloc leaders into a street gang similar to the tough New York gangs portrayed in the popular musical and film *West Side Story*. In *MAD*'s version, the Reds revolt against Khrushchev, and his wife escorts him back to the

Soviet Union. In 1967, when internal unrest threatened to tear the nation apart, *MAD*'s "The Preamble Revisited" showed photographs of the Ku Klux Klan, police arresting strikers, a lynching, and the aftermath of a riot, comparing these images to scenes from Nazi Germany thirty years before. *MAD* called itself "high-level trash" and lambasted its own readers for wasting time reading the "idiotic garbage." *MAD*'s official mascot was gap-toothed quintessential nerd Alfred E. Neuman, whose slogan was "What, me worry?" Its indiscriminate hilarity was echoed on television by comedians such as Sid Caesar and Steve Allen.

**Impact** Americans, particularly teenagers and college students, loved to hate *MAD* or hated to love it because it exposed absurdity in the culture. It alerted readers to what was happening in advertising, the consumer movement, and the mass media. By 1960, circulation reached one million. It was read by 58 percent of all college students and 43 percent of all high school students. However, all was not fun and games publishing a humor magazine. In the early 1960's, two troubling court cases drained *MAD*'s creative energies.

In 1960, the Music Publishers Protective Association, representing such composers as Irving Berlin, Cole Porter, and Richard Rodgers, filed a $25 million lawsuit for copyright infringement of twenty-five songs. The plaintiffs said that only the copyright owners had the right to parody their work. In 1963, a district court ruled that twenty-three songs were completely different from the originals; however, two songs were too similar to the originals to be considered legitimate parodies. A court of appeals in 1964 ruled in favor of *MAD*'s right to publish all the songs. Judge Irving R. Kaufman said, "While the social interest in encouraging the broad-gauged burlesques of *MAD* magazine is admittedly not readily apparent, we believe that parody and satire are deserving of substantial freedom—both as entertainment and as a form of social and literary criticism." That same year, the Supreme Court upheld the lower court's decision.

The magazine's other court battle was in Oklahoma, at the beginning of the decade, when the prevailing Cold War mentality made drug stores and newsstands reluctant to sell unpatriotic publications. Clyde J. Watts, a lawyer and retired brigadier general, was reported to have called *MAD* "the most insidious

communist propaganda in the United States today." His statement caused *MAD* to be pulled from stores throughout Oklahoma, resulting in a drop in sales. In 1961, the publisher filed a $1.5 million libel and slander suit against Watts, who countersued for $250,000 for libel. The matter was settled in 1962 when Watts publicly stated that he never referred to the magazine as communistic. The case was closed, and each side paid its own legal fees.

Some of *MAD*'s other enemies were conservatives and reactionary groups such as William F. Buckley, Jr., the Ku Klux Klan, and the John Birch Society. In 1963, at the height of the Cold War, its political satire tended to favor liberals although its main targets were extremists on both sides. *MAD* found a middle ground in a society polarized between the squeaky clean suburban lifestyle and the perceived menaces of communism, ethnicity, and rock and roll. It dared to drill holes in the American Dream. Critics believe that *MAD*'s main accomplishment was to strike down the barriers of black and white—conservative or liberal—and establish the possibility of gray.

**Related Works** *Spy* and *National Lampoon* are similar magazines with outrageous satire that were published years after *MAD*'s debut.

**Additional Information** For an illustrated look at *MAD* magazine, see *Completely MAD: A History of the Comic Book and Magazine* (1991) by Maria Reidelbach. *MAD* magazine, although not as popular as it was in the 1960's, had a U.S. circulation of 584,684 in 1996.

*Marian Wynne Haber*

**See also** Bruce, Lenny; Buckley, William F., Jr.; Cold War; Conservatism in Politics; John Birch Society; Ku Klux Klan (KKK); Liberalism in Politics; Literature; Social Satires.

---

# ■ Maddox, Lester

**Born** September 30, 1915, Atlanta, Georgia

*Segregationist, restaurant owner, and governor of Georgia from 1967 to 1971. Maddox gained national notoriety by defying the Civil Rights Act of 1964.*

Born into a working class family in Atlanta, Lester Garfield Maddox labored in defense plants before starting his first business in the early 1940's. In 1947, Maddox opened the Pickrick restaurant. Two years later, he gained local attention by placing in Atlanta newspapers a series of "Pickrick Says" advertisements in which he trumpeted conservative political views and defended segregation.

Maddox defied the Civil Rights Act of 1964 by brandishing a pickax handle at demonstrators in front of the Pickrick. After losing several suits in federal court, Maddox closed his restaurant rather than serve African American customers. He claimed that his stance was motivated not by racism but by states' rights, free enterprise, and Christianity. In 1966, he parlayed his notoriety into victory in the race for governor. His policies proved surprisingly progressive: He increased funding for education and appointed African Americans to state offices.

Maddox was elected lieutenant governor in 1970 but lost a second bid for the governorship in 1974.

**Impact** His campaign theatrics and governorship were indicative of the political turmoil in the South in the wake of the Civil Rights movement. Although race baiting could still attract enough disaffected white voters to defeat moderate Democrats, economic needs demanded progressive policies.

**Additional Information** Compare Maddox's own story, *Speaking Out: The Autobiography of Lester Garfield Maddox* (1975), with Bruce Galphin's *The Riddle of Lester Maddox* (1968).

*Robert E. McFarland*

**See also** Civil Rights Movement; School Desegregation; Wallace, George.

---

# ■ Mailer, Norman

**Born** January 31, 1923, Long Branch, New Jersey

*One of the nation's most important novelists and journalists. Mailer shocked the literary community when he stabbed his second wife at a party meant to launch his campaign for mayor of New York City.*

**Early Life** Norman Kingsley Mailer grew up in Brooklyn, New York, graduated from Harvard University, and served in the Philippines in World War II. In 1948, he became a best-selling author with the publication of his first novel, *The Naked and the Dead*. His second novel, *Barbary Shore* (1951), which concerned Cold War politics, received a mixed reception, and his third novel, *The Deer Park* (1955), an exposé of Hollywood, also failed to match the success of his first novel. He turned to journalism, experimental fiction, and politics in the 1960's, hoping to recoup his reputation and to make an impact on public affairs.

**The 1960's** In the 1960's, Mailer found a new voice in essays such as "Superman Comes to the Supermarket," which suggested that John F. Kennedy had the personality of a box-office star. This influential essay persuaded Mailer that he could shape the country's political destiny. Like many writers of the 1960's, his writing became confessional, and he believed he could speak to the new generation, young people who were overturning the status quo of the boring, conserva-

*Segregationist Lester Maddox, who closed his Pickrick restaurant rather than integrate it in 1964, sells an autographed pickax handle similar to the one he waved at protesters in front of his restaurant. He became governor of Georgia three years later. (AP/Wide World Photos)*

tive 1950's. Mailer was drinking heavily and smoking marijuana—both of which, along with chronic insomnia, made him irritable and prone to lose control. At a party meant to show he had the clout to become mayor of New York City, a drunken Mailer, when goaded by his second wife, Adele Morales, stabbed her twice (in front and back), barely missing her heart. She recovered, and after a psychiatric evaluation, Mailer was released from Bellevue Hospital. His wife did not press charges, but this incident and Mailer's reputation as an irresponsible 1960's radical and male chauvinist did him lasting harm.

Mailer produced two remarkable novels, *An American Dream* (1964) and *Why Are We in Vietnam?* (1967), and two outstanding works of reportage, *Armies of the Night* (1968) and *Miami and the Siege of Chicago* (1968).

**Later Life**  His work in the 1970's was equally distinguished. *The Fight* (1975) is his riveting account of the Muhammad Ali versus George Foreman heavyweight title fight, and *Marilyn* (1972), his biography of Marilyn Monroe, has had a lasting influence on popular culture studies. *The Executioner's Song* (1979), his account of executed murderer Gary Gilmore, has become a nonfiction classic. His subsequent work has received a mixed reception. Mailer married his sixth wife, Norris Church, in 1980.

**Impact**  Mailer became a symbol of the politically active writer in the 1960's when he was jailed for protesting the war in Vietnam. He also became a symbol of the excesses of the 1960's, attacked for his womanizing and wife abuse. He played a large part in the culture's tendency to turn writers into celebrities with his appearances on interview programs such as *The Dick Cavett Show*, on which he demonstrated his fighting talents in a boxing ring.

**Subsequent Events**  In 1997, Adele Morales Mailer published *The Last Party: Scenes from My Life with Norman Mailer*, her own account of the stabbing, adding gruesome details about the Mailers' lives in the 1960's, including Mailer's desire to humiliate her and to participate in wife-swapping.

**Additional Information**  In 1991, Carl Rollyson published *The Lives of Norman Mailer: A Biography*, which has a detailed account of the stabbing, linking it to other events in Mailer's life.

*Carl Rollyson*

**See also**  Kennedy, John F.; Literature.

## ■ Malcolm X

**Born** May 19, 1925, Omaha, Nebraska
**Died** February 21, 1965, New York, New York

*Prominent leader of the African American community, social activist, civil rights advocate, and minister in the Nation of Islam. Malcolm X's outspoken promotion of black separatism and criticism of the evils of institutionalized racism placed these issues in the forefront of the Civil Rights movement.*

**Early Life**  Malcolm X, born Malcolm Little, was raised in poverty in the urban North unlike other civil rights activists such as Martin Luther King, Jr., who came from upper-middle-class southern families of professional standing. Malcolm's father, Earl Little, died tragically when Malcolm was five years old, and his mother, Louise Little, suffered a nervous breakdown when Malcolm was fourteen. Malcolm and his seven siblings were separated and placed in foster homes or with family members across the country. Malcolm's teenage years were spent between Boston, Massachusetts, and New York City. After working for a short period in a menial job in the service sector, he turned to street life and criminal pursuits. In 1946, Malcolm was convicted of burglary and sentenced to prison, where he converted to the Nation of Islam, a separatist black Muslim sect. During this period, Malcolm abandoned his family surname for the letter "X," which he said represented the evils of slavery that stripped blacks of their African heritage. Upon his parole in 1952, Malcolm X worked as a minister for the Nation of Islam under the leadership of Elijah Muhammad. In 1958, he married Betty Sanders with whom he had six children.

**The 1960's**  During the 1950's and 1960's, Malcolm X was a driving force for the Nation of Islam, which grew from a minuscule religious movement of four hundred members to a sect of national prominence with forty temples, ten thousand members, a media system of radio stations and a newspaper, and a network of businesses owned and operated by African Americans. Founded in 1930, the Nation of Islam advanced a racial theology that held that blacks were Allah's chosen race and that whites were the race of Satan. The group believed that whites had constructed a false history to justify their exploitation of blacks. It was the Nation of Islam's expressed goal to awaken African Americans to their

*Malcolm X, a powerful speaker, promoted the Nation of Islam and its message of black separatism until his assassination in 1965.* (AP/Wide World Photos)

true heritage by freeing them of the values of white culture and directing them on a grand historical quest for freedom, justice, and equality. Unlike the gradualism and pacifism of King's civil rights followers, the Nation of Islam promoted immediate black self-determination through an increasingly militant stance that totally excluded whites as potential allies. Malcolm became the group's most productive recruiter in northern ghettoes because of his power as a public speaker, his leadership through his exemplary spartan personal life, and his escalating verbal outrage at overt acts of white racism. By 1963, Malcolm had emerged as the chief rival to King for leadership of the Civil Rights movement. In 1964, Malcolm formally left the Nation of Islam because of a rift with its leader, Muhammad, over strategic policy and personal codes of conduct for the Nation of Islam's inner ruling circle. Following a celebrated pilgrimage to Mecca (the Holy Land of Islam), Malcolm recanted his universal indictment of whites as inherently evil racists and formed the Organization of Afro-American Unity (OAAU) to transform the struggle for civil rights into a universal struggle for human rights. He changed his name to el-Hajj Malik

el-Shabazz and, in 1965, crisscrossed the globe seeking international support for the OAAU. Drawing increased wrath from the Nation of Islam, Malcolm suspected an assassination plot had been ordered against him by Muhammad. On the afternoon of February 21, 1965, the thirty-nine-year-old Malcolm was speaking at an OAAU rally in a hotel ballroom in New York City when he was assassinated. Three fringe members of the Nation of Islam were later convicted of the murder, but no formal proof linking the killing to the Nation of Islam has been found.

**Impact** Malcolm X represented the cutting edge of the radical elements in the Civil Rights movement. Generally viewed as the antithesis of King, he strategically used inflammatory rhetoric and manipulated the U.S. news media for coverage in an attempt to get his message across.

In the early 1960's and after Malcolm's death, young northern blacks entrapped in the vicious cycle of ghetto life came to perceive Malcolm as an apostle in the battle against the evils of white racism.

**Subsequent Events** The late 1980's saw the emergence of a tremendous revival of interest in Malcolm as a cultural force for African American identity and pride. This interest culminated in Spike Lee's motion picture, *Malcolm X* (1992).

**Additional Information** *The Autobiography of Malcolm X* (1965), by Malcolm X and Alex Haley, should be read in conjunction with Bruce Perry's revisionist biography, *Malcolm* (1991).

*Ronald Lettieri*

**See also** Black Power; Civil Rights Movement; King, Martin Luther, Jr.; Nation of Islam.

# ■ Malone, Vivian

**Born** 1942, Mobile, Alabama

*One of two African American students registering at the University of Alabama in June, 1963, despite Governor George Wallace's strong, personal opposition. She became the first African American to graduate from the university.*

**The 1960's** Vivian Malone has long been linked with Alabama governor George Wallace's defiant symbolic stand at the schoolhouse door. Wallace, who had proclaimed "Segregation now, segregation tomorrow, segregation forever" in his inaugural speech in 1963, vowed to personally block the deseg-

*African American Vivian Malone graduates from the University of Alabama, which she and James Hood integrated in June, 1963, despite Governor George Wallace's disapproval.* (National Archives)

regation of the University of Alabama. In expression of his opposition to desegregation of the school, Wallace stood in a doorway of the administration building, but Malone and James Hood, accompanied by the federalized National Guard, registered for the summer quarter in June, 1963. Another African American, Autherine Lucy, had entered the University of Alabama in 1956 but was expelled after three days for accusing the university administration of complicity in the riots occurring upon her arrival.

Although Hood soon dropped out, Malone completed her degree in personnel management. Although she experienced some difficulty with white students, she also enjoyed several close friendships at the university. Finishing with an above-B average, Malone entertained many job offers after graduation. Malone later married physician Mack Jones and changed her name to Vivian Malone Jones.

**Later Life** Malone's professional work focused on improving the lives of other African Americans. She worked for the Justice Department, the Veteran's

Administration Hospital in Atlanta, and the Environmental Protection Agency (EPA) as director of civil rights and urban affairs. She also served as executive director of the Voter Education Project in Atlanta. Malone retired from the EPA in 1996.

In 1996, Malone met with former governor Wallace, who apologized for the 1963 confrontation, expressing deep regret over his and others' political actions before awarding Malone the first Lurleen B. Wallace Award of Courage, an award honoring women who made major improvements in the state. Wallace commended Malone, noting the importance of her role in the 1963 desegregation of the state's flagship university: "Vivian Malone Jones was at the center of the fight over states' rights and conducted herself with grace, strength, and, above all, courage. She deserves to be rewarded for her actions in that air of uncertainty."

**Impact** The desegregation of the University of Alabama in 1963 was part of a continued assault on segregation in the Deep South. Malone's perform-

*Police escort Charles Manson, charged with killing actress Sharon Tate and six others, to a Los Angeles courtroom, where his trial was set to begin on March 30, 1970. (AP/Wide World Photos)*

ance and completion of her program at the university, coupled with the graduation of other prominent African American students at southern universities, struck at popular notions of the intellectual capabilities of African Americans and demonstrated that state university admission policies, despite the 1954 *Brown v. Board of Education* ruling, continued to be racially discriminatory, and additionally, antiintellectual.

**Additional Information** E. Culpepper Clark's *The Schoolhouse Door: Segregation's Last Stand at the University of Alabama* (1993) describes the 1963 confrontation between Malone and Wallace. Malone's later life is described in "What Ever Happened to . . . Vivian Malone?" in the December, 1978, issue of *Ebony* magazine.

*LeeAnn Bishop Lands*

**See also** Civil Rights Movement; Holmes, Hamilton, and Charlayne Hunter; Meredith, James H.; School Desegregation.

## ■ Manson Murders

**Date** August 8-9, 1969

*Perhaps the most gruesome, sensational murders of the 1960's. The bizarre and brutal nature of the slayings and the perpetrators' haunting lack of remorse shocked the people of Los Angeles and the rest of the country.*

**Origins and History** Charles Manson, thirty-three years old, was the ex-convict leader of a nomadic group called the Family that originated in the Haight-Ashbury district of San Francisco. Through carefully orchestrated sexual orgies, organized drug use, and his own religious and mystical teachings, Manson exercised considerable power over his followers, who believed him to be the Messiah and obediently followed his commands.

**The Murders** On the night of August 8, 1969, Manson dispatched five Family members, Patricia Krenwinkle, Susan Atkins, Charles "Tex" Watson, Leslie Van Houten, and Linda Kasabian, to an estate in the Hollywood Hills rented by film director Roman Polanski and his wife, actress Sharon Tate. After shooting visitor Steve Parent in the driveway, all but Kasabian entered the house, where, under Manson's orders, they savagely murdered its four occupants. Tate, eight months pregnant, was stabbed sixteen times. Jay Sebring, a celebrity hair stylist, was stabbed seven times and shot once. Abigail Folger, heiress to the Folger coffee fortune, was stabbed twenty-eight times, and her boyfriend, Voytek Frykowski, was stabbed fifty-one times, shot twice, and bludgeoned over the head thirteen times. The word "PIG" was printed in Tate's blood on the door of the house.

The following night, August 9, Manson again ordered his followers to murder, though this time he accompanied them to their destination, the home of grocery-chain owner Leno LaBianca and his wife, Rosemary. Manson entered the house and bound his victims, then instructed Watson, Van Houten, and Krenwinkle to kill the couple. Leno was strangled and stabbed twenty-six times; Rosemary was stabbed forty-one times. The words "RISE," "DEATH TO PIGS," and "HEALTER SKELTER" (sic) were written in the victims' blood on the walls and refrigerator.

The group was charged with the murders several months later after Atkins, in jail on a separate charge, confessed to a cellmate. Following a lengthy and bizarre trial that included the murder of defense attorney Ronald Hughes, Manson, Krenwinkle, Van Houten, and Atkins were found guilty of first-degree murder and conspiracy to commit murder; Watson was tried separately and similarly convicted. All were sentenced to death, but upon the California Supreme Court's abolishment of the death penalty in 1972, their sentences were commuted to life in prison with the possibility of parole.

Prosecutor Vincent Bugliosi's search for a motive eventually led him to Manson's professed belief in the coming of Helter Skelter, an apocalyptic race war that would ultimately conclude in Manson's ascendance to world leadership. The Tate-LaBianca murders were apparently intended to incite Helter Skelter.

**Impact** The savage brutality of the murders sent a shockwave of fear through the ranks of Hollywood's elite, many of whom relocated temporarily. Aspects of the Family's appearance, lifestyle, and antiestablishment politics affiliated them with hippie culture, causing a detectable backlash against hippies throughout the country.

**Additional Information** A complete account of the murders, titled *Helter Skelter* (1974), was published by Bugliosi and Curt Gentry.

*Alice A. Dailey*

**See also** Crimes and Scandals; Cults; Hippies.

## ■ Mantle, Mickey

**Born** October 20, 1931, Spavinaw, Oklahoma
**Died** August 13, 1995, Dallas, Texas

*One of the greatest major league baseball players of all time. Mantle retired after the 1968 season with numerous records and honors.*

Mickey Charles Mantle joined the New York Yankees in 1951, replacing the legendary Joe DiMaggio in center field. Mantle's combination of speed and batting power quickly elevated him to stardom. Known for his long home runs, Mantle won a triple crown in 1956 and Most Valuable Player awards in 1956 and 1957.

Mantle began the 1960's by leading the American League in homers in 1960 and batting over .300 the next four years. He challenged Babe Ruth's single-season homer record in 1961, won Most Valuable Player honors in 1962, and played in the World Series from 1960 to 1964. Injuries, alcohol abuse,

and age combined to erode his skills after 1964, culminating in his retirement after the 1968 season. Among the records he set were most homers by a switch-hitter (536); most World Series homers (18); and most games played by a Yankee (2,401).

In 1974, Mantle was inducted into the National Baseball Hall of Fame. In 1994, he was diagnosed as suffering from a variety of liver ailments; although he received a controversial transplant, he died shortly thereafter.

**Impact** Mantle's lasting legacy transcended statistical accomplishments. Mickey's name had a magical quality to it—ask anyone who found a Mantle in a pack of baseball cards—and he had an aura about him that granted Mantle heroic status in a decade punctuated by strong antihero sentiments.

**Additional Information** Sportswriter Maury Allen and photographer Bob Olen combine to present a warm portrait of Mantle in *Memories of the Mick* (1997).

*Paul J. Chara, Jr.*

**See also** Baseball; DiMaggio, Joe; Koufax, Sandy; Maris, Roger; Sports.

## ■ March Against Death

**Date** November 13-15, 1969

*One of the most emotionally potent, large-scale protests of the antiwar movement. Forty-five thousand Americans marched single file past the White House in witness to those who had died in the Vietnam War.*

**Origins and History** The events of November 13-15, 1969, were the result of collaborative planning between the New Mobilization Committee to End the War in Vietnam (MOBE) and the Vietnam Moratorium Committee (VMC). MOBE planned what turned out to be the largest antiwar demonstration in U.S. history on November 15, and the VMC sponsored two days of no business as usual as part of its moratorium. The March Against Death was proposed by American Friends Service Committee leader Stewart Meacham as part of the weekend's actions.

**The March** The March Against Death began in the early evening on Thursday, November 13, at the west end of the Arlington Memorial Bridge. Led by six drummers beating a slow funeral cadence and by

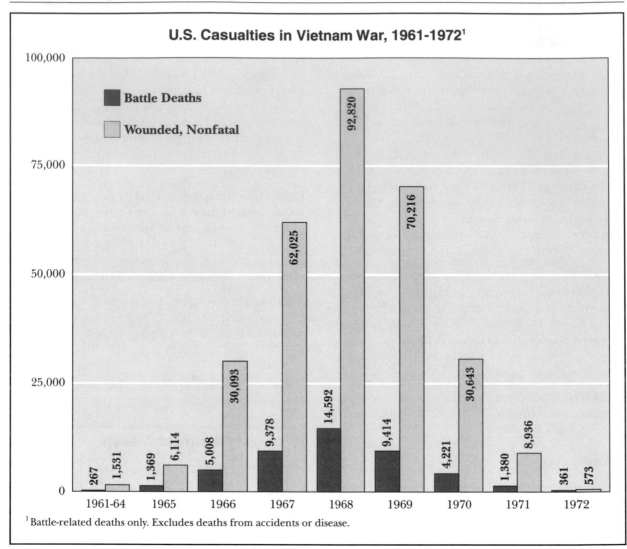

U.S. Casualties in Vietnam War, 1961-1972[1]

■ Battle Deaths

Wounded, Nonfatal

[1] Battle-related deaths only. Excludes deaths from accidents or disease.

*Source:* U.S. Department of Defense

close relatives of war dead, marchers proceeded silently and in single file across the bridge—at a rate of about twelve hundred people an hour—and past the front gate of the White House. Each marcher wore a placard around his or her neck bearing the name of an American soldier killed in the war or the name of a Vietnamese village destroyed by U.S. firepower. As marchers approached the space directly in front of the White House, they turned, called out the name on the placard, and placed the placard in one of twelve wooden coffins at the base of the Capitol steps.

Sustained by bus loads of protesters arriving at about three-minute intervals, the march continued

through weather conditions that included rain, biting wind, bitter cold, and bright sun for approximately thirty-six hours. During the nighttime, each marcher carried a lit candle; the glare of spotlights facing away from the White House added to the eeriness of the experience. At the massive Saturday march and demonstration, the twelve coffins were carried by "pallbearers"—again to the cadence of drums. Throughout the weekend's activities, the White House was barricaded by locked gates and ringed by a solid wall of buses. Despite the feeling of being under siege by the protesters, the White House was so intent on presenting a business-as-usual face that President Richard M. Nixon informed the press that he planned to watch a football game during the afternoon's activities.

**Impact** Participants in the march described their experience with terms such as "haunting," "overwhelming," and "emotionally powerful." The march also captured some national media attention early in the weekend, though it was quickly displaced by the massive Saturday demonstration and its more confrontational spin-offs. Symbolically, the march reflected the antiwar movement's compassion for U.S. and Vietnamese dead. However, the central theme of the march was later obscured by images—and propaganda attacks—that suggested a protest that was antipathetic to soldiers.

**Additional Information** For information on background planning of the march and related activities see Tom Wells's *The War Within: America's Battle over Vietnam* (1994); for an account of the atmosphere surrounding the march, see Nancy Zaroulis and Gerald Sullivan's *Who Spoke Up? American Protest Against the War in Vietnam, 1963-1975* (1984).

*Edward P. Morgan*

**See also** Moratorium Day; National Mobilization Committee to End the War in Vietnam (MOBE); Vietnam War.

# ▪ March on Selma

**Date** March 7-25, 1965

*The demonstration bringing the greatest amount of attention to the lack of voting rights for African Americans.*

**Origins and History** One of the many goals of the Civil Rights movement was to increase the number of African Americans registered to vote in the South. For more than a year, the Student Nonviolent Coordinating Committee (SNCC) had been working in Selma, Alabama, where only 2.5 percent of eligible African Americans were registered voters. During the early weeks of 1965, small groups of local African Americans marched to the Dallas County courthouse, but none were permitted to register. Its funds were dwindling, so SNCC called Martin Luther King, Jr., and the Southern Christian Leadership Conference (SCLC) for assistance.

*On March 21, 1965, a group of people, led by Martin Luther King, Jr. (third from right, holding the hand of his wife, Coretta) and other civil rights activists, began a five-day march from Selma, Alabama, to Montgomery to help secure voting rights for African Americans.* (AP/Wide World Photos)

**The March** In an effort to bring national attention to police brutality and voter registration efforts in Alabama, King and local civil rights leaders decided to lead a march from Selma to the state capital in Montgomery. The fifty-four mile march brought five to six days of publicity to civil rights efforts in the South. Alabama governor George Wallace banned the demonstration. However, on March 7, the march began as six hundred men, women, and children left Brown's Chapel Methodist Church and quietly walked out of town. As marchers attempted to cross the Edmund Pettus Bridge, they were met by approximately one hundred state troopers and police. Troopers, ordered by Governor Wallace to stop the march and armed with horses, whips, clubs, and tear gas, advanced on the approaching crowd. Offering no resistance, demonstrators turned back across the bridge. The police pursued, injuring dozens of marchers as the crowd fled. The incident, which became known as Bloody Sunday, was broadcast later that evening on national television. Viewers watched as nightsticks rose and fell on march participants, who could be seen through the cloud of tear gas.

The sight of Bloody Sunday encouraged hundreds of Americans to flock to Selma, eager to participate in a second march. U.S. District Court Judge Frank Johnson temporarily barred the march until a hearing could be held. On March 9, King again led marchers toward Montgomery. Demonstrators crossed the Pettus Bridge, where they were met by state troopers. Not wishing to defy a federal ban, King waited, hoping for police protection for marchers. The demonstrators prayed, then turned around and walked back to Selma, which had erupted in demonstrations and violence.

On March 15, Judge Johnson ruled that the march from Selma could take place. President Lyndon B. Johnson federalized eighteen hundred members of the Alabama National Guard to protect thirty-two hundred marchers as they left Selma on March 21. By the time the long walk ended four days later, twenty-five thousand people had participated. The event culminated in a speech given by King on the steps of the Alabama statehouse.

**Impact** The march from Selma to Montgomery brought national attention to the plight of African Americans in the South. On August 6, President Johnson signed the Voting Rights Act of 1965. Its passage, promised during the march, gave the federal government stronger authority to enforce voting rights within state boundaries.

**Additional Information** A detailed history of the march, which focuses primarily on its legal and social implications, can be found in Charles E. Fager's *Selma 1965: The Town Where the South Was Changed* (1974).

*Leslie Stricker*

**See also** Civil Rights Movement; King, Martin Luther, Jr.; Southern Christian Leadership Conference (SCLC); Student Nonviolent Coordinating Committee (SNCC); Voting Rights Legislation.

---

# ■ March on Washington

**Date** August 28, 1963

*One of the most memorable demonstrations of the 1960's. It culminated with Martin Luther King, Jr.'s "I Have a Dream" speech.*

**Origins and History** A. Philip Randolph, the head of the Brotherhood of Sleeping Car Porters, first conceived of staging a massive March on Washington in 1941. Reforms enacted by President Franklin D. Roosevelt prompted Randolph to call off this march. In early 1963, Randolph revived the idea, calling for a march for jobs and freedom. Initially, President John F. Kennedy opposed the idea, fearing the march would turn violent. However, after Randolph and other civil rights leaders warned that if those dedicated to nonviolence were not allowed to lead the march, other, more militant activists would (a not-so-thinly veiled allusion to Malcolm X), they won Kennedy's blessing for the protest.

**The March** The March on Washington took place on a hot and humid August day. All the major civil rights organizations, the Southern Christian Leadership Conference (SCLC), National Association for the Advancement of Colored People (NAACP), Congress of Racial Equality (CORE), Student Nonviolent Coordinating Committee (SNCC), and National Urban League (NUL) and numerous liberal allies and entertainers headed the march. After gathering near the Washington Monument, more than two hundred thousand men and women, black and white, set out for the Lincoln Memorial, brandishing banners demanding voting rights, decent housing and jobs, and an end to segregation. At the Lincoln

*Crowds packed the Lincoln Memorial area during the 1963 March on Washington for jobs and freedom. The march, headed by all the major civil rights groups, culminated in Martin Luther King, Jr.'s famous "I Have a Dream" speech. (AP/Wide World Photos)*

Memorial, they listened to music performed by Mahalia Jackson and Joan Baez and speeches by clergymen, prominent liberals, and civil rights leaders. Among the most memorable speeches were those by Walter Reuther, the president of the United Automobile Workers union, and John Lewis, the chairman of SNCC. Although Lewis modified his address at the last minute to appease moderates, his speech still stood out for its stridency. King stirred both those assembled and those in radio and television audiences with his description of his "dream" that one day black children and white children would "walk together as sisters and brothers" and that the nation would "rise up and live out the true meaning of its creed." The march took place without any violence, much to the credit of Bayard Rustin, who attended to every detail, from the coordinating of speakers to feeding the hungry.

**Impact** The march won public support for the Civil Rights movement, worldwide admiration for King, and legitimized protest in the nation's capital. Although Malcolm X derided the event as the "farce" on Washington and conservatives proclaimed that communists had organized the demonstration, years later a broad array of Americans agreed that King's speech was a classic and that the march stood as one of the high points of the Civil Rights movement and the 1960's.

**Additional Information** The march and the Civil Rights movement are examined in Thomas Gentile's *March on Washington: August 28, 1963* (1983) and Juan Williams's *Eyes on the Prize: America's Civil Rights Years, 1954-1965* (1987).

*Peter B. Levy*

**See also** Baez, Joan; Civil Rights Movement; Congress of Racial Equality (CORE); "I Have a Dream" Speech; King, Martin Luther, Jr.; Malcolm X; National Association for the Advancement of Colored People (NAACP); Southern Christian Leadership Conference (SCLC); Student Nonviolent Coordinating Committee (SNCC).

# ■ Marijuana

*A preparation of the cannabis plant containing a psychoactive agent that produces euphoria. Marijuana, also called weed, pot, reefer, and grass, emerged as the drug of choice among young Americans during the development of a rebellious counterculture in the 1960's.*

The hemp plant, or *Cannabis sativa*, originated in Asia and contains tetrahydrocannabinol (THC), a hallucinogenic agent. The plant was first harvested for its fiber, which was made into rope and clothing. In 2737 B.C., emperor and pharmacologist Shen Nung recorded descriptions of the plant's medical

*Marijuana became the drug of choice for many young people during the 1960's. This ten-foot plant grew outside the home of a Pendleton, California, couple, who had no idea what the plant was until their visiting son told them. (AP/Wide World Photos)*

uses. Although the Chinese forbade use of cannabis for its intoxicating nature, the peoples of India, the Arab nations, Europe, and Africa were drawn to its mind-altering effects. Cannabis was used in the New World before Columbus arrived, but it did not gain popularity in the United States until the early 1920's, when it was brought across the border by Mexican laborers. During the 1930's, tales of crime and violence allegedly induced by smoking marijuana were widely publicized. A 1936 movie, *Reefer Madness*, which showed casual use leading to murder, rape, madness, and death, created panic among the public. Controversy surrounded marijuana's use as a social drug, and legislation in 1937 attempted to curb its popularity by making it illegal.

**Marijuana Use Spreads** Before the 1960's, marijuana use appeared to be deeply ingrained in certain segments of the population—Mexican farm laborers, African American jazz musicians, and some members of the Beat generation. However, the average, law-abiding American usually got "high," or intoxicated, through alcohol. In the 1960's, marijuana use spread to members of the hippie counterculture, antiwar protesters, and other young people.

Why so many young people began to use marijuana is unclear. Reasons cited include the baby boomers coming of age, the influence of television, and the breakdown of the family. Many researchers trace the spread of marijuana use to the student unrest associated with the birth of the Free Speech movement in Berkeley, California, in 1965. This unrest became joined with the growing dissatisfaction young people felt with U.S. policy in Vietnam and with American society in general. A generation of young people began to reject their parents and their values. They set out to create their own world, a counterculture delineated by symbols of rebellion such as long hair, rock music, and marijuana.

During the late 1960's, marijuana use spread outside the counterculture and antiwar movement. Marijuana was typically baked in brownies and ingested or rolled in cigarette papers and smoked, with users inhaling deeply and holding their breath as they passed the marijuana cigarette (or "joint") on to the next person in a small group. It came to be enjoyed by those people seeking an escape from reality or just the drug's relaxing euphoria as well as by those trying to make a statement. College students were enticed by its pleasurable effects.

**Marijuana and the Law** As the popularity of marijuana grew, efforts to legalize its use began. The first demonstrations urging the legalization of marijuana had been held by 1964. The law-reform movement gained momentum, and by 1966, chapters of LeMar (Legalize Marijuana) had been established in Cleveland, Ohio; Detroit, Michigan; and Berkeley. Controversy over the dangers and effects of marijuana escalated. One faction claimed that marijuana was an insidious "killer weed" that caused addiction, crime, violence, and raging sexual desires and therefore was a menace to life and health. The other end of the spectrum claimed that marijuana was not mentally or physically addicting, did not incite violent activity, and was a harmless social relaxant.

In 1968, Richard M. Nixon did not include drugs as an issue in his presidential campaign, but in 1970, he declared a much publicized war on marijuana and other drugs to fulfill his campaign promises for law and order. The crusade against drugs was fanned by political agendas that targeted marijuana as an apparent source of the moral and social deterioration in the United States.

**Impact** Marijuana was originally used by subcultures within minorities and restricted social circles as an expression of rebellious and subversive behavior; however, the 1960's marked the beginning of the drug's popularity with an entire generation. An inexpensive, readily available, euphoriant, marijuana became the trademark of a counterculture that rejected traditional standards, and its use gradually spread into other factions of society.

Marijuana, as a symbol of transformation, carried with it myths and misconceptions. Controversy over its effects confused the public and led to fear. Its association with activists, rebels, hippies, and the onset of the sexual revolution indicated a seeming degradation of social mores that was unacceptable and apparently unavoidable. It also became known as a gateway drug for its ability to lead to use of harder, more harmful drugs such as heroin. The use of marijuana also led to increasing use of illegal drugs among the youth of the United States. For these reasons, marijuana became the target of political, social, and legal action and the focal point for the United States' war on drugs.

**Subsequent Events** Widespread use and misconceptions about marijuana's effects initiated scientific inquiry. Research dispelled many of the myths surrounding marijuana use and sparked interest in the drug's medicinal uses. Although originally used in Asia to treat everything from beriberi to absentmindedness, marijuana's medical properties had been ignored for many centuries. Renewed interest, spurred by wide use of the drug in the 1960's, initiated research into marijuana as medicine. Some researchers found that marijuana may provide relief for patients suffering from glaucoma and asthma and for the nausea and vomiting of cancer chemotherapy, but the use of marijuana as a medicine is still controversial.

**Additional Information** An in-depth discussion on this topic can be found in *High in America: The True Story Behind NORML and the Politics of Marijuana* (1981), by Patrick Anderson, and Edward Bloomquist's *Marijuana: The Second Trip* (1971). Additional information is available in Peggy Mann's *Pot Safari: A Visit to the Top Marijuana Researchers in the U.S.* (1985).

*Carol J. Sample*

**See also** Counterculture; Drug Culture; LSD; People's Park, Berkeley.

# ■ Mariner Space Program

*One of the most important undertakings of the U.S. space program. The Mariner interplanetary probes examined the three nearest planets, Venus, Mercury, and Mars, revolutionizing scientific understanding of those worlds.*

During the late 1950's and 1960's, both the United States and the Soviet Union inaugurated programs to explore the Moon and other planets with automated spacecraft. The U.S. programs were called Ranger, Surveyor, Pioneer, and Mariner. The Jet Propulsion Laboratory (JPL) in Pasadena, California, which is jointly operated by the California Institute of Technology and the National Aeronautics and Space Administration (NASA), managed the Mariner space program. The Mariner spacecraft carried cameras and scientific instruments powered by solar panels to radio their findings back to Earth. Ten Mariner probes were launched on Atlas-Agena or Atlas-Centaur rockets. Two of these probes failed during launch, and another failed after reaching Earth orbit. Mariner 11 and Mariner 12 were renamed Voyager 1 and Voyager 2 and visited the outer planets during the 1970's and 1980's.

**Venus** The first Mariner spacecraft was launched on July 22, 1962, using an Atlas-Agena B rocket. Normally, a guidance signal from the ground directed the rocket's ascent; however, the signal failed, causing an onboard computer to take over. A programming mistake—an omitted hyphen—caused the rocket to veer to the left, toward shipping lanes and populated areas. A range safety officer was forced to detonate an explosive charge within the rocket, destroying it minutes after liftoff.

A second attempt on August 27, 1962, was successful, and Mariner 2 headed toward Venus, the planet nearest to Earth and almost the same size. Venus is covered with a thick layer of clouds that no telescope has ever pierced. Before the 1960's, some speculated that a tropical world or a searing desert lay beneath the clouds. On December 14, 1962, Mariner 2, the first successful interplanetary probe, flew by Venus. The probe determined that Venus possessed neither radiation belts nor a magnetic field. Four days after passing Venus, the electronics on Mariner 2 failed because of the heat of the Sun.

In 1967, the Soviets achieved their first success with interplanetary probes. The Soviets launched many more probes than the United States did but were plagued by persistent failures at launch or during the long journey to other planets. Soviet probes were mass-produced, and the Soviets attempted to maintain Earth-like conditions within their large spacecraft. U.S. spacecraft were produced individually, and each component was rigorously tested and designed to work in the vacuum of space. As the Soviet Venera 4 flew by Venus on October 18, 1967, it dropped a probe into the atmosphere. Higher-than-expected atmospheric pressures crushed the probe before it reached the planet's surface.

Mariner 5, launched June 14, 1967, arrived at Venus only a few days after the Soviet probe. Soviet and U.S. spacecraft often arrived at their destinations at about the same time because interplanetary probes had to be launched during a short window of time when Earth and the target planet were in the right positions. When Mariner 5 passed behind Venus, its radio signal passed through the planet's atmosphere. U.S. astronomers measured the strength of the returning signal to learn the density of the atmosphere. Venus has a surface atmospheric pressure one hundred times greater than that of Earth. The surface temperature was a scorching 800 degrees Fahrenheit. On Venus, carbon dioxide

clouds retain the sun's heat, creating a runaway greenhouse effect. Later Soviet Venera probes succeeded in reaching the surface of Venus and transmitting scientific readings, as well as a limited number of television pictures. Venera probes were also the first to orbit Venus in the 1970's.

**Mars** Early astronomers imagined that Mars might be covered with canals. Seasonal changes in surface color were thought to indicate the waxing and waning of vegetation. Mars also had white polar caps that changed in size as the seasons passed, just as the polar ice caps on Earth do. However, by the 1960's, astronomers had concluded that Mars was probably a barren planet, though the planet still captured the imaginations of astronomers and science-fiction fans. Scientists later determined that the northern polar cap is mostly water ice, and the southern polar cap is mostly carbon dioxide ice.

On November 5, 1964, Mariner 3, the first flyby mission to Mars, failed when the shroud protecting the probe during ascent did not eject from the probe. A backup probe, Mariner 4, was launched less than a month later on November 28 with a redesigned shroud. Mariner 4 flew by Mars on July 15, 1965, coming within 6,200 miles of the surface. A television camera took 21 pictures. The murky pictures transmitted to Earth revealed a cratered surface much like that of Earth's moon. By analyzing the strength of Mariner 4's radio signals as they passed through the Martian atmosphere, scientists determined the surface pressure of the atmosphere. Their analysis showed the atmosphere to be very thin, with a surface pressure equal to less than 1 percent of Earth's atmosphere at sea level. The atmosphere was discovered to be mostly carbon dioxide, with only a tiny amount of water vapor.

Mariner 6 and Mariner 7 (launched February 24 and March 27, 1969) passed by Mars on July 31, 1969, and August 5, 1969, respectively, coming as close to the planet's surface as 2,100 miles. Mariner 6 returned 75 pictures, and Mariner 7 returned 126 pictures. Even with these pictures, only one-tenth of the planet's surface had been photographed. The probes confirmed the atmosphere's low pressure and determined that Mars did not possess a magnetic field. A temperature reading of the southern polar cap revealed the temperature to be -190 degrees Fahrenheit. Though the surface of Mars was cold and cratered, scientists still hoped that Mars had once possessed a denser atmosphere and that life had thrived then.

**Impact** The Mariner space program, which continued into the 1970's, entirely remade scientific understanding of Venus, Mars, and later Mercury. Although the Mariner program helped advance study in astronomy and other sciences, the primary motivation for the program was the space race between the United States and the Soviet Union. The competitiveness that marked the space race in the early 1960's gradually gave way to cooperation between the superpowers' space scientists as relations between the two countries improved. In 1971, the United States and the Soviet Union agreed to share the information gained by the Mariner 9 and Mars 2 and 3 missions.

**Subsequent Events** In the 1970's, probes continued to investigate Mars and Venus, then flew by Mercury, the planet closest to the Sun. Mariner 8 and Mariner 9 were twice the mass of earlier probes and contained additional scientific instruments. On May 8, 1971, the second stage of an Atlas-Centaur failed to ignite during ascent, causing Mariner 8 to crash into the sea. Mariner 9, launched on May 30, 1971, entered orbit around Mars on November 13, 1971. However, a great dust storm obscured the surface of the planet, and ground controllers had to reprogram Mariner 9 to wait about a month until the storm cleared. Among the 7,239 pictures returned were some that showed what looked like ancient dry riverbeds and runoff channels. This indicated that free-flowing water must have existed on Mars in the past. Among the many discoveries was Valles Marineris, a great canyon that stretched a quarter of the way around the planet.

Shortly after Mariner 9 reached Mars, Soviet probes Mars 2 and Mars 3 arrived, dropping descent modules to examine the surface before going into orbit around the planet. Both descent modules failed, and the Soviet probes circled the planet, operating on automatic programs and taking useless pictures of the dust storm.

Mariner 10, launched November 3, 1973, flew by Venus on February 5, 1974, then went into orbit around the Sun, passing Mercury, the planet closest to the Sun, three times, on March 29, 1974, September 21, 1974, and March 16, 1975. Mariner 10 found that Mercury possessed a slight magnetic field and no atmosphere. The first flyby took the probe within

435 miles of the surface of the planet's dark side. The second flyby went past the sunlit side of the planet. The final encounter passed only 125 miles from the darkside. Pictures returned by the probe showed a surface covered with craters and ancient lava flows.

In 1976, two U.S. Viking orbiters reached Mars, and each released a lander. These landers returned pictures from the surface of the planet that revealed a red, rocky landscape. An onboard laboratory tested the Martian soil and failed to find traces of bacterial life. Spacecraft from the United States and the Soviet Union have continued to explore Venus and Mars. Two other programs, Pioneer and Voyager, explored the outer planets.

**Additional Information** *Journey into Space: The First Three Decades of Space Exploration* (1989), by Bruce Murray, a scientist at the Jet Propulsion Laboratory; *Exploring Space: Voyages in the Solar System and Beyond* (1990), by William E. Burrows; and *The Illustrated Encyclopedia of Space Technology: A Comprehensive History of Space Exploration* (1981), by Kenneth Gatland, provide a closer look at Mariner and other exploratory programs. Duncan Brewer's *Mercury and the Sun* (1992) takes a closer look at the planet Mercury, and William Sheehan's *The Planet Mars: A History of Observation and Discovery* (1996) focuses on Mars.

*Eric G. Swedin*

**See also** Science and Technology; Space Race.

---

# ■ Maris, Roger

**Born** September 10, 1934, Hibbing, Minnesota
**Died** December 14, 1985, Houston, Texas

*A baseball star best known for breaking Babe Ruth's single-season home run record. Maris was voted American League Most Valuable Player in 1960 and 1961.*

Roger Eugene Maris, who moved to North Dakota as a child, was good at many sports, including basketball, football, and baseball. In high school football, he excelled both offensively and defensively, and University of Oklahoma coach Bud Wilkinson recruited him for the school's team. Maris rejected the offer and instead in 1953 signed a contract to play professional baseball with the Cleveland Indians organization, for whom he made his major league debut in 1957.

In 1958, he was traded to the Kansas City Athletics; two seasons later, the Athletics traded him to the

New York Yankees. A slugging left-handed out-fielder, Maris won the first of his consecutive most valuable player awards in his first season with the Yankees, hitting thirty-nine home runs and driving in 112 runs for the league champions. In 1961, he far exceeded even these accomplishments, as he and teammate Mickey Mantle pursued Babe Ruth's 1927 record of sixty home runs in a single season. Mantle was injured and fell off the pace, finshing with fifty-four home runs; Maris, though, entered the final day of the season tied with Ruth. On October 1, 1961, Maris broke the record with a fourth-inning home run off Tracy Stallard of the Boston Red Sox.

The feat, however, became a point of controversy. Baseball commissioner Ford Frick ruled that a special note would be placed in the record book because Maris had set the record in 162 games, whereas Ruth had set his record in only 154 games. Maris played five more seasons with the Yankees and two with the St. Louis Cardinals before retiring from baseball following the 1969 season.

In the 1970's, Maris often visited former teammates at preseason games, participated in Old Timers games, and owned a business in Florida. After Maris was diagnosed with cancer in 1984, the New York Yankees honored him with a special day. On July 21, 1984, Maris was presented with a plaque in recognition of his baseball accomplishments.

**Additional Information**  In 1986, sportswriter Maury Allen wrote a book entitled *Roger Maris: A Man for All Seasons*, which describes Maris's life and career.

*Joseph R. Paretta*

**See also**  Baseball; Koufax, Sandy; Mantle, Mickey; Mays, Willie; Sports.

---

# ■ Marriage

*A basic, age-old institution that came under assault in the 1960's. The decade's various movements set in motion changes that weakened the male-dominated and role-bound model of marriage but enabled couples to chose their own marital lifestyle.*

Most human societies have at least one form of marriage, a recognized bond for producing and bringing up children and securing social cohesion through family ties. In the United States, marriage is typically a monogamous and voluntary union of two individuals. Other expectations may vary with social class, ethnicity, and individual couples. In the 1950's, television and the consumer economy promoted a traditional model of marriage: a breadwinner husband as "head of household" and a homemaker wife. Not long after marriage, the couple would start a family, having two or more children.

As the 1960's opened, this traditional model, at least as an ideal, was largely unchallenged. Suburban growth and widespread prosperity made it possible for many people to follow this model, and the backyard barbecue party replaced the vine-covered cottage as a symbol of marital bliss. On the national scene, newly elected president John F. Kennedy and his wife, Jacqueline Bouvier Kennedy, exemplified this modern, glamorous ideal of marriage and family: a powerful, achieving man married to a gracious woman whose dedication to her husband's career and their children had superseded her desire for a career.

**Trouble in Paradise**  Beneath the idyllic surface, however, stress lines were forming. Seemingly unrelated events subtly, but effectively, cast doubt on this one-size-fits-all ideal. Books such as Vance Packard's *The Hidden Persuaders* (1957) had already shown how advertisers equated "wife" with "nonstop consumer." Although the salaries and job outlook for college-educated men were still promising, their average income began to drop in the early 1960's relative to that of blue-collar workers, and periodic job shortages developed in some fields such as engineering. As if recognizing these almost hidden facts, university guidance counselors urged women students—the likely future spouses of such men—to aspire to their own professional careers. The Presidential Commission on the Status of Women (1961) issued its report before the publication of the explosive book *The Feminine Mystique* (1963), by Betty Friedan, but both documented that a typical woman's position was one of an unequal partner in the economy and in marriage.

The human potential movement founded by psychologists such as Carl Rogers and Dorothy Jongeward, who along with Muriel James wrote *Born to Win: Transactional Analysis with Gestalt Experiments* (1971), gained popularity in the 1960's. It defined creativity, self-knowledge, and continued growth as markers of healthy adulthood. For some women, these values directly clashed with those of adjustment and self-sacrifice that they had used to justify their unhappy marriages or their lack of a career.

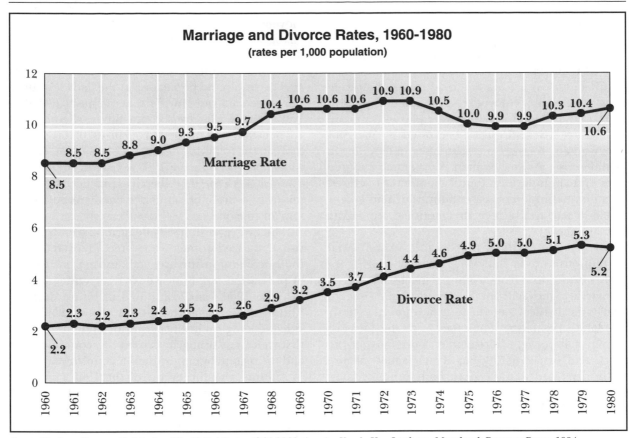

### Marriage and Divorce Rates, 1960-1980
#### (rates per 1,000 population)

Marriage Rate

Divorce Rate

*Source:* Kurian, George, *Datapedia of the United States, 1790-2000, America Year by Year.* Lanham, Maryland: Bernam Press, 1994.

At the same time, young Americans' exposure to other cultures as Peace Corps volunteers or foreign exchange students helped them—and also their elders—recognize that marriage could take different forms.

**Sex and Marriage** The rigid—if often hypocritical—sexual rules and taboos thought to uphold the sanctity of marriage suffered a long series of attacks during the 1960's. The birth control pill, first made available in 1960, had a major impact. Although fairly reliable contraceptives already existed, the pill was easy to use and entirely under the woman's control. It gave married women the ability to plan and space their childbearing without having to depend on their husbands' cooperation. For unmarried women, the pill cut the risks of premarital sex enormously. The advent of the pill did not result in a sudden change in behavior (statistics show no sudden increase in premarital sex) but did make unmarried women more willing to admit to previously taboo sexual experiences.

Literature and science both challenged the prevailing wisdom about women's and marital sexuality. The first unpurgated edition of D. H. Lawrence's *Lady Chatterley's Lover* (privately published in 1928) was published in the United States in 1959. The novel dealt explicitly with a woman's sexual desires and responses. Similar themes were treated in many 1960's novels. Significantly, married sex lost its protected status within fiction; according to Elizabeth Benedict in *The Joy of Writing Sex* (1996), unambiguous scenes from the marital bedroom were not published until the 1960's. In 1966, the study *Human Sexual Response* by William H. Masters and Virginia E. Johnson destroyed the myths of incurable frigidity and the vaginal orgasm.

**Discontented Spouses** All these developments put enormous stresses on many marriages. From a wife's perspective, it was easy to feel that she had been "sold a bill of goods"—if not about marriage as an institution, at least in entering her own imperfect marriage.

However, the culture of the 1960's also contained many elements that spurred husbands' discontent with marriage. The first wave of adult baby boomers (born 1946-1964) created several well-publicized youth cultures, among them a group of upscale single men who enjoyed fast cars and expensive stereos and the hippies, who were part of the counterculture. These lifestyles beckoned to many an overworked, fortyish married man undergoing a midlife crisis. As the Vietnam War became a source of moral anguish, men found themselves confused by a new definition of masculinity, which no longer equated warfare, bluster, or emotional impassivity with manhood.

By the latter half of the decade, several social revolutions were in full swing, each challenging society's institutions from a new perspective. Criticism of marriage moved from the specific to the general, and radical voices called the institution hopelessly outdated. Feminists denounced it as the locus of patriarchal power, where women bore most of the work and responsibility but men claimed all the authority. Many young people, both within and outside the counterculture, judged their own parents' union to be hollow and marriage itself to be an obstacle to intimacy. The sexual revolution dared to question verities such as the need for monogamy. As the Civil Rights movement showed that limiting rights and privileges by race was wrong, rights and privileges based on gender or marital status also became suspect.

New remedies for these ills abounded. Divorce, while not new, came to be viewed as a logical and even creative outcome of marital problems rather than a slightly disreputable solution for extreme cases. Cohabitation—living together without marriage, formerly largely limited to bohemian and other fringe groups—became thinkable to average middle-class Americans. Experiments such as open marriage (in which spouses are free to have other relationships outside the marriage), swinging (consensual sexual sharing with other couples), and group marriage were touted as ways to revitalize stale marriages. Those seeking a wider and deeper web of relationships founded or joined communes.

**Impact** All in all, the 1960's were a hard time for marriages. Probably only elderly couples in long-established unions avoided experiencing new stresses and reevaluations. However, the various movements and changes resulted in more dramatic changes in thought patterns than in behavior. Americans did not stop getting married; in fact, the marriage rate continued to climb, reaching a high of 10.6 per thousand population at the decade's end, a rate exceeded only in the years immediately after World War II. The divorce rate did rise slightly, from 2.2 per thousand in 1960 to 3.5 in 1970; it rose even more in the following decades. Cohabitation was not widely practiced in the 1960's. Late in the decade, *The New York Times* described it as practiced by a "tiny minority"—probably an understatement but not an implausible one.

The two certain, steady behavioral trends were a rise in married women who were employed outside the home and in the acceptability and occurrence of premarital sex. Both trends were under way before the 1960's and continued in future decades. Although the social revolutions of the 1960's provided ideological justifications for these trends, the first trend was primarily caused by economic shifts and the second by cultural and technological forces.

Another way the events of the 1960's changed marriage was through the law. The Equal Pay Act of 1963 and the Civil Rights Act of 1964 prescribed gender equality in the public sphere, altering the power balance in many marriages. In addition, Supreme Court rulings struck down long-accepted provisions of domestic law. For example, *Loving v. Virginia* (1967) voided all state laws against racially mixed marriages, and *Levy v. Louisiana* (1968) abolished legal disadvantages for children born out of wedlock.

The birth control pill and antidiscrimination laws gave women a more equal playing field on which to make their life and career decisions. For many American couples, the new ideal became marriage as a partnership entered into by equals rather than as a role-bound institution.

**Subsequent Events** Sexual and lifestyle innovations from the 1960's lasted into the 1970's, although many ultimately disappeared or became less prominent. Of the alternatives to traditional marriage that author Edgar W. Butler examines in *Traditional Marriage and Emerging Alternatives* (1979), only singlehood, cohabitation, and homosexuality proved to have staying power beyond the 1970's. Swinging, group marriage, communes, and open marriage as lifestyles have retreated to the social margins. However, nonsexual open marriage, in which spouses forgo total togetherness and instead share their hobbies and recreational interests with like-minded third parties, is widely practiced.

**Additional Information**   Steven Mintz and Susan Kellogg's *Domestic Revolutions* (1988) and Elaine Tyler May's *Homeward Bound: American Families in the Cold War Era* (1988) examine marriage in the 1960's insightfully if briefly. Stephanie Coontz's *The Way We Really Are* (1997) traces connections between economic and historical events and marital behavior with unparalleled acuity. *Statistical Handbook on the American Family* (1992), by Bruce Chadwick and Tim Heaton, provides statistical data.

*Emily Alward*

**See also**   Birth Control; Civil Rights Act of 1964; Communes; Equal Pay Act of 1964; *Feminine Mystique, The*; Friedan, Betty; *Human Sexual Response*; Interracial Marriage Laws; Pill, The; Pop Psychology; Sexual Revolution; Women in the Workforce; Women's Identity.

# ■ Marshall, Thurgood

**Born** July 2, 1908, Baltimore, Maryland
**Died** January 24, 1993, Bethesda, Maryland

*One of the prime legal movers in the struggle for civil rights in the United States. After years of trying cases for the National Association for the Advancement of Colored People (NAACP), Marshall became the first African American to serve on the United States Supreme Court.*

**Early Life**   The son of a club steward and a schoolteacher, Thurgood Marshall was named for his grandfather, a freed slave. After he was graduated first in his class at Howard University Law School, Marshall briefly practiced law privately before joining Charles Houston as special counsel to the National Association for the Advancement of Colored People (NAACP). Together, the two pursued a strategy of convincing the federal courts that separate but equal educational facilities were inherently unconstitutional, winning *Missouri ex rel. Gaines v. Canada* in the U.S. Supreme Court in 1938. It was the

*Thurgood Marshall became the first African American to serve on the U.S. Supreme Court in 1967.* (Sam Falk/New York Times Company/Archive Photos)

first of twenty-nine Supreme Court victories (out of thirty-two cases) for Marshall, who would also argue the seminal case of *Brown v. Board of Education of Topeka, Kansas* (1954) before the Court, finally winning an official declaration that "separate but equal" was no longer the law of the land.

**The 1960's** In 1961, President John F. Kennedy nominated Marshall to serve on the Second Circuit Court of Appeals. The confirmation battle was prolonged, and Marshall had already been on the bench for eleven months before he was officially confirmed. During the four years he served as a federal appellate judge, he accumulated a stellar record, with none of the ninety-eight opinions he delivered for the court majority subsequently overturned by the Supreme Court. In 1965, Kennedy named Marshall the first African American solicitor general, and Marshall won fourteen of the nineteen cases he argued for the government before the Supreme Court.

Finally, in 1967, President Lyndon B. Johnson decided to name an African American to sit on the nation's highest court, and Marshall was the obvious choice. Despite his distinguished career, Marshall was once again subjected to racially motivated attacks, but after a nearly four-month confirmation battle, on October 2, 1967, he finally joined the Supreme Court headed by Chief Justice Earl Warren. Marshall immediately joined the liberal voting bloc headed by Warren, who would lead the Court for only two more years. Although Marshall would remain on the Court for almost twenty-four years, the most significant opinion he ever wrote for the majority was *Benton v. Maryland* (1969), a decision handed down during the final term of the Warren Court. *Benton v. Maryland* extended protections against double jeopardy to state criminal defendants and was an important element of the "due process revolution" that made the guarantees of the Bill of Rights applicable at the state as well as the federal level. It was a decision that clearly reflected Marshall's own liberal orientation and grounding in civil rights.

**Later Life** When Warren was succeeded by Chief Justice Warren Burger, and Burger by William Rehnquist, the Supreme Court became increasingly conservative. No longer in the majority, Marshall sided most often with another holdover from the Warren years, Justice William Brennan, particularly in death penalty cases, in which the two invariably voted against the imposition of capital punishment.

Marshall hoped to remain on the Court long enough to have his successor appointed by a Democratic (and presumably more liberal) president. Failing health, however, forced him to retire in June, 1991, while President George Bush was still in office. Marshall continued, however, to serve occasionally on federal appellate courts until his death in January, 1993.

**Impact** Although the Reverend Martin Luther King, Jr., was the moving spirit behind the nonviolent struggle for civil rights in the 1960's, Marshall's contribution to the liberation of African Americans cannot be overstated. As the director of the NAACP Legal Defense and Education Fund and the architect of the winning strategy in *Brown v. Board of Education*, Marshall was the individual most responsible for enlisting the crucial support of the federal courts in enforcing the dictates of a nation founded in the belief that all persons are created equal.

**Subsequent Events** In July, 1991, Bush appointed Clarence Thomas to replace Marshall. After a stormy confirmation process, the highly conservative Thomas eventually became the second African American Supreme Court justice in U.S. history.

**Additional Information** Marshall's life is covered in Carl T. Rowan's *Dream Makers, Dream Breakers: The World of Justice Thurgood Marshall* (1993), and Michael D. Davis and Hunter R. Clark's *Thurgood Marshall: Warrior at the Bar, Rebel on the Bench* (1992).

*Lisa Paddock*

**See also** Burger, Warren; Civil Rights Movement; National Association for the Advancement of Colored People (NAACP); Supreme Court Decisions.

# ■ Max, Peter

**Born** October 19, 1937, Berlin, Germany

*An artist whose works represented an unusual blending of cultural symbolism. Max used an intense, vivid color palette to create bold, expressive, improvisational, cosmic landscapes in the 1960's.*

**Early Life** Peter Max was born in Germany and raised in Shanghai, Israel, Tibet, and France. His multicultural background imparts a rich, artistic character to his work, in which influences as diverse as popular comic books, European expressionism, classical Western art, American jazz, and the ancient, traditional culture of China are evident. As a young artist, Max worked to refine his skills as a realistic painter.

**The 1960's**  In the early 1960's, Max and a partner opened a graphic arts studio, but after a few years, he decided to cut back on his work to study Eastern religions. Max was affected by the social, cultural, and technological changes that were taking place, and in 1967, he burst upon the art scene with his brilliantly colored cosmic imagery—stars, flowers, unusual lettering—that would become known as "Max style" and spread across the United States and the world. During the late 1960's, his celestial images and graphics adorned mass-produced items such as posters, book jackets, and record covers, including the cover for the Beatles' *Yellow Submarine* album. Max has been credited with capturing the sensibility of a generation with his psychedelic designs. His innovative, artistic expressions celebrate the American experience and revel in popular American iconography.

**Later Life**  As a passionate environmentalist and defender of human and animal rights, Max has often directed his artistic energy toward noteworthy causes. In 1992, he created the official postage stamps commemorating the first Environmental Summit held in Rio de Janeiro, Brazil, and in 1995, he was named official artist for Earth Day. He has created numerous works celebrating freedom and democracy, including his famous Statue of Liberty paintings and series of U.S. flags.

**Impact**  Max, whose mass-produced posters sold in the millions in the 1960's, is widely recognized as one of the most important visual pioneers and innovators of the twentieth century. The artist's colorful imagery, which combines cultural icons with a vivid and colorful palette, has reached millions globally and exerted a sweeping influence in the world of art. His works are in the permanent collection of many museums, including the Museum of Modern Art in New York.

**Additional Information**  More on the artist and his works in the 1960's can be found in *The Peter Max Poster Book* (1970) and *The Peter Max Superposter Book* (1971), both by Peter Max.

*Patricia Jessup-Woodlin*

**See also**  Art Movements; Pop Art.

*Peter Max, pictured in his home in 1968, used brilliantly colored stars, flowers, and lettering to create graphics that adorned posters, book jackets, and record covers. (Santi Visalli Inc./Archive Photos)*

## ■ Mays, Willie

**Born** May 6, 1931, Westfield, Alabama

*One of the greatest baseball players of all time and an American icon. Mays was the first African American team captain in the major leagues.*

Willie Howard Mays, Jr., played his first professional baseball game at the age of seventeen with the Birmingham Black Barons team of the Negro National League. In 1950, he signed a contract with the National League (NL) New York Giants organization. After he performed impressively at two minor league stops, the Giants brought the twenty-year-old Mays to the major leagues in the middle of the 1951 season. He helped spark the club to a dramatic pennant victory and was named the NL's rookie of the year. He was drafted the following year and spent most of the 1952 and 1953 seasons in the U.S. Army,

*Willie Mays of the San Francisco Giants possessed a wide range of skills that enabled him to be a great all-around player.* (Sporting News/Archive Photos)

but he returned after his discharge in 1954 to lead the Giants to another pennant and a World Series championship. That year, he also won the NL batting title and was named the league's most valuable player.

A fast, graceful, and powerful center fielder, Mays earned recognition as the classic "complete" baseball player, one who could do everything well. He hit for high averages with great home-run power, he was a fast and aggressive base runner, and he was perhaps the best defensive outfielder in the game's history. In the 1954 World Series, he made a spectacular running catch that is often cited as the best ever. His popularity was further enhanced by the evident enthusiasm with which he played.

In 1958, the Giants moved to San Francisco. Although Mays later recalled that he was never as comfortable playing there as he had been in New York, he remained one of the game's greatest stars. In 1962, he led the Giants to another pennant, and in 1964 he was named the major leagues' first African American team captain. In 1965, he hit a career-high fifty-two home runs and won his second most valuable player award.

In 1972, Mays returned to New York when the Giants traded him to the Mets in mid-season. He retired after the 1973 season and was inducted into the Baseball Hall of Fame in 1979.

**Impact** Mays's 660 career home runs placed him third on the all-time list, behind Babe Ruth and Hank Aaron. In addition to his two most valuable player awards and rookie of the year award, he won twelve Gold Gloves for fielding excellence and played in a record twenty-four All-Star Games. His diverse skills and consistent long-term excellence have led many experts to rate him as the greatest all-around player in the game's history.

**Subsequent Events** After retiring, Mays worked in public relations for the Mets. Later, he became a special coach for the Giants.

**Additional Information** Mays and Lou Sahadi's *Say Hey: The Autobiography of Willie Mays* (1989) relates Mays's many accomplishments in addition to numerous events from his childhood and adolescence.

*Jennifer Raye James*

**See also** Baseball; DiMaggio, Joe; Koufax, Sandy; Mantle, Mickey; Maris, Roger.

## ■ Media

*A crucial, formative era in the history of American media. Television moved to the forefront of U.S. politics and popular culture and helped to shape the events and public memory of the 1960's.*

The world of communications media—newspapers, popular magazines, books, radio, television, and, eventually, the Internet—was enormously transformed in the years between World War II and the end of the twentieth century. Typically, more than 80 percent of all newspapers were independently owned in 1945, a proportion that was more than reversed fifty years later when more than 80 percent of all newspapers were owned by corporate chains or conglomerates. Reflecting its enormous commercial potential and the political clout of communications corporations, television was introduced to the American public in 1946 and rapidly became an advertising-supported medium. Television made significant inroads into the popularity of entertainment radio during the 1950's. Suburban family life was idealized through popular situation comedies such as *Father Knows Best* (1954-1963), *The Adventures of Ozzie and Harriet* (1952-1966), *Leave It to Beaver* (1957-1963), and *The Donna Reed Show* (1958-1966). In public memory, these shows came to epitomize the innocent and sanitized United States of the 1950's. During this time, television came into its own as a potent vehicle for spreading the ideology of mass consumption.

**A Unifying Power** Riveting images and moments in the Civil Rights movement were crucial catalysts in forming a national consciousness for racial justice and ultimately producing the Civil Rights Act of 1964 and Voting Rights Act of 1965. The sight of police dogs and fire hoses being used against civil rights protesters in Birmingham, Alabama, and the brutal attack on the Selma, Alabama, march of 1965 were pictures that the nation could not ignore. Images of brutality against nonviolent protesters appeared in newspapers worldwide, and the Birmingham direct action was called a "masterpiece in the use of media" to get a point across. News coverage of the attack on Selma marchers broke into television's airing of *Judgment at Nuremberg* (a television drama about Nazi war crimes), helping to draw hundreds of additional volunteers to subsequent efforts in Selma.

Similarly, the personable magnetism of John F. Kennedy —the first television president—helped spawn a personal attachment to Kennedy and his rhetoric on the part of many young people. Kennedy's media success also proved a catalyst for image manipulation in later political campaigns. Perhaps more than any other event in the decade, the Kennedy assassination revealed the full universalizing potential of a televisual media culture, as a stunned nation grieved in front of its television sets.

**A Divisive Force** However, as the decade progressed and the Vietnam War became increasingly visible through media coverage, the unifying effect of early-1960's events faded from view. The United States became increasingly polarized by the war, and the media accentuated the polarization.

For virtually the entire span of United States involvement in Vietnam, the national media echoed the official government rationale of defending the nation of South Vietnam against aggression from North Vietnam in framing news stories. Before 1967-1968, by which time elite opinion was sharply divided, the news media largely conveyed official pronouncements on the war's progress to the American public, tempered by reports that challenged official

optimism. From 1967, especially after the sweeping Tet Offensive was viewed by American audiences, the media became increasingly critical of the war as a failed policy. After the atrocity at My Lai came to light in 1969 (after a year of media silence), the news media became more attentive to the horrific side of the war. By war's end, the media had become part of the controversy swirling around the war, particularly as war architects sought to blame the failed war on external forces.

In contrast to civil rights coverage, the news media reports on antiwar protests had a more contradictory impact on efforts to bring the war to an end. On one hand, antiwar demonstrations attracted media attention, thus giving the movement visibility; on the other, the media tended to systematically undercount protest numbers, to attempt to balance reports of antiwar activists by covering counterprotesters even if their numbers were minuscule, and to frame antiwar rallies with the viewpoint of political officialdom. More problematic for antiwar organizers, media coverage also tended to attract and magnify the more sensational, sometimes violent spinoffs of large rallies; in several cases, coverage of violence by a handful of street militants obscured the significance and message of huge numbers of people peacefully gathering to oppose the war. In effect, the acts of the antiwar activists became the news focus, supplanting the antiwar movement's substantive arguments about the war.

**Covering Culture** Hence, by late in the decade, a politics of statement came to dominate public discourse about the war. A similar tendency became readily apparent in the media's coverage of the spreading counterculture of the late 1960's. Attracted by the more bizarre styles and visual images of areas such as San Francisco's Haight-Ashbury, media coverage of much-hyped events, including the Summer of Love, drew hundreds of thousands of younger adolescents into a culture of drug use, uninhibited sexual relations, and rock music—in the process, driving out much of the original bohemian culture of these locales. Simultaneously, and for the same market reasons, advertisers discovered the economic potential of this new "youth culture" and began to sell "rebellion" and "revolution" through consumer goods that appealed to the young. By decade's end, the media culture was littered with images of a nation coming apart through excess; meanwhile, 1960's activists began to gravitate quietly toward more personal and local issues of gender relations and ecology, occasionally rallying against the latest revelation of horror in Vietnam.

Even television studios reflected the anything-goes dynamic of mass media in the 1960's. Shows such as *The Smothers Brothers Comedy Hour* (1967-1969), *Rowan and Martin's Laugh-In* (1968-1973), and *The Dick Cavett Show* (1968-1972) picked up on the zaniness of the times—at least for a while.

**Impact** Overall, the mass media tended to portray events from a market-driven, national perspective, thereby constructing an increasingly national media culture. From this vantage point, dramatic political events and images that were compatible with market imperatives and consensual political ideology, such as civil rights in the South, tended to be given sympathetic coverage. Events and images that challenged consensual political ideology, such as antiwar mobilization, tended to be covered in ways that were, in effect, unsympathetic, thanks in part to the behavior of some young rebels. By decade's end, the media, particularly television, seemed a constrained forum for sorting out the inconsistencies and horrors of the war. The new national media of communications appeared to be inadequate to the task of democratic public discourse.

**Subsequent Events** The mass media of the 1960's left behind a provocative collage of powerful imagery and social turbulence. It remained to opinion makers of all stripes, but particularly those backed by ample resources, to try to explain the meaning of the decade. For the most part, television continued to be propelled by commercial imperatives. As social turbulence continued in the early 1970's, popular television shows, notably *All in the Family* (1971-1983), *M\*A\*S\*H* (1972-1983), *The Mary Tyler Moore Show* (1970-1977), and *The Mod Squad* (1968-1973), capitalized on 1960's disenchantment to portray, and make safe, a range of controversial issues that had been tearing the nation apart. Television in the 1970's has been described as a "contested terrain," yet media retrospectives of 1960's events, along with advertising and Hollywood films, began to strip 1960's phenomena of their political context and meaning. The groundwork was being laid for a period of political and ideological retrenchment in the 1980's.

**Additional Information** For an account of the political economy of television's evolution, see Douglas Kellner's *Television and the Crisis of Democracy* (1990) and Todd Gitlin's *Inside Prime Time* (1985). On Vietnam and the media, see Daniel C. Hallin's *The Uncensored War: The Media and Vietnam* (1986), Todd Gitlin's *The Whole World's Watching* (1980), and Melvin Small's *Covering Dissent: The Media and the Anti-Vietnam War Movement* (1994). On the commercial discovery of "hip," see Thomas Frank's *The Conquest of Cool: Business Culture, Counterculture, and the Rise of Hip Consumerism* (1997).

*Edward P. Morgan*

**See also** Communications; *Smothers Brothers Comedy Hour, The*; Television; *Tonight Show, The*; Underground Newspapers.

# ■ Medicare

*A federally funded program that guaranteed health insurance coverage for Americans age sixty-five and older. Medicare and Medicaid, a similar entitlement program designed to provide health insurance to the needy, were established through amendments to the Social Security Act of 1935.*

The necessity and feasibility of a national health care program, first proposed by President Harry S Truman in 1945, were the subject of heated political debate for two decades. Surveys from 1943 until the early 1960's revealed that a consistent two-thirds of Americans favored some form of federal financing of health care. Additional support for government-funded health care came from liberal politicians and consumer and senior-citizen groups. A health insurance plan proposed by congressmen Cecil King and Clinton Anderson in 1961 met stiff opposition from the American Medical Association, which feared losing control over health care and labeled Medicare as impersonal "socialized medicine" in a nationwide campaign. The plan also sparked opposition from insurance companies, which viewed it as competition for private insurance plans. The legislation was tabled.

In 1963, a government survey revealed that only about 50 percent of elderly people in the United States had health insurance of any kind, although more than 75 percent of those under age sixty-five had some form of health insurance. Many older Americans could not afford private coverage, and many of those who attempted to obtain coverage were denied on the basis of age or preexisting conditions. This survey helped renew interest in health care legislation. In 1965, President Lyndon B. Johnson reintroduced Medicare legislation as part of his Great Society programs. The program was to be funded by an increase in the Social Security tax, which drew opposition from political conservatives.

On July 30, 1965, Johnson signed into law the amendments to the Social Security Act of 1935 that established Medicare and Medicaid. Medicare, formally enacted as Title XVIII of the 1965 Social Security Amendments, went into effect July 1, 1966, and authorized compulsory health insurance for American citizens age sixty-five and older who were entitled to receive Social Security or Railroad Retirement benefits (approximately nineteen million people). Medicaid was established by Title XIX of the 1965 amendments, Grants to States for Medical Assistance Programs, as a means-tested entitlement program to provide medical assistance to low-income individuals who were aged, blind, disabled, or pregnant; to members of families with dependent children; and to other groups of needy children.

Medicare's basic benefits package consists of Part A (hospital insurance) and Part B (supplemental medical insurance). Part A is an earned benefit for most Americans and requires no premium upon eligibility, but Part B is voluntary and requires a monthly premium. Part A covers inpatient hospital care for the first sixty days less a deductible, inpatient psychiatric care, nursing care or rehabilitation after hospitalization, home health care prescribed by a physician, and hospice care for the terminally ill. Part B pays about 80 percent of physician and out-

*On July 30, 1965, President Lyndon Johnson signed legislation establishing the Medicare and Medicaid health care programs. Seated next to Johnson is former president Harry S. Truman, and Lady Bird Johnson and Hubert Humphrey and his wife, Bess, stand behind the president.* (AP/Wide World Photos)

patient services after a deductible is met. Prescription drugs (except those received during a hospital stay), hearing aids, eyeglasses, and long-term nursing home care are not covered.

The Medicaid program increased federal grants to the states and called for additional care for children in low-income families. States were required to provide medical assistance to those on welfare. The program also set limits on the amount that physicians and medical facilities were reimbursed for various services. By 1968, forty-eight states had Medicaid programs.

**Impact** The passage of Medicare and Medicaid marked the beginning of numerous major changes in the health care industry. The federal government became involved in areas such as establishing suitable fees for health care, a process that had been based entirely on a private discussion between the physician and patient, and the training of physicians and other health care professionals. The insurance industry expanded in an attempt to be competitive with the federal government, and insurance, which had covered only in-hospital care, came to cover inpatient care in subacute facilities such as nursing homes.

Historians rate Medicare and Medicaid as being among the most successful of President Johnson's Great Society programs in that they did help enable the elderly and poor to obtain medical care. However, Medicare and Medicaid did not cover medical care for some low-income patients or address certain needs such as outpatient prescription drugs, and some physicians and health care facilities refused to treat Medicaid patients because of the limits placed on fees. In addition, by the late 1960's, these programs had become substantially more expensive than originally anticipated and reports of fraud and abuse had begun to emerge.

**Subsequent Events** Amendments to the Social Security Act in 1972 were the first major attempts to limit expenditures. These amendments included cost containment measures such as patient cost sharing and eliminating the goal of comprehensive health care coverage for individuals with low incomes. These same amendments, however, extended coverage to most beneficiaries of the Supplemental Security Income program. In 1984, Congress created amendments to Medicaid that required individual states to cover all infants and pregnant

women below poverty level with their eligibility determined by an index based upon income level and family size.

The Medicare Catastrophic Coverage Act of 1988 attempted to require Medicare beneficiaries to pay the full cost of expanded benefits through an income-related tax surcharge and a flat premium. Elderly citizens organized groups in intense opposition to premium funding, leading to repeal of the act one year later.

In 1997, the Department of Health and Human Services issued a report on its audit of the Health Care Financing Administration, concluding that during fiscal year 1996, net Medicare overpayments totaled about $23.2 billion (about 14 percent of the $168.6 billion in processed Medicare fee-for-service payments). Objectives of this study were to determine if Medicare payments were furnished by certified providers to eligible beneficiaries, reimbursed by Medicare contractors in accordance with the program's laws and regulations, and for medically necessary procedures that were accurately coded and sufficiently documented. This landmark report concluded that Medicare is "inherently vulnerable" to incorrect provider billing practices, and that improper payments were caused by anything from inadvertent mistakes to outright fraud and abuse.

**Additional Information** The often-referenced historical text, *Medicare* (1970), by Robert J. Myers, contains chapters on legislative proposals between 1935 and 1965, the 1965 enactment of Medicare and Medicaid, and subsequent developments such as the problems involved in actuarial cost estimates for health benefits.

*Daniel G. Graetzer*

**See also** Aid to Families with Dependent Children (AFDC); Great Society Programs; Inflation; Medicine; Unemployment.

---

# ■ Medicine

*The 1960's was a time of tremendous research and clinical breakthroughs in pharmaceutical and surgical therapies and practice. This medical progress was possible because of the concurrent rapid advancements seen in several related fields of science and technology.*

Medical research and practice in the 1960's were strongly influenced by two monumental discoveries in the previous decade. The 1953 description of the structure of deoxyribonucleic acid (DNA) by American biochemist and geneticist James Dewey Watson and British biophysicist Francis Harry Compton Crick led to their 1962 Nobel Prize and initiated several lines of research during the 1960's into the genetic causes of many common diseases and the development of new treatments based on the body's response to harmful agents. The 1956 report of the first successful trials of a birth control pill (developed at the urging of social activist Margaret Sanger) by American experimental biologist Gregory Pincus helped usher in the sexual revolution of the 1960's.

**Surgery**  The tremendous surgical breakthroughs of the 1960's were possible only because of the concurrent rapid strides in related fields of science and technology. Surgical firsts in the decade included the creation in 1960 of a fully implantable pacemaker for heart block by William M. Chardack and a shielded ball-valve prosthesis for mitral heart valve replacement by Albert Starr and M. Lowell Edwards. Other heart-related developments included coronary arteriography by Frank Mason Sones and Earl K. Shirley in 1962 and percutaneous transluminal coronary arteriography by C. T. Dotter and M. P. Judkins in 1964, both of which provided ways for physicians to visualize arteries using X rays. In 1963, Thomas J. Fogarty and coworkers were responsible for the balloon catheter embolectomy (the removal of an abnormal particle circulating in the blood). The first human heart transplant was performed in 1967 by South African surgeon Christiaan Barnard, with the patient surviving for eighteen days after surgery, and the first coronary artery autograft bypass was performed by R. G. Favaloro in 1968.

Other major developments in surgery include the total hip joint replacement known as the Charnley arthroplasty by John Charnley in 1961, liver transplantation between humans by Thomas Earl Starzl in 1963, reattachment of a completely severed human limb by Ronald A. Malt and Charles Freemont McKhann in 1964, and Canadian (also called Shouldice) repair for inguinal (groin-area) hernia by Edwin W. Shearburn and Richard N. Myers in 1969. Other significant progress in medical research included the experimental transmission of leprosy to animals by Charles Carter Shepard in 1960, immunoglobulin molecule sequencing by Gerald Maurice Edelman in 1969, and the first in vitro fertilization of human oocytes in 1969 by Robert Geoffrey Edwards, B. D. Bavister, and Patrick Christopher Steptoe.

**Treatments, Tests, and Vaccines**  Pharmaceutical breakthroughs were highlighted by the development of an inexpensive, safe, and reliable contraceptive pill that contained a combination of estrogens and progestogens that suppressed ovulation without interfering with menstruation. In 1964, British pharmacologist James Whyte Black used his discovery of beta-blockers to produce the heart drug propranolol, which prevented hormones from triggering undesirable reactions.

The early 1960's saw the opening of the Salk Institute for Biological Studies in California, radioimmunoassay of the hormone insulin by Rosalyn Sussman Yallow, and significant improvements in hemodialysis (the process of removing blood from an artery, purifying it by dialysis, and returning it to a vein) by indwelling Teflon-Silastic arteriovenous shunts. The mid-1960's saw the first use of amniocentesis for in utero diagnosis of genetic disorders and Nobel Prizes for work on the genetic control of enzyme and virus synthesis, hormonal treatment of cancer, and elucidation of hormone-dependent tumors.

Medical progress was advanced by the first live-virus vaccine against measles by John Franklin Enders and colleagues in 1960, the first ethambutol attempts in treatment of tuberculosis by J. P. Thomas in 1961, elucidation of the chemical structure of prostaglandins by Sune Bergstrom and coworkers in 1962, and isolation of the rubella virus by several investigators in 1962. The Epstein-Barr virus, a human herpesvirus implicated in Burkitt's lymphoma, was discovered by Michael Anthony Epstein and Y. M. Barr in 1964 and shown to be the causal agent in infectious mononucleosis in 1968.

The late 1960's was marked by the development of more powerful antibiotics and research focusing on advanced understanding of the immune system to conquer diseases such as rheumatic fever, rheumatoid arthritis, and lupus erythematosus. The discovery that many cancer cells are capable of combining with unique antibodies led to research into the possibility that some cancers may someday be dealt with through immune-related methods such as vaccines. Earlier in the twentieth century, the worldwide disappearance of smallpox through immunization stimulated better treatment methods and reduced

# Medical Milestones

| 1960 | Researcher William M. Chardack develops the pacemaker, which enables those with ailing hearts to live longer. |
|------|---------------------------------------------------------------------------------------------------------------|
|      | The Food and Drug Administration approves the anti-anxiety drug Librium. |
|      | G. D. Searle Company introduces Enovid, a birth control pill, the first major advance in contraceptive devices in decades. |
|      | Frances Kelsey, a researcher at the Food and Drug Administration, delays the approval of thalidomide, a tranquilizer used to treat morning sickness, because it may cause birth defects. |
| 1961 | The Food and Drug Administration approves the sale of acetaminophen tablets, an analgesic that provides an alternative to aspirin. |
|      | New York physician Jack Lippes develops an intrauterine birth control device (IUD), the Lippes Loop. |
| 1962 | Opthamologist Charles Campbell and his colleagues are the first to use the laser to perform eye surgery on humans. |
|      | The muscle relaxant Valium, produced by Roche Laboratories, is introduced in the United States. |
| 1963 | American physician Michael De Bakey develops an artificial heart that can be used to circulate a patient's blood during heart surgery. |
|      | Doctors perform the first human liver transplant in Denver, on forty-seven-year-old William Grigsby, who lived three weeks. |
| 1964 | The Surgeon General's Report links cigarette smoking to lung cancer and other ailments. |
| 1965 | Developmental psychologist Harry Harlow's experiments show that infant monkeys deprived of maternal contact become emotionally impaired. |
|      | Scientists develop soft contact lenses. |
| 1967 | The first successful heart transplant is performed in South Africa by surgeon Christiaan Barnard on fifty-five-year-old grocer, Louis Washkansky, who lives eighteen days. |
| 1968 | The American Medical Association develops a new definition of death, brain death, in answer to questions raised by doctors seeking donor organs for transplants. |
| 1969 | The Food and Drug Administration, citing a risk of cancer, removes cyclamates, an artificial sweetener, from the market. |
|      | Denton A. Cooley, a surgeon in Houston, implants the first artificial heart in a patient, forty-seven-year-old Haskell Karp, who dies thirty hours after undergoing the procedure. |

occurrences of other childhood diseases such as poliomyelitis, rubeola (measles), rubella (German measles), diphtheria, and mumps. Vaccines for influenza and other diseases were developed, but the numerous virus varieties and their capacity to mutate made them much more difficult to control.

**Pain Management**  In 1967, Britain's Cicely Saunders, who worked in both nursing and social work before becoming a physician, established Saint Christopher's in London, the first hospice dedicated to care of the dying. Saunders pioneered research into the control of intractable pain and the psychological issues encountered by the dying, leading to much more aggressive pain management programs for the terminally ill. With her outreach and teaching programs rapidly reaching an international audience, Saunders promoted the realization that medicinal care needs to emphasize comfort as well as cure, which has continued to become increasingly important as the elderly population escalates in proportion within developed countries.

**Thalidomide and Disillusion**  In the late 1950's and early 1960's, obstetricians noticed phocomelia (grossly shortened long limb bones) in newborns whose mothers had taken thalidomide in early pregnancy. The drug was banned in late 1961, with subsequent legal action enabling many of the estimated ten thousand thalidomide babies to receive financial compensation. This event triggered an escalating trend of patients bringing lawsuits against their personal physicians, particularly obstetricians and surgeons, and encouraged the practice of medical contingency litigation, whereby lawyers were paid a percentage of damages awarded but were not paid for an unsuccessful verdict.

Societal disillusionment with modern medicine initiated by the thalidomide incident continued to escalate during the mid-1960's because of public knowledge that the increasing varieties of drugs being developed could have serious side effects that could not be predicted or prevented no matter how rigorous the testing. Rapidly increasing medical care costs resulted in financial hardship to both insured and uninsured individuals seeking coverage and to the government as the proportion of the gross national product devoted to health care continued to rise. Many Americans felt that physicians were becoming less interested in their patients as human beings and much more interested in the discovery

of disease mechanisms and the potential for their own personal advancement upon finding a cure. The 1960's was marked by the questioning of established institutions and protests against medical research, particularly that involving animals, which took place on university medical school campuses in combination with demonstrations against the Vietnam War and the atomic bomb.

**Impact**  In the 1970's, Thomas McKeown, professor of social medicine at the University of Birmingham, wrote several widely read critiques of medicine that have remained extremely influential within the medical community. McKeown's major controversial contention was that improvements in human health and longevity may not be directly related to recent developments in medicine. Using statistical evidence of cure, McKeown maintained that reductions in childhood death rates due to disease were more influenced by better nutrition and sanitation than by immunization with vaccines and antibiotics. McKeown stated that historically the predominant risks to life and health have occurred in three major phases: injuries and accidents; infectious diseases, many transmitted from animals when people and animals began living in close contiguity; and the degenerative diseases of longevity, largely caused by rises in living standards and better hygiene. Many revolutionary breakthroughs in medicine that Western society has continued to enjoy since the 1960's have produced a tremendous increase in the number of elderly persons, resulting in increased demand for expensive medical care and associated costs of long-term maintenance of their lives within the community.

**Subsequent Events**  Researchers first began to take the possibility of mapping the entire human genome seriously in the 1960's, leading to the 1990 beginning of the Human Genome Project. This project is a fifteen-year research effort focusing on the analysis of the structure of DNA, the determination of the precise location of an estimated one hundred thousand human genes, and the complete sequence of an estimated three billion DNA subunits (bases).

The unsuccessful heart transplant from chimpanzee to human in 1964 performed by James Daniel Hardy provided valuable information about reactions to transplants. This led in 1982 to the implantation of the first permanent artificial heart in American Barney Clark, who survived 112 days after the surgery. In 1984, American surgeon Leonard Bailey performed the first transplant of an animal heart to a human when he transplanted a baboon heart into a baby, who later died from a blood mismatch.

**Additional Information** An exhaustive year-by-year compilation of significant events in medicine and its supporting fields is available in *A Chronology of Medicine and Related Sciences* (1997), by Leslie T. Morton. *Heroes of Medicine,* a fall, 1997, *Time* magazine special issue, provides an excellent history of medicine from the Greek physician Hippocrates to contemporary genetic engineers.

*Daniel G. Graetzer*

**See also** Birth Control; Cancer; Cyclamates; Genetics; Heart Transplants; Kidney Transplants; Medicare; Nobel Prizes; Pill, The; Science and Technology; Thalidomide.

---

# ■ *Medium Cool*

**Released** 1969
**Director** Haskell Wexler (1926-      )

*A motion picture that uses fiction and documentary to explore the political mood in the United States in 1968. It follows the life and work of a television news cameraman in Chicago before and during the tumultuous 1968 Democratic National Convention.*

**The Work** *Medium Cool* opens with cameraman John Cassellis (Robert Forster) and his sound technician filming a car wreck for their Chicago television station. Only after they get their footage do they call an

*Cameraman John Cassellis (Robert Forster) films a car wreck for a television station before calling an ambulance in the 1969 film* Medium Cool, *which examines the issues facing the nation and the media's role in reporting them.* (Museum of Modern Art/Film Stills Archive)

ambulance. This famous scene is the first of many that examine the issues of 1960's American life and the role the media play in reporting it.

As the film unfolds, Cassellis defends his profession against cocktail-party critics who blame television news for superficiality and violence, films the funeral of Robert F. Kennedy; and covers the National Guard's crowd-control exercises as they prepare for the 1968 Democratic National Convention. Throughout these activities, Cassellis is the essence of cool, professional detachment.

A warming of his attitude is demonstrated by two events. Cassellis tries to pursue a human-interest story about an African American taxi driver who returns ten thousand dollars that someone has left in his cab. This story gets him fired by bosses who want more protester footage (which they share with Federal Bureau of Investigation dissident hunters). An accomplished professional, Cassellis quickly finds a job covering the convention floor.

In his private life, Cassellis finds himself becoming involved with a Vietnam widow from West Virginia coal country (Eileen, played by Verna Bloom) and her introspective, adventurous boy. When her son disappears from home at the height of the rioting that surrounds the Democratic National Convention, Eileen enters the riot-torn hell of Grant Park but cannot find her son. She calls Cassellis for help, and they leave the convention in his car. On the road, they have a blowout and crash. A family drives by without stopping; a child in the car takes a snapshot as they pass, giving the film an ironically symmetrical conclusion.

**Impact** This issue-oriented film looks at the role of the media in shaping or misshaping the nation's view of itself, the damage done to individuals and society by the Vietnam War, and the lives of the urban poor, both African Americans and newcomers from Appalachia.

Director Haskell Wexler, a cinematographer for most of his career, combined semi-improvisational fictional scenes with vivid, documentary-style location shooting to give a cinema verité feel to his film. One sequence shows an intense group of African American militants lecturing Cassellis on the media's shallow coverage of African American issues. The heart of the film shows Eileen searching downtown Chicago and Grant Park during the protests and riots of the convention's final day. Wexler shot

hours of dangerous live footage that were intercut with location sequences with Eileen. The result is a heightened dramatic realism that is effective as social commentary and adventurous, committed cinema.

In the film's final shot, a cameraman (Wexler himself) pans from John and Eileen's wrecked car toward the audience, challenging Americans to take responsibility for what a watching world will see through the media's omnipresent lens.

**Related Works** For a European view of similar issues see Michelangelo Antonioni's *Blow-up* (1966) and *Zabrieski Point* (1969).

**Additional Information** Ethan Mordden's *Medium Cool: The Movies of the 1960's* (1990) places Wexler's film in its historical context.

*Roger J. Stilling*

**See also** *Blow-up*; Democratic National Convention of 1968; Film; Media.

## ■ *Memoirs v. Massachusetts*

*United States Supreme Court case that resulted in the adoption of a three-part test for obscenity. Afterward, the Court overturned all but the most explicit obscenity convictions in the nation.*

Early U.S. law made it a crime to publish an obscene book. In 1821, a Boston court convicted two booksellers of obscenity for selling John Cleland's *Memoirs of a Woman of Pleasure* (1749, also known as *Fanny Hill*); the convictions were upheld on appeal although no legal definition of obscenity existed at the time. By the late 1800's, obscenity was defined as that which has a tendency "to deprave and corrupt those whose minds are open to such immoral influences." This definition survived until *Roth v. United States* (1957), when the U.S. Supreme Court, although accepting that obscenity was not protected by the First Amendment, adopted a new test for obscenity as "whether to the average person, applying contemporary community standards, the dominant theme of the material taken as a whole appeals to the prurient interest."

In 1964, *Memoirs of a Woman of Pleasure* was again declared obscene in the Massachusetts courts. The appeal to the U.S. Supreme Court is formally called *A Book Named "John Cleland's Memoirs of a Woman of Pleasure" v. Attorney General of Massachusetts* (1966), but is typically referred to as *Memoirs v. Massachusetts.* The case is a landmark one in which the Court adopted a new, three-part test for obscenity. To be judged obscene, a work had to be judged obscene according to the "prurient interest" test of *Roth*; "patently offensive because it affronts contemporary community values," and "utterly without redeeming social value."

Only three justices accepted the three-part *Memoirs* test at the time: Justices William Brennan, who wrote the opinion, and Abe Fortas and Chief Justice Earl Warren. Justice William O. Douglas wrote a concurring opinion in which he agreed that *Memoirs* was protected by the First Amendment. Douglas and Justice Hugo Black were First Amendment "absolutists" who argued that all speech, even that which is obscene, is protected by the First Amendment. Rejecting the test entirely and arguing that *Memoirs* was obscene were Justices Thomas Clark, John M. Harlan, and Byron White, who wrote individual dissenting opinions in the case.

**Impact** Immediately, however, the justices jettisoned any single test and decided obscenity cases by applying their own individual definitions. Thus, when an obscenity case came before the Court, Brennan and his followers would use the *Memoirs* test, Black and Douglas would declare all obscenity protected, and others would use their own individual tests. Because the three *Memoirs* test adherents could count upon Douglas and Black to create a majority, only the most explicit materials were deemed obscene.

**Subsequent Events** The election of President Richard M. Nixon in 1968 on a platform opposing the nation's declining moral values led to his appointment of four conservative justices to the Court. Those four, joined by White, replaced the *Memoirs* test with a conservative one that would allow for more obscenity convictions (*Miller v. California*, 1973).

**Additional Information** An examination of *Memoirs v. Massachusetts* can be found in Charles Rembar's *The End of Obscenity* (1968).

*Michael W. Bowers*

**See also** Censorship; *Jacobellis v. Ohio*; Supreme Court Decisions.

# ■ Mercury Space Program

*The United States' first manned space program. The Mercury program succeeded in lifting two men into suborbital flight and four more into orbit around Earth in the early 1960's.*

The Mercury man-in-space program began in 1958, just after the National Aeronautics and Space Administration (NASA) began operation and more than a year after the spectacular, and to Americans, shocking success of *Sputnik 1*, launched by the Soviet Union. NASA named its program after the ancient Greek messenger of the gods, whose winged feet carried him between the heavens and earth with ease. Roger Gilruth, a NASA engineer who had been working on the design of a piloted spacecraft, became the head of a space task group responsible for the Mercury flights.

On October 4, 1957, the Soviet satellite *Sputnik 1*, which weighed only 183 pounds, had orbited Earth every ninety minutes and sent back radio signals identifying itself, allowing ground trackers to monitor its position. The Soviets had quickly followed up on the satellite's success, lofting *Sputnik 2* into orbit on November 3, 1957, just a month later. *Sputnik 2* weighed 1,120 pounds and carried a dog, Laika, into orbit for almost two hundred days. To hoist a 180-pound satellite into orbit was one thing; to launch a human-made object weighing a half ton and achieve orbit at seventeen thousand miles per hour, with a live animal on board, was quite another. *Sputnik 2* astounded scientists the world over and sent a message that the Soviet space effort was more advanced than that of the Americans.

Facing a clear and daunting challenge, Gilruth and other NASA scientists decided on a three-phase attack. Instead of building rockets from scratch, NASA engineers would use existing technology, modify the nose cones, and begin with what seemed the modest goal of launching a man in an arching suborbital trajectory some three hundred miles downrange from Cape Canaveral, the U.S. spaceport on the eastern coast of Florida. Phase one of the Mercury program envisioned putting a manned capsule atop a Redstone rocket, a type of military rocket that had been in use since 1953, had a range of five hundred miles, and could carry a small warhead. NASA's first space voyager would just skim the edges of the void and return within fifteen minutes. In

*The first American in space, Alan B. Shepard, Jr., smiles as he sits in the tiny Mercury spacecraft in 1961.* (AP/Wide World Photos)

phase two, the capsule would make longer suborbital flights after being sent aloft by a slightly larger, more powerful booster, the Jupiter. Finally, in phase three of the Mercury program, an Atlas intercontinental ballistic missile would launch an astronaut into orbit. Gilruth projected that the third phase would take

place within two years of the start of the program.

This was an ambitious plan, and Gilruth and the Mercury team almost achieved it. The Mercury capsule, only eleven feet long and six feet wide at the base, was built by the McDonnell Aircraft Corporation. The pilot, an astronaut chosen after a rigorous selection process, was a man with long experience as a test pilot for the armed forces. He sat, facing backward, in a cramped cockpit jammed with instrument panels, an onboard computer for automatic timing of the capsule's return to Earth, and a small periscope.

This tiny spacecraft was used not only for the first suborbital flight but also for the longer orbital flights around Earth. The first U.S. manned flight took place on May 5, 1961, three years after NASA had begun its quest for parity in the space race and almost five years after the first *Sputnik* had been launched.

The 7 young astronauts chosen to become Mercury space voyagers were selected through an arduous process from a group of 508 highly talented fliers who also happened to be engineers. The final 7 made their debut before the U.S. public on April 9, 1959.

The first American in space, Alan B. Shepard, Jr., and the second, Virgil I. "Gus" Grissom, rode Redstone boosters on short, suborbital flights. A mishap on landing caused Grissom's *Liberty Bell 7* to sink into the Atlantic Ocean, although Grissom was safely plucked from the sea by helicopter. The third Mercury flight was the first to orbit Earth. An Atlas booster carried John Glenn into orbit on February 20, 1962, inside the capsule he had named *Friendship 7*. Glenn circled Earth three times before returning to splash down in the Atlantic near the Bahamas. His flight was not without problems: His capsule's heat-resistant shield, designed to protect him from the searing three-thousand-degree Fahrenheit heat of reentry, came loose during liftoff from Cape Canaveral, and Glenn had to ride *Friendship 7* back to Earth with his retrorockets strapped to the shield. Glenn, a Marine Corps flier, watched a spectacular shower of flames shoot by his cockpit window as the capsule descended into the atmosphere. At times during reentry, he was unsure whether he was about to become a shooting star himself.

The Mercury program made three more orbital flights around Earth in 1962 and 1963. Navy Lieutenant M. Scott Carpenter completed a three-orbit flight on May 20, 1962; Lieutenant Commander Walter M. Schirra circled Earth six times on October 3, 1962; finally, on May 15-16, 1963, just six months before President John F. Kennedy's assassination, Captain L. Gordon Cooper of the Air Force completed a twenty-two orbit flight in thirty-four hours.

The seventh astronaut, Air Force Captain Donald "Deke" Slayton never flew aboard a Mercury capsule because NASA grounded him after physicians discovered a slight heart murmur in a preflight examination.

**Impact**  The Mercury program set the stage for further U.S. manned exploration of space. The United States also boosted its prestige, in question after a long series of Soviet space successes. Through the program, NASA engineers had solved the basic problems of manned space flight: lifting a human being into orbit, keeping the pilot alive in space, and returning capsule and crew safely to Earth. With the successful completion of this early program, the United States had committed itself to a long-term presence in outer space.

**Subsequent Events**  The next U.S. effort, the Gemini program of 1965-1966, launched two-person capsules into orbit around Earth. Although most of the original Mercury astronauts did not fly in space again, Grissom piloted the first Gemini mission on March 23, 1965. Then, in culmination of a decade-long effort, Apollo missions to the Moon began in 1968 with an Earth-orbit test mission and continued until December, 1972. Grissom died in a fire aboard the first Apollo capsule as it sat on a launch pad atop a huge Saturn 5 booster rocket on January 27, 1967. It was an Apollo capsule that later, on July 20, 1969, successfully landed the first human on the moon.

In the mid-1970's, after a decade and a half of competition, the United States and the Soviet Union shifted focus and began cooperative efforts in space. Slayton flew aboard a joint Apollo-Soyuz mission with the Soviets on July 17, 1975. Slayton died of cancer in June, 1993.

Shepard died at a hospital outside Monterey, California, in July, 1998.

**Additional Information**  A highly readable account of the early U.S. space effort, including the Mercury program, can be found in *Moon Shot: The Inside Story of America's Race to the Moon* (1994), by astronauts Shepard and Slayton. *We Seven, by the Astronauts Themselves* (1962), a collection of first-person narratives by the seven Mercury astronauts, takes the reader inside key missions. Roger D. Launius's *NASA: A History of the U.S. Civil Space Program* (1994) provides an overview of the space effort.

*Benjamin Zibit*

**See also**  Apollo 1 Disaster; Apollo Space Program; Gemini Space Program; Mariner Space Program; Space Race; Science and Technology.

# ■ Meredith, James H.

**Born** June 25, 1933, Kosciusko, Mississippi

*Student who integrated the University of Mississippi. Meredith's decision to apply to the previously all-white "Ole Miss" focused attention on the state and gave momentum to the Civil Rights movement.*

**Early Life**  James Howard Meredith, a native Mississippian from a farming family, saw that his economic opportunities were limited in his home state and joined the United States Air Force in 1951. After a nine-year stint, he returned to Mississippi, hungry for a superior education.

**The 1960's**  Meredith enrolled at an all-black state college but soon deemed it inferior to the University of Mississippi in Oxford, the state's flagship university. He was the first African American to publicly make such claims. Meredith fought through state and federal courts for nearly two years to gain admission to "Ole Miss," which he entered in the fall of 1962. His arrival on campus set off what became known as the "battle of Oxford," a serious test of American federalism.

As the courts rejected a string of appeals from the University of Mississippi to deny Meredith admission, Mississippi governor Ross Barnett, a strong proponent of segregation, began to urge defiance of constitutional authority. When a federal court finally ordered in late September, 1962, that Meredith be enrolled immediately, a crowd of "toughs," some of them University of Mississippi students but most of them outside agitators, assembled on campus, intending to keep the university segregated by any means necessary. Flanked by Chief U.S. Marshal James P. McShane and John Doar of the United States Justice Department, Meredith arrived in Oxford on September 30.

More than five hundred U.S. marshals with special riot training circled a campus building where Meredith was to register on his first day of classes. At sundown, the white mob, estimated at two to four thousand, began throwing bricks and Molotov cocktails at the forces. The marshals attempted to disperse the crowd with tear gas but failed; President John F. Kennedy eventually had to dispatch twenty-three thousand soldiers to Oxford to restore order. In the aftermath of the rioting, Meredith literally stepped past burned-out cars and through rubble on his way to his first class (appropriately enough, in U.S. history).

After graduating from the University of Mississippi in 1963, Meredith left the state for three years. In 1966, his March Against Fear, a solitary walk from Memphis, Tennessee, to Jackson, Mississippi, that was halted when Meredith was shot, brought the state's tense racial climate even more notoriety.

**Later Life**  Meredith, always something of a puzzle in that his motives were not always easy to understand,

*James H. Meredith, whose admission to the University of Mississippi in 1962 brought about its desegregation, appears the following year on the television program* Meet the Press. *(Library of Congress)*

confounded African Americans and liberals when he went to work as an aide for Senator Jesse Helms, a conservative Republican from North Carolina, in the late 1980's.

**Impact** Meredith and the federal government won the war of wills at the University of Mississippi but at an exorbitant price: A French journalist and an Oxford bystander were killed, and more than one hundred marshals were seriously wounded. Unfortunately, many politicians interpreted the incident as evidence of federal "tyranny," and used it to rally whites across the South against the federal government and the Civil Rights movement. However, African American Mississippians drew strength from Meredith's courageous example, even though they knew they would gain little from his efforts in the short term. Meredith's desegregation of the University of Mississippi was not a tactic in the larger strategy of the Civil Rights movement in the state, but the attention it brought to southern African Americans in their struggle for justice was invaluable. Finally, it began to be perceived as more of a national issue than a local one.

**Additional Information** Meredith published *Three Years in Mississippi*, an account of his trials and tribulations at the University of Mississippi, in 1966.

*J. Todd Moye*

**See also** Civil Rights Movement; Holmes, Hamilton, and Charlayne Hunter; Kennedy, John F.; Malone, Vivian; School Desegregation.

---

# ■ Merriam, Eve

**Born** July 19, 1916, Philadelphia, Pennsylvania
**Died** April 11, 1992, New York, New York

*Poet, playwright, and prose writer. Merriam's many poems for children, her public addresses, and her essays about poetry made her an important influence on how children's literature was taught in the late twentieth century.*

**Early Life** A lover of the sound of poetry from her earliest childhood, Eve Merriam (born Eva Moskovitz) began writing poems at the age of seven and published her first works in high school. After graduating from college, she wrote radio scripts for the Columbia Broadcasting System. Her first book of poetry, *Family Circle* (1946), earned for her the Yale Younger Poets Prize. Over the next fourteen years,

she published more poetry, fiction, a fictionalized biography of Emma Lazarus, and her first feminist nonfiction book, *The Double Bed from the Feminine Side* (1958).

**The 1960's** Merriam established her importance as a children's poet with her first volumes of children's poetry: *There Is No Rhyme for Silver* (1962), *It Doesn't Always Have to Rhyme* (1964), and *Catch a Little Rhyme* (1966). All were named Junior Literary Guild selections, bringing her celebration of the sound of words to a wide audience. Her poems, read and studied in classrooms across the country, were instantly recognized as intelligent and fun—works to be read aloud and enjoyed. She also wrote several books of juvenile prose during this decade.

Although she had a lifelong concern for gender equality, in her early career she had revealed this belief only occasionally, consciously avoiding the label "feminist writer." The children's book *Mommies at Work* (1961) depicted women in nontraditional roles and was followed by adult books including *After Nora Slammed the Door* (1964), *Man and Woman* (1968), and *Equality, Identity, and Complementarity* (1968). She turned to political commentary and satire in *The Inner City Mother Goose* (1969) and *The Nixon Poems* (1970).

**Later Life** In the 1970's, Merriam wrote numerous books for children, which increasingly dealt with social issues. In books such as *I Am a Man: Ode to Martin Luther King, Jr.* (1971) and *Boys and Girls, Girls and Boys* (1972), she attempted to erase gender-based divisions. During this decade, she concentrated on writing plays, which she saw as a natural extension of her interest in the sounds of poetry. Her first play, *Out of Our Father's House* (1975), was based on her book *Growing Up Female in America: Ten Lives* (1971). She wrote seven more plays, including the Obie Award-winning *The Club* (1976). In 1981, she was presented the National Council of Teachers of English Award for excellence in poetry for children. This award recognizes a poet's entire body of work rather than a single poem or volume of poems.

**Impact** One of the most prolific poets for children of the later twentieth century, Merriam helped young audiences recognize poetry's ability to bring pleasure to daily life through its musicality and magic. She taught that poetry is fun. Merriam became one of a handful of poets whose poems appeared in every major anthology of poetry for children and whose work was both respected by educators and enjoyed by readers.

**Additional Information** Merriam explained her philosophy of poetry in "Some Pearls from Eve Merriam on Sharing Poetry with Children" in the journal *Learning85* (volume 14, September, 1985).

*Cynthia A. Bily*

**See also** Education; Literature; Poetry.

# ■ Metafiction

*A work of fiction that focuses on the nature or creation of fiction itself. Writers of the 1960's did much to develop this experimental form of writing, also known as self-reflexive fiction.*

Because traditional literary forms did not adequately reflect the social upheaval of the 1960's, experimental authors chose to go beyond the idea that fiction should mimic reality. Instead, postmodernist writers embraced a kind of self-conscious fiction that examined the very process by which fiction is created. Few notable examples of metafiction existed before the late 1950's. One rare early model is *Tristram Shandy* (1759-1767) by Laurence Sterne. André Gide's seminal novel *The Counterfeiters* (1926) uses a predecessor to postmodernist experimentalism, the *mise-en-abyme* method (a method in which a continual internal duplication exists within a literary work).

Metafiction in the United States was inspired by work in nonliterary artistic fields. In visual art, cubists, Dadaists, and expressionists provided impetus for metafictional writers by seeking to obliterate the paradoxical falsity of reality in their art, just as metafictional writers wanted to tear away facades in their fiction. In philosophy, eighteenth century philosopher Immanuel Kant's suggestion that humanity's relationship to the world is defined by subjective sensory perceptions and that humans create their own reality prompted writers to diverge from traditional realistic fiction. Epistemological theories based on Kant pointed out that empirical evidence cannot exist, and thus life itself becomes a form of metafiction. These ideas impelled European authors such as Franz Kafka, Jean-Paul Sartre, and Samuel Beckett to focus on existentialism and litera-

ture of the absurd; they in turn were catalysts for the experimental fiction movement in the United States. In the late 1950's, U.S. writers William Gaddis and John Hawks worked with experimental forms and influenced later writers in the metafictional vein, contributing to the scant metafictional canon before 1960.

Despite these sparse antecedents, much celebrated metafiction was written throughout the 1960's. The heyday of postmodernist experimental fiction began as a reflection of social turbulence; novelists who felt that absolute truth was too elusive to be fettered by realistic writing turned inward and explored a personal version of reality. The chaos of that personal reality was mimicked in the antinovel (an experimental novel that dispenses with traditional elements such as characterization and a sequential plot) by an increasing emphasis on internal fictional technique. Some authors highlighted the concept that fiction resembles a game, illustrating its playful quality by writing stories sustained by an internally supported system of logic without ever linking their words to a universal reality (mainly because metafictional writers believed that truth can be grounded only in personal sensory experiences and thus does not exist universally). In other words, the fiction's style became superior to its plot and characters; the manner of writing evolved into the theme and meaning of the story.

*Ficciones* (1962) by Argentinean Jorge Luis Borges served as one of the most notable models of metafiction and broadened its influence as a genre. In 1963, Thomas Pynchon published *V.*, a masterful example of self-reflexive technique that stylistically resembles a series of mazes. In 1966, John Barth published *Giles Goat-Boy*, a sweeping allegory set in the world of academia. Barth's short work, "Lost in the Funhouse" (1968), a much anthologized piece depicting the mind of a fiction writer, is a textbook example of metafiction technique. Two other writers, Donald Barthelme and Robert Coover, helped shape experimental fiction throughout the 1960's. Barthelme's collection, *Come Back, Dr. Caligari* (1964) played with narrative voice and irony in mimetic prose, and Coover's novel *The Universal Baseball Association, Inc., J. Henry Waugh, Prop.* (1968) dealt with fantasy and its role in creating and sustaining fiction. Other notable authors working with metafiction in the 1960's, such as Richard Fariña, Gilbert Sorrentino, William Gass, Joseph McElroy, and George Herbert, contributed to the mood of metasensibility present in that decade.

**Impact** The experimental writers once shunned by the academic mainstream soon found their way into the traditional intellectual community. Once established as a legitimate genre, metafiction merged with other experimental techniques and with traditional literary methods. New structural devices in fiction—the use of typography as a literary tool, the portrayal of accepted reality as fantasy, the inclination of authors to freely exhibit their fictional natures, and the introduction of multiple and paradoxical viewpoints—became more conventional. This medley of literary styles generated a resurgence of romanticism and renewed dependence on personal insight for creative inspiration.

**Subsequent Events** Metafiction retained its popularity throughout the 1970's. Experimental writers who had first published in the 1960's continued to contribute to the growing canon of metafiction. Gass objectified some ideas about the nature of metafiction in his *Fiction and the Figures of Life* (1970), a text that legitimized the innovative fiction techniques of the 1960's and became an important reference for critics of self-reflexive fiction. Pynchon published another experimental novel, *Gravity's Rainbow* (1973). Sorrentino's *Mulligan Stew* (1979) portrayed the author as a character surrounded by other writers who were aware that they were characters in that novel. Coover's controversial *The Public Burning* (1977) examined the association between humankind's fictional schemes and reality. The general openness to new literary ideas in the 1960's spawned creative output in the decades thereafter.

**Additional Information** A study of modern experimental fiction with an emphasis on metafiction can be found in *Fabulation and Metafiction* (1979), by Robert Scholes. Larry McCaffery's *The Metafictional Muse* (1982) focuses specifically on the works of Coover, Barthelme, and Gass. *The Concise Oxford Dictionary of Literary Terms* (1990), by Chris Baldick, and *A Handbook to Literature* (1992), edited by C. Hugh Holman and William Harmon, offer basic definitions of metafiction.

*Valerie Brown*

**See also** Literature; Theater of the Absurd.

# ■ Microwave Ovens

*An electronic device used to heat and cook food. Because of their high efficiency and low cost, microwave ovens became an important cooking tool in modern kitchens.*

In October, 1945, Percy Spencer, a physics engineer working at Raytheon, a world leader in radar equipment, applied for a U.S. patent for a device that would eventually evolve into the modern microwave oven. His work was a result of studies by British scientists Sir John Randell and H. A. Boot, who, in 1940, had developed an electron tube that generated microwaves. This tube, known as a magnetron, was first put to practical use improving radar defenses during World War II. Spencer observed that the magnetron generated considerable heat and on one occasion melted a candy bar in his pocket. He further tested the heating power of the device by putting some popcorn in a paper bag and placing the bag near the tube. The popcorn immediately popped. Raytheon patented its microwave cooking device as the Radar Range. Heavy, awkward, and expensive, the appliance was originally intended for use solely in hospitals and military canteens.

By 1952, the Tappan Company had marketed the first household microwave ovens, which cost as much as fifteen hundred dollars. In 1967, the Japanese developed an improved electron tube that allowed the production of small, affordable microwave ovens. They quickly found their way into residential kitchens as prices fell to less than five hundred dollars. These ovens expose food to microwaves, which are absorbed by water, fat, sugar, and other molecules in the food, causing the molecules to vibrate and generate the heat that cooks the food. They are portable, clean, and compact and cook food faster than a conventional oven. They also allow rapid defrosting of frozen foods and efficient reheating of precooked foods.

**Impact** As more and more women entered the workforce in the 1960's, the market for the quick-cooking microwave oven grew. The ovens also boosted the development of the frozen-dinner industry, which got its start in 1954. Prices of basic models had fallen to a little more than one hundred dollars by the 1990's, and microwave ovens could be found in most kitchens, many offices, and even some dormitory rooms.

**Additional Information** A detailed account of the operation of microwave ovens can be found in *The Microwave Oven* (1973), by Helen J. Van Zante.

*Nicholas C. Thomas*

**See also** Science and Technology.

## ■ *Midnight Cowboy*

**Released** 1969
**Director** John Schlesinger (1926-      )

*The breakthrough film that best illustrates the increased freedom of the screen in American commercial cinema in the 1960's. The film was a milestone in the mature and responsible treatment of sexuality, particularly the self-contained world of the homosexual, in a Hollywood film.*

**The Work** *Midnight Cowboy* tells the story of Joe Buck (Jon Voight), a Texan who comes to New York City in the hope of becoming a stud for rich and lonely ladies but winds up hustling men instead. He makes friends with Ratso Rizzo (Dustin Hoffman), a repulsive-looking bum who is suffering from tuberculosis, and the two take refuge in each other's friendship. Although their relationship is not homosexual, Joe and Ratso move in a milieu largely inhabited by homosexuals. When both men begin to realize that Ratso's illness is fatal and he is never going to recover, Joe frantically turns to hustling men to acquire the money needed to take Ratso to Florida before he dies. They head for Florida, but Ratso dies aboard the bus just before they reach their destination. The ending, nonetheless, is not pessimistic. Having experienced genuine friendship and companionship with Ratso, Joe is ready to embark on a more mature way of life; his adolescent illusions about the easy life are now shattered.

**Impact** *Midnight Cowboy* was the first film made by a major commercial studio in Hollywood to give the general public a glimpse of the world of the male hustler. In commercial films up to that time, homosexuality was treated with extreme reticence if it was depicted at all. Consequently, *Midnight Cowboy* marked a step forward in the treatment of homosexuality on the screen. In presenting an uncompromising picture of the homosexual milieu in a mainstream Hollywood film, director John Schlesinger said his intent was not just to push back the frontiers of what was acceptable subject matter for a Hollywood film but also to enrich the film with thought-provoking thematic implications. Thus, this film has an interesting religious dimension, a fact that is often overlooked by scholars. In a televised sermon, a bishop asks rhetorically, "Is God dead?" It might appear that this is true—at least in the corrupt world in which Joe finds himself, among the lowlife of New York's slums. Admittedly, Joe does not have his faith in God strengthened in any explicit way in the picture. However, through his friendship with Ratso, he does have his faith in humankind restored, and that in itself is significant. *Midnight Cowboy* was looked upon almost from the beginning as a major cinematic landmark of the 1960's, as evidenced by the fact that the film won Academy Awards for Best Director and for Best Picture.

**Related Work** *Advise and Consent* (1962) directed by Otto Preminger, which deals with a United States senator with a homosexual past, is another ground-

*Texan Joe Buck (Jon Voight) and Ratso Rizzo (Dustin Hoffman) develop a surprising friendship in New York City in the 1969 film* Midnight Cowboy. *(Museum of Modern Art/Film Stills Archive)*

breaking portrayal of homosexuality in a Hollywood film.

**Additional Information** For further analysis of *Midnight Cowboy* as a representative film of the 1960's, see *The Films of the Sixties* (1990), by Douglas Brode, and *The Lavender Screen: Homosexuality on Film* (1993), by Boze Hadleigh.

*Gene D. Phillips*

**See also** Censorship; Film.

---

## ■ Mills, Billy

**Born** June 30, 1938, Pine Ridge, South Dakota

*Native American who stunned the world with a record-breaking running performance. Mills, with a tremendous burst of speed, sprinted to a ten-foot win, establishing an Olympic record for the 10,000-meter run in 1964.*

*At the 1964 Tokyo Olympics, Native American Billy Mills beat the favored runners to set a record and take the gold in the 10,000-meter event. (AP/Wide World Photos)*

William Mervin "Billy" Mills was born June 30, 1938, to Sidney and Grace Mills on the Oglala Sioux Reservation, Pine Ridge, South Dakota. Mills, who is half Sioux, was orphaned at age twelve and was sent to the Haskell Institute for Native Americans in Lawrence, Kansas, for guidance and further education. In high school, he concentrated on running cross-country events and seldom lost a competition. In 1957, Mills received an athletic scholarship to the University of Kansas. For the next four years, he competed in both indoor and outdoor track events, bringing home honors in both, although he did not show his true running potential until after he was graduated.

After returning to Pine Ridge in 1962, Mills joined the U.S. Marine Corps and stopped all competitive running. He took a two-year hiatus from the sport, then returned to competition in early 1964 and qualified for two running events—the 10,000 meters and the marathon—on the United States Olympic team. At the 1964 Olympic Games, there were no qualifying heats, so thirty-eight runners crowded into the 10,000-meter event. Mills was a virtual unknown and was not expected to do well in the race. In one of the biggest upsets of the Olympic Games, Mills won and set the 10,000-meter record by beating the favorites, Mohamed Gamoudi of Tunisia and Ronald Clarke of Australia, in 28 minutes, 24.4 seconds.

In 1972, he was named one of American's Ten Outstanding Young Men. In 1976, he was inducted into the National Track and Field Hall of Fame and in 1984 into the U.S. Olympic Hall of Fame.

**Impact** In 1912, another American Indian, Lewis Tewanima, had won the silver medal in the 10,000-meter event, but Mills was the first American Indian to win a gold medal in the event. He returned to the United States a hero, admired for his ability to triumph over adversity.

**Additional Information** In 1994, Mills published *Wokini: A Lakota Journey to Happiness and Self-Understanding*; though fiction, the work expresses the author's own philosophies. The 1983 film *Running Brave*, directed by D. S. Everett and starring Robby Benson, was based on Mills's life and career.

*Earl R. Andresen*

**See also** Olympic Games of 1964; Ryun, Jim.

# ■ Minimalism

*A musical style based on simple melodic materials and repeated patterns. Minimalism was controversial because of its hypnotic repetitions, which some critics called excruciatingly boring, yet it became an influential force in modern music.*

In the 1950's young composers began questioning the foundations of music. Composer John Cage reduced music to nothing with a piece entitled "Four Minutes and Thirty-three Seconds" (1952), in which the performer remains silent for that length of time. Other composers created pieces that were essentially performance art, with no traditional musical content. Minimalism, using simple tones, familiar harmonies, and regular rhythms, arose against this musical anarchy.

The music now known as minimalism (that term was not commonly used until the late 1970's) grew from a variety of experimental ideas from a number of composers, many of whom worked in New York City, knew each other, and performed together. One important type of experimental music was "process music," in which the composer merely set up a system and then let the music develop in its own way. An example is Terry Riley's "In C" (1964), in which the performers were given a set of musical figures to play, and the authority to decide how long to repeat each figure and when to change to the next one. Steve Reich also worked with process music and, with "It's Gonna Rain" (1965), introduced the technique of "phasing," using two tape recorders playing the identical fragment over and over at slightly different speeds, so that the sounds moved out of and then back into phase with each other, creating unexpected rhythms and patterns. In contrast, Philip Glass retained control of his music, carefully scoring his pieces, using limited tones and constant rhythms, creating interest by gradually altering, adding to, or subtracting from his musical material. These and other minimalist composers employed long time periods and gradual changes to focus the listener's attention on the musical development.

**Impact** Minimal music was part of the experimental art scene of the 1960's that included visual art, "happenings," and performance art. It was influenced by and, in turn, influenced artists working in other media. It was still in its infancy as a musical form, though, and was little noticed beyond the music schools and performance spaces of New York and the West Coast.

**Subsequent Events** Minimal music continued to develop in the 1970's and 1980's, becoming more complex and more accessible to general audiences. Glass achieved commercial success with his cycle of operas *Einstein on the Beach* (1975), *Satyagraha* (1980), and *Akhnaten* (1984). Reich composed ensemble and orchestral pieces that entered the repertory of contemporary orchestras. The influence of minimal music could be heard in the works of later composers such as John Adams and Michael Nyman and in pop music, film scores, and even television commercials.

**Additional Information** Two good introductions to minimal music are *American Minimal Music* (1980) by Wim Mertens and the more musically technical *Experimental Music: Cage and Beyond* (1974) by Nyman.

*Joseph W. Hinton*

**See also** Art Movements; Music.

# ■ Miniskirts

*A skirt that fell between two and nine inches above the knee. The miniskirt, which reflected the changing moral climate and shifting views about female sexuality, gained widespread popularity among young Americans during the 1960's.*

Miniskirts were first worn by fashionable young women during the early 1960's. A British fashion designer, Mary Quant, is usually credited with creating the first miniskirts, but French designers André Courrèges and Pierre Cardin also played a large role in promoting miniskirts.

The early 1960's mod culture, created by young people in London, resulted in the evolution of fashions that promoted feminine liberty. Young people played a huge role in fashion development during this turbulent decade by wearing clothes that expressed their rebellious attitudes against the establishment. Miniskirts, shockingly revealing to many people who had matured during the 1940's and 1950's, came to symbolize their youthful rebellion. Faddish models such as Twiggy, Jean Shrimpton, and Penelope Tree popularized miniskirts by posing in skirts made from a variety of fabrics and in flamboyant colors.

**Impact** Miniskirts remained in vogue throughout the 1960's and subsequent decades. Other related fashions such as minidresses, minicoats, and mini-pants were introduced in the late 1960's. Additional revealing styles for women have enjoyed widespread popularity partly because of the fashion revolution that occurred during the 1960's.

**Additional Information** Further discussion of the miniskirt can be found in Yvonne Connikie's *Fashions of a Decade: The 1960's* (1990).

*Valerie Brown*

**See also** British Invasion; Fashions and Clothing; Mod; Quant, Mary; Twiggy.

# ■ Minutemen

*A right-wing secret paramilitary organization opposing a feared communist takeover in the United States. The Minutemen's penchant for secrecy about its members and activities brought the group media and law enforcement attention disproportionate to its small size.*

**Origins and History** Minutemen mythology suggests that Robert Bolivar DePugh, a chemist from Norborne, Missouri, was inspired to form this organization during a 1960 duck hunt when he fantasized about sportsmen forming guerrilla bands in a future United States under communist domination. More likely, DePugh was influenced by the widely available literature of such groups as the John Birch Society, American Nazi Party, and Liberty Lobby. The Minutemen followed a policy of organizational secrecy. Squads of five to twenty-five were to be organized, with no lists of members maintained. State commanders would know only the squad leaders. These precautions were meant to avert infiltration by authorities or "neutralization" in case of the take-over they anticipated. Ironically, most members were already known to authorities from their membership in other radical right-wing organizations, which were heavily infiltrated by law enforcement agencies. The organization differed from other extremist groups in that it did not emphasize racism and anti-Semitism but merely anticommunism and paramilitary exercises. Targeted by media and government for its terrorist potential, the Minutemen suffered from low membership, factionalism, embezzlement by officers, and the repeated prosecution of DePugh on numerous charges. Another weakness was the willingness of members to divulge information to authorities in plea-bargain arrangements.

**Activities** Described as "essentially a paper organization," attracting people through the promise of violence and the lure of military weapons, the Minutemen had fewer than two thousand members at any time. Between 1966 and 1968, Minutemen attempted bombings against targets such as a pacifist community in Voluntown, Connecticut. Members also tried to assassinate Marxist historian and activist Herbert Aptheker in 1967. All of these efforts were intercepted by law enforcement agencies. DePugh published two books that still circulate: *Blueprint for Victory* (1966) and *Can You Survive?* (1968). The subject of repeated prosecutions on charges ranging from firearms violations to sexual exploitation of a minor, DePugh once successfully fought a subpoena demanding membership lists by getting legal assistance from the American Civil Liberties Union. As an inmate, he published *Behind the Iron Mask* (1970), a call for liberal prison reform.

**Impact** Erratic, ineffective, the creation of a man discharged from the U.S. Army in 1944 for "psycho-neurosis . . . anxiety and depressive features and schizoid personality," the Minutemen were an embarrassment even to other right-wing extremist groups. A one-time member called the erstwhile guerrilla patriots "the damndest collection of blab-bermouths, paranoids, ding-a-lings and f—kups." DePugh craved the attention of the media and law enforcement agencies but accomplished nothing and even lost money on his activities. By 1973, the organization was moribund.

**Additional Information** J. Harry Jones, Jr.'s *The Minutemen* (1968) is a contemporaneous source. A more recent source of information is the Anti-Defamation League of B'nai B'rith's *Extremism of the Right: A Handbook* (1983).

*Thomas P. Carroll*

**See also** American Nazi Party; Conservatism in Politics; John Birch Society; National States Rights Party.

# ■ *Miranda v. Arizona*

*The Supreme Court's most controversial case involving self-incrimination. Despite the ruling's intent to clarify the voluntary nature of a prisoner's confession, it has given rise to further cases questioning the circumstances in which suspects must be informed of their rights.*

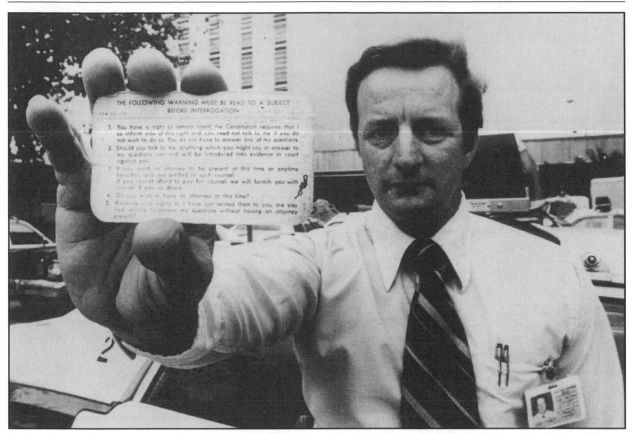

*A Miami official holds a copy of the Miranda rights, guidelines that inform suspects of their Fifth Amendment rights. These rights were created as a result of the Supreme Court's ruling in the* Miranda v. Arizona *case in 1966. (AP/Wide World Photos)*

The Fifth Amendment to the United States Constitution protects individuals from being forced to give evidence against themselves or to testify against themselves at trial. Before the Supreme Court decision in the *Miranda v. Arizona* case, the admissibility of a prior confession as evidence at a trial depended on whether it was made voluntarily. This question had to be decided on the basis of the facts in each case. Outcomes were very uneven, leading to dissatisfaction with this standard. At the same time, awareness of the plight of the poor and uneducated in the justice system began to grow. In 1963, the Supreme Court held that states had to provide a lawyer to anyone who was accused of a felony but could not afford legal counsel. This ruling provided little help, however, to those who were not aware of it before questioning and who, without a lawyer present, might be intimidated into confessing to a lesser crime to avoid prosecution for a more serious offense.

The *Miranda* case began when Phoenix police arrested Ernesto Miranda, a poverty-stricken twenty-three-year-old, on suspicion of rape and kidnapping. After being questioned for two hours, Miranda voluntarily signed a confession, which was placed in evidence against him at his trial. Miranda was convicted on all counts. He appealed, and the case reached the Supreme Court.

The Supreme Court ruled on June 13, 1966, five to four, in favor of Miranda. Chief Justice Earl Warren, who authored the majority opinion, argued that the rights to remain silent and have an attorney present during questioning were absolutely necessary to preserve the constitutional right against self-incrimination. He further argued that the requirement that these rights be clearly explained to the accused would not deter effective law enforcement. Justice Thomas Clark disagreed, arguing that conventional due-process analysis, not the right against self-incrimination, should be the basis for deciding whether a confession was voluntary. Justice John M. Harlan proclaimed his astonishment at the ruling; he believed that the right against self-incrimination did not extend outside the courtroom to the police station. Justice Byron White wrote a separate dissent, lambasting the majority for reaching an opinion that had no precedential basis and which, in his opinion, weakened law enforcement.

The ruling resulted in the Court creating guidelines, which became known as Miranda rights, for informing suspects of their Fifth Amendment rights. The Court held that before questioning suspects, police must inform them that they have the right to remain silent, anything they say may be used against them in court, they have the right to have a lawyer with them during questioning, and if they cannot afford a lawyer, one will be provided for them without charge. If police obtain a statement from a suspect in custody without informing the individual of these rights, it is not admissible evidence in a trial.

**Impact** Miranda rights have been heavily criticized as a legal loophole through which the guilty can sometimes return to the streets. Many critics agree with the dissenting justices, who felt that the decision was wrong as a matter of constitutional law. As a matter of policy, the issue is even more controversial. The outcome of the Miranda decision undoubtedly hinders police work and sometimes results in criminals going free. Whether the protection provided to individuals is worth the price is a matter of ongoing and heated debate.

**Subsequent Events** Later cases narrowed the circumstances in which Miranda rights must be read to suspects, holding that they are not required if, for example, a suspect comes to the police station voluntarily, a person who is not under arrest is questioned at a friend's home, or a person is stopped but not arrested for a traffic violation. The requirement that individuals be informed of their rights before questioning can also be waived "in a situation posing a threat to the public safety," (*New York v. Quarles*, 1984). Exactly what constitutes interrogation and thus necessitates the reading of the Miranda rights is a subject of ongoing litigation.

**Additional Information** Wayne R. Law Fave and Jerold H. Israel explain Miranda rights and related legal issues in heavily footnoted detail in the second edition of their legal textbook, *Criminal Procedure* (second edition, 1992). For an outlook limited to the 1960's but written for the average person, try Rich-

ard James Medalie's *From Escobedo to Miranda: The Anatomy of a Supreme Court Decision* (1966).

*Jean McKnight*

**See also** Supreme Court Decisions.

---

# ■ Miss America Pageant of 1968

**Date** September 7, 1968

*Hours before the 1968 Miss America pageant began, television images of women protesters crowning a sheep in mockery of the crowning of the next Miss America were broadcast across the nation. An astonished public was witnessing the dramatic debut of the women's liberation movement.*

**Origins and History** Robin Morgan and other members of New York Radical Women believed that the 1968 Miss America pageant presented the ideal opportunity to send an unmistakable message to the public about the sexual objectification and patriarchal oppression of women in American society. Radical feminists believed that the incremental, legislation-oriented approach taken by moderate groups such as the National Organization for Women (NOW) was not enough and that women would become equals only after major changes in the structure of society.

**The Protest** Just hours before the final competition began at the Miss America Pageant on September 7, 1968, about one hundred women gathered outside the pageant center in Atlantic City, New Jersey. The protest was organized by New York Radical Women member Robin Morgan, who had invited women from Detroit, New York, Washington, D.C., Boston, and Florida to participate.

The women marched along the boardwalk chanting, "Atlantic City is a town with class. They raise your morals and judge your ass." In mock tribute to the contestants, they sang, "Ain't she sweet? Makin' profit off her meat." Some carried signs. One read "Welcome to the Miss America cattle auction." An effigy of Miss America was auctioned off by protester Peggy Dobbins. Dobbins, dressed like a stockbroker, shouted to the crowd, "Gentlemen, I offer you the 1969 model. She's better every year. She walks. She talks. She smiles on cue. *And* she does housework."

In a symbolic act of liberation, protesters gathered around a large receptacle that they labeled "Freedom Trash Can." Into it they threw bras and girdles, curlers and high-heeled shoes, and copies of *Playboy*, *Vogue*, *Cosmopolitan*, and *The Ladies' Home Journal*, all of which protesters said were symbols of female bondage and representative of the second-class status of American women. The protest culminated in the crowning of a live sheep. With a bow on its tail, the sheep was led up the boardwalk, draped with a Miss America banner, then crowned the new Miss America in mockery of the crowning that would take place later that night. Many in the crowd were unsympathetic. Some called the protesters "screwy, frustrated women." Others accused them of being lesbians. Some women's rights activists were also unsympathetic. Gloria Steinem, for example, later said the event and others like it were inappropriate.

The New York Radical Women had been searching for ways to increase awareness of what they perceived as sexism in the culture and bring about changes in society. Morgan suggested a protest at the Miss America pageant, which the radical feminists felt symbolized women's oppressed status. In Morgan's "No More Miss America," one of a number of essays collected in *Sisterhood Is Powerful: An Anthology of Writings from the Women's Liberation Movement* (1970), edited by Morgan, the feminist explained that Miss America contestants, like most women, "allowed a patriarchal society to use them." She believed that through protest, the public could be made aware that patriarchal oppression of Miss America contestants was symbolic of the patriarchal oppression of women in general.

Morgan also said Miss America represented the American ideal of feminine beauty. Based upon "ludicrous beauty standards," it was an ideal that enslaved and degraded women. To counter that detrimental image, Morgan invited what she termed "normal, de-plasticized women" to protest against the "degrading, mindless, Boobie-girl symbol" embodied in Miss America.

**Impact**  The widely covered protest of the 1968 Miss America pageant made the public aware of women's liberation efforts and created the impression that support for women's liberation was growing. This brought more women into the movement. However, the protest, which even some feminists viewed as too extreme, cast women's liberation efforts in a negative light that persisted for years. For example, although none of the items thrown into the trash can

were burned during the protest, the media, in describing the event, called the women "bra-burners." This unflattering label was frequently applied to women liberationists, much to their dismay.

**Additional Information**  Morgan's "No More Miss America," in *Sisterhood Is Powerful: An Anthology of Writings from the Women's Liberation Movement* (1970), discusses the mobilization for and protest of the 1968 Miss America Pageant.

*Susan Green Barger*

**See also**  Feminist Movement; *SCUM Manifesto*; Women's Identity.

---

# ■ Mississippi Freedom Democratic Party (MFDP)

*An alternative political party. Its aim was to enable African Americans to participate fully in the Mississippi state political process.*

**Origins and History**  Mississippi's 1890 constitution had disenfranchised its African American citizens, allowing only a tiny percent to register to vote. Potential voters were prevented from exercising their rights through intimidation and taxes at the polls and registration laws requiring applicants to read and copy any section of the state constitution on request, give a "reasonable" interpretation of the section, and demonstrate a "reasonable" understanding of the duties and obligations of citizenship under a constitutional form of government. Illiterate whites often passed by just "signing the book," however, blacks were often told they had failed but were not permitted to see test results. In the mid-1950's, an effort to restrict registration even further by adding a "good moral character" requirement was initiated in response to the U.S. Supreme Court school desegregation ruling; this amendment was successful in 1962.

The Mississippi Freedom Democratic Party (MFDP) was founded April 24, 1964, in Jackson, Mississippi, by African Americans as an alternative to a segregationist state Democratic Party. Profoundly grassroots in both promise and practice, the MFDP was chaired by Lawrence Guyot with vice chair Ed King; its legal council was attorney Arthur Kinoy. It pledged loyalty to the National Democratic Party and sought its base among poor Mississippians of all races.

*Fannie Lou Hamer of the Mississippi Freedom Democratic Party addresses the Democratic National Convention's credentials committee in an effort to have her party's delegates recognized at the convention.* (AP/Wide World Photos)

**Activities** In the summer and fall of 1964, MFDP "freedom registrars," building on a fall, 1963, voter registration campaign, collected more than sixty thousand registrations on simplified unofficial forms. The MFDP and others also worked under the umbrella of the Council of Federated Organizations (COFO) to help people register on official rolls. Prevented from participating in the regular Democratic state convention, the MFDP held its own state convention on July 26, 1964, and elected delegates and alternates to the Democratic National Convention. The MFDP also nominated the first African American candidates to run for Congress since Reconstruction: Fannie Lou Hamer, Second District; Annie Devine, Fourth District; and Victoria Gray, Fifth District.

At the Democratic National Convention in Atlantic City in August, the MFDP challenged seating of the official delegation from Mississippi. Televised coverage of the MFDP's activities at the Democratic National Convention favorably affected public perception of the justice of the group's challenge. How-ever, its challenge was rejected by the party's credentials committee. In turn, the MFDP rejected a proposed compromise, linked to Hubert Humphrey, that promised that the Democratic Party would seat a racially balanced Mississippi delegation in 1968.

In January, 1965, the MFDP challenged the seating of Mississippi's newly elected congressional delegation. Depositions about voting irregularities collected in support of that challenge during the following months further publicly disgraced the state's segregationist political leadership although the MFDP's congressional challenge finally died in a House vote on September 17, 1965.

**Impact** The MFDP failed to unseat the official delegation at the 1964 Democratic National Convention but was effective in local consciousness raising and in increasing national disaffection with Mississippi's segregationist voter registration practices. In April, 1965, a federal court injunction ordered Sunflower County's registrar to operate on a nondiscriminatory basis. In August, 1965, Mississippi reformed its voter registration application process. Mississippians of all races began to register with increasing success, and racial diversity increased among elected officials. In 1968, a racially integrated Mississippi delegation was seated, as promised, at the Democratic National Convention. The MFDP was absorbed into a liberal coalition known as the Mississippi Loyal Democrats in 1968. By the late 1970's, there were more African Americans registered in Mississippi than in any other state.

**Additional Information** More information on the party can be found in the U.S. Government publication "Restrictions on Negro Voting in Mississippi History: Appendix to Brief of ACLU, *Amicus Curiae*," Publication No. 73 of the Supreme Court of the United States, October Term, 1964.

*Barbara Roos*

**See also** Civil Rights Movement; Democratic National Convention of 1968; Humphrey, Hubert; Voting Rights Legislation.

# ■ Mitford, Jessica

**Born** September 11, 1917, Batsford, Gloustershire, England
**Died** July 23, 1996, Oakland, California

*A civil rights activist, social critic, and muckraking journalist. Mitford's scathing attack on the undertaking business, published in 1963, became a model of watchdog journalism and agitation on behalf of the consumer.*

**Early Life** Jessica Mitford was born into a noted aristocratic British family, numbering among her siblings biographer and author Nancy Mitford. When sisters Diana and Unity embraced fascism in the 1930's, contrarian Jessica went to Spain to support the anti-Fascists during the Spanish Civil War. She migrated to the United States in 1939, working jobs from bartending and sales to investigator for the Office of Price Administration during World War II. She moved to Oakland, California, with second husband and union lawyer Robert E. Treuhaft after the war.

**The 1960's** When her husband's work with the estates of union employees revealed exploitative practices by the funeral industry, Mitford spotlighted the problem in the article "Saint Peter, Don't You Call Me" (*Frontier*, November, 1958). After further research, the article evolved into *The American Way of Death* (1963), a blistering exposé and indictment of the undertaking business, which became an instant best-seller.

Her next book, *The Trial of Dr. Spock* (1969), focused on the federal prosecution in Boston of famous baby doctor Benjamin Spock and four others for conspiracy to promote violations of the Selective Service Act. She focused on the politics of prosecution, arguing that the defendants had been denied a fundamental right not to be tried for dissent. Following conviction of four of the five, she asserted that political use of federal conspiracy laws meant that all Americans are not as free as they think they are.

**Later Life** With wry humor, Mitford continued to ridicule practices that "victimize people in odd little ways." She attacked a required oath of loyalty to the California constitution while at San Jose State University in "My Short and Happy Life as a Distinguished Professor" (*Atlantic*, 1974) by noting, "Do I uphold and defend, for example, Article 4, Section $25\frac{3}{4}$, limiting boxing and wrestling matches to fifteen rounds? I don't know."

Major works included *Kind and Unusual Punishment: The Prison Business* (1971) and a study of the role of politics and money in national health care, *The American Way of Birth* (1992).

**Impact** Along with seminal works such as Rachel Carson's *Silent Spring* (1962) and Ralph Nader's *Unsafe at Any Speed: The Designed-in Dangers of the American Automobile* (1965), Mitford's writings helped inaugurate a new era of legal protection from big business and big government. Legislators split by the Vietnam War could find common ground here, and in the 1960's, concern for consumers' rights became a permanent part of the American psyche.

**Subsequent Events** Although funeral directors from all over the country offered their services when the "Queen of the Muckrakers" succumbed to lung cancer, her family provided what she wanted—a sensible and dignified cremation.

**Additional Information** In 1979, Mitford published *Poison Penmanship: The Gentle Art of Muckraking*, in which she explored the approach and methods used in creating each of her key works. It is a virtual course in investigative journalism.

*Gary A. Olson*

**See also** Boston Five Trial; Carson, Rachel; Nader, Ralph; Spock, Benjamin.

# ■ Mod

*The 1960's term for young and stylish. It became a byword for the pop culture of the decade, particularly between 1967 and 1972.*

"Mod," shortened from the word "modern," originally referred to the group of British young people who in the 1960's rebelled against the establishment with outrageous clothing, long hair, and flamboyant behavior.

In the United States, the word "mod" became a symbol of post-World War II modernity and the counterculture of the hippies. An outgrowth of the 1950's Beat generation, the hippies banded together around political issues, advocating a lifestyle that included free love and hallucinogenic drugs. The mod era embraced the youth culture as a response to the coming-of-age of the postwar baby boomers (born 1946-1964), whose earliest members turned twenty in 1966. The term also referred to a style of clothing rendered in colors such as neon orange, acid green, and hot pink. One television show, *The Mod Squad*, a police drama featuring three young undercover "hippie cops" that ran from 1968 through 1973, used the word in its title. The mod movement was reflected in art such as that of Peter Max, which employed bright colors and wild designs, and even toys such as the Barbie doll, which sported an entire line of mod clothing, including miniskirts, go-go boots, and bell-bottom pants.

**Impact** Mod epitomized the youth culture of the 1960's—modern, hip, and groovy. Elements of the mod style were incorporated into later trends, but the style was replaced by other trends by the early 1970's.

**Additional Information** William O'Neill's *Coming Apart: An Informal History of America in the 1960's* (1971) and *Gates of Eden: American Culture in the '60's* (1977) are insightful sources for further investigation.

*Michaela Crawford Reaves*

**See also** Barbie and Ken Dolls; British Invasion; Counterculture; Fashions and Clothing; Hippies; Max, Peter.

# ■ Monkees

*Stars of a television comedy series about a rock-and-roll band. The Monkees quickly developed into a true band, releasing five chart-topping albums in two years.*

In 1965, Columbia Pictures selected four young men to star in a half-hour comedy show patterned after the Beatles' 1964 film *A Hard Day's Night. The Monkees* would feature the zany adventures of a struggling rock-and-roll band and serve as a promotional tool for professionally produced albums recorded by studio musicians and released under the Monkees name. After auditioning hundreds of actors and musicians, the producers selected the four Monkees—Mickey Dolenz, David Jones, Michael Nesmith, and Peter Tork—for their personalities and screen chemistry rather than their musical talent.

The program ran for two seasons, 1966-1967 and 1967-1968. Each episode combined a wacky and cartoonish plot with sight gags, outtakes, and lip-synched performances of the band's hits. Bolstered by the popularity of the television show, the Monkees' first two albums, *The Monkees* and *More of the Monkees*, both reached number one on the *Billboard* charts and generated three number-one singles ("Daydream Believer," "I'm a Believer," and "Last Train to Clarksville").

The group was criticized when public performances revealed that they could not play their instruments as well as the musicians heard on their records. Led by Nesmith, the group fought for permission to play on their own albums. Subsequent releases such as the 1967 *Headquarters* and *Pisces, Aquarius, Capricorn, and Jones*, which both reached number one on the *Billboard* charts, and 1968 *The Birds, the Bees, and the Monkees*, which reached number three, showcased the band as musicians, songwriters, and vocalists.

When their television show was canceled in 1968, the group starred in the film *Head*, lampooning their own prefabricated origins and rise to fame. The film was a commercial failure as was a television special aired later the same year, *33 1/3 Revolutions per Monkee*. Tork left the group, and the remaining Monkees disbanded in 1969.

**Impact** In spite of their prefabricated beginnings, the Monkees developed into an innovative and remarkably successful pop group. They sold millions of records and were professionally linked to many

*The Monkees—from left to right, David Jones, Peter Tork, Mickey Dolenz, and Michael Nesmith—began as the stars of a weekly television show then gradually became a real rock-and-roll band.* (AP/Wide World Photos)

notable figures in 1960's music and popular culture. Dolenz was one of the first musicians to experiment with the Moog synthesizer. Jimi Hendrix was introduced to U.S. audiences as an opening act for the Monkees; Jack Nicholson coauthored *Head*. Their hit songs were written by well-known composers such as Carole King and Neil Diamond. Nesmith's compositions were recorded by other groups including the Stone Poneys (with Linda Ronstadt) and the Nitty Gritty Dirt Band.

**Additional Information** Dolenz's *I'm a Believer: My Life of Monkees, Music, and Madness* (1993) offers a behind-the-scenes account of the group's career. More recent accounts are Glenn A. Baker's *Monkeemania: The True Story of the Monkees* (1986) and *Hey, Hey, We're the Monkees* (1996), edited by Harold Bronson.

*Maureen Puffer*

**See also** Beatles; Music.

## ■ Monroe, Marilyn

**Born** June 1, 1926, Los Angeles, California
**Died** August 5, 1962, Los Angeles, California

*Film star and pinup of the 1950's who died at age thirty-six. The consummate sex symbol's drug overdose made her one of the first "casualties" of the 1960's.*

**Early Life** The childhood of Marilyn Monroe (born Norma Jean Mortenson) was virtually Dickensian: an illegitimate daughter whose mother was confined to

*Glamorous movie star Marilyn Monroe appeared at President John F. Kennedy's birthday celebration in 1962, giving rise to rumors that the two were romantically linked.* (Archive Photos)

a mental hospital, Monroe lived in a series of foster homes where she suffered from neglect and possibly sexual abuse. She became a photographer's model in the 1940's, appearing in advertisements, on magazine covers, and in nude photos that would resurface when her film career took off. A Hollywood contract player from the late 1940's, she quickly became a star, going from bit parts in B-pictures to featured roles in films such as *All About Eve* (1950) to starring in *Niagara, How to Marry a Millionaire,* and *Gentlemen Prefer Blondes* (all 1953). These roles and her appearance on the cover and as the centerfold for the first *Playboy* magazine in 1953 made her the embodiment of sexuality as it was expressed and understood during that decade. Marriage to baseball hero Joe DiMaggio (1954-1955) and intellectual playwright Arthur Miller (1956-1960), as well as forays into method acting and liberal politics, did little to change her sex symbol image.

**The 1960's** Despite critical and commercial acclaim in the 1950's when she starred in *The Seven Year Itch* (1955), *Bus Stop* (1957), and *Some Like It Hot* (1959),

Monroe's career began to wane. Following two commercial failures, the musical comedy *Let's Make Love* (1960) and the Miller-penned drama *The Misfits* (1961), Monroe began filming *Something's Got to Give* for financially troubled Twentieth Century Fox in April, 1962. Strapped by years of mismanagement and extravagant spending on the set of its only other production, *Cleopatra* (1963), starring Elizabeth Taylor, Fox fired Monroe from the film for excessive absences in June, 1962. She was negotiating a return to the film when she died.

Monroe's off-screen activities during the early 1960's are less clearly documented. After she and Miller divorced, Monroe purchased her first home in a suburb of Los Angeles. Her appearance at John F. Kennedy's 1962 birthday celebration at Madison Square Garden fed rumors that the president and the star were romantically linked. She was treated by a number of physicians and psychiatrists, many of whom prescribed amphetamines, barbiturates, and other drugs.

On the morning of August 5, 1962, Monroe's housekeeper, Eunice Murray, and her psychiatrist, Ralph Greenson, found Monroe in her bed, clutching her telephone—dead of an overdose of barbiturates. Initial speculation centered on whether Monroe's death was an accident or a suicide; the police investigation concluded that she had killed herself. She was buried in Los Angeles at a private service organized by DiMaggio.

**Impact** The question of who was responsible for Monroe's death has inspired a variety of biographers, historians, journalists, and conspiracy theorists in the years since her death. Their answers tend to reveal more about the authors than about their subject. Among those who accept the suicide verdict, blame is assigned to Hollywood (Norman Mailer), capitalism (the Soviet Union's *Pravda*), the drug culture (Jacqueline Susann's *Valley of the Dolls*), and prefeminist misogyny (Gloria Steinem). Post-Watergate investigations in the 1970's postulated murder conspiracies involving President Kennedy and Attorney General Robert F. Kennedy, organized crime boss Sam Giancana, the Teamsters' Jimmy Hoffa, U.S. or Soviet agents, and others. Monroe's death has been interpreted as signaling a break from the innocence (and prurience) of the 1950's and the promise of the Camelot era.

In death, Monroe remains a powerful American

icon. Her image has been appropriated by artist Andy Warhol, novelist Mailer, pop singer Madonna, and commercial interests worldwide. Surges of interest in her life and death, heralded by new "evidence" regarding her death or novel interpretations of her life, occur periodically. In 1973, Mailer published *Marilyn*, the first of his two book-length studies of the actress; the same year, singer Elton John released "Candle in the Wind," a song memorializing her. In 1982, the Los Angeles District Attorney's office reinvestigated her case as a possible murder. Although the district attorney was satisfied that it was a case of suicide, others were less convinced. Anthony Summers's spectacular allegations surrounding her involvement with the Kennedy brothers, published in 1985, sparked yet another wave of interest in Monroe and the early 1960's.

**Additional Information** Monroe's life has been the subject of more than eighty celebrity biographies, ranging from the lucid to the lurid; among the best known are Fred Lawrence Guiles's *Norma Jean* (1969) and Summers's *Goddess: The Secret Life of Marilyn Monroe* (1985).

*Susan McLeland*

**See also** DiMaggio, Joe; Film; Kennedy, John F.; Kennedy, Robert; Mailer, Norman; Organized Crime; Steinem, Gloria; Susann, Jacqueline; Taylor, Elizabeth; Women's Identity.

---

# ■ Monterey Pop Festival

**Date** June 16-18, 1967

*The event that inaugurated the 1967 Summer of Love. The Monterey, California, event—the nation's first large-scale rock music festival—became the model for many later music extravaganzas.*

**Origins and History** The Monterey International Pop Festival was the brainchild of two Los Angeles businesspeople who raised money and secured a lease to the fairgrounds where it was held. However, after John Phillips of the Mamas and Papas and his producer-manager, Lou Adler, became involved, they assumed the job of organizing the festival. They created a board of governors that included musicians Paul McCartney, Paul Simon, William "Smokey" Robinson, and Brian Wilson and established a plan to donate the proceeds to charities. The aim of the festival was to showcase the most impor-

tant musical acts of the period, particularly California bands.

**The Festival** On a weekend in June, 1967, a crowd of fifty thousand gathered in Monterey for the first and only Monterey Pop Festival. Despite initial fears, the event took place without any major problems. The Friday evening show was a mixture of new and veteran performers. The Paupers, an unknown Canadian group, gave a surprising performance; Eric Burdon debuted his new version of the Animals; and Johnny Rivers appeared. However, the highlight of the evening was the singing of Simon and Garfunkel.

Saturday afternoon was devoted to the blues, with Los Angeles band Canned Heat starting the show, followed by Country Joe and the Fish, the Paul Butterfield Blues Band, and the Steve Miller Band. Al Kooper played a solo number on the piano, and Mike Bloomfield, formerly of the Butterfield band, introduced the Electric Flag, who gave a rousing performance. The highlight of the afternoon was the inspired singing of Janis Joplin, lead singer of Big Brother and the Holding Company. She made such an impression that her band was asked to play again on Sunday night. That second performance is captured in D. A. Pennebaker's film, *Monterey Pop* (1969). Saturday night's proceedings began with Moby Grape, followed by the Byrds and the Jefferson Airplane, featuring new singer Grace Slick. Otis Redding, however, stole the show with a dynamic version of "Try a Little Tenderness."

Sunday afternoon featured a two-and-a-half-hour performance by Indian sitarist Ravi Shankar, who hypnotized an audience largely unfamiliar with his ragas. On Sunday evening, Blues Project opened, followed by the Buffalo Springfield and the Grateful Dead. The Who, a band that had enjoyed only limited success in the United States, worked itself into a frenzy of smashed guitars, smoke bombs, and feedback that stunned the crowd. Two sets later, the Jimi Hendrix Experience made its U.S. debut. Hendrix topped the Who's antics when he lit his guitar on fire and smashed it into his amplifier. The Mamas and Papas closed the show with a selection of the group's most popular songs.

**Impact** The festival was a seminal event in the history of American rock and roll. Although annual folk and jazz festivals took place across the country, the Monterey event was the first carefully organized rock festival. Before the Monterey event, typically a

*In addition to rock and blues artists such as the Jefferson Airplane, Grateful Dead, the Who, Paul Butterfield Blues Band, Janis Joplin, and Jimi Hendrix, the Monterey Pop Festival featured Indian sitar player Ravi Shankar.* (Fotos International/Archive Photos)

collection of bands toured a number of cities, putting on predictably choreographed performances. However, the concept of a collection of bands performing over a number of days was repeated at events in Miami, Fort Lauderdale, Atlanta, the Isle of Wight, and Woodstock.

After the festival, San Francisco became an established music capital, with its own recording studios and a thriving community of musicians and producers. The Monterey Pop Festival brought widespread attention to a host of bands that had been known primarily in San Francisco. The festival boosted the sales of albums that had been released by the Jefferson Airplane, the Grateful Dead, and Moby Grape, and Quicksilver Messenger Service, the Steve Miller Band, Electric Flag, and Big Brother and the Holding Company managed to parlay their appearances into recording contracts. Other artists also found themselves with an instant reputation and lucrative contracts, most notably Hendrix, Redding, and the Who.

The best aspect of the festival was the spirit of good will. The crowds were especially appreciative of the bands and remarkably tolerant of each other, and many band members calmly mingled with their fans. To most observers, this behavior seemed the perfect embodiment of the hippie ethos of peace and love, and it set the tone for the remarkably docile spirit of the 1969 Woodstock Music and Art Fair.

**Additional Information** The most comprehensive treatment of the festival is Joel Selvin's *Monterey Pop* (1992). Other important accounts include Robert Christgau's *Any Old Way You Choose It: Rock and Other Pop Music, 1967-1973* (1973), Jack McDonough's *San Francisco Rock: The Illustrated History of San Francisco Rock Music* (1985), Gary Herman's *Rock 'n' Roll Babylon* (1982), and D. A. Pennebaker's film, *Monterey Pop* (1969).

*David W. Madden*

**See also** Altamont Music Festival; Grateful Dead; Hendrix, Jimi; Jefferson Airplane; Joplin, Janis; Music; San Francisco as Cultural Mecca; *Sgt. Pepper's Lonely Hearts Club Band*; Summer of Love; Woodstock Festival.

## ■ Moon Landing

**Date** July 20, 1969

*Humans visit the Moon and return safely. On July 20, 1969, Neil A. Armstrong became the first person on the Moon.*

**Origins and History**  Books such as Jules Verne's *From the Earth to the Moon* (1865) and H. G. Wells's *War of the Worlds* (1898) made a profound impact upon generations of youthful stargazers such as physicist Robert Goddard and engineer Wernher von Braun.

These scientists' dreams became reality with the successful flights of Mercury, Gemini, and Apollo.

On May 25, 1961, President John F. Kennedy committed Americans to landing astronauts on the Moon before the end of the decade. Kennedy used

*On July 20, 1969, Neil A. Armstrong and Edwin E. "Buzz" Aldrin become the first men to walk on the Moon.* (National Aeronautics and Space Administration)

the lunar goal to demonstrate to the world the technological growth and social vitality of the United States. He wanted to restore the nation's pride and self-confidence, which had been badly shaken by Soviet space achievements. The Apollo flights did capture international public attention.

**The Landing** Nearly one million onlookers came to view the launch. Millions more watched through television relayed by satellites at 9:32 A.M., July 16, 1969, when the 3,817-ton spacecraft, propelled by a gigantic Saturn 5 launch vehicle, slowly rose above the launch tower and lifted out over the Atlantic Ocean. Astronaut Michael Collins got a view of the fast-receding Earth—brilliant white clouds, a faint trace of green jungles, a noticeable smear of rust from North African deserts, and blue sea slid by majestically and silently.

On the fourth day of flight, the astronauts—Collins, Neil A. Armstrong, and Edwin E. "Buzz" Aldrin—swung the spacecraft around to face the Moon. The Moon appeared three-dimensional with two distinct central regions: one nearly black and the other basked in the whitish light reflected from the surface of Earth.

The next day, July 20, the astronauts prepared for the lunar landing. All three suited up. As Armstrong and Aldrin took off in the lunar module *Eagle*, Collins stayed to monitor and fly the command module *Columbia* around the Moon. Collins said the lunar module was a weird contraption. Its four legs awkwardly jutted out above a body with neither symmetry nor grace; however, it performed admirably. Armstrong had to manually steer the craft away from many craters but selected a good area on the Sea of Tranquillity before running out of fuel. Armstrong announced, "Houston, Tranquillity Base here. The *Eagle* has landed."

At 10:56 P.M., July 20, 1969, via satellite television, Armstrong shared with the world the first human footstep on the Moon. His unforgettable words, "That's one small step for man, one giant leap for mankind," immortalized the moment.

An estimated 600 million people watched first Armstrong and then Aldrin on the lunar surface. Aldrin described the lunar landscape as "magnificent desolation." The astronauts retrieved some fifty pounds of lunar rocks, ending the first walk on the Moon after only two hours and twenty-one minutes.

**Impact** Collins suggests that the greatest benefit from the lunar landing was that human beings were drawn together for one fleeting moment: It was not Americans who accomplished this feat; it was humankind. Nevertheless, the United States had won the race to the Moon and had firmly established its dominance in science and technology. It was at once an accomplishment for humanity and an American triumph in the Cold War.

**Subsequent Events** The United States successfully launched Skylab, the nation's first space station, in 1973-1974. The 1975 Apollo-Soyuz Test Project marked the first U.S.-Soviet collaboration in space.

**Additional Information** For further information on the lunar landing and U.S. space programs, see *U.S. Space Gear* (1994), by Lillian D. Kozloski; . . . *The Heavens and the Earth* (1987), by Walter A. McDougall; and *Carrying the Fire* (1974) and *Liftoff* (1988), by astronaut Collins.

*Lillian D. Kozloski*

**See also** Apollo 1 Disaster; Apollo Space Program; Gemini Space Program; Mercury Space Program; Space Race.

# ■ Moratorium Day

**Date** October 15, 1969

*A nationwide protest against the Vietnam War. The Moratorium made opposing the war more acceptable and popular and spread the protest from Washington, D.C., to communities and campuses.*

Moratorium Day was launched in April, 1969, at a meeting of Mass. PAX, a Massachusetts peace group whose chair, Jerome Grossman, suggested the notion of a general deadline strike. The call for student participation read, "If there is no firm commitment to American withdrawal or a negotiated settlement, on October 15, participating members of the academic community will spend the entire day organizing against the war and working in the community to get others to join us in an enlarged and lengthened moratorium in November."

Besides Grossman, a successful fifty-five-year-old businessperson, organizers ranged from Marty Peretz, a Harvard University teacher who would eventually become publisher of *The New Republic* magazine, to Sam Brown, an Iowa native who had been president of the Young Republicans at Redlands University before becoming active in the National Student Association and Eugene McCarthy's 1968 presidential campaign. Brown, national director of the Moratorium, operated out of a modest headquarters on Vermont Avenue in Washington, D.C., where his committee included Ken Hurwitz, Adam Walinsky, Dick Lavine, Dave Hawk, Marge Sklencar, and David Mixner, according to Hurwitz.

With a simple slogan, Work for Peace, by June 30, the Moratorium had ninety-six endorsements from student leaders who asked for a change in the U.S. government's Vietnam policy, demanded the creation of opposition political candidates, or expressed their doubt or anger about the war.

Groups of doctors and lawyers placed supportive advertisements in newspapers, and city councils passed resolutions calling for an end to the war. Moratorium committees were formed not just at schools but also in government agencies in Washington, in media companies in New York, and among secretaries and laboratory workers at the Massachusetts Institute of Technology in Boston. Labor unions such as the United Automobile Workers and Teamsters endorsed the action; seventy-nine college presidents signed a public appeal to the White House for quick withdrawal of U.S. troops from Vietnam.

Hundreds of thousands of Americans from coast to coast participated in teach-ins, marches, rallies, candlelight vigils, and other activities.

*On October 15, 1969, Moratorium Day, hundreds of thousands of Americans, like these college students marching on the federal building in New Orleans, protested against U.S. involvement in Vietnam.* (AP/Wide World Photos)

**Impact** Although Moratorium Day did not directly lead to an immediate withdrawal of U.S. troops, the protest was successful in revealing the extent of public discontent with the war and encouraging citizen involvement with the issue. It made opposition to the war a more popular and acceptable viewpoint and broadened the antiwar movement's base of support. By 1971, more than five hundred thousand people had demonstrated in Washington, D.C.

Conceived as a general strike against the Vietnam War, Moratorium Day eventually was tempered by leaders who "liked the idea of political action but not the threat of a strike," according to *The New York Times*, and expanded to a November march on Washington.

Some critics seemed to dislike the growing popularity of antiwar sentiment: In *The Paper Revolutionaries* (1972), Laurence Leamer wrote that "liberal politicians usurped the peace movement, transforming it into their symbolic, emotive, and inconsequential ritual." Indeed, taking part was a bipartisan group of senators and representatives including such mainstream figures as New York Democrat Allard Lowenstein, diplomat Averell Harriman, economist John Kenneth Galbraith, Cardinal Cushing, and even Columbia Broadcasting System (CBS) news anchor Eric Severeid, who on the night of October 15 said that Moratorium Day had earned its place in history.

**Additional Information** Ken Hurwitz, one of the Moratorium Day committee members, wrote a first-person memoir of the protest in *Marching Nowhere* (1971).

*Bill Knight*

**See also** March Against Death; National Mobilization Committee to End the War in Vietnam (MOBE); Pentagon, Levitating of the; Vietnam War.

# ■ Motion Picture Association of America Rating System

*A voluntary, self-regulating film rating system adopted by Hollywood. The Motion Picture Association of America introduced the system in the 1960's to provide parents with information on a film's content.*

The Motion Picture Association of America (MPAA) was established in 1922 as the Motion Picture Producers and Distributors of America (MPPDA) under the leadership of Will H. Hays, former United States postmaster general. The association's goal was to police and govern the film industry without federal and state interference and to actively promote a positive image of the industry among the American public. The MPPDA initiated self-censorship when it established the Motion Picture Production Code in 1930. The Code, as it became known, was regulated by the Production Code Administration (PCA). In the mid-1940's, the MPPDA changed its name to the Motion Picture Association of America.

After World War II, domestic and foreign films increasingly began to reflect important social, political, religious, and moral issues that denied them the PCA seal of approval. Frustrated filmmakers mounted legal challenges to the whole concept of PCA censorship. The U.S. Supreme Court rulings on censorship, obscenity, and cinema's constitutional status, along with sweeping societal changes, gave the Code a negative public image. In 1966, newly selected MPAA president Jack Valenti initiated a reexamination of the Code.

In 1968, Valenti abolished the controversial Code and introduced a self-regulating, voluntary rating system under the MPAA Classification and Rating Administration. This system established four categories: G, general audiences, all ages admitted; M, mature audiences, parental guidance suggested but all ages admitted; R, restricted, children under sixteen not admitted without accompanying parent or adult guardian; and X, no one under sixteen admitted. The MPAA, as part of its continuing self-regulatory procedure, checked all advertising to ensure that films carried a rating and examined the content of all film trailers so that they were shown only to appropriate audiences.

**Impact** The impact on the U.S. film industry and the public was immediate. Motion picture theater owners liked the new rating system and generally adhered to the stated admission policies. Parents approved because it gave them advance information on a film's content. To make sure that the rating system remained effective, the MPAA conducted a yearly poll through the Opinion Research Corporation of Princeton.

**Subsequent Events** The MPAA film rating system remains in effect but has undergone slight changes. In 1970, the age restriction on films rated R and X was raised to seventeen. The M category became PG for parental guidance suggested, then in 1984, the system gained a new category, PG-13, which did not restrict admittance to the film but warned parents that it contained some material that may be inappropriate for children under age thirteen. Six years later, the X category was changed to NC-17, for no one under seventeen admitted.

**Additional Information** In 1996, the MPAA reissued its pamphlet "The Voluntary Movie Rating System" by Jack Valenti, which covers all aspects of the rating system from its beginnings to how it is applied and regulated.

*Terry Theodore*

**See also** Censorship; Film; *Midnight Cowboy*.

# ■ Motor Vehicle Air Pollution Act of 1965

*Added federal controls for motor vehicle emissions to the Clean Air Act of 1963. The Environmental Protection Agency sets automotive emission standards and regulates motor fuels and additives.*

Historically, automobile manufacture had been largely unregulated. In the late 1950's, the Department of Health, Education, and Welfare (HEW) studied causes of air pollution and determined that the automobile engine was the largest single contributor of pollutants, particularly hydrocarbons, to the air.

The automobile industry was opposed to any program that might increase costs and reduce sales; more research was urged. The environmental community wanted controls to protect public health from pollution and smog. The administration of President Lyndon B. Johnson, while concerned with auto exhaust, initially opposed an air pollution bill introduced into the Senate by Edmund Muskie as premature but switched when "flexibility" in setting standards and deadlines was given to HEW.

In 1965, Congress enacted the Motor Vehicle Air Pollution Act, legislation designed to control air pollution caused by automobiles by requiring exhaust controls on all new cars within two years. Subsequent legislation mandated higher standards in emission controls.

**Impact** To meet emission standards, equipment to reduce or eliminate air pollution from crankcase, exhaust, fuel tank, and carburetor systems had to be produced. Some of these devices added weight and reduced fuel economy, hurting another environmental goal. Improvement in air quality was slow because many older cars were still on the road, but gradually the air in cities improved. Hydrocarbon emissions in San Francisco fell 25 percent from 1967 to 1976, and other cities, such as New York, reported decreases in air pollutants.

**Subsequent Events** In the 1970's, the Environmental Protection Agency (established in 1970) moved toward requiring engines to run on unleaded fuel. Catalytic converters became the primary method of controlling automobile emissions. States were required to develop implementation plans that involved the measurement of mobile source pollutants, vehicle inspections, and transportation control plans.

**Additional Information** Lawrence J. White's *Regulation of Air Pollutants, Emissions from Motor Vehicles* (1982) discusses various federal laws regarding air pollution caused by motor vehicles.

*Stephen B. Dobrow*

**See also** Air Pollution; Automobiles and Auto Manufacturing; Environmental Movement.

## ■ Motown

*A black-owned and family-operated music recording company. Motown Record Corporation developed a unique and significant musical sound to become the most profitable African American recording company in the United States.*

Motown—a contraction of Motortown, for the automotive industry in Detroit, Michigan, where the record company was founded—began in 1959 in a two-story house identified as "Hitsville USA." Founder Berry Gordy, Jr., a musician, lyricist, entrepreneur, and former autoworker, defined the Motown sound as a combination of "rats, roaches, and love." Under his guidance, Motown's music transformed from established soul music into a blend of unpolished southern soul and sophisticated rhythm and blues.

Motown experimented with a revolutionary resistance to traditional recording methods. Engineers mixed bright new voices with touches of classical music to develop a smooth modern sound. Employing echoes, recording on wider ranges of tracks, adding instruments and vocals to previously recorded songs, multitracking, and overdubbing in no way overshadowed the original beat of soul and rhythm and blues.

In an effort to maintain established ethnic audiences while attracting white, middle-class listeners, Motown marketed its new music as "The Sound of Young America." Performers dressed up their productions by wearing formalized and colorful attire and added choreographed dance steps, classical arrangements, and stringed instruments.

Motown drew its talent and technical expertise from Detroit natives and residents. Its operation was a precise and well-designed machine, and its employees were "interchangeable parts" that could function during every stage of a recording session. William "Smokey" Robinson, lead singer of the Miracles, was also a composer and producer, providing music and technical assistance to other Motown artists as well as his own group. He wrote and produced Marvin Gaye's "I'll Be Doggone" (1965) and "Ain't That Peculiar" (1965). Star performers Valerie Simpson and Nick Ashford wrote lyrics and composed music for "Ain't No Mountain High Enough," performed by Gaye and Tammi Terrell in 1966 and later recorded by Diana Ross. However, the major impetus behind Motown hits was the Holland-Dozier-Holland writing and production team composed of Lamont Dozier and brothers Brian and Eddie Holland. These three were largely responsible—individually or together—for the success of the Four Tops, Temptations, Supremes, Martha and the Vandellas, Gaye, and others. Gaye and Gordy also contributed to Motown's top records as composers and producers.

**Impact** Motown proved that a company owned by African Americans could be successful in a previously white-dominated industry. It also set a pattern of success for soloists and groups, particularly fostering the rise of "girl groups." The seasoned Motown professionals and future stars monopolized the recording industry, introducing innovative arrangements and new styles, and consistently topped pop and rhythm-and-blues charts. Backed by the Miracles, Robinson's falsetto delivery of mostly self-composed songs scored high on the charts. Gaye's

musical and technical background produced a natural stage presence that shaped future stars throughout the industry. A collage of multitalented Motown performers—Michael Jackson, Stevie Wonder, Gladys Knight and the Pips, Ross, and other Motown alumni—contributed much to the entertainment world.

**Subsequent Events** In 1967, Motown established a branch in Los Angeles but maintained its headquarters in Detroit. Some Motown artists and talents, including the Holland-Dozier-Holland production team, left the studio, although some eventually returned. In 1969, the California contingent became Motown's official headquarters and the company began to produce television specials and films. Ross starred in the Gordy-inspired films *Lady Sings the Blues* (the life of Billie Holiday), *Mahogany*, and *The Wiz.* By the 1980's, competition from major entertainment corporations had begun to lessen Motown's profits, so Gordy signed a distribution agreement with MCA. In 1993, Gordy sold Motown to

*Berry Gordy, Jr., (right) founder of Motown Record Corporation, receives an award from the National Association for the Advancement of Colored People in 1968.* (AP/Wide World Photos)

Polygram—one of several major record companies controlling nearly 90 percent of the market—for a record $301 million.

**Additional Information**  A history of Motown is documented in *Where Did Our Love Go: The Rise and Fall of the Motown Sound* (1985), by Nelson George, and references to Motown can be found in *A Generation in Motion: Popular Music and Culture in the Sixties* (1979), by David Pichaske.

*Adolph Dupree*

**See also**  Detroit Riot; Music; Supremes.

## ■ *Mountain of Gold*

**Published** 1967
**Author** Betty Lee Sung (1924-      )

*One of the first books to trace and analyze the history of the Chinese in the United States. Sung examines family and community life, anti-Chinese legislation, and the many contributions and accomplishments of Chinese Americans.*

**The Work**  In *Mountain of Gold: The Chinese in America*, Sung directly challenged prevalent stereotypes of Chinese as "unassimilable aliens" who supposedly could not become respectably productive, fully integrated members of American society. Drawing on individual case studies, social surveys, demographic reports, popular media, and a wide range of scholarship, Sung argued that the "Chinese have been able [in the 1960's] to utilize their abilities in this country to their fullest extent." She also documented the hardships endured by Chinese from 1848 to the mid-1960's in their struggle for civil and legal rights. Overall, Sung attempted to show that "the experiences of this group, once hated and persecuted, may serve as a guide to dealing with present-day minority problems and peoples." Accordingly, she emphasized the courageous pioneer spirit of early immigrants who built the Central Pacific railroad and transformed California wilderness into farmland, the harshly tested strength of Chinese who remained in the United States during periods of public persecution and anti-Chinese legislation, and the remarkable achievements of second-, third-, and fourth-generation Chinese Americans who proved that their people were as capable as any other. Sung carefully researched such aspects of Chinese American history as the causes, forms, and consequences of anti-Chinese sentiment; changing

attitudes among the general public toward Chinese Americans (officially marked by the 1943 repeal of the 1882 Chinese Exclusion Act); and the often painful experiences of Chinese Americans trying to reconcile traditional and modern values.

**Impact**  *Mountain of Gold*'s basic themes reflect the 1960's concern with recognizing and reinforcing minority groups' rights as citizens of a democracy. Sung realized that Chinese Americans, like other minority groups, were generally misunderstood by the American public. To counter perceptions of Chinese Americans as "foreigners" who could not fit into American society, she composed a history of their experiences that reached a wide audience. Moreover, she set Chinese Americans apart from other minorities, claiming that they "were never so belligerent or pushy as to challenge the white majority's position, nor so submissive and servile as to invite contempt." Reviews of *Mountain of Gold* in the 1960's were consistently favorable. *Best Sellers* magazine, for example, noted, "Any American who professes a humane interest in Civil Rights has an obligation to read[this book]."

**Related Works**  Other perspectives on the history of the Chinese in the United States are provided by Thomas Chinn's *A History of Chinese in California* (1969) and Sien-Woo Kung's *Chinese in America* (1962).

**Additional Information**  For general readers, substantial studies of Chinese American history include Ruthann Lum McCunn's *Chinese American Portraits* (1988) and Ronald Takaki's *Strangers from a Different Shore* (1989).

*Mary Louise Buley-Meissner*
**See also**  Civil Rights Movement; Demographics of the United States; *Eat a Bowl of Tea*; Immigration.

## ■ Music

*The many styles of popular songs and serious music that defy unequivocal categorization or tidy summation. The music of the 1960's was as tumultuous, contradictory, and thrilling as the complicated culture that gave it birth.*

Born in the 1950's as an alternative to the tame popular music of the day, rock and roll inspired impassioned debate. Critics dismissed its lyrics as mindless, condemned its unremitting beat as sexually suggestive, and deplored the fissure it opened between parents and children as dangerous to the social order. For them, it was subversive. Its champions defended it as an emotional outlet for life-affirming energies, justified it as a generation's natural and irrepressible search for identity, and prized it as the unfettered quest of young people for a good time. For them, it was liberating. An alchemical brew of country, rhythm and blues, and black gospel music, rock and roll had no single creator but was the work of many, including Buddy Holly, Bill Haley, Chuck Berry, Little Richard Penniman, Jerry Lee Lewis, Bo Diddley, and Elvis Presley, who rocketed to the forefront of American music in 1956.

**Commercialized Rock**  In the first three years of the 1960's, rock and roll became increasingly commercialized and less daring as many artists solidified careers and polished the musical styles that had made them famous. Dance crazes, especially Chubby Checker's "The Twist" (1960), provided much of what excitement there was. Presley, newly discharged from the army, plunged into a series of lame films and mediocre soundtracks. The singer of "Heartbreak Hotel" (1956) wasted his enormous talents on throwaways such as "There's No Room to Rhumba in a Sports Car" (1963). Not until an acclaimed television special in late 1968 did Presley resurface, his talent and charisma surprisingly intact. At age twenty, Phil Spector was one of the few innovators, founding Phillies Records in 1961 and beginning a long run of hits. Many instrumentalists began their careers as studio musicians erecting the famous Spector "wall of sound" behind the Crystals, the Ronettes, the Righteous Brothers, Darlene Love, and Ike and Tina Turner.

**Folk**  In part as a backlash against rock and roll, folk music enjoyed a revival in the early 1960's. The Kingston Trio, the New Christie Minstrels, Joan Baez, and Peter, Paul and Mary sang traditional folk songs as well as original and socially relevant music. Most important, Bob Dylan, whose first album was released in 1962, emerged from the urban avant-garde wing of folk. Popular mainly with university students and social activists, Dylan drew on Woody Guthrie's music and 1950's Beat poetry, and even though some reckoned his singing intolerably grating, many judged him to be a genius, the voice of a generation. His songs were poetically elusive and seemingly too politically abrasive to be commercially attractive (for example, "Hard Rain's a-Gonna Fall" and the prophetic "The Times They Are a-Changin'"). However, when covered by Peter, Paul and Mary, Dylan's "Blowin' in the Wind" reached number two on the charts in 1963 and became an anthem for social change and racial justice. Recorded by at least sixty artists, it reached number one on the rhythm-and-blues charts in 1966 thanks to Stevie Wonder. Dylan also paved the way for progressive folk music such as that of Simon and Garfunkel who, more polished in performance than Dylan and even more self-consciously literary, enjoyed a widespread following after the release of "The Sounds of Silence" in 1965.

**The British Invasion**  The death of President John F. Kennedy on November 22, 1963, had little direct effect on popular music but nevertheless approximates a watershed in musical culture, for three months after the president's assassination, in February, 1964, the Beatles appeared on *The Ed Sullivan Show* and changed popular music profoundly, marking the true beginning of 1960's music. Already riding high after issuing the best-selling single in British history ("She Loves You," 1963), the Beatles swept Bobby Vinton's "Blue Velvet" from number one with "I Want to Hold Your Hand" and in April occupied the first five spots on the *Billboard* charts. Until their breakup in 1970, the Beatles remained the most powerful force in American music and indeed in the nation's popular culture, influencing style, language, film, art, and more.

Hard on their heels, a legion of British groups rushed to capitalize on the newly acquired American taste for the Liverpool sound. Manfred Mann, the Dave Clark Five, Chad and Jeremy, Herman's Hermits, the Hollies, and the Merseybeats were among the first wave of the British Invasion. After the initial blow, American groups such as the Beau Brumels and Paul Revere and the Raiders slavishly adopted the style of their attackers, the former attired in Edwardian finery and the latter in Revolutionary War uniforms. Even more obviously contrived, the Monkees owed their existence to a television show of the same name in 1966.

The Beatles and their imitators wore suits or theatrical costumes, sported long but neat hair, and projected an air of puckish good humor. Although the Beatles were capable of high-energy rock and roll (John Lennon and Paul McCartney adored Presley and Chuck Berry), their sound was basically up-tempo pop, inspiring hysterical reactions from teenage audiences but bafflement rather than alarm from their parents. Very soon, however, a more provocative breed of British musician joined the invasion. First, the Animals, whose "House of the Rising Sun" related misadventures in a house of ill-repute, led the charts during the summer of 1964. Harsh sounding and unsmiling on stage, the group's lead singer Eric Burdon was no McCartney lookalike. Even raunchier was the convulsive posturing of Mick Jagger, lead singer of the Rolling Stones, a group whose manager Andrew Oldham positioned them in every way in opposition to the Beatles. The coy, wise-cracking Fab Four just wanted to hold hands; the Rolling Stones posed as testosterone-crazed degenerates whose sympathies were for the devil and whose intentions were unabashedly libidinous: "I Just Wanna Make Love to You" (1964). The nastiness of the Rolling Stones may have been a marketing ploy, but the musical styles of the two groups represented genuinely hostile poles of popular music—pop and rock—and social divisions among fans. Arriving after the Rolling Stones, the Who featured an angry stage show full of adolescent fury, culminating with the destruction of drums and guitars, and produced a memorable testament for those who claimed not to trust anyone over thirty. "Hope I die before I get old," they snarled contemptuously in "My Generation" (1966).

**West Coast Creations** As stunned as American musicians were by the tidal force of British performers, two West Coast composers and producers rose to the moment: Brian Wilson of the Beach Boys and Roger McGuinn of the Byrds. The Beach Boys had been turning out widely imitated surfing and car songs since 1962. In 1965, Wilson's songs took a more serious turn with the extraordinarily original "Good Vibrations." Wilson was only an adequate lyricist, but his melodies lingered in the mind, his harmonic language was the most inventive in all of popular music, and his arrangements were the equal of Spector's. In 1966, he produced the first "concept album," *Pet Sounds,* a song cycle meant to be heard from beginning to end. At once ebullient and tragic, full of youthful longing and broken-hearted anguish, the album was a breathtaking work of art but a commercial disappointment. Still, such was its reach that the Beatles used it as a creative springboard for their own stunning concept album, *Sgt. Pepper's*

*Lonely Hearts Club Band* (1967). Like Wilson, McGuinn stretched existing musical forms. In 1965, he formed the Byrds and recorded Bob Dylan's "Mr. Tambourine Man," the genesis of folk rock.

**A Synthesis of Styles** In 1965, Dylan released *Bringing It All Back Home,* which featured a rock-and-roll backup band, and accompanied himself on electric guitar at the Newport Folk Festival to the disgust of folk purists. Folk rock merged rock and roll's energy with folk's social conscience and set off a synthesizing trend in the second half of the decade. Again, the Byrds were groundbreakers, recording *Sweetheart of the Rodeo* in 1968, a blend of country and rock that flourished into the 1970's. Often touring with the Byrds, Buffalo Springfield joined the movement, as did Poco and then the Flying Burrito Brothers in 1968. Even Dylan enlisted in the country crusade with *Nashville Skyline* (1969). Ironically, Ray Charles, the legendary rhythm-and-blues singer, had been singing country music since at least 1962 when his "Born to Lose" sold more than a million copies. The country music establishment, however, mostly ignored rock. Complacently lounging in the long shadow of Hank Williams (who died in 1953), the Nashville recording companies promoted Grand Ole Opry luminaries and younger honky-tonk singers, notably Loretta Lynn, Dolly Parton, Tammy Wynette, George Jones, and Merle Haggard. Beneath the surface, less traditional artists such as Willie Nelson, Waylon Jennings, and Kris Kristofferson billed themselves as outlaws and burned to take country music in a new direction.

Extending rock's fusion with other styles, Mike Bloomfield formed the Electric Flag in 1967, which, although short-lived, sparked jazz rock. Al Kooper's Blood, Sweat, and Tears followed in 1968 but broke up at the crest of its popularity after producing just two albums. Chicago Transit Authority (later Chicago) stayed together for decades after their first album in 1969. In 1967, Procol Harum's "A Whiter Shade of Pale" welded baroque-sounding organ music to pretentiously obscure lyrics and sold two and a half million copies in just a few weeks. In 1969, the Flock added classical music to jazz rock, as did the Dutch group Focus. Significantly, the decade closed with the Who composing a rock opera, *Tommy* (1969).

**Classical Music** For classical music, the 1960's was largely the decade of Leonard Bernstein, whose compositions, recordings, books, and television specials did more to promote serious music in the United States than the efforts of any one else. Moreover, just as popular musicians experimented with classical forms and sounds, Bernstein narrowed the gap between classical and pop audiences. During three nationally televised Young People's Concerts in 1964, 1965, and 1966, Bernstein used Beatles' songs to illustrate points about classical music.

Like Bernstein, Ward Swingle lured popular music listeners to the classics, beginning a vogue for the music of Johann Sebastian Bach in transcription by arranging instrumental compositions for voices, drums, and bass. The result was *Bach's Greatest Hits* (1963), followed in 1964 by the Grammy Award-winning *Going Baroque*. In 1969, Walter Carlos recorded the first classical album performed on electronic synthesizer, *Switched-on Bach*, which sold more than a million copies, won three Grammys, and led classical music sales for ninety-four weeks. Two of the best-selling selections of the decade were from film soundtracks: Richard Strauss's "Thus Spake Zarathustra" from *2001: A Space Odyssey* (1968) and Wolfgang Amadeus Mozart's Piano Concerto in C Major from *Elvira Madigan* (1967). Bernstein's vigorous conducting with the New York Philharmonic helped spark a renewed appreciation of the music of Gustav Mahler, but despite his efforts, classical music ranged only between 5 percent and 10 percent of record sales.

Several young American musicians solidified major careers in the 1960's. Van Cliburn, winner of the Tchaikovsky Competition in Moscow in 1958, showed skeptics he could play more than Tchaikovsky's First Piano Concerto, branching out with recordings of the piano music of Ludwig van Beethoven, Mozart, and Frederic Chopin. Almost as popular on the concert circuit as Cliburn was André Watts. Of mixed Hungarian and African American heritage, Watts, in his teens, owed much of his success to an appearance on one of Bernstein's Young People's Concerts in 1963. Beverly Sills, who had a promising career in the 1950's, broke through to opera stardom after singing the role of Cleopatra in George Frederic Handel's *Giulio Cesare* in 1966 at the New York City Opera. Given the shameful treatment of Marion Anderson during the 1940's and 1950's by opera companies and impresarios, the success of young black opera singers was especially noteworthy. Leontyne Price debuted at the Metropolitan Opera in 1961 as Donna Anna in Giuseppe Verdi's *Il Trova-*

*tore* and sang a lead role in Samuel Barber's *Anthony and Cleopatra* at its first performance in 1966. Martina Arroyo, who grew up in Harlem, broke into the Metropolitan Opera by audition and, by 1968, had an international following. Similarly, Grace Bumbry became the first African American to appear at Bayreuth, where in 1961 she sang Venus in Richard Wagner's *Tannhausser*. Her Metropolitan Opera premiere came in 1965. By 1969, African American conductors also began to land major positions: Henry Lewis conducted the New Jersey Symphony, Paul Freeman was appointed associate conductor of the Dallas Symphony, and George Byrd became an assistant conductor of the American Ballet Theater.

**Transformations** As in popular music, a generation gap of sorts existed among serious compositions. Although Samuel Barber composed *Anthony and Cleopatra* during this period, the greatest works of the older generation of American composers, such as Virgil Thomson and Aaron Copland, were behind them, and younger avant-garde composers flowered in this hot-house decade of musical innovation. Milton Babbitt, John Cage, Elliot Carter, and Roger Sessions composed complex twelve-tone, microtonal, and polytonal compositions, some of them playable only on electronic instruments similar to Carlos's Moog synthesizer, and two composers in their twenties—Philip Glass, influenced by Indian music, and Steve Reich, by West African and Balinese music—were pioneering the reductionist style of minimalism.

Not surprisingly this decade of radical musical transformation witnessed a revolution in acoustical engineering and recording technology, changes that helped give popular and classical music much of its experimental flavor. In 1960, most listeners depended on AM radio, jukeboxes, or rudimentary home record players. Records were seven, ten, or twelve inches in diameter, overwhelmingly monophonic, and played at 33, 78, or 45 revolutions per minute. By 1970, many popular and classical radio stations had switched to FM for greater fidelity, jukeboxes were rare, and record players gave way to elaborate sound systems with powerful amplifiers, lighter cartridges and tone arms, and speakers that produced flatter frequency responses. Recorded in true stereo high fidelity rather than mono or binaural sound and standardized at 33 revolutions per minute on long-playing twelve-inch platters, music sounded more convincingly live.

**Impact** Musicians in the 1960's varied immensely in vision and motive, often placing profits ahead of social comment. However, some were in the vanguard of a cultural revolution. For instance, as African Americans founded production companies and retained their own publishing rights, they took control of their own financial and artistic destinies, as when Berry Gordy, Jr., launched Motown Records in Detroit in 1959. Thanks to the poetic brilliance and musical sensitivity of William "Smokey" Robinson and to the astute writing and producing of Eddie Holland, Lamont Dozier, and Brian Holland, Motown quickly developed its trademark sound: meticulously produced, easy-to-remember three-minute dance masterpieces. Throughout the decade, Motown brought together appealing singers (among them Martha and the Vandellas, the Supremes, Gladys Knight and the Pips, the Four Tops, the Temptations, Marvin Gaye, and the Jackson Five), provided them with infectious soul songs of intentional crossover potential, backed them with the most talented house musicians of any U.S. recording company, and toured them to exhaustion in justly renowned and impressively choreographed stage shows. The result was an aesthetically vibrant and commercially successful empire that, along with Atlantic, Chess, Stax\Volt and other studios, ensured a prominent place for African American capitalists in the music business and provided the security for African American artists to express racial pride in songs such as Sam Cooke's "Change Is Gonna Come" (1964), Curtis Mayfield's "Keep on Pushin'"(1964), and James Brown's "Say It Loud, I'm Black and I'm Proud" (1968).

During the last half of the 1960's, underground bands such as the Doors sealed the historic alliance of sex, drugs, and rock and roll. The Doors were a Los Angeles band with a hit single, "Light My Fire" (1967), and a lead singer, Jim Morrison, who was responsible for the most blatantly Oedipal song ever written, "The End" (1967), used to haunting effect in the film *Apocalypse Now* (1979). Morrison was arrested at a concert in Miami in 1969 for public indecency and died of heart failure in Paris in 1971. Meanwhile, in the Haight-Ashbury district of San Francisco and inspired by the Grateful Dead, the counterculture found its musical voice. The Jeffer-

son Airplane's *Surrealistic Pillow* (1967) appeared just before the Summer of Love and epitomized much of the hippie ethos: "Somebody to Love" was a clarion call for sexual revolution and "White Rabbit" a paean to psychedelic drugs. In an age dominated by male musicians, the Jefferson Airplane was unusual for being fronted by a woman, Grace Slick, as was another San Francisco band, Big Brother and the Holding Company. On Big Brother's *Cheap Thrills* (1968) and especially in live performance, Janis Joplin was a heart-stopping blues singer, a feverish incarnation of pain and dissipation. What Joplin did to raise the voice to its emotional apex, Jimi Hendrix did for the guitar. A virtuoso of staggering originality, Hendrix cut *Are You Experienced?* (1967) and appeared at the Monterey International Pop Festival, where he both figuratively and literally set his guitar ablaze. A year after performing at the Woodstock Art and Music Fair in 1969, Hendrix died of inhalation of vomit after barbiturate intoxication, and within a few months of his death, Joplin died of a heroin overdose.

As the decade ended, the Vietnam War had divided the nation musically as much as politically. Kingston Trio's "Where Have All the Flowers Gone?" (1962), Dylan's "Masters of War" (1963), Barry McGuire's apocalyptic "Eve of Destruction" (1965), and Simon and Garfunkel's "Scarborough Fair" (1966) had all protested war generally. When the Cold War turned hot in Vietnam in 1965, antiwar music became more focused. Yet Phil Ochs's "I Ain't Marchin' Anymore" and "Draft Dodger Rag" (1965) were not hit songs; Sergeant Barry Sadler's "Ballad of the Green Berets," however, went to number one in 1966. In 1968, Lennon pleaded "Give Peace a Chance," and at Woodstock in 1969, Hendrix played a wild, psychedelic version of the national anthem. Still, as late as 1969 and 1970 pro-war songs such as Merle Haggard's "Okie from Muskogee" and "Fightin' Side of Me" sold well by blasting every aspect of the counterculture on behalf of "the silent majority." Perfectly symbolizing the rift within the nation, "Fightin' Side of Me" was number one on the country charts in 1970, while Edwin Starr's "War" (which asked what war was good for and answered "Absolutely nothin' ") was first on the pop charts.

**Additional Information** Three contemporary chronicles are invaluable: Lillian Roxon's *Rock Encyclopedia* (1969) is witty, lively, and brimming with information. In 1969 and 1970, the editors of Rolling Stone magazine compiled reviews and essays in a two-volume set, *The Rolling Stone Record Review*. Filled with irreverent and passionate reviews and essays, each volume makes for entertaining and enlightening reading. A generation later, Patricia Romanowski and Holly George-Warren published a more detached but exhaustively detailed study, *The New Rolling Stone Encyclopedia* (1995). For candid firsthand accounts by the musicians, see Timothy White's *Rock Lives: Interviews* (1990).

*David Allen Duncan*

**See also** Baez, Joan; Beach Boys, The; Beatles, The; Bernstein, Leonard; British Invasion; Brown, James; Doors; Dylan, Bob; Folk Music; Grateful Dead; Hendrix, Jimi; Jagger, Mick; Jefferson Airplane; Joplin, Janis; Minimalism; Monkees; Monterey Pop Festival; Motown; Newport Folk Festivals; Presley, Elvis; Price, Leontyne; Protest Songs; Rock Operas; Rolling Stones; *Sgt. Pepper's Lonely Hearts Club Band*; Simon and Garfunkel; Supremes; *Switched-on Bach*; Thomson, Virgil; *Tommy*; Twist; Woodstock Festival.

*Liberal Democrat Edmund Muskie was presidential candidate Hubert Humphrey's running mate in the 1968 elections. (Archive Photos)*

# ■ Muskie, Edmund

**Born** March 28, 1914, Rumford, Maine
**Died** March 26, 1996, Washington, D.C.

*One of the most effective environmental legislators in congressional history. Muskie served as governor of and senator from Maine and as secretary of state.*

**Early Life** Edmund Sixtus Muskie, who attended Bates College in Lewiston, Maine, by virtue of scholarships and summer jobs, graduated Phi Beta Kappa in 1936. He received a law degree from Cornell University in 1939 and in 1940 opened a law office in Waterville, Maine. During World War II, he served on destroyer escorts in the Atlantic and Pacific theaters. He resumed his law practice in 1945. The following year, he was elected to the Maine House of Representatives, where he served three terms. In 1954, Muskie, the son of a Polish immigrant, became Maine's first Catholic governor. Two years later, the voters awarded him another term. In 1958, he became his state's first popularly elected Democratic senator.

**The 1960's** In the Senate, Muskie's record on domestic issues marked him as a liberal Democrat. He supported bills providing for school aid, civil rights, antipoverty programs, Medicare, and establishment of the Department of Housing and Urban Development. He also introduced amendments to the Model Cities Act of 1966, part of President Lyndon B. Johnson's Great Society, and guided the legislation through the Senate.

Muskie's greatest achievement, however, was in environmental regulation. When he came to Washington, D.C., in 1959, no broadly based environmental constituency existed. As chairman of the subcommittees on air and water pollution, Muskie held hearings in major cities across the country in 1963, 1964, and 1965 to help create such a constituency. He also sponsored and maneuvered through the Senate two important environmental laws—the Clean Air Act of 1963 and the Water Quality Act of 1965.

Aware of the senator from Maine's accomplishments and reputation, Hubert Humphrey chose Muskie as his running mate in the 1968 presidential campaign. Humphrey and Muskie were narrowly defeated by the Richard M. Nixon-Spiro T. Agnew ticket in November.

**Later Life** After the 1968 campaign, Muskie returned to the Senate. He added to his growing reputation as "Mr. Clean" by sponsoring legislation that led to the establishment of the Environmental Protection Agency in 1970. However, his attempt to secure the Democratic presidential nomination in 1972 was unsuccessful.

Between 1974 and 1980, Muskie was the first chairman of the Senate budget committee. As chairman, he developed a complex system to track federal spending. Though a Senate insider, Muskie left that body when President Jimmy Carter appointed him secretary of state in 1980.

**Impact** When Muskie entered the Senate in 1959, no federal legislation existed to regulate the nation's air and water quality. The Great Lakes and other bodies of water in the United States were under severe stress from pollution. When Muskie left the Senate in 1980, three-quarters of the rivers were swimmable and fishable, the Great Lakes were considerably cleaner, and more than 95 percent of the lead had been removed from the country's air. Muskie could claim a substantial share of the credit for this environmental progress.

**Additional Information** For background on Muskie's life and career, consult Bernard Asbell's *The Senate Nobody Knows* (1978).

*Richard P. Harmond*

**See also** Air Pollution; Environmental Movement; Great Society Programs; Humphrey, Hubert; Presidential Campaign of 1968; Water Pollution.

---

# ■ My Lai Incident

**Date** March 16, 1968

*Massacre of Vietnamese civilians by a company of U.S. soldiers at My Lai in South Vietnam. The incident, which came to light in 1969, is the most prominent example of U.S. atrocities committed during the Vietnam War.*

**Origins and History** Army intelligence had reported the presence of Viet Cong in Son My village in the province of Quang Ngai in the Republic of Vietnam (South Vietnam). Consequently, a search-and-destroy operation was planned for the area. On the morning of March 16, 1968, Charlie Company approached Son My under the command of Captain Ernest Medina.

**The Incident** The first platoon of Charlie Company, under Lieutenant William L. Calley, Jr., entered the hamlet of My Lai 4 in Son My village without taking fire or seeing weapons. Some Vietnamese were in front of their homes cooking rice. None attempted to run away, knowing that to do so would invite being shot as Viet Cong. The second platoon began gathering villagers for interrogation, and Paul Meadlo was directed to take them to Calley for questioning. Meanwhile, men in Calley's first platoon also began rounding up Vietnamese.

The killing apparently began spontaneously. An eyewitness recalled one young soldier who stabbed a man in the back with a bayonet and then threw a second man down a well, tossing a grenade in after him. Meadlo had been left by Calley with a group of about forty Vietnamese. According to Meadlo, Calley told him, "You know what I want you to do with them." When Calley returned to find Meadlo still guarding the villagers, he asked, "Haven't you got rid of them yet? I want them dead." Meadlo said that Calley started shooting and ordered Meadlo to join in. According to Army eyewitnesses, Calley personally machine-gunned three groups of villagers.

Another group of villagers was driven into an open area and ordered to sit. A machine gun was set up, and despite the villagers' pleas for mercy, the shooting began. As the massacre accelerated, terrified Vietnamese frantically tried to escape the carnage. As they ran, helicopter gunships opened fire on them.

U.S. soldiers indiscriminately killed between two hundred and five hundred unarmed Vietnamese civilians. Women were raped, and children, including infants, bayoneted or shot. Fifteen to twenty women and children praying outside a temple were shot in the head. Witnesses also testified to the participation of Medina and members of the third platoon.

A helicopter pilot, Hugh Thompson, repeatedly landed his helicopter to rescue villagers, including a baby pulled from a pile of bodies. At one point, Thompson placed himself in front of Vietnamese to protect them from Calley and his men. Thompson ordered his door gunners to fire on U.S. soldiers if they attempted to shoot the Vietnamese he was trying to rescue.

The incident might never have come to light if former infantryman Ron Ridenhour, who had heard of the massacre while in Vietnam, had not written to

*This aerial view of part of the Tu Cung and My Lai hamlets in South Vietnam, photographed in November, 1969, shows where on March 15, 1968, U.S. soldiers massacred Vietnamese civilians.* (AP/Wide World Photos)

civilian and military officials in March, 1969. Ridenhour reported that "something rather dark and bloody did indeed occur sometime in March, 1968, in a village called 'Pinkville' [My Lai] in the Republic of Vietnam." The formal inquiry that followed ultimately concluded that many war crimes had been committed, among them "individual and group acts of murder, rape, sodomy, maiming, and assault on noncombatants."

Thirteen men were charged with war crimes, but only six were brought to trial. Medina and four others were acquitted, and Calley was convicted in March, 1971, of the first-degree murder of at least twenty-two Vietnamese civilians. Calley was sentenced to life in prison, a sentence reduced by President Richard M. Nixon to twenty years in response to a widespread perception that the low-ranking Calley had been made a scapegoat. Calley served three years under house arrest at Fort Benning, Georgia, before being paroled on March 19, 1974.

As punishment for failing to conduct an appropriate investigation, Major General Samuel Koster,

superintendent of the U.S. Military Academy (West Point) and former commander of the Americal Division, was demoted from two-star to one-star rank; and his assistant divisional commander at the time of the incident, Brigadier General George Young, lost his distinguished service medals. Both men also were issued letters of censure.

**Impact** My Lai gave increased impetus to the antiwar movement as activists argued that the massacre confirmed their worst fears about U.S. involvement in Vietnam. Many members of the military and Congress expressed outrage over the violations of moral behavior and military law that My Lai represented and lamented the harm that the incident caused to the reputations of U.S. soldiers, most of whom had fought with honor and distinction in Vietnam.

The My Lai incident also focused attention on such issues as military justice, following orders as a defense against criminal charges, and the psychological effect on soldiers of fighting a war where the enemy is hard to identify, the terrain and climate are radically different from anything they had experienced, and sudden death by booby trap or ambush is a constant fear.

**Subsequent Events**  In 1998, Thompson and two of his comrades, Lawrence Colburn and Glenn Andreotta (killed in battle three weeks after My Lai), received Soldiers Awards for their heroic actions in My Lai.

**Additional Information**  The official report on the My Lai massacre by the U.S. Army's Board of Inquiry was issued in 1970 and published in 1976 as *The My Lai Massacre and Its Cover-Up: Beyond the Reach of Law?*

with Lieutenant General William R. Peers as principal author. Other reports include Richard Hammer's *The Court Martial of Lieutenant Calley* (1971); Seymour M. Hersh's *My Lai 4: A Report on the Massacre and Its Aftermath* (1970); *Lieutenant Calley: His Own Story*, as told to John Sack (1971); and *Facing My Lai: Moving Beyond the Massacre* (1998), edited by David L. Anderson.

*Edward J. Rielly*

**See also**  National Mobilization Committee to End the War in Vietnam (MOBE); Vietnam War; War Resisters League.

# *N*

## ■ Nader, Ralph

**Born** February 27, 1934, Winsted, Connecticut

*A leading consumer advocate who became popular during the 1960's. Nader's activism led to passage of federal safeguards to protect citizens.*

**Early Life** Ralph Nader, the youngest of four children, practiced law in Connecticut after being admitted to the bar in 1958. He appeared on the scene as a brash, young lawyer in an ill-fitting suit who took up the cause against big industry and big government.

*Consumer advocate Ralph Nader, whose 1965 book* Unsafe at Any Speed *revealed that some American automobiles were dangerously designed, speaks before Congress.* (Library of Congress)

**The 1960's** A graduate of Princeton and Harvard Law School, Nader was a part-time lecturer in history and government from 1961 to 1963 at the University of Hartford. He first came to national attention with the release and subsequent promotion of his book, *Unsafe at Any Speed: The Designed-in Dangers of the American Automobile* (1965), which claimed that faulty American automotive design was a major contributing factor in accidents and injuries. Despite the book's outright condemnation of the subcompact Corvair produced by General Motor (GM), it was not refuted by GM until July, 1996, eight months after its release. GM's response made *Unsafe at Any Speed* a best-seller. The book's opening chapter, "The Sporty Corvair," documented the rear-engine car's tendency to skid out of control and even overturn.

GM hired a private investigator to probe into Nader's private life in an effort to discredit him, and the company president was forced to apologize for this harassment during a televised traffic-safety subcommittee hearing. This action, coupled with Nader's continual condemnation of Detroit's auto industry, propelled the consumer advocate into his long-held role as the country's number-one whistleblower. Thanks to Nader's testimony, in 1966, Congress passed the National Traffic and Motor Vehicle Safety Act, which gave federal control to automotive design. The Corvair, after sales declined following the publication of Nader's book, was discontinued in 1969. Although GM, the largest automotive company of the decade, was the main target of Nader's attacks, Nader also found fault with cars ranging from the Volkswagen (defective fuel tanks and steering columns) to the Rolls-Royce (defective door catches).

Nader, who had been a freelance magazine writer earlier in the 1960's, had traveled to Europe, the Soviet Union, Africa, and Latin America and had a knowledge of how the media functioned, which he effectively used to enhance his cause. Often holding press conferences on weekends—typically slower news days—he reached a wide national audience. He continued to use his press-management skills as he branched into other worthy projects including efforts to ban smoking on airline flights and to expose faulty hospital equipment and the higher doses of radiation that were given to African Americans. He assisted journalists with their story assignments by his understanding of what was newsworthy. He attacked big business on behalf of the average citizen, with sensational quotations and documented charges. He knew that he would have more success with the media if he could localize stories for particular markets. Such strategies worked when he attacked the meat industry for unsafe state inspection standards. By December, 1967, his efforts were rewarded with passage of the Wholesome Meat Act. Other federal legislation he worked for during the decade included the Natural Gas Pipeline Act of 1968, the Radiation Control for Health and Safety Act of 1968, the Wholesome Poultry Act of 1968, and the Coal Mine Health and Safety Act of 1969. American university students, identifying with the young lawyer's uncompromising idealism and antigovernment sentiment during the 1960's, were quick to join his investigation teams. Nicknamed "Nader's Raiders," these groups of mostly college-age adults looked into the role of state and federal regulatory agencies. They came under the umbrella of the Center for Study of Responsive Law, founded by Nader in 1969. Royalties from the sale of their many investigative reports were returned to the center.

**Later Life** Nader's later activities on behalf of consumers led to the installation of seat belts and airbags in automobiles and the freedom of information act. He was the 1996 Green Party candidate for president in a handful of states, garnering about 1 percent of the popular vote, despite refusing campaign contributions.

**Impact** Nader was largely responsible for fostering the consumer movement and popularizing consumer advocacy. He encouraged whistleblowers to reveal industry practices that were unfavorable for consumers and created consumer advocacy groups called Public Interest Research Groups (PIRGs) on college campuses throughout the nation. Nader and his associates investigated many products and consumer-related issues including baby food, insecticides, mercury poisoning, pension reform, insurance rates, radiation hazards control, and coal-mine and natural gas pipeline safety.

**Additional Information** Two sources about Nader's activities in the 1960's are Robert F. Buckhorn's *Nader: The People's Lawyer* (1972) and Charles McCarry's *Citizen Nader* (1972).

*Randall W. Hines*

**See also** Automobiles and Auto Manufacturing.

---

# ■ Naked Ape, The

**Published** 1967
**Author** Desmond Morris (1928-    )

*A book that explores humans as members of the ape family. Morris discusses* Homo sapiens *from a zoological perspective to help humans understand some of their biologically destructive limitations as a species.*

**The Work** Desmond Morris, in his introduction to *The Naked Ape: A Zoologist's Study of the Human Animal*, says that of the 193 species of monkeys and apes, all but one is covered with hair. He identifies *Homo sapiens*, the self-named ape, as the exception. In the seven chapters that follow, Morris studies humans from a zoological perspective, focusing on origins, sexual behavior, rearing, exploration, fighting, feeding, and comfort. The final chapter explores humans as they relate to other animals.

From a zoological perspective, Morris rejects the idea of a homocentric universe. He contends that humans' biological nature has shaped their social structure and not the reverse. He argues that the human reproductive cycle has the potential to overpopulate the world, and therefore, those opposing birth control are engaged in "dangerous war mongering." Finally, he cautions people that humans may destroy themselves if they do not control population and aggression and the resulting environmental damage both to other species and to the earth.

**Impact** *The Naked Ape*'s view that the behavior of humans was determined largely by their biology and that humans share many characteristics with animals, particularly apes, was offensive to many readers and enlightening to others. Nevertheless, the book had an effect on teachings in psychology, sociology, and history. Although Christian fundamentalists and other groups objected to the book, many young people found in its pages a justification for the sexual revolution.

**Related Work**  In 1973, Playboy produced *The Naked Ape*, a film version of the best-selling book, starring Victoria Principal.

**Additional Information**  *Naked Ape or Homo Sapiens?* (1969), by John Lewis and Bernard Towers, presents a reply from a scientific and philosophical perspective to Morris's *The Naked Ape*.

*Carol Franks*

**See also**  *Human Sexual Response*; Science and Technology.

# ■ Namath, Joe

**Born** May 31, 1943, Beaver Falls, Pennsylvania

*Flamboyant professional football quarterback. He led the New York Jets to a shocking upset victory in Super Bowl III.*

A native of Beaver Falls, Pennsylvania, Joseph William "Joe" Namath quarterbacked his high school team to an undefeated season in his senior year. In 1960, Namath accepted an athletic scholarship to attend the University of Alabama. Injuries plagued Namath during his senior year (1964), but Alabama was undefeated during the regular season and was declared national champion in several polls.

In 1965, the New York Jets of the American Football League (AFL) signed Namath to a three-year contract for the unprecedented sum of $427,000. The AFL was in competition with the older National Football League (NFL), and signing high-profile players such as Namath was imperative. During his years in New York, Namath earned the nickname "Broadway Joe" for his playboy lifestyle.

In 1968, Namath led the Jets to the AFL championship and into Super Bowl III against the NFL champion Baltimore Colts. The Jets were 17-point underdogs, but Namath brashly guaranteed that his team would win. On January 12, 1969, "Broadway Joe" quarterbacked the Jets to a stunning 16-7 victory. Namath was named Super Bowl Most Valuable Player and became a national celebrity.

Namath retired from football in 1977 and was later inducted into the Pro Football Hall of Fame. Since retiring, he has appeared in numerous commercials and several movies and television shows.

**Impact**  By combining athletic success and flamboyance on a national stage, Namath helped usher in a new generation of athletes who reflected the changing cultural climate in the United States.

**Additional Information**  A special edition of *Sports Illustrated* (September 19, 1994) contains a good overview of Namath's significance.

*Charles H. Evans*

**See also**  Brown, Jim; Football; Super Bowl.

# ■ Nation of Islam

*The most visible and controversial of the black nationalist organizations before 1965. This religious group grew out of a social movement among economically dispossessed inner-city African Americans and helped popularize a defiant cry for black separatism and self-determination.*

The Nation of Islam, also known as Black Muslims, was created in Detroit in the 1930's during the Great Depression when large numbers of southern blacks who had moved to the nation's cities were struggling against social and economic discrimination. Attacked initially as a "voodoo cult," the Nation of Islam was founded by a mysterious itinerant peddler named W. D. Fard who taught that the white man was a devil and that blacks were of divine stature. Elijah Poole, the son of a Georgia sharecropper who as an autoworker remained largely unemployed, became the leading minister, assuming the name Elijah Muhammad along with the leadership of the Nation of Islam by the time of Fard's unexplained disappearance in 1934. Fard was quickly elevated by his followers to the status of divinity and proclaimed the Messenger of Allah. The Nation of Islam by the 1940's also included a paramilitary division known as the Fruit of Islam, a Muslim girls training class, and a variety of educational institutions for children and adults. The Nation of Islam became nationally recognized in 1959 when a television documentary entitled *The Hate That Hate Produced* publicized the group's doctrines of black nationalism, retaliation against white racism, and scorn for the symbols of U.S. democracy and the Christian religion that it judged to be long tarnished by the nation's history of racial bigotry and repression.

**Growth and Malcolm X**  From 1954 to 1964, the Nation of Islam experienced explosive growth, with new temples opened in major cities from Los Angeles to New York and Atlanta. By the early 1960's, Malcolm X had risen to the rank of national representative of the Messenger (Fard), though the authoritarian nature of the Nation of Islam still concentrated organizational control in the hands of Elijah Muhammad and his "royal family." Membership by this time had risen to between 65,000 and 100,000, primarily because of the charismatic influence of Malcolm X as field organizer. As spokesperson for the Messenger, Malcolm X became one of black America's most visible figures. He frequently spoke on college campuses, made guest appearances on radio and television talk shows, and engaged in highly publicized debates with civil rights leaders, praising the Messenger while spurning integration and nonviolence. The minister of the Nation of Islam became a familiar prophet of doom, crying the portents of an ultimate Armageddon in which Allah would destroy the white race.

Civil rights leaders criticized Malcolm X and his followers, charging that they had no real program of action. However, the Nation of Islam's militant rhetoric along with the grim spectacle of the organization's soldiers in uniform helped to focus attention on the problem of the inner cities, which the civil rights leadership had largely failed to address.

**Internal Division**  Schism within the Nation of Islam through the mid-1960's grew out of personal antagonism between Malcolm X and Elijah Muhammad's inner circle, a conflict that was nourished and exploited by domestic and foreign counterintelligence programs sponsored by the Federal Bureau of Investigation (FBI) and the Central Intelligence Agency. The Nation of Islam had been largely composed of the hard-core unemployed, former convicts, illiterates, and others from the lowest income levels, but after Malcolm X became a spokesperson for the organization, its membership had become increasingly youthful and middle class. Malcolm X had helped to found and develop *Muhammad Speaks*, the Nation of Islam's top publication, a biweekly newspaper that grew in circulation to become the most widely read African American newspaper in the United States. The financial success of *Muhammad Speaks* provided capital for a wide range of the organization's investments, creating a financial empire tightly controlled at the top by Elijah Muhammad and his immediate circle of relatives.

On March 8, 1964, the split between Malcolm X and the Nation of Islam became official. Only a handful of the Nation of Islam members partici-

*Elijah Muhammad led the black nationalist group the Nation of Islam from 1934 until his death in 1974.* (Archive Photos)

pated in Malcolm's newly formed orthodox, reform Muslim Mosque, Inc., and his departure did not cause an immediate deep fissure within the organization. However, the controversy surrounding Malcolm X's assassination in February, 1965, would plague the Nation of Islam throughout the remainder of the 1960's. Beginning in 1967, J. Edgar Hoover's FBI undertook a massive counterintelligence campaign against all alleged "black nationalist hate groups," resulting in continued turmoil within the Nation of Islam until 1972.

**Impact**  The role played by Malcolm X and the Nation of Islam helped alter the course of the Civil Rights movement in midstream. After Malcolm X's murder, from 1965 through the early 1970's, more than three hundred race riots occurred in U.S. cities, demonstrating that the era of nonviolence was at an end. Although the Nation of Islam had never embraced political or civil rights activism, the followers of Malcolm X could claim to have contributed to the final destruction of Jim Crow. Major civil rights organizations such as the Congress for Racial Equality and the Student Nonviolent Coordinating Committee both underwent a black nationalist-separatist ideological transformation after 1965, and militant nationalist groups flourished. Through the 1960's, the Nation of Islam message of success through self-help, moral uplift, black pride, and racial separation won increasing acceptance among black youth as urban revolt and white backlash transformed the consciousness and culture of African Americans.

**Subsequent Events** Before his death in 1974, Elijah Muhammad retained full control of the highly centralized religious order. However, the excommunication of favorite son Wallace Muhammad, who remained in sympathy with the fallen Malcolm X, encouraged the rise of minister Louis Farrakhan as national spokesperson. Wallace Muhammad, who reconciled with his father before 1974, assumed control of the organization after his father's death and installed reforms that would create the World Community of Al-Islam in the West. The reforms rejected Fard as Allah and embraced the teaching of orthodox Sunni Islam, thereby bringing growing acceptance of the World Community of Al-Islam with encouragement from official sources of international Islam. However, Farrakhan along with a supporting group within the "royal family" rejected the reforms beginning in 1977, leading the Nation of Islam away from orthodox Islam and toward the restoration of its original doctrines.

**Additional Information** Helpful studies of the Nation of Islam and related topics include Mattias Gardell's *In the Time of Elijah Muhammad: Louis Farrakhan and the Nation of Islam* (1996), C. Eric Lincoln's *The Black Muslims in America* (1961), Clifton E. Marsh's *From Black Muslims to Muslims: The Transition from Separatism to Islam, 1930-1980* (1984), and Bruce Perry's *Malcolm: The Life of a Man Who Changed Black America* (1991).

*John L. Godwin*

**See also** Black Christian Nationalist Movement; Black Power; Civil Rights Movement; Congress of Racial Equality (CORE); Malcolm X; Student Nonviolent Coordinating Committee.

# ■ National Association for the Advancement of Colored People (NAACP)

*First civil rights organization established in the United States. The NAACP was the primary organization committed to full equality and civil rights for African Americans and a major player in the struggle for full social, economic, and political equality.*

**Origins and History** The National Association for the Advancement of Colored People (NAACP) was formally founded in May, 1910. Most of the charter members were white, although membership included African Americans who had been part of the 1905 Niagara Movement. The organization's goals were to eliminate all de jure segregation and specifically to obtain equal education for all children, the right to vote for African Americans, and full enforcement of the Fourteenth and Fifteenth Amendments regarding citizenship and voting rights, respectively. The NAACP initiated a number of programs that would enhance the status of and quality of life for African Americans by aiding economic development, fostering job opportunities, enhancing police protection in the South, and creating initiatives against lynching, rioting, and mob formation, all of which often victimized African Americans.

Early tension within the NAACP centered on whether the organization should pursue a social agenda of equality and civil rights or one of economic development and independence; this debate became a public issue. Joel E. Spingarn, who became president of the NAACP in 1930, felt that racial inequality and racism had to be addressed before African Americans could build a foundation in the educational and economic arenas. On the other hand, W. E. B. Du Bois, one of the prominent founders of the NAACP, argued that African Americans needed higher education and that a small group of educated people could lead the masses in the fight for equality. He believed that the political power they gained would lead to economic progress. Du Bois often clashed publicly with his archrival Booker T. Washington, who felt that African Americans should not be concerned about racial equality but should accept their subservient status and position in American society. Washington, the founder and president of Tuskegee Institute, advocated vocational education and training and felt that economic development would gradually lead to racial equality.

During the first two decades of its existence, the NAACP won three court victories. Its attorneys addressed the grandfather clause in voting and segregation in housing and obtained a retrial for an African American man convicted by an all-white jury in Arkansas. Its biracial team of lawyers also won legal victories before the high court involving restrictive covenants, the white primary, and the "separate but equal" doctrine. After the death of the white primary in the South in 1944, the NAACP began to organize local voter leagues. These leagues were short-lived, however, because of repression from local governments and the White Citizens Council, which destroyed the NAACP in the South.

**Activities**  In the 1960's, the NAACP continued to push for civil rights and racial integration, but it also began to undertake more political activities and often acted as an interest group in concert with other civil rights organizations to obtain its goals. Under the leadership of Roy Wilkins, the organization was one of the major players in planning and organizing the 1963 March on Washington with the Southern Christian Leadership Conference and other entities. The NAACP was part of a strong lobbying effort for passage of the Civil Rights Act of 1964, an act designed to end discrimination in every aspect of American society and integrate public places such as eating facilities, motels and hotels, and motion picture theaters.

However, the NAACP soon realized some of the limitations of the 1964 act and led a major drive to flood the Equal Employment Opportunity Commission with discrimination complaints to underline the fact that the agency was understaffed and lacked the resources to handle complaints emanating from Title VII of the 1964 Civil Rights Act.

The organization also continued its legal battles in court. In the case of *Griggs v. Duke Power Company*, the NAACP supported a class-action suit brought by thirteen of the fourteen African American workers at the Dan River steam station located near Draper, North Carolina. After passage of the Civil Rights Act of 1964, which forbade discrimination in hiring and promoting workers, the power company began using a standardized test developed by professionals that was unrelated to job performance, with the rationale that it needed to upgrade the educational level of the workforce because of the hazards of their jobs. Few blacks could pass the test because the quality of the education they had received was inferior to that received by whites. After the case wound its way through federal district and circuit courts, in 1971, the U.S. Supreme Court ruled in favor of the African American workers, stating that what mattered was whether the practice resulted in discrimination not whether its intent was to discriminate. In a state known for its separate and inferior education for African Americans, the use of a standardized test resulted in discrimination in the workplace.

During the 1960's, the NAACP came to support the quest for community control of educational institutions, although this position contradicted the organization's traditional tenets relating to racial integration. In the Ocean Hill-Brownsville dispute involving striking teachers in New York City in 1968-1969, the NAACP, in its official publication, *The Crisis*, argued that a community-controlled local school board and the teachers that replaced the striking ones should be reinstated after being fired by the board of education. The NAACP took the position that the school district's African Americans—rather than whites who did not live in the community—should be able to set the public school agenda.

In the 1960's, after the dissolution of the voter leagues, regional or local mobilization of NAACP supporters was minimal in the South. However, the Student Nonviolent Coordinating Committee (SNCC) and the Congress of Racial Equality (CORE) were active in this region, playing vital roles in the fight against white supremacy and racial injustice. Their activities resulted in important economic and political gains.

**Impact**  As the oldest civil rights organization, the NAACP amassed an impressive record of victories that have benefited African Americans and American society. Before the 1960's, it was successful in improving the legal, social, economic, and political status of African Americans, resulting in greater respectability for this group in American society. The NAACP played a major part in victories such as advancing voting rights (ending the grandfather clause, the white primary, and discriminatory residential covenants), eliminating Jim Crow in the South and segregation in places of public accommodation and education, and the safeguarding of courtroom rights in a hostile legal environment.

The support of the NAACP, along with other civil rights organizations, and several tragic events involving civil rights activists were partially responsible for Congress passing the Civil Rights Act of 1964, which significantly changed the social structure in the United States, particularly in the South. Because of the NAACP's litigation and advocacy in the Griggs case, it became easier for plaintiffs to prove discrimination in hiring and promotions in the job sector. The organization's activities changed the fundamental nature of American society and social arrangements.

**Subsequent Events** The NAACP, like a number of other civil rights organizations, stagnated after the 1960's. Although its sister organization, the NAACP Legal Defense Fund, continued the struggle in the courtroom, the NAACP lost the influence it once commanded. Beginning in 1995, the organization began a comeback with the election of Myrlie Evers Williams as the chair of the board of directors and former congressman Kweisi Mfume as the executive director.

**Additional Information** Obie Clayton, Jr.'s *An American Dilemma Revisited* (1996), Harold Cruse's *Plural but Equal* (1987), and Kenneth W. Goings's *The NAACP Comes of Age* (1990) provide detailed information on the NAACP. Jack Greenberg's "NAACP Legal Defense and Education Fund," in *Civil Rights and Equality* (1989), edited by Leonard W. Levy, Kenneth L. Karst, and Dennis J. Mahoney, examines the organization's legal and education funds, and B. Joyce Ross's *J. E. Spingarn and the Rise of the NAACP* (1972) looks at the NAACP's early history.

*Mfanya Donald Tryman*

**See also** Civil Rights Act of 1964; Civil Rights Movement; Congress of Racial Equality (CORE); March on Washington; Student Nonviolent Coordinating Committee (SNCC); Voting Rights Legislation.

# ■ National Commission on the Causes and Prevention of Violence

*A United States government commission established by President Lyndon B. Johnson in 1968. For eighteen months, it studied both the antecedents of violence and public policy to change these circumstances.*

In the 1960's, Americans were troubled by escalating levels of public unrest. The developing mass media had begun covering these disturbing, violent events, which, through television, were viewed in the homes of increasing numbers of citizens. By the late 1960's, the federal government deemed it important to play a visible role in decreasing public violence, so President Lyndon B. Johnson established a commission to study its roots and possible remedies.

The National Commission on the Causes and Prevention of Violence, established in June, 1968, consisted of thirteen members headed by Milton S. Eisenhower. Its task was to synthesize research concerning "lawless acts of violence" and "violent disruptions of public order" and to suggest policy directions for change. In December, 1969, this assignment was completed with the publication of a final report entitled *To Establish Justice, To Insure Domestic Tranquility: Final Report of the National Commission on the Causes and Prevention of Violence*.

**Impact** The commission found that a "subculture of violence" existed within the urban ghettos and that public policy initiatives directed toward the improvement of inner-city conditions would decrease the violence.

Government funding of police forces, courts, and prisons continued, but changes in public policy meant to address social inequities and violence were inadequate; hence, public unrest continued into the 1970's.

**Additional Information** Lynn A. Curtis edited updated submissions by former commission members in *American Violence and Public Policy* (1985), which provides a historic perspective on the commission's role.

*Susan J. Wurtzburg*

**See also** Assassinations of John and Robert Kennedy and Martin Luther King, Jr.; Crimes and Scandals; New York Riots; Oakland Riot.

# ■ National Indian Youth Council (NIYC)

*Native American activist organization. The National Indian Youth Council used political activism and public protests to garner attention and support for American Indian causes.*

Angered by the poor treatment that Native Americans received in the United States and frustrated with the conservative stance of many tribal leaders, American Indian college students meeting in Gallup, New Mexico, in August, 1961, founded the National Indian Youth Council (NIYC). The organization declared that Indians had the right to determine the futures of their communities and promoted aggressive political activity on behalf of Native Americans.

In 1964, the NIYC took part in "fish-ins" in the Pacific Northwest to protest violations of Indian fishing rights guaranteed in treaties. These protests gained the support of hundreds of Indians and several celebrities, which resulted in significant press coverage. The NIYC also participated in the 1968 Poor People's Campaign in Washington, D.C. The group published a newspaper, *Americans Before Columbus*, to spread its message.

**Impact**  By the standards of the early 1960's, the NIYC was a radical organization. It legitimized the use of civil disobedience and other protest strategies within the Indian community, thus paving the way for later activist organizations such as the American Indian Movement (AIM).

**Additional Information**  For a discussion of NIYC activities, see *Like a Hurricane: The Indian Movement from Alcatraz to Wounded Knee* (1996), by Paul Chaat Smith and Robert Allen Warrior.

*Thomas Clarkin*

**See also**  Alcatraz Island Occupation; American Indian Civil Rights Act of 1968; American Indian Movement (AIM); Native American Fishing Rights; Poor People's March.

---

# ■ National Mobilization Committee to End the War in Vietnam (MOBE)

*An umbrella organization for protest against the Vietnam War. MOBE played a key role in protest activities between 1966 and 1969.*

**Origins and History**  The National Mobilization Committee to End the War in Vietnam (MOBE) grew out of a 1966 conference of pacifist, liberal, student, religious, and Marxist organizations opposed to the war in Vietnam. The conference adopted Sidney Peck's plan for a national mobilization in New York City and San Francisco on April 15, 1967, and formed the Spring Mobilization (Committee) to End the War in Vietnam to carry it out. A. J. Muste, a leading pacifist, became chair, and David Dellinger and Peck were among the vice chairpersons. The organization's principles emphasized nonexclusion, that is, its membership would include not only socialists but also communists. The organization stressed the practice of nonviolent, legal protest.

**Activities**  At a conference in Washington, D.C., May 20-21, 1967, to assess the April march, those present decided to issue a call for civil disobedience on October 21 in Washington, D.C. At this point, the committee renamed itself the National Mobilization Committee to End the War in Vietnam (MOBE). The MOBE began to change when Dellinger asked Jerry Rubin to help with the October event. Rubin suggested a march on the Pentagon rather than a rally at the capitol. Rubin also enlisted the help of the counterculture, which led to Abbie Hoffman's idea of levitating the Pentagon. The march on the Pentagon in 1967 became one of the best-known protests of the 1960's. Activities in 1968 focused primarily on the Democratic National Convention to be held in August in Chicago. Ideas about nonviolent, legal protests were undermined by ambivalent statements by Rennie Davis and Tom Hayden, both formerly in the Students for a Democratic Society (SDS). Davis and Hayden were in charge of the Chicago office of the MOBE. Hayden came to believe a prerevolutionary situation existed. The involvement of the Yippies, led by Hoffman and Rubin, further complicated matters. The Democratic National Convention marked the nadir of the MOBE. Relatively few participated, and most activities ended in police violence and wholesale arrests.

The MOBE collapsed in 1969. Reorganized as the New Mobilization Committee to End the War in Vietnam (also known as the MOBE), it sponsored a huge protest on November 15, 1969, in Washington, D.C., in cooperation with the Vietnam Moratorium Committee. It was also active in demonstrations in May, 1970, against the U.S. incursion into Cambodia but declined not long afterward.

**Impact**  Events in Chicago created the impression that the United States was close to revolution, but radicals made little headway in U.S. political life. Instead, broad-based movements such as the MOBE continued to stage most protests against the war. Nevertheless, in the long term, neither the efforts to build broad-based reform movements nor to support revolutionary groups had much chance in the changing political atmosphere of the 1970's.

**Additional Information** Two informative books on antiwar efforts are *Who Spoke Up? American Protest Against the War in Vietnam, 1963-1975* (1984), by Nancy Zaroulis and Gerald Sullivan, and *The War Within: America's Battle over Vietnam* (1994), by Tom Wells.

*Michael Richards*

**See also** Democratic National Convention of 1968; March Against Death; Pentagon, Levitating of the; Yippies.

# ■ National Organization for Women (NOW)

*A feminist mass-membership organization. Its stated purpose is "to take action to bring women into full participation in the mainstream of American society now, to exercise all of the privileges and responsibilities thereof in truly equal partnership with men."*

**Origins and History** The origins of the National Organization for Women (NOW) can be traced to the summer of 1966 when Betty Friedan, author of *The Feminine Mystique* (1963), met informally with fifteen concerned women who were attending the third national Conference on the Status of Women. They met in Friedan's hotel room in Washington, D.C., to discuss the possibility of organizing a feminist movement in reaction to passage of Title VII of the Civil Rights Act of 1964, which banned sex discrimination in employment. Twenty-eight concerned women continued the discussion over lunch the next day, contributed five dollars each, and launched the National Organization for Women.

**Activities** NOW announced its incorporation on October 29, 1966, and elected Friedan president. Friedan accepted, vowing "to use every political tactic available to end sex discrimination against women." NOW's three hundred charter members drew up a statement of purpose, which stated that they not only believed that it was time for a new Civil Rights movement to work toward true equality for all women in the United States but that they also saw themselves as part of a worldwide revolution of human rights.

On August 30, 1967, NOW picketed *The New York Times* to protest the policy of separate male-female help-wanted ads. At the second NOW National Conference, held in Washington, D.C., on November 18-19, 1967, members drew up a bill of rights for women, calling for passage of the Equal Rights Amendment and for a repeal of all existing abortion legislation and laws restricting access to contraception. NOW also supported enforcement of laws banning sex discrimination in employment, maternity-leave rights in employment and in social security benefits, tax deductions for child care expenses for working parents, the establishment of more child care centers, equal and unsegregated education, and equal job training opportunities and allowances for women in poverty. NOW organized the first national demonstration on women's rights since the suffrage movement on December 14, 1967, against the Equal Employment Opportunity Commission and on February 15, 1968, filed formal suit against the commission. Other NOW activities included filing discrimination cases against thirteen hundred of the largest corporations; testifying against federal and local sex discrimination in education, employment, welfare, and public accommodations; and lobbying for federal funds for child care centers.

**Impact** NOW organized a political agenda to end discrimination against women. It filled not only the organizational need for a strong political lobby for women's rights but also the philosophical need for a forum in which to address new feminist ideas. NOW initiated and supported action to end prejudice and discrimination against women in government, industry, churches, political parties, the judiciary, labor unions, education, science, medicine, law, religion, and the family. NOW was the first and largest national feminist mass-membership organization of the 1960's that vowed to secure women's rights and end discrimination against them; however, in the late 1960's and subsequent decades, thousands of feminist organizations, many specialized rather than umbrella organizations and some more radical, have emerged to assist with this task.

**Additional Information** Amy Swerdlow's *Women Strike for Peace: Traditional Motherhood and Radical Politics in the 1960s* (1993) is a study of various aspects of the women's movement in the 1960's that contains detailed information on the role of NOW.

*Garlena A. Bauer*

**See also** Equal Rights Amendment; *Feminine Mystique, The*; Feminist Movement; Friedan, Betty; SCUM Manifesto; Women's Identity.

# ■ National States Rights Party

*A white supremacist and neo-Nazi organization founded in 1958 by Edward Fields. The National States Rights Party was involved in racist and anti-Semitic activity in the South during the Civil Rights movement of the 1960's.*

**Origins and History** The National States Rights Party (NSRP) was organized in 1958 in Jeffersonville, Indiana, by Edward Fields, who served as national secretary of the party. Fields was joined by Jesse B. Stoner, a lawyer and former Klan organizer. At one time, both Stoner and Fields were leaders of the

Christian Anti-Jewish Party. Soon after its founding, the NSRP moved to Birmingham, Alabama, then to Augusta, Georgia, and finally to Marietta, Georgia. The NSRP differed from most right-wing extremist groups in that it did not oppose government programs such as Medicare and Social Security. The major purpose of the group was to propagate white racism and anti-Semitism. The party became associated with other neo-Nazis with similar agendas, including Matt Koehl and James Warner, both of whom once belonged to the American Nazi Party.

**Activities** The National States Rights Party peaked in the 1960's during the Civil Rights movement. The party nominated segregationist candidates for the presidency and other political offices. It also published a newspaper called *The Thunderbolt*, a racist

*National States Rights Party attorney Jesse B. Stoner (second from left) leaves criminal court in Baltimore in 1966 with three party officials—left to right, Joseph Carroll, Richard B. Norton, and Connie Lynch—who received jail sentences for inciting a riot.* (AP/Wide World Photos)

and anti-Semitic publication edited by Fields and claiming to have a circulation of 125,000 in the 1960's. The party also held rallies and was involved in violent confrontations in several southern states. In Saint Augustine, Florida, in 1964, a mob attacked civil rights demonstrators and injured forty of them. A Florida legislative investigating committee later reported that the NSRP had played a key role in the riots and that the Reverend Connie Lynch, the party's official policy speaker, and Stoner were instrumental in causing the violence. In 1966, Lynch and four other party members were convicted on charges of inciting a riot in Baltimore. In 1968, NSRP members were involved in a confrontation near Berea, Kentucky, which left two people dead.

**Impact** In 1970, Fields claimed that the NSRP had twelve full-time employees and a membership of more than two thousand. Although these figures are probably high, the organization did have about thirty chapters. In general, the NSRP appealed to lower- and working-class whites. The party received publicity because of its strident racism and anti-Semitism, but it never attracted continuous widespread support.

**Subsequent Events** During the 1970's, Stoner ran statewide for political office in Georgia five times on a racist platform. In 1980, he was convicted in Alabama in connection with the 1958 bombing of the Bethel Baptist Church in Birmingham and served three and one half years of a ten-year prison sentence. In 1983, while Stoner was in prison, dissident members expelled Fields from the NSRP. Within a year, the party was defunct.

**Additional Information** John George and Laird Wilcox discuss the National States Rights Party in *Nazis, Communists, Klansmen, and Others on the Fringe* (1992), and information on Fields and Stoner can be obtained in a publication by the Anti-Defamation League entitled *Danger: Extremism* (1996).

*William V. Moore*

**See also** American Nazi Party; Church Bombings; Civil Rights Movement; Ku Klux Klan (KKK).

---

# ■ Native American Fishing Rights

*Native Americans along Puget Sound in Washington militantly protected their fishing rights. The protests, based on treaties negotiated in the 1850's, reached a peak in the* 1960's, *leading to judicial recognition of fishing rights in* 1974.

To the Northwest Indian nations, the salmon was central to economic life. For example, fish made up 80 percent to 90 percent of the Puyallup diet. However, salmon was more than food; it was the center of a way of life. A cultural festival accompanied the first salmon caught in the yearly run. The fish was barbecued over an open fire, and bits of its flesh were parceled out to all. The bones were saved intact and were carried by a torch-bearing, singing, dancing, and chanting procession back to the river, where they were placed in the water, the head pointed upstream, symbolizing the spawning fish and ensuring that the run would return in later years. In treaties in the 1850's, the Indians had agreed to give up large amounts of land in exchange for the right to fish at their "usual and accustomed places."

In the late 1950's, American Indians in Washington were accused of "overfishing," although their catch accounted for less than 1 percent of the total state harvest. By the early 1960's, state fishery officials were conducting wholesale arrests of Indians, confiscating their boats and nets. The Indians took their treaty-rights case to state courts and found these courts solidly in support of non-Indian commercial interests.

The tribes pursued their claim at the federal level. During the 1960's and early 1970's, they also militantly protected their rights in the face of raids by state fishery authorities. Fishing rights activists took to their boats in several locations along Puget Sound, from Franks Landing, near Olympia, to Tulalip, near Everett, north of Seattle. State fishery police descended on the Indian fishers as the legal battle continued in the courts. Vigilante sports fishers joined state fishery police in harassing the Indians, stealing their boats, slashing their nets, and sometimes shooting at them. Tribal elders and women joined the young Indian men in their protests, and many non-Indians, including actor Marlon Brando, also lent support.

**Impact** By 1965, the United States Supreme Court had ruled that Indians had a right to fish at their "usual and accustomed places" but that the state had the right to regulate Indian fishing through its courts. That ruling, and a few federal court rulings after it, had little practical effect as long as the state, whose fishery managers were adamantly opposed to

On May 13, 1966, members of the Muckleshoot tribe in Washington began a thirteen-mile march from Auburn to Federal Way to protest the state's interfering with their fishing rights. (AP/Wide World Photos)

any fishing by Indians, held enforcement power.

The protests, dubbed "fish-ins," continued until February 12, 1974, when United States District Court Judge George Boldt ruled that Indians were entitled to an opportunity to catch as many as half the fish returning to off-reservation sites that had been the "usual and accustomed places" when the treaties were signed.

**Additional Information** The fishing-rights protests are described in more detail in *Wasichu: The Continuing Indian Wars* (1979), by Bruce Johansen and Roberto Maestas.

*Bruce E. Johansen*

**See also** Alcatraz Island Occupation; American Indian Movement (AIM).

## ■ New York Riots

**Date** July 18-23, 1964; July 26, 1967

*Riots injuring many in New York City during the 1960's. The race-related riots in the streets of the city exemplify the turmoil throughout the nation over civil rights issues.*

**Origins and History** The Civil Rights movement, in bringing attention to the inequality of legally imposed segregation in the South, also highlighted the de facto discrimination that affected the economic status and living conditions of African Americans in northern and western cities. Many African Americans became somewhat frustrated with the slow pace of the struggle for civil rights.

**The Riots** On July 16, 1964, New York Police Department Lieutenant Thomas Gilligan shot and killed James Powell, a fifteen-year-old African American. The officer's claim that he acted in self-defense when Powell allegedly threatened him with a knife was not accepted by many African Americans. The Congress of Racial Equality (CORE) held a rally in Harlem two days later that turned into the 1964 New York riot. Three years later, on July 26, 1967, with racial tensions still high from a riot in the Puerto Rican area of East Harlem on July 23-25, about two hundred African Americans became involved in a riot after a rock concert in Central Park The New York riots of 1964 and 1967 were typical of the urban unrest that accompanied the racial tensions of the decade. By 1964, African Americans were demanding equality, especially in the South where they faced legally imposed (de jure) discrimination, and to a lesser extent in the North, where they suffered from de facto discrimination. The U.S. Congress was considering new civil rights legislation, but many African Americans were angered by the more subtle discrimination and the economically bleak situation in the nation's northern and western inner cities.

The killing of Powell was simply a spark that served to ignite a dangerous situation. After the CORE rally on July 16, 1964, protesters marched to the police station, and rioting broke out. African Americans roamed the streets, breaking store windows and throwing bottles at police officers. The rioting continued until July 23, 1964. One African American was killed, five others were shot and wounded, eighty-one civilians and thirty-five police officers were injured, one hundred and twelve stores were looted, and one hundred and eighty-five people were arrested.

On July 26, 1967, around two hundred African Americans marched down Fifth Avenue in New York

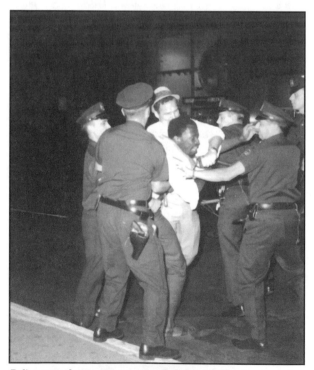

*Police struggle to arrest a man on July 26, 1967, when an urban racial riot broke out on Fifth Avenue in New York City. (AP/Wide World Photos)*

City, looting stores and breaking windows after a concert in Central Park. An estimated twenty-six thousand dollars worth of goods was stolen, and twenty-two youths were arrested. Later, on July 29, 1967, more violence broke out but was quickly controlled.

**Impact** The riots called national attention to the discrimination that affected African Americans in New York City. After the 1964 riots, which were the first urban race-related riots of the decade, President Lyndon B. Johnson ordered the Federal Bureau of Investigation (FBI) to detect any possible violations of federal laws and to search for possible communist influence. Paul Screvane, the acting mayor of New York in 1964 declared that the Powell killing would go to trial and that more African American police officers would work in the area where the conflict took place.

In 1967, race-related unrest erupted in cities all across the nation. The looting of New York City's Fifth Avenue did not escalate into a major incident the way the 1964 unrest did because the city's officers were better trained on how to handle the situation. The New York Police Department had begun to employ a large number of African Americans on the force to prevent racial tensions from becoming overwhelming.

**Additional Information** The Kerner Commission Report (1968) contains important information on race-related riots and the conditions that produced them, and *The New York Times* provides detailed accounts of both the 1964 and 1967 riots.

*Theresa R. Doggart*

**See also** Chicago Riots; Civil Rights Movement; Congress of Racial Equality (CORE); Detroit Riot; Kerner Commission Report; New York Riots; Newark Riot; Watts Riot.

---

# ■ *New York Times Company v. Sullivan*

*A 1964 landmark libel case. The Supreme Court held for the first time that an award of damages for libel of a public official violated freedoms of speech and press guaranteed by the First Amendment.*

The press, particularly in the northern states, extensively covered the early 1960's civil rights struggle in the South. Newspapers printed photographs showing Alabama police meeting protesters in Selma, Montgomery, and Birmingham with harsh resistance, including physical violence, threats, and intimidation. The South was portrayed as a stronghold of racism, existing outside of constitutional law. Retaliation against the press usually took the form of lawsuits. One such libel suit was filed against the New York Times Company.

On March 29, 1960, *The New York Times* printed an advertisement entitled "Heed Their Rising Voices" to raise funds for civil rights workers, particularly Martin Luther King, Jr., a minister in Montgomery. The advertisement stated that King had been arrested seven times, Montgomery's African American student protesters were expelled after singing "My Country 'Tis of Thee" on the steps of the state capitol, and the students' school dining hall was padlocked in an attempt to starve them into submission.

L. B. Sullivan, Montgomery commissioner of safety and police department supervisor, sued *The New York Times* for libel, claiming that the advertisement reflected on him and contained errors in its text. Sullivan pointed out that King had been arrested only four times, the students sang the national anthem, and the dining facility was locked. Sullivan sued for and was awarded $500,000 by a jury in the circuit court of Montgomery County in 1962, and the state supreme court affirmed the judgment, ruling that the statements in *The New York Times* were libelous per se, false and therefore not privileged, and that the evidence showed malice. It was further ruled that the First Amendment did not protect libelous publications. Other Montgomery officials, including the governor of Alabama, also sued over the advertisement, claiming damages up to $2.5 million. The Alabama supreme court allowed Sullivan to recover damages for minor errors in a newspaper advertisement that did not name him.

On March 9, 1964, the U.S. Supreme Court unanimously reversed the Alabama court's decision. Justice William J. Brennan, writing for the court, held that the state court's ruling failed to provide the safeguards for freedoms of speech and press guaranteed by the First Amendment in libel cases brought by public officials against critics of their official conduct, and it also did not allow a qualified privilege for honest misstatement of facts.

**Impact** The decision in the *New York Times Company v. Sullivan* profoundly affected the law. For years,

public officials in libel cases were denied recoveries. The ruling was extended to criminal libel and, in 1967, to well-known public figures such as athletes, film stars, and businesspeople (in *Curtis Publishing Company v. Butts* and *Associated Press v. Walker*). Previously, constitutional freedoms of speech and press had offered no protection to libelous statements. For the first time, the Supreme Court established that the constitutional guarantee of freedoms of speech and press precluded public officials recovering damages for publication of a defamatory statement, even when statements were false, unless officials proved they were made with actual malice (with knowledge that the statement was false or with reckless disregard of its veracity). The verdict established and set forth the five tenets that plaintiffs must prove in libel cases: defamation, publication, identification, negligence and/or malice, and damages.

**Subsequent Events** In 1974, in *Gertz v. Robert Welch, Inc.*, the Court ruled that the First Amendment did not protect the press in libel cases brought by private individuals, even when a matter of "public concern" was involved.

**Additional Information** The Libel Defense Resource Center of New York City wrote an enlightening tribute to Justice Brennan, *Heed Their Rising Voices, a Tribute to Justice William J. Brennan, Jr.: New York v. Sullivan and the Judicial Role in the Advancement of Free Expression and Peaceful Social Change* (1992).

*Pearlie Strother-Adams*

**See also** Censorship; King, Martin Luther, Jr.

---

# ■ New York World's Fair

**Date** April 22-October 18,1964; April 21-October 17, 1965

*A showcase for technology. Held in conjunction with the city's three-hundredth anniversary, the 1964-1965 New York World's Fair transported an empty Flushing Meadows field into the future.*

**Origins and History** The idea to hold another world's fair in New York came from lawyer Robert Koppel, who felt that such an event would teach children in the United States about other nations. In May, 1960, Robert Moses, New York City's park commissioner and a veteran of the 1939-1940 New York World's Fair, replaced Koppel as the Fair Corporation president.

*A crowd of people visit the New York World's Fair soon after its opening in April, 1964. The fair featured the Unisphere, a 140-foot-high steel globe.* (AP/Wide World Photos)

The Bureau of International Expositions did not sanction the New York World's Fair because world fairs are limited to one-year runs, and the United States had just hosted a world's fair in Seattle in 1962.

**The Fair** Dedicated to "man's achievements on a shrinking globe in an expanding universe," the fair covered more than six hundred acres and featured one hundred and forty pavilions. The visual theme of the fair was the Unisphere, a 140-foot-high, 900,000-pound steel globe encircled by three giant rings. Viewed from the edge of the structure's pool, the Unisphere had the dimensions Earth would have if viewed from a height of six thousand miles.

Because the Bureau of International Expositions did not sanction the event, most European and Communist bloc countries did not participate. Those that did included Belgium, whose pavilion replicated a walled nineteenth century town built out of stone, and Spain, which exhibited paintings by Francisco de Goya, Diego Velázquez, El Greco, Joan Miró, and Pablo Picasso.

Concern about the lack of religion in the 1939-1940 New York World's Fair led Moses to offer rent-free pavilions to religious groups of all denominations. Fifteen accepted, including the Vatican, which displayed Michelangelo's *Pieta* for the first time outside of St. Peter's Church in Rome.

Strong corporate involvement created a showcase for new technology. Primitive computers matched first-time users with foreign pen pals and helped them choose colors for redecorating their homes. The two-acre United States Space Park featured the Mercury capsule flown on the second U.S. manned orbital flight and full-scale models of other U.S. spacecraft and satellites. The U.S. Atomic Energy Commission took visitors to Atomsville, USA, where they could test remote "hot cell" manipulators for handling radioactive materials and run a simulated reactor.

Moses recruited Walt Disney to design major displays for four commercial pavilions, including Pepsi Cola's tunnel-of-love-style water ride. It's a Small World—A Tribute to UNICEF featured animated figures in global settings, all singing in different languages. When the fair ended, the small world pavilion was moved to Disneyland in Anaheim, California, and opened there in 1966.

**Impact** The 1964-1965 New York World's Fair lost nearly as much money as the 1939-1940 fair had and did not reach its attendance goal of seventy million people. Moses's conservative tastes dictated that the amusement zone would feature culturally oriented entertainment instead of the thrill rides and risqué amusements of years past. After suffering losses in the first year, Moses relented, and sixty-nine bars and nine "go-go" (dance) clubs were added for the 1965 season.

**Additional Information** For an overview, see the *Official Souvenir Book of the 1964-65 New York World's Fair* (1964), published by Time-Life books.

*P. S. Ramsey*

**See also** Science and Technology; Seattle World's Fair.

# ■ Newark Riot

**Date** July 12-17, 1967

*One of a series of major civil disorders of the 1960's. In 1967, more than one hundred U.S. cities experienced riots, mostly in ghettos, directly affecting African American communities, law enforcement officials, and the entire nation.*

**Origins and History**  Although riots had occurred in the Watts section of Los Angeles in 1965 and in several cities in the summer of 1967, the disturbance in Newark, New Jersey, best illustrated the "tinderbox" concept—an eruption of violence lit by a slow burning fuse. By 1967, Newark had the highest daytime population turnover, venereal disease and maternal mortality rates, and population density in the nation. It had changed from being 85 percent white in 1940 to nearly 50 percent African American by 1965. During the three years before the 1967 riot, a series of incidents of police brutality, some involving deaths of young African American men, had occurred. In July, 1967, twenty-four thousand unemployed African Americans lived within Newark's boundaries, an area of twenty-four square miles. Newark had proportionally the largest police force of any major city, yet its crime rate was among the highest.

**The Riot**  On July 12, another incident involving apparent police brutality occurred, the beating of cab driver John Smith, who had been stopped for traffic violations. Word of the incident traveled quickly through the taxi radio network and throughout the African American community, and the rumor spread that the police had killed Smith. Although this rumor was false, it was believable because of previous fatal incidents involving the police.

Soon angry crowds developed outside the police station where the officers had taken Smith. Rocks, bottles, and Molotov cocktails were thrown at the police station. The police rushed out of the station in a show of force, setting off days of rock throwing, window smashing, looting, car burning, and fire-bombing of businesses. Civil rights leaders and moderate African American ministers intervened and mediated, hoping to achieve a meaningful peace. Mayor Hugh Addonizio made some concessions to the group's demands for reform. More militant elements of the community, including black nationalists and members of the Nation of Islam, denounced

a commission appointed to examine what it termed "this isolated incident." City police were called in, and although they made many arrests, the situation soon was out of control.

On July 14, the mayor asked Governor Richard J. Hughes to send in state troopers and the National Guard. The 475 state troopers, 4,000 National Guardsmen, and 1,300 city police officers experienced immediate coordination and communications problems. The National Guard units had not been trained in riot control, and when sniper fire rang out, the troops, unable to pinpoint the origin of the shots, overreacted, spraying bullets throughout the congested area, hurting many innocent bystanders. At times, the three law enforcement groups mistakenly shot at each other, creating even more hysteria. During the course of three nights, law enforcement officers shot into buildings that bore signs indicating they were owned by African Americans.

On July 17, Governor Hughes ordered an end to the state of emergency and removed the National Guard from Newark. Casualties included the deaths of 1 firefighter, 1 police officer, and 23 African Americans; 145 law enforcement officers and 580 civilians had been injured. In addition, 1,465 people were arrested, including 1,394 African Americans,

*Firefighters put out a Broad Street fire believed to have been started by a firebomb during rioting in Newark, New Jersey, in July, 1967. (AP/Wide World Photos)*

50 whites, and 21 Puerto Ricans. Property damage exceeded fifteen million dollars. The major participants were predominantly somewhat educated, unemployed young African American men. Rioters directed their hostility toward property; the only people they injured were police officers.

**Impact** The Newark riot was followed later that month by rioting in Detroit, Michigan, in which forty-three people died. President Lyndon B. Johnson established the National Advisory Commission on Civil Disorders, chaired by Illinois governor Otto Kerner, to determine the cause of the rioting, find ways to control it, and determine the role of law enforcement. In 1968, the Kerner Commission, as it was commonly known, concluded that typically, a series of tension-heightening incidents over time led to one "triggering or precipitating event" that set off the riots. The nationwide study concluded that police in Newark and elsewhere were involved in more than half of the incidents that preceded riots and led to an escalation of violence. Newark's law enforcement efforts were found deficient. City police practices of overenforcement and harassment of people on the streets negated positive initiatives (such as mandatory human relations training and police community councils) taken by Director of Police Dominick Spina. Also, National Guard troops were found to be ill-prepared for crowd control, unable to contain violence in densely populated areas, and far too eager to discharge their weapons. The Newark riot nationally dramatized the severe condition of people living in the nation's ghettos.

**Additional Information** Nathan Wright, Jr.'s classic *Ready to Riot* (1968) stresses the underlying causes and anatomy of the Newark riot from a community perspective, terming the disturbance a "racial rebellion." The Kerner Commission Report (1968) presents the government commission's findings from its nationwide study on the causes of riots and its prescriptions for prevention and change.

*G. Thomas Taylor*

**See also** Chicago Riots; Detroit Riot; Kerner Commission Report; New York Riots; Washington, D.C. Riots; Watts Riot.

# ■ Newport Folk Festivals

*The summer gathering of prominent folk musicians that took place in Newport, Rhode Island, nine times between 1959 and 1969. It became the most popular such celebration of its era.*

In July, 1954, Boston pianist George Wein presented an outdoor jazz festival at Newport, Rhode Island. Blossoming into an annual summer event, and featuring renowned performers such as Dizzy Gillespie and Oscar Peterson, it proved a financial, as well as artistic, success. Five years later, recognizing the nationwide commercial appeal of folksingers Peter, Paul and Mary and the Kingston Trio, Wein decided to supplement his jazz festival revenue with a folk festival also held in Newport. Albert Grossman co-produced the event, and thirteen thousand folk aficionados watched performers such as the Kingston Trio, Odetta, Earl Scruggs, and the New Lost City Ramblers at the first Newport Folk Festival in 1959.

In spite of the appearance of high-quality performers, Wein discontinued the festival after only two years (1959 and 1960). Two factors contributed to this decision. First, the festival was losing money, and second, the 1960 Newport Jazz Festival riots had bankrupted Wein's corporation. The incidents of unruly behavior had been increasing since the mid-1950's and were blamed on lax enforcement of alcohol-purchasing laws.

Folksinger Pete Seeger, having performed in the earlier concerts, saw possibilities of folk music development and enrichment when artists of varying ages and background came together and demonstrated their talents. Seeger, with the active support of Theodore Bikel, convinced Wein to institute the Newport Folk Foundation, Inc. This was to be a nonprofit organization whose proceeds were to be used for folk music research, workshops, and scholarships. The seven members of the board of directors were from the cream of the crop of the folk world. The festival was to be held annually during the third week in July.

The first nonprofit Newport Folk Festival was held in 1963, and forty thousand attended the three days of concerts. Included in the billing were Joan Baez, Seeger, Judy Collins, and possibly the most popular folksinger and songwriter of the 1960's, Bob Dylan. At the 1964 festival, Canadian-born, full-blooded Cree Buffy St. Marie sang her self-authored "Cripple Creek" and "Universal Soldier" before seventy thousand people.

The attendance apex was reached in 1965 when more than eighty thousand people, many booing,

*The Watson Family with Doc Watson (center) opened the Newport Folk Festival of 1964. The nine festivals spanned most of the decade and showcased artists such as Joan Baez, Judy Collins, Pete Seeger, Bob Dylan, B. B. King, and James Taylor.* (AP/Wide World Photos)

watched pure folk idol Dylan transform himself into an electric-guitar-playing folk rocker. Dylan discarded his acoustical guitar for an electric one and played songs from his most recent albums, *Another Side of Bob Dylan* (1964) and *Bringing It All Back Home* (1965). In addition to the radical introduction of electrified instruments, Dylan's music abandoned the arena of social concern for introspection. Songs such as "All I Really Want to Do" and "It Ain't Me Babe" spoke more of how Dylan was feeling about himself than about the state of the society. Although the general public embraced the artist's new works, many at Newport felt betrayed and greeted his renditions with hisses and catcalls. Dylan defended himself, saying that acoustical protest songs were no longer a means of musical growth for him, and without growth, he could not continue as a performing artist.

By the late 1960's, rowdy elements were beginning to put fear in the heart of music concert pro-

moters; however, the musicians at the Newport Folk Festival still reflected the nation's pulse. B. B. King and Janis Joplin reigned in 1968, and James Taylor stole the show the following year. Dylan and most of the earlier performers could be counted on to showcase their most recent songs year after year. Every summer, the crowds flocked to Newport; however, drugs were endemic, and the larger the crowds, the greater the opportunity for harmful and sometimes fatal overdoses. In a nationally publicized incident at a 1969 concert headlined by the Rolling Stones in Altamont, California, an African American spectator was murdered by members of the Hell's Angels motorcycle gang who were providing security at the event. The decade of peace and love was coming to a less-than-peaceful ending.

**Impact** The Newport Folk Festival took place on nine July weekends between 1959 and 1969. The first two years, it was produced as a commercial venture, then from 1963 on, the festival was a nonprofit attempt to revitalize and revamp folk music. It is widely recognized that the nonprofit version succeeded in meeting its goals. The festival functioned as a lightning rod for the dynamic forces shaping folk music during the 1960's. The greatest names in the genre appeared there, rubbed shoulders and developed new directions as a result of their interaction. What happened at Newport made news throughout the country and even internationally.

**Subsequent Events** In 1970, the Newport City Council pressured the Newport Folk Foundation to cancel the festival that year. The official reasons given by the foundation were that crowd problems at the earlier jazz festival necessitated increased police protection and the building of a hurricane fence, thus depleting the foundation's coffers. The following year, again in response to jazz festival lawlessness, the city council rescinded the foundation's license. Wein then moved the jazz festival to New York and eliminated the folk festival.

*For most of the 1960's, Jack Nicklaus, a very popular and successful golfer, was Arnold Palmer's main rival.* (Ralph W. Miller Golf Library)

**Additional Information** A description of the inception and production of the Newport Folk Festival may be found in *Folk Music, More Than a Song* (1976), by Kristin Baggelaar.

*James Heaney*

**See also** Altamont Music Festival; Dylan, Bob; Folk Music; Monterey Pop Festival; Music; Woodstock Festival.

---

# ■ Nicklaus, Jack

**Born** January 21, 1940, Columbus, Ohio

*One of the greatest golfers of all time. Nicknamed "the Golden Bear," Nicklaus was the key rival of Arnold Palmer for most of the 1960's.*

Jack William Nicklaus, a versatile young athlete, chose golf and won the Ohio Open in 1956. In 1959 and 1961, he won the U.S. Amateur. Already married, he left college and turned professional. In 1962, he won the U.S. Open, which he had nearly won as an amateur in 1960. This playoff win began a decade of friendly but intense rivalry between the stoical Nicklaus and the charismatic Arnold Palmer, with media hype orchestrated by their manager Mark McCormack.

Nicklaus's longest run of victories was from 1959 to 1967, when he won nine major championships and was in the top three in ten others while winning numerous lesser titles. By 1966, he had won each professional major at least once, a feat matched by only three other men; eventually, he won each major at least three times. In 1968-1969, Nicklaus had a dry spell in the majors and was challenged by Gary Player and Lee Trevino for the number-one position, but his popularity grew as fans belatedly appreciated his sportsmanship and character.

**Impact** Nicklaus's dramatic success in the 1960's set the stage for his remarkably durable career. He regained his best form in the early 1970's and was again in great form in the 1980's. By 1986, Nicklaus had won twenty major championships, many other victories worldwide, and several money-winning titles. Later, he was a force on the Seniors Tour, playing only part-time because of pressures of health and business. He always built his year around the majors, entering every professional major from 1962 to 1997. His moral legacy to golf also includes a dignified demeanor and a well-lived, balanced life.

For example, upon turning pro, he promised his wife, Barbara, that he would never be away from home more than two weeks despite the lures of money and competition.

**Subsequent Events** In the 1990's, Nicklaus competed less frequently, but he became a leading golf-course architect, and his Golden Bear Corporation became a major producer of golf paraphernalia.

**Additional Information** See Nicklaus's candid autobiography, *My Story* (1997) for further details on his life.

*Tom Cook*

**See also** Golf; Palmer, Arnold; Rawls, Betsy; Wright, Mickey.

## ■ Nixon, Pat

**Born** March 16, 1912, Ely, Nevada
**Died** June 22, 1993, Park Ridge, New Jersey

*First Lady of the United States, 1969-1972. Nixon supported her husband, Richard M. Nixon, thirty-seventh president of the United States, throughout his political career, including during his resignation as president in 1974.*

**Early Life** The youngest of three children, Pat Nixon was born Thelma Catherine Patricia Ryan on March 16, 1912, in the mining town of Ely, Nevada. Her father was the son of Irish immigrants and her mother was an immigrant from Germany. Her father called her "Pat" from the start because she was born on the eve of St. Patrick's Day. In later life, she had her name legally changed to Pat. In 1914, the Ryans moved to a small farm in Artesia, California, outside of Los Angeles. When Pat Ryan was thirteen, her mother died of cancer. Four years later, in 1930, her father died of tuberculosis.

In 1937, Ryan completed her degree in merchandising at the University of Southern California and became a teacher in the business department of Whittier High School in Whittier, California. She met Richard M. Nixon when they were performing in a Whittier community play in 1938. They were married on June 21, 1940. In February, 1946, their daughter Tricia was born. Their second daughter, Julie, was born in July, 1948.

**The 1960's** Nixon devoted herself to raising her daughters, following her husband's rise in the Re-

publican Party, and supporting him in all his endeavors. For many years, Nixon, fearful that she might say or do something that might ruin her husband's career, had adopted a rigidly controlled manner. As a result the media gave her nicknames such as "Plastic Pat" or "Pat the Robot."

During her husband's first term as president, Nixon worked hard to make the White House more accessible. She redecorated and added antiques to fourteen rooms of the White House. She also advocated volunteerism by encouraging Americans to get involved in social work. She traveled widely with her husband, notably on his 1969 tour of the world.

**Later Life** During her husband's second term in office, Nixon traveled with him on his 1972 visit to China. Nixon's tenure as First Lady ended in August, 1974, after her husband resigned as a result of the Watergate scandal, following the break-in at the National Democratic Party headquarters in the summer of 1972.

Nixon's health remained unpredictable in later years. She suffered strokes in 1976 and 1983. In 1987, she had a malignant tumor removed from her mouth. She died on June 22, 1993, of lung cancer at the age of eighty-one.

**Impact** Nixon became the most widely traveled First Lady in history, having taken trips to eighty countries. She was also the first incumbent First Lady to support the Equal Rights Amendment publicly. The readers of *Good Housekeeping* magazine expressed their admiration for her by four times voting her America's Most Admired Woman.

**Subsequent Events** Nixon's husband died on April 22, 1994, less than a year after his wife, at the age of eighty-one.

**Additional Information** In 1986, Julie Nixon Eisenhower, Nixon's daughter, published a biography of her mother, *Pat Nixon: The Untold Story*.

*Eddith A. Dashiell*

**See also** Nixon, Richard M.

## ■ Nixon, Richard M.

**Born** January 9, 1913, Yorba Linda, California
**Died** April 22, 1994, New York, New York

*One of the dominant U.S. political leaders from 1947 to 1974. The zenith of Nixon's life and career was his election in November, 1968, as the thirty-seventh president of the United States.*

**Early Life** Richard Milhous Nixon was raised in Whittier, California. In 1934, he graduated from Whittier College and in 1937 received his law degree from Duke University Law School. Nixon enlisted in the Navy in 1942 and served as a naval officer in the Pacific theater during World War II. Upon his discharge in 1946, he embarked on his political career, winning a seat in the U.S. House of Representatives from California. In those early Cold War years, he soon gained recognition as a staunch anticommunist. Working with Joseph McCarthy, he played a major role in the Alger Hiss investigation. This experience propelled Nixon to the U.S. Senate in 1950 and to the office of vice president under President Dwight D. Eisenhower.

**The 1960's** Nixon entered the 1960's with high hopes of becoming the next president of the United States. His eight years as vice president had given him valuable experience in foreign affairs, especially in dealing with the Soviet Union after the death of Joseph Stalin. His tenure also covered the rise of Nikita Khrushchev, the intense nuclear arms race of the 1950's, and the beginnings of space exploration. In addition, while President Eisenhower was recovering from two heart attacks, Nixon had gained experience in executive leadership in the White House. The most important political asset that Nixon had in 1960 was, perhaps, a name and face recognition far beyond that of any potential rival. Possible roadblocks between Nixon and the White House included disillusionment with Republican leadership during the late 1950's, a weak economy, and Cold War victories by the Soviet Union, such as the first space satellite in 1957, Fidel Castro and communism in Cuba in 1959, and the downing of an American U-2 reconnaissance plane over the Soviet Union in 1960.

*Presidential candidate Richard M. Nixon (left) speaks with Minnesota governor Harold Levander before addressing the crowd during his 1968 campaign.* (National Archives)

Nixon easily won the Republican nomination in 1960 but lost the closest election in the second half of the twentieth century to Democratic nominee John F. Kennedy. Public perception of the candidates in the first televised presidential debate played a major role in that election. In 1962, Nixon lost the California gubernatorial race, seemingly ending his political career. In a press conference after his defeat, he said, "You won't have Nixon to kick around any more." However, he was able to rebuild his political reputation during the mid-1960's, and in 1968, he defeated Democrat Hubert Humphrey to become the thirty-seventh president of the United States.

During Nixon's first term as president, the complexity of his personality, which some have interpreted as a "dark side," began to unfold. His first priority had to be the Vietnam War, which had consumed the presidency of his predecessor, Lyndon B. Johnson. Although known to favor a military solution, he saw the futility of it and began the gradual withdrawal of U.S. troops. Although remaining a staunch anticommunist, he was the first U.S. president to visit the communist capitals of Beijing and Moscow, opening the doors of trade with China and the Soviet Union. Nixon further shocked the world by supporting the admission of the People's Republic of China to the United Nations, even to the exclusion of Taiwan, a longtime U.S. ally.

**Later Life** President Nixon easily won a second term in 1972. However, during the months following his second inauguration, stories began to emerge concerning his direct involvement in the Watergate scandal, the burglarizing of Democratic Party headquarters at the Watergate Hotel in Washington, D.C. On June, 17, 1972, a group of men working for Nixon's reelection committee broke into the Watergate office of the Democratic Party. The intrigue and cover-up that followed, including taped conversations that revealed that Nixon had participated in the cover-up, led to Nixon's humiliating resignation in August, 1974.

Nixon retired to his secluded home in San Clemente, California, where he anguished over his uncertain future and attempted to settle into the normal life of a former president. In September, 1974, he accepted President Gerald Ford's full pardon for any crimes he may have committed. The pardon was accompanied by a statement of contrition from Nixon. As the years passed, his life became very

routine. By the mid-1980's, he sought to assume the role of an elder statesman and traveled around the world, in 1986, visiting Moscow to meet the new Soviet leader, Mikhail Gorbachev.

After leaving the White House, Nixon wrote eight books, several of which reveal his continued interest in foreign affairs. *Real War* (1980) and *Real Peace: A Strategy for the West* (1984) were the major books dealing with foreign affairs. *Leaders* (1982) gives an interesting view of the qualities Nixon felt that a good leader should have. Nixon's final book, his evaluation of the post-Cold War period, is *Seize the Moment: America's Challenge in a One-Superpower World* (1992).

**Impact** Nixon arguably fulfilled most of his domestic and foreign policy goals as president. His greatest success was in foreign policy. His role in removing U.S. troops from Vietnam, his establishment of peaceful ties with China, and his leadership in Middle East peace making are the high points of that success. All his triumphs, however, have been overshadowed by the Watergate scandal and his resignation from the presidency.

**Additional Information** *Richard Milhous Nixon: The Rise of an American Politician* (1990), by Roger Morris, covers Nixon's life up to when he became vice president in 1953. Jonathon Aitken's *Nixon: A Life* (1993) gives a detailed description of the twenty years after Watergate and Nixon's resignation. An additional source for an overall evaluation of Nixon is Gerald and Deborah Strober's *Nixon: An Oral History of His Presidency* (1994). After years of legal battles, the Watergate tapes were finally published in *Abuse of Power: The Nixon Tapes* (1997), edited by Stanley I. Kutler. This book put to rest many questions about Nixon's direct involvement in the burglary and cover-up. It also proved extremely revealing about his character and personality.

*Glenn L. Swygart*

**See also** Cold War; Humphrey, Hubert; Johnson, Lyndon B.; Kennedy, John F.; Kennedy-Nixon Debates; Nixon, Pat; Paris Peace Talks; Vietnam War.

# ■ Nobel Prizes

*Prestigious achievement awards given to thirty-one Americans in the 1960's. Americans received Nobel Prizes in five categories—physics, chemistry, physiology or medicine, peace, and literature.*

The Alfred Nobel Foundation awards prizes honoring achievement in physics, chemistry, physiology or medicine, peace, literature, and economics. The first prizes were awarded in 1901, and Europeans dominated all categories before World War II. After the war, however, Americans accounted for an increasing proportion of the winners, especially in the sciences. In part, the recognition reflected the great expansion of U.S. science during the war. Many U.S. Nobel laureates were refugees from Nazi persecution in Germany or scientists who had immigrated to the United States in search of jobs in the nation's universities.

During the 1960's, thirty-one Americans, nine of them foreign born, won or shared Nobel Prizes: ten for physics, five for chemistry, thirteen for physiology or medicine, two for peace, and one for literature. (The first Nobel Prize for Economics was awarded in 1969 but not to an American.) Americans formed 40 percent of the seventy-eight new laureates during the decade.

**Physics** The ten physics prizes went for research in detecting or explaining the properties of nuclear physics or elementary particles or for creating new technology based on the discoveries. Donald D. Glaser (1960) invented the bubble chamber; Richard Hofstadter (1961) probed the nucleus with an electron-scattering technique; and Luis W. Alvarez (1968) developed the hydrogen bubble chamber, particle-tracking equipment, and related computer programs. Their work, all performed in the 1950's, enabled physicists to discover many new elementary particles. Charles Hard Townes (1964) constructed the first workable maser (acronym for microwave amplification by stimulated emission of radiation); the techniques of optical pumping and stimulated emission later led to the laser (acronym for light amplification by stimulated emission of radiation). Hungarian-born Eugene P. Wigner (1963), German-born Maria Goeppert Mayer (1963), and German-born Hans Albrecht Bethe (1967) plumbed the structure of the nucleus and the reactions among its constituent particles; Bethe was also honored for explaining how stars produce nuclear energy. Two of the most famous physical theories of the twentieth century won Nobel recognition in the 1960's. Richard Feynman and Julian Schwinger (1965, both shared with Japanese theorist Shinichiro Tomonaga) formulated quantum electrodynamics, which describes electrons, positrons, photons, and their interactions. Murray Gell-Mann (1969) explained how families of particles are related and predicted the existence of a new type of elementary particle, quarks, the beginning of quantum chromodynamics.

**Chemistry** The five chemistry prizes, all unshared, recognized scientists who discovered chemical techniques and fundamental processes. Williard Frank Libby (1960) devised a way to date matter by measuring its carbon 14 content; this radiocarbon-dating technique greatly helped other specialists, particularly geologists and archeologists, establish the age of Earth and human cultures. Melvin Calvin (1961) explained how plants assimilate carbon dioxide during photosynthesis, a basic biological mechanism. Robert Burns Woodward (1965) pioneered techniques for synthesizing organic compounds. Robert S. Mulliken (1966) helped explain how chemical bonds form in the electron structure of molecules. Finally, Norwegian-born Lars Onsager (1968) elucidated the thermodynamics of irreversible chemical processes.

**Physiology or Medicine** The most famous of the thirteen laureates for physiology or medicine were selected for explaining aspects of genetics. James D. Watson (1962) shared his prize with Francis Crick and Maurice Wilkins, both English, for deciphering the molecular structure of deoxyribonucleic acid (DNA), among the most celebrated scientific detective stories of the century. Marshall W. Nirenberg, Indian-born Har Gobind Khorana, and Robert W. Holley (1968) interpreted the role of the genetic code in protein synthesis. Italian-born Salvador E. Luria, German-born Max Delbrück, and Alfred D. Hershey (1969) discovered how viruses replicate and determined their basic genetic structure. Francis Peyton Rous (1966) won a prize for work he had done fifty-five years earlier, isolating viruses that cause tumors; he shared the prize with Charles Brenton Huggins, who developed a hormone treatment for prostate cancer. Hungarian-born Georg Von Békésy (1961) explained how sound stimulates the cochlea in the inner ear, and George Wald and Haldan Keffer Hartline (1967) explained the principal chemical and physiological mechanisms of the eye. German-born Konrad E. Bloch (1964) clarified the production and regulation of cholesterol and fatty acids.

**Peace and Literature** The two U.S. Nobel Peace Prize laureates were controversial figures. Linus Pauling (1962) received the prize for his outspoken opposition to nuclear arms, opposition that had incurred retaliation from the U.S. government, which refused to issue him a passport. (It was Pauling's second unshared prize; his first, for chemistry in 1954, rewarded his explanation of chemical bonding.) Martin Luther King, Jr. (1964), the best-known leader in the nation's Civil Rights movement, guided the Southern Christian Leadership Conference in its attempt to end discrimination against African Americans.

The lone American literature prize winner was John Steinbeck (1962). His fiction portrayed the underclasses of the nation's society with sympathy and often with humor, notably his novel *The Grapes of Wrath* (1939).

**Impact** The Nobel Prizes enhanced the reputation of the United States, especially in the natural sciences. Following the embarrassment over the Soviet launch of Sputnik 1 in 1957, which made the United

States look like a runner-up in the space race, the steady flow of Noble Prizes assured the public that U.S. researchers were not falling behind in science and technology. The prizes also attracted talented students from all over the world to U.S. universities and prompted government and private foundations to spend more liberally on research.

**Additional Information** *The Who's Who of Nobel Prize Winners, 1901-1995* (1996), edited by Bernard S. Schlessinger and June H. Schlessinger, provides information about the prize winners.

*Roger Smith*

**See also** Genetics; King, Martin Luther, Jr.; Lasers; Medicine; Science and Technology.

## ■ Nuclear Reactors

*Devices in which uranium or plutonium atoms are split apart in a process called fission that releases large amounts of heat energy. Usually this energy is used to make steam that drives a turbine, which ultimately produces electrical power.*

*One of the nuclear power plants operating in the 1960's was Consolidated Edison's Indian Point nuclear steam-electric generating station at Buchanan, New York.* (AP/Wide World Photos)

In 1934, Enrico Fermi was bombarding uranium atoms with neutrons. Although he expected the neutrons to be absorbed and result in heavier atoms, the chemical properties of the atoms he produced were not what he expected. Finally, Otto Hahn realized that instead of being absorbed into the uranium 235 nucleus, the neutrons were causing that nucleus to split roughly in half. The result was two lighter atoms rather than one heavier one. Under the direction of Fermi, the first nuclear reactor was built at the University of Chicago. It consisted of tubes of naturally occurring uranium imbedded in large blocks of graphite. On December 2, 1942, this reactor "went critical" for the first time. A reactor is said to be "critical" when the number of fissions in one second is the same as the number in each second that follows.

**Nuclear Plants** Nuclear reactors generated a great deal of enthusiasm in the early and mid-1960's. Early estimates suggested that nuclear reactors would make electricity so cheaply that electric meters could be eliminated. By the end of the decade, however, people became aware of the problems regarding safety, pollution, and radioactive waste disposal.

The first civilian nuclear reactor used to generate electricity began operation at Shippingport, Pennsylvania, in December, 1957. It was soon followed by Commonwealth Edison's Dresden Number One plant in August, 1960. Although the Atomic Energy Commission's Cooperative Power Reactor Demonstration Program offered heavy federal subsidies to utility companies, only a handful of civilian reactors had been built by 1963. Most of those constructed had experienced problems, and the future of civilian nuclear power looked gloomy. Then Jersey Central Power and Light signed a contract with General Electric to build the Oyster Creek facility. Economic analyses by the Jersey utility showed that this nuclear plant would generate electricity more cheaply than a coal-using power plant at the same location.

By 1965, General Electric and Westinghouse were flooded with orders for nuclear plants, and in April, 1968, there were about one hundred such plants on order, under construction, or in operation. During the late 1960's, more than half of the new generating plants being ordered were nuclear fueled. The Oyster Creek plant generated half a million kilowatts of electricity, and later plants had larger and larger capacity. By 1968, contracts were being signed for one-million-kilowatt plants.

**Nuclear Ships and Submarines** During the 1960's, nuclear reactors were also being used to propel ships. In ships, the steam produced by the reactor drove a turbine that was connected directly to the propeller. The U.S. Navy's first nuclear-powered submarine, the *Nautilus*, was commissioned in 1954, and the nuclear submarine fleet grew rapidly during the 1960's. An attempt was made to use nuclear reactors to power commercial ships as well. The nuclear merchant ship *Savannah* made its maiden voyage in August, 1962. This ship continued in service throughout the 1960's and was decommissioned in 1971. *Savannah* was intended to demonstrate that nuclear power was feasible for commercial ships.

**Nuclear Accidents** At least two serious reactor accidents occurred in the United States during the 1960's. In 1961, three men were killed when a small research reactor in Idaho exploded. Some radioactivity was released into the sparsely populated surrounding area. Late in 1966, a serious accident occurred in the Enrico Fermi reactor at Lagoona Beach, Michigan. Some of the uranium in the reactor core overheated and melted. Fortunately, very little radiation was released, and no one was injured.

**Impact** By the end of the 1960's, it appeared as if nuclear reactors would take over the business of generating electric power. Forecasts made at that time estimated that five hundred thousand megawatts of electrical power would be generated in nuclear plants by 1990. The actual capacity in 1990 was about one hundred thousand megawatts. Nuclear-powered submarines were a great success; they rapidly replaced conventionally powered submarines in the U.S. Navy during the 1960's. Because nuclear submarines can travel at high speeds under water and remain submerged for several months, their existence drastically changed the nature of undersea warfare. No additional nuclear-powered merchant ships were built in the United States during the 1960's, and none have been built in the decades that followed.

**Subsequent Events** On March 28, 1979, a major accident occurred in reactor number two at the Three Mile Island facility near Harrisburg, Pennsylvania. Through a series of errors by operating personnel at the facility, the flow of cooling water over the fuel rods was not maintained, and later, part of the core was not even submerged in water. As a result, much of the core overheated and melted. Although a core meltdown is a very serious event, exposure of people outside the reactor complex to radioactivity was negligible.

**Additional Information** Sheldon Novick's *The Careless Atom* (1969) takes a negative view of nuclear power. *Nuclear Choices* (1991), by Richard Wolfson, is a more recent and more balanced view of the subject. *Atomic Energy in Cosmic and Human Life* (1947), by George Gamow, contains beautifully clear explanations of the basic physics of nuclear fission. *Introduction to Nuclear Power* (1987), by John Collier and Geoffrey Hewitt, contains excellent drawings of reactors and detailed descriptions of major accidents. *Nuclear Power and the Environment* (1973), published by the American Nuclear Society, addresses a wide range of issues in question-and-answer format.

*Edwin G. Wiggins*

**See also** Arms Race; SANE (National Committee for a Sane Nuclear Policy); Science and Technology; *Scorpion* Disappearance; *Thresher* Disaster; *Triton* Submarine.

*President John F. Kennedy signs the 1963 Nuclear Test Ban Treaty.* (AP/Wide World Photos)

---

## ■ Nuclear Test Ban Treaties

**Dates** 1963, 1967, 1968

*A set of international arms-control agreements involving nuclear weapons. These treaties, signed in 1963, 1967, and 1968, were designed to reduce the chance of nuclear war, lower the levels of destruction if such a war occurred, and minimize the cost of existing military establishments.*

**Origins and History** In the 1950's and early 1960's, the United States and the Soviet Union began talks on limiting nuclear testing because of public concern about radioactive fallout and the growing number of countries that possessed nuclear weapons. The comprehensive test ban treaty negotiations, which focused on preventing underwater, outer-space, underground, and atmospheric tests and on stopping the proliferation of nuclear weapons, signaled the beginning of major arms-control talks between the two superpowers.

**The Treaties** In the late 1950's and early 1960's, the United States and the Soviet Union embraced the global arms-control movement. The nuclear arms race was out of control, and the superpowers began talks to reduce the danger of nuclear war. On August 5, 1963, the United States, the Soviet Union, and the United Kingdom formally signed the Nuclear Test Ban Treaty, which prohibited nuclear-weapons testing in the atmosphere, outer space, and under water but allowed underground testing. The danger of nuclear war between the United States and the Soviet Union during the Cuban Missile Crisis of 1962 and the failure of communication between the superpowers, among other strategic conditions, provided the momentum for the treaty.

After the treaty was signed in 1963, relations between the United States and the Soviet Union remained fairly stable. On January 27, 1967, the two superpowers, along with sixty other nations, signed the Outer Space Treaty, which prohibited using outer space for military purposes, including those involving nuclear weapons.

On July 1, 1968, the two superpowers and fifty-eight other nations signed the Nuclear Non-Proliferation Treaty, which prohibited nonnuclear nations from manufacturing and testing nuclear weapons. This treaty was the first international arms-control agreement that applied to nations that did not possess nuclear weapons. In return for their cooperation, the nonnuclear nations received commitments from the nuclear powers that they would seek an end to the nuclear arms race and pursue other disarmament measures.

**Impact** The impact on U.S. society of the nuclear test ban treaties was positive; most Americans reacted favorably. However, the strategic nuclear arms competition between the superpowers became more heated, intensifying the threat of nuclear war.

**Subsequent Events** The nuclear test ban treaties inspired the 1971 Seabed Treaty, the U.S.-Soviet 1974 Threshold Test Ban Treaty, and the U.S.-Soviet Peaceful Nuclear Explosion Treaty. More important, the superpowers agreed to reduce their strategic offensive nuclear systems and to limit their deployment of antiballistic missile sites in the Strategic Arms Limitation Talks (SALT I), signed in May, 1972. In November, 1979, SALT II was signed, extending the 1963 treaty banning nuclear testing and further limiting the deployment of antiballistic missile sites.

**Additional Information** An excellent study on nuclear test ban treaties can be found in *International Arms Control: Issues and Agreements* (1984), edited by Coit D. Blacker and Gloria Duffy.

*Michael J. Siler*

**See also** Arms Race.

# ■ Nureyev Defection

**Date** June 16, 1961

*The flight to freedom by a rebellious Soviet ballet dancer. The handsome, talented artist's escape from his strict communist homeland was viewed as a Cold War victory for the Western world.*

**Origins and History** Rudolf Nureyev, born March 17, 1938, decided to become a dancer soon after seeing his first ballet at age six in Ufa in eastern Russia. At age seventeen, Nureyev became a student of the prestigious Kirov Ballet school in Leningrad. In 1958, he first performed with the company, in the principal male role in *Laurencia*. Nureyev's daring, innovative, energetic dancing style and his intense, somewhat arrogant personality attracted attention and alienated some Kirov dancers and teachers. In 1961, the Kirov Ballet planned to tour France, London, and the United States as part of an attempt by Soviet premier Nikita Khrushchev to soften the Soviet Union's harsh image.

**The Defection** The rebellious Nureyev, already being watched by the Soviet secret police, was allowed at the last minute to travel to Paris and opened with the Kirov Ballet on May 22. In Paris, Nureyev was allowed unusual freedom, making friends with local ballet dancers and Clara Saint, the twenty-one-year-old daughter of a Chilean painter. On the morning of June 16, 1961, after the ballet company reached Le Bourget airport, scheduled to travel to London for the next part of the tour, Konstantin Sergeyev, a male dancer with the company, informed Nureyev that his mother was ill and that he was to return to Moscow immediately. Nureyev managed to get word to Saint, who came to the airport and found the dancer in an airport bar, guarded by two representatives of the Soviet embassy. He asked her to help, and Saint enlisted the aid of two French police. She informed Nureyev of the officers' presence, and he ran to them, shouting, "Protect me!" In the airport police office, Nureyev declared to Soviet officials that his decision to defect from his homeland was made in "full liberty." He was granted asylum by France and joined the International Ballet of the Marquis de Cuevas two days later.

**Impact** Nureyev's "leap to freedom," as his defection became known, was regarded by many Westerners as proof of the harsh rigidity of the Soviet system and the superiority of Western democracy. The Soviets, displeased by their Cold War defeat, claimed Nureyev's defection was based not on politics but on his desire to be with Saint. In actuality, Nureyev's flight to freedom was most likely inspired by both his devotion to his art and his homosexuality, which the dancer never publicly acknowledged. Some historians believe that the secret police may have allowed Nureyev relative freedom in Paris so that he would reveal his homosexuality, a serious crime in the Soviet Union. Nureyev is believed to have made advances to Yuri Soloviev, a male dancer with whom he roomed in Paris. The Soviets tried Nureyev in absentia in January, 1962, declaring him a "traitor" and sentencing him to seven years of hard labor if he ever returned to the country. In 1987, Nureyev was allowed to visit the Soviet Union to see his dying mother.

As a dancer, Nureyev's exotic appearance and presence, which included a hint of sexuality, and his energetic style, which incorporated powerful jumps, gave a new prominence to the male dancer's role. He is best remembered for his longtime pairing with ballerina Dame Margot Fonteyn with the Royal Ballet in London. He became ballet director of the Paris Opéra in 1983 and served as its principal choreographer from 1989 until 1992. He died of AIDS in January, 1993.

**Additional Information**  A good source of information on the dancer's early years is his autobiography, *Nureyev: An Autobiography with Pictures* (1963). A mid-career perspective is given by *Nureyev: Aspects of the Dancer* (1975), by John Percival, and Otis Stuart's

*Ballet dancer Rudolf Nureyev, who fled the Soviet Union in 1961, demonstrates his energetic style in this flying leap in 1969. (The Times/Archive Photos)*

*Perpetual Motion: The Public and Private Lives of Rudolf Nureyev* (1995) provides a look at the dancer's career and private life.

*Rowena Wildin*

**See also**  Cold War; Radio Free Europe.

# O

## ■ Oakland Riots

**Dates** October 17 and October 20, 1967

*Violence erupted on two days of a five-day protest against the Vietnam War and the military draft at the induction center in Oakland, California. Dubbed riots, the incidents resulted in numerous injuries and arrests but no deaths and limited property damage.*

**Origins and History** The Stop the Draft movement, a group of people opposed to the military draft and the Vietnam War, targeted Oakland, California, as the focal point for five days of protest because it was the site of a large military induction center.

**The Riots** From October 16-20, 1967, dubbed "Stop the Draft Week," people from all over Northern California converged on the Oakland Induction Center to physically shut it down. The leaders of the Stop the Draft movement had the stated goal of rejecting nonviolent action and wanted to "muck up" the whole draft process.

The plan was to completely close the Oakland Induction Center at Fifteenth and Clay to prevent any inductees and, more important, any armed services members from entering the building. A massive call went out for protesters to gather by 6:00 A.M at the induction center on Monday, October 16, and every day during the week. The protesters were prepared for a violent response from the police. They smeared their faces with petroleum jelly to take the sting out of any Mace, an irritating chemical, that might be sprayed at them and carried gas masks and garbage can lids that they could use as shields. They used bullhorns and shouted at the police "We order you to disperse—we are the people of California" and the ubiquitous "Hell no, we won't go," used to voice young men's objection to being drafted and sent to Vietnam. They displayed signs bearing antidraft slogans and hammer-and-sickle flags and carried cans of spray paint. However, the movement's ranks had been infiltrated by undercover police officers, and on the first day of the protest, the protesters were met by twenty-seven county and city police departments from nine Bay Area counties and the California Highway Patrol.

Three of the five planned days of protest were peaceful, including October 16, when Joan Baez sang, but violence erupted on Tuesday, October 17, dubbed "Terrible Tuesday," and Friday, October 20. On these two days, termed riots by the media, the protesters overturned parked vehicles, deflated tires, ripped wires from cars, strew tacks and garbage across the streets, sat in front of the induction center, and spray painted and shouted antiwar slogans. On October 20, an estimated ten thousand demonstrators were involved in the protests, with men outnumbering women four to one. One thousand officers were present and three hundred police officers were on call. Twenty-three people were injured and ten jailed.

**Impact** Nearby businesspeople complained of physical damage to their stores and lost business because the protesters, in blocking entrance to the induction center, also prevented customers from entering their stores. Police arrested 277 people during the five days of protest. Minor clashes with police occurred daily, and many people viewed the police as the instigators of the violence. Most of the protesters' injuries were the result of being clubbed, kicked, or teargassed.

An informal survey of experienced reporters found that the majority of the crowd came merely to watch not to protest. The protesters were unable to close the induction center but produced delays as buses of inductees had to be rerouted.

**Subsequent Events** The "Oakland Seven"—Michael Smith, Steven Hamilton, Robert Mandel, Reese Erlich, Frank Bardacke, Jeff Segal, and Terence Cannon—were arrested and tried on numerous criminal charges including trespassing, obstructing public sidewalks, interfering with officers, creating a general public nuisance, and conspiracy. The police and prosecutors alleged that the dowels used for the picket signs were in fact weapons. The Oakland Seven, represented by defense lawyer Charles Gar, were acquitted of all charges in 1969.

**Additional Information** For more information about the protests and the trial of the Oakland Seven, see Todd Gitlin's *The Sixties: Years of Hope, Days of Rage* (1987).

*Akilah Monifa*

**See also** Boston Five Trial; Chicago Seven Trial; Days of Rage; Draft Resisters; National Mobilization Committee to End the War in Vietnam (MOBE); Vietnam War; War Resisters League; Weathermen.

## ■ Oates, Joyce Carol

**Born** June 16, 1938, Lockport, New York

*One of the nation's most distinguished and prolific fiction writers. Her novel* them *(1969) won the National Book Award and capped her career in the 1960's, solidifying her reputation as a writer of violence and bleak psychological and social realism.*

**Early Life** Joyce Carol Oates's childhood poverty and family violence influenced the themes she explores in her fiction; Erie County, New York, where she grew up, is the Eden County of her early fiction. Her father, Frederic Oates, quit school during the Depression after his father deserted the family. Oates's mother, Carolyn Bush, was adopted as an infant when her father was murdered in a bar brawl. Oates, the first in her family to finish college, earned a master's degree from the University of Wisconsin in 1961. One of the United States' most honored writers, Oates began publishing in the 1960's.

**The 1960's** Oates taught at the University of Detroit (1961-1967) and the University of Windsor, in Ontario (1967-1978). Her early short-story collections and novels quickly earned her a reputation as a rising literary star. *By the North Gate* (1963) is a collection of Oates's undergraduate stories, set in the ironically renamed Eden County of her childhood. Together with *Upon the Sweeping Flood* (1966), these stories marked Oates as a regional writer and contain repeated themes of youthful rebellion and violence. Oates describes her early characters as having "extreme but normal and desirable" reactions and "straining against the too-close confines of a personality now outgrown or a social 'role' too restrictive." In the novels Oates wrote in the 1960's, she established herself as a realist fascinated by the destructive personal and social worlds her characters inhabit. *With Shuddering Fall* (1965) is an intense story of a

destructive love affair between a sheltered seventeen-year-old girl and a rough race-car driver and includes rape, a car wreck, murderous fights, miscarriage, riot, suicide, and insanity. *A Garden of Earthly Delights* (1967) covers three generations, featuring a girl raised in migrant worker camps who later marries into middle-class security, experiences explosive violence, and finally declines in a nursing home. *Expensive People* (1968) tells the story of an obese eighteen-year-old genius; stifled by an affluent suburban environment and cynical parents, he commits matricide and attempts liberation as an anonymous sniper, terrorizing his community. *them* (1969) was Oates's fourth novel and sixth book in as many years. At thirty-one, she won the National Book Award for *them*, engendering widespread praise for her skill as a novelist, shock at her violent imagination, and surprise at her frail, feminine appearance. *them* is the story of a poor family who survives the Depression only to face the horror of inner-city rioting in Detroit in 1967. The characters in *them* face the difficulties of love and its true opposite, apathy, an emptiness that invites violence.

**Later Life** Oates, a prolific writer, continued to write in the following decades, turning out numerous short-story collections, poems, essays and critical writings, and novels. Some of the better-known works include *Do with Me What You Will* (1973), and a parodic Gothic series: *Bellefleur* (1980), *A Bloodsmoor Romance* (1982), and *Mysteries of Winterthurn* (1984).

**Impact** Oates's bleak fiction boldly addresses the inner and outer turmoil of the 1960's through her troubled, often violent protagonists and social settings. In Oates's intensely realistic fictional world, "Violence can't be singled out from an ordinary day; . . . everyone must live through it again and again." Oates's characters reflect an aspect of American consciousness in the 1960's. Burdened by psychological and social pressure, they are subject to unpredictable violence, inevitable imbalance, and apocalyptic death.

**Additional Information** For more themes of violence in Oates's fiction, see Mary Kathryn Grant's *The Tragic Vision of Joyce Carol Oates* (1987).

*Linda Kearns Bannister*

**See also** Literature.

# ■ Office of Minority Business Enterprise (OMBE)

*A federal agency charged with coordinating the government's efforts at promoting minority business enterprise. The OMBE embodied President Richard M. Nixon's commitment to "black capitalism."*

**Origins and History**  During the 1960's, riots erupted in a number of cities in the United States, prompting politicians to develop policies to stabilize conditions in the inner city. Many observers blamed the riots on a growing sense of frustration with the slow pace of economic progress being made by African Americans. Although inner-city residents were predominantly black, most of the businesses were owned by whites. Advocates of minority business argued that the creation of a African American middle class would provide role models for inner-city youth and thus help to soothe their discontent.

In April, 1968, Republican presidential candidate Richard M. Nixon delivered a radio address promising African Americans a "piece of the action" in business. On March 5, 1969, Nixon issued an executive order establishing the Office of Minority Business Enterprise (OMBE) within the department of commerce. The OMBE's goal was to create "equal opportunity at the top of the ladder" by urging other federal agencies to provide loans, grants, and government contracts to minority businesses.

The OMBE was not the first federal agency to get involved in promoting minority business enterprise. In 1963, the Small Business Administration (SBA) launched a pilot program to assist African American entrepreneurs in Philadelphia. One year later, Congress authorized the SBA to make "economic opportunity loans" to ghetto entrepreneurs. By 1968, SBA Administrator Howard Samuels was aggressively pursuing a policy of "compensatory capitalism," a form of affirmative action for African American businesses. By pledging to support "black capitalism," Nixon co-opted an idea that already had wide appeal.

**Activities**  Nixon directed the OMBE to mobilize existing resources within the federal government, but the office lacked the authority to order agencies to provide assistance to minority-owned companies. The OMBE's relations with the SBA soured as the two agencies bickered over jurisdictional issues. The OMBE was also hindered by economic realities; a tight money supply discouraged banks from making loans to minority businesses.

**Impact**  The OMBE got off to a painfully slow start, leading critics to charge that the Nixon administration was not really serious about its commitment to minority enterprise. Although its short-term impact was limited, the OMBE embodied a bipartisan consensus that the federal government should grant preferential treatment to minority businesses. Between 1969 and 1991, federal financial assistance to minority businesses increased thirty-five-fold and federal procurement dollars awarded to minority firms increased two hundred-fold.

**Subsequent Events**  The OMBE was later renamed the Minority Business Development Administration. During the 1970's, the minority enterprise programs became embroiled in scandals, and congressional investigations revealed that many of the beneficiaries were minority members who fronted for white business owners. Very few of the companies participating in OMBE-or SBA-sponsored programs were ever able to wean themselves from government assistance. Those companies that prospered did so by serving markets that were far removed from the inner city.

**Additional Information**  Arthur Blaustein and Geoffrey Faux examine the early years of the OMBE in *The Star-Spangled Hustle* (1972), a highly critical account of the Nixon administration's "black capitalism" programs.

*Jonathan J. Bean*

**See also**  Affirmative Action; Nixon, Richard M.; Prosperity and Poverty; Watts Riot.

---

# ■ *Oh, Calcutta!*

**Produced** 1969
**Author** Kenneth Tynan (1927-1980)

*The Broadway play that best reflects the sexual revolution of the 1960's. It is comical, musical, and both a celebration and a satire of the sexual preoccupations of the era.*

**The Work**  In *Oh, Calcutta!: An Entertainment with Music,* five men and five women act out thirteen comic and musical sketches that often include dance, invariably focus on sexual issues, and usually involve disrobing to total nudity. Kenneth Tynan collected or recruited the sketches from figures as famous and diverse as Samuel Beckett, Jules Feiffer, John Lennon, and Sam Shepard. Many of the sketches involve dysfunctional lovers. For example, "Dick and Jane" takes place in a darkened bedroom where the man and woman give each other instructions on how to make love more effectively, but neither is satisfied by the coaching. Finally, Dick suggests acting out a sexual fantasy that involves a mask, a whip, high-heeled boots, a basketball, a bicycle, a watermelon, paint, balloons, a tub, a department-store mannikin, a light show with deafening rock music, and an umbrella. When the cacophony of his fantasy ends, his pleasure is exquisite, but Jane has disappeared. Similarly, the humor of many of the sketches celebrates sexual freedom while at the same time satirizing sexual excesses.

**Impact** *Oh, Calcutta!* premiered Off-Broadway on June 17, 1969, at the Eden Theater. The critical reception was mixed, but the show's phenomenal commercial appeal carried it to a notorious success, running for 704 performances at the Eden before transferring to Broadway's Belasco Theater for 610 additional performances. Revived in 1976 at the Edison Theater, it ran for nearly 6,000 more performances, closing in 1989 as the second longest running musical in Broadway history. The play was successful partly because of its entertainment value and partly for its slightly salacious nature; some theater-goers got "peep show" thrills without enduring the social stigma of loitering near the sleazy pornography houses of Forty-Second Street, and at a certain point late in its Edison Theater run, the show was notorious for catering to out-of-town businessmen looking for a night of fun in New York City. The production celebrated the new-found sexual freedom of the 1960's and opened the way for a more relaxed attitude toward nudity on the public stage while stimulating nationwide debate on censorship, morality, and taste in the theater.

**Related Work** *Human Sexual Response* (1966), by William H. Masters and Virginia E. Johnson, was a widely read and very influential book that described in detail the body's response to erotic stimulation and helped to make open discussion of sex more acceptable.

**Additional Information** For a detailed portrait of eroticism on stage in two contrasting periods—1890 to 1910 and 1950 to 1972—along with a sophisti-

cated analysis of changing social attitudes toward such eroticism, read *Erotic Theater* (1974), by John Elsom.

*Terry Nienhuis*

**See also** Free Love; *Hair*; *Human Sexual Response*; Sexual Revolution; Theater.

---

# ■ O'Hair, Madalyn Murray

**Born** April 13, 1919, Pittsburgh, Pennsylvania

*The self-proclaimed first lady of atheism, once known as the most hated woman in the United States. O'Hair was active in eliminating prayer and Bible studies from public schools.*

**Early Life** Much information about the childhood and early adult years of Madalyn Murray O'Hair, nee Mays, is unclear. She met William Murray while serving in the Women's Army Corps during World War II, and the couple had two sons. O'Hair credited her atheism to having found the Bible unbelievable when she read it through at the age of thirteen. She attended several colleges before receiving a bachelor's degree from Ashland College in Ohio and a law degree from South Texas College of Law in 1953.

**The 1960's** In October, 1959, when William, her eldest son, objected to required participation in daily Bible reading and recital of the Lord's Prayer at the Baltimore, Maryland, junior high school he attended, Murray wrote a letter requesting that he be excused from this observance. Eventually the school granted her request, but Murray said she was subjected to abuse, both verbal and physical. She filed suit in city court, asking that "sectarian opening exercises" be eliminated from Baltimore's public schools.

The case of *Murray v. Curlett* reached the United States Supreme Court, and on June 17, 1963, the Court ruled in Murray's favor. The Court held that by requiring students to recite a prayer and read aloud from the Bible, the school violated the ban on the establishment of religion created by the First and Fourteenth Amendments. Murray followed her victory by pursuing a total separation of church and state, focusing her efforts on eliminating the tax-exempt status for church property and on having the word "God" struck from the pledge of allegiance.

In 1965, after marrying Richard Franklin O'Hair, she founded the American Atheist Center and the Society of Separationists. She later began a weekly

*Madalyn Murray (later O'Hair) stands with her first son William and second son Garth in front of the Supreme Court building in Washington, D.C., in February, 1963, before the Supreme Court ruled in her favor.* (AP/Wide World Photos)

radio series and published a number of books defending atheism.

**Later Life**  O'Hair continued to espouse atheism and planned to sue to have the words "In God we trust" removed from U.S. currency. She denounced her son William when he became a Christian in 1980. In September, 1995, O'Hair, along with her younger son Jon Garth and granddaughter Robin, whom she had formally adopted, disappeared from their home in Austin, Texas. It was subsequently reported that more than $627,000 had also disappeared from bank accounts belonging to two of the atheist societies O'Hair had founded.

**Impact**  In the early 1960's, there were several court cases involving prayer in public schools, including *School District of Abington Township v. Schempp.* O'Hair's case garnered public attention partly because of her aggressive personality and her continued attacks on practices that impressed her as uniting church with state. She provided a focal point for those on either side of the issue.

**Additional Information**  O'Hair published her account of the events that led to the lawsuit in *An Atheist Epic* in 1970; Lawrence Wright's 1993 work, *Saints and Sinners,* takes a negative view of the famous atheist.

*Linda Pratt Orr*

**See also**  *Engel v. Vitale*; Prayer in Schools.

---

# ■ Olympic Games of 1960

**Date** Winter Games, February 18-28; Summer Games, August 26-September 11

*An amateur athletic competition between various nations. Cold War mentality permeated the 1960 Olympics, and many Americans viewed the Games as an arena for competition between the United States and the Soviet Union.*

The Olympic Games of 1960 were held in the heat of the Cold War. The tension between the Soviets and the Americans was heightened when a U.S. spy plane was shot down over the Soviet Union between the Winter and Summer Games. The United States, which was forced to compete against the highly subsidized athletes of Eastern Bloc countries, continued to insist on complete amateur status for Olympic athletes. In both the winter and summer competitions, the United States fell far short of the Soviet Union in the number of medals won, although many memorable performances were recorded.

**The Winter Games**  The eighth Winter Olympics was held in Squaw Valley, California, from February 18 to 28. The opening and closing ceremonies were directed by Walt Disney and featured five thousand participants, including a twenty-six-hundred-voice chorus and a thirteen-hundred-piece band. More than eight hundred athletes representing thirty nations competed in seventeen events in the Winter Games, generally recognized as one of the most successful and efficient Olympics ever held. The United States finished second to the Soviet Union, winning ten medals to the Soviets' twenty-one.

The most publicized competition and the most memorable of the Winter Games was the stunning gold medal performance of the unheralded U.S. hockey team. In this "miracle on ice," the Americans upset the highly favored Soviet team, 3-2, and then defeated Czechoslovakia, 9-4, for the gold medal. Other top American athletes included Carol Heiss,

# American Olympic Medalists in Popular Events

## 1960 Winter Olympics

### Alpine Skiing

| | | |
|---|---|---|
| Penny Pitou | Women's Downhill | Silver |
| Penny Pitou | Women's Giant Slalom | Silver |
| Betsy Snite | Women's Slalom | Silver |

### Figure Skating

| | | |
|---|---|---|
| Dave Jenkins | Men's | Gold |
| Carol Heiss | Women's | Gold |
| Barbara Ann Roles | Women's | Bronze |
| Nancy and Ronald Ludington | Pairs | Bronze |

### Speed Skating

| | | |
|---|---|---|
| William Disney | Men's 500 Meters | Silver |
| Jeanne Ashworth | Women's 500 Meters | Bronze |

### Hockey

| | | |
|---|---|---|
| USA Team | Ice Hockey | Gold |

## 1960 Summer Olympics

### Boxing

| | | |
|---|---|---|
| Quincelon Daniels | Light Welterweight | Bronze |
| Skeeter McClure | Light Middleweight | Gold |
| Eddie Crook | Middleweight | Gold |
| Cassius Clay | Light Heavyweight | Gold |

### Diving

| | | |
|---|---|---|
| Bob Webster | Men's Platform | Gold |
| Gary Tobian | Men's Platform | Silver |
| Gary Tobian | Men's Springboard | Gold |
| Sam Hall | Men's Springboard | Silver |
| Paula Jean Pope | Women's Platform | Silver |
| Paula Jean Pope | Women's Springboard | Silver |

### Swimming

| | | |
|---|---|---|
| Lance Larsen | Men's 100-meter Freestyle | Silver |
| Chris von Saltza | Women's 100-meter Freestyle | Silver |
| Chris von Saltza | Women's 400-meter Freestyle | Gold |
| George Breen | Men's 1,500-meter Freestyle | Bronze |
| Frank McKinney | Men's 100-meter Backstroke | Silver |
| Robert Bennett | Men's 100-meter Backstroke | Bronze |
| Lynn Burke | Women's 100-meter Backstroke | Gold |
| Bill Mulliken | Men's 200-meter Breaststroke | Gold |
| Carolyn Schuler | Women's 100-meter Butterfly | Gold |
| Mike Troy | Men's 200-meter Butterfly | Gold |
| J. David Gillanders | Men's 200-meter Butterfly | Bronze |
| USA Team | Women's 4x100-meter Freestyle Relay | Gold |
| USA Team | Men's 4x200-meter Freestyle Relay | Gold |
| USA Team | Men's 4x100-meter Medley Relay | Gold |
| USA Team | Women's 4x100-meter Medley Relay | Gold |

### Track and Field—Running

| | | |
|---|---|---|
| Dave Sime | Men's 100 Meters | Silver |

*(continued)*

| | | |
|---|---|---|
| Wilma Rudolph | Women's 100 Meters | Gold |
| Lester Carney | Men's 200 Meters | Silver |
| Wilma Rudolph | Women's 200 Meters | Gold |
| Otis Davis | Men's 400 Meters | Gold |
| Lee Calhoun | Men's 110-meter Hurdles | Gold |
| Willie May | Men's 110-meter Hurdles | Silver |
| Hayes Jones | Men's 110-meter Hurdles | Bronze |
| Glenn Davis | Men's 400-meter Hurdles | Gold |
| Clifton Cushman | Men's 400-meter Hurdles | Silver |
| Dick Howard | Men's 400-meter Hurdles | Bronze |
| USA Team | Men's 4x400-meter Relay | Gold |
| USA Team | Women's 4x100-meter Relay | Gold |
| **Track and Field—Jumping and Throwing** | | |
| John Thomas | Men's High Jump | Bronze |
| Ralph Boston | Men's Long Jump | Gold |
| Irv Roberson | Men's Long Jump | Silver |
| Don Bragg | Men's Pole Vault | Gold |
| Ron Morris | Men's Pole Vault | Silver |
| Al Oerter | Men's Discus Throw | Gold |
| Dick Babka | Men's Discus Throw | Silver |
| Dick Cochran | Men's Discus Throw | Bronze |
| Bill Nieder | Men's Shot Put | Gold |
| Parry O'Brien | Men's Shot Put | Silver |
| Dallas Long | Men's Shot Put | Bronze |
| Earlene Brown | Women's Shot Put | Bronze |

| | | |
|---|---|---|
| **Track and Field—Decathlon** | | |
| Rafer Johnson | Men's Decathlon | Gold |
| **Basketball** | | |
| USA Team | Men's Basketball | Gold |
| **1964 Winter Olympics** | | |
| **Alpine Skiing** | | |
| Billy Kidd | Men's Slalom | Silver |
| Jim Heuga | Men's Slalom | Bronze |
| Jean Saubert | Women's Giant Slalom | Silver |
| Jean Saubert | Women's Slalom | Bronze |
| **Figure Skating** | | |
| Scott Allen | Men's | Bronze |
| **Speed Skating** | | |
| Terry McDermott | Men's 500 Meters | Gold |
| **1964 Summer Olympics** | | |
| **Boxing** | | |
| Robert Carmody | Flyweight | Bronze |
| Charles Brown | Featherweight | Bronze |
| Ronald Harris | Lightweight | Bronze |
| Joe Frazier | Super Heavyweight | Gold |
| **Diving** | | |
| Bob Webster | Men's Platform | Gold |
| Ken Sitzberger | Men's Springboard | Gold |
| Francis Gorman | Men's Springboard | Silver |
| Larry Andreasen | Men's Springboard | Bronze |
| Lesley Bush | Women's Platform | Gold |
| Jeanne Collier | Women's Springboard | Silver |
| Mary Willard | Women's Springboard | Bronze |
| **Swimming** | | |
| Don Schollander | Men's 100-meter Freestyle | Gold |

*(continued)*

| | | | | | | |
|---|---|---|---|---|---|---|
| Sharon Stouder | Women's 100-meter Freestyle | Silver | | Carl Robie | Men's 200-meter Butterfly | Silver |
| Kathleen Ellis | Women's 100-meter Freestyle | Bronze | | Fred Schmidt | Men's 200-meter Butterfly | Bronze |
| Don Schollander | Men's 400-meter Freestyle | Gold | | Dick Roth | Men's 400-meter Individual Medley | Gold |
| Ginny Duenkel | Women's 400-meter Freestyle | Gold | | Ray Saari | Men's 400-meter Individual Medley | Silver |
| Marilyn Ramenofsky | Women's 400-meter Freestyle | Silver | | Donna de Varona | Women's 400-meter Individual Medley | Gold |
| Terri Lee Stickles | Women's 400-meter Freestyle | Bronze | | Sharon Finneran | Women's 400-meter Individual Medley | Silver |
| John Nelson | Men's 1,500-meter Freestyle | Silver | | Martha Randall | Women's 400-meter Individual Medley | Bronze |
| Cathy Ferguson | Women's 100-meter Backstroke | Gold | | USA Team | Men's 4x100-meter Freestyle Relay | Gold |
| Ginny Duenkel | Women's 100-meter Backstroke | Bronze | | USA Team | Women's 4x100-meter Freestyle Relay | Gold |
| Jed Graef | Men's 200-meter Backstroke | Gold | | USA Team | Men's 4x200-meter Freestyle Relay | Gold |
| Gary Dilley | Men's 200-meter Backstroke | Silver | | USA Team | Men's 4x100-meter Medley Relay | Gold |
| Robert Bennett | Men's 200-meter Backstroke | Bronze | | USA Team | Women's 4x100-meter Medley Relay | Gold |
| Chester Jastremski | Men's 200-meter Breaststroke | Bronze | | **Track and Field—Running** | | |
| Claudia Kolb | Women's 200-meter Breaststroke | Silver | | Bob Hayes | Men's 100 Meters | Gold |
| | | | | Wyomia Tyus | Women's 100 Meters | Gold |
| Sharon Stouder | Women's 100-meter Butterfly | Gold | | Edith McGuire | Women's 100 Meters | Silver |
| | | | | Henry Carr | Men's 200 Meters | Gold |
| | | | | Paul Drayton | Men's 200 Meters | Silver |
| Kathleen Ellis | Women's 100-meter Butterfly | Bronze | | Edith McGuire | Women's 200 Meters | Gold |

*(continued)*

| | | | | | | |
|---|---|---|---|---|---|---|
| Mike Larrabee | Men's 400 Meters | Gold | | Jenny Fish | Women's 500 Meters | Silver |
| Bob Schul | Men's 5,000 Meters | Gold | | Dianne Holum | Women's 500 Meters | Silver |
| Bill Dellinger | Men's 5,000 Meters | Bronze | | Mary Meyers | Women's 500 Meters | Silver |
| Billy Mills | Men's 10,000 Meters | Gold | | Dianne Holum | Women's 1,000 Meters | Bronze |
| Hayes Jones | Men's 110-meter Hurdles | Gold | | **1968 Summer Olympics** | | |
| Blaine Lindgren | Men's 110-meter Hurdles | Silver | | **Boxing** | | |
| Rex Cawley | Men's 400-meter Hurdles | Gold | | Harland Marbley | Light Flyweight | Bronze |
| USA Team | Men's 4x100-meter Relay | Gold | | Alfred Robinson | Featherweight | Silver |
| | | | | Ronnie Harris | Lightweight | Gold |
| USA Team | Men's 4x400-meter Relay | Gold | | Alfred Jones | Middleweight | Bronze |
| USA Team | Women's 4x100-meter Relay | Silver | | George Foreman | Super Heavyweight | Gold |
| **Track and Field—Jumping and Throwing** | | | | **Diving** | | |
| John Thomas | Men's High Jump | Silver | | Edwin Young | Men's Platform | Bronze |
| John Rambo | Men's High Jump | Bronze | | Bernie Wrightson | Men's Springboard | Gold |
| Ralph Boston | Men's Long Jump | Silver | | | | |
| Fred Hansen | Men's Pole Vault | Gold | | James Henry | Men's Springboard | Bronze |
| Al Oerter | Men's Discus Throw | Gold | | Ann Peterson | Women's Platform | Bronze |
| Dave Weill | Men's Discus Throw | Bronze | | Sue Gossick | Women's Springboard | Gold |
| Dallas Long | Men's Shot Put | Gold | | Keala O'Sullivan | Women's Springboard | Bronze |
| Randy Matson | Men's Shot Put | Silver | | **Swimming** | | |
| **Basketball** | | | | Ken Walsh | Men's 100-meter Freestyle | Silver |
| USA Team | Men's Basketball | Gold | | | | |
| **1968 Winter Olympics** | | | | Mark Spitz | Men's 100-meter Freestyle | Bronze |
| **Figure Skating** | | | | Don Schollander | Men's 200-meter Freestyle | Silver |
| Peggy Fleming | Women's | Gold | | | | |
| Tim Wood | Men's | Silver | | Jan Henne | Women's 100-meter Freestyle | Gold |
| **Speed Skating** | | | | | | |
| Terry McDermott | Men's 500 Meters | Silver | | | | |

(*continued*)

| | | | | | |
|---|---|---|---|---|---|
| Susan Pedersen | Women's 100-meter Freestyle | Silver | Kaye Hall | Women's 100-meter Backstroke | Gold |
| Linda Gustavson | Women's 100-meter Freestyle | Bronze | Mitchell Ivey | Men's 200-meter Backstroke | Silver |
| John Nelson | Men's 200-meter Freestyle | Bronze | Jack Horsley | Men's 200-meter Backstroke | Bronze |
| Debbie Meyer | Women's 200-meter Freestyle | Gold | Pokey Watson | Women's 200-meter Backstroke | Gold |
| Jan Henne | Women's 200-meter Freestyle | Silver | Kaye Hall | Women's 200-meter Backstroke | Bronze |
| Jane Barkman | Women's 200-meter Freestyle | Bronze | Don McKenzie | Men's 100-meter Breaststroke | Gold |
| Mike Burton | Men's 400-meter Freestyle | Gold | Sharon Wichman | Women's 100-meter Breaststroke | Bronze |
| Debbie Meyer | Women's 400-meter Freestyle | Gold | Brian Job | Men's 200-meter Breaststroke | Bronze |
| Linda Gustavson | Women's 400-meter Freestyle | Silver | Sharon Wichman | Women's 200-meter Breaststroke | Gold |
| Debbie Meyer | Women's 800-meter Freestyle | Gold | Doug Russell | Men's 100-meter Butterfly | Gold |
| Pamela Kruse | Women's 800-meter Freestyle | Silver | Mark Spitz | Men's 100-meter Butterfly | Silver |
| Jane Swagerty | Women's 800-meter Freestyle | Bronze | Ross Wales | Men's 100-meter Butterfly | Bronze |
| Mike Burton | Men's 1,500-meter Freestyle | Gold | Ellie Daniel | Women's 100-meter Butterfly | Silver |
| John Kinsella | Men's 1,500-meter Freestyle | Silver | Susan Shields | Women's 100-meter Butterfly | Bronze |
| Charles Hickox | Men's 100-meter Backstroke | Silver | Carl Robie | Men's 200-meter Butterfly | Gold |
| Ron Mills | Men's 100-meter Backstroke | Bronze | John Ferris | Men's 200-meter Butterfly | Bronze |
| | | | Ellie Daniel | Women's 200-meter Butterfly | Bronze |

*(continued)*

| | | | | | | |
|---|---|---|---|---|---|---|
| Charles Hickcox | Men's 200-meter Individual Medley | Gold | | Wyomia Tyus | Women's 100 Meters | Gold |
| Gregory Buckingham | Men's 200-meter Individual Medley | Silver | | Barbara Ferrell | Women's 100 Meters | Silver |
| John Ferris | Men's 200-meter Individual Medley | Bronze | | Tommie Smith | Men's 200 Meters | Gold |
| | | | | John Carlos | Men's 200 Meters | Bronze |
| Claudia Kolb | Women's 200-meter Individual Medley | Gold | | Lee Evans | Men's 400 Meters | Gold |
| | | | | Larry James | Men's 400 Meters | Silver |
| Susan Pedersen | Women's 200-meter Individual Medley | Silver | | Ronald Freeman | Men's 400 Meters | Bronze |
| | | | | Thomas Farrell | Men's 800 Meters | Bronze |
| Jan Henne | Women's 200-meter Individual Medley | Bronze | | Madeline Manning | Women's 800 Meters | Gold |
| | | | | Jim Ryun | Men's 1,500 Meters | Silver |
| Charles Hickcox | Men's 400-meter Individual Medley | Gold | | George Young | Men's 3,000-meter Steeplechase | Bronze |
| Gary Hall | Men's 400-meter Individual Medley | Silver | | | | |
| Claudia Kolb | Women's 400-meter Individual Medley | Gold | | Willie Davenport | Men's 110-meter Hurdles | Gold |
| Lynn Vidali | Women's 400-meter Individual Medley | Silver | | Erv Hall | Men's 110-meter Hurdles | Silver |
| | | | | USA Team | Men's 4x100-meter Relay | Gold |
| USA Team | Men's 4x100-meter Freestyle Relay | Gold | | USA Team | Men's 4x400-meter Relay | Gold |
| USA Team | Women's 4x100-meter Freestyle Relay | Gold | | **Track and Field—Jumping and Throwing** | | |
| USA Team | Men's 4x200-meter Freestyle Relay | Gold | | Dick Fosbury | Men's High Jump | Gold |
| | | | | Ed Caruthers | Men's High Jump | Silver |
| USA Team | Men's 4x100-meter Medley Relay | Gold | | Bob Beamon | Men's Long Jump | Gold |
| | | | | Ralph Boston | Men's Long Jump | Bronze |
| USA Team | Women's 4x100-meter Medley Relay | Gold | | Bob Seagren | Men's Pole Vault | Gold |
| | | | | Al Oerter | Men's Discus Throw | Gold |
| | | | | Randy Matson | Men's Shot Put | Gold |
| **Track and Field—Running** | | | | George Woods | Men's Shot Put | Silver |
| | | | | **Basketball** | | |
| Jim Hines | Men's 100 Meters | Gold | | USA Team | Men's Basketball | Gold |
| Charles Greene | Men's 100 Meters | Bronze | | | | |

who became immensely popular after winning a gold medal in women's figure skating; Dave Jenkins, who won a gold medal in men's figure skating; and Penny Pitou, who won two silver medals in downhill skiing.

**The Summer Games**   The seventeenth Summer Olympics was held in Rome, Italy, from August 26 to September 11. The ancient city offered a spectacular mixture of old and new architecture; events were held in centuries-old structures and modern buildings. The event was larger than any previous Olympics, with more than five thousand athletes from eighty-three nations taking part. The Olympics was the first covered by a U.S. network, the Columbia Broadcasting System. The United States finished a distant second to the Soviet Union in number of medals won, one hundred and three to seventy-one.

The United States did not produce a large number of medals in the Summer Games, but some of the most memorable achievements were made by Americans. One of the nation's favorite athletes was eighteen-year-old Cassius Clay, nicknamed the "Louisville Lip," who won the light heavyweight boxing gold medal. The appeal of Clay, who later became Muhammad Ali, went beyond his boxing ability. He bantered constantly with the Roman crowds, quoted poetry, and was a favorite of the press.

In track and field, Wilma Rudolph, unable to walk without a brace on her left leg until age eleven, became one of the world's best-known female athletes when she won gold medals in the 100-meter and 200-meter events and as anchor of the 400-meter relay. The United States won the men's long jump for the eighth consecutive time when Ralph Boston broke Jesse Owen's twenty-four-year-old Olympic record. Don Bragg took the eleventh consecutive gold medal for the United States in the pole vault. In one of the more publicized competitions, Rafer Johnson of the United States defeated his best friend and University of California at Los Angeles, teammate, C. K. Yang of Taiwan, in a very close battle in the decathlon to take the gold medal.

Gold medal winners included the U.S. basketball team, featuring Jerry West, Oscar Robertson, and Jerry Lucas; Gary Tobian, who won the ninth-straight gold medal for the United States in springboard diving; and the U.S. swimming relay teams, which captured the gold in two men's relays and two women's relays. Carolyn Schuler took the gold in the 100-meter butterfly, defeating teammate Carolyn Wood whose excellent performance in the trial had made her the favorite to win.

**Impact**   Despite the pregame tensions between the United States and the Soviet Union, the 1960 Olympic Games were recognized for the goodwill and sportsmanship displayed by the athletes. Following the Winter Games, the virtually unknown resort of Squaw Valley emerged as one of the premier ski resorts in the world, and figure skating champion Heiss gained considerable fame as a professional skater. Clay (Ali) became heavyweight champion and one of the most recognized sports figures in the world. Rudolph was recognized as the top female athlete of the decade and was very active in the Civil Rights movement, and ten of the members of the basketball team went on to play professionally in the National Basketball Association. U.S. Olympic officials were becoming acutely aware that the insistence on complete amateur status was placing American athletes at a disadvantage in international competition.

**Additional Information**   The Olympics are covered in more detail in *An Approved History of the Olympic Games* (1984), by Bill Henry and Patricia Henry Yeomans.

*Joe Blankenbaker*

**See also**   Ali, Muhammad; Basketball; Heiss, Carol; Olympic Games of 1964; Olympic Games of 1968; Rudolph, Wilma; Sports.

# ■ Olympic Games of 1964

**Date**   Winter Games, January 29-February 9; Summer Games, October 10-24

*An arena for international athletic rivalry, particularly between the United States and the Soviet Union. The Summer Games in Tokyo were the first Olympics to be held in Asia.*

The Americans had participated in all the Olympic Games held since the modern games were established in Athens, Greece, in 1896. After the Soviet Union's first entry into the games in 1952, they had come to be viewed as a worldwide competition for athletic superiority between the superpowers. The 1964 Tokyo Summer Games were the first to be held in Asia, and Japan spent more than two billion dollars preparing for the Games.

*American Don Schollander (center) poses for photographs with the silver and bronze medalists after receiving the gold medal—his third during the 1964 Olympics—for the 400-meter freestyle.* (AP/Wide World Photos)

**The Winter Games** The ninth Winter Olympics was held in Innsbruck, Austria, January 29 to February 9. About one thousand athletes from thirty-six nations competed in thirty-four events. Traditionally, the Alpine and Nordic European nations had outperformed the United States, and in 1964, the United States followed tradition. The United States won only one gold medal—Terry McDermott's Olympic record-setting victory in the 500-meter speed skating event—far behind the Soviet Union's eight gold medals.

**The Summer Games** The eighteenth Summer Olympics was held in Tokyo, Japan, from October 10 to 24. The Games were to have been held in that city in 1940, but Japan's invasion of China caused the event to be canceled. Japan spent lavishly in preparing for the Games, even creating a new expressway for the occasion. More than five thousand athletes representing ninety-three nations participated. The United States proved to be a powerful force in To-

kyo, winning ninety medals, and was especially dominant in track and field and swimming, two of the premier Olympics sports. Although the National Broadcasting Company had paid $1.5 million for the rights to the Games, the network attempted only one live telecast and delayed broadcast of the Games until after *The Tonight Show*.

In track and field, U.S. men won gold medals in nine of the fifteen running events and three of the nine field events. Led by double gold medal winners Bob Hayes, Mike Larrabee, and Henry Carr, U.S. athletes took first place in all sprint events. Even in the distance running events, not a traditional area of strength, the United States garnered two gold medals, including a major upset by the previously unknown Billy Mills in the 10,000-meter event. Al Oerter won his third consecutive discus gold medal. Other U.S. gold medalists were Bob Schul, 5,000 meters; Hayes Jones, 110-meter hurdles; Rex Cawley, 400-meter hurdles; Fred Hanson, pole vault; Dallas Long, shot put; and the 400- and 1,600-meter U.S.

relay teams. U.S. women won two gold medals. Sprinters Wyomia Tyus and Edith McGuire were victorious in the 100 meters and 200 meters, respectively.

U.S. men and women dominated the swimming and diving competition, winning thirty-seven of the fifty-six medals awarded. Don Schollander won three gold medals, and Dick Roth, Ken Sitzberger, Ken Webster, Ginny Duenkal, Sharon Stouder, Cathy Ferguson, Donna de Varona, and Lesley Bush were also U.S. gold medal winners in swimming and diving individual events. Americans also captured the four relay events contested.

In all other sports, the Americans won only six gold medals. In basketball, the U.S. team defeated the Soviets for a third consecutive Olympiad to win the gold. Boxer Joe Frazier launched his rise to fame with a win in the heavyweight division. Gary Anderson and Lones Wigger won gold in shooting events, and the pairs and eight oars were victors in rowing. The Soviets were able to make up for their disappointing showing in track and field in other venues. The Cold War athletic competition between the superpowers was a virtual tie, with the Americans outpacing the Soviets thirty-six to thirty in gold medals, and the Soviets leading in total medals, ninety-six to ninety.

**Impact** The 1964 Olympics marked the end of an era. The Cold War athletic rivalry between the United States and the Soviet Union had reached its height. Increasingly, Americans accused the Soviets of ignoring the amateur code of the Olympic Games. They claimed that governmental support of Soviet athletics made them professionals, resulting in an unfair advantage.

By the mid-1960's, Americans had begun to devote more time and money to professional sports such as football. However, although overall fan interest in amateur sports may have peaked in 1964, the Tokyo Olympics was the last time that the media presented the Olympics in a secondary role, delaying broadcast in favor of a regularly programmed show. The interest in amateur athletics began to be driven not by the fans but by television, which began to direct the public's tastes in Olympic competition by focusing on certain athletes, often relatively unknown, just before the Games. The fame of these Olympic athletes was minimal and fleeting when compared with that of professional ath-

letes in non-Olympic sports that were televised on a regular basis.

**Additional Information** *The Story of the Olympic Games, 776 B.C. to 1976* (1977), by John Kieran, Arthur Daley, and Pat Jordan, gives a fairly detailed history of the Olympics, and the *World Book Year Book* (1965) provides information on the gold medal winners along with a brief account of the 1964 Olympics.

*Paul J. Zbiek*

**See also** Frazier, Joe; Mills, Billy; Olympic Games of 1960; Olympic Games of 1968; Sports.

## ■ Olympic Games of 1968

**Date** Winter Games, February 6-18; Summer Games, October 12-27

*Politicized Olympic Games in a watershed year. The Olympics, particularly the Summer Games, featured great performances by U.S. athletes and striking political statements that challenged many people's notions of the connection between sports and society.*

By the 1968 Olympics, the Cold War issue had faded somewhat, eclipsed by the question of whether athletes from South Africa, where apartheid was practiced, should be allowed to compete. African Americans threatened to boycott the Games if South Africans participated, and the International Olympic Committee was forced to rescind its invitation to athletes from that nation. In addition, shortly before the start of the event, student unrest erupted in Mexico City, the host city for the Summer Games. More than two hundred people were killed during the rioting. The 1968 Olympics also brought expanded television coverage, as networks and marketers began to realize the potential for exploitation. Olympic products flooded stores, and athletes increasingly lent their names to product endorsements.

The Summer Games took place at an altitude of 7,347 feet, leading to eighteen new world records in the sprint events and generally poor performances in endurance events. U.S. athletes captured 114 medals (46 gold, 33 silver, and 35 bronze) in events ranging from figure skating to boxing, more than any other nation.

**The Winter Games** The tenth Winter Games were held in Grenoble, France, a four-time Olympic host, February 6-18. More than twelve hundred competitors representing thirty-seven nations participated.

The events were televised and viewed by millions of people worldwide.

The two most famous athletes to emerge from the competitions in Grenoble were U.S. figure skater Peggy Fleming and French alpine skier Jean-Claude Killy. Both dominated their events thoroughly. Fleming established a commanding lead during the compulsory figures part of the competition and expanded it. She captured all nine of the judges' first-place votes on her way to the gold medal. Killy, competing near his hometown of Val d'Isère, won gold medals in all three alpine events, the downhill, slalom, and giant slalom. In addition to Fleming's gold, Americans won six medals, five silver and one bronze.

**The Summer Games** The nineteenth Summer Olympics were held in Mexico City, Mexico, October 12-27. More than fifty-five hundred athletes representing one hundred and twelve nations partici-

pated. Mexico City's altitude, the highest for any Summer Games, dampened the speeds of the endurance events and played a role in establishing most of the eighteen world records, especially those set in track and field sprints and horizontal jumps, events where the thin air is advantageous. U.S. athletes set eight of the eleven marks while winning the men's 100-, 200-, 400-meter dashes and the 400- and 1,600-meter relays. U.S. women also set records in winning the 100-meter dash and the 400-meter relay. Three of the records, those set in the men's 400-meter dash, the 1,600-meter relay, and long jump, are particularly noteworthy. Lee Evans came to Mexico City holding the world record in the 400 meters, 44.0 seconds, which he lowered to 43.86 seconds, and the silver medalist, Larry James, posted a 43.97, also faster than the old record. The Americans swept the 400-meter event, with Ronald Freeman taking the bronze. Their success led spectators to have great expectations for the U.S. 1,600-meter relay team:

*American runners—(from left) Larry James, silver; Lee Evans, gold; and Ronald Freeman, bronze—wave black berets to the crowd after sweeping the 400-meter run.* (AP/Wide World Photos)

Evans, James, and Freeman, joined by Vincent Matthews, won the race in 2:56.16, an improvement of more than two and one-half seconds over the old record. In spite of those accomplishments, many sport scholars regard the men's long jump competition as the most amazing of all the summer events. In his first jump of the competition, Bob Beamon produced the greatest jump of his career, leaping to a new record of 8.90 meters (29.2 feet). With this single jump, Beamon moved the record 55 centimeters (21.8 inches), even though the world record had moved only 22 centimeters (8.5 inches) between 1935 and 1968.

Two track and field athletes, Tommie Smith and John Carlos, who won gold and bronze medals, respectively, for their performance in the 200-meter dash, staged a protest at the awards ceremony. The pair, who had been part of the group opposed to participation by South Africans, raised clenched fists and wore only black socks on their feet to demonstrate their support of black power. They were sent home after this display.

In swimming, the United States won 73 out of a possible 104 medals. Debbie Meyer won gold medals in the 200-, 400-, and 800-meter freestyle events, as did Claudia Kolb in the 200- and 400-meter individual medley events. Another double gold medalist was Mike Burton, who was victorious in the 400- and 1,500-meter freestyle events, and Charles Hickcox won gold medals in the 200- and 400-meter individual medley events and a silver in the 100-meter backstroke event. Jan Henne received a gold medal in one freestyle event and a silver in another, plus a bronze in an individual medley event. Other women taking home gold medals were Kaye Hall, Pokey Watson, and Sharon Wichman.

Swimmer Mark Spitz won four medals in 1968 (two gold in relays, one silver and one bronze). Four years later he would win seven gold medals while setting new world records in each event at the Munich Olympics in 1972. Other memorable U.S. Olympians included Al Oerter, who won the discus throw for the fourth consecutive time; Dick Fosbury, whose winning high jump technique (he went over the crossbar backward and head-first) revolutionized the event; and George Foreman, who won the Super Heavyweight boxing competition.

**Impact** The success of the 1968 U.S. Olympic athletes affected both politics and sports. For some observers, the fact that U.S. athletes won more total medals at the Games than the Soviets did (114 to 104) and also more gold medals (46 to 34) demonstrated the superiority of U.S. political, economic, and social systems over those of the Soviet Union. In addition, the athletic records established in the thin air at the Mexico City Olympics remain very significant. Evans's world record in the 400-meter dash lasted twenty years, Beamon's long jump mark was not bested until 1991, and the 1,600-meter relay team's record was not surpassed for thirty years.

The Summer Games, taking place during a turbulent year in the United States, were permeated by politics. Many spectators cheered the Czechoslovakian athletes, who had endured recent political turmoil in their country. Because of the student riots that had just taken place in Mexico City, guards were called in to protect the athletes and spectators during opening ceremonies. The controversy surrounding the participation of South African athletes raised awareness in the United States of the practice of apartheid. However, many people felt that the Olympics was not an appropriate venue for Smith and Carlos's political statement. Despite the highly charged atmosphere, the Summer Games were not marred by the kind of politically based violence that resulted in the deaths of eleven Israeli athletes in Munich, Germany, in 1972.

**Additional Information** *The Complete Book of the Olympics*, a publication produced by David Wallechinsky in the year before each Olympics, provides the most comprehensive coverage of the Olympic Games.

*E. A. Reed*

**See also** Black Power; Czechoslovakia, Soviet Invasion of; Fleming, Peggy; Olympic Games of 1960; Olympic Games of 1964; Smith, Tommie, and John Carlos; Sports.

# ■ One Flew over the Cuckoo's Nest

**Published** 1962
**Author** Ken Kesey (1935- )

*The novel that became famous for its exposure of electroshock treatments and patient abuse in mental wards. Through his three major characters, Kesey attacked the dehumanizing effects of 1960's technology and warned against the dangers of mindless conformity.*

*Jack Nicholson (center) starred in the 1975 film adaptation of Ken Kesey's 1962 novel* One Flew over the Cuckoo's Nest. *(Museum of Modern Art/Film Stills Archive)*

**The Work**  *One Flew over the Cuckoo's Nest* is narrated by Chief Bromden, a Native American mental patient who hides himself in a hallucinatory fog of his own making. Chief Bromden, a long-term patient in the psychiatric ward of an Oregon veterans hospital, has survived more than two hundred shock treatments and has learned to act as if he is deaf and dumb in a world that never hears him. In his delusion, he fears world control by the "Combine," a machinelike entity that will eliminate all individuality just as the icy head nurse, Nurse Ratched, has eliminated all dissent on the ward. Into this scene bursts Randle Patrick McMurphy, a logger, brawler, and con artist who has feigned insanity to escape his sentence on a work farm. He brings a breath of the untamed natural world to the sad inmates through his powerful physical presence and his rowdy humor, and he treats the other patients like human beings and teaches them to laugh again. He gives them the

confidence and courage to rebel against the control of the formidable Nurse Ratched. When she retaliates by ordering punitive shock treatments and a lobotomy for McMurphy so that she can maintain her authority, he becomes a symbolic savior to Chief Bromden, who escapes to freedom.

**Impact**  The 1962 novel established Kesey's literary reputation overnight by calling public attention to the conditions and potential for abuse in the nation's mental hospitals, where electroshock therapy and even lobotomy were still standard practices. Kesey's own experience as a night attendant on the psychiatric ward of a Menlo Park, California, veterans hospital added credibility to his charges, as did later rumors of the illegal shock treatment he took under the guise of research. His remark that the character of Chief Bromden had appeared to him in a peyote-induced vision fueled interest and controversy, especially when he revealed that he had volunteered for government-sponsored experiments that introduced him to a variety of psychomimetic drugs, including LSD (lysergic acid diethylamide) and psilocybin. Chief Bromden's hallucinations echoed Kesey's continued fascination with mind-altering substances and created a psychedelic style new to fiction. The ominous figure of the head nurse captured public imagination as did that of the irrepressible McMurphy, who personified the 1960's concept of rebellion against conformity.

**Related Work** A film version of *One Flew over the Cuckoo's Nest* was released in 1975.

**Additional Information** Tony Tanner's *City of Words: American Fiction 1950-1970* (1971) provides a discussion of how the themes of Kesey's first two novels were embodied in his life as the leader of the Merry Pranksters and in his involvement with LSD in the 1960's.

*Joanne McCarthy*

**See also** Drug Culture; *Electric Kool-Aid Acid Test, The*; Literature, LSD.

## ■ Ono, Yoko

**Born** February 18, 1933, Tokyo, Japan

*Avant-garde artist and wife of Beatle John Lennon. Ono's personal and professional partnership with Lennon led to her widespread reputation as "the woman who broke up the Beatles."*

**Early Life** Born into a prominent Tokyo banking family, Yoko Ono's childhood was secure until World War II, when she and her younger siblings were evacuated to the Japanese countryside, where she looked after herself and her siblings. After the war, her family moved to Scarsdale, New York, where Ono attended Sarah Lawrence College, continuing her interest in the arts. First marrying a musician and then a filmmaker, Ono moved into underground artistic circles in New York's Greenwich Village, staging avant-garde performances in her loft and experimenting with poetry, music, art, and film.

**The 1960's** Ono became a member of the conceptual art movement known as "Fluxus" but remained little known until she met Beatle John Lennon at an exhibition of her concept art in London in 1968. Their marriage a year later was soon followed by the breakup of the Beatles, leading to the perception that it was Ono who had undermined the most phenomenal and influential rock group of its time. With her exotic looks and all-black outfits, Ono was viewed as a dangerous interloper with a mannish, domineering personality. However, Lennon saw Ono as his partner and soulmate and worked with her on musical and other projects, producing provocative albums such as *Two Virgins* (1968), which featured a nude photo of the couple on its cover. Together, Lennon and Ono were an unconventional couple who very much lived by their own lights. They were also at home in an increasingly influential counterculture known for its experimentation with lifestyles and psychotropic drugs. The couple shared the counterculture's political idealism, using their fame to stage events in the service of causes such as world peace.

**Later Life** After a time of instability, Ono and Lennon spent most of the 1970's living quietly in New York City, where she gave birth to their son, Sean, and where they began to work together on record albums. After a period of mourning following Lennon's murder in 1980, Yoko remained in New York, raising their son and continuing to work on musical and artistic projects.

**Impact** Ono has had a widespread influence on other artists and musicians, but it was through her relationship with Lennon that she made her greatest impact. For Lennon himself, she was a liberating force and kindred spirit, however, for many, she was the heartless "dragon lady" who broke up the Beatles. She remains a mysterious and controversial presence on the pop culture scene.

**Additional Information** A number of interviews, essays, and other materials pertaining to Lennon and Ono have been collected by Jonathan Cott and Christine Duedna in *The Ballad of John and Yoko* (1982).

*Margaret Boe Birns*

**See also** Art Movements; Beatles, The; *Sgt. Pepper's Lonely Hearts Club Band*.

## ■ Op Art

*An art form based on various visual effects. Op, or optical, art was a very approachable kind of art that reflected an age dominated by advertising, television and film images, and science and technology.*

The origins of op, or optical, art can be traced to the work of post-Impressionist artists such as Wassily Kandinsky, Henri Matisse, and Vincent van Gogh. These artists' interest in pure color, along with the focus on geometric abstraction in the works of the constructivists, Futurists, and cubists, provided the foundation for op art.

In the 1960's, many Americans and Western Europeans fully experienced the affluence of the postwar era. This age of mass production and mass consumption, of widespread advertising images, and of mass media such as film and television, created a rich landscape for a group of artists who made op art. These artists explored and exploited the nature of human vision to produce hard-edged, large-scale works that seemed mechanical and precisely planned.

Op artists drew their motifs from several contemporary forces within their own culture. As science and technology played increasingly large roles in the age of affluence, op artists used mathematical series, numerical progressions, and grids to represent energy and forces and a space-time continuum. At a time when nuclear technology transformed matter into energy, op art used tricks of the eye to transform colors and shapes on a canvas into a surface that gave a viewer a sense of energy and movement. These artists replicated the force of the television and print images from mass media advertising with their simple, direct forms and shapes, their sharp-edged boundaries, and their uniform and intense colors. Drawing on new paint technology, they used store-shelf acrylic and emulsion paints to provide the viewer with a uniform, homogeneous colored surface that mimicked the effect of slick, glossy advertisements. These artworks, bearing no hint of a brush stroke or personal characteristics, were reproduced mechanically in much the same way as mass-produced consumer items found in a society increasingly dependent on large-scale technology.

Op art also reflected the egalitarian thrust of the 1960's. At a time when more and more people sought a voice in the forces that shaped their lives and their futures, op art required only that a viewer observe the images on the canvas. Neither a trained eye nor specialized knowledge was needed for a viewer to experience the optical effects of these works. They were very approachable in their directness and in their celebration of mass-culture images, a trait op art shared with the pop art of the 1960's.

American-based artists such as Joseph Albers, Richard Anuszkiewicz, Ellsworth Kelly, and Larry Poons depicted several visual effects in their works. Among the devices or effects they used to draw a viewer into the world of changing perception were the ordered repetition of simple geometric forms; after-images; irradiation or blurring; the phi phenomenon (the sense that fixed dots or other fixed images seem to move); moiré patterns; and the optical effects of color. Theoretically, a viewer's active and patient participation brought the reward of finding various visual images and effects in one work. This was an art of movement and energy created by stationary forms and shapes and by the artists' awareness of the physics of color and light.

**Impact** Because it reflected the images of a modern industrial Western culture, op art influenced and was influenced by the culture that produced it. This style affected other artists; its influence on the post-painterly abstractionists, who flourished during and after the 1960's, can be seen in their simple, direct use of geometry and color. The influence of op art on advertising and other media can still be seen. The best example of this is the Woolmark logo used by the clothing industry to indicate wool fabric. The style continues, in part, as a rational, high-tech art that has been given additional exposure as computer-generated art replicates the visual imagery of several op artists who used geometric abstraction as their motif. The pervasive use of images that arrest the viewer's gaze, especially in mass media advertising, stands as testament to the op artists' awareness that an art that communicates directly to the viewer through the visual "tricks" of geometry and color is a powerful mass medium in itself.

**Additional Information** For more information and many illustrations of op art, see Cyril Barrett's *Op Art* (1970) and Rene Parola's *Optical Art: Theory and Practice* (1969).

*H. J. Eisenman*

**See also** Art Movements; Media; Pop Art.

## ■ Organized Crime

*Large criminal "families" that controlled many legal and illegal activities in New York, Chicago, and other major cities. The 1960's was a turning point for organized crime because of the large numbers of arrests and extensive negative public exposure.*

Organized criminal activity gained a foothold in the United States around 1900. In its early manifestations, organized crime consisted of small extortion, prostitution, and burglary rackets. In 1919, the passage of the Eighteenth Amendment and the Volstead Act, both designed to prohibit the sale of alcoholic beverages, created a new and lucrative business for organized crime. From 1920 to 1933, gangs sprang up in the nation's major cities to cash in on the bootlegging and speakeasy trade that flourished during Prohibition.

**The "Families"** In the early thirties, the Italian gangs in New York broke into five "families." These families, along with gangs in Chicago and the rest of the country, created a "commission," a governing board that settled territory and policy disputes. After the repeal of Prohibition, organized crime consolidated and got involved in gambling, labor racketeering, and extortion. In 1950, a Senate investigation of gambling led by Senator Estes Kefauver created sensational television coverage. In 1957, law enforcement officers raided an upstate New York meeting of numerous organized crime bosses from around the country. This incident proved the existence of a national organized crime syndicate and led to congressional and Federal Bureau of Investigation (FBI) pressure for its destruction. Organized crime suffered a severe reversal in 1959 when Fidel Castro closed down its lucrative Havana casinos.

During the 1960's, organized crime concentrated on its well-known rackets of gambling, extortion, and labor racketeering. The New York families also became involved in heroin smuggling. The most powerful organized crime figure in the country during the decade was Carlo Gambino, head of the Gambino family in New York and a powerful voice on the syndicate's commission. Gambino controlled the New York docks and had investments in pornography and labor unions. Another leading organized crime figure of the 1960's was Chicago boss Sam Giancana, who led a flamboyant life compared with the reserved Gambino. Giancana became involved with the Central Intelligence Agency in the late 1950's and early 1960's in an abortive effort to kill Cuban leader Fidel Castro. Giancana fled the country in 1966 to avoid testifying to a grand jury. Other leading organized crime figures around the country were Nick Civella in Kansas City, who had interests in Las Vegas and the Teamsters Union, Carlos Mar-

*Jimmy Hoffa, president of the Teamsters Union, appears before the Senate Investigations Subcommittee in Washington, D.C., in 1961 to answer questions about his dealings with New York mobster Anthony Corallo.* (AP/Wide World Photos)

cello in New Orleans, Santos Trafacante in Florida, and Jimmy Fratiano in Los Angeles.

**Damaging Testimony** One of the events that had the most effect on organized crime during the 1960's was the testimony of Joe Valachi, a low-level member of the Genovese crime family in New York who had been involved in organized crime since 1931. After he went to prison in 1959 on drug charges, Valachi became convinced that his boss, Vito Genovese, also serving time in prison, had ordered his murder. After killing another inmate who he mistakenly believed was tailing him, Valachi made a deal in which he agreed to testify for the government in investigations of organized crime. Valachi's testimony before a U.S. Senate committee in September and October, 1963, broke the crime syndicate's code of silence and revealed many details about the structure of organized crime. His memoirs, *The Valachi Papers*, were published in 1969, the same year Valachi died of cancer.

**Funding the Families** One of organized crime's most lucrative pursuits during the 1960's was the management of several Las Vegas casinos. Organized crime had been a part of Las Vegas since 1946 when Benjamin "Bugsy" Siegel built the Flamingo hotel and casino. By 1960, the Chicago crime family, called the "Outfit," controlled the Desert Inn, Stardust, and Riviera casinos. Other crime families were associated with the Sands and the Tropicana hotels. Organized crime would take cash directly from the hotels, a practice called "skimming," and transport the money back to syndicate headquarters. The skimming of Las Vegas was a significant source of profit for organized crime until newspaper exposure created unwelcome publicity in the mid-1960's. In 1967, billionaire Howard Hughes moved to Las Vegas and bought out most of the hotels connected with organized crime.

Much of organized crime's Las Vegas adventure was funded with loans from the Central States Teamsters pension fund. The link between organized crime and the Teamsters union became public in the late 1950's during Senate hearings on labor racketeering. One target of those hearings was Teamster president, Jimmy Hoffa. Hoffa's election as head of the Teamsters in 1955 led to a running battle with Attorney General Robert F. Kennedy. Hoffa was convicted of jury tampering and pension fund abuse in 1964. His appeals ran out in 1967, and he served prison time until 1975.

Much of the pressure brought to bear on organized crime during the 1960's was a result of the efforts of Attorney General Kennedy. Kennedy supported federal investigations of organized crime figures and pursued greater wiretapping authority. Kennedy had been chief counsel to the Senate committee investigating labor racketeering in 1958-1959. As attorney general, he urged the reluctant FBI director, J. Edgar Hoover, to give organized crime cases higher priority.

**Subsequent Events** Organized crime began a slow steady decline during the 1970's and 1980's because of new racketeering laws, wiretaps, and informants. By the mid-1990's, most organized crime families had either disbanded or were under extreme pressure from law enforcement officials.

Hoffa disappeared soon after his release from prison in 1975. That same year, Giancana, recently returned from Mexico, was murdered in his Chicago home. In the early 1980's, a "mob war" broke out in Philadelphia after the murder of longtime boss Angelo Bruno. In 1985, many of New York City's top organized crime figures were arrested in what became known as the "commission case." A leading figure in the case, Gambino boss Paul Castellano, was killed on the streets of Manhattan in September,1985. All of the other defendants in the commission case were convicted and received long prison sentences. Many Chicago-area organized crime figures were convicted in 1980 of charges stemming from the skimming of the Stardust hotel and casino.

**Additional Information** An excellent overview of organized crime is provided in Robert Lacey's biography of Meyer Lansky, *Little Man* (1991). Also in 1991, two FBI agents, Joseph O'Brien and Andris Kurins, published *Boss of Bosses*, the story of the agency's efforts to convict Gambino boss Castellano.

*Charles C. Howard*

**See also** Crime and Scandals; Hoover, J. Edgar.

## ■ Oswald, Lee Harvey

**Born** October 18, 1939, New Orleans, Louisiana
**Died** November 24, 1963, Dallas, Texas

*The alleged killer of President John F. Kennedy. Much speculation has arisen as to whether he acted alone or was part of a conspiracy.*

**Early Life** Lee Harvey Oswald was born two months after the death of his father. His mother, unable to provide for him, placed Oswald in an orphanage until she was able to return and claim him. Oswald and his mother lived in various cities in Texas and Louisiana, then, in 1952, they moved to New York City. School records in New York indicate that Oswald's grades suffered as a result of chronic truancy. Psychiatric records indicate that he experienced emotional problems in his youth. When doctors suggested that he needed psychiatric treatment, Oswald's mother refused their recommendation and returned to New Orleans. After completing the ninth grade, Oswald dropped out of school and joined the Marine Corps. In 1959, he was released from the Marines after claiming hardship; Oswald stated that his mother's ill health and poor financial situation required his release. Less than a month after being discharged, he went to the Soviet Union.

*Lee Harvey Oswald, accused killer of President John F. Kennedy, (center) grimaces as he is fatally shot by Dallas nightclub owner Jack Ruby on November 24, 1963.* (Library of Congress)

**The 1960's** Oswald remained in the Soviet Union from 1959 until 1962. He married a Soviet woman, Marina Nikolaevna Prusakova, and applied for Soviet citizenship but was refused. Frustrated with his circumstances, he tried to return to the United States with his wife and baby daughter but was detained by the Soviets. After the authorities released him, Oswald went to New Orleans to participate in pro-Castro activities. He later surfaced in Dallas, where he was hired by the Texas School Book Depository. Less than one month later on November 22, 1963, he allegedly fired three shots from a window on the sixth floor of the depository, killing President John F. Kennedy and seriously wounding Governor John B. Connally of Texas. It was later revealed that Oswald, using an assumed name, had ordered a 6.5-caliber rifle and a Japanese telescopic sight from a Chicago mail-order catalog some months earlier. Forty-five minutes after shooting

Kennedy, Oswald also allegedly shot and killed a Dallas police officer who was trying to bring him in for questioning. When captured, Oswald denied everything. Two days later, while being transferred to another holding facility, he was shot and killed by Dallas nightclub owner Jack Ruby. Ruby was found guilty of murder and sentenced to death the following year. However, Ruby's conviction was overturned in 1966 on the grounds that illegal testimony had been allowed by the trial judge. Ruby died in 1967 before his new trial began.

**Impact** The assassination of President Kennedy and the subsequent deaths of Oswald and Ruby led to much speculation about a possible conspiracy. Many people believed that Oswald was working for the Cuban and Soviet governments or perhaps even the Central Intelligence Agency. Such speculation did little to improve the already strained relations between the United States and the Soviet Union and Cuba.

**Subsequent Events** President Lyndon B. Johnson established a commission to investigate the events leading to Kennedy's death. Chief Justice Earl Warren, who led the investigation, reported in September, 1964, that Oswald had acted alone. However, a congressional committee that later reexamined the evidence concluded, in its 1979 report, that the assassination was probably a conspiracy.

**Additional Information** A multitude of books have been published on the role of Oswald in the death of President Kennedy. One of the best-researched is *Oswald's Tale: An American Mystery* (1995), by Pulitzer Prize-winning author Norman Mailer.

*Donald C. Simmons, Jr.*

**See also** Assassinations of John and Robert Kennedy and Martin Luther King, Jr.; Kennedy, John F.; Warren Report.

# P

## ■ Palmer, Arnold

**Born** September 10, 1929, Youngstown, Pennsylvania

*A top professional golfer of the early 1960's. Palmer was the first golf star of the television era and later became one of the founders of the senior professional golf circuit.*

A muscular greenskeeper's son, Arnold Daniel Palmer attended Wake Forest University but left to join the Coast Guard. He then returned to college but did not finish. Soon after winning the 1954 U.S. Amateur, Palmer turned professional.

By 1960, Palmer was the leading player on the professional tour, a role he shared with Jack Nicklaus after the mid-1960's without any loss of his immense personal popularity. Palmer and Nicklaus each won twice as many major pro championships in the decade as any other professional golfer did. Their rivalry, as promoted by the media, initiated a golf boom that continues today.

**Impact** Palmer won sixty-one pro tournaments, not counting senior or non-U.S. wins. He won six major championships from 1960-1964 but none thereafter, though he later won a number of Senior Tour majors. Palmer's dramatic victory in the 1960 U.S. Open and his Masters victories in 1958, 1960, 1962, and 1964 are among the leading events in the history of golf in the United States, and they helped to establish Palmer as a media celebrity and golf as a television attraction. In 1961 and 1962, Palmer won the British Open and helped to restore the prestige of the venerable championship. He also led the professional money winners in 1958, 1960, 1962, and 1963, although he never won the Professional Golfers' Association (PGA) Championship.

**Subsequent Events** Palmer won less frequently in the 1970's, as a new generation of stars emerged. In the 1980's however, he became one of the leading stars of the new PGA Senior Tour, which owed its success in large part to his continuing popularity. Health problems limited Palmer's success in the 1990's. However, even after cancer surgery, he con-

tinued to play the senior tour with the same verve that made a final-round "Palmer Charge" a feared event in his heyday and "Arnie's Army" the largest golf gallery of its era.

**Additional Information** Curt Sampson's discussion of Palmer in his 1992 book *The Eternal Summer: Palmer, Nicklaus, and Hogan in 1960, Golf's Golden Year* provides information about Palmer in the 1960's and his later years.

*Tom Cook*

**See also** Golf; Nicklaus, Jack; Rawls, Betsy; Wright, Mickey.

*Arnold Palmer, along with rival Jack Nicklaus, was one of the top golfers during the 1960's.* (Ralph W. Miller Golf Library)

# ■ Paris Peace Talks

**Date** 1968-1969

*The first serious effort of both the United States and North Vietnamese governments to negotiate an end to the Vietnam conflict. However, both sides' failure to compromise on a variety of issues stalled the talks by late 1969.*

**Origins and History** The Paris Peace Talks began as a result of the backlash from the Tet Offensive of early 1968. Tet shocked the U.S. government and public; subsequently, many Americans believed the war in Vietnam could not be won. For North Vietnam, Tet was a military defeat but a psychological victory because the offensive caused the U.S. government to rethink its policy in Vietnam.

**The Talks** Three days after President Lyndon B. Johnson's March 31, 1968, speech, in which he spoke of peace in Vietnam and announced his decision not to seek another term as president, the North Vietnamese government of Ho Chi Minh agreed to open negotiations with U.S. and South Vietnamese officials. Talks began in Paris on May 12. From the U.S. side, chief negotiator Averell Harriman and Secretary of Defense Clark Clifford led the move to extricate the United States from Vietnam. They offered to stop the bombing campaign in exchange for reciprocal North Vietnamese army troop withdrawals from South Vietnam. North Vietnam, however, argued for an unconditional halt of U.S. bombing north of the demilitarized zone.

From the start, both sides revealed reasons for coming to the negotiating table. For the United States, the goal was to get its forces out of Vietnam as it gradually transferred the job of fighting to the South Vietnamese military (a process called "Vietnamization"). Johnson's original objective of securing an independent, noncommunist South Vietnam remained intact despite the realization that the United States could no longer fight the war for the South Vietnamese. For North Vietnam, the peace talks functioned as part of the nation's new strategy for winning the war. Its army had suffered greatly during the Tet Offensive, and the country desperately needed a break from the constant bombing. In addition to these concerns, the North Vietnamese realized that what occurred on the battlefield had caused, and could continue to cause, internal dissension between U.S. policymakers and the American public. Therefore, the North Vietnamese

instituted a policy of *danh va dam*, or "fighting while negotiating."

The Paris talks stalled the remainder of 1968, and the fighting in Vietnam continued. U.S. and South Vietnamese forces maintained constant pressure on the Viet Cong and North Vietnamese forces. Vietnamization gradually intensified. A minor breakthrough occurred in the fall of 1968 when President Johnson agreed to halt the bombing campaign in return for minor concessions. Harriman convinced North Vietnamese negotiators to drop their unconditional stance against cessation. While agreeing unofficially, the North Vietnamese insisted that the National Liberation Front (NLF) be allowed to participate in the talks. The South Vietnamese government rejected the proposal, causing yet another impasse just as the talks appeared to be making some progress. The South Vietnamese responded to pressure from Republicans in the United States who were concerned that progress in the peace talks might result in a Democratic victory in the November, 1968, presidential election. The South Vietnamese decided to take their chances with Richard M. Nixon and the Republicans in 1969. The North Vietnamese, for their part, agreed to open "serious" talks once the bombing stopped. Johnson halted the bombing campaign unconditionally on October 31.

The talks stalled again over the shape of the negotiating table, delaying substantive negotiations for weeks. By the time the table issue was settled, the Johnson administration was out of office. President Nixon proved too uncompromising to make any real progress in negotiations during 1969. Instead, he turned to a peace-through-coercion approach that included bombing of Viet Cong sanctuaries in Cambodia. In May, 1969, Nixon unveiled a new peace plan, which included the phased withdrawal of U.S. forces from South Vietnam, leaving an independent South Vietnam. This plan, in reality, was nothing new, leading the North Vietnamese to reject it.

**Impact** Despite the peace talks, the continuing war in Vietnam served only to feed the antiwar movement in the United States. The movement manifested itself primarily on college campuses throughout the country, where protests against U.S. involvement in Vietnam grew increasingly intense and violent, culminating in the shooting deaths of four Kent State University students by National Guardsmen in 1970. In Vietnam, more Americans and Vietnamese were killed and wounded as Nixon ordered the invasion of Cambodia. In all, it took the Nixon administration four years to achieve "peace with honor" to end the U.S. involvement in the Vietnam War. Two years later, in 1975, South Vietnam fell.

**Additional Information** See Ronald Spector's *After Tet: The Bloodiest Year in Vietnam* (1993) and George C. Herring's *America's Longest War, 1950-1975* (1996).

*William Allison*

**See also** Johnson, Lyndon B.; March Against Death; Moratorium Day; Nixon, Richard M.; Presidential Election of 1968; Tet Offensive; Vietnam War.

# ■ Patterson, Floyd

**Born** January 4, 1935, Waco, North Carolina

*Olympic middleweight and professional world heavyweight boxing champion.*

Reared in Brooklyn, New York, Patterson was a juvenile delinquent. The police introduced him to boxing as a form of rehabilitation, and he was discovered by legendary trainer Cus D'Amato. He captured the 1952 Olympic middleweight gold medal, and in 1956 became the youngest world heavyweight champion ever. He made four successful defenses before losing to Ingemar Johansson in 1959.

In a rematch on June 20, 1960, Patterson knocked out Johansson to become the first man to ever regain the heavyweight championship. He twice defended his title before suffering first-round knockouts at the hands of Sonny Liston in 1962 and in a 1963. In 1965, he again attempted to recapture the title from new champion Muhammad Ali but was knocked out in the twelfth round. During the last half of the decade, he continued to fight successfully but lost to contenders Jerry Quarry (1967) and Jimmy Ellis (1968).

Patterson retired in 1972 with a professional record of 55-8-1. In 1974, he co-authored an instructional manual for beginning boxers entitled *Inside Boxing*. He was elected to the Boxing Hall of Fame in 1977 and to the Olympic Hall of Fame in 1987.

**Impact** Patterson's record as the youngest man to hold the heavyweight title was not eclipsed for three decades, when it was broken by Mike Tyson, another D'Amato protege. Patterson's successful use of the "peek-a-boo" style has been copied by numerous subsequent fighters, including Tyson.

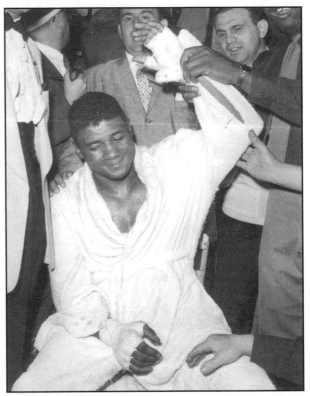

*Boxer Floyd Patterson smiles after regaining the heavyweight championship in June, 1960, a title he would lose to Sonny Liston in 1962.* (AP/Wide World Photos)

**Additional Information** More information about Patterson's life and career can be found in Greg Garber's *Boxing Legends* (1994).

*Akim D. Reinhardt*

**See also** Ali, Muhammad (Cassius Clay); Frazier, Joe; Griffith-Paret Fight; Liston, Sonny.

# ■ Peace Corps

*A U.S. government overseas assistance agency. The Peace Corps attracted thousands of young Americans to serve as goodwill ambassadors and agents of development throughout the developing world during the 1960's.*

**Origins and History** Although legislative proposals for a Peace Corps had been put forward in the late 1950's, John F. Kennedy gave the idea impetus in the last week of his presidential campaign on November 2, 1960, when he proposed it as one way to rejuvenate U.S. foreign policy by promoting goodwill and peace using a volunteer corps of young Americans. One of the earliest acts of the Kennedy administration's New Frontier policy was the signing of an Executive Order on March 1, 1961, by which the Peace Corps was officially inaugurated. President Kennedy appointed R. Sargent Shriver director of the corps. The Peace Corps attracted a number of young, prominent, energetic government officials who worked tirelessly from their offices in the Maiatico Building in Washington, D.C., overlooking Lafayette Park, to build an organization equal to the ideals set for it by President Kennedy. The Peace Corps, established as an independent agency, was to provide newly independent countries of the Third World with trained manpower to help those being served to better understand Americans and to help Americans better understand foreign peoples and cultures.

Growth in the early years of the Peace Corps program was remarkable. In 1961, only five hundred volunteers served in eight countries, but by 1963, seven thousand volunteers served in forty-five countries, and by 1966, the Peace Corps achieved its high point with more than fifteen thousand volunteers serving abroad.

Underlying the Peace Corps philosophy and program was the idea that the United States needed to combat the expansionist development programs of the communist bloc. Thus, the Peace Corps was partly a child of the Cold War. It aimed at improving the United States' image abroad and overcoming the "Ugly American" stigma by establishing a people-to-people style diplomacy. Peace Corps volunteers were to become ambassadors of goodwill from the United States to the peoples of the developing world. The political dimension of Peace Corps work, then, remained an ever-present reality. When U.S. involvement in the Vietnam War escalated in the late 1960's, the Peace Corps tended to attract many who sought to avoid the draft, unleashing a domestic controversy over abuses in Peace Corps recruitment. However, overall recruitment tended to decline at this time as many young Americans came to question not only U.S. foreign policy in general but also the role of the Peace Corps.

**Activities** Peace Corps volunteers worked in a variety of capacities. A very large percentage engaged in

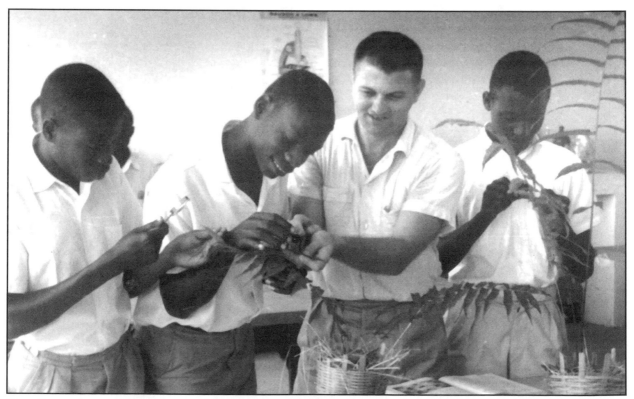

*Peace Corps volunteer George Coyne, a schoolteacher from New Jersey, (center) works with students in Sunyani, Ghana, in 1963.* (AP/Wide World Photos)

educational activities, including teacher training, vocational and technical education, and sometimes university-level teaching. Others worked in community development or social welfare programs such as child care, family planning, nutrition, sanitation and health projects, and small-scale rural development activities such as vegetable gardening, animal husbandry, fisheries projects, and development of water resources. Still others focused on public-works activities such as road building, housing and school construction, and rural electrification. Those volunteers involved in more specific and technical posts tended to have better experiences than their counterparts who worked in more vague community development activities where they needed to define for themselves how they could contribute to the communities they served.

**Impact** The vast majority of volunteers during the 1960's were college graduates with general credentials. Some specialists were recruited, but most volunteers went abroad without highly technical skills. This tended to limit the impact of volunteers on the overall development of host countries, although it may have contributed somewhat to the other goals of promoting intercultural contact and understanding. A common complaint of early volunteers was that they were often sent abroad without explicit instructions and so had to devise their own ways of being useful to a rural community. Still, the vast majority of Peace Corps volunteers reported their experiences abroad as having been personally rewarding. Most returning volunteers came back to the United States with enriched understandings of peoples from other parts of the world, but some experienced anti-United States sentiments overseas, and early resignations were not uncommon in the late 1960's. Some former volunteers became involved in protest activities against U.S. foreign policy and the Vietnam War, particularly the Committee of Returned Volunteers, which moved to the forefront of anti-Vietnam War protest after its formation in 1966, giving the impression to patriotic Americans that the Peace Corps was populated not only by draft dodgers but also by political radicals. As disillusionment with U.S. foreign policy increased, fewer young Americans volunteered for the Peace Corps.

**Subsequent Events** Under President Richard M. Nixon, the Peace Corps was made part of a new bureaucratic unit. The position of Peace Corps di-

rector became a revolving door, and the organization's administration lost continuity. Not until 1981 did the Peace Corps regain its independence under the direction of Loret Miller Ruppe. By that time, about five thousand volunteers per year served overseas, barely one-third of the number that had served during the heyday of the Peace Corps in 1966. After the reorientation of the Peace Corps in the 1980's, the average age of volunteers increased and the number of volunteers with specific technical skills rose. The agency experienced renewed vitality in the late 1980's and 1990's, having weathered the political storms of the 1970's and having matured as an agency of overseas assistance.

**Additional Information** For a critical assessment of the success of the Peace Corps by two prominent former volunteers see Kevin Lowther and C. Payne Lucas's *Keeping Kennedy's Promise: The Peace Corps—Unmet Hope of the New Frontier* (1978). Another systematic study of the founding and work of the Peace Corps in the 1960's is Gerard T. Rice's *The Bold Experiment: JFK's Peace Corps* (1985). Other useful works that incorporate much oral history are Coates Redmon's *Come as You Are: The Peace Corps Story* (1986) and Karen Schwarz's *What You Can Do for Your Country: An Oral History of the Peace Corps* (1991).

*Robert F. Gorman*

**See also** Cold War; Kennedy, John F.; Vietnam War.

## ■ Pentagon, Levitating of the

**Date** October 21, 1967

*One of the most colorful antiwar demonstrations of the 1960's. The surreal attempt by hippie protesters to use their mind power to levitate the Pentagon and exorcise its demons suggested how bizarre the actions of some opponents to U.S. military involvement in Vietnam had become.*

**Origins and History** Frustrated that peaceful demonstrations seemed unable to change U.S. policy in Vietnam, David Dellinger of the National Mobilization Committee to End the War in Vietnam (MOBE) organized a large, potentially violent demonstration for October, 1967, and invited many different groups of dissidents.

**The Levitating** On the morning of Saturday, October 21, 1967, roughly fifty thousand demonstrators gathered around the Lincoln Memorial in Washington, D.C., for a march on the Pentagon. After a series of speeches and some jostling among prominent members of the antiwar movement for a spot in the front line of the march, the protesters filed into the north parking lot of the Pentagon. There they encountered a stage set up by the dissident rock-and-roll band, the Fugs, who had helped plan the event since September, when maverick radical Jerry Rubin, who worked as coproject director of the march, invited hippie leader Abbie Hoffman to participate. Hoffman suggested that twelve hundred demonstrators encircle the Pentagon and use their mental powers to levitate the building three hundred feet above the ground. He applied for a permit for the event, and a witty general services administrator granted it, allowing levitation up to ten feet only and prohibiting complete encirclement by limiting the participants to the parking lot.

The Fugs, dressed in orange, yellow, and rose capes, told the demonstrators what to do. As a triangle and a cymbal were sounded, a leaflet explaining the event was distributed. The gathered demonstrators would use their minds to raise the Pentagon, which would levitate, turn orange, and vibrate until all its evil emissions had fled as a result of this exorcism. Then, the war in Vietnam would end.

In reality, after much chanting, praying, and singing, the Pentagon did not rise by even a fraction of an inch. Some demonstrators charged the military police who guarded the Pentagon but were beaten back. More violence ensued, and six demonstrators briefly entered the building. Two hundred fifty protesters were arrested, but most were fined and released the next day.

**Impact** Although it was unsuccessful, the surrealist approach of the hippies indicated how widespread opposition to U.S. involvement in Vietnam had become. The large number of protesters at the march, which came at the end of a week of violent antiwar protests and riots all over the United States, and the ensuing violence revealed a deeply divided society. Public opposition such as this march led President Lyndon B. Johnson to downplay the seriousness of the Vietnam War; and after the Tet Offensive showed the extent of U.S. involvement, Johnson decided not to run for reelection. In the end, popular opposition caused the United States to abandon its allied nations in Southeast Asia, and Vietnam fell to the communists' relentless onslaught in the spring of 1975.

**Additional Information** Norman Mailer, who participated in the levitating of the Pentagon, wrote about it in *Armies of the Night* (1968).

*Bophasy Saukam*

**See also** *Do It! Scenarios of the Revolution*; Hippies; Music; National Mobilization Committee to End the War in Vietnam (MOBE); Oakland Riot; Protest Songs; Tet Offensive; Vietnam War; Yippies.

## ■ People's Park, Berkeley

*A one-block park in Berkeley, California, created April, 1969, by residents seeking to create a community commons.*

Berkeley's Telegraph Avenue neighborhood, near the University of California, Berkeley, was a center of activism in the late 1960's. Under the banner of "urban renewal," the university began buying up property in the neighborhood. Although the university's stated purpose was to build additional student facilities, the underlying agenda was to displace the hippies and radicals who had collected in the area. In July, 1967, with funding from conservative state politicians, the university bought a block bounded by the streets of Telegraph, Haste, Dwight, and Bowditch and demolished the old houses on the property.

The university announced plans for a playing field at the site in April, 1969. Activists responded by claiming the land for a public park and called for a gathering there on April 20. Hundreds of people arrived with shovels and wheelbarrows to transform the razed block into a community commons, lay sod, and plant a vegetable garden. In the early hours of May 15, the University of California evicted the gardeners, bulldozed the plantings, and fenced off the area. That afternoon, following a rally at Sproul Plaza on the Berkeley campus, thousands marched to the site. Police responded with tear gas, and sheriff's deputies fired live ammunition. At least 50 (and by some accounts as many as 110) people were shot; one man, James Rector, was killed. Governor Ronald Reagan sent in the National Guard, who occupied Berkeley for seventeen days. Although it was illegal for more than three people to congregate, several marches drawing thousands took place in the ensuing days. On May 30, more than twenty-five thousand people peacefully marched to People's Park; shortly thereafter, the Guard was withdrawn.

**Impact** The occupation of the streets of Berkeley by the National Guard, coming as it did at the height

*National Guardsmen watch from inside the steel mesh fence erected around People's Park in May, 1969, as protesters pass by.* (AP/Wide World Photos)

of the Vietnam War, led to analogies about the "war at home." People's Park challenged the sanctity of property rights and heralded the environmental movement and neighborhood-based organizing in the 1970's.

**Subsequent Events** Frequent and sometimes violent conflicts over the park continued between the University of California and Berkeley residents. In 1972, antiwar protesters tore down the fence; attempts by the university to build on the site were met with protests, sit-ins, or sabotage. In 1991, the University of California and the city of Berkeley agreed to jointly manage the site. The university succeeded in building a volleyball court at the park in 1991 over strenuous opposition, but because of disuse, it was demolished in 1997. On June 20, 1997, the university turned the site into a soccer field and parking lot, kept under round-the-clock guard.

**Additional Information** W. J. Rorabaugh's *Berkeley at War* (1989) describes the evolution of the conflict and includes photographs of demonstrators and National Guard troops. Todd Gitlin's *The Sixties:*

*Years of Hope, Days of Rage* (1987) provides a look at the motivations of protesters.

*Vanessa Tait*

**See also** Counterculture; Environmental Movement; Urban Renewal.

# ■ Percy Murder

**Date** September 18, 1966

*The murder of a politician's daughter in her own bedroom. It shocked the nation, drawing attention to seemingly random, violent crimes, and remains unsolved.*

**Origins and History** The 1966 U.S. senatorial campaign of Charles H. Percy was abruptly interrupted when Valerie Jeanne Percy, one of his twenty-one-year-old twin daughters, was found bludgeoned and stabbed in her bedroom. The murder occurred in the Percy mansion in Kenilworth, Illinois, a suburb of Chicago. No one was ever arrested for the crime, and the identity of the actual killer will probably never be known.

**The Murder** On September 18, 1966, at about 5:00 A.M., Percy's wife, Jeanne, was awakened by the sounds of moaning. She followed the noise to the bedroom of one of her twin daughters, where she saw a figure standing over the bed of her daughter, Valerie. The intruder shined a flashlight into Jeanne Percy's eyes, blinding her, and then fled, escaping down the stairs of the house. A screaming Jeanne Percy then woke her husband, who immediately sounded an audible burglar alarm. Charles Percy then proceeded to Valerie's room, where he found his daughter, barely alive. She died a short time later. Her skull had been crushed by a blunt object, and she had been stabbed numerous times in her chest, throat, and abdomen. The crime scene provided little evidence.

After questioning fourteen thousand people and investigating more than thirteen hundred leads, the authorities were able to narrow the list of suspects, focusing their efforts on the most likely suspects, Frederick Malchow and Frank Hohimer. They were professional burglars who had worked together with Mafia fence Leo Rugendorf on several occasions. Malchow supposedly told a cell mate sometime after the murder that he feared a pair of bloody trousers might implicate him in the Percy murder if the police discovered them. The police did find the blood-stained pants, but it was too late to draw any conclusive scientific evidence from them. In 1967, Malchow died when he fell from a railroad trestle while running from police after escaping from a Pennsylvania prison.

The other prime suspect, Hohimer, who in 1971 became a government witness in several organized crime prosecutions, was later implicated in the murder by his former cohort, Rugendorf. Hohimer's younger brother also made statements against him. The brother described the way Hohimer acted the day after the murder and recounted statements Hohimer had made about the Percy murder.

**Impact** Charles Percy resumed his campaign and went on to win the election. Some speculated that the murder of his daughter elicited the sympathy of voters. His defeated opponent, however, admitted that Percy had been pulling ahead of him since the summer of 1966. Due to the lack of physical evidence, officials have admitted that they will probably never know exactly who killed Valerie Percy. A fifty-thousand-dollar reward for information, once offered by Senator Percy, has been withdrawn.

**Additional Information** Suspect Hohimer wrote *The Home Invaders* (1975), the story of his criminal career. In the book, he denies any involvement in the murder of Valerie Percy.

*Trent Marshall*

**See also** Boston Strangler; Career Girl Murders; Crimes and Scandals; Genovese Murder; Speck Murders.

## ■ Photocopying

*A process that produces one or multiple copies of any document. The first office machine to make good, permanent copies on ordinary paper, the Xerox 914, was introduced in 1960 and rapidly transformed business and scholarly practices.*

Before xerography, making copies was tedious and chancy. Carbon copies, hectographs, and mimeographs, the methods used in the mid-twentieth century, required special care and materials. Expensive photostats were needed to copy a preexisting document. Scholars took copious notes from research materials by hand. In the 1950's, an office copier, the Thermo-Fax, was introduced, which used rolled, heavy paper and made dark, fading copies.

Meanwhile, the Haloid Company of Rochester, New York, was working on a copier based on a selenium-coated drum, which used opposing electrical charges to create a duplicate image. Building a new machine from this principle was a daunting task for a small company. At one point Joseph Wilson, Haloid's president, offered International Business Machines (IBM) the chance to develop it jointly. IBM, convinced five thousand copiers was the market ceiling, turned him down.

However, the Xerox 914 was an immediate success. At first, the company could make only five copiers a day, and orders almost exceeded their capacity. Haloid's 1959 revenues of 32 million dollars exploded to more than 500 million dollars by 1966. The machine produced permanent, sharp images of an original. Using plain, white paper kept per-copy costs low, and making copies was so simple a child could do it. (One early television commercial showed a little girl making copies for her businessman father.) As its capacities became known, almost every business, library, and office wanted a "Xerox machine." The company developed new models that improved on the desk-sized 914 and became the Xerox Corporation, one of the great business success stories of the 1960's.

By the decade's end, the office copier was firmly established in American worklife and lore. Among twentieth century inventions, its rapid adoption was matched only by that of television a few years earlier.

**Impact**  The copier expanded communication. Businesses kept more records, sent more notices and bills, and—sometimes—disseminated data more quickly and widely. This contributed to the "information explosion" and, coincidentally, created the modern office memo.

Journalists, whistleblowers, and protesters copied documents that revealed the secrets of the "establishment," such as universities' informal racial quotas. Copied flyers and manifestos helped movements emerge and develop, and amateur production of small-press publications became practical.

Professors provided their students with relevant copied articles. This spurred the teaching of current controversies and up-to-date scientific discoveries but raised copyright issues because permission was seldom sought from the copyright holders.

**Subsequent Events**  Photocopying influenced the Copyright Act of 1976, which permitted individuals to copy a work once for study or research. Successful lawsuits were brought against copy shops that mass-copied protected material for profit.

Xerox's patents expired in 1972, allowing other companies to market similar copiers. The technology expanded to create color copiers, fax machines, and ultimately, computer functions such as scanners.

**Additional Information**  David Owen's "Copies in Seconds," in *The Atlantic Monthly* 257 (February, 1986), is the most accessible account of the development of the photocopier.

*Emily Alward*

**See also**  Communications; Education; Science and Technology.

# ■ Photography

*Major changes occurred in art photography of the 1960's. The development of the "snapshot aesthetic," a new form of photographic realism, challenged traditional aesthetic norms and practices of art photography.*

In the 1890's, photography first began to be considered a form of art, thanks largely to the work of New Yorker Alfred Stieglitz. In 1896, Stieglitz was instrumental in founding the Camera Club of New York and later formed a new society, the Photo-Secession, in New York to promote art photography. In 1903, the group began publishing *Camera Work*, an impressive international quarterly that highlighted the art of photography. The Photo-Secession also loaned its members' works for exhibits.

Under the Photo-Secessionists, art photography evolved from pictorialism, which emphasized the manipulation of images so that they emulated modernist paintings, to straight, or pure, photography. The straight images emphasized the content and function of an image rather than form. By the 1920's, the solid composition and clarity in subject matter of straight photography had replaced the abstractions of pictorial photography. Straight art photography and documentary photography also grew closer from the 1920's to the 1960's, led by photographers such as Arthur Rothstein, Dorothea Lange, Berenice Abbott, and Walker Evans.

**Art Photography Redefined**  In the 1950's and early 1960's, challenges to traditional straight photography began to mount as changes occurred in the understanding of how photographs conveyed meaning. Led by scholars such as the French semiotician Roland Barthes and curators and writers such as George Eastman House's Nathan Lyons, those who studied or practiced art photography began to question the ability of the photograph to directly and simply convey universal truth. *The Photographer's Eye* (1966) by John Szarkowski, the director of the department of photography of the Museum of Modern Art, added to these new perspectives through historical and theoretical explorations of the uniqueness of photographic communication.

Also, the work of two European photographers who had emigrated to the United States in the 1930's and 1940's influenced the new critical views and introspective practices of art photography. Lisette Model, an Austrian who moved to New York in 1937, began teaching photography in the 1950's at New York City's New School for Social Research. Model, whose photographs appeared in *PM, Harper's Bazaar,* and art museums, became a central figure in the redefinition of art photography in the 1960's through teaching star pupils such as Diane Arbus. Swiss-born

Robert Frank, who emigrated to the United States in 1947, greatly influenced the new 1960's generation of art photographers with his book, *The Americans* (1959). The book, consisting of eighty-three photographs taken while Frank traveled the United States on a Guggenheim Fellowship in 1955 and 1956, was first published in France and reached U.S. bookstores in January, 1960. Frank's images defied traditional straight and social documentary photography. He did not present an indictment or a celebration of American society but rather his own ironic, detached view. His subjective vision as an outsider to American society dominated his images, making it possible for him to transform the undetected visual norms of American pastimes and institutions into the bizarre. He was able to explore issues such as racism, consumerism, poverty, and religion by focusing on the facetiousness and irony in his subjects' expressions, gestures, and social contexts. He irreverently disregarded the traditional aesthetics of straight photography by presenting images that were often blurred, erratically framed, or unposed.

**The Snapshot Aesthetic** Therefore, because of the work of Szarkowski, Lyons, Model, Frank, and others, by the mid-1960's, photography was seen by many in the art world as not an objective distillation of reality but as a constructed, subjective mediation of reality with a grammar all its own. For art photographers, the photograph became an internal, individual exploration connected to the external world but not determined by it. Adherence to the traditional aesthetics of straight photography's composition and exposure was abandoned by many of the new photographers. In following Frank, the new photographers deliberately highlighted the artifice of photographic practice by presenting images that were harshly lighted, unfocused, or framed in confounding manners, such as with distracting foregrounds or backgrounds. This trend came to be known as the "snapshot aesthetic."

Photographers such as Arbus, Lee Friedlander, Garry Winogrand, Bruce Davidson, Danny Lyon, Mary Ellen Mark, and Richard Avedon used the irreverence of the snapshot aesthetic to explore the changing cultural climate of the United States in the 1960's. They blurred the distinctions between art and documentary photography more than ever before. The eccentric, ordinary, and banal merged in the ironies and metaphors of their visual explorations of social elements such as crime, poverty, insanity, suburban life, consumerism, death, work, protest, and loneliness.

**Three Talented Photographers** Curators, editors, and critics began to pay an increasing amount of attention to the new art photography, especially after the *New Documents* exhibition of 1966 and 1967. The work of three of the most talented and prolific new photographers—Arbus, Friedlander, and Winogrand—was showcased in *New Documents,* curated by Szarkowski of the Museum of Modern Art. The exhibition, considered one of the landmark shows of the 1960's, received numerous exceedingly good reviews. Not only were new art photographers Arbus, Friedlander, and Winogrand receiving acclaim, they were also receiving financial support through Guggenheim Fellowships.

For example, Arbus, who began her career as a fashion photographer, switched to art photography after studying under Model in 1959. Many of her images were published in *Harper's Bazaar* and *Esquire.* Guggenheim Fellowships in 1963 and 1966 helped support her passion for seeing the bizarre in the ordinary or the ordinary in the bizarre. She quickly drew attention from the artistic community through her images of people in parks or homes, the wealthy, the poor, and particularly midgets, giants, transvestites, and the insane—the "freaks," as she called them. Many of Arbus's subjects were sharply lighted by direct flash and looked directly at her camera, seemingly confronting viewers.

Friedlander studied at the Art Center in Los Angeles from 1953 to 1955 and worked as a freelance commercial photographer and university teacher in the late 1950's. His work also appeared in *Esquire* and other periodicals. By the early 1960's, he was promoting the snapshot aesthetic through his numerous offhanded urban views and self-portraits. He abandoned formal conventions, making such images as undramatic, seemingly flat photographs taken from automobiles. He was awarded Guggenheim Fellowships twice, in 1960 and 1962, and was featured in George Eastman House exhibitions in 1963 and 1966.

Winogrand, who began photographing while in the United States Air Force in 1946 and 1947, attended City College, Columbia University, and the New School for Social Research in New York City. During the 1960's, he worked as a freelance advertising photographer and photojournalist and was published regularly in national magazines such as *Collier's*. Winogrand received two Guggenheim Fellowships, in 1964 and 1969, and exhibited his work at the George Eastman House and the Museum of Modern Art. In 1969, he published a book titled *The Animals*, which was based on outstanding photographs he took at the Coney Island Aquarium and New York City zoo. Because of his repeated use of tilted framing and wide-angle lenses, Winogrand's images of crowded parties or public spaces often appeared uncomposed, random, or accidental to the uninitiated.

**Impact**  By the end of the 1960's, photography was no longer considered a straightforward, simple, objective practice. The new photography had proved photographs to be subjective and layered with meaning. The 1960's snapshot aesthetic of the new art photographers also contributed to the development of the ideals and practices of the counterculture that became so prevalent during the period. The new photographers, like so many who were questioning mainstream values and beliefs, considered themselves outside the traditional. The new photography complemented and therefore strengthened similar movements in other areas of communications and art, such as New Journalism writing, cinema verité filmmaking, and the popular-culture graphic artistry of Andy Warhol.

**Subsequent Events**  Although traditional straight photography survived the 1960's, primarily through the work of Minor White and landscape photographers such as Ansel Adams, the snapshot aesthetic did not disappear but developed into a significant genre of art photography. The snapshot aesthetic, with its focus on the subjective, helped fuel the postmodernist theories and practices of the 1980's and 1990's.

**Additional Information**  Excellent comprehensive discussions of 1960's art photography and photographers can be found in *Decade by Decade: Twentieth-Century American Photography from the Collection of the Center for Creative Photography* (1989), edited by James Enyeart; *A World History of Photography* (1984), by Naomi Rosenblum; and *The International Center of Photography Encyclopedia of Photography* (1984), with editorial direction by Cornell Capa.

*Charles Lewis*

**See also**  Arbus, Diane; Art Movements; Op Art; Pop Art; Warhol, Andy.

---

## ■ Piercy, Marge

**Born** March 31, 1936, Detroit, Michigan

*One of the most socially and politically concerned writers in the nation. Piercy has written poems, novels, and essays about women's issues, history, politics, commerce, and the effects of industrialization.*

**Early Life**  Marge Piercy spent her formative years in a small house in a working-class neighborhood. She almost died from the German measles and then caught rheumatic fever halfway through grade school. She looked to books for consolation and became a voracious reader. At age seventeen, she won a scholarship that paid her tuition to the University of Michigan. In 1956, she received the Avery and Jule Hopwood Award for Poetry and Fiction and, in 1957, received the same award for poetry. The same year, she earned a bachelor of arts degree from the University of Michigan. In 1958, she earned a master's degree from Northwestern University.

**The 1960's**  From 1960 to 1962, Piercy taught literature, freshman composition, and research methods at the Gary extension of Indiana University. At the end of that period, she and her second husband grew increasingly troubled by the Vietnam War, and Piercy became an active member of Students for a Democratic Society (SDS) from 1965 to 1969 and a member of the North American Congress on Latin America from 1966 to 1967.

During breaks in political organizing, Piercy worked on her first book of poems, *Breaking Camp* (1968), in which she explored the ideas of racial and gender equity and nature versus industry. In her first novel, *Going Down Fast* (1969), she addressed political concerns of the time, particularly in regard to race and socioeconomic class. Her second book of poems, *Hard Loving* (1969), showed her continuing interest in feminist issues, especially the ways that women view their bodies and are viewed by others.

**Later Life**  When *Dance the Eagle to Sleep* was published in 1970, Piercy was still frustrated by the ongoing Vietnam War, which she and many others had been opposing for eight years. She also continued her involvement in the women's movement, organizing consciousness-raising groups and writing articles.

Piercy's work continues to describe the dynamics of male-female relationships and the human need for intimacy. In her book of poems *What Are Big Girls Made Of?* (1997), she discusses both the personal and political implications of sexual harassment and other subjects including her Jewish heritage.

Moving to Wellfleet, Massachusetts, on Cape Cod in 1971 made Piercy even more aware of the relationship between people and nature and how the environment must be protected. Her work examines the ways in which humanity is negligent and cruel in its treatment of nature, including animals.

Piercy explored new territory in her novel, *City of Darkness, City of Light* (1996), portraying the French revolution as the beginning of modern politics and feminism and an example of a capitalist society in which the rich get richer, the poor get poorer, and the middle class is disproportionately taxed.

**Impact** One of the most politically progressive writers of her time, Piercy has helped to make nontraditional poetic subjects such as sexuality and the domestic realm acceptable and even celebrated in literature. In her poetry and novels, she explores how the lives of common women are uncommonly rich and complex and how ethnic heritage plays a crucial role in the development of one's identity.

**Additional Information** *Parti-Colored Blocks for a Quilt* (1982), a book of interviews, reviews, and essays by Piercy, presents this writer's approach to writing and the issues with which she is concerned.

*Holly L. Norton*

**See also** Feminist Movement; Literature; Poetry; Students for a Democratic Society (SDS); Vietnam War.

# ■ Pill, The

*An oral contraceptive containing the female reproductive hormones estrogen and progesterone. It reduces the risk of pregnancy to one in one thousand.*

In 1959, the American Public Health Association alerted all levels of government to the need to address the issue of population growth and its effect on health. The worldwide population explosion and growing scarcity of resources became the impetus for social, political, medical, and economic action. President Lyndon B. Johnson pledged to find new ways to deal with these problems. Introduction of the birth control pill in 1960 became a key component in working to solve these problems.

The birth control pill, which contains the hormones progesterone and estrogen, prevents contraception by blocking ovulation, preventing implantation of a fertilized egg, and increasing mucous production, making the cervix more hostile to sperm. In May, 1960, the first oral contraceptive, the G. D. Searle Company's Enovid, was made available to the public. Initially, a strict criteria governed distribution of birth control pills: Prescriptions were given only to married women, eighteen years of age or older. Controversy erupted around the country regarding the morality of providing the pill to unmarried women. Some people felt that access to the birth control pill would encourage immoral sexual behavior and lend fuel to the already growing sexual revolution. Others argued that women had a right to control their own bodies. However, the moral controversy soon faded, partly because of government initiatives intended to reduce population growth, and women, regardless of marital status, gradually were able to obtain the pill.

In part to address the developing concern about overpopulation, the Department of Health, Education, and Welfare and the Office of Economic Opportunity provided funds to community groups for health and welfare programs. Governmental agencies and health professionals created family planning programs that made it easier for low-income women to receive birth control pills.

**Impact** The birth control pill—an effective, easy means of contraception that cannot be detected during the act of sexual intercourse—helped women gain more complete control of their bodies and reproductive functions. It gained ready acceptance among women, and the numbers of users swelled until some serious health risks regarding high-dosage pills were uncovered in the late 1960's. Use of the pill, a key player in the sexual revolution, contributed to social and cultural changes by providing sexual freedom for single women.

**Subsequent Events** The high-dosage pills of the early 1960's have been replaced by safer, lower-dosage versions. Years of research on side effects and long-term effects resulted in chemical improvements that increase the benefits and reduce the risks. The pill continues to be one of the most effective contraceptives on the market.

**Additional Information**  A more thorough discussion of the pill can be found in "Prescribing the Pill: Politics, Culture, and the Sexual Revolution in America's Heartland," by Beth Baily in the 1997 issue of the *Journal of Social History*.

*Carol J. Sample*

**See also**  Abortion; Birth Control; Feminist Movement; Sexual Revolution; Women's Identity.

---

# ■ *Planet of the Apes*

**Released** 1968
**Director** Franklin J. Schaffner

*A motion picture that envisions an authoritarian society ruled by apes. It is a biting satire of the bureaucratic mind, scientific progress, and race relations.*

**The Work**  The film *Planet of the Apes* is based on a book with the same title by Pierre Boulle, first published in French in 1963 as *Le planète des singes* and translated into English the same year. In the book, the story revolves around French journalist Ulysse Mérou, who is part of an expedition to an Earth-like planet where the roles of apes and humans are reversed. He and his companions are captured by the apes, who use them as zoological specimens.

During the course of his stay, Ulysse learns to communicate with two chimpanzee scientists, Cornelius and Zira, and convinces them of his intelligence. He civilizes a woman who has reverted to a primitive lifestyle and eventually names her Nova. The bureaucratic orangutan, Zaius, sees Ulysse as a threat and devises a scheme to get rid of him. Ulysse, with the help of the two scientists, escapes on his rocketship with Nova and their child and returns to Paris.

In his book, Boulle attacks bureaucracy as seen in the form of the inflexible Zaius. Ulysse discovers that the human decivilization of the Earth-like planet was brought about through people's failure to use their minds.

The 1968 film is less abstract in its themes and reflects the concerns of 1960's audiences. In the film, the action centers around astronaut George

*George Taylor (Charlton Heston) gazes out from his cage at chimpanzee scientists Zira (Kim Hunter) and Cornelius (Roddy McDowall) in the 1968 film* Planet of the Apes. *(Museum of Modern Art/Film Stills Archive)*

Taylor. The misanthropic Taylor and his two companions, Dodge, the curious scientist, and Landon, the egocentric explorer, suffer karmic fates: Dodge is killed and placed in a museum, Landon becomes a lobotomized pet, and Taylor realizes that humankind is greater than the ape. The film also explores racism by making it clear that the scientist chimpanzees inhabit the lowest rungs of ape society and delves into the contradictions of mixing religion and science. In the film, Zaius is portrayed as a fanatical, scripture-quoting hypocrite, more interested in maintaining the status quo than in expanding the knowledge of his society.

The most striking image in both the film and the book is when the two heroes discover the fate of Earth. Ulysse returns to Paris, where, although Ulysse has been gone less than ten years, seven hundred years have passed. Earth has also evolved into a planet of the apes, so Ulysse escapes, leaving an account in a bottle that is found by two chimpanzees. In the film, Taylor, in an ending that reflects 1960's fears, runs off into the wasteland where he finds the top of the Statue of Liberty sticking out of the sand and realizes that the Earth-like planet of the apes is actually Earth. His contemporaries had destroyed themselves in a nuclear holocaust, leaving the apes to develop their own society.

**Impact** The book and the film were meant as cautionary tales bearing messages about racism, corruptive power, and the inevitability of fate by drawing parallels between the apes and people. In both versions, the apes, unlike humans, have been able to achieve a utopian society where there is no war, but they, like humans, have developed stratified societies that have become too conservative to accept new knowledge and are evolving toward disaster. The idea of a disastrous destiny appealed to many people during the turbulent 1960's and in subsequent decades, preserving the popularity of the book and film. The film spawned several sequels in the 1970's and a television series.

**Related Work** *Stranger in a Strange Land* (1961), by Robert Heinlein, uses a similar theme involving a man alienated from the society in which he finds himself. In Heinlein's work, however, the man, raised by Martians, is alienated from his own people.

C. A. Wolski

**See also** Film; Literature; Social Satires; *Stranger in a Strange Land.*

# ■ *Plum Plum Pickers, The*

**Published** 1969
**Author** Raymond Barrio (1921-     )

*One of the most poignant depictions of the Mexican American farmworker. The book is a major representative work of the Chicano movement of the late 1960's and early 1970's.*

**The Work** Set in California's Santa Clara County during the summer and fall harvest season, *The Plum Plum Pickers* takes place in and around the fictional town of Drawbridge and more specifically at the Western Grande Company's migrant housing project. The novel presents the dehumanized conditions of the mostly Mexican plum plum, or prune, pickers at the hands of the fruit company representatives, Mr. Quill, the grounds boss, and his superior and company owner, Mr. Turner. The squalor of the migrant camps is a major element of the narrative and enhances the brutalized relations between not only Anglo bosses and Mexican laborers but also between different groups within the farmworkers' Mexican community. The harsh reality of conditions is brought to the forefront in large part by the contrapuntal techniques employed in the narrative (which allow for contrasting views of the same topic) and the frequent attributing of animal qualities to individual characters.

**Impact** Barrio published *The Plum Plum Pickers* privately in 1969. Its publication coincided with the unionizing activities of César Chávez, and the book appeared to illustrate the very conditions that Chávez sought to improve. The book was therefore an immediate popular success, although it received little critical attention, perhaps because of the poor quality of print and paper employed in its first printing. The novel has since maintained its position as one of the key novels of the Chicano movement of the late 1960's and early 1970's. A major reason is Barrio's use of an unusual narrative form, which incorporates such items as newspaper clippings, radio announcements, handwritten notes, and even a government agricultural manual. *The Plum Plum Pickers* set a new standard for Chicano fiction to follow.

**Related Works** Roughly contemporary with *The Plum Plum Pickers* are two other major novels: *Chicano* (1970), by Richard Vasquez, an epic history of the Chicano experience; and . . . *y no se lo tragó la tierra* (and the earth did not part, 1971), by Tomas Rivera, which more closely resembles Barrio's work in terms of technique.

**Additional Information** Except for a few doctoral dissertations, works that treat this novel in depth are few. For a brief but good discussion of the work in the context of the Chicano novel, see *Understanding Chicano Literature* (1988), by Carl and Paula Shirley, and Teresa McKenna's "Three Novels: An Analysis," in the fall, 1970, issue of *Aztlán*.

*St. John Robinson*

**See also** Chávez, César; Chicano Movement; Grape Workers' Strike.

# ■ Poetry

*The transformation of an academic discipline into a universal medium of expression. During the 1960's, the idea that poetry had to follow the form of great English poems of earlier centuries was challenged by poets writing in the language and rhythms of American vernacular speech.*

U.S. literary history has followed two essentially separate approaches to poetry. Poets such as Anne Bradstreet, Phillis Wheatley, and William Cullen Bryant followed a dominant tradition that was based on the British masters of conventional forms and assumed that poetic art depended on formal diction and specific structures; however, at the same time, many poets pursued a countercurrent based on Henry David Thoreau's contention that "Poetry is nothing but healthy speech" and Walt Whitman's declaration that the old British poetic forms had no place in the New World.

As with many other social and cultural movements, the seeds of the poetry of the 1960's were planted in previous decades. The artists who spearheaded the Beat scene, William S. Burroughs, Jack Kerouac, and Allen Ginsberg, met in New York in the 1940's, and by the time Ginsberg's landmark poem "Howl" was published in 1956, their work was already making an impact on a growing counterculture, preparing the ground for a full-scale transformation in perceptions about poetry and the other arts. Although the work of poets who continued to write in the fashion approved by academic arbiters was not necessarily diminished, an "opening of the field" (as poet Robert Duncan put it) was taking place. Instead of gradually polishing a poem, Ginsberg suggested as a principle of composition

termed "first thought, best thought." He called attention to the work of "young minstrels" who "think not only in words but in music simultaneously," insisting that the lyrics of songwriters such as Bob Dylan, John Lennon, and Leonard Cohen were a valid type of poetry. Poet Robert Creeley challenged the whole concept of established form when he maintained, "There's an appropriate way of saying something inherent in the thing to be said. . . . [f]orm is never more than an extension of content."

Instead of restricting poetic diction to the particular vocabulary of well-educated British gentlemen, American poetry in the 1960's convincingly demonstrated the poetic qualities of Thoreau's "healthy speech." The work of numerous poets used slang, argot, profanity, many dialects, archaisms, neologisms, and similar coinages that had previously been excluded as somehow unpoetic. Traditional stanzas such as the quatrain opened out into long lines, word clusters and other arrangements emphasized measure instead of meter as a rhythmic determinant.

The changing political landscape of the 1960's also altered both public perceptions about poetry and the relationship of poetry to power. Robert Frost, perhaps the most celebrated poet in the nation's history, read a poem at John F. Kennedy's inaugural. Robert Lowell, another New Englander recognized as a poet of national prominence, refused an invitation to the White House from Lyndon B. Johnson as a protest against government policies in Vietnam, and by the end of the decade, Lawrence Ferlinghetti's "Tyrannus Nix," a caustic criticism of President Richard M. Nixon, was representative of many poems and songs of protest against foreign and domestic governmental actions. Similarly, the growing sense of black power and black consciousness was reflected in the work of men such as LeRoi Jones (Amiri Baraka) and Haki Madhubuti (whose Third World Press was founded to encourage the work of African American writers) and women such as Nikki Giovanni and Sonia Sanchez, whose writing also expressed the concerns and experience of women who had been effectively excluded from nearly all the groups and channels of poetic creativity. Although minority groups were slowly gaining a voice, the major poetry anthologies continued the pattern of including only a few women. The three primary subdivisions (or schools) demarked in *The New American Poetry*—the Projectivists, the New York group, and the Beats—maintained a ratio of about ten to one, effectively isolating women such as Adrienne Rich or Denise Levertov whose work in the 1960's was arguably the equal of many men who were much better known and considerably more prominent.

**Impact** The kind of poetry approved by academia in the years after World War II was overwhelmed in the 1960's by what scholar Charles Molesworth termed "a poetry of immersion" that entailed "an embrace of the raw and chaotic energies of contemporary life." Frost's death in 1963 was emblematic of the passing of an era, and although Frost's poetry continued to draw a large, enthusiastic audience, so did Ginsberg's, whose readings at universities were avidly attended by a new generation that also listened to the Beatles and the Rolling Stones. The proliferation of individual voices and styles was summarized by Beat poet Gary Snyder's assertion that his peers were not searching for new forms but seeking "a totally new approach to the very idea of form." Poets found that the comfort provided by the university was also a kind of confinement, and in the tradition of Walt Whitman, small, self-published journals and broadsides proliferated, and the popularity of readings in large arenas and small coffee shops, saloons, and city streets and on records and tapes restored the classic balance between the voice and the page.

**Additional Information** Informative discussions of the poetry of the 1960's include Charles Molesworth's *The Fierce Embrace* (1979); Charles Altieri's *Enlarging the Temple: New Directions in American Poetry During the 1960's* (1979); *The Craft of Poetry: Interviews from the New York Quarterly* (1974), edited by William Packard; and *Contemporary Poetry in America* (1974), edited by Robert Boyers.

*Leon Lewis*

**See also** Brautigan, Richard; Beat Generation; Dylan, Bob; Ferlinghetti, Lawrence; Ginsberg, Allen; Giovanni, Nikki; Literature; Sanchez, Sonia.

---

# ■ Poor People's March

**Date** April 28-May 13, 1968

*Unsuccessful attempt to broaden the Civil Rights movement into a campaign to reduce poverty. Its failure reflected the public's lack of interest in the complex problem of economic injustice and the difficulty of solving such a problem.*

**Origins and History** In 1967, after passage of federal laws designed to end racial segregation and disenfranchisement of African American voters, including the Civil Rights Act of 1964 and Voting Rights Act of 1965, the Southern Christian Leadership Conference (SCLC) decided that federal legislation was needed to address joblessness and homelessness.

**The March** To draw attention to the problems of poor Americans and push Congress to pass laws to expand employment and low-income housing opportunities, SCLC developed plans for a nonviolent march to Washington, D.C., in the spring of 1968. The march would be followed by the construction of Resurrection City, a temporary community for poor people, on federal property in Washington. SCLC hoped that these actions, labeled the Poor People's Campaign, would unify impoverished people of various ethnic and racial backgrounds. Although Martin Luther King, Jr., strongly supported the campaign, others in SCLC were critical of it and argued that Congress was unlikely to respond to the protesters. Public support for marches had faded considerably since 1965, partly because people believed that protest marches tended to provoke urban rioting.

On April 4, 1968, with the march just weeks away, King was assassinated in Memphis, Tennessee. Although his death represented a tremendous loss to SCLC and march organizers were in mourning, plans for the Poor People's Campaign continued. Ralph Abernathy, King's successor as leader of SCLC, became spokesperson for the march. On April 28, groups of poor people left their communities to travel to Washington, D.C. Although some southern participants actually walked from town to town en route to Washington, others from the North, Midwest, and West Coast traveled by bus toward the nation's capitol. Marchers made designated stops during their journeys to hold rallies and recruit additional participants.

Marchers began to arrive in Washington on May 11, and on May 13, the Poor People's March officially marked its end with Abernathy driving a construction stake into the grounds of a fifteen-acre section of West Potomac Park that became Resurrection City, where the marchers would live during the next phase of the campaign. The demonstrators erected wooden shacks and tents designed to draw the government's attention to the plight of poor people. On

*Participants in the Poor People's Campaign slowly make their way from the Washington Monument (in background) toward the Lincoln Memorial on June 19, Solidarity Day.* (AP/Wide World Photos)

June 24, police moved in with tear gas and razed the buildings. Abernathy and a group of followers held a march in protest of the destruction of Resurrection City and were arrested.

**Impact** The Poor People's March drew media attention to SCLC's decision to focus national attention on the need for federal legislation to address the problems of people living in poverty. However, neither the public nor Congress responded with support for new programs for the poor. The failure of the Poor People's Campaign reflected the loss of King's leadership and a shift in public attention from problems of racism and poverty to the war in Vietnam and the 1968 presidential campaign.

**Additional Information** Charles Fager, who observed the march, wrote about it and the Poor People's Campaign in *Uncertain Resurrection: The Poor People's Washington Campaign* (1969). "The Promised Land" in the Public Broadcasting System's *Eyes on the Prize* video series contains footage of the march and interviews with participants.

*Beth Kraig*

**See also** Abernathy, Ralph; King, Martin Luther, Jr.; Southern Christian Leadership Conference (SCLC).

## ■ Pop Art

*An art form reflecting the popular culture of the affluent postwar Western world. It employed the symbols and methods of a consumerist society to celebrate and criticize the culture created by mass production and consumption.*

In the early twentieth century, several artists used commonplace images and objects in their works. For example, in the 1920's, Marcel Duchamp displayed "ready-mades," including a snow shovel and typewriter cover, as art objects. Fernand Leger filled his canvases with ordinary, everyday objects such as a pair of trousers. American artist Stuart Davis produced paintings containing commercial images such as a pack of cigarettes or a soap box. This celebration of popular culture in the early part of the twentieth century provided a precedent for the pop art movement in the 1960's.

Pop art celebrated the popular cultural icons of the United States' affluent consumer society, often called the "ad/mass society." These icons included images from advertising, billboards, and other commercial imagery; from film, television, and popular publications; and from symbols of the 1960's lifestyle such as cars, food, and stores. Pop artists embraced the techniques of this mass production/mass consumption culture by replicating mechanization and standardization with art that was either machine-made or appeared to be machine-made. Using both repetition and uniformity, pop artists reflected the technological society of the 1960's with their commonplace images and motifs.

**Ordinary Objects and Stars** As Americans in the 1960's turned to the supermarket and shopping malls for access to the products of their affluent society, pop artists such as Andy Warhol, Roy Lichtenstein, Wayne Theibaud, Claes Oldenburg, and Tom Wesselmann, used subjects such as Campbell soup cans, Coca-Cola bottles, and other brand-name food products as repetitive or large-scale images in paintings. These depictions of the ready-made objects of an assembly-line world were direct and simple images immediately identifiable by viewers. The mechanical process of silk screening, used by several pop artists, yielded works that replicated the processes of mass production; many artists deliberately sought to create a machine-made art for the machine-made age. The serial imagery of several pop artists, who created a canvas full of repeating images, hinted strongly at a society of nearly identical mass-produced products from foods to automobiles to mass media publications, releases, and broadcasts.

Pop art also celebrated the luminaries of popular culture. Pop artists focused on a new set of heroes and heroines, including Marilyn Monroe and Elvis Presley, for the affluent 1960's. Employing repetitive, mechanically produced images based on the techniques used in films, magazines, or television, they rendered the men and women of popular culture as mass-produced objects intended for the mass marketplace. With their bright colors, sharp edges, and photograph-like images, these works seemed little different from the original popular culture product or mass media advertisements that served as a source of imagery. The distinction between popular culture and fine art was blurred by pop art.

**New Techniques and Materials** This blurring of popular and fine art was apparent in the techniques used by many pop artists. For example, Lichtenstein's signature Ben-Day dots, based on industrial printing technology, became as much a subject of his paintings and sculptures as the images he presented. Warhol used a silk-screen technique to replicate images. James Rosenquist used billboard painting styles to produce sharp-edged, large-scale images that mirrored the slick, glossy advertisements that permeated the ad/mass culture of the 1960's. For these artists, process gained equal footing with subject in their work, which celebrated and criticized Americans' affluent lifestyle.

Many pop artists also used the materials and products of the 1960's to create their works. Traditional oil paints gave way to bright, intense acrylic paints. Hand-drawn images or figures became photographs or dots of color merged into photograph-like images. Other materials, among them metal, cardboard, plaster, vinyl, and plastic, appeared in pop art. The distinction between painting and sculpture dimmed as artists such as Robert Rauschenberg and Jim Dine used actual store-bought products in their newly conceived "combine paintings," attaching these three-dimensional objects to their canvases. Everyday, ordinary products became worthy subjects of or part of paintings or sculpture.

**The Ordinary as Art** As an art movement celebrating the urban landscape and lifestyle, pop art mirrored the great urban and suburban growth of the 1960's. Artists created works that grew out of a lifestyle of shopping at the mall and supermarkets, going to films, watching television, and driving around in a car. Traditional artists celebrated classical heroes and heroines, idyllic landscapes, and historical moments, but pop artists replaced images of nature—trees, mountains, rivers, and seascapes—with urban images of skyscrapers, billboards and other commercial signs, store-front window displays, supermarkets, and pop stars. The mundane scenes of everyday urban life became noble; the hero on horseback became a Brillo soap pad box or a giant hamburger that hinted at food from a drive-in restaurant. A bowl of fruit became an item that symbolized a 1960's kitchen: a Campbell's soup can. The commonplace features of ordinary people and their lives were a rich source of subjects for pop art. Using them celebrated the richness and comfort of modern affluence.

Through larger-than-life images, subjects that were photographs and symbols of the ad/mass, and common materials, pop artists grabbed the attention of the viewing public. These artists sought to criticize as well as praise the affluent American culture that had developed. Repetition in their art touched on the banality of experiences and images in a consumerist culture. Large-scale reproductions of ordinary objects asked a viewer to question the impact of these objects on people's lives. The use of imagery from advertising, television, and film raised the issue of the real versus the created image; was the public misled by the larger-than-life persona of a Hollywood star or the value placed on celebrity status? In some ways, these pop artists were asking citizens of the 1960's whether there was any depth or lasting meaning to the symbols of affluence that surrounded them and whether the technological culture had transformed humans into machines of consumption. Their art was meant to challenge as well as to comfort its viewers.

**Impact** Just as pop art imitated life through the symbols of the 1960's, so life in the 1960's imitated pop art. The imagery of this art movement appeared on clothing, various mass-produced products, posters, and advertisements. This very process of life imitating an art that imitated life attests the popular success and impact of pop art. Its presence was felt within the art world, transformed by its use of vernacular imagery that celebrated an egalitarian and technological culture. Almost any object became a possible subject of art. Outside the art world, ordinary citizens recognized and related to the objects and lifestyles celebrated in pop art. Pop art played a key role in making Americans evaluate and appreciate the affluent culture in which they lived.

**Subsequent Events** Pop art's influence waned in the 1970's as a backlash developed against the world of comfort, mass production, and technological supremacy. Members of the counterculture debated the value of the ad/mass society and the art it produced. However, by the 1980's, some artists had returned to the imagery of pop art, and their works, along with those of many other artists, provided audiences with a spectrum of styles. Pop art images remained in the marketplace—on the canvas, in sculpture, and in mass merchandise. In the 1980's and 1990's, consumers wore clothing with ad/mass images such as trademarks, designer names, and celebrity photos. This visual and cultural linkage to the icons of a consumerist culture is, perhaps, pop art's most lasting influence.

**Additional Information** Sidra Stich's *Made in USA: An Americanization in Modern Art, the 1950's and 1960's* (1987) is a thorough treatment of pop art in the United States. Other treatments of pop art and its place in the art of the 1960's include Lucy R. Lippard's *Pop Art* (1966); Lawrence Alloway's *American Pop Art* (1974); and Nicholas Calas and Elena Calas's *Icons and Images of the Sixties* (1971).

*H. J. Eisenman*

**See also**  Art Movements; Lichtenstein, Roy; Media; Op Art; Warhol, Andy.

---

# ■ Pop Psychology

*A movement emphasizing the actualization of human potential. Popular trends in psychology during the 1960's shifted from models of neurosis and adjustment to those facilitating personal growth and a fuller life.*

During the 1950's, behaviorism dominated psychology in the United States. By focusing on observable behavioral responses to stimuli, behaviorists aimed to demonstrate that psychological life was the mechanistically determined result of cause-effect sequences to be explained from a purely external viewpoint, without recourse to concepts of consciousness or any other notions of mental life. In clinical settings, psychoanalysis provided an alternative, but it also was governed by a mechanical view of psychological life, envisioning all motivation, feeling, and action to be the outcomes of instincts and other unconscious drives. However, although behaviorism and psychoanalysis dominated the 1950's, three psychologists, Abraham Maslow, Carl Rogers, and Rollo May, were laying the groundwork for the alternative vision that would emerge in the 1960's.

**Maslow, Rogers, and May** Maslow's *Motivation and Personality* (1954) showed that people are not only reactive but also proactive and that human striving is not exhausted by coping with environmental stimuli but has "farther reaches," including an intrinsic interest in actualizing all potential. Maslow's specification of this tendency toward "self-actualization" subsequently became a cornerstone in the emergence of a pop psychology devoted to fostering such self-actualization.

Simultaneously, Rogers was developing an alternative approach to psychotherapy. Rather than manipulating the client's responses (as behaviorists would) or interpreting what they "really" meant (as psychoanalysts would), Rogers advocated a "nondirective" approach, one that would remain "client centered" in order to facilitate a deepening of the clients' own self-understanding of their experience. His first book, *Client-Centered Therapy* (1951), had a profound impact as the pace of change quickened in the 1960's.

May, trained as a psychoanalyst, contributed significantly by introducing European existentialism and phenomenology to American psychology. These philosophies provided powerful ways to attend to the experience of the person and were already used in psychoanalysis in Europe by renowned practitioners such as Ludwig Binswanger and Medard Boss. In *Man's Search for Himself* (1953) and *Existence* (1958), May introduced American readers to a new vision of the human psychological capacity for deeply meaningful experience in a time pervaded by a sense of emptiness, loneliness, and boredom.

In the 1960's, these isolated voices of protest began to gather momentum and advance a fundamental alternative to psychology's starkly behaviorist landscape. In place of the prevailing psychology of adjustment, pop psychology proposed a psychology of fulfillment. The larger sociocultural relevance of this change drew an enormous popular response from people attracted by the movement's timely rejection of narrow ways of living and its aspiration to develop the full range of human possibility.

**New Techniques** An early development was the start of "T-groups"—human-relations training for managers in business. These were much influenced by Rogers, who served as a consultant. They took the form of what later became more generally known as encounter groups and emphasized sensitivity training—procedures for learning to become more aware of one's actual experience in the moment and those of others. Beyond the corporate world, the prospect of developing fuller capacities for human relations sparked widespread interest, and growth centers were instituted, offering a wide variety of seminars, workshops, and exercises. The most well-known of these is the Esalen Institute in California.

A profusion of techniques soon emerged: transactional analysis, sensory awareness, Gestalt, body work, meditation, psychosynthesis, and even nude marathon encounter sessions. The human potential movement was born. Although its procedures were disparaged as "touchy-feely" by mainstream psychology, one of its central concepts, the idea of "getting in touch with one's feelings," had a wide appeal.

**The Value of Consciousness** The value the movement placed on immediate experience recognized the worth of a person's consciousness and so provided a potent antidote to the conformism of the previous era, which sought validation outside the individual. As long as psychology denied validity to consciousness (as behaviorism had done in the 1950's), norms could be kept at the extrinsic level. Pop psychology's highlight on consciousness made the intrinsic level a frontier for exploration, with books such as Clark Moustakas's *Creativity and Conformity* (1967), May's *Love and Will* (1969), and Maslow's *Toward a Psychology of Being* (1962, second edition 1968) and *Religion, Values, and Peak Experiences* (1964).

In place of the 1950's conformist norm of social adjustment, pop psychology promoted a deeper purpose: the development of intrinsic, creative capacities of consciousness. Such an aspiration necessarily departed from any notions of one-size-fits-all thinking. For example, Maslow's research on those who had contributed significant innovations clearly showed that their intrinsic motivation was quite distinct from the adjustment model's reliance on "deficiency needs" as the basis for human striving.

Pop psychology reached beyond the prevailing assumption of a narrow self that just wants to feed its mouth and focused attention on the larger, transcendent self by speaking to the best in humans. For instance, Rogers's client-centered therapy incorporates the insight that the power to heal is already within each person. R. D. Laing, a British psychiatrist, contributed powerfully to this vision with his insightful understanding that even psychosis could be a journey of the human psyche toward fulfillment. His scholarly books during the 1960's, especially *The Divided Self* (1960) and *The Politics of Experience* (1967) became anthems for a vast American audience. His scathing criticism of the medical model's prevailing tendency to view the psychotic patient only in organic terms revised the understanding and treatment of mental illness. Various

American psychiatrists, most notably Thomas Szasz, joined in elaborating this critique.

Pop psychology's strongest message about the larger realm of human potential stressed its nonexclusive nature: Human potential is not the preserve of the elite or the wealthy. This popularizing movement brought previously elite values to everyone, proffering psychological growth beyond mere adjustment as a universal potentiality. Rather than seeing the average person as deficient, pop psychology addressed an innate potential in all to manifest superior capacity. Furthermore, personal growth was depicted as something that could be cultivated by the individual. In sharp contrast to the behavioristic and psychoanalytic reliance on expert authorities as the necessary agents of change, pop psychology showed that higher levels of human development are attainable by the self or with the help of other laypersons, support groups, or growth centers because of the ultimate ability of all people to come to insights on their own.

**Impact** During the 1960's, pop psychology changed both mainstream psychology and society at large. Its societal impact was largely in leading people to question what they had taken for granted, to examine their own experience, and to reclaim responsibility for themselves as autonomous agents rather than mechanistic robots. These influences reverberated beyond the field of psychology, conjoining and infusing larger social movements such as the antiwar movement, the Civil Rights movement, and the women's movement.

Within academia, pop psychology also left its mark, as humanistic organizations, scholarly conferences, and journals appeared. Early on the scene were the Association for Humanistic Psychology, founded in 1962, and the *Journal of Humanistic Psychology*, begun in 1961. In 1964, this ferment culminated in a meeting at Old Saybrook, Connecticut, bringing together many of psychology's most prominent thinkers to formulate a vision for a "new psychology." These included Gardner Murphy, Gordon Allport, May, Rogers, Maslow, James Bugental, George Kelly, Moustakas, Henry Murray, Charlotte Buhler, and Jacques Barzun.

Perhaps the most significant long-term impact was the establishment of various graduate programs that taught the foundational insights of pop psychology to the next generation of psychologists. Universities that incorporated humanism into their programs include Brandeis University, under Maslow's direction; the University of Florida, under Sid Jourard's leadership; and the Merrill-Palmer Institute, with Clark Moustakas. These various programs built an institutional base to introduce to psychology the study of previously neglected dimensions of human existence such as values, subjectivity, and experience.

Perhaps the high-water mark during the 1960's was reached when Rogers and then Maslow were elected president of the American Psychological Association (APA), the major mainstream psychology organization in the country.

**Subsequent Events** Pop psychology flourished in the 1970's. In 1971, the APA established an interest group, the Division of Humanistic Psychology, for its members, providing humanism with a home and a platform. This division subsequently launched a journal, *The Humanistic Psychologist*. More graduate programs began to incorporate humanistic psychology, and psychology began to import insights from the East, particularly from Hinduism, Taoism, and Buddhism. Although humanistic organizations, journals, and schools are still thriving, the momentum that brought them into being has shifted. Pop psychology was the work of multiple leaders, had various levels, and was interpreted various ways and, therefore, had an ephemeral quality.

With the passing of the larger social ethos of the 1960's, the pop psychology movement receded from center stage. However, it left enduring legacies in a variety of areas. In academic psychology, it has become respectable to talk about consciousness. In psychotherapy, the trend toward empowering people and using self-help and support groups continued, as have the forms of professional psychotherapy this trend promulgated. Beyond psychology, the influence of the movement can be seen most clearly in the fields of education and business. Rogers's emphasis on students' intrinsic interest (*Freedom to Learn*, 1969, and *Freedom to Learn in the 1980's*, 1983) inspired a humanistic education movement that fundamentally altered the terms of the pedagogical debate. In business, Maslow applied his ideas to the newly emerging field of organizational development, with books such as *Eupsychian Management* (1965). He introduced new notions of "bottom-up" rather than "top-down" management that have become the cornerstone of subsequent management theories.

**Additional Information** Key books in the pop psychology movement during the 1960's included Rogers's *On Becoming a Person* (1961), Maslow's *Toward a Psychology of Being* (1962), Eric Berne's *Games People Play* (1964), Laing's *The Politics of Experience* (1967), Thomas Harris's *I'm OK—You're OK* (1967), J. F. T. Bugental's *Challenges of Humanistic Psychology* (1967), and May's *Love and Will* (1969). Detailed surveys of that movement that appeared soon after the 1960's include Severin Peterson's *A Catalog of the Ways People Grow* (1971) and Henryk Misiak and Virginia S. Sexton's, *Phenomenological, Existential, and Humanistic Psychologies* (1973).

*Christopher M. Aanstoos*

**See also** Medicine; Sexual Revolution; Women's Identity.

# ■ Powell, Adam Clayton, Jr.

**Born** November 29, 1908, New Haven, Connecticut
**Died** April 4, 1972, Miami, Florida

*A flamboyant and controversial political and religious leader. Powell, elected in 1944 from Harlem, was the first African American member of the House of Representatives from the East.*

Adam Clayton Powell, Jr., grew up in New York City's Harlem, where his father served as pastor of the Abyssinian Baptist Church. Powell received a bachelor's degree from Colgate University in 1930 and a master's degree from Columbia University in 1932. When Powell became his father's successor as pastor of Abyssinian Baptist Church in 1937, he was already known as a champion for racial justice.

In 1961, Powell became the first African American to chair the House Committee on Education and Labor. The flamboyant politician spearheaded more than fifty major laws related to social legislation. In 1967, he was expelled from Congress because of mismanagement of public funds. Powell was reelected to Congress in 1968. In June, 1969, the Supreme Court ruled that Powell's expulsion from Congress had been unconstitutional.

By the summer of 1969, Powell was suffering from a type of lymph malignancy. When Powell failed to win the Democratic primary election in 1970, his political career ended. His health steadily declined, and Powell died on April 4, 1972.

**Impact** Powell strongly opposed all forms of segregation and discrimination. He organized numerous successful boycotts and demonstrations, which helped to promote social reforms and break racial barriers. His expulsion from Congress was widely regarded as a setback for the Civil Rights movement.

**Additional Information** Robert E. Jakoubek wrote a very informative book entitled *Adam Clayton Powell, Jr.* (1988).

*Nila M. Bowden*

**See also** Supreme Court Decisions.

# ■ Power Failure of 1965

**Date** November 9-10, 1965

*The largest electric power failure in history. A small, local disturbance cascaded into a massive blackout that affected more than thirty million people in Canada and the northeastern United States.*

**Origins and History** A large interconnected network of power plants and high-voltage transmission lines provides electricity to the northeastern United States and Canada. On November 9, 1965, a faulty circuit breaker triggered a sequence of events that brought the whole system to a halt within ten minutes.

**The Blackout** Four hundred miles north of New York, the Sir Adam Beck power plant was supplying electricity to the Toronto area. A defective relay sensed an overload in one of five transmission lines and opened a switch to shut down that line. The power was automatically diverted to the other four lines, which then became overloaded and shut down. Immediately, the lights went out in Toronto.

All the power that had been flowing toward Canada suddenly was rerouted south into the U.S. network. This power surge caused automatic safety devices to shut down the main transmission line from Niagara Falls to New York City. Generators in the New England system automatically cut off from the network to protect them from damage. Within minutes, an eighty-thousand-square-mile area was left without electricity.

When the power went off at 5:15 P.M. during rush hour, more than six hundred thousand people were

*On November 9, 1965, the first night of the blackout, the darkened skyscrapers of New York City loom over the Hudson River, where the only light is from ships.* (AP/Wide World Photos)

stranded in subway trains. Passengers had to be evacuated along unlighted tunnels. Skyscrapers lost power, and thousands of elevators came to a stop, leaving people trapped between floors. Automobile traffic became snarled when stop lights ceased to function, and many commuters were stranded in the darkened cities of the Northeast.

Hospitals and airports discovered their vulnerability to a power failure. Babies were delivered and operations had to be completed by candlelight. Lights went out at airport runways, and air-traffic controllers lost contact with incoming planes. Major accidents fortunately were avoided by establishing telephone communication with alternate airports to divert planes from the blackout region.

It took more than four hours to restore power in Boston and thirteen hours in New York City because auxiliary power was not available. Fortunately, one small plant on Staten Island was still running. It was used to restart a second plant and to restore power to its immediate area. Other plants were brought back into service one by one. Not until the next morning was the power grid back to normal.

**Impact** The power failure created widespread anxiety that an act of sabotage, terrorism, or simple vandalism could immobilize a whole region of the country. In the aftermath of the Northeast blackout of 1965, the Federal Power Commission (FPC) convened a panel of experts to study how the reliability of electric service could be improved. Their report contained an extensive list of recommendations, many of which were adopted.

To deal with unexpected power outages, the FPC determined that airports and hospitals should install emergency generators and recommended that public buildings provide emergency lighting in stairwells and elevators. It urged that backup battery power be available for communications equipment and suggested that coal-burning power plants ready a source of auxiliary power.

The FPC recommended that a better balance be developed between the number of power plants and the network of transmission lines. In 1965, the Northeast had ample generating capacity but not enough interconnecting lines, so the power that was available could not be rerouted along alternate pathways. The commission advocated the increased use of computers for rapid on-line analysis and control and better emergency training of control-room operators.

**Additional Information** The November 19, 1965, issue of *Life* magazine contains Theodore H. White's "What Went Wrong? Something Called 345 KV," an excellent article on the power failure, as well as many photographs.

*Hans G. Graetzer*

**See also** Science and Technology.

## ■ Prayer in Schools

*Constitutional issue based on the religion clauses of the First Amendment. Cases decided by the U.S. Supreme Court banned school prayer as unconstitutional interference by the government in religious matters.*

At the beginning of the 1960's, school prayer and Bible study—voluntary and compulsory—was the norm in more than thirty states. Challenges had

arisen, however, in a number of states through the efforts of Roman Catholics and Jews who protested the overly Protestant nature of many of those programs. Consequently, in New York, the state's board of regents composed and distributed a "denominationally neutral" prayer, but its recitation was challenged by a group of Christians and Jews who believed the exercise to be a violation of religious liberty. The resulting case, known as *Engel v. Vitale* (1962), was the first of several landmark Supreme Court decisions that outlawed school prayer as a violation of the establishment clause of the First Amendment, which prohibits the founding of a state church.

In 1963, the Supreme Court repeated its ruling, again forbidding public schools from sponsoring the reading of selected passages from the Bible in *School District of Abington Township v. Schempp*, which involved students in a Pennsylvania school, and reading Bible verses and reciting prayers in *Murray v. Curlett*, a case involving the outspoken atheist Madalyn Murray (later Madalyn Murray O'Hair). Murray

*Instead of starting the day with a quote from the Bible, Pittsburgh elementary teacher Mildred Gold uses a literary quote from* The School Day Begins. (Library of Congress)

challenged the policy of the Baltimore, Maryland, School District after learning that her son was participating in school prayer exercises. Although the suit she brought was not the first nor technically the most important of the school prayer cases, it did perhaps more than any of the others to bring national attention to the school prayer debate.

Participants in the school prayer cases did not break down along clear or distinct lines. Protestants, Catholics, and Jews could be found on both sides of the issue; however, more conservative Catholics and evangelical Protestants were usually in favor of school prayer, and mainline Protestant denominations, more liberal Catholics, and most Jews were typically opposed. Ecumenical organizations such as the National Council of Churches were mostly opposed to school prayer, as were the American Civil Liberties Union and various atheist groups.

In deciding these cases, the Supreme Court went farther than ever before in linking school districts to government sponsorship. By the Court's reasoning, because children are required by state laws to attend a minimum number of years of public or private schooling, they are a "captive audience." Therefore, public schools, which are the instruments for the implementation of these attendance laws, fall under the jurisdiction of the establishment clause. The Court considered school prayer to be coercive, even if defined as voluntary, because children had no real choice but to be present where prayer was being offered. The Court also declared that school prayer, in all its forms, was being carried out solely for the purpose of "advancing religion" rather than for any secular purpose and was thus an unconstitutional intrusion of government into the sphere of religion.

**Impact**  The school prayer cases had three major impacts. First, in deciding the cases, the Supreme Court increased individual and minority rights, requiring maximum protection from unwarranted government interference. Second, it redefined the relationship of the two religion clauses of the First Amendment, making the establishment clause predominate over the free exercise clause for perhaps the first time in U.S. history. Historically, the establishment clause had been interpreted as preventing the government from preferring one particular religion over another, but after these rulings, it was also seen as preventing the government from preferring religion over nonreligion, even if the majority of

citizens in any particular location supported public religious exercises. Third, the school prayer cases ignited a firestorm of reaction among conservative Americans who now demanded a constitutional amendment to allow prayer in schools. Although no such amendment has ever passed, one has been proposed nearly every year since the original cases were decided.

**Subsequent Events**  After the Supreme Court's rulings on school prayer, some states have attempted to circumvent the Court's ban by enacting "moment of silence" laws, based on the presumption that silence is not necessarily religious. All such laws have been overruled by the Court, based primarily on the *Engel v. Vitale* decision. The Court has also ruled against high school baccalaureate services, invocations at graduation ceremonies, and religious displays at schools and other public buildings. The school prayer issue was also one of the reasons for the passage, in 1993, of the Religious Freedom Restoration Act, which was designed to return the understanding and interpretation of the First Amendment religion clauses to their earlier status.

**Additional Information**  The importance of the school prayer issue is discussed in Robert Alley's *School Prayer: The Court, the Congress, and the First Amendment* (1994), and the *Engel v. Vitale* case is covered in *Engel vs. Vitale: Separation of Church and State* (1994), by Carol Hass. An interesting personal perspective on the *Murray v. Curlett* case can be found in William Murray's *Let Us Pray* (1995).

*Robert C. Davis*

**See also**  *Engel v. Vitale*; O'Hair, Madalyn Murray; Religion and Spirituality; Supreme Court Decisions.

---

## ■ Presidential Election of 1960

*One of the closest presidential elections in U.S. history. It was especially significant because of the youth and Catholicism of the winning Democratic candidate, John F. Kennedy, and his very narrow margin of victory in popular votes.*

Dwight D. Eisenhower, a Republican, won the 1952 and 1956 presidential elections by wide margins. In order for the Democratic Party to win the presidential election of 1960, it needed to nominate presidential and vice presidential candidates who could attract many of the independents and Democrats

## Presidential Elections of 1960, 1964, 1968

| | Presidential Candidates | Party | Popular Vote (1,000) | Popular Vote % | Electoral Votes | Voter Turnout[1] |
|---|---|---|---|---|---|---|
| 1960 | John F. Kennedy | Democratic | 34,227 | 49.7 | 303 | 62.8 |
| | Richard M. Nixon | Republican | 34,108 | 49.5 | 219 | |
| 1964 | Lyndon B. Johnson | Democratic | 43,130 | 61.1 | 486 | 61.9 |
| | Barry Goldwater | Republican | 27,178 | 38.5 | 52 | |
| 1968 | Richard M. Nixon | Republican | 31,785 | 43.4 | 301 | 60.9 |
| | Hubert Humphrey | Democratic | 31,275 | 42.7 | 191 | |
| | George Wallace | American Independent | 9,906 | 13.5 | 46 | |

[1]Votes cast for president as a percentage of the all U.S. residents of voting age, including noncitizens.

*Source:* U.S. Bureau of the Census. *Statistical Abstract of the United States: 1996* (116th edition). Washington, D.C.: Government Printing Office, 1996.

who had voted for Eisenhower, especially Catholics and southern whites. Encouraged by his landslide reelection to the Senate in 1958, Democratic Senator John F. Kennedy of Massachusetts continued to develop a campaign organization and a national network of supporters for his presidential candidacy. By 1960, Kennedy was the front-runner for his party's presidential nomination, although he still had to compete with Democratic Senators Hubert Humphrey of Minnesota, Wayne Morse of Oregon, Stuart Symington of Missouri, and Lyndon B. Johnson of Texas. Kennedy's decisive victories in the West Virginia and Wisconsin primaries made his receipt of the presidential nomination more likely. Meanwhile, Vice President Richard M. Nixon faced no significant opposition for the Republican presidential nomination, especially after Governor Nelson A. Rockefeller of New York announced that he would not run for president.

**The 1960's** After being nominated for president at the Democratic National Convention, Kennedy chose Johnson as his vice presidential candidate in order to attract the votes of southern whites and unite his party. Kennedy's campaign theme, called the New Frontier, stressed that the United States must improve its economy and domestic and foreign policies to compete better against the Soviet Union in the Cold War. Nixon stressed his experience as

vice president and his identification with the popular Eisenhower. Public opinion polls often showed that Kennedy and Nixon were roughly even in their voter appeal until the first of four nationally televised debates between them was held. To many viewers, Kennedy appeared confident and articulate while Nixon seemed uneasy and uncertain at times. Kennedy won the election by receiving 303 electoral votes and a popular vote margin of approximately 120,000 votes over Nixon.

**Impact** The narrowness of Kennedy's victory margin, the Republican gain of twenty seats in the House of Representatives, and Kennedy's focus on foreign policy crises made him initially cautious and selective about introducing liberal, controversial legislation, especially his civil rights bill.

**Subsequent Events** President Kennedy was assassinated in Texas in 1963 during a trip to raise campaign funds for the 1964 election. After becoming president and during the 1964 presidential campaign, Johnson emphasized continuity with Kennedy's ideas and policies.

**Additional Information** The most thorough and best-known book about the 1960 election is *The Making of the President: 1960* (1961), by Theodore White.

*Sean J. Savage*

**See also** Humphrey, Hubert; Johnson, Lyndon B.; Kennedy, John F.; Kennedy-Nixon Debates; Nixon, Richard M.; Rockefeller, Nelson A.

# ■ Presidential Election of 1964

*The election that gave Democratic candidate Lyndon B. Johnson the nickname of "Landslide Lyndon." It was especially important because of the wide margin of Johnson's victory and the deep divisions within the Republican Party at that time.*

Some conservative activists in the Republican Party blamed Richard M. Nixon's narrow loss to John F. Kennedy in the 1960 presidential elections on his moderate rhetoric and platform. In 1964, these Republicans wanted a presidential candidate who was clearly more conservative than Presidents Kennedy and Lyndon B. Johnson and who opposed civil rights laws and advocated a more aggressive foreign policy toward communism, much less federal spending, states' rights, and fewer regulations on the economy. Referring to his presidential candidacy as "choice, not an echo," Senator Barry Goldwater of Arizona became the favorite candidate of conservative Republicans and the front-runner for the Republican presidential nomination. President Lyndon B. Johnson had no significant opposition for the Democratic nomination.

Conservative organizations such as the John Birch Society and Young Americans for Freedom and conservative journals such as the *National Review* grew in prominence during the 1960's. The growth of the conservative movement was especially prominent in the South and West. More and more conservative Americans found the racial unrest, liberal Democratic policies and Supreme Court decisions, the youth culture, rising crime rates, and the anti-Vietnam War movement to be threats to traditional morality, patriotism, states' rights, and capitalism. The conservative activists' success in gaining control of the Republican Party in 1964 was evident in Goldwater's success in receiving the Republican nomination and the defeat of his chief rival, Governor Nelson A. Rockefeller of New York, who represented the policy positions of many moderate and liberal Republicans.

Goldwater opposed the Civil Rights Act of 1964 and such popular federal programs as Social Security and the Tennessee Valley Authority. He also implied a greater willingness to use nuclear weapons. These controversial positions sharply distinguished Goldwater from President Johnson, the Democratic platform, and many moderate and liberal Republican and independent voters. Consequently, the Democratic campaign portrayed Goldwater as a dangerous extremist and Johnson as an experienced, responsible, unifying leader.

Johnson received 486 electoral votes, carried forty-four states, and received 61 percent of the popular vote.

**Impact** President Johnson perceived these election results to be a public mandate for his Great Society legislation. Congress soon passed bills for such major new programs as Medicare and Head Start. For the next few years, most Democrats assumed that Johnson would run for reelection in 1968. The Republicans realized that they needed a more moderate candidate in order to win the presidential election of 1968.

**Subsequent Events** Shortly after the presidential election of 1964, President Johnson substantially increased U.S. military involvement in the Vietnam War. With the Vietnam War arousing greater public and congressional opposition, Johnson announced on March 31, 1968, that he would not seek reelection.

**Additional Information** A comprehensive study of the 1964 election is *The Making of the President: 1964* (1965), by Theodore White.

*Sean J. Savage*

**See also** Conservatism in Politics; Goldwater, Barry; Great Society Programs; Johnson, Lyndon B.; Liberalism in Politics; Rockefeller, Nelson A.

# ■ Presidential Election of 1968

*Both a pivotal and a tragic presidential campaign and election. In a year marred by two political assassinations, this election changed the direction of both the foreign and domestic policy of the United States.*

Between 1945 and 1968, the United States witnessed four contrasting styles of presidential leadership. The death of President Franklin D. Roosevelt in April, 1945, initiated the confrontational leadership of Harry S Truman. This was replaced in 1953 by the restrained, fatherly style of Dwight D. Eisenhower. In 1961, John F. Kennedy, epitomizing the liberalism of the eastern establishment, ushered in aggressive, future-oriented leadership. His assassination in November, 1963, thrust Lyndon B. Johnson, with his chief legislator style, into the leadership of the nation.

The 1964 election gave President Johnson the mandate he needed to pursue his own agenda, including the Civil Rights Act of 1964 and the escalation of the Vietnam War. Opposition to his Vietnam policy, especially from within the Democratic Party, caused great distress for President Johnson, but it was still assumed that he would run for reelection in 1968. However, as the election drew nearer and as antiwar demonstrations grew more numerous and more violent, that assumption evaporated. On March 31, 1968, the president shocked the nation by announcing that he would neither seek nor accept his party's nomination for another term in the White House.

The wave of political assassinations that began in 1963 with the killing of President Kennedy soon marred the 1968 campaign. On April 4, civil rights leader Martin Luther King, Jr., was killed in Memphis, Tennessee. James Earl Ray confessed and was convicted of that murder. Shortly after midnight on June 5, the winner of that day's California primary, Democrat Robert F. Kennedy, was assassinated by a Jordanian immigrant named Sirhan Sirhan, apparently because of Kennedy's support of Israel.

The Democratic National Convention in Chicago that summer, marred by violent antiwar demonstrations, nominated Vice President Hubert Humphrey for president. The Republican National Convention chose former vice president Richard M. Nixon, who had narrowly lost to John F. Kennedy in 1960. Alabama governor George Wallace organized his new American Independent Party to protest civil rights policy and to promote a military victory in Vietnam. The November election gave Nixon the victory with 301 electoral votes; compared with 191 for Humphrey and 46 for Wallace.

**Impact** In 1968, opposition to President Johnson's Vietnam policy cost the Democrats the White House that they had won by a landslide in 1964. President Nixon, who had previously supported the war policy, realized that a military victory was impossible. He therefore began a gradual disengagement and eventual withdrawal of U.S. forces; which was completed in 1973.

**Subsequent Events** As President Nixon prepared for reelection in 1972, the Watergate break-in of the Democratic Party headquarters began one of the most traumatic periods of U.S. history. This included the unrelated forced resignation of Vice President Spiro Agnew in 1973 and climaxed with the resignation of the president in August, 1974.

**Additional Information** A detailed analysis of the political climate and the political figures of the 1960's can be found in *The Growth of the American Republic*, volume two (1980), by Samuel Eliot Morison, Henry Steele Commager, and William Edward Leuchtenburg.

*Glenn L. Swygart*

**See also** Agnew, Spiro; Democratic National Convention of 1968; Humphrey, Hubert; Johnson, Lyndon B.; Nixon, Richard M.; Wallace, George.

---

# ■ Presley, Elvis

**Born** January 8, 1935, Tupelo, Mississippi
**Died** August 16, 1977, Memphis, Tennessee

*One of the greatest American entertainers of the twentieth century. Presley established the supremacy of rock and roll in pop music in the United States.*

**Early Life** Elvis Aron Presley's childhood in Tupelo, Mississippi, was overshadowed by poverty. When he was thirteen, he and his parents moved to Memphis, Tennessee. In 1953, Presley, singing and playing his guitar, performed impressively on his high school stage. He went on to place second at a talent show in Meridian, Mississippi, and then to cut his first record. His flashy clothing, sideburns-and-ducktail hairstyle, and country rock and blues singing punctuated by bump-and-grind body movements fashioned the accoutrements of a youth rebellion. His increasingly marketable recordings for Sun Records in 1954 led to a three-year contract with RCA Victor in 1955. By April, 1956, his recording of "Heartbreak Hotel" became a number-one hit. At the age of twenty-one, Presley had reached the top and had become a symbol of 1950's-style youthful rebellion.

**The 1960's** Concluding his army service in Germany early in 1960, Presley sustained his popularity with three gold-record albums and six gold singles. He began to distance himself from his early rebellious, sensual style and delivery and move closer to a conservative, mainstream easy-listening style. Frank Sinatra, overcoming or overlooking his initial disgust with Presley's rebel rock—he had referred to rock-and-roll artists as cretinous goons—played host to Presley on a television special on May 12, 1960. From 1960 through 1968, Presley turned away from live concerts and instead released a series of singles and albums, chiefly culled from his lightweight but popular film musicals. "Can't Help Falling in Love," from the 1961 film *Blue Hawaii,* was a major success and became his signature close at performances in later years. On December 3, 1968, he appeared in a very successful television special, dressed in the black leather of motorcycle gangs with his long sideburns restored. He reasserted his musical direction with "Guitar Man" and exhibited some of his early rebellious sensuality.

Songs such as "In the Ghetto" and "Clean Up Your Own Back Yard," released in 1969 following three 1968 films—*Stay Away, Joe*; *Flaming Star*; and *Charro!*—contain a message of social protest in deference to minority groups, but they did not effectively champion American Indians or the underprivileged. Presley's real influence on the 1960's was his propagation of an existentialistic authenticity: Be what you are and do what you want to do. He loved hymns, law and order, and Cadillacs, but it was the emotional freedom of his love, not the objects of his love, that reflected the 1960's.

**Later Life** During the 1970's, Presley changed his costume from black to white and his major provenance from the studio to the stage: He became the undisputed king of rock and roll. His satellite television special from Hawaii on January 14, 1973, during which Presley wore the white costume that would later be duplicated by numerous impersonators, was seen by an estimated one billion viewers. In his final years, Presley suffered from obesity and became the subject of tabloid headlines. His death at forty-two, the passing of a cultural hero, was marred by reports of prescription drug abuse.

**Impact** As an uninhibited and individualistic performer, Presley symbolized 1950's youthful rebellion. Presley's superbly controlled intimations of licentiousness and cool indifference to convention were the keynotes to modern culture's swing to

*Elvis Presley, idol of 1950's rebellious youth, performs at the International Hotel in Las Vegas in 1969.* (Fotos International/Archive Photos)

pervasive permissiveness. Checked by Colonel Tom Parker's entrepreneurship, however, Presley settled into an accommodation of the prevalent cultural standards. By the latter half of the 1960's, Presley was part of mainstream popular music; rebellious teenagers had turned first toward the protest songs of Bob Dylan, then the group sounds of the Beatles and the Rolling Stones, and finally the psychedelic rock of the Jefferson Airplane, Grateful Dead, and Jimi Hendrix.

Presley gained posthumous canonization—in books, memorabilia, an Elvis-impersonation entertainment industry, scores of reissued recordings, and virtual worship—as the liberator of the young and the young at heart.

**Subsequent Events** The U.S. Postal Service issued a very popular Presley commemorative stamp in

1993. Presley's Memphis home, Graceland, became the site of constant pilgrimage.

**Additional Information** Lee Cotten's *All Shook Up: Elvis Day by Day, 1954-1977* (1985), includes an informative personal and musical chronology.

*Roy Arthur Swanson*

**See also** Film; Music.

## ■ Price, Leontyne

**Born** February 10, 1927, Laurel, Mississippi

*A highly renowned African American opera singer. Price's extraordinary voice enabled her to become the first African American international opera superstar.*

Leontyne Price (born Mary Violet Leontine Price) had an unforgettable musical experience at age nine when her mother took her to Jackson, Mississippi, to attend a recital by African American contralto Marian Anderson, who became Price's idol. She played piano and sang regularly as a young girl. In 1948, Price received a bachelor of arts degree from Central State College in Ohio. From 1949 to 1952, she pursued graduate studies at the Juilliard School of Music in New York. Subsequently, she sang in several operas, including the role of Bess in George Gershwin's *Porgy and Bess* (1955) with costar William Warfield, whom she married but later divorced.

By 1960, Price had performed with many leading opera companies in the United States and Europe. In 1961, she first appeared at the Metropolitan Opera in New York, where she sang the part of Leonora in Giuseppe Verdi's *Il Trovatore* and received a standing ovation lasting forty-two minutes. From 1961 to 1969, Price made 118 Metropolitan performances. During the 1960's, she continued to expand her repertoire. In 1966, she performed in Samuel Barber's *Antony and Cleopatra* at the opening of the new Metropolitan Opera House.

After 1969, Price reduced the number of her Metropolitan appearances. On September 3, 1985, she ended her operatic career after performing Aida's role in Verdi's *Aida* at the Metropolitan.

**Impact** Price opened the doors for other African American opera singers when in February, 1955, she performed on national television the role of Floria Tosca in the NBC Opera Company production of Giacoma Puccini's *Tosca*.

**Additional Information** Sylvia B. Williams's *Leontyne Price: Opera Superstar* (1984) is a heavily illustrated biography of the operatic superstar.

*Nila M. Bowden*

**See also** Music.

## ■ Prosperity and Poverty

*Poverty amid affluence, leading to social and economic stratification. In the 1960's, the federal government attempted to achieve full employment and economic equity.*

In the 1930's and 1940's, the federal government made a major effort to address the social concerns of the electorate. President Franklin D. Roosevelt's New Deal, particularly the Social Security Act of 1935, gave the government greater responsibilities. The post-World War II period was a time of relative prosperity marked by large increases in consumer demand and in the standard of living. By the 1960's, it was obvious that this affluence failed to reach many demographic groups and geographic regions. The divisiveness of such inequality reached a critical threshold.

**Family Incomes** In 1960, the unemployment rate was 5.5 percent, low by historical standards, but by 1969, it had fallen to the unprecedented level of 3.5 percent. Real gross domestic product (in 1992 dollars) increased from $2.3 trillion in 1960 to $3.4 trillion in 1969. In both 1960 and 1969, the federal budget showed a surplus, and prices increased at an annual rate of just over than 2 percent. Real hourly earnings increased from $6.79 in 1960 to $7.98 in 1969. These macroeconomic indices hid what Michael Harrington termed "the other America" in his 1963 book, which employed the phrase as its title. In 1960, 22.2 percent of the population lived below the poverty level. In 1966, 12.2 percent of whites and 41.8 percent of blacks were below the poverty level. More than a third of people over age sixty-five, 20.6 percent of white children under age eighteen, and 66.7 percent of black children under age eighteen fell into this group. The problems were particularly severe in urban ghettos and rural areas such as Appalachia.

Some social researchers, including Robert Lampman, argued that a prosperous economy would benefit everyone and lessen the need for special targeted programs. However, many of the least well-off individuals lacked education, making

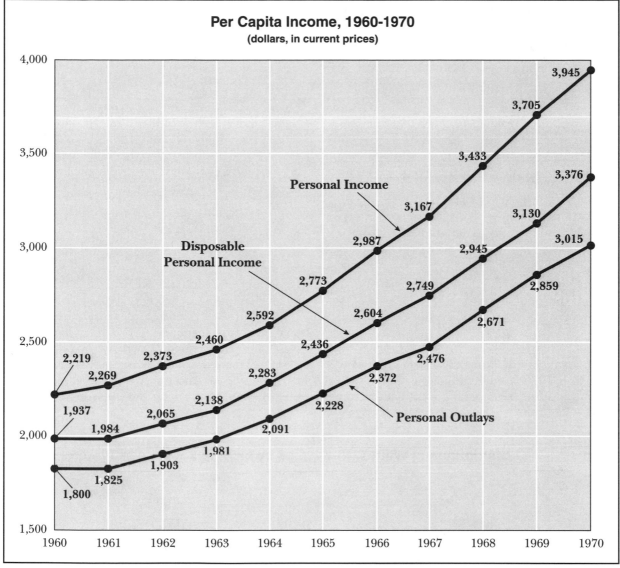

**Per Capita Income, 1960-1970**
(dollars, in current prices)

*Source:* Kurian, George, *Datapedia of the United States, 1790-2000, America Year by Year.* Lanham, Maryland: Bernam Press, 1994.

their upward mobility unlikely. In 1964, 2.7 percent of whites had less than five years of education, but 11.6 percent of nonwhites had less than an elementary education. Median years of school completed for whites was 12.2, but for other races it was 10.1. Only 19.1 percent of nonwhite men had a high school education, compared with 32.4 percent of white men. Among women, 43 percent of those who were white had completed high school compared with 26.6 percent of those who were of other races.

Although total unemployment was low, unemployment was concentrated in certain segments of the population. Therefore, the duration of unemployment increased, as shown by the rise in the numbers of individuals without a job for more than twenty-seven weeks. The unemployment compensation system, intended to address short-term cyclical unemployment, was inappropriate for these individuals, described as "hard core" unemployed. In 1961, the average duration of unemployment in weeks was 15.6; the highest it had been since 1948. In 1964, the aggregate unemployment rate was 5.2 percent; however, it was 4.6 percent for whites and 9.6 percent for blacks. Among young men age sixteen to nineteen, the unemployment rate was 14.7 percent for whites and 24.3 percent for blacks. For young women age sixteen to nineteen, the unemployment rate was 14.9 percent for whites and 31.6 percent for blacks.

Even by the end of the 1960's, in the five southern states of Alabama, Georgia, Mississippi, North Carolina, and South Carolina, 25.5 percent of the households were below the poverty line, 44.7 of those more than twenty-five years old had less than one year of high school, and the median years of school completed was 9.6.

Among the minority groups, Hispanics were especially disadvantaged. At the start of the 1960's, 34.1 percent of families were below the poverty line. Among households headed by a woman, 33.9 percent of Anglo Americans and 54.8 percent of Hispanics lived in poverty. Finally, it is estimated that in 1962, 47 percent of families headed by a person more than sixty-five years old were below the poverty level.

**Government Efforts** From the election of John F. Kennedy in 1960 through the administration of Lyndon B. Johnson, the federal government assumed the responsibility of waging a War on Poverty in the United States. The war was waged on a number of fronts. The passage of the Equal Pay Act of 1963, Title VII of the Civil Rights Act of 1964, and President Kennedy's 1961 executive order on affirmative action set the stage for an attempt to integrate all Americans in the economic mainstream. The civil rights leader Martin Luther King, Jr., pressed the cause of the downtrodden until his assassination in 1968. The constitutional rights of individuals had been established in the early 1960's, and leaders had come forward to articulate the rights of the oppressed.

Between 1960 and 1970, social welfare expenditures increased from $14.3 billion to $45.2 billion, a real increase of 143 percent. During the Johnson administration, real expenditures on education, manpower, and social services increased 38 percent, and expenditures on health increased 57.2 percent. During the same period, real expenditures on low-income groups increased 35.3 percent and in-kind expenditures increased 71 percent. Among the earliest programs were the Manpower Development and Training Act and the Area Redevelopment Act that targeted individuals and areas most in need.

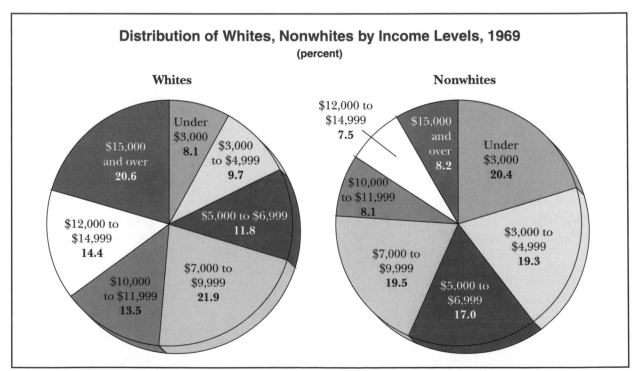

*Source:* U.S. Bureau of the Census. *Historical Statistics of the United States, Colonial Times to 1970.* New York: Basic Books, 1976.

These were followed by Community Action Programs, Job Corps, Head Start, Upward Bound, legal aid to the poor, neighborhood health centers, food stamps, and many other programs, most of which were revised and amended. The Democratic congressional landslide in 1964 enabled the passage of guaranteed health insurance—Medicare for the elderly and Medicaid for the poor. For a time, at least, the focus of the national agenda was on the effect of programs on the poor.

After Richard M. Nixon was elected president in 1968, he tried to rein in the job programs, particularly those that provided public service employment, but subsequent increases in unemployment made cuts more difficult. Nixon also extended the food stamp program. In 1969, he recommended funding be increased from $340 million to $610 million. He also supported increases in nutritional programs for children and the elderly.

Because of the nation's general prosperity and the graduated tax system, it was possible to generate tax revenues to fund these social welfare programs. The programs came to be thought of as "entitlements," implying an obligation on the part of more prosperous individuals to provide the financing through their taxes. It was believed that once the cycle of poverty was broken, the need for such expenditures would decline. The idea that welfare leads to dependency, creates incentives to shirk work or be irresponsible, and encourages illegitimacy and teenage pregnancies, if articulated, went unheard in the 1960's.

**Impact** In 1959, 20.8 percent of the population was living below the poverty level; by 1969, the percentage had fallen to 10.4. The percentage of blacks living below the poverty level fell from 56.2 in 1959 to 32.2 in 1969. Children under age eighteen living in poverty fell from 26.9 percent in 1959 to 13.8 percent in 1969. For black children under age eighteen, the percentage fell from 66.7 to 39.6. Median years of school completed rose from 10.6 years in 1960 to 12.1 in 1970. For blacks, the median years of school completed increased from 8.0 to 9.8.

Most people would agree that the programs initiated in the 1960's helped provide greater opportunities for the least well-off. However, these welfare programs, the increasing expenditures for the war in Vietnam, and a decline in aggregate economic activity ultimately led to a period of rising prices, interest rates, and unemployment. The prosperity of Johnson's Great Society gave way to the "stagflation" of the 1970's. In the 1980's and 1990's some of the progress toward greater equality in income and earnings reversed as technological advances increasingly placed a premium on highly skilled and specialized workers. Unlike in the 1960's, however, fewer of the differences in earnings arise because of a lack of opportunity due to race, gender, or status.

**Additional Information** Few books were as instrumental in creating public awareness of the poverty amid 1960's affluence as Michael Harrington's *The Other America* (1963). *The Distributional Impacts of Public Policies* (1988), edited by Sheldon H. Danziger and Kent E. Portney, describes the evolution of the federal programs designed to achieve greater equality. *The Battle Against Unemployment and Inflation*, edited by Martin N. Baily and Arthur M. Okun, originally published in 1965 and updated in 1972 and 1982, is helpful in understanding the economic paradigm that lay beneath the surface. The alternative view of the role of government is admirably stated in *Capitalism and Freedom* (1962) by Milton Friedman.

*John F. O'Connell*

**See also** Business and the Economy; Great Society Programs; Johnson, Lyndon B.; Kennedy, John F.; Unemployment; War on Poverty; Welfare State.

## ■ Protest Songs

*Songs that attack prevailing political and social attitudes and conditions. Protest songs provided a soundtrack for the civil rights and antiwar struggles of the 1960's and helped establish an atmosphere in which it was acceptable to question and criticize the status quo.*

Protest songs—also known as topical songs—have long been a part of the musical heritage of the United States. Songs accompanied the nation's rebellion against Britain, agitated for the abolition of slavery, and urged the enfranchisement of women. In the 1940's, protest songs, often set to traditional folk tunes, became one vehicle through which the Left advanced the interests of the working class. Prominent in that effort were Woody Guthrie and Pete Seeger, who performed together as part of the Almanac Singers, a group dedicated to the creation of a singing labor movement. In 1950, Seeger helped start *Sing Out!* magazine, a periodical devoted to the promulgation of "people's music," which it defined as all music that served the "common cause of humanity." Later in the 1950's, blacklists, fueled by anticommunist hysteria, deprived Seeger and his colleagues of meaningful avenues of communication. It appeared, for a time, that the forces of the status quo had silenced all songs of social change.

**Topical Songs Emerge**  In the early 1960's, the growing commercial popularity of folk music, along with a relaxation of the more conservative mores of the previous decade, provided an opportunity for Seeger and other folk performers interested in political song to return to public prominence. Believing that many people were writing topical songs, Seeger decided that they needed an outlet. He lent advice and some funds to a new publication, *Broadside*, founded by two of his old friends, Agnes "Sis" Cunningham and her husband, Gordon Friesen. *Broadside*, subtitled "a handful of songs about our times," debuted in February, 1962. The premier

*Folksinger and songwriter Pete Seeger combined music with social activism throughout the 1960's.* (AP/Wide World Photos)

issue included the words to "Talkin' John Birch," by the still unknown Bob Dylan, who would soon become a legend through his socially conscious song lyrics. It was the first publication of a Dylan song, but by the end of 1963, Dylan had published twenty-one songs in the pages of the new periodical.

When the first issue of *Broadside* appeared, the nation as a whole was unaware of any burgeoning topical song movement. However, in the spring of 1962, the Kingston Trio had a minor hit record with the Seeger composition "Where Have All the Flowers Gone?" It was the first time in roughly a decade that Seeger received significant radio play, albeit as a composer. Though the song's political message—war is terrible—was benign, it is unlikely that radio would have played it only a few years earlier, when Seeger was in open conflict with the House Committee on Un-American Activities, a Congressional investigating committee. In the fall of 1962, folksingers Peter, Paul and Mary had a hit with "If I Had a Hammer," a song composed by Seeger and his activist colleague, Lee Hays. Though written at least a dozen years earlier, the song's cry for "justice," "freedom," and "love between my brothers and my sisters" was plainly applicable to the civil rights battle then gripping the nation.

**Activism Gains a Voice**  It was through the Civil Rights movement that the nation as a whole began to link songs with social activism. On August 20, 1962, *The New York Times* ran a front-page story entitled "Songs a Weapon in Rights Battle," which described how African American folk music had become a "vital force" in the ongoing battle for integration. The songs, the article stated, reflected the activist attitude of a younger generation who were no longer thinking "about pie in the sky, in the bye and bye, but a piece of that pie now." Peter, Paul and Mary's next big hit, the Dylan composition "Blowin' in the Wind," expressed this mood of discontent unequivocally. The song, which dominated the airwaves in the summer of 1963, asked bluntly, "How many years can some people exist before they're allowed to be free?" In the world of popular music, such lyrics were revolutionary. In the song's wake, the still largely unknown Dylan became a star and went on to compose a body of stirring protest songs that attacked injustice, war, and conformity and that signaled the vocal emergence of a new culture founded on youthful idealism.

Dylan was not the only young composer of the 1960's whose lyrics challenged the status quo. In July, 1963, *Time* magazine noted that performers had not sung about current events "in such numbers or with such intensity" since the Civil War. That same month, *Look* magazine reported that a "whole generation of young Americans" was singing, listening to, and buying records of protest songs. In the realm of folk music, Phil Ochs, Tom Paxton, and Woody Guthrie's son, Arlo Guthrie, achieved fame with songs that commented upon the racial and antiwar struggles of the decade. Other genres of popular music also contributed to the decade's canon of protest material. Some of the better known songs in this vein were Barry McGuire's "Eve of Destruction," which decried the seemingly omnipresent threat of nuclear annihilation; James Brown's "Say It Loud, I'm Black and I'm Proud," which reflected the more militant attitude of the late 1960's Black Power movement; and "Volunteers," in which the rock band Jefferson Airplane urged revolution and declared that U.S. leaders had turned the nation's youth into "outlaws."

**Impact** One can never be certain if the political songs of the 1960's, by themselves, actually motivated large numbers of people to take to the streets in protest. The songs did, however, unify and energize those who were politically active. More important, the songs demanded that people think, and their popularity contributed to the atmosphere of open commentary, questioning, and criticism that characterized the 1960's. After 1963, the pop music of the decade was never the same. Increasingly, pop songs ceased being merely the commercial product of professional songwriters as listeners demanded that performers write their own songs and express their own viewpoints, both politically and personally.

**Additional Information** David Pichaske's *A Generation in Motion: Popular Music and Culture in the Sixties* (1989) examines the social and political impact of music throughout the decade. Ray Pratt's *Rhythm and Resistance: The Political Uses of American Popular Music* (1994) and Reebee Garofalo's anthology, *Rockin' the Boat: Mass Music and Mass Movements* (1992), provide broader surveys of the political uses of popular song, with discussion of the 1960's and later decades.

*Michael F. Scully*

**See also** Dylan, Bob; Folk Music; Newport Folk Festivals; Youth Culture and the Generation Gap.

## ■ *Pueblo* Incident

**Date** January 23, 1968

*Capture of the USS* Pueblo *by North Korean naval personnel. Internment and torture of the ship's crew provoked a diplomatic crisis and severe criticism of the U.S. Navy.*

**Origins and History** The USS *Pueblo*, a U.S. Navy freighter equipped with electronic intelligence equipment, was on an information-gathering mission off the coast of North Korea when it was captured.

**The Incident** The USS *Pueblo*, under the command of Lieutenant Commander Lloyd Bucher, was intercepted by North Korean naval forces while traveling off the North Korean coast. When confronted and harassed by the North Koreans, Bucher reacted by asserting the *Pueblo*'s rights as a vessel in international waters. When the Koreans became more aggressive, he called for help and began destroying classified materials. After one man was killed and several wounded by shelling, he surrendered. The ship was forcibly boarded and towed to Wonsan January 21-23, 1968. Bucher and eighty-one crew members were imprisoned, tortured, and forced to broadcast espionage confessions. Lengthy negotiations ensued, with the United States and North Korea periodically holding talks at Panmunjom. After the United States apologized for spying, an apology that it repudiated in advance, the *Pueblo* crew members were released December 23, 1968; however, North Korea kept the ship. A Court of Inquiry, convened January 20, 1969, recommended Bucher's court-martial. The commander of the Pacific Fleet reduced the sentence to a letter of reprimand. The Secretary of the Navy, however, dropped all charges.

**Impact** South Korea was displeased that it was not included in President Lyndon B. Johnson's early negotiations with North Korea and felt that the United States was not showing enough concern for South Korea's welfare. The United States, which viewed the seizure of the *Pueblo* as a sign of North Korea's continuing aggression, eventually increased its support of South Korea, granting an additional $100 million in military aid and moving additional aircraft to that nation. In the United States, a debate ensued over whether the *Pueblo* had been in international waters as the U.S. government claimed or within North Korean territorial waters, engaging in

*USS* Pueblo *crew members are taken into captivity after the intelligence-gathering ship was captured by North Koreans in 1968.* (AP/Wide World Photos)

espionage. The ship's capture was an election year embarrassment to Johnson's administration. Many Americans asserted that the *Pueblo* should have resisted capture, fighting until it sunk, and that the crew and captain violated their duty in confessing to espionage. Other Americans criticized the military for inadequately preparing and supporting the *Pueblo* and for not forcibly retaliating after the seizure.

**Additional Information**  Bucher presents his story in *Bucher: My Story* (1970). Admiral Daniel Gallery's *The Pueblo Incident* (1970) criticizes the *Pueblo*'s crew, the authorities, and the general public.

*Ralph L. Langenheim, Jr.*

**See also**  *Liberty* Incident.

## ■ Pulsating Radio Waves

*Rapidly repeating radio signals from space emitted by objects called pulsars. At first, these highly regular pulses were thought possibly to be signals from aliens but were eventually identified as pulsating radio waves produced by rapidly rotating neutron stars.*

Radio astronomy was pioneered in the United States in the 1930's. After the development of radar in World War II, the field grew rapidly. During the 1960's at Cambridge University, Antony Hewish and his students built a large radio telescope array containing 2,048 radio antennas covering nearly five acres of land to study compact radio sources. Unexpected clocklike radio pulses from space were first recorded on November 28, 1967, by graduate student Jocelyn Bell. At first, the Cambridge group could not explain the strange periodic signals from space because the pulses did not originate from any known astronomical object, so they delayed publication of their discovery. When they realized that the short duration of the pulses (on the order of 20 milliseconds) implied that the source could not be larger than Earth (according to arguments based on the travel time of light), they briefly entertained the possibility that the signals might be from an extraterrestrial civilization and whimsically designated them LGM (Little Green Men) signals. However, they could not discern any recognizable code in the signals, and when they detected three more similar pulsating sources, they concluded that the pulses must be natural phenomena.

Hewish, Bell, John Pilkington, Paul Scott, and Robin Collins announced the discovery of the first pulsar (PSR 1919+21, coordinate designation) in an article in the February 24, 1968, issue of the journal *Nature*. Bell had analyzed some four hundred feet of chart recordings each week and by August, 1967, had observed a fluctuating source that led her to install a special high-speed detector to record rapid intensity changes. Three months later, this recorder revealed that the source was emitting periodic bursts of radio noise every 1.337 seconds to an accuracy of one part in a million. In their *Nature* article, the scientists suggested that the source might be a pulsating white dwarf or neutron star, leading them to call it a pulsating radio source, or pulsar, although it was later shown that the signals come from rotation rather than periodic expansion and contraction of the source.

The first four pulsars discovered by the Cambridge group were soon confirmed by other scientists using large radio telescopes, and several new pulsars were discovered by researchers in Australia and the United States. The fifth pulsar was discovered by a group from Harvard University observing at Green Bank, West Virginia, with a 92-meter dish telescope, and researchers in Arecibo, Puerto Rico, discovered two more with a 305-meter spherical reflector. In late 1968, researchers at Arecibo discovered two more pulsars near the Crab Nebula, which was known to be the remnant from a supernova. One was found to be near the center of the Crab Nebula and to have a very short period of only 33 milliseconds that slowly increased at a rate of about one part in two thousand per year. These observations suggested that pulsars are probably related to supernovas.

**Impact**  The discovery of pulsars had an immediate impact on astronomers and theorists throughout the world. Within a few weeks, most of the large radio telescopes in the world were directed at PSR 1919+21. By the end of 1968, more than one hundred technical papers were published reporting observations and interpretations of pulsars. The first dozen pulsars that were discovered had similar periods between 0.25 and 1.96 seconds. However, the discovery of millisecond pulsars posed a special challenge to theorists.

Even before the discovery of millisecond pulsars, Thomas Gold at Cornell University had published a paper postulating their existence, theorizing that they might be caused by the rapid rotation of a neutron star (in which atomic electrons are absorbed by the nucleus to form neutrons) with a strong magnetic field that transfers rotational energy into electromagnetic radiation in the form of a rotating beacon. He successfully predicted that the loss of rotational energy would result in a slowing of the pulsar repetition rate as confirmed by the Crab Nebula pulsar.

**Subsequent Events**  The discovery of pulsars not only stimulated research and interest in astronomy but also dramatized the growing contribution of women in science. When the Nobel Prize was awarded to Antony Hewish in 1974 for the discovery of pulsars, objections were raised that Jocelyn Bell Burnell should have shared the prize for her contribution. In 1987, she became the first recipient of the American Astronomical Society's Beatrice M. Tinsley Prize.

**Additional Information**  Exhaustive studies of pulsars can be found in two books, both published in 1977 and both entitled *Pulsars*, one by F. G. Smith and the other by Richard Manchester and Joseph Taylor.

*Joseph L. Spradley*

**See also**  Lasers; Quasars, Discovery of; Science and Technology.

# Quant, Mary

**Born** February 11, 1934, London, England

*Creator of the miniskirt and recognized leader of the 1960's fashion world. British designer Quant's affordable, distinct styles defined the "mod" clothing of the decade.*

*Mary Quant, a young British fashion designer, was largely responsible for the popularity of the miniskirt. (Library of Congress)*

**Early Life** The daughter of Welsh schoolteachers, Mary Quant was interested in clothing even as a young child and held definite opinions regarding fashion. Economy dictated that she must wear clothes passed down from a cousin, but she took them apart and made them over to suit her own sense of style. Quant has often said her sense of style was influenced by an older girl in her dance class who wore very short black skirts, white ankle socks over black tights, and black patent leather shoes with ankle straps. At age sixteen, while studying art on a scholarship at Goldsmith's College in London, Quant met Alexander Plunket Greene, her future husband and business partner. In 1955, Quant, Greene, and partner Archie McNair opened Bazaar, a boutique selling unusual clothing and accessories on King's Road in the Chelsea district of London.

**The 1960's** Unable to find enough of the styles she wanted to feature in Bazaar, Quant began sewing her own designs for sale. She could not keep up with the demand for her products and soon employed a number of seamstresses who worked out of her small apartment. In those early days, she was so lacking in knowledge of retail and wholesale business practices that she bought her fabric from Harrod's department store. The look she eventually made famous, often called the "Chelsea girl" look, included skinny, ribbed sweaters, hipster belts, colored tights, high boots, and most important, the miniskirt.

Mass production of Quant styles began in the early 1960's when U.S. retailer J. C. Penney, in an effort to update its somewhat staid and stodgy fashion image, contracted with Quant to supply it with four collections per year. A contract with Butterick Patterns soon followed. Quant began experimenting with makeup that would complement her clothes, and, in 1966, introduced the Mary Quant makeup line. That same year, the British government recognized her achievements by making her an officer of the British Empire. She was the first female designer to be so honored.

**Later Life** In 1970, Quant gave birth to a son, Orlando, and in 1971, she closed Bazaar, which had by that time expanded to three London locations. The family moved to the country, and Quant began designing household items such as sheets and wall coverings while she continued to expand her cosmetics line. In 1990, she was named to the Hall of Fame of the British Fashion Council, and in 1994, at age sixty, she once again opened a London boutique, the Mary Quant Colour Shop.

**Impact** Mary Quant led the fashion segment of the 1960's "British invasion" of the United States. She designed clothes that rejected the status quo in a decade known for that sentiment. Her creations brought designer-label clothing out of the confines of haute couture and into the closets of young, average income women.

**Additional Information** *Quant by Quant,* the designer's 1965 autobiography, provides interesting details on the designer's unconventional personal life and her rise in the fashion industry.

*Linda Pratt Orr*

**See also** British Invasion; Fashions and Clothing; Miniskirts; Mod.

---

# ■ Quasars, Discovery of

**Date** 1963

*One of the most puzzling discoveries in the history of astronomy. The evidence that quasars were the strongest, though smallest, sources of energy yet detected in the universe implied that there might be great defects in the understanding of astronomy and physics.*

**Origins and History** In the 1940's, astronomers found that radio telescopes could be constructed to detect distant sources of radio waves that were beyond the reach of visible light. During the 1950's and 1960's, astronomers used radio interferometers, which combined the resources of several radio telescopes, to determine the precise positions of the strongest radio sources.

**The Discovery** When viewing the locations of radio sources with optical telescopes, astronomers occasionally saw what they thought to be a star within the same galaxy as Earth. Because the spectrum of a star's light can reveal much about its composition, Allan Sandage, at the Hale Observatory in 1960, photographed the spectrum of one such "star." He was surprised to discover that the spectrum contained emission lines that no one could identify.

In 1963, Maarten Schmidt at the California Institute of Technology discovered that the emission lines of one of these starlike objects were identical to hydrogen lines, except they were situated farther toward the red end of the spectrum. Schmidt used the same logic employed by Edwin Hubble, who in the 1920's noted that because the emission lines of spectrum light from other galaxies were redshifted, the wavelengths of such light must be longer, meaning the galaxies were moving away from Earth. Schmidt decided that his "star" was rapidly moving away from Earth, at the enormous speed of about forty-five thousand kilometers per second, or about 15 percent of the speed of light. Using Hubble's law for determining distance, Schmidt found that this "star" was far outside the galaxy, nearly three billion light years away.

Many more of these starlike objects were discovered during the 1960's. They acquired the name "quasi-stellar object," later shortened to "quasar," because they resemble stars when viewed with an optical telescope. Astronomers decided that if the distance determined by redshift was accurate, quasars could typically emit light about a hundred times as bright as the largest galaxy then known. However, because the intensity of light from a quasar could fluctuate from one night to the next, the size of a quasar could be very small, comparable to that of the solar system containing Earth.

**Impact** The discovery of quasars created a powerful dilemma among astronomers. They could not come to a consensus that reconciled the conflict between the apparent size of a quasar and its luminosity. Any denial of Hubble's interpretation of redshift would compromise many widely accepted beliefs based on his conclusions, such as the expanding universe.

Throughout the 1960's, the nature of quasars remained unclear. To account for theoretical contradictions, astronomers in later years attempted both to analyze quasars without using redshift and to offer multiple interpretations of redshift, such as the presence of an intense gravitational field. Even decades after the discovery of quasars, however, none of the diverse solutions to the problem received universal acceptance.

**Additional Information**  A description of the quasars discovered in the 1960's and a discussion of various theories about them can be found in William J. Kaufmann III's *Galaxies and Quasars* (1979).

*Jacob Darwin Hamblin*

**See also**  Pulsating Radio Waves; Science and Technology.

# R

## ■ Radio Free Europe

*In an age of social turbulence, the revelation that Radio Free Europe, an organization built on the ideals of "truth" and "freedom of expression," was funded by the CIA caused surprisingly little public turmoil compared with that produced by other issues of the times.*

**Origins and History** In 1947, the United States became concerned about the weakness of the nation's intelligence apparatus and the welfare of the thousands of European refugees from communist states who had fled to camps in West Germany and to Paris, London, New York, and Washington, D.C. This concern resulted in the creation of the Free Europe Committee by the Central Intelligence Agency (CIA). The committee planned to employ the refugees and help them experience democracy in action by having them use shortwave radio transmitters to project signals—carrying broadcasts in their own languages—across the Iron Curtain to the countries from which the refugees had fled.

Radio Free Europe began functioning at the height of the Cold War on July 4, 1950, and its sister station, Radio Liberation, later to be called Radio Liberty, began broadcasting on March 1, 1953. The

*In 1967, it was revealed that Radio Free Europe was largely financed by the Central Intelligence Agency rather than by American citizens' donations.* (Archive Photos)

radio station signals were picked up in Bulgaria, Hungary, Poland, Romania, and Czechoslovakia. Former Eastern Bloc and Soviet Union citizens made the stations' broadcasts, which always began with the assertion: "We present the news, good or bad, but always true." The stations were listed in international catalogs as "private" and "noncommercial" agencies and were said to be financed by the voluntary contributions of Americans. Their headquarters were in Munich, West Germany, and their original transmitters were in West Germany, Spain, Portugal, and Taiwan. Radio Free Europe's stated purpose was "waging total psychological warfare to subvert the communist regimes." Its programs were designed to promote democracy, destabilize communist regimes, and to provide accurate information to citizens of communist countries.

**Activities** Radio Free Europe owes its creation to Americans' fears about the Soviet Union's rapid and deep incursions into Central and Western Europe. Radio Free Europe had no precedent anywhere in the world. Unlike at the British Broadcasting Corporation and the Voice of America, at Radio Free Europe, the refugees who read the broadcasts also prepared them. The programs contained pro-Western propaganda and informational segments on events in the broadcast area and worldwide that might be censored or presented in a biased manner within the target nation. The broadcasts also included serious and popular music, drama, and cultural readings. Radio Free Europe broadcast all day and well into the night. Referred to as "surrogate broadcasting" or "home radio service broadcasting," Radio Free Europe provided an essential archival service for researchers, academics, and those interested in events in communist countries where media were thought to be weak, inflammatory, corrupt, or unreliable.

Radio Free Europe reported extensively on the 1962 Cuban Missile Crisis and the 1963 assassination of President John F. Kennedy. In February, 1967, a disgruntled National Students Association member discovered that the CIA supported Radio Free Europe and took the story to *Ramparts* magazine, a San Francisco counterculture publication. The magazine ran a detailed investigative report in its March, 1967, issue, explaining how the CIA used "dummy" corporations to conceal its role in funding. Shortly after the *Ramparts* article appeared, a piece in *The New York Times* indirectly revealed to the public

that Radio Free Europe was financed by the CIA, a fact that had been kept secret since 1949. A Columbia Broadcasting System television documentary brought the story into a wider light, and much controversy in the press followed.

**Impact** Millions of Americans who had contributed to Radio Free Europe and sent "truth dollars" and pennies from schoolchildren's funding drives to "keep freedom alive in Eastern Europe" had taken pride and a sense of satisfaction in contributing to the effort. Their money did not mean much if the CIA was channeling funds to Radio Free Europe. The media reports caused the public to mistrust both the CIA and Radio Free Europe. Surprisingly, however, this story caused little if any public disturbance, perhaps because it was overshadowed by the turmoil of the late 1960's. In 1969, Radio Free Europe's staff and budget began to be severely reduced.

In 1956, Radio Free Europe broadcasts had both calmed workers in a Polish union strike and agitated freedom fighters in Hungary after that nation was invaded by the Soviets. Although its broadcasts did not result in the demise of any communist regimes, it did encourage refugees to flee and perhaps enabled citizens of troubled nations to obtain a better view of the situation in their own countries. In 1968, Radio Free Europe did play a moderating role during the turmoil in Czechoslovakia.

**Subsequent Events** Radio Free Europe continues to operate, still publicly funded, although its budget has been reduced and its mission has had to be redefined in view of the general decline of communism in the area.

**Additional Information** See *Subversion by Radio: Radio Free Europe and Radio Liberty* (1974), by Aryom Panfilow and Yuri Karchevshy, and *America's Other Voice: The Story of Radio Free Europe and Radio Liberty* (1983), by Sig Mickelson.

*Patricia Leigh Gibbs*

**See also** Cold War.

## ■ Rawls, Betsy

**Born** May 4, 1928, Spartanburg, South Carolina

*An early star of women's pro golf. Rawls was a leader in promoting the Ladies' Professional Golf Association.*

Elizabeth "Betsy" Rawls started playing golf at age seventeen. While a physics student at the University of Texas, from which she would be graduated Phi Beta Kappa, she won many local, state, and regional amateur events and placed second in the 1950 U.S. Women's Open.

In 1951, Rawls turned professional, launching a career that would span three decades. She won at least one tournament every year from 1954 through 1965. Throughout her career, she won fifty-five tournaments and more than $300,000. In 1959, she won ten tournaments and set a new money record. Her major victories included four U.S. Opens (1951, 1953, 1957, 1960) and two Ladies' Professional Golf Association (LPGA) championships (1959 and 1969), these being the only women's majors at the time. In 1959, she won the Vare Trophy. She was LPGA Player of the Year in 1963. She was twice LPGA president and was inducted into the LPGA Hall of Fame, confirming her status as a role model for two generations of women pro golfers.

**Impact** Rawl's success, along with that of fellow golfer Mickey Wright, helped to preserve the LPGA for later generations of women golfers.

**Subsequent Events** Her last victory was in 1972. In 1975, she left regular competition to become the LPGA's tournament director.

**Additional Information** Liz Kahn's *The LPGA, The Unauthorized Version: The History of the Ladies Professional Golf Association* (1996) provides information about the lives of many women involved in the LPGA in addition to giving a history of the organization.

*Tom Cook*

**See also** Golf; Nicklaus, Jack; Palmer, Arnold; Wright, Mickey.

# ■ Reapportionment Revolution

*The transformation of legislative representation ending rural domination of almost all U.S. legislatures. In 1962, the Supreme Court declared that malapportioned state legislatures could be corrected by court action.*

The Supreme Court requires legislative districts to be equal in population, but a serious problem of malapportionment had arisen before the 1960's. The U.S. Constitution requires the number of representative in the U.S. House of Representatives shifted with the population after the national census

*Golfer Betsy Rawls won at least one tournament per year from 1954 through 1965.* (Archive Photos)

taken once every ten years, but the various state legislatures have the responsibility to draw congressional and state legislative district lines within their own state boundaries.

For more than 150 years, small disparities were either repaired or ignored, but after 1945 an accelerating movement from rural to urban areas left rural areas depopulated but still overrepresented in the legislature. Because rural incumbents almost everywhere benefitted from this and held a majority of seats, there was little the urban legislators, who represented a much larger population, could do to solve the inequity.

**The Court Rules** This malapportionment seemed to have no solution before the reapportionment revolution because rural-dominated legislators would not reapportion to their own political disadvantage, and the Supreme Court refused to act until the *Baker v. Carr* decision in 1962. This case arose in Tennessee where the state legislature had not redistricted itself since 1900 despite a specific requirement in the

Tennessee constitution to do so after every election. The disparity between the largest and smallest district was such that the largest district had sixteen times more voters than the smallest district. The Supreme Court decision technically applied to only the lower house of the Tennessee legislature, but its implications were broader, opening the doors wide to further litigation to establish proper redistricting procedures. The decision also established that the federal courts can enter the state arena to correct districting imbalances, and it did not take the courts long to extend a requirement everywhere it was practical to uphold such a rule.

**One Person, One Vote** In *Reynolds v. Sims* (1964), the Supreme Court specifically set out a one-person, one-vote rule to apply to both houses of the state legislatures. This rule applied even when a state's constitution allowed its senate districts to be unequal in size (as happened when a state mimicked the U.S. Constitution and treated its counties as if they were analogous to states, allowing one senator per county). Up to this point, court decisions did not directly affect the federal legislature, so the Supreme Court did not have to risk conflict with a coequal branch of the national government.

In *Wesberry v. Sanders* (1964), however, the Supreme Court applied the same requirements to the state legislatures that were drawing U.S. House of Representative districting boundaries. Still technically affecting only state actions, the Court was reaching closer to a conflict with the U.S. Congress. Subsequently, the Court has mandated almost exactly equal districts under the one-person, one-vote doctrine for all election districts (except the U.S. Senate where the constitutionally mandated equal representation of each state means admittedly unequal representation according to population).

With the one-person, one-vote standard enunciated, the question remained how close to mathematical equality the district lines within each state had to be drawn. This question was resolved in the *Kirkpatrick v. Preisler* (1969) decision, in which the Court said it would accept minimum acceptable variance in population size. Thereafter, all U.S. legislative districts of any kind (except for the U.S. Senate) were to be as mathematically equal as possible.

**Impact** Before the reapportionment revolution, many scholars hypothesized a dramatic change in U.S. politics because they believed that once the

rural domination of legislators was broken, the impact of the equalized urban vote would be in a liberal and democratic direction. Some Republicans, led by Republican Senate Majority Leader Everett Dirksen, even attempted a failing effort to amend the U.S. Constitution to stop the one-person, one-vote principle from being adopted. They did not need to be so fearful. True, urban voters were somewhat more liberal, but the real shift was from rural area to suburban areas, in which the voters were more conservative. To be sure, more representation was provided for nonrural areas, but the expected shift in a liberal direction never developed.

Even with districts of equal size, gerrymandering, or the drawing of district lines for partisan benefits, was still possible. Gerrymandering is the process by which the party controlling the legislature attempts to draw district boundaries to favor its own candidates. Although citizens may vote contrary to the intention of those who draw the lines, there has been enough stability in the history of precinct and county voting that a skilled political cartographer has a reasonable chance of creating districts favorable to either party. Any general region of a state can be made to produce a high likelihood of either a solid Democratic or Republican majority by the simple expedient of drawing the lines.

Most incumbents prefer the "bipartisan gerrymandering" type of districting, or "loaded" districts, for everyone, thereby virtually ensuring their own reelection. In fact, the toughest fights during redistricting are usually among members of the same party who are competing to receive the strongest areas of support.

**Subsequent Events** Although courts have ruled that districts cannot be drawn to disadvantage obvious minorities such as African Americans, the Supreme Court has been reluctant to enter the very difficult area of gerrymandering for political purposes. Particularly when so many observers are lamenting the regularity with which incumbents are being reelected, it is remarkable that so little is said about the phenomenon of gerrymandering. The Supreme Court has apparently believed the solution lies in population equality of the district alone, but this is clearly inadequate.

**Additional Information** R. B. Dixon's *Democratic Representation* (1968) remains the most comprehensive book setting out the reapportionment revolution at the end of the decade. R. C. Cortner's *The Apportionment Cases* (1970) similarly gives a decade-long perspective. G. E. Baker's *The Reapportionment Revolution* (1966) is also a good source of detailed information.

*Richard L. Wilson*

**See also** Demographics of the United States; Supreme Court Decisions; Voting Rights Legislation; Warren, Earl.

## ■ Religion and Spirituality

*Enormous changes in religious beliefs, institutions, and spirituality. A religious and spiritual revival with long-lasting consequences occurred in the 1960's.*

In the decades leading up to the 1960's, religion was characterized by high levels of active involvement and interest, and after World War II, religious involvement increasingly was linked to a sense of civic duty that went along with being a good citizen. In 1954, the words "under God" were added to the pledge of allegiance to the flag. Going to church and voting were intertwined in the American consciousness as expressions of religiosity. Spirituality was synonymous with institutional membership and carrying out the obligations entailed by that membership.

**The Winds of Change** Underneath the religious and spiritual calm that seemed to characterize U.S. society at mid-century, change was beginning. Theologians and scholars were debating biblical inerrancy (whether the bible was infallible). People were beginning to question the authority of the church and the power of bureaucratic religious institutions. Traditional religious practices and rituals seemed antiquated and irrelevant as the United States entered the latter half of a century that had seen the creation of the atomic bomb, the beginnings the exploration of space, and other remarkable scientific and technological discoveries and inventions. People were wondering what the function and purpose of religion was in the face of all these new developments.

By the beginning of the 1960's, the Roman Catholic Church and Protestant churches were already experiencing the effects of challenges from liberal theologians as they struggled with political issues and modern scientific issues such as evolution and birth control. Pope John XXIII called the Second Vatican Council, which lasted from 1962 through 1965 and resulted in profound changes for Ameri-

can Catholics who were used to ritual, practices, and beliefs that were essentially unchanged since the Council of Trent in 1545. Protestant Christianity was undergoing its own modernization. Protestant theologians "demythologized" the Bible, expanded on the Social Gospel (which demanded that churches pay special attention to the poor and create a more equitable society in line with the gospel values of love, compassion, and justice), and demanded that the churches involve themselves in politics to avoid charges of irrelevancy and hypocrisy from young people.

During the 1960's, Judaism in the United States was continuing to develop four divisions—Orthodox, Conservative, Reformed, and Reconstructionist—with separate religious beliefs, practices, and rituals. Escalation of the conflict between Arabs and Jews into the Six-Day War in 1967 made Jewish Americans more conscious of their identity and culture and more wary of its disappearance as Jewish people were being assimilated into the greater American culture. This secularization of American Judaism provoked a renewed interest in religion as a way to define the Jewish identity. Many American Jews demonstrated a renewed interest in some form of Judaism; still others looked to Jewish mysticism and converted to Hasidism.

The social upheavals of the 1960's presented a challenge to already changing Christian and Jewish religious traditions and organizations, resulting in further movement toward modernization or a return to more stringent traditional practices and a corresponding loss or gain in members. Young people increasingly challenged American society and the churches to respond to national problems such as racism, sexism, and militarism, and respected religious leaders such as the Reverend Martin Luther King, Jr., became politically involved in hopes of effecting radical social change. Inspired by members of the Beat generation, young people criticized American values and started to pursue alternative lifestyles that included nontraditional religious beliefs and spiritual values. Mainstream churches and denominations began to lose members to these alternative faiths.

**Religion and Social Movements** During the 1960's, many of the mainstream denominations became involved in or were affected by political and social movements, particularly the Civil Rights, peace, and

## Membership in Religious Bodies, 1969
### (percent)

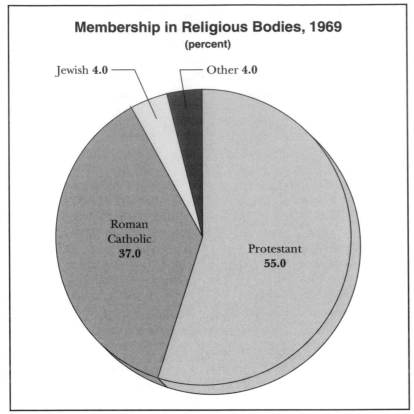

Source: Kurian, George, *Datapedia of the United States, 1790-2000, America Year by Year.* Lanham, Maryland: Bernam Press, 1994.

women's movements. African American churches such as the African Methodist Episcopal and Protestant denominations such as the Baptist and Methodist churches actively supported the Civil Rights movement. As the movement gained strength, more liberal Protestant churches and even the Roman Catholic Church joined the cause with varying degrees of commitment from clergy and church members. These churches supported the Southern Christian Leadership Conference and formed the core support of the Civil Rights movement, performing tasks such as raising money, registering voters, and participating in boycotts all over the South.

An outgrowth of the Civil Rights movement, the Black Power movement, prompted many young African Americans to join the Nation of Islam, a group founded by Elijah Muhammad (Wallace D. Fard) in the 1930's. Malcolm X's charismatic leadership drew many followers, and many members adopted Muslim names to show their allegiance to the faith. The well-known boxer Cassius Clay joined the Nation of Islam in 1964, changing his name to Muhammad Ali.

The peace movement, although a political movement, had the active support of many religious groups, including the Catholic Peace Fellowship, the Catholic Worker, and Clergy and Laity Concerned About the War in Vietnam (an ecumenical group). These groups all had close ties to liberal Catholic and Protestant churches. Two Roman Catholic priests, Daniel and Philip Berrigan, were radical activists and leaders in the peace movement.

The women's movement had an impact on church structure, religious beliefs, and spirituality. Although some denominations ordained women or used them in church leadership, the mainstream Christian and Jewish groups were perceived to be male-dominated because they offered women very few alternatives to unpaid, volunteer work and excluded them from ordination and the rabbinate. They were challenged to change by religious women whose consciousness was raised by the women's movement. These women wanted a more feminine spirituality and more equal participation in church leadership. They wanted a more inclusive language for rituals, prayers, and Bible translations. For example, some of the alternatives they proposed were using "humankind" instead of "mankind," including stories of women in the Bible in rituals and prayers, rejecting biblical passages that demeaned women, and recognizing that there is a feminine as well as masculine component in God, that is, seeing God as mother as well as father. Some women left the traditional churches, calling themselves "post-Christian feminists." They became involved in the neopagan movement and in Wicca groups led by or more inclusive of women. Goddess worship, which was already part of the counterculture, seemed to be a more feminist form of spirituality than the traditional male-dominated religions.

Not all church members and their leaders agreed on the churches' response to these major social issues. Disagreements over the social and political movements of the 1960's caused deep conflict and bitter controversy in mainstream Christian and Jewish groups.

**Alternative Religions**  Alternative religious groups, sometimes called cults, were a hallmark of religious ferment in the 1960's. These new religious movements took various forms depending on the background of the founder and members. Some movements were founded as a direct result of social changes occurring in the 1960's, and others had roots that extended back thirty years or more but were new and attractive to young Americans. For example, the Holy Spirit Association for the Unification of World Christianity (Unification Church) was founded by Reverend Sun Myung Moon in 1936 but did not begin to gain momentum in the United States until the late 1960's. Similarly, the Church of Scientology was founded in the 1950's but did not receive wide recognition until the 1960's. Other religious groups were the product of increased interaction with believers in other parts of the world. Zen Buddhism, Transcendental Meditation, and the International Society for Krishna Consciousness (ISKCON, also known as Hare Krishnas) are good examples of religious imports. These new religious movements fall into three overall categories: the imports, the psychic and New Age religions, and offshoots of mainstream churches formed either in response to an increased religious fervor that found no outlet in the established organization or in reaction to the social and religious changes of the 1960's.

The imported religions include faiths that were brought by immigrants from Asia or enthusiastic converts. Jack Kerouac and Allen Ginsberg of the Beat generation popularized Zen Buddhism in their writing and poetry. Alan Watts added to this interest with his writings and lectures on Zen and Christian mysticism. Religious leaders such as Maharishi Mahesh Yogi, a native of India who introduced Transcendental Meditation to the United States in 1957 and founded the Students' International Meditation Society in 1966, were very influential, partly because of their association with celebrities such as the Beatles and the 1960's counterculture.

Psychic religions have roots in the nineteenth century enthusiasm for extrasensory perception (ESP), telepathy, clairvoyance, and psychokinesis. These religions base their beliefs on a supernatural world and often involve interpretation of dreams, astral travel, communication with the dead, and

various occult practices. New Age religions share many beliefs with the psychic religions, such as belief in an astral plane and the power of objects such as amulets and charms. However, many were also influenced by more modern scientific developments and recent research into psychology and anthropology. In *The Aryan Christ* (1997), Richard Noll attributes the rejuvenation of the occult during the 1960's to New Age religious leaders tapping into C. G. Jung's work on dreams, myths, and the collective unconscious of universal archetypes. Other groups organized around a combination of Zen Buddhism, metaphysics, New Age beliefs in the power of crystals and pyramids, or adaptations of American Indian beliefs. Reincarnation often served as a central tenet for these New Age groups. One such group is ECKANKAR, the Ancient Science of Soul Travel, founded by Paul Twitchell in 1965. Influenced by Hinduism, Twitchell developed a process whereby a master leads the believer through various spiritual or astral realms, leaving their bodies to reach the spiritual city of Agam Des. Esoteric Christian beliefs from Gnosticism and ancient Egyptian and Greek mystery religions are often used in these New Age religions. In addition, a few groups employed drugs in their religious practices and rituals, following the tradition of the ancient Greeks and American Indians, who used various substances to attempt to alter consciousness. The use of drugs in search of spiritual enlightenment was not limited to antiquity or Native American culture, however. At the end of the nineteenth century, scholar William James mentions using nitrous oxide to stimulate mystical consciousness. In the 1950's and 1960's, Aldous Huxley's writings about his experiments with LSD (lysergic acid diethylamide) and his criticism of modern society as empty and aimless (*Eyeless in Gaza*, 1936, and *The Doors of Perception*, 1954) influenced the 1960's counterculture. Former Harvard professor Timothy Leary's teachings about LSD inspired some religious cults to use LSD as a sacrament in their rituals, including the Neo-American Church, founded in 1964 by psychologist Arthur Kleps. Many people reported mystic and religious awakenings under the influence of LSD or other mind- and mood-altering drugs such as peyote. The American Indians' use of peyote was described in Carlos Castaneda's book, *The Teachings of Don Juan: A Yaqui Way of Knowledge* (1968). In the late 1960's, the space age gave rise to religious groups organized around stories of alien landings, abduction by aliens, and unidentified flying object (UFO) sightings.

In the 1960's, a number of religious groups emerged that were offshoots of mainstream religious organizations. They arose from a resurgence of religious fervor that developed in reaction to the continued revitalization of mainstream religions and the major social transformations that were sweeping the country. In the latter half of the 1960's, the large number of baby boomers (people born between 1946 and 1964) in Protestant and Roman Catholic churches brought energy to traditional religious organizations but also forced them to change to attempt to retain these young people as members. Many churches modified their practices and structures, becoming more liberal, but followers still left to join alternative religions. Charismatic and evangelical groups developed and extended programs to the young. Many of these groups not only updated church practices but also incorporated elements drawn from the social and political movements that were sweeping the country, including the Civil Rights, women's, peace, and environmental movements. Many of these groups seemed better able to deal with the violence, drug abuse, racial unrest, and sexual promiscuity of the decade, issues that traditional churches seemed ill-equipped to handle.

Many young people became part of the Jesus people movement that emerged in California in the late 1960's. One of the most radical groups to emerge from this movement was the Children of God (also known as the Family of Love or the Family), founded by David "Moses" Berg in California in 1968. This group explored various living arrangements and recruitment methods in its pursuit of Christian socialism.

Other Christian-based religious groups pursued communal living. One of these was the Peoples Temple, founded by Jim Jones in the 1950's. This group, which followed a combination of Fundamentalism and Jones's own philosophy and was affiliated with the Disciples of Christ, settled near Ukiah in Northern California in the mid-1960's. It flourished, establishing churches in San Francisco, Los Angeles, and Jonestown, Guyana, where the group committed mass suicide in 1977.

Many conservative religious believers felt that the more liberal, mainstream churches were losing followers, especially the young, to alternative religions because during the process of modernization, they had lost their sense of structure. Evangelical and Pentecostal religious groups reassessed their beliefs and practices and renewed their commitment to their traditions, hoping to draw young people into religious organizations that offered them structure and direction after the chaos of the counterculture.

**Impact** The consequences of the modernization of traditional religious groups, the development and growth of alternative religious groups, and the revitalization that occurred as a result of evangelical, Pentecostal, and charismatic groups, both old and new, are enormous. Conflicts raised in churches and denominations over women's participation, social justice issues, sexuality, the family, and politics altered religious and spiritual life in fundamental and profound ways. These transformations were watersheds for the religious denominations and for society as a whole. During the 1960's, religions began to ordain women and homosexuals, allowed birth control and divorce, converted their rituals and prayers into contemporary language, altered their power and authority structure and organizational bureaucracy, and made other far-reaching and permanent changes.

Alternative religious groups formed or expanded during the 1960's survived or disappeared depending on their ability to adapt. Some, like the Peoples Temple, self-destructed. Others became more institutionalized, turning into organizations that seem, in retrospect, much like other religious groups. Others remain small cults, perhaps never destined to appeal to more than a small group of believers because of their very esoteric, mystical teachings.

On the whole, organized religion emerged from the 1960's revitalized yet smaller. By the 1990's, although most people, more than 90 percent, continued to express a belief in some sort of supreme being, far fewer were actively involved in organized religion. Surveys estimate only 40 percent to 60 percent attend church or synagogue regularly. Spirituality, on the other hand, emerged as a vital force in life in the United States although as an individualized response to the sacred and the transcendent in the lives of Americans. Religion and spirituality continue to interest many Americans.

**Additional Information** An overview of religious denominations in the 1960's can be found in Robert Wuthnow's *The Restructuring of American Religion* (1988), and William A. Au's *The Cross, the Flag, and* *the Bomb* (1985) discusses the conflict within the churches over the issues of peace and war. Ronald B. Flowers's *Religion in Strange Times: The 1960's and 1970's* (1984) is an excellent source on the development of cults in the 1960's, and Robert S. Ellwood's *Alternative Altars: Unconventional and Eastern Spirituality in America* (1979) provides an excellent historical perspective on the influence of Eastern religion on American spirituality. His subsequent two books, *The 1960's Spiritual Awakening: American Religion Moving from Modern to Postmodern* (1994) and *Religious Spiritual Groups in Modern America* (1988), with Harry B. Portin, are invaluable resources for understanding religion and spirituality in the 1960's. A good source of information on religious issues relating to women is *Women in New Religions* (1997), by Elizabeth Puttick.

*Susan A. Farrell*

**See also** Berrigan, Daniel, and Philip Berrigan; Counterculture; Cults; Hare Krishnas; Nation of Islam; Southern Christian Leadership Conference (SCLC); *Teachings of Don Juan, The*; Vatican II; Women's Identity.

---

# ■ Rock Operas

*The literary zenith of the rock lyric. The development of the rock opera demonstrated rock music to be a viable medium for expressing ideas and ideological concepts.*

The rock lyric developed rapidly in the 1960's as a literary form. The vacuous lyrics of pop and bebop, which were subservient to the driving beat of rock and roll, were giving way to lyrics that reflected the social concerns of the developing counterculture.

In 1965, when Bob Dylan joined socially significant folk music lyrics with rock music, the result was a rapidly evolving rock lyric with a new intellectual respectability. Rock music rapidly developed subgenres such as psychedelic and progressive rock. In 1967, the Beatles expanded the boundaries of the independent psychedelic and progressive rock song by creating the "concept album." The album *Sgt. Pepper's Lonely Hearts Club Band* unified its component songs on a central theme that reflected the counterculture and presented an optimistic social statement of a future realized through self-discovery and love. This album took the music world by storm and has even been credited with unifying, at least briefly, the fragmented minds of Western youth.

Pete Townshend of the Who was inspired by *Sgt. Pepper* to create an album that outlined the story of a young man's personal search for morality and that functioned on both symbolic and real levels. Although Townshend's narrative was developed in the rock idiom, it most closely resembled the opera form. *Tommy* (1969) is credited with being the first rock opera and was an international hit in its album and concert formats. Even though *Tommy* was never presented as a staged musical or opera because it was not theatrically cohesive, the Who received the unprecedented honor of performing it in opera houses throughout Europe and finally in New York's prestigious Metropolitan Opera House. A spokesperson for the Met described *Tommy* as an opera in a new language.

While Townshend was creating *Tommy*, two other young British musicians were experimenting independently. Andrew Lloyd Webber, a classically trained musician who aspired to write for the theater, and Tim Rice, who had an encyclopedic knowledge of rock and roll with a desire to write rock lyrics, had been invited to write a short cantata on a religious theme. The result was *Joseph and the Amazing Technicolor Dreamcoat* (1968), in which they discovered they could tell a story using popular musical styles without a narrative line, creating a kind of opera. When a recording of *Joseph and the Amazing Technicolor Dreamcoat* unexpectedly became a hit album in England, the two decided to attempt to tell the story of Jesus's last seven days entirely in rock music. The resulting rock opera, *Jesus Christ Superstar* (1969), was released as a double album in England and the United States, selling more than three million copies within two years.

**Impact** The emergence of the rock opera in 1969 had very different effects on rock music and musical theater. Rock musicians, in general, did not seize upon the rock opera format even though the rock lyric was proven to be an effective medium for the communication of complex issues and ideas. The rock opera did establish the acceptability of rock in the musical theater. It quickly changed the way traditional musicals were written and performed, requiring amplified sound and modern orchestrations even for musical comedy revivals.

**Subsequent Events** Townshend completed a second rock opera, *Quadrophenia* (1973), a study in spiritual desperation against the background of the

British Mod subculture. Although *Quadrophenia* did not achieve the international success of its predecessor, it climbed to number two on the charts, providing the Who with their highest chart rating. When *Jesus Christ Superstar* opened on Broadway in 1971, its impact was unexpected and unprecedented. The rock opera attracted a new, young audience that began to revitalize the Broadway theater. In London, *Jesus Christ Superstar* became the longest running musical in English history. The contemporary rock opera became the most successful theatrical genre and shifted the center of musical theater from New York City to London. A theatrically restructured *Tommy*, complete with one new song, was finally produced on Broadway in 1993, completing the transformation from rock-opera album to staged rock opera.

**Additional Information** Paul Friedlander examines the development of Townshend's rock operas in

*Liberal Republican Nelson A. Rockefeller was unable to win nomination as his party's presidential candidate in 1964 or 1968.* (AP/Wide World Photos)

*Rock and Roll: A Social History* (1996), and Michael Walsh details the establishment of rock opera on the stage in *Andrew Lloyd Webber: His Life and Works* (1989).

*Gerald S. Argetsinger*

**See also** British Invasion; Dylan, Bob; Music; *Sgt. Pepper's Lonely Hearts Club Band*; *Tommy*.

---

## ■ Rockefeller, Nelson A.

**Born** July 8, 1908, Bar Harbor, Maine
**Died** January 26, 1979, New York, New York

*A prominent New York state and national official. As governor of the state of New York throughout the 1960's, he advocated and secured the passage of much progressive social and welfare legislation for the state.*

**Early Life** Nelson Aldrich Rockefeller was born into one of the United States' wealthiest families. Shortly after graduating from Dartmouth College in 1930, he married Mary Todhunter Clark, a socially prominent Philadelphian. He was subsequently employed in various Rockefeller companies. By 1940, his interests had turned to foreign affairs, particularly South America. In that year, President Franklin D. Roosevelt named him head of the Office of Inter-American Affairs, and in 1944, he was appointed assistant secretary of state for Latin America. Subsequently Rockefeller aided a succession of presidents in a variety of appointive jobs. President Harry S Truman named him chairman of the International Development Advisory Board, and he counseled the president on the Point Four Program. He was a special assistant to President Dwight D. Eisenhower in a number of foreign and domestic areas. For, example, Rockefeller planned and set up a new U.S. Department of Health, Education, and Welfare and became the first undersecretary of that agency in 1954. He resigned in 1956 and devoted much of his attention to what he considered to be the most pressing social problems facing the nation. A book, *Prospect for America* (1961), was the result of this effort.

**The 1960's** In 1958, Rockefeller campaigned as a liberal Republican for the governorship of New York. He defeated the incumbent Democratic governor, W. Averell Harriman, and was reelected to the office in 1962, 1966, and 1970. During the early years of his tenure, he successfully pushed through the state legislature the creation of a statewide university system. Rockefeller secured passage of civil rights legislation, minimum wage laws, a liberalized welfare program, and an increase in New York's public housing program. He inaugurated a state medicaid plan and led a fight for the liberalization of abortions. Rockefeller was a major supporter of the nascent environmental movement and was largely instrumental in the setting up of a New York department to deal with environmental problems.

During Rockefeller's first two terms as governor, these programs were largely paid for by increases in taxes. New York legislators, however, became increasingly reluctant to vote for ever-higher taxes or to borrow money to pay for new programs. Partially because of this development plus his increasing interest in national presidential politics, Rockefeller became more conservative in his last years as governor. In 1971, he presented the legislature with an "austerity" budget that called for a tightening up of welfare payments and medicaid allowances. Such actions and his tough suppression of the Attica prison riot in 1971 drew severe criticism from liberals.

Rockefeller was frustrated in attempts to secure the Republican nomination for president. In 1964, he lost to Senator Barry Goldwater and in 1968 to Richard M. Nixon. In 1973, he resigned as governor and in 1974, following the resignation of President Nixon who was succeeded by Vice President Gerald Ford, he was nominated for vice president by President Ford and was overwhelmingly confirmed in that office by the Congress.

**Later Life** Until his term expired in January, 1977, Vice President Rockefeller's major activities included the heading of a White House Domestic Council and a special commission to investigate the Central Intelligence Agency. Turning from politics in 1977, he picked up on a lifelong interest in art. In 1939, he had served as president of the Museum of Modern Art; in 1957, he founded the Museum of Primitive Art; and he sponsored and wrote the introduction to the pictorial *Masterpieces of Primitive Art* (1977). In the course of his life, Rockefeller had gathered together an extensive collection of modern and primitive paintings, sculpture, and other art forms. Shortly before his death, he was engaged in the creating and selling of reproductions from this collection.

**Impact** Rockefeller had his greatest influence in social and welfare legislation and in art. He secured

the passage of liberal social and welfare programs at the state level, which later influenced events at the national level. In addition, Rockefeller, an articulate financial backer of modern and primitive art throughout his life, greatly encouraged public interest in and support for art.

**Additional Information** In 1982, Joseph E. Perico, a long-time aide to Rockefeller, published an interpretive biography, *The Imperial Rockefeller: A Biography of Nelson.*

*Joseph C. Kiger*

**See also** Central Intelligence Agency (CIA); Goldwater, Barry; Nixon, Richard M.; Presidential Election of 1964; Presidential Election of 1968.

## ■ Rolling Stones

*Vanguard British musical group. The Rolling Stones brought rhythm and blues to a young, white audience by mixing it with mainstream rock and roll.*

The revived friendship between childhood friends Mick Jagger and Keith Richards, who had met again by chance in 1960, marked the birth of the Rolling Stones. Vocalist Jagger and guitarist Richards, both rhythm-and-blues fanatics, joined with fellow blues lover and guitarist Brian Jones in 1962. Working with temporary bandmates, they played the Ealing Blues Club and the Richmond Station Hotel. Bass player Bill Wyman and drummer Charlie Watts joined the group just as it was establishing a loyal following. They played their first date as the Rolling Stones on July 12, 1962, at the Marquee Club. They soon became the house band at the Crawdaddy Club, owned by Giorgio Gomelsky, their first manager.

Andrew Loog Oldham, an employee of Beatles' manager Brian Epstein, saw the band's commercial potential. He and industrialist Eric Easton managed the Rolling Stones in the mid-1960's. Oldham transformed the group into the "anti-Beatles" by having them do publicity stunts that created a rebellious image that hinted of drugs, sex, androgyny, violence, and occultism. Lending credence to this image were songs such as "(I Can't Get No) Satisfaction," "Let's Spend the Night Together" (which they performed on *The Ed Sullivan Show* in January, 1967, mumbling or changing the controversial lyrics), and "Sympathy for the Devil."

"The Last Time" became their first top-ten U.S. hit in January, 1965. They followed that success with

*The Rolling Stones, who cultivated a bad-boy image to differentiate them from the early Beatles, perform at a Christmas show in London in December, 1969.* (AP/Wide World Photos)

more hit songs, including "Get Off My Cloud" and "(I Can't Get No) Satisfaction," and during the next two years had numerous hits, such as "Ruby Tuesday," "Paint It Black," "Nineteenth Nervous Breakdown," and "Mother's Little Helper." Their 1967 album, *Their Satanic Majesties Request*, a psychedelic album released in answer to the Beatles' *Sgt. Pepper's Lonely Hearts Club Band* (1967), although successful, received a mixed reaction from critics. In 1968, the group released the hit song "Jumpin' Jack Flash" and album *Beggar's Banquet*, which critics praised. In 1969, the group's "Honky Tonk Woman" was a number-one hit, and the *Let It Bleed* album, which contained "Gimme Shelter," became a gold record.

One aspect of the group's bad-boys image—drugs—drew police attention. In a 1966 *News of the World* interview, Jones (misidentified as Jagger) admitted drug use. After the interview was published, Jagger sued for libel. On February 12, 1967, police raided Richards's house, arresting him and Jagger on drug possession charges. Several months later,

Jones was arrested. At about the same time, Jones lost his girlfriend, Anita Pallenberg to bandmate Richards, and his drug use escalated. By 1969, he was a liability to the band and a lure for police surveillance. The convictions of Jagger and Richards were overturned, but Jones was repeatedly arrested.

In June, 1969, Jones released a public statement citing his desire to pursue a different musical direction, and he was replaced by Mick Taylor. On July 3, 1969, Jones's girlfriend, Anna Wohlin, found him dead in his swimming pool. Mysteries surround his demise, but the coroner's report stated "death by misadventure." Taylor first played live as a member of the Rolling Stones at Jones's memorial concert on July 5.

The band launched its U.S. tour, countering criticism of high ticket prices by promising to play at a free festival on December 6. The site was Altamont Speedway near San Francisco, and the Hell's Angels motorcycle gang was hired to provide security. Early on, the bikers clashed with the audience and performers. When the Rolling Stones performed, brawls were constant, and sometime after they played the disturbing "Sympathy for the Devil," audience member Meredith Hunter got into a fight with members of the motorcycle gang. The documentary film *Gimme Shelter* (1970) captures Hunter being stabbed to death.

**Impact** High-profile trials linked the Rolling Stones to drug use. Their lyrics flouted British standards of sexuality, and lurid allegations at the drugs trials hinted at decadent personal lives. Their conviction on drug charges in the late 1960's raised a public outcry, which showed that views of "milder" drugs were softening. Social critics felt the band was being persecuted for the decade's changing morals. Representatives of freer sexuality, members of the group lived with their girlfriends, had illegitimate children, and adopted androgynous stage personae. When Jagger's girlfriend, Marianne Faithfull, announced her pregnancy, she was denounced by the Archbishop of Canterbury. The decade that saw the band epitomize "sex, drugs, and rock and roll" was ending, but not the Rolling Stones.

**Subsequent Events** The members of the Rolling Stones changed over the years, but the group continued to record and perform. Drug arrests and scandals did not put off the band's multigenerational audience, which stayed loyal through the 1990's. Some of their 1970's hits were "Brown Sugar" and "Wild Horses" (from the 1971 *Sticky Fingers* album), "Angie," and "It's Only Rock 'n' Roll." Hits from the 1980's include the albums *Tattoo You* (which contained "Start Me Up" and "Waiting on a Friend"), *Undercover* (1983), and *Dirty Work* (1986). The group received a Grammy Award for its 1994 album, *Voodoo Lounge.*

**Additional Information** *The Rolling Stones: The First 20 Years* (1981), by David Dalton, gives an excellent chronology of the band. Robert Greenfield's *STP: A Journey Through America with the Rolling Stones* (1974) shows the band at the height of its popularity. Stanley Booth's 1985 volume, *The True Adventures of the Rolling Stones*, is a personal account mixed with history and interviews.

*Cynthia R. Kasee*

**See also** Altamont Music Festival; British Invasion; Jagger, Mick.

# ■ *Rosemary's Baby*

**Released** 1968
**Director** Roman Polanski (1933-      )

*The controversial film about the conception and birth of Satan's son. Some people believed it exemplified the nation's moral decline; others felt it redefined the horror genre; and still others saw it as a product of the social, religious, and political turmoil of the 1960's and a harbinger of further chaos.*

**The Work** In *Rosemary's Baby*, a young New York couple, Rosemary and Guy Woodhouse, become friends with an older couple, Minnie and Roman Castevet, living in their apartment building. Rosemary has a vivid nightmare of a satanic ritual culminating in her rape by a demonic figure. She dismisses it as just a dream—until she becomes pregnant, her struggling actor husband suddenly becomes successful, and the Castevets take an unusual interest in the welfare of the unborn child. Soon Rosemary is convinced she is carrying the devil's child and is trapped in a web of conspiracy involving Guy, the Castevets, and even her obstetrician. Although she was informed that her baby was born dead, Rosemary discovers it in the Castevets' apartment in a black-swathed cradle with a crucifix hanging upside down above it. The Castevets and other Satanists hail the coming of Satan in the flesh as Rosemary wails in despair. Yet Rosemary's motherly instinct prevails, and she agrees to care for the child. The film ends with her gently rocking the cradle and singing softly to the baby.

**Impact** *Rosemary's Baby*, based on Ira Levin's novel of the same name published in 1967, was released in 1968, the year the new Motion Picture Association of America rating system went into effect, clearing the nation's screens for more adult-oriented material. The film's discreet nudity, the bloody aftermath of a suicide, and its fairly explicit rape scene shocked viewers unaccustomed to such sights in films. Just the screen treatment of Satanism (especially with the Satanists triumphant at the end) outraged enough people that the film's producer, William Castle, received death threats and had to be hospitalized. The film redefined the horror genre by dealing with formerly taboo topics and eschewing the on-screen monsters typical of earlier 1960's films for a never-seen yet more terrifying menace. Many audience members gave grisly descriptions of the baby, fully

*Mia Farrow plays Rosemary, the young woman who gives birth to Satan's son, in the 1968 Roman Polanski film* Rosemary's Baby. (Museum of Modern Art/Film Stills Archive)

believing they had seen it, although it is never actually shown in the film. Rosemary's torment, the conspiracy she suspects but can't quite prove, and the promise of more chaos and horror to come ("Here's to the year one!" Roman Castevet declares) can easily be seen as reflecting the anguish the United States was experiencing on so many levels during the 1960's. The then-popular motto of youth, Trust No One Over Thirty, is perfectly mirrored in the vast age difference between Rosemary and the elderly Satanists.

**Related Works** *The Exorcist,* released in 1974, is the most closely related work in terms of content and theme. Note that the film that Chris MacNeil is making before her daughter becomes possessed by a demon is a typical 1960's youth rebellion film. In

1997, Ira Levin published *Son of Rosemary: The Sequel to Rosemary's Baby.*

**Additional Information** A more detailed discussion of the book and film can be found in Douglas Fowler's *Ira Levin* (1987).

*Charles Avinger*

**See also** Film; Motion Picture Association of America Rating System.

## ■ Roth, Philip

**Born** March 19, 1933, Newark, New Jersey

*One of the most successful and important American postwar novelists. Roth's fiction defines many aspects of Jewish American experience.*

**Early Life** Roth was born into a lower-middle-class Jewish family, and his memories of the social stratification of his home have found their way into his fiction. He attended Rutgers University and in 1954 received his bachelor's degree from Bucknell University and the next year his master's degree from the University of Chicago. From 1956 to 1957, he studied at the University of Chicago, and some of those experiences were transformed into his second novel, *Letting Go* (1962). His writing career began with the publication of *Goodbye, Columbus* (1959), a novella and five stories, that won him a number of awards and signaled the emergence of a new, compelling voice in American letters.

**The 1960's** In 1960, Roth won the National Book Award and spent much of the decade as a writer-in-residence at a number of American universities. With the publication of *Portnoy's Complaint* (1969), Roth's career changed dramatically. The novel was a best-seller and brought Roth recognition and financial security. However, popularity brought a severe critical backlash, with some critics labeling him anti-Semitic.

The novel is a *Bildungsroman* that chronicles the tortured exploits of a successful young man who wrestles with his Jewish heritage. Alexander Portnoy involves himself with a succession of non-Jewish women, the most ardent of whom is one he nicknames Monkey, an ignorant model who adores him. Portnoy feels oppressed by his parents and upbringing and seeks to rebel but manages only to inflict pain on himself and those closest to him. The novel is by turns a hilarious and touching portrait of personal freedom and cultural assimilation, and Roth saw the work as a liberating opportunity to give his comic impulses free rein. The comic mode became Roth's characteristic form of expression in successive novels such as *Our Gang* (1971), *The Breast* (1972), and *The Great American Novel* (1973).

**Later Life** Beginning with *My Life as a Man* (1974), Roth's fiction turns to seriocomic examinations of Jewish American experience, and usually the protagonist is a literate, highly intelligent man. The novel is furthermore significant for introducing Roth's fictional projection of himself—Nathan Zuckerman—and the persistent theme of living life or a fictional projection of life. In the Zuckerman quartet, *Zuckerman Bound* (1985), Roth develops this character more fully than any of his other creations.

The obsession with Zuckerman continues in the metafictional *The Counterlife* (1986).

**Impact** Roth is concerned not only with Jewish American assimilation but also with keen social observation. Nothing is beyond his consideration—the sexual revolution, baseball, the Richard M. Nixon administration, and the intellectual and moral malaise of the 1970's and 1980's. Beginning with *Portnoy's Complaint*, he has challenged notions of what constitutes taboo subjects, and his comic inventiveness has expanded the possibilities for serious fiction.

**Additional Information** Roth's autobiography, *The Facts* (1988); a memoir of his father, *Patrimony* (1991); and a collection of nonfiction, *Reading Myself and Others* (1975), offer interesting personal details, as does Claire Bloom's unflattering portrait in *Leaving a Doll's House* (1996).

*David W. Madden*

**See also** Literature; Metafiction; Sexual Revolution; Social Satires.

# ■ Route 66

*The Main Street of America. Also known as the "Mother Road," this highway, dedicated in 1926, was the first unbroken, fully paved highway from Chicago to Los Angeles.*

By the 1920's, the automobile had captured America's imagination, and the resultant public demand for better roads spurred Congress to modify the 1916 Federal Highway Act in 1921. The new law provided federal money to states for a system of interconnected interstate highways and required states to designate as much as 7 percent of their roads as national highways. This was the beginning of a federal interstate highway system that included Route 66. Dedicated in 1926 and completed in 1937, Route 66 was more than twenty-four hundred miles long and traversed three time zones and eight states—Illinois, Missouri, Kansas, Oklahoma, Texas, New Mexico, Arizona, and California. It was the best way to see some of the scenic wonders of the United States, including the Grand Canyon and the Pacific Ocean.

By the 1960's, the nation's love affair with Route 66 was well entrenched. The highway had been immortalized in the Depression era songs of Woody Guthrie and Pete Seeger and in Bobby Troup's popular hit "Get Your Kicks on Route 66" recorded by Nat King Cole in 1946, and Jack Kerouac's 1955 novel *On the Road*. However, the construction of a new 42,500-mile interstate highway system supported by President Dwight D. Eisenhower and made possible by the Federal Highway Act of 1956 led to the inevitable bypassing of the old road. The U.S. Highway 66 Association tried to prevent the total destruction of America's Main Street, and many sections of it were kept as service roads for the new interstates.

In 1960, the Columbia Broadcasting System created a television show entitled *Route 66*. It starred Martin Milner as Tod Stiles and George Maharis as Buz Murdock, two men who crisscrossed the country in a red Corvette helping people resolve various problems in towns and cities along Route 66. The TV show, which ran until 1964, revived many fond memories in the minds of Americans, many of whom had traveled Route 66 during the Depression, during World War II, or as vacationers in the 1950's. This nostalgia and the efforts of the U.S. Highway 66 Association, other preservationists, and historians has meant that many of the original signage has been maintained and many of the motels, cafés, gas stations, and tourist attractions along the old road are still in operation. The lore of the road—stories about motels with buildings shaped like tepees, a jack rabbit mounted on the roof of a trading post, "real Indians" selling their wares along the roadside, and the natural wonders of the Meramec Caverns, the desert, and the Grand Canyon—spurred the preservation of as much of the road as possible. Parts of the original road can be found in each of the eight states Route 66 crossed. Even stories about the many and terrible automobile accidents that happened along Route 66 have become part of the road's folklore.

**Subsequent Events** Many of the stories of Route 66 businesses and travelers have been documented in the 1980's and 1990's. The old guide books have been reprinted, and many historians, preservationists, and private citizens as well as the National Park Service are working to protect those sections of the route that are still viable and to restore others that have declined to no more than weed-infested gravel or dirt pathways. In the stretches where people can walk along remnants of the road, the old road is creating stories for new travelers.

**Additional Information** In 1990, Michael Wallis published *Route 66: The Mother Road*, which provides a thorough discussion of the road and excellent photographs. *Route 66: The Highway and Its People* (1988), by Susan Croce Kelly with a photographic essay by Quinta Scott, discusses the history of the highway from its birth through the building of the interstate that bypassed much of it.

*Maureen K. Mulligan*

**See also** Interstate Highway System; Travel.

---

# ■ Rubinstein, Arthur

**Born** January 28, 1887, Lodz, Poland
**Died** December 20, 1982, Geneva, Switzerland

*Renowned concert pianist. Rubinstein's performances produced an enduring standard of virtuosity and a popular following worldwide.*

A child prodigy, Arthur Rubinstein studied under the most notable music teachers of his time. Early in his career, he toured throughout Europe, South America, and the United States, becoming a U.S. citizen in 1946.

In the 1960's, Rubinstein, already in his seventies, experienced one of his most active and productive periods of performances and recordings. Commanding a formidable repertoire of French, Spanish, German, Russian, and even Brazilian composers, he enthralled audiences with his refined, assured technique and delicate yet vigorous interpretations. Governments and organizations around the world bestowed awards, commendations, and honors upon him.

Rubinstein performed well into his eighties. In 1982, after becoming increasingly deaf and almost blind, he died of cancer. The Arthur Rubinstein International Music Society, in Tel Aviv, Israel, has maintained a research center devoted to the pianist's life and work since 1980.

**Impact** Through recordings of his performances, Rubinstein remains a formidable standard for interpretations of Beethoven, Brahms, and especially Chopin.

**Additional Information** *Rubinstein: A Life* (1995), by Harvey Sachs, includes a valuable discography. Rubinstein published an autobiography in two volumes, *My Young Years* (1973) and *My Many Years* (1980).

*Edward A. Riedinger*

**See also** Bernstein, Leonard; Music; Price, Leontyne; Thomson, Virgil.

## ■ Rudolph, Wilma

**Born** June 23, 1940, St. Bethlehem, Tennessee
**Died** November 12, 1994, Brentwood, Tennessee

*Fastest woman in history. Rudolph was the first American woman to win three Olympic gold medals in track and field.*

When four years old, Wilma Glodean Rudolph, unable to walk because of polio, was fitted with a brace. Although told she would never walk, she learned to walk with the brace and eventually was able to discard the device. At age twelve, she began playing basketball, and during her high school years, she competed in basketball and track. In 1956, her relay team won a bronze medal at the Olympics in Melbourne, Australia.

In 1960, the Tennessee State University student competed in the Olympic Games in Rome, setting a world record in the 200 meters during the trials and in the 100 meters during the Games. She won gold medals in the 100-, 200-, and 400-meter relays, just as her hero, Jesse Owens, had in Nazi Germany in 1936. She was the first American woman to win three gold medals in track and field. Rudolph, hailed as the "fastest woman in history," broke her own world record in the 100 meters in 1961.

In 1962, she retired and established the Wilma Rudolph Foundation to train young, underprivileged athletes. That same year, she received the Zaharias Award for being the Most Outstanding Athlete in the World. In 1974, Wilma was inducted into the National Track and Field Hall of Fame. She died in 1994 of a brain tumor.

**Impact** Rudolph instilled hope in athletes, especially young women, African Americans, and those with physical impediments. The tall, slender sprinter also popularized the sport of track running

*American Wilma Rudolph won three gold medals in track and field at the 1960 Olympic Games in Rome.* (AP/Wide World Photos)

by lending it a sort of glamour through her elegant style.

**Additional Information** Rudolph wrote an autobiography, *Wilma*, in 1978 and a volume about her sport, *Wilma Rudolph on Track*, in 1980.

*Myrna Hillburn-Clifford*

**See also** Olympic Games of 1960.

# ■ Rusk, Dean

**Born** February 9, 1909, Cherokee County, Georgia
**Died** December 20, 1994, Athens, Georgia

*Secretary of state from 1961 to 1969, under both John F. Kennedy and Lyndon B. Johnson. Rusk played an instrumental role in international relations, particularly U.S. involvement in the Vietnam War.*

**Early Life** After spending his boyhood years in Georgia, (David) Dean Rusk attended Davidson College in Davidson, North Carolina, where he graduated Phi Beta Kappa in 1931. As a Rhodes Scholar, Rusk went to St. John's College of Oxford University and earned a master of arts degree in philosophy, politics, and economics in 1934. Upon returning to the United States, Rusk taught at Mills College in Oakland, California. In 1937, Rusk married Virginia Foisie; they had two sons and a daughter. In 1940, Rusk was called to active duty from his position as an Army Reserve officer and served until 1946 in the Pacific theater and in Washington, D.C. From 1946 until 1951, Rusk was employed in various capacities by both the Department of State and Department of War. In 1952, Rusk became the president of the Rockefeller Foundation and remained in that position until 1961.

**The 1960's** Having spent much of his early career in the State Department (1946 to 1952), Rusk had the background as a diplomat and was a strong candidate for secretary of state. In 1961, President John F. Kennedy appointed Rusk secretary of state, a position Rusk would hold for eight years.

Under Kennedy, Rusk led U.S. foreign policymakers through two crises involving Cuba. The first was the 1961 Bay of Pigs invasion. Rusk opposed the invasion of Cuba but voiced his concerns to Kennedy only in private meetings and on nonmilitary grounds and deferred to the decision made by the president and his other advisers. The second problem involving the island nation in which Rusk played

a role was the 1962 Cuban Missile Crisis. On October 19, after five days of debate, Rusk, along with Secretary of Defense Robert McNamara, advised Kennedy to order a partial blockade of Cuba. Kennedy followed their advice, coupling the blockade with the threat of military force, and the Soviet Union removed the missiles from Cuba.

In 1963, Lyndon B. Johnson retained Rusk as his secretary of state. Under Johnson, Rusk's time and energy was consumed by the escalating conflict in Vietnam. Rusk believed that the United States had committed to helping South Vietnam and was determined that the United States would fulfill its promise. Rusk continually defended the nation's Vietnam policy to Congress and the American public. As the war lingered into the late 1960's, Rusk became the target of antiwar protesters, including his estranged son, Richard Rusk, at public appearances. Despite his earlier stance of remaining dedicated to U.S. involvement in Vietnam, Rusk recommended in March, 1968, that the United States stop enlarging its forces in South Vietnam and slow its bombing of North Vietnam.

**Later Life** Soon after Richard M. Nixon was sworn in as president in 1969, Rusk left the Department of State. He took a teaching position at Athens Law School at the University of Georgia in 1970 and taught international law there until he retired in 1984. Following his retirement, Rusk wrote his memoir, *As I Saw It* (1990), with the help of his son Richard, with whom he had reconciled after the end of the Vietnam War. Looking back on the Vietnam War, Rusk said his policy was flawed in two ways. First, he believed he had underestimated the resolve of the Viet Cong (South Vietnamese Communists) and the North Vietnamese in fighting for an independent and unified Vietnam. Second, he felt that he overestimated the patience with which the United States public would wait for an eventual victory.

**Impact** Rusk, one of the leading advocates for continued U.S. involvement in the Vietnam War, helped prolong the nation's tour of duty in Southeast Asia. Although initially reserved in providing his opinion to Kennedy, he had no problem voicing his position on U.S. foreign policy during his tenure under Johnson. His recommendations to both presidents affected the United States' world position during the following decades.

**Additional Information** Warren Cohen's *Dean Rusk* (1980), volume 19 of *The American Secretaries of State and Their Diplomacy*, provides deeper insight into Rusk and his policies.

*David Buck*

**See also** Bay of Pigs Invasion; Cuban Missile Crisis; Johnson, Lyndon B.; Kennedy, John F.; McNamara, Robert; Vietnam War.

---

# ■ Russell, Bill

**Born** February 12, 1934, Monroe, Louisiana

*Bill Russell of the Boston Celtics throws a shot over the heads of two Syracruse Nationals players at Boston Garden in 1962.* (AP/Wide World Photos)

*Basketball player. Russell led Boston to eleven National Basketball Association (NBA) championships and became the first African American head coach in major U.S. professional sports.*

Born in Louisiana, William Felton "Bill" Russell grew up in West Oakland, California, where he attended McClymonds High School. Although he played varsity basketball in his last two years of high school, he was not a star. Following graduation, he joined a traveling team and was able to perfect his

skills by playing daily. In 1952, he received a scholarship to play at the University of San Francisco (USF), a small school without a gymnasium. Russell led USF to national championships in 1955 and 1956. He was an All-American both years, and he led the 1956 Olympic team to the gold medal.

Following college, Russell joined the Boston Celtics of the National Basketball Association (NBA) and led the team to eleven championships in thirteen seasons, including eight consecutive from 1959 to 1966. He was a five-time Most Valuable Player (1958, 1961-1963, 1965). He averaged 22.5 rebounds per game during his career, and once had 51 rebounds in a game, still a record. In 1967, Russell was named to succeed Red Auerbach as Celtics coach, making him the first African American head coach in the NBA. He served as player and coach from 1967 to 1969 and led Boston to the 1968 and 1969 championships.

**Impact** Russell practically invented the concept of defensive basketball. Before him, basketball games were won by having a better offense than the other team. Russell showed that defense could win championships.

**Additional Information** In 1979, Russell coauthored his autobiography with Taylor Branch entitled *Second Wind: The Memoirs of an Opinionated Man.*

*Dale L. Flesher*

**See also** Alcindor, Lew (Kareem Abdul-Jabbar); Basketball; Chamberlain, Wilt; Sports.

*Jim Ryun, the first high school student to run a mile in less than four minutes, wins a pre-Olympic meet at Walnut, California, in 1968.* (AP/Wide World Photos)

## ■ Ryun, Jim

**Born** April 29, 1947, Wichita, Kansas

*One of the world's greatest middle-distance runners. In 1964, Ryun became the first high school student to break the four-minute mile.*

In the fall of 1962, as a sophomore, James Ronald "Jim" Ryun made his high school cross-country team. In his first two-mile race, he finished fourth on the school's "B" team; by the end of the season, Ryun led his varsity team to the state championship.

In spring, 1963, Ryun ran his first mile race, finishing second behind the defending state champion. A few weeks later, he won the state championship with a time of 4:16.2. In 1964, he became the first high school student to run a four-minute mile, and he made the U.S. team for the 1964 Tokyo

Olympics. The media rallied around the seventeen-year-old Olympian who still had a paper route. Although outclassed at the Olympics, a year later Ryun beat gold medalist Peter Snell. In 1967, he broke the world record with a time of 3:51.1, a mark that would stand for eight years.

Ryun won the 1968 Olympic trials, but the altitude of Mexico City was tough to overcome, and he finished second behind Kip Keino. The 1968 silver medal was Ryun's only Olympic medal. In the 1972 Munich games, he was tripped 550 meters from the finish.

In 1996, Ryun was elected to Congress as a Republican from the second district of Kansas.

**Impact** Ryun popularized running in the United States. As more Americans took up the sport, he became the godfather to whom others looked for motivation.

**Additional Information** In 1984, Ryun published his autobiography, *In Quest of Gold.*

*Dale L. Flesher*

**See also** Mills, Billy; Olympic Games of 1964; Olympic Games of 1968; Rudolph, Wilma.

# S

## ■ San Francisco as Cultural Mecca

*A city that attracted numerous elements of the counterculture of the 1960's. San Francisco, with its history of cultural diversity and tolerance, attracted followers of various movements for social change.*

In the 1960's, the port city of San Francisco, California, was a cosmopolitan city of world renown, a fitting stage on which to carry out the many cultural, social, and political dramas of the decade. At the start of the decade, beatniks gathered in the North Beach area of the city. The word "beatnik" had been coined in the 1950's by a columnist for the *San Francisco Chronicle* to describe a group of writers who led an unconventional lifestyle expressed in their works. The leading figures of this group were novelist Jack Kerouac, who wrote *On the Road*; poet Allen Ginsberg, author of "Howl"; and Lawrence Ferlinghetti, poet and founder of City Lights, a bookstore/publishing company and gathering place for members of the Beat generation.

In the middle of the decade, a new group of young people, dubbed "hippies" by a writer for the *San Francisco Examiner*, appeared in the city. They settled in the Haight-Ashbury district, an area surrounding the intersection of Haight and Ashbury, where cheap housing, mainly for students, was available. Hippies believed in eliminating sexual inhibitions, allowing free, even communal, love, and advocated peace in the midst of the Cold War and the escalating war in Vietnam. The hippie culture was also shaped by an emerging drug culture in which young people, often college students, used marijuana and psychedelic drugs such as LSD (lysergic acid diethylamide). The banner of these hippies, or flower children, was "peace and love," and they listened to the messages and rhythms of musical groups such as the Beatles, Grateful Dead, and Jefferson Airplane.

Landmark hippie events included the early 1967 Gathering of the Tribes for a Human Be-in (a free gathering featuring concerts, political rallies, and theatrical "happenings") in Golden Gate Park, attended by thousands, and the Summer of Love that followed it. Thousands of young Americans moved to San Francisco, drawn by the counterculture that had spawned there. As the war in Vietnam escalated, both Beat and hippie opposition to the war grew. Antiwar demonstrations, which had been taking place throughout the decade, increased in size and frequency, and massive protests were held in Golden Gate Park.

Many forces opposed the young people's advocacy of drugs, free love, and peace. An older generation seemed intent on exterminating the boisterous youth culture that had developed in San Francisco. The repression of demonstrations in the city often resulted in charges of police brutality. Most indicative of the period's tensions and ensuing conflicts was a series of strikes and riots at San Francisco State College from 1968 through 1969.

Other elements also marked the cultural ferment of San Francisco during the 1960's. The October, 1961, performance of comedian and social satirist Lenny Bruce resulted in his arrest and trial on obscenity charges. Though acquitted in San Francisco, Bruce would be arrested and tried in other cities during the decade. Theater and politics mixed in the audacious performances of the San Francisco Mime Troupe. In 1969, Native Americans claiming Alcatraz Island occupied it and began broadcasting as Radio Free Alcatraz. They would hold the island until June, 1971.

The 1960's was a unique decade for San Francisco, marking its coming-of-age as a point of origin for cultural movements and innovation. The decade left a legacy that is part of the affection many people feel for the city. This sentiment is often recalled in a song by Tony Bennett, "I Left My Heart in San Francisco." Appropriately enough, he first recorded it in 1962.

**Impact** After the 1960's, San Francisco remained an influential cultural center although it lacked some of the decade's vigorous originality. Its already numerous cultural activities and features grew to include an increasing number of art festivals, ballet and dance companies, libraries, museums, opera programs, orchestras, and schools and universities. The mixing of ethnicities and cultures in the city continued, and by the end of the 1980's, less than 50 percent of San Franciscans were white and no single group dominated the city's population. In the vanguard spirit of the city, its large homosexual community became a leader in advancing gay rights, especially after the onslaught of AIDS in the 1980's.

**Additional Information**  Charles Perry's *The Haight-Ashbury: A History*, published in 1984, examines the neighborhood where the hippie culture flourished. Warren French analyzes the origins of beatnik literary culture in *The San Francisco Poetry Renaissance, 1955-1960*, which was published in 1991.

*Edward A. Riedinger*

**See also**  Alcatraz Island Occupation; Beat Generation; Be-ins and Love-ins; Cults; Drug Culture; Flower Children; Free Love; Grateful Dead; Haight-Ashbury; Hippies; Jefferson Airplane; Sexual Revolution.

---

# ■ Sanchez, Sonia

**Born** September 9, 1934, Birmingham, Alabama

*An African American poet of the 1960's Black Arts movement. She used black English, colloquial terminology, and dramatization of personal situations to capture her anger on behalf of the African American community.*

**Early Life**  Born Wilsonia Benita Driver in Birmingham, Alabama, she lost her mother, Lena Jones Driver, at age one and was raised by her grandmother and later her father. In 1943, she and her sister moved to Harlem, New York, to live with her father, Wilson L. Driver, a musician. Through him, she was exposed to jazz artists such as Billy Holiday, Art Tatum, and Count Basie, whose music influenced her poetic style. She studied poetry and political science at Hunter College, where she received her bachelor's degree in 1955. She continued studying poetry under professor Louise Bogan at New York University.

**The 1960's**  The Black Power movement, particularly Malcolm X, influenced Sanchez, who began publishing her poetry in African American and left-wing periodicals such as *Liberator* and *The Journal of Black Poetry*. In addition, her poetry was featured in Hoyt Fuller's *Negro Digest* (later renamed *Black World*), a prominent journal of the period. In 1969, *Homecoming*, a collection of poems that was her first book, was published by Broadside Press.

Sanchez's other interests included education. She held numerous positions in the field, starting as a staff member of the New York City Downtown Community School from 1965 to 1967. During this period, she also worked with the Congress of Racial Equality (CORE) and helped establish the first black studies program nationwide at the university level. In the late 1960's, Sanchez married poet Etheridge Knight, divorcing him soon after. She had two children, Morani and Mungu Neusi.

**Later Life**  Sanchez joined the Nation of Islam in 1972, leaving three years later because of their views on women. She wrote thirteen books, including short stories, plays, and children's stories, and received numerous awards, including the PEN Writing Award in 1969, and the Tribute of Black Women Award from the Black Students of Smith College in 1982. In addition, *homegirls and homegrenades* (1984), received an American Book Award in 1985.

**Impact**  The poetry of Sanchez, a supporter of African American nationalism, promoted the strengthening of ties within the African American community. Additional themes include drug abuse, love, and the reverence of leaders such as Malcolm X. Her poetic style, which some critics have called revolutionary, consists of imitating African American English through devices such as slashes (for example, "im/mi/grant") and the omission of letters (for example, "cept"). She also employs derogatory terms such as "nigger" in her work.

**Additional Information**  Among Sanchez's writings, *Homecoming* captures her unusual poetic style. *A Blues Book for Blue Black Magical Women* (1973) reveals her Muslim bent with poetry that supports the tenets of her beliefs. *Does Your House Have Lions?* (1997) revolves around her brother's life and death from acquired immunodeficiency syndrome (AIDS).

*Dolores Lopez*

**See also**  Giovanni, Nikki; Malcolm X; Nation of Islam.

# ■ SANE (National Committee for a Sane Nuclear Policy)

*An activist organization that sought a comprehensive nuclear test ban treaty, global disarmament, and a shift in the priorities of nations from military to human needs.*

**Origins and History** In the 1950's, writer Norman Cousins joined with leaders of influential peace organizations to form a committee (which became known as the Committee for a Sane Nuclear Policy, or SANE) to oppose what the group termed the "insanity" of nuclear weapons. The organization was publicly announced on November 15, 1957. Because of widespread concern about carcinogenic radioactivity from nuclear tests, SANE soon gained many enthusiastic members. This initial success was compromised by Cousins's confused response to Senator Thomas J. Dodd's charge that communists had infiltrated SANE. When President John F. Kennedy defused public anxiety about fallout with the partial Nuclear Test Ban Treaty of 1963, it accelerated the decline in the organization's membership. In seeking another issue to increase membership and funding, SANE chose the Vietnam War, which proved destructively divisive. Disagreements within SANE led to the resignations of such key officials as Cousins. To resolve the organization's problems, its new leaders enlisted the aid of public figures such as pediatrician and author Benjamin Spock, who had become spokesman for the organization in 1962. In 1969, the organization's name was changed to National Committee for a Sane Nuclear Policy (SANE). With the new name came a new focus: a campaign against U.S. and Soviet construction of antiballistic missile (ABM) systems.

**Activities** In the early 1960's, the Soviet Union resumed testing of nuclear weapons. SANE condemned this action, called for worldwide protests, and tried in vain to prevent the United States from following the Soviet example. After the peaceful resolution of the Cuban Missile Crisis in 1962, Cousins acted as unofficial liaison between the United States and the Soviet Union to break impasses in the negotiations for a test ban treaty. After the partial Nuclear Test Ban Treaty was signed in 1963, SANE helped get it ratified in the U.S. Senate. In the mid-1960's, SANE's programs centered on ending the Vietnam War, but this divided its membership, and in 1969, SANE returned to its traditional antinuclear-weapons focus.

**Impact** The years of greatest influence for SANE were the late 1950's and early 1960's when its arguments about the dangers of nuclear tests energized the public. Increased membership and numerous local committees meant increased financial stability, which heightened SANE's impact. The Dodd Committee hearings regarding communist infiltration, the loss of prominent members, and the foray into Vietnam War protests attenuated SANE's influence, and even though the group tried to recoup its losses by returning to its traditional antinuclear activities, its ability to affect U.S. defense policies remained enfeebled.

**Subsequent Events** In the 1970's, SANE opposed mobile basing of MX missiles, but a financial crisis led to new leaders, who augmented the membership of the organization (renamed A Citizens' Organization for a Sane World, or SANE, in 1983) to a high of one hundred thousand in 1984. With the expansion of the nuclear arms race during the administration of President Ronald R. Reagan, SANE, along with Freeze and other peace organizations, proposed a halt to the production, testing, and deployment of new nuclear weapons. In 1987, SANE merged with Freeze, making it the largest peace organization in U.S. history, and in 1992, SANE/FREEZE: Campaign for Global Security adopted the name Peace Action.

**Additional Information** In 1986, Milton S. Katz published *Ban the Bomb: A History of SANE, The Committee for a Sane Nuclear Policy, 1957-1985*; the book provides a sympathetic analysis of SANE from its founding to its work with Freeze.

*Robert J. Paradowski*

**See also** Cuban Missile Crisis; Fallout Shelters; Nuclear Test Ban Treaties.

# The Sixties in America

# ■ List of Entries by Category

**Subject Headings Used in List**

Arts
Asian Americans
Business and the Economy
Civil Rights
Crimes and Scandals
Drug Culture
Environment and Demographics
Film
Gender Issues
Government and Politics
Health and Medicine

Hippies and the Counterculture
International Affairs
Latinos
Laws and Acts
Literature
Media
Music
Native Americans
Organizations and Institutions
Science and Technology
Sexual Revolution

Social Revolution
Social Welfare
Space
Sports
Supreme Court Cases
Theater
Vietnam War
Visual Arts
Women's Issues

**Arts**

Albee, Edward
Arbus, Diane
Architecture
Art Movements
Baldwin, James
Brautigan, Richard
Brooks, Gwendolyn
*Catch-22*
*Cat's Cradle*
Cheever, John
*Chicano: Twenty-five Pieces of a Chicano Mind*
*City of Night*
*Confessions of Nat Turner, The*
Dances, Popular
*Death of a President, The*
Didion, Joan
*Eat a Bowl of Tea*
Federal Aid to the Arts Bill
Ferlinghetti, Lawrence
Ginsberg, Allen
Giovanni, Nikki
Hansberry, Lorraine
Hesse, Eva
*House Made of Dawn*
*Indians*
Lichtenstein, Roy
Literature
*Lucky Come Hawaii*
McKuen, Rod
Max, Peter

Merriam, Eve
Metafiction
*Midnight Cowboy*
*Mountain of Gold*
Oates, Joyce Carol
*Oh, Calcutta!*
*One Flew over the Cuckoo's Nest*
Op Art
Photography
Piercy, Marge
Poetry
Pop Art
Roth, Phillip
Sanchez, Sonia
Silko, Leslie Marmon
Simon, Neil
*Slaughterhouse-Five*
Social Satires
*Stranger in a Strange Land*
Susann, Jacqueline
*Teachings of Don Juan, The*
Teatro Campesino, El
Terry, Megan
Theater
Theater of the Absurd
*To Kill a Mockingbird*
*2001: A Space Odyssey*
Tyler, Anne
Updike, John
Warhol, Andy
*Way to Rainy Mountain, The*
*Who's Afraid of Virginia Woolf?*

**Asian Americans**

*Eat a Bowl of Tea*
Immigration
*Lucky Come Hawaii*
*Mountain of Gold*

**Business and the Economy**

Agriculture
Automobiles and Auto Manufacturing
Branch Banks
Business and the Economy
Corporate Liberalism
Credit and Debt
Economic Oppportunity Act of 1964
*Economy of Cities, The*
Gross National Product (GNP)
Inflation
International Trade
Japanese Imports
Motor Vehicle Air Pollution Act of 1965
Office of Minority Business Enterprise (OMBE)
Prosperity and Poverty
Unemployment
Unions and Collective Bargaining
Urban Renewal
War on Poverty

## Civil Rights

Abernathy, Ralph
Affirmative Action
Assassinations of John and
    Robert Kennedy and Martin
    Luther King, Jr.
Baldwin, James
Birmingham March
Black Christian Nationalist
    Movement
Black Liberation Front
*Black Like Me*
"Black Manifesto"
Black Panthers
Black Power
Black United Students
Bond, Julian
Brooks, Gwendolyn
Brown, H. Rap
Brown Berets
Busing
Carmichael, Stokely
Chávez, César
Chicago Riots
Chicano Movement
Church Bombings
Civil Rights Act of 1960
Civil Rights Act of 1964
Civil Rights Act of 1968
Civil Rights Movement
Cleaver, Eldridge
*Confessions of Nat Turner, The*
Congress of Racial Equality
    (CORE)
Davis, Angela
Detroit Riot
Evers, Medgar
Freedom Rides
Freedom Summer
Hampton-Clark Deaths
*Heart of Atlanta Motel v. the United
    States*
Holmes, Hamilton, and
    Charlayne Hunter
Housing Laws, Federal
"I Have a Dream" Speech
*In the Heat of the Night*
Jackson, Jesse
*Katzenbach v. McClung*
Kerner Commission Report

King, Martin Luther, Jr.
Ku Klux Klan (KKK)
League of Revolutionary Black
    Workers
Maddox, Lester
Malcolm X
Malone, Vivian
March on Selma
March on Washington
Marshall, Thurgood
Meredith, James H.
Nation of Islam
National Association for the
    Advancement of Colored
    People (NAACP)
New York Riots
Newark Riot
Poor People's March
Sanchez, Sonia
School Desegregation
Schwerner, Goodman, and
    Chaney Deaths
Sit-ins
Smith, Tommie, and John Carlos
    Protest
Southern Christian Leadership
    Conference (SCLC)
Student Nonviolent Coordi-
    nating Committee (SNCC)
Voting Rights Legislation
Washington, D.C., Riots
Watts Riot
Young, Andrew
Young Lords

## Crimes and Scandals

Agnew, Spiro
Air Force Academy Cheating
    Scandal
Assassinations of John and
    Robert Kennedy and Martin
    Luther King, Jr.
Baker Resignation
Boston Strangler
Career Girl Murders
Chappaquiddick Scandal
Chessman, Caryl
Crimes and Scandals
Eichmann, Adolf
Estes, Billie Sol

Fitzpatrick Drug Death
Fortas, Abe
Genovese Murder
Haynsworth, Clement, Jr.
*In Cold Blood*
Kennedy, Edward "Ted"
Mailer, Norman
Manson Murders
Monroe, Marilyn
Nixon, Richard M.
Organized Crime
Oswald, Lee Harvey
Percy Murder
Powell, Adam Clayton, Jr.
Radio Free Europe
Sheppard, Sam
Sinatra Kidnapping
Skyjackings
Speck Murders
Texas Tower Murders
U-2 Spy Plane Incident

## Drug Culture

*Alice's Restaurant*
Be-ins and Love-ins
Beat Generation
Counterculture
Death of Hippie
Drug Culture
East Village
*Easy Rider*
*Electric Kool-Aid Acid Test, The*
Fitzpatrick Drug Death
Flower Children
Ginsberg, Allen
Grateful Dead
Haight-Ashbury
*Hair*
Hippies
Jefferson Airplane
Leary, Timothy
LSD
Marijuana
Manson Murders
San Francisco as Cultural Mecca
*Sgt. Pepper's Lonely Hearts Club
    Band*
Summer of Love
*Teachings of Don Juan, The*
Trips Festival

McGovern, George
McNamara, Robert
Marshall, Thurgood
Medicare
*Memoirs v. Massachusetts*
*Miranda v. Arizona*
Mississippi Freedom Democratic
  Party (MFDP)
Muskie, Edmund
My Lai Incident
National States Rights Party
Nixon, Pat
Nixon, Richard M.
Nuclear Test Ban Treaties
Nureyev Defection
Paris Peace Talks
Peace Corps
Powell, Adam Clayton, Jr.
Presidential Election of 1960
Presidential Election of 1964
Presidential Election of 1968
*Pueblo* Incident
Radio Free Europe
Reapportionment Revolution
Rockefeller, Nelson A.
Rusk, Dean
Six-Day War
Smith, Margaret Chase
Supreme Court Decisions
Tet Offensive
Vietnam War
Wallace, George
War on Poverty
Warren, Earl
Warren Report

**Health and Medicine**
Abortion
Agent Orange Controversy
Birth Control
Cancer
Cyclamates
Genetics
Heart Transplants
*Human Sexual Response*
Kidney Transplants
Lasers
Medicare
Medicine
Pill, The

Sex-Change Operations
Sexual Revolution
Silicone Injections
Thalidomide
Weight Watchers
World Health Organization
  (WHO)

**Hippies and the Counterculture**
*Alice's Restaurant*
Altamont Music Festival
Be-ins and Love-ins
Beat Generation
Communes
Counterculture
Cults
Death of Hippie
Drug Culture
East Village
*Easy Rider*
*Electric Kool-Aid Acid Test, The*
Fashions and Clothing
Fitzpatrick Drug Death
Flower Children
Free Love
Ginsberg, Allen
Grateful Dead
Greenwich Village
Haight-Ashbury
*Hair*
Hairstyles
Happenings
Hippies
Jefferson Airplane
Joplin, Janis
Leary, Timothy
LSD
Marijuana
Manson Murders
Monterey Pop Festival
San Francisco as Cultural Mecca
*Sgt. Pepper's Lonely Hearts Club
  Band*
Summer of Love
*Teachings of Don Juan, The*
Trips Festival
Underground Newspapers
Woodstock Festival
Youth Culture and the
  Generation Gap

**International Affairs**
Arms Race
Bay of Pigs Invasion
Berlin Wall
Biafran War
Castro, Fidel
Central Intelligence Agency
  (CIA)
Cold War
Cuban Missile Crisis
Czechoslovakia, Soviet Invasion
  of
Dominican Republic, Invasion of
Gulf of Tonkin Incident
International Trade
Japanese Imports
*Liberty* Incident
My Lai Incident
New York World's Fair
Nuclear Test Ban Treaties
Nureyev Defection
Paris Peace Talks
Peace Corps
*Pueblo* Incident
Radio Free Europe
Seattle World's Fair
Six-Day War
Space Race
Tet Offensive
Vietnam War
World Health Organization
  (WHO)

**Latinos**
Brown Berets
Chávez, César
Chicano Movement
*Chicano: Twenty-five Pieces of a
  Chicano Mind*
Grape Workers' Strike
*Plum Plum Pickers, The*
Teatro Campesino, El
United Mexican American
  Students (UMAS)
Young Lords

**Laws and Acts**
American Indian Civil Rights Act
  of 1968
Bilingual Education Act
Civil Rights Act of 1960

Supremes
*Switched-on Bach*
Thomson, Virgil
Tiny Tim
*Tommy*
Trips Festival
Twist
Wolfman Jack
Woodstock Festival
Zappa, Frank

**Native Americans**
Alcatraz Island Occupation
American Indian Civil Rights
  Act of 1968
American Indian Movement
  (AIM)
*House Made of Dawn*
Mills, Billy
National Indian Youth Council
  (NIYC)
Native American Fishing
  Rights
Silko, Leslie Marmon
*Teachings of Don Juan, The*
Wauneka, Annie Dodge
*Way to Rainy Mountain, The*

**Organizations and Institutions**
American Indian Movement
  (AIM)
American Nazi Party
Black Liberation Front
Black Panthers
Black United Students
Brown Berets
Central Intelligence Agency
  (CIA)
Congress of Racial Equality
  (CORE)
Hare Krishnas
Hell's Angels
Job Corps
John Birch Society
Ku Klux Klan (KKK)
League of Revolutionary Black
  Workers
Minutemen
Mississippi Freedom Democratic
  Party (MFDP)
Nation of Islam

National Association for the
  Advancement of Colored
  People (NAACP)
National Commission on the
  Causes and Prevention of
  Violence
National Indian Youth Council
  (NIYC)
National Mobilization
  Committee to End the War in
  Vietnam (MOBE)
National Organization for
  Women (NOW)
National States Rights Party
Office of Minority Business
  Enterprise (OMBE)
Radio Free Europe
SANE (National Committee for
  a Sane Nuclear Policy)
Southern Christian Leadership
  Conference (SCLC)
Student Nonviolent Coordi-
  nating Committee (SNCC)
Students for a Democratic
  Society (SDS)
United Mexican American
  Students (UMAS)
War Resisters League
Weathermen
Weight Watchers
White Panthers
World Health Organization
  (WHO)
Yippies
Young Americans for Freedom
Young Lords

**Science and Technology**
Air Pollution
Apollo 1 Disaster
Apollo Space Program
Arms Race
Birth Control
Cancer
Communications
Computers
Concorde
Condon Report
Cyclamates
Environmental Movement

Gemini Space Program
Genetics
Geodesic Domes
Heart Transplants
Kidney Transplants
Lasers
Mariner Space Program
Medicine
Mercury Space Program
Microwave Ovens
Moon Landing
*Naked Ape, The*
New York World's Fair
Nobel Prizes
Nuclear Reactors
Photocopying
Pill, The
Power Failure of 1965
Pulsating Radio Waves
Quasars, Discovery of
SANE (National Committee for
  a Sane Nuclear Policy)
Science and Technology
*Scorpion* Disappearance
Sealab
Seattle World's Fair
Sex-Change Operations
Silicone Injections
Space Race
Supersonic Jets
Telecommunications Satellites
Thalidomide
*Thresher* Disaster
Travel
*Trieste* Dive
*Triton* Submarine
*2001: A Space Odyssey*
Unidentified Flying Objects
VCRs
Water Pollution
Weather Satellites
World Health Organization
  (WHO)

**Sexual Revolution**
Abortion
Birth Control
Censorship
*City of Night*
Counterculture